5TH EDITION

DEVELOPING MANAGEMENT SKILLS

A COMPREHENSIVE GUIDE FOR LEADERS

A special thank you to David Whetten and Kim Cameron. Thank you for giving us access to such excellent material. Thank you to my co-author. It continues to be an honour and a privilege to work with you.

Thank you to my family. You are the light in my life.

James Carlopio

Thanks for the foundation, David and Kim. I greatly value the history of my collaboration with James.

Thanks, Susan, my partner in all things.

Graham Andrewartha

JAMES CARLOPIO and
GRAHAM ANDREWARTHA

Adapted from the text by
Whetten and Cameron

5TH EDITION

DEVELOPING MANAGEMENT SKILLS

A COMPREHENSIVE GUIDE FOR LEADERS

Pearson Australia
Unit 4, Level 3
14 Aquatic Drive
Frenchs Forest NSW 2086

www.pearson.com.au

Authorised adaptation from the United States edition, entitled *Developing Management Skills*, 8th Edition, ISBN: 0136121004 by Whetten, David A. and Cameron, Kim S., published by Pearson Education, Inc., publishing as Prentice Hall, Copyright © 2011

Fifth adaptation edition published by Pearson Australia Group Pty Ltd, Copyright © 2012

Acquisitions Editor: Judith Bamber
Project Editor: Liz de Rome
Editorial Coordinator: Camille Layt
Production Administrator: Rochelle Deighton
Copy Editor: Robyn Flemming
Proofreader: Ron Buck
Copyright and Pictures Editor: Helen Cross
Indexer: Garry Cousins
Cover design by Simon Rattray
Typeset by Midland Typesetters, Australia

Printed in Malaysia (CTP-VP)

1 2 3 4 5 16 15 14 13 12

National Library of Australia
Cataloguing-in-Publication Data

Author:	Carlopio, James R.
Title:	Developing management skills : a comprehensive guide for leaders / James Carlopio and Graham Andrewartha ; adapted from the text by Whetten and Cameron.
Edition:	5th ed.
ISBN:	9781442547629 (pbk.)
Notes:	Includes bibliographical references and index.
Subjects:	Management—Study and teaching—Australia. Management—Australia—Problems, exercises, etc.
Other Authors/ Contributors:	Andrewartha, Graham.
Dewey Number:	658.40071194

Foreword

I am delighted to write the foreword for the fifth edition of *Developing Management Skills: A Comprehensive Guide for Leaders*, by James Carlopio and Graham Andrewartha. This book is a significant adaptation of the successful US text by David Whetten and Kim Cameron and continues to consolidate its reputation as a key resource on management skill development in the Asia-Pacific region for managers and business academics. This new edition builds on the strengths of the fourth edition and contains updated chapters plus new material on business ethics and creative problem solving. There are many texts that emphasise the development of hard skills for managers, but this book focuses on the soft management skills, and provides a context of examples and research with an emphasis on experiential learning.

The combination of practitioner and academic talent that is evident in this book is especially welcome. James Carlopio is the Director of the Bond University Centre for Executive Education, and Graham Andrewartha is an Adjunct Research Fellow at the School of Management UniSA and a well-known management and business consultant operating his own business. This combination of practitioner and academic experience and resources strengthens the book and makes it suitable for management development programs both within enterprises and in more traditional educational settings. Overall, it is an excellent mix of theory and practical reality.

I congratulate the authors for their valuable and ongoing contribution to management education and development in the Asia-Pacific region.

Peter J. Dowling, PhD, LFAHRI, FANZAM
Professor of International Management and Strategy
School of Management
La Trobe University
Melbourne

President of Australia and New Zealand International Business Academy

Contents

Preface

This fifth edition of *Developing Management Skills* has involved a redesign of the chapters, updated references and some completely new material.

Chapter 1 has been redesigned and includes a considerably expanded section on management and business ethics.

Developing Management Skills focuses on developing skills identified by research as being critically important. Not only are the skills presented in this book important skills, but researchers have identified them as *distinguishing* skills—those that set outstanding managers apart from merely effective managers (see Boyatzis 1982; Carnevale, Gainer & Meltzer 1989; Dowd & Liedtka 1994; Goleman 1998). Each chapter discusses a cluster of related skills, and each skill area overlaps with other skill areas. No skill stands alone.

Part 1 of the book contains four chapters on personal skills: 'Management essentials', 'Developing self-awareness', 'Managing stress' and 'Solving problems analytically and creatively'. Part 2 focuses on interpersonal skills: 'Communicating supportively', 'Motivating others' and 'Managing conflict'. These skill areas also overlap—managers must rely on parts of many skills areas in order to perform any one skill effectively. Part 3 has three chapters on group skills: 'Empowering and delegating', 'Building effective teams' and 'Managing change'. These chapters overlap substantially with one another as well as with the skill areas in Parts 1 and 2. Thus, as we progress from personal to interpersonal to group skills, the core competencies developed in the previous area help to support successful performance of the new skill area.

Part 4 contains two chapters: 'Making oral and written presentations' and 'Conducting interviews'. These chapters are contained in the online supplement at **www.pearson.com.au/highered/carlopio** and cover specialised communication skills that are particularly relevant for students who have had little managerial experience or skill training in these areas. They also foster the skill development needed to implement assignments typically included in a management skill-building course. Writing reports, giving class presentations and interviewing are all prerequisites for building skills in the core management skill areas, so material has been provided on these three topics that students will find helpful.

Chapters are organised on the basis of the learning model summarised in the table in the introduction. Each chapter begins with skill assessment instruments. Their purpose is to help you focus attention on areas of personal competence, as well as areas needing improvement in both knowledge and performance.

An explanation of the key behavioural guidelines, as well as a rationale for why these guidelines work, is found in the skill learning sections. These sections explain the core behavioural principles associated with each skill. A model of each skill is presented, along with evidence from research that the principles identified are effective in practice. The objective is to provide a sound rationale for the action guidelines summarised at the end of the section.

The skill analysis sections provide brief case histories that illustrate effective and/or ineffective applications of the behavioural principles. The purpose of these sections is to bridge the gap between intellectual understanding and behavioural application. Critiquing a manager's performance in a real-life case enhances your understanding of the skill learning material. Each case provides a model of effective performance and helps to identify ways that the skill can be adapted to your personal style.

The skill practice sections provide exercises, problems and role-play assignments. The goal of these sections is to provide opportunities to practise the behavioural guidelines in simulated managerial situations and to receive feedback from peers and instructors. Practising these managerial skills in a classroom setting is not only safer and less costly than in a real-life management job, but others' observations and feedback can be timely and more precise.

The last section of each chapter is skill application and scoring keys for each assessment. These contain forms to help you generate your own improvement agenda, as well as assignments and ideas for applying the skill in an out-of-class situation. The purpose of these assignments is to help you transfer behavioural guidelines into everyday practice. You may be directed to teach the skill to someone else, consult with another manager to help resolve a relevant problem, or apply the skill in an organisation or a family.

Practice and application

The philosophy of this book is that improvement in management skills is primarily the learner's responsibility. If the principles covered in this book are not conscientiously applied outside the classroom, little or no progress can be achieved. The authors' intention, therefore, is to have the course carry over into the life activities of learners. Effectiveness in management is no different from effectiveness in most other human enterprises. The same kinds of skills are required to live a productive and successful life as for managing people effectively. That is why, even though some users of this book may not presently be managers of other employees, and indeed may never become managers, they should neither dismiss these skills as irrelevant nor wait until they become managers before attempting to practise them.

Psychological research has confirmed that, when people are forced to perform under stress, they rely on what is called a 'dominant response pattern' (Staw, Sandelands & Dutton 1981). That is, they rely on the behaviour patterns that are most deeply ingrained in their response repertoire. For example, if a person who has been accustomed to responding to conflict combatively, but who has recently begun practising a more supportive response pattern, is faced with an intense emotional confrontation, they may begin by reacting supportively. But, as pressure mounts, they are likely to revert to the more practised, combative style.

Thus, it is important for learners not to make the mistake of thinking they can delay applying skill training until they become managers. When problems and conflicts do occur, it is too late for learners to change their behaviour to handle issues effectively. Learners, therefore, should practise the skills discussed in this book and apply them to part-time jobs, friendships, student organisations, families, social groups and so forth. Employees, of course, will want to use the guidelines provided here with their co-workers, managers, employees and customers. With conscientious practice, following the behavioural guidelines will become second nature.

A second reason that non-managers should not delay the application of management skills is that individuals learn faster and remember better what they experience both intellectually and emotionally. In other words, people learn best when they are affected, and they feel affected by something if they see an immediate effect on their lives. For example, individuals can more quickly acquire a working knowledge of a foreign language and retain it longer if they spend some time living in the country where the language is spoken than if they merely take a language course in their own country.

Simply stated, application is a crucial component of the skill improvement process, but it generally takes extra effort and ingenuity to make application exercises effective and worthwhile. We encourage you to put that extra effort into improving your management skills.

Developing Management Skills is intended for individuals and students who plan to enter managerial positions or who currently manage organisations. It is also meant to help people in general manage many aspects of their lives and relationships more effectively. In fact, John Holt (1964: 165) succinctly summarised the intention of this book by equating management skill to intelligence (see also Goleman

1998; Mant 1993). When we talk about intelligence, we do not mean the ability to get a good score on a certain kind of test, or even the ability to do well in your studies; these are, at best, only indicators of something larger, deeper and far more important. By 'intelligence' we mean a style of life, a way of behaving in various situations. The true test of intelligence is not how much we know how to do, but how we behave when we do not know what to do. Fostering the development of such intelligence is the goal of *Developing Management Skills*.

Acknowledgments

The publisher would like to thank the following academics for their valuable feedback and advice for this edition:

Joanne Pimlott, University of South Australia
David Pender, University of Adelaide
Michael John Segon, RMIT University
Kylie Redfern, University of Technology, Sydney

About the authors

James Carlopio is Associate Professor of Management, Faculty of Business, Technology and Sustainable Development, Bond University, Gold Coast Queensland.

During the past twenty years he has worked on projects for numerous Australian and international corporations, such as Rio Tinto, Vodafone, the ABC, Westpac and Deloitte—and most recently in the areas of organisational and management development and strategy implementation and planning. He regularly conducts programs in organisational and personal change, strategy and technology implementation, creativity and strategy design, communication and interpersonal skills, and organisational behaviour.

James has published many articles and several books on various socio-technical issues and is a regular contributor to the Australian *Financial Review BOSS* magazine.

Graham Andrewartha is an Adjunct Research Fellow with the School of Management at the University of South Australia (UniSA). He is also a clinical and organisational psychologist and Director of the psychological and consultancy management organisation, McPhee Andrewartha.

For over 30 years, Graham has provided executive coaching, leadership and management skills development training, performance and change management, strategic planning, workplace investigation, and mediation for numerous national and international universities and organisations within both the public and private sectors, including the Asian Development Bank and AusAID.

Graham is an author of a leading managerial textbook, along with several other books and articles on communication and human resource management, and has developed an online leadership and communication tool that is utilised in Australia and overseas.

Introduction

Do management skills still matter?

To answer this question let us examine some contemporary survey information and other research data on management and business.

Leaders and job satisfaction

Starting at the top, Tusing's (2011) survey of the attitudes and perceptions of top executives in Australia found the following: while 49 per cent were satisfied with their current employer, 47.4 per cent indicated they were likely to look for new opportunities within the next year; 42.5 per cent said they changed jobs because work no longer engaged them or provided a challenge; and 22 per cent said they moved because they did not like their last employer. Intrinsic benefits were valued more highly than extrinsic rewards, such that a majority of 36.6 per cent considered work/life balance as most important, compared to only 14.2 per cent who valued a generous base salary most highly. Workplace bullying was encountered by 31.5 per cent, and workplace discrimination in general was encountered by 55.4 per cent, at least once in their work-life. Finally, 50.9 per cent thought training was essential to progress their career, but were not satisfied with the resources provided by their employers.

An Aon Hewitt report (*HR Leader*, April 2011) found that only 51 per cent of workers said they agreed, or strongly agreed, that their boss was an effective leader. No particular style of leadership was favoured, the respondents instead indicating that they preferred a more individualised approach. (See the discussion of matching in Chapter 1.) This dissatisfaction was considered to be contributing to a significant loss of productivity.

Workers and job satisfaction

'Most Australian workers want to quit their jobs' was the headline by staff writers in News.com.au on 16 March 2011. The article suggested that job satisfaction is at a new low, with 82 per cent of Australian workers wanting a new job. Interestingly, men want as much flexibility in the workplace as women. Longer hours, inadequate resources and a reluctance by organisations to increase salaries are factors driving workers to hand in their resignation, according to a Careerone.com.au survey.

Tingwell (2011: 1) found that the intense focus being placed on profit by organisations in the post global financial crisis environment is taking its toll on worker satisfaction and loyalty:

> *Australian workers are less satisfied with their jobs across all the measures used in the research not only compared to last year but even since 2008. Women are traditionally more active in pursuing new roles, however 54 per cent of workers on the move in the past year were men, the research shows. For the first time in the history of our four-year research we are seeing flexibility become a unisex desire among job hunters, including highly educated and qualified men.*

In a separate study in the US and Canada, half of the respondents reported being fatigued at the end of the week, and 40 per cent of all age groups said their jobs made them depressed. A recent online survey by Linkedin and Right Management Inc. found that just 47 per cent almost always take a daily lunch break. Of the remainder, 20 per cent usually eat at their desk, 19 per cent take a break only occasionally, and 13 per cent rarely break for lunch.

In their book *Well-being*, Rath and Harter (2010) claim that two-thirds of workers are just waiting for the working day to end. The fundamental need of humans is to have a close friendship, and the authors suggest that everyone needs social time each day to increase their sense of well-being and minimise stress. They argue that the most successful managers show how much they care about what is happening in the personal lives of their people at work. Research from the National Time Accounting: The Currency of Life survey of 2008 found that, for a majority of respondents, spending time with their boss was two to four times as unpleasant as spending time with friends.

Productivity and stress

Researchers from the Department of Innovation, Industry, Science and Research (Management Matters 2011) surveyed 439 manufacturing firms in Australia to examine the link between their management practices and their productivity performance. The survey is an extension of a study developed by the London School of Economics, Stanford University and McKinsey & Co., which has assessed more than 4000 firms across 16 countries. The survey rates management based on three core components: (1) operations, (2) performance and targets, and (3) people.

The findings indicated that there is a strong positive relationship between good management practices and firm productivity. Better management is positively associated with various measures of success, including: sales, productivity, employee numbers and market valuation.

Australia ranks sixth overall among the 16 countries that have participated in the study. Australian firms were found to be relatively good at performance and operations management, but less effective at people management. Businesses with higher levels of education and skills in management and non-management positions tend to exhibit superior management performance. Finally, managers in Australian manufacturing firms were found to be poor at self-assessment, tending to overestimate their own performance.

A Gallup consulting survey conducted in 2009 suggested that about 80 per cent of people in Australian workplaces are not fully engaged at work, with a corresponding direct impact on productivity costing businesses more than $33 billion a year.

In a recent study (Rafter 2010), 81 per cent of human resource managers agreed that fatigue is a bigger problem than in years past. A workforce management and workforce software survey of 820 US companies found the major culprits are reduced headcount, lack of boundaries between home life and work, second jobs, and a culture of wanting to do it all. More than half the respondents reported feeling fatigued at the end of the workday, and at least 40 per cent said their jobs made them depressed. 'Doing more with less is a pretty unsustainable model.'

Training and management skill development

Erker and Thomas (2011) found that only 11 per cent of managers are promoted through a formal development program; 45 per cent of managers described their first year as 'challenging'; 57 per cent say they learned their leadership skills through trial and error; only 56 per cent of managers in their first year have a good understanding of the job; and 30 per cent of managers spend most of their time on administrative tasks, compared to 15 per cent on coaching direct reports and 18 per cent on execution.

Global scandals

McManus and White (2008) argue that the moral obligations of corporations have escalated following the failure of financial services firm Lehman Brothers and scandals involving companies such as

Adelphia Communications, Bernard L. Madoff Investment Securities LLC, Arthur Andersen, Enron and WorldCom. They suggest that moral obligations and business ethics are an integral and important part of the strategic management process and management skills.

These sorts of issues are challenging and demanding even more effective skills from managers. Financial pressures and poor behaviours tempt firms to consider reactive downsizing and other superficial cost-cutting measures. The rapid spread of smart phones, iPads and all forms of electronic communication increase the blurring of lines between work and home, as well as the blurring of lines between privacy and business. Laws to punish bullying and harassment are being formulated as a direct result of perceived increases in these practices in our organisations. The trite mantra of 'work smarter not harder' is only increasing the pressure and distress for employees, as well as reducing the amount of time and thoughtfulness that goes into effective strategic planning and performance management. Increasingly, chief executives are recruited, retained or fired on a very short-term goal of return on investment. These CEOs and other executives also often bring with them a small team from their previous firms, so a wedge of a new culture is driven into the firm that hires them. More chief executives and senior managers are heavily pressured from both sides; from their boards and bosses on the one hand, and from their subordinates and employees on the other. These issues require foundation principles of managerial skills and behaviour from which to take effective decisions and actions.

Observations by Sutton (2010) on his best leader beliefs are a good introduction to the leadership character behind the management skills portrayed in the rest of this book:

- *I have a flawed and incomplete understanding of what it feels like to work for me.*
- *My success—and that of my people—depends largely on being the master of obvious and mundane things, not on magical, obscure, or breakthrough ideas or methods.*
- *Having ambitious and well-defined goals is important, but it is useless to think about them much. My job is to focus on the small wins that enable my people to make a little progress every day.*
- *One of the most important, and most difficult, parts of my job is to strike the delicate balance between being too assertive and not assertive enough.*
- *My job is to serve as a human shield, to protect my people from external intrusions, distractions, and idiocy of every stripe—and to avoid imposing my own idiocy on them as well.*
- *I strive to be confident enough to convince people that I am in charge, but humble enough to realize that I am often going to be wrong.*
- *I aim to fight as if I am right, and listen as if I am wrong—and to teach my people to do the same thing.*
- *One of the best tests of my leadership—and my organization—is 'what happens after people make a mistake?'*
- *Innovation is crucial to every team and organization. So my job is to encourage my people to generate and test all kinds of new ideas. But it is also my job to help them kill off all the bad ideas we generate, and most of the good ideas, too.*
- *Bad is stronger than good. It is more important to eliminate the negative than to accentuate the positive.*
- *How I do things is as important as what I do.*
- *Because I wield power over others, I am at great risk of acting like an insensitive jerk—and not realizing it.*

A recent definition of global leadership is 'influence across national and cultural boundaries' (Mobley & Dorfman 2003: 3). Influence skills are the building blocks of broad management and leadership styles, which understandably vary across cultures. It is this aspect of influence and 'best fit' in teams, inside organisations, within our culture and between our nations that is sorely needed. Global leadership relies in part on creating a 'teachable point of view', and leadership development must include communication learning (quoted in Boudreau, Ramstad & Dowling 2003: 68), which is what Maturana and Varela (1987) call 'structural coupling'.

Developing management skills is like the Chinese proverb: Unless you keep rowing the boat forwards, the current will take you backwards. You cannot stand still, only go forwards or backwards (Mobley & Dorfman 2003: xiii).

There is an overwhelming need for ethical relationships, trust and effective people-management skills as a fundamental part of business life. Fukuyama (1996: 21) says:

> *We know now, however, that in any information society neither governments nor corporations will rely exclusively on formal bureaucratic rules to organize people. Instead they will decentralize and devolve power, and rely on the people over whom they have nominal authority to be self-organizing. The precondition for such self-organization is internalized rules and norms of behavior, a fact that suggests that the world of the 21st century will depend heavily on such informal norms.... Social virtues such as honesty, reciprocity, and the keeping of commitments are not worthwhile just as ethical values; they also have a dollar value and help the groups that practice them to achieve shared ends.*

Organisational culture and individual culture are again being considered. The fact that organisations are centres of human social contact is being rediscovered. The organisation is itself a community. This is sometimes overlooked by its executives and leaders, but never by the employees. The fundamental issue, regardless of organisation, system, country, gender or race, is how to work productively and professionally with our fellow human beings. For 'with management comes the responsibility and excitement of realising the human potential in one's organisation' (Van der Heijden 1997: 1).

The core competency for good mature management is the use of *matching*. The word 'competence' means 'to be suitable or fit'. 'Matching' means finding 'a person who equals or resembles another, or who fits with another'. Being able to fit in and be effective, given the diversity and changing complexity alluded to above, is the fundamental skill that is addressed in this book.

Contemporary management skills enable managers to achieve world-class organisational performance. The emphasis is on 'soft' skills as much as 'hard' skills—personal abilities and interpersonal skills are to the forefront. The development of a continuous, on-the-job, experiential learning program is emphasised, rather than rote learning; a superficial four-step technique to being a successful manager is *not* presented. The main focus is on developing adaptable, flexible distinctions about how to handle continuously changing human interactions in the workplace.

There are several misconceptions about management. For example: 'management is neat and definable', 'management is soft and easy', 'managers are not important', 'management is only about productivity and controlling resources' and 'people are just a means to an end'. For most of us, work is the main place for interpersonal relationships. Consistent, close human contact is a significant feature and requirement of our workplaces. The amount of time shared with family and friends has dramatically diminished in relation to the time we spend interacting with our work colleagues. It is inescapable that the practice of management primarily involves the handling of these personal interactions. Management is strategic, thoughtful influence through goal setting and motivation to ensure the achievement of the organisation's objectives.

Improving management skills

The *Macquarie Dictionary* (1991) defines 'manage' as 'to bring about; to succeed in accomplishing; to take charge or care of; to dominate or influence (a person) by tact, address or artifice; to handle, direct, govern, or control in action or use; to succeed in accomplishing a task, purpose, etc.; to contrive to get along'. The term has its origins in Latin and Italian, where it refers to the management of horses: *maneggio* means a riding school and the literal sense is a handling, from *manum*, the hand. 'Skill' is defined as 'the ability that comes from knowledge, practice, aptitude; to do something well, or competent excellence in performance or understanding'. Essentially, management is concerned with handling the problems of people. It is social psychology. As Peter Block (1993) says, it is a question of stewardship. For Goleman (1998), it is a matter of emotional intelligence.

The context for management practice includes all organisations: private business, government, family, sports, religious and not for profit. *Developing Management Skills* reflects all these meanings and contexts. It is the intention of the authors that when you complete this book you will have acquired excellence in management performance, so that you will be able to bring about successful outcomes in your organisation. The fundamental goal of managers is to recruit and promote excellent people, enable excellent performance of individuals and teams, and collaborate effectively with other stakeholders inside and outside the organisation.

Changes in structural and personal relationships in our workplaces have resulted in confusion about goals and directions. Leadership is required not just at the top of the organisation but from every employee, especially managers. Most importantly, management skill development must meet continuously changing organisational needs and goals.

Developing highly competent management skills is much more complicated than developing the skills associated with a trade (for example, welding) or a sport (for example, kicking goals). Management skills are:

- linked to a more complex knowledge base than other types of skills
- inherently connected to interaction with other (frequently unpredictable) individuals.

A standardised approach to welding or kicking goals might be feasible, but no standardised approach to managing human beings is possible.

Management is a professional practice that is the foundation of organisational success. Evidence suggests that many managers are not as competent as they need to be in the area of people skills. This criticism does not mean that organisations should throw managers out with the structural bath water. Reactive downsizing and reorganisation are short-sighted at best (see Cascio 1993). The findings about managers' skills in recent research, however, do support the purpose of this book: to provide comprehensive development in a range of people-management skills to increase the effectiveness of managers.

Skills improve through practice. Any approach to developing management skills, therefore, must involve a significant element of practical application. At the same time, practice without the necessary conceptual knowledge is sterile, ignoring the need for flexibility and adaptation to different situations. Developing skill competency is inherently tied to both conceptual learning and behavioural practice.

The method that has been found most successful in helping individuals develop management skills is based on social learning theory (Bandura 1977; Davis & Luthans 1980). This approach combines rigorous conceptual knowledge with opportunities to practise and apply observable behaviours. Variations on this general approach have been used widely in on-the-job supervisory training programs (Goldstein & Sorcher 1974) as well as in allied professional education classrooms such as teacher development and social work (Rose, Crayner & Edleson 1977; Singleton, Spurgeon & Stammers 1980). This learning style is similar to adult learning principles or the action learning propounded by Reg Revans (1982).

As originally formulated, this learning model consisted of four steps:

- the presentation of behavioural principles or action guidelines, generally using traditional instruction methods
- demonstration of the principles by means of cases, films, scripts or incidents
- opportunities to practise the principles through role-plays or exercises
- feedback on performance from peers, instructors or experts.

'Most of what managers learn derives from the context of the management job itself' and 'One must learn by doing the thing; for though you think you know it, you have no certainty until you try' (Karpin 1995: 78, 83).

The authors' own experience in teaching complex management skills has convinced them that three important modifications are necessary for this model to be most effective. First, the behavioural principles must be grounded in social science theory and in reliable research results. Common-sense generalisations and panacea-like prescriptions appear regularly in the popular management literature. To ensure the validity of the behavioural guidelines being prescribed, the learning approach must include scientifically based knowledge about the effects of the management principles being presented.

Second, individuals must be aware of their current level of skill competency and be motivated to improve on that level in order to benefit from the model. Most people receive very little feedback about their current level of skill competency. Most organisations provide some kind of annual or semi-annual evaluation (for example, grades in university or performance appraisal interviews in firms), but these evaluations are almost always infrequent and narrow in scope, and they fail to assess performance in most critical skill areas. To help a person understand what skills to improve and why, an assessment activity must be part of the model.

In addition, most people find change uncomfortable and therefore avoid taking the risk to develop new behaviour patterns. Assessment activity in the learning model helps to encourage people to change by illuminating their strengths and limitations. People then know where their limitations lie and what things need to be improved. In this book, assessment activities take the form of self-evaluation instruments, case studies, or problems that help to highlight personal strengths and limitations in a particular skill area.

Third, an application component is needed in the learning model. Most management skill training takes place in a classroom setting where feedback is immediate and it is relatively safe to try out new behaviours and make mistakes. Transferring this learning to an actual job setting is often problematic. Application exercises help to apply classroom learning to examples from the real world of management. Application exercises often take the form of an outside-of-class intervention, a consulting assignment or a problem-centred intervention, which the student then analyses to determine its degree of success or failure.

In summary, evidence suggests that a five-step learning model is the most effective for helping individuals to develop management skills (see Cameron & Whetten 1984). The following table outlines such a model.

TABLE 0.1 A model for developing management skills

Components	Contents	Objectives
1 Skill assessment	Survey instruments Role-plays	Assess current level of skill competence and knowledge; create readiness to change.
2 Skill learning	Written text	Teach correct principles and present a rationale for behavioural guidelines.
3 Skill analysis	Cases	Provide examples of appropriate and inappropriate skill performance. Analyse behavioural principles and reasons they work.
4 Skill practice	Exercises	Practise behavioural guidelines. Adapt principles to personal style. Receive feedback and assistance.
5 Skill application	Assignments (behavioural and written)	Transfer classroom learning to real-life situations. Foster ongoing personal development.

Step 1 involves the assessment of current levels of skill competency and knowledge of the behavioural principles. Step 2 consists of the presentation of validated, scientifically based principles and guidelines for effective skill performance. Step 3 is an analysis step in which models or cases are made available in order to analyse behavioural principles in real organisational settings. This step also helps to demonstrate how the behavioural guidelines can be adapted to different personal styles and circumstances. Step 4 consists of practice exercises in which experimentation can occur and immediate feedback can be received in a relatively safe environment. Step 5 is the application of the skill to a real-life setting outside the classroom, with follow-up analysis of the relative success of that application. One part of this is the application of the skill to real human resource issues in the organisation.

Research on the effectiveness of training programs using this general learning model has shown that it produces results superior to those based on the traditional lecture–discussion approach (Burnaska 1976; Latham & Saari 1979; Moses & Ritchie 1976; Porras & Anderson 1981; Smith 1976). 'Learning' is often resisted by managers because it is not seen as directly related to performance and productivity. But this view is changing. Dr Peter Honey sees learning itself as an area of competence that underlies all others—it is the most fundamental skill. He believes that 'learning from experience is the most important of all the life skills' (Karpin 1995: 1112).

One way of helping managers to understand their own learning is to understand the learning cycle. The HONEY learning cycle is based on action (having an experience), reflection (reviewing and pondering on that experience), knowledge (reaching conclusions) and planning (planning to do something better). Implementation becomes the next experience (Karpin 1995: 1114). The model of learning in this book reflects a similar approach. Abundant research shows that managers will learn a lot more if they understand their own learning style and how to maximise learning from opportunities provided by their work roles. This is combined with the skill development process of each chapter, which emphasises practising management skills in order to achieve an integrated range of management competencies in the work context. The book has been organised with this specific approach in mind.

References

Preface and Introduction

Australian (from correspondents in London), 'Bosses perceived as poor decision makers', 6 August 2007, p. 16.

Australian Financial Review (AAP Report), 'Workers give their bosses poor appraisals', 3 August 2007.

Bandura, A. 1977, *A Social Learning Theory* (Englewood Cliffs, NJ: Prentice Hall) (New York, Harper & Row, 1985).

Block, P. 1993, *Stewardship: Choosing Service over Self-interest* (San Francisco: Berrett-Koehler Publishers).

Boudreau, J. W., P. M. Ramstad and P. J. Dowling 2003, 'Global talentship: Toward a decision science connecting talent to global strategic success', in W. H. Mobley and P. W. Dorfman, *Advances in Global Leadership*, vol. 3 (Oxford, UK: Elsevier Science Ltd), pp. 63–100.

Boyatzis, R. E. 1982, *The Competent Manager* (New York: Wiley).

Burnaska, R. F. 1976, 'The effects of behavioral modeling training upon managers' behavior and employees' perceptions', *Personnel Psychology*, 29, pp. 329–35.

Cameron, K. S. and D. A. Whetten 1984, 'A model for teaching management skills', *Organizational Behavior Teaching Journal*, 8, pp. 21–27.

Carnevale, A. P., L. J. Gainer and A. S. Meltzer 1989, *Workplace Basics: The Skills Employers Want* (US Department of Labor Employment and Training Administration).

Cascio, W. 1993, 'Downsizing: What do we know? What have we learned?', *Academy of Management Executive*, 7(1), pp. 95–104.

Davis, T. W. and F. Luthans 1980, 'A social learning approach to organizational behavior', *Academy of Management Review*, 5, pp. 281–90.

Dowd, K. O. and J. Liedtka 1994, 'What corporations seek in MBA hires: A survey', *Magazine of the Graduate Management Admission Council*, Winter.

Erker, S. and Thomas, B. 2011, 'Finding the first rung: A study on the challenges facing today's frontline leader' (DDI).

Fukuyama, F. 1996, *Trust: The Social Virtues and the Creation of Prosperity* (New York: The Free Press).

Goldstein, A. P. and M. Sorcher 1974, *Changing Supervisor Behavior* (New York: Pergamon).

Goleman, D. 1998, *Working with Emotional Intelligence* (New York: Bantam).

Holt, J. 1964, *How Children Fail* (New York: Pitman).

Karpin, D. S. 1995, *Enterprising Nation: Report of the Industry Task Force on Leadership and Management Skills* (Canberra: Australian Government Publishing Service).

Latham, G. P. and L. P. Saari 1979, 'Application of social learning theory to training supervisors through behavioral modeling', *Journal of Applied Psychology*, 64, pp. 239–46.

McManus, J. and D. White 2008, 'A governance perspective', *Journal of Management Services*, 52(3), pp. 14–20.

Macquarie Dictionary, The 1991 (ed. A. Delbridge et al.), 2nd ed. (Sydney: Macquarie Library).

Management Matters in Australia Study Fact Sheet 2011 (Department of Innovation, Industry, Science and Research).

Mant, A. 1993, *Leaders We Deserve* (Carlton, Vic: Australian Commission for the Future).

Maturana, H. and F. Varela 1987, *The Tree of Knowledge: The Biological Roots of Human Understanding* (Boston: Shambhala Publications Inc.).

Mobley, W. H. and P. W. Dorfman (eds) 2003, *Advances in Global Leadership*, vol. 3 (Oxford, UK: Elsevier Science Ltd).
Moses, J. L. and R. J. Ritchie 1976, 'Supervisory relationships training: A behavioral evaluation of a behavioral modeling program', *Personnel Psychology*, 29, pp. 337–43.
Porras, J. I. and B. Anderson 1981, 'Improving managerial effectiveness through modeling-based training', *Organizational Dynamics*, 9, pp. 60–77.
Rafter, M. 2010, 'The yawning of a new era', *Workforce Management Archives*, 8 December, pp. 1–30.
Rath, T. and J. Harter 2010, *Well-being: The Five Essential Elements* (New York: Gallup Press).
Revans, R. W. 1982, *The Origins and Growth of Action Learning* (Bromley, UK: Chartwell-Bratt).
Rose, S. D., J. J. Crayner and J. L. Edleson 1977, 'Measuring interpersonal competence', *Social Work*, 22, pp. 125–9.
Singleton, W. T., P. Spurgeon and R. B. Stammers 1980, *The Analysis of Social Skill* (New York: Plenum).
Smith, P. E. 1976, 'Management modeling training to improve morale and customer satisfaction', *Personnel Psychology*, 29, pp. 351–9.
Staw, B. M., L. Sandelands and J. Dutton 1981, 'Threat-rigidity effects in organizational behavior: A multi-level analysis', *Administrative Science Quarterly*, 26, pp. 501–24.
Sutton, R. 2010, *Good Boss, Bad Boss: How to Be the Best ... and Learn from the Worst* (New York: Business Plus).
Tingwell, D. 2011, 'Hidden hunters', in CareerOne.com.au's annual report (Adelaide: News Corporation).
Tusing, P. 2011, 'The perception, opinion and behaviour of executives and high-income earners in Australia', *The Executive Monitor*.
Van der Heijden, K. 1997, *Scenarios: The Art of Strategic Conversation* (Chichester, UK: John Wiley & Sons).

PART 1

PERSONAL SKILLS

CHAPTER 1

MANAGEMENT ESSENTIALS

OBJECTIVES

- **Understand the development of modern management practice and what constitutes effective management**
- **Learn the principles and nature of management**
- **Explore the ethical and cultural aspects of management practice**
- **Consider the fundamental management skill of matching**
- **Understand the importance of management assessment and development**

1

CHAPTER OUTLINE

Skill assessment

Evaluative surveys for establishing management skills
- How ethical are you?
- Personal assessment of management skills
- What does it take to be an effective manager?
- Does your organisation have a strong ethical management culture?
- Management communication skills

Skill learning

Developing the management discipline: A brief history of theorists, theories and thinking
Effective management
Principles and practice of management
Leadership and management
Ethical management
Cross-cultural management considerations
Management and productivity
Matching skills for managers
Management assessment: The start of management skill development

Skill analysis

Case study involving management skills
- The best candidate

Skill practice

Exercise in applying management skills
- Asian Electronics' in-basket
- Ethics code
- Ethics case studies

Skill application
- Application plan and evaluation

Scoring keys and supplementary materials

References

Skill assessment

Evaluative surveys for establishing management skills

Tip: These surveys at the beginning of each chapter in the book are designed to maximise your learning and the development of your management skills. Some of the questions are probing and personal. Thoughtful, accurate and honest answers will increase your learning and development.

How ethical are you?

Given how critical management ethics has become, we commence the book with an ethics skill assessment.

Complete the answers to this survey. The survey is difficult to answer because it goes to the heart of our subtle internal thoughts and reactions. Be very honest and thoughtful about these questions. When answering, consider your internal response and your unspoken thoughts and feelings, rather than your intentions or behaviour.

Rating scale
1 Almost never
2 Rarely
3 Sometimes
4 Mostly
5 Almost always

______ 1. I tend to react to people according to their appearance.
______ 2. I feel a little uncomfortable if the person I am speaking to is too tall (short, fat, young, strongly accented, hesitant, and so on).
______ 3. I prefer to speak to people who have similar interests to me in sport, politics and the arts.
______ 4. I tend to avoid people in the organisation who seem a bit on the outer.
______ 5. On a selection panel I tend to favour an applicant I feel comfortable with.
______ 6. An unresolved argument with a colleague in the past would get in the way of me offering them a new work opportunity.
______ 7. I believe that my contribution in a workgroup is more significant than others really appreciate.
______ 8. I tend to work harder and more skilfully than most of my colleagues.

Scoring keys for each of these surveys are found at the end of the chapter, beginning on page 43.

In relation to the ethics survey, you may also wish to access the Implicit Association Test (IAT) developed by Tony Greenwald, Professor of Psychology, University of Washington, at <www.buster.cs.yale.edu/implicit> or <www. tolerance.org/hidden_bias/index.html>.

Personal assessment of management skills

Step 1: To get an overall profile of your level of skill competence, respond to the following statements using the rating scale below. Please rate your behaviour as it is, not as you would like it to be. If you have not engaged in a certain activity, answer according to how you think you would behave, based on your experience in similar activities. Be realistic; this instrument is designed to help you tailor your learning to your specific needs. After you have completed the survey, the scoring key at the end of the chapter (page 43) will help you to generate an overall profile of your management skill strengths and weaknesses.

Step 2: Use copies of the associates' version of this instrument. An alternative version has been provided on page 44 that uses 'he or she' instead of 'I' in the questions. Give copies to at least three people who know you well or who have observed you in a managerial situation. They should complete the instrument by rating your behaviour. Bring the completed surveys back to class and compare your own ratings to your associates' ratings, your associates' ratings to the ratings received by others in the class, and the ratings you received to those of a national norm group.

Subsections of this instrument appear in each chapter throughout the book.

Rating scale

1 Strongly disagree
2 Disagree
3 Slightly disagree
4 Slightly agree
5 Agree
6 Strongly agree

In regard to my level of self-knowledge:

______ 1. I seek information about my strengths and weaknesses from others as a basis for self-improvement.

______ 2. In order to improve, I am willing to share my beliefs and feelings with others.

______ 3. I am very much aware of my preferred style in gathering information and making decisions.

______ 4. I have a good sense of how I cope with situations that are ambiguous and uncertain.

______ 5. I have a well-developed set of personal standards and principles that guide my behaviour.

When faced with stressful or time-pressured situations:

______ 6. I use effective time-management methods such as keeping track of my time, making to-do lists and setting task priorities.

______ 7. I frequently confirm my priorities so that less important things do not drive out more important things.

______ 8. I maintain a program of regular exercise for fitness.

______ 9. I maintain an open, trusting relationship with someone with whom I can share my frustrations.

______ 10. I know and practise several temporary relaxation techniques such as deep breathing and muscle relaxation.

______ 11. I strive to redefine problems as opportunities for improvement.

When I approach a typical, routine problem:

______ 12. I always define clearly and explicitly what the problem is.

______ 13. I always generate more than one alternative solution to the problem.

______ 14. I keep problem-solving steps distinct; that is, I make sure that the processes of formulating definitions, generating alternatives and finding solutions are separated.

When faced with a complex or difficult problem that does not have a straightforward solution:

______ 15. I try to be flexible in the way I approach the problem; I do not just rely on conventional wisdom or past practice.

______ 16. I try to unfreeze my thinking by asking lots of questions about the nature of the problem.

______ 17. I frequently use metaphors or analogies to help me analyse the problem and discover what else it is like.

______ 18. I strive to look at problems from different perspectives so as to generate multiple definitions.

______ 19. I do not evaluate the merits of each alternative solution to the problem until I have generated many alternatives.

When trying to foster more creativity and innovation among those with whom I work:

______ 20. I make sure there are divergent points of view represented in every problem-solving group.

______ 21. I try to acquire information from customers regarding their preferences and expectations.

______ 22. I provide recognition not only to those who are idea champions but also to those who support others' ideas and who provide resources to implement them.

______ 23. I encourage informed rule breaking in pursuit of creative solutions.

In situations where I have to provide negative feedback or offer corrective advice:

______ 24. I help others recognise and define their own problems when I counsel them.

______ 25. I understand clearly when it is appropriate to offer advice and direction to others and when it is not.

______ 26. I always give feedback that is focused on problems and solutions, not on personal characteristics.

______ 27. My feedback is always specific and to the point, rather than general or vague.

______ 28. I am descriptive in giving negative feedback to others—that is, I objectively describe events, their consequences and my feelings about them.

______ 29. I take responsibility for my statements and point of view by using, for example, 'I have decided' instead of 'They have decided'.

______ 30. I convey flexibility and openness to conflicting opinions when presenting my point of view, even when I feel strongly about it.

______ 31. I do not talk down to those who have less power or less information than I.

______ 32. I do not dominate conversations with others.

In a situation where it is important to obtain more power:

______ 33. I always put forth more effort and take more initiative than expected in my work.

______ 34. I am continually upgrading my skills and knowledge.

______ 35. I strongly support organisational ceremonial events and activities.

______ 36. I form a broad network of relationships with people at all levels throughout the organisation.

______ 37. In my work I consistently strive to generate new ideas, initiate new activities and minimise routine tasks.

______ 38. I consistently send personal notes to others when they accomplish something significant or when I pass along important information to them.

______ 39. I refuse to bargain with individuals who use high-pressure negotiation tactics.

______ 40. I always avoid using threats or demands to impose my will on others.

When another person needs to be motivated:

______ 41. I always determine if the person has the necessary resources and support to succeed in a task.

______ 42. I use a variety of rewards to reinforce exceptional performances.

______ 43. I design task assignments to make them interesting and challenging.

______ 44. I make sure that the person gets timely feedback from those affected by task performance.

______ 45. I always help the person establish performance goals that are challenging, specific and time-bound.

______ 46. Only as a last resort do I attempt to reassign or release a poorly performing individual.

______ 47. I consistently discipline when effort is below expectations and capabilities.
______ 48. I make sure that people feel fairly and equitably treated.
______ 49. I provide immediate compliments and other forms of recognition for meaningful accomplishments.

When I see someone doing something that needs correcting:
______ 50. I avoid making personal accusations and attributing self-serving motives to the other person.
______ 51. I encourage two-way interaction by inviting the respondent to express his or her perspective and to ask questions.
______ 52. I make a specific request, detailing a more acceptable option.

When someone complains about something I have done:
______ 53. I show genuine concern and interest, even when I disagree.
______ 54. I seek additional information by asking questions that provide specific and descriptive information.
______ 55. I ask the other person to suggest more acceptable behaviours.

When two people are in conflict and I am the mediator:
______ 56. I do not take sides but remain neutral.
______ 57. I help the parties generate multiple alternatives.
______ 58. I help the parties find areas on which they agree.

In situations where I have an opportunity to empower others:
______ 59. I help people feel competent in their work by recognising and celebrating their small successes.
______ 60. I provide regular feedback and needed support.
______ 61. I try to provide all the information that people need to accomplish their tasks.
______ 62. I exhibit caring and personal concern for each person with whom I have dealings.

When delegating work to others:
______ 63. I specify clearly the results I desire.
______ 64. I specify clearly the level of initiative I want others to take (for example, wait for directions, do part of the task and then report, do the whole task and then report, and so forth).
______ 65. I allow participation by those accepting assignments regarding when and how the work will be done.
______ 66. I avoid upward delegation by asking people to recommend solutions, rather than merely asking for advice or answers when a problem is encountered.
______ 67. I follow up and maintain accountability for delegated tasks on a regular basis.

When I am attempting to build and lead an effective team:
______ 68. I help team members establish a foundation of trust among one another and between themselves and me.
______ 69. I help members learn to play roles that assist the team in accomplishing its tasks as well as building strong interpersonal relationships.
______ 70. I encourage a win-win philosophy in the team—that is, when one member wins, every member wins.
______ 71. I encourage the team to achieve dramatic breakthrough innovations as well as small continuous improvements.
______ 72. I manage difficult team members effectively, through supportive communication, collaborative conflict management and empowerment.

What does it take to be an effective manager?

The purpose of this exercise is to help you gain an in-depth picture of the role of a manager and the skills required to perform that job successfully.

Your assignment is to interview at least three managers who are employed full-time. You should use the questions below in your interviews, but you are not restricted to them. The purpose of these interviews is to give you a chance to learn about critical managerial skills from those who have to use them.

Please treat the interviews as confidential. The names of the individuals do not matter—only their opinions, perceptions and behaviours. Assure the managers that no one will be able to identify them from their responses.

Keep notes on your interviews. These notes should be as detailed as possible so you can reconstruct the interviews for your class. Be sure to keep a record of each person's job title and a brief description of his or her organisation.

1. Please describe a typical day at work.
2. What are the most critical problems you face as a manager?
3. What are the most critical skills needed to be a successful manager in your line of work?
4. What are the main reasons managers fail in positions like yours?
5. What are the outstanding skills or abilities of other effective managers you have known?
6. If you had to train someone to replace you in your current job, what key abilities would you focus on?
7. On a scale of 1 (very rarely) to 5 (constantly), can you rate the extent to which you use the following skills or behaviours during your workday?
   ______ Managing personal stress
   ______ Managing time
   ______ Facilitating group decision making
   ______ Making personal decisions
   ______ Recognising or defining problems
   ______ Using verbal communication skills
   ______ Appraising others' performance
   ______ Motivating others
   ______ Managing conflict
   ______ Personal reflection
   ______ Gaining and using power
   ______ Orchestrating change
   ______ Delegating
   ______ Setting goals
   ______ Listening
   ______ Counselling others
   ______ Interviewing
   ______ Empathising
   ______ Team building
   ______ Solving problems
   ______ Conducting meetings
   ______ Negotiating

Does your organisation have a strong ethical management culture?

Rate your organisation for each of the following questions.

Rating scale
1 Almost never
2 Rarely
3 Sometimes
4 Mostly
5 Almost always

______ 1. People at all levels are encouraged and supported to speak openly and honestly about what they think.
______ 2. There is genuine conversation—managers listen to what people say.
______ 3. Many people are encouraged to take the lead and express their ideas and visions, and managers are responsive to these new ideas.
______ 4. Values, goals and actions are determined and shared by people at all levels of the organisation.
______ 5. Each manager is a reflection and example of the vision, mission and values shared by people at all levels in the organisation.
______ 6. Managers are genuinely committed to learning and building their expertise.
______ 7. People at all levels are acknowledged and valued as individual members and contributors.
______ 8. People's plans and actions within the organisation are motivated by their common values and shared vision.
______ 9. The organisation succeeds primarily because of the vision and empowerment of people at all levels.
______ 10. People at all levels understand their key responsibilities. People are encouraged to think for themselves and take responsible action based on what they understand to be important for the organisation's success.
______ 11. As long as their intentions and actions are mostly in the right direction, people are allowed to make mistakes. Mistakes are considered important feedback for how to improve, and people are prepared to try something and then assess its effectiveness.
______ 12. People's plans and actions within the organisation are primarily motivated by their alignment with common values and passion to reach a shared vision.

Source: Adapted from A. Deering, R. Dilts and J. Russell, 'Leadership cults and cultures', *Leader to Leader*, 28, Spring 2003, pp. 36–43.

Management communication skills

Answer the following questions:

Rating scale
1 None of the time
2 Some of the time
3 A lot of the time
4 All the time

______ 1. I watch people closely when I talk with them.
______ 2. I put a lot of energy into my communication.
______ 3. I think about the best way to make myself understood.
______ 4. I pay attention to the speed of the person's communication.
______ 5. I get a sense of the other person before raising my proposition.
______ 6. I use some of the way they see the world in my communication with them.
______ 7. I plan what I want to say before my meeting.
______ 8. I plan the way I want to present my communication before the meeting.
______ 9. I consciously adjust my presentation style according to the nature of the other person's communication.
______ 10. I am comfortable with silence during my discussions.
______ 11. I feel good about myself when I am talking with others.
______ 12. I attempt to give the other person a sense of their worth when I talk to them.
______ 13. I am curious about the other person's presentation.
______ 14. I am patient in my communication.
______ 15. Later on, I reflect back positively on my communications.

Skill learning

Developing the management discipline: A brief history of theorists, theories and thinking

So much of what we call management consists in making it difficult for people to work.

—Peter Drucker (1967)

In this opening section we will trace the origins of management thinking from its roots in 2000-year-old philosophy to contemporary theories of management. A more comprehensive picture of some of this material is available in *The History of Management Thought* by Daniel Wren (2005).

As Drucker (1998: 4) has said, 'Basic assumptions about reality are the paradigms of a social science. These assumptions about reality determine what the discipline focuses on.' Given that management is a social science first and foremost, its reality is shaped and focused by the theorists and authors who have contributed to its history. Management and leadership had its origins in the armed forces and started with an analysis of ways of defeating the enemy—the derivation of the word 'strategy' (Wren 2005: 377). Confucius, Lao Tzu, Empress Wu Zetian, Agamemnon, Hannibal, Alexander the Great, Genghis Khan and Machiavelli were all precursors of modern management thought.

The East has made significant contributions to management thought. In the work of Confucius there is a rich foundation for contemporary management practice. For excellence in governance, Confucius identified five qualities to pursue and four evils to avoid. The qualities were: (1) being generous without having to spend; (2) making people work without making them groan; (3) having ambition but no rapacity; (4) having authority but no arrogance; and (5) being stern but not fierce. The evils were: (1) terror, which rests on ignorance; (2) tyranny, which expects results without proper preparation; (3) extortion, which is achieved through contradictory directions; and (4) bureaucracy, which denies people their rightful entitlements (Leys 1997: 100).

The Tao is more than 2000 years old but is still relevant today. Twelve management abilities identified in the Tao are:

- Know the character of people.
- Handle people with respect.
- Focus on the core business.
- Be well organised.
- Be agile and flexible.
- Be diligent and prudent.
- Choose the best person for the job.
- Articulate clearly.
- Be shrewd in acquisition.
- Solve problems and handle conflicts effectively.
- Initiate and lead by example.
- Be far-sighted. (Wee 2001: 8)

It is instructive to contrast these management abilities with the key skills identified in this book. The Eastern way is a philosophical and indirect means of imparting knowledge compared to the Western way of teaching people how to manage in an analytical and systematic manner. But voices in the West, too, have been raised against this 'dictatorship of reason' (Saul 1993).

The first systematic application of management principles in the West was, according to Drucker (1998), the reorganisation of the US Army in 1901 by Elihu Root, Theodore Roosevelt's Secretary of War. The first management congress was held in Prague in 1922 and was organised by Herbert Hoover (then US Secretary of Commerce) and Thomas Masaryk (the founding president of the new Czechoslovak Republic). In Europe and the United States, the first management theorists were practising businesspeople such as John D. Rockefeller Sr, J. P. Morgan and Andrew Carnegie. The first job to which the term 'manager' in its present meaning was applied was not in business but was the large city manager or city administrator. The first truly modern corporation was General Motors, led by the first professional manager, Alfred Sloan, from 1923 to 1946.

Frederick W. Taylor (1856–1915), author of *Shop Management* and then, more famously, *Principles of Scientific Management*, became the yardstick for the scientific management discipline in the West. Taylor started the process of a systematic study that drew in other theorists, including psychologists. This was a time when the concept of organisational structure was not understood at all well. Large-scale business organisations were just beginning to develop and their managers had to create their discipline as they went along. Throughout his career, Taylor focused on 'the owners and their helpers' and not on organisational structures, and this non-organisation concept persisted well into the 20th century. Taylor and, later, Chester Barnard (in around 1938) treated business management as a subspecies of general management. A contemporary, M. L. Cooke, determined that it was not the scientific system itself, but the confidence that people had in the system, that was most important.

Meanwhile, in Europe, Henry Fayol (1841–1925) recognised the importance of management capabilities to organisational outcomes. He developed a set of principles of management and defined the basic elements of management that are common terms used today. Some of these elements included planning (unity, continuity, flexibility, precision), organising (selection, evaluation and training of personnel), command (knowledge of the staff, removing poor performers, setting a good example), coordination (harmonising and integrating) and control (precursor of quality control). Fayol saw management's overall task as guiding the enterprise towards its objectives. He also laid down the principle that there was one right structure for every enterprise, and this inhibited for a long time the concept of working with flexible structures.

Writing at the same time, Max Weber (1864–1920) focused on the size of the organisation and how it could function systematically. He stressed a systematic management practice that was logical and efficient. From him arose the concept of bureaucracy, and the word itself, as well as the beginnings of organisational theory. He suggested there were three types of authority: rational–legal authority (obedience to an established position), traditional authority (obedience to the person who occupied the position) and charismatic authority (obedience due to personal trust in the person). Only the first, he argued, ensured continuity of administration, selection based on competence and clearly defined authority. Like Taylor, Weber considered that 'management meant the exercise of control on the basis of knowledge' (Wren 1987: 194). Scientific management initiated formal analysis of management practice and established the study of organisational behaviour.

The famous experiment into workplace illumination and worker productivity in the Western Electric Company, conducted by Elton Mayo and known as the Hawthorn effect, is symbolic of the era and a legend of management theory. The Hawthorn effect (Parsons 1974) demonstrated that improved performance was not due to the scientific management method but to the impact of the research personnel themselves. It was this experiment that led to the human relations investigations of management practice and worker performance. The pendulum began to swing strongly the other way.

Mary Parker Follett (1868–1933) proposed that improved performance was related to better understanding of, and between, employees. While unpopular at the time, her views are now commonplace. Her focus was on the group in the workplace, which resulted in Gestalt psychologists and sociologists (Pareto, Alfred Marshall, Durkheim and Talcott Parsons) contributing to the theory of management. This introduced theories of group dynamics, employee participation, leadership, motivation, organisational development, social needs hierarchy and socialisation to management theory and practice. Thus the connection between people, management, organisational structure and function was formed.

The Elton Mayo School attempted to connect productivity and satisfaction around these social elements, while other theorists focused more on the organisation and its structure and function. All approaches were searching for a more definitive theory and model of management. Naturally, from the

Hawthorn experiment and the behavioural research that followed, focus was placed on dynamic leaders and the meaning, nature and origins of leadership. Likert (of Likert scale fame) suggested that leading people was the central and most significant aspect of all the tasks of management that encouraged a sense of participative or consultative management. It was his work that formed the basis for Blake and Mouton's managerial grid. The human relations movement focused on human interaction and people skills, rather than technical skills. A sense of belonging to a group was considered important, as was developing participants' feeling of sharing power in an organisation. Trust was considered important for effective management. Financial incentives were seen as significant but were not the whole picture.

After 1945, alliances and competition between the United States and Japan led to W. Edwards Deming and the quality management movement. Long-range planning came into vogue, which developed into strategic planning and then strategic management.

In 1954, Douglas McGregor asserted that managers had to choose between two, and only two, ways of managing people—the theory X and theory Y manager model. Theory X assumes that people do not want to work, so they must be coerced and controlled. Theory Y assumes that they really do want to work and require only proper motivation. Abraham H. Maslow (1908–70), famous for the hierarchy of needs pyramid, showed conclusively in his book *Eupsychian Management* that people have to be managed differently. Tannenbaum and Schmidt, Vroom and Yetton, and House and Dessler also reflect this sense of flexibility rather than one particular way of managing or leading. This is known as contingency theory—the idea that there is no one right way of managing, making decisions or doing anything. Our behaviour needs to be adjusted to best suit the situation, the people involved and other contingency factors. Different people need to be managed uniquely—which is the proposition presented in this book.

Peter Drucker is an icon of management thinking and management development. In a *Forbes* survey conducted in 2001 he was voted, by an élite group of 50 management gurus, the most significant management theorist of his time. He foreshadowed so many developments and remains the leading light of management theory. He has always written about management, not leadership, and only refers to leadership as a sub-behaviour of management. Examination of a multitude of studies on leadership indicates there is no clear or agreed understanding of what qualities actually constitute leadership (Stogdill 1974: xvii).

In one of his first works, Drucker (1954) described management as having three broad functions—namely, (1) managing the business, (2) managing managers, and (3) managing workers and work. In 1957, he was also the first writer to introduce the concept of the knowledge worker:

> *One who knows more about his or her job than anybody else in the organization.... For thousands of years, the economy was based almost exclusively on manual work ... but within the last few decades, knowledge work has become the primary economic focus. In fact, knowledge workers now account for almost half of the US workforce. This means that there have been major changes in the way work is performed. Knowledge workers face new and different challenges. (Drucker 1998: 78)*

From the interest in organisations the idea of 'fit', or a match between individuals and organisations, developed. From this naturally followed corporate culture and the ideas of culture and cultural fit. Peters and Waterman (1982) advanced the art of management over the science of management, and by this time the variety and focus of management theories had become numerous and complicated. One researcher (Koontz 1980) identified 11 schools and approaches to management:

- operational school
- managerial roles
- contingency or situational school
- empirical school
- human behaviour school (interpersonal behaviour)
- human behaviour school (group behaviour)
- sociotechnical systems

- cooperative social systems
- systems approaches
- decision theory
- management science school.

In the last decade or so, knowledge management has grown in popularity. Profiles of theories by Sveiby on tacit and explicit knowledge, Ulrich and also Huang on intellectual capital, and many others, can be found in Cortada and Woods' *The Knowledge Management Yearbook 1999–2000* (1999).

The other significant growth area linked to knowledge management that impacts directly upon management skill and practice has been the work of the organisational learning theorists, beginning with Argyris (1992) and Senge (1990). Their work has captured particularly the essence of human behaviour within an organisational system. Concepts of short-term easy fixes versus long-term intricate interventions, single- and double-loop learning, systemic error versus human error, and thinking in an integrated future-focused or systems manner have been valuable additions to the management skill set.

Kibok Baik (2003) has developed an outstanding new theory of management, called issue leadership. The crux of issue leadership theory lies in the definition of issues and their role in the leadership context. An issue is created when someone attaches significance or meaning to a situation or perceived 'problem'. Issues may be routine, incidental or innovative. Anyone can play a leader's role if he or she serves the audience better than others. The one who handles an issue the most effectively will emerge as the leader. Therefore, managers and executives of organisations need to be prepared with skills to effectively develop and handle issues in order to become leaders. The leader-versus-followers dichotomy is not useful. The concept of 'audience' means that the relationship is circular, with the leader at the centre, surrounded by the audience. The audience includes superiors, peers and subordinates in an organisation, as long as they relate to the issues at hand. A person may serve in a leadership role for one issue and play an audience role for another. Issue leadership is composed of three distinctive behaviours: (1) issue creating, (2) audience persuading, and (3) issue implementing.

Having reviewed the historical background, let us now consider what current research reveals about effective management.

Effective management

Research to identify what constitutes effective management was conducted by Cameron and Whetten (1984). (Similar results were found in Karpin's (1995) *Enterprising Nation* research.) Cameron and Whetten identified individuals who were rated as highly effective managers in their own organisations. They contacted organisations in the fields of business, health care, education and state government, and asked senior officers to name the most effective managers in their organisations. They then interviewed these managers to determine what attributes they associated with managerial effectiveness. They also reviewed studies conducted by other researchers that attempted to identify the characteristics of effective managers.

In their study, 402 highly effective managers were identified by their peers and superiors. The questions they were asked included the following:

- How have you become so successful in this organisation?
- Who fails and who succeeds in this organisation, and why?
- If you had to train someone to take your place, what knowledge and skills would you ensure that person possessed?
- If you could design an ideal course or training program to teach you to be a better manager, what would it contain?
- Think of other effective managers you know. What skills do they demonstrate that explain their success?

The analysis of the interviews produced about 60 characteristics of effective managers. The ten identified most often are listed in Table 1.1.

TABLE 1.1 The most frequently cited skills of effective managers

1. Verbal communication (including listening)
2. Managing time and stress
3. Managing individual decisions
4. Recognising, defining and solving problems
5. Motivating and influencing others
6. Delegating
7. Setting goals and articulating a vision
8. Self-awareness
9. Team building
10. Managing conflict

Notice that these ten characteristics are all behavioural skills. They are not personality attributes or styles, or generalisations such as 'luck' or 'timing'. Nor are they very surprising. The characteristics of effective managers are not a secret.

More recently, a study of 1300 American managers found a very similar skills set (Kabacoff 2002), and Kambil (2010) found there were five key traits associated with effective leaders: curiosity, courage, perseverance, personal ethics, and confidence.

Table 1.2 lists the results of several studies using a variety of respondents. Regardless of whether respondents are CEOs or first-line supervisors, or whether they work in the public or private sector, their skills are generally well marked and agreed upon by observers. It is not hard to identify and describe the skills of effective managers. More recently, research by Goleman (1998) indicated that the best-performing managers excelled in emotional competencies. This included skills such as self-awareness, empathy and emotional management. Outstanding or star performers were found to significantly outperform their peers on these types of management skills. Tellingly, poorly performing managers exhibited two compelling traits: (1) they were inflexible; and (2) they had poor people relationship skills.

Three notable aspects of management skills can be identified from this research:

- Skills are behavioural.
- Skills are paradoxical.
- Skills are interrelated.

TABLE 1.2 Identifying critical management skills: A sample of studies

STUDY/RESPONDENTS/FOCUS	RESULTS	
Prentice (1984) • 230 executives in manufacturing, retail and service firms • Critical skills for managing organisations?	Listening Communication Leadership Problem solving Time management	Interpersonal relations Formal presentations Stress management Adaptability to change
Margerison and Kakabadse (1984) • 721 chief executive officers in US corporations • Most important things you have learned in order to be a chief executive?	Communication Managing people Delegation Patience Respect Control Understanding people Evaluating personnel Tolerance Team spirit	Strategic planning Decision making Self-discipline Analytical abilities Hard work Flexibility Financial management Time management Knowledge of the business Clear thinking

STUDY/RESPONDENTS/FOCUS	RESULTS	
Margerison and Kakabadse (1984) • 721 chief executive officers in US corporations • Key management skills to develop in others to help them become senior executives?	Human relations Communication Planning and goal setting People management and leadership Teamwork	Decision making Financial management Entrepreneurial skills Delegating Broad experience
Cameron and Whetten (1984) • 50 consultants, professors, management development experts and public administrators • Critical management skills needed by state government managers?	Managing conflict Motivating others Managing stress and time Decision making Delegation	Goal setting Problem solving Job design Gaining and using power Career planning
Luthans, Rosenkrantz and Hennessey (1985) • 52 managers in three organisations • Participants' observation of skills demonstrated by most effective versus least effective managers	Managing conflict Building power and influence Communicating with outsiders	Decision making Communicating with insiders Developing employees Processing paperwork Planning and goal setting
Benson (1983) • A survey of 25 studies in business journals • A summary of the skills needed by students entering the professions	Listening Written communication Oral communication Motivating/persuading	Interpersonal skills Informational interviewing Group problem solving
Curtis, Winsor and Stephens (1989) • 428 members of the American Society of Personnel Administrators • (1) Skills needed to obtain employment? • (2) Skills important for successful job performance?	(1) Verbal communication Listening Enthusiasm Written communication Technical competence Appearance	(2) Interpersonal skills Verbal communication Written communication Persistence/determination Technical competence
• (3) Skills needed to move up in the organisation?	(3) Ability to work well with others\one-on-one Ability to gather information and make a decision Ability to work well in groups Ability to listen and give counsel Ability to give effective feedback Ability to write effective reports Knowledge of the job	 Ability to present a good image for the firm Ability to use computers Knowledge of management theory Knowledge of finance Knowledge of marketing Knowledge of accounting Ability to use business machines

Skills are behavioural

Skills are not personality attributes or stylistic tendencies. They consist of an identifiable set of actions that are performed by individuals and lead to certain outcomes. An important implication, therefore, is that individuals can learn to perform these actions and improve their current level of performance. Although people with different styles and personalities may apply the skills differently, there is, nevertheless, a core set of observable attributes of effective skill performance that is common across a range of individual differences. Effective management skills can be learned, practised and enhanced.

Skills are paradoxical

Skills are neither all soft and humanistic in orientation, nor all hard-driving and directive. They are oriented neither towards teamwork and interpersonal relations exclusively, nor towards individualism and entrepreneurship exclusively. A variety of skills is present.

To illustrate, Cameron and Tschirhart (1988) assessed the skill performance of more than 500 mid-level and upper-middle managers in about 150 organisations. They used the 25 most frequently mentioned management skills taken from Table 1.1, as well as from research by Ghiselli (1963), Katz (1974), Livingston (1971), Mintzberg (1975), and Boyatzis (1982). Through statistical analyses, Cameron and Tschirhart discovered that the skills could be sorted into four main groups.

One group of skills focused on participative and human relations skills (for example, supportive communication and team building), while another group focused on just the opposite—competitiveness and control (for example, assertiveness, power and influence skills). A third group focused on innovativeness and entrepreneurship (such as creative problem solving), while a fourth group emphasised the opposite types of skills—namely, maintaining order and rationality (for example, managing time and rational decision making).

One conclusion from this study was that effective managers are required to demonstrate paradoxical skills. That is, the most effective managers are both participative and hard-driving, both nurturing and competitive. They were able to be flexible and creative while also being controlled, stable and rational. The second characteristic associated with effective management, then, is the mastery of diverse and seemingly contradictory skills. Handy (1995) explored the complexities of paradox for managers and organisations in some detail. This is further supported by the work of Senge (1990) and Argyris (1992).

The core capability is the capacity to select and utilise the most appropriate management skills for the particular situation.

Skills are interrelated

No effective manager performs one skill or one set of skills independently of others. For example, in order to motivate others effectively, skills such as supportive communication, influence and delegation are required. To resolve a conflict in a culturally diverse team, skills such as matching, creative problem solving and change management are needed. Effective managers, therefore, develop a constellation of skills that overlap and support one another, and allow flexibility in managing diverse situations.

These three aspects are captured in a leadership skill guide adapted from the work of Michael Yapko (2009), who proposes five guidelines:

1. Your work colleagues are not just like you. A manager needs to recognise that everyone is different and has different motivations, styles, and ways of being understood. It is useful to pay attention to frames of reference, flexibility and acceptance of others.
2. Clearly define your expectations and work relationship with your colleagues. This requires a level of self-awareness, some thought about the context and the organisation's goals, as well as a careful explication of your expectations.
3. You are always on duty. As a manager, it is your job to lead. You are the model of the expected attitudes and successful outcomes. Your colleagues are not your friends or family. Be aware of your behaviour, and use it always as a model of excellent management practice.
4. Build self-awareness and encourage honest feedback. As managers we can delude ourselves about our image and about the impact we are having upon others. It is a vital element of management skills to develop and maintain good self-awareness and an understanding of how you are coming across to others. Find ways of receiving genuine feedback by a trusted colleague, 360-degree appraisal, and team and staff surveys.
5. Draw professional lines. Part of defining your expectations above should include defining carefully your personal and professional boundaries with your colleagues and then sticking to this. It is skilful to be a friendly manager but not have close friendships in the workplace.

Having considered these qualities of effective management we now identify the underlying principles of management on which this book is based.

Principles and practice of management

1. *Responsibility.* This means to take ownership of, and accept the consequences of, our actions; it means to willingly accept being answerable and accountable. In this way, we are known to be reliable. The focus in this book is on the individual manager's responsibility to develop such maturity.
2. *Self-knowledge.* This principle of management holds that the more managers are aware of their strengths and limitations, prejudices and biases, delights and disappointments, skills and abilities, the more they are able to develop flexibility and competence as managers. They can more appropriately make distinctions and handle personal and business issues that arise in the workplace. An increasing number of researchers and training organisations advocate self-knowledge as a central tool for effective leaders. As David De Vries of the Centre for Creative Leadership puts it, 'You cannot manage others until you can manage yourself' (Karpin 1995: 1211).
3. *Creating opportunities, such that the organisation's goals will be achieved.* This means that managers will be able to be direct and authoritative when the circumstances require it, and indirect and facilitative when it is appropriate. They will help to establish and encourage a workplace environment in which employees are motivated to develop their own direction, initiative and goals.
4. *The need to make mistakes.* This is a principle about management and also about learning. Effective management and effective learning can take place only where there is an understanding that errors need to occur in order to provide information that can lead to adjustments to future actions. Being wrong a few times is an essential part of the process of being right (see Schulz 2010). It is important for risk taking and initiative. Mistakes can also be in the eye of the beholder. Honest feedback is the mechanism that supports and enables this principle.
5. *All reality is subjective.* This is the managerial equivalent of fuzzy logic. It rests on the assumption that there is no black or white answer, no right or wrong option, nor a single best way. In different situations with different people there are always different approaches and techniques that can be just as successful as any other approach. It affirms that people's perceptions are their genuine beliefs about their world. Understanding ourselves and others' perceptions is crucial to effective management.
6. *People like to be liked*—good management uses this as a principle of motivation, not as an inhibitor of action. Effective managers are not swayed by the need to be liked, nor by friendships. Honest feedback that is critical is provided when needed, and positive feedback that is supportive is offered wherever possible. Goleman's research (1998) clearly demonstrates that good managers are in fact popular, but they are also fair and honest.

These principles are encapsulated in our definition of management and leadership:

The capacity to create a work environment in such a way that each person is uniquely motivated to achieve the organisational goals, and feels recognised for so doing.

Leadership and management

It is important to discuss the place of leadership in this volume. We have taken the position that management and leadership are, for all intents and purposes, the same thing. This is because of our approach to the theory of leadership and management, as much as a consequence of the research about management. Historically, as we saw above, a large number of writers have considered leadership to be a key task of management practice. Some modern writers differentiate between the concepts of 'leadership' and 'management' (Bennis 1989; Bennis & Goldsmith 1997; Kotter 1990; Nahavandi 1997; Selznick 1957; Shriberg et al. 1997; Zaleznik 1977). Leaders are supposed to be strategic and to inspire and energise their followers. Managers, on the other hand, allegedly take care of managing people and tasks, and attend to the routine details. However, Ng (2011) insists that management means 'getting things done effectively through people', and that 21st-century managers must possess all the attributes of both leaders and managers.

These varying approaches have motivated us to be clear at the outset of this volume about what we mean by 'management' and why we believe that it encompasses 'leadership' as typically defined. We subscribe to Drucker's (1998, 2001) view that management is a discipline that subsumes and incorporates leadership skills.

Traditionally, the term 'leadership' is used to describe what certain individuals do under conditions of change. Leadership can exist without an organisation, whereas management develops out of the organising of others. When organisations are dynamic and undergoing transformation, people at the top are supposed to exhibit leadership. Management, on the other hand, has traditionally been used to describe what executives do under conditions of stability. Thus, management has been linked with the status quo. In addition, leadership is sometimes defined as 'doing the right things', while management is defined as 'doing things right' (see Bennis & Nanus 1985: 21). Leaders have been said to focus on direction setting, articulating a vision and creating something new. Managers have been said to focus on monitoring, directing and refining current performance. Leadership has been equated with dynamism, vibrancy and charisma; management with hierarchy, equilibrium and control.

Such distinctions between leadership and management have no meaning in today's global and constantly changing organisational life. Managers cannot be successful without being good leaders, and leaders cannot be successful without being good managers. 'The general research conclusion is that most managers show some leadership skills, while most leaders find themselves managing at times' (Karpin 1995: 1210).

No longer do organisations and individuals have the luxury of holding on to the status quo, of worrying about doing things right but failing to do the right things, of keeping the system stable instead of leading change and improvement, of monitoring current performance instead of formulating a vision of the future, of concentrating on equilibrium and control instead of vibrancy and charisma. Effective management and leadership are inseparable. The skills required to do one are also required of the other. No organisation in a post-industrial, competitive environment will survive without executives and managers who are capable of providing both management and leadership. Effective leaders achieve optimum organisational performance by astutely combining individual competencies in their job role with developing and enhancing their managerial style in keeping with the organisational climate (*Fortune*/Hay Group 1999).

Because our circumstances are constantly changing and expectations for performance are continually escalating, the traditional definition of management is outmoded and irrelevant today. This book, therefore, focuses on management skills, because effective management subsumes effective leadership. Each skill contained in this book is just as essential for an effective leader as for an effective manager. Leadership and management, from our perspective, are indistinguishable.

Based on this introduction to effective management skills, it is now appropriate to examine the crucial aspect of ethical management.

Ethical management

A superior person thinks of what is right. An inferior person thinks only of what is profitable.

—Confucius

Without ethics there can be no effective management skills. This reality has been noted by many of the foundation management theorists discussed earlier, including Taylor, Barnard and Drucker. Early management thought and contemporary views follow Kant's moral law to always treat people as a means and never as an end in themselves. Taylor (1947: 184–5) argued:

> *No system of management, however good, should be applied in a wooden way. The proper personal relations should always be maintained between the employers and men; and even the prejudices of the workmen should be considered in dealing with them. The employer who talks to his men in a condescending or patronizing way, or else not at all, has no chance whatever of ascertaining their real thoughts or feelings. Each man*

should be encouraged to discuss any trouble which he may have, either in the works or outside, with those over him.

Drucker's (1954) theory of management centres on three ethical arguments:

1. Profits, although important, are not the purpose of business.
2. Corporations are social institutions and therefore have social responsibilities.
3. Business has special responsibilities towards its employees.

He continues:

[I]t requires of the manager that he assume responsibility for the public good, that he subordinates his actions to an ethical standard of conduct, and that he restrain his self-interest and his authority wherever their exercise would infringe upon the commonwealth and upon the freedom of the individual. (Drucker 1954: 382–3)

Drucker strongly believed that a manager was responsible first for the public good and should follow an ethical standard so as not to misuse his authority.

Schwartz (2007) suggests that management theory should not be taught without discussing both the business ethics implications and the business ethics content inherent in the theory. An understanding of both early management theory and its ethical ramifications, and business ethics issues, is essential for developing effective management skills.

Business and management theorists have tended to deviate from ethical academic theorists over the years, but the global financial crisis, the BP oil rig disaster, Enron, and many other recent displays of unethical behaviour have reinforced the importance of ethics in business as a natural part of ethics in society as a whole. Such poor behaviours and human-caused disasters arise from complex systems errors (see Dekker 2011). Managers are people working within a complex social system in the workplace within a community. An ethical foundation is the ingredient that holds diverse complex systems together and minimises the likelihood of such poor practices.

In the workplace as elsewhere in life, trust is fundamental to our relationships with each other. Integrity depends upon trust, and trust engenders ethical behaviour (Provis 2001). Every single managerial action is affected by ethical considerations. Hiring and firing, needs analysis, job description preparation, self-awareness, performance management, team development, downsizing, outsizing, rewards and recognition, occupational health and safety, team development, communication, managing conflict, task allocation, project management, decision making, change management, motivation, career development and strategic planning all require managers to behave ethically. In short, every element of this textbook on management skills is driven by, and based upon, the foundation of ethical principles.

Ethics is defined in multiple ways. A Christian definition is: 'Moral principles that govern a person's or group's behaviour.' Gowdy (2010) describes an ethic as 'a singular, logically deduced, self-created, self-chosen choice to think and behave as deemed most correct to the individual' and virtue as 'the sum creation of good ethics applied'.

Business ethics (or 'corporate ethics') considers ethical principles and moral problems that arise in a business environment. It relates to the conduct of individuals and organisations. MacDonald (2011) describes business ethics as 'the critical, structured examination of how people and institutions should behave in the world of commerce. In particular, it involves examining appropriate constraints on the pursuit of self-interest, or (for firms) profits, when the actions of individuals or firms affects others'. MacDonald sees both the critical and the structured parts of those definitions as being important. He considers ethics to be a process of examining and critiquing our moral beliefs and behaviours, and assessing which ones are more important in different contexts. It is an attempt to establish a higher-order set of principles to guide our actions:

- *Ethics is* critical *in the sense of having to do with* examining *and* critiquing *various moral beliefs and practices. ('Morality', by contrast, is just the word for the more-or-less shared collection of norms and values according to which we act and judge each other's actions.) Ethics involves looking at particular norms and values and behaviours and judging them, asking whether various norms and values are mutually contradictory, and asking which ones matter more in what sorts of situations.*

- *Ethics is* structured *in the sense that it is not just about having an opinion about how people should behave. Everyone has opinions. Ethics involves attempting, at least, to find higher-order principles and theories in an attempt to rationalise and unify our diverse moral beliefs.*

Solomon defines ethics as 'the art of mutually agreeable tentative compromise. Insisting on absolute principles is, if I may be ironic, unethical' (Solomon 1997: 11). Elsewhere, he discusses ethics in connection to values and trust:

> *Values have to be translated into action, and that means acting according to our values cannot merely be an abstract obligation but must be built into our ways of dealing with the world; that is what a virtue is, and that is what good business and business ethics is. (Solomon 1999: xix)*

The three most basic business virtues, according to Solomon, are honesty, fairness and trustworthiness.

Provis (2001) considers trust in management in more detail. While many authors argue that trust is important as a means to an end, to gain certain business outcomes, Provis postulates that trust is valuable in and of itself. In the workplace as well as in social contexts, trust is intimately associated with the quality of our relationships with those we work with and it has an impact upon the quality of our lives.

Trust not only promotes good business, but is inherently good, Provis argues. He suggests that a Balanced Scorecard analysis of work performance should incorporate the promotion of trust under one of the four perspectives discussed further in Chapter 6: (1) customer focus, (2) financial focus, (3) internal processes, and (4) people and growth.

Many authors, including Provis, identify that ethical issues are closely tied to our perceptions, judgment and reasoning. Thus, as we identified earlier, ethics underlies managerial decisions and actions of every kind.

Rawls (1971: 24, 171) states that ethical principles are, in essence, the basic rules required to maintain a good society. The rules define right and wrong and are intended to minimise harm caused to individuals and their society.

> *... the doctrine behind ethical analysis is linked to the view that ethical principles are not subjective measures that vary with cultural and economic conditions; in essence they are the basic rules or first principles to ensure a good society.*
>
> ...
>
> *Morality is concerned with the norms, values and beliefs embedded in social processes that define the right and wrong for an individual community. Moral problems are concerned with the harms caused or brought about by others, and particularly with the harms caused or brought to others in ways that are outside their own control. Harming others rarely promotes the most good, and the prevention of harm is the promotion of good in many cases.*

The prevention of harm is an ethical skill required for all managers.

Hollan (2002) suggests that ethical issues are those which relate to the grey areas between what is accepted as right and wrong. Ethical skills in his study are associated with judgment, integrity, courage and humanity. The first two skills are fundamental, but require courage to enable them. Humanity provides resilience and respect. Hollan is concerned that legalistic approaches to ethical problems fail to permit options and may in fact condone unethical behaviour.

> *The first two are considered as primary requirements for ethical decision-making and courage a necessary precursor. Humanity may contribute to judgement before a decision is made and an important element in resilience to stressors associated with both choices and consequences. The predominant use of a legalistic mode of decision-making is of some concern as it may fail to identify ethical options and condone or permit unethical behaviour. (Hollan 2002: 868)*

We consider that ethics involves the development of a principles-based knowledge of what is right and wrong, and of doing what is right. Given this understanding of ethics, it is useful now to consider the practical aspects of good ethical behaviour in the workplace.

Ethical management in practice

The work environment poses a quandary for effective managers. As Martin Luther King is said to have remarked, 'You cannot legislate the heartless.' Ethical behaviour at work, as we have seen above, is impacted by values, perceptions and culture. Legislation is in place for offensive behaviour, and recently in Victoria for offensive behaviour involving bullying and harassment. However, no rules and laws can enable ethical behaviour, but only attempt to punish unethical behaviour. As Collins and Wray-Bliss (2005: 820) observed in their study of ethics in the workplace, 'We end by being as concerned by the capacity of ethical discourse to enable and legitimise discrimination as we are reassured by its utility to enable us to discriminate right from wrong behaviour in organisations.'

The literature is full of efforts to define ethical frameworks and guidelines. Human resource management efforts abound in developing codes of conduct, enterprise bargaining agreements, guides for recruitment and selection, performance management, and so on. As a basic minimum, a good manager needs to operate in an organisational environment where there are human resource management procedures which define and direct proper behaviour for all employees; where there is an effective code of conduct; where regular and publicised training in ethical behaviour is made available to all; where all forms of discrimination, nepotism and unethical behaviour are dealt with immediately and with procedural fairness.

One such framework of business ethics can be found in a paper by Svensson and Wood (2011). Their framework brings together experience from many organisations and posits that a true learning organisation needs to build ethical structures and performance in order to ensure good ethical behaviour within the organisation.

Heitzman (2005) also has made a significant contribution to developing a comprehensive understanding of, and practical approaches to, managing ethics in the workplace. As is necessary in this area of management skills, the approach needs to start with being clear about what are the unethical or poor behaviours that need to be prevented before the ethical and good behaviour can be enabled. Heitzman begins by identifying ethical issues in the workplace in terms of their risk.

Figure 1.1, adapted from Heitzman (2005), divides various ethics issues into high and low risk against high and low occurrence. Apart from a few notably famous cases, harassment has a low risk profile along with most human rights abuses, which reinforces the need for good effective management and good effective organisational procedures and policies.

	Low occurrence	High occurrence
High risk	• Improper grants and political donations • Gross waste or corruption • Abuse of position/human rights	• Unethical contract • Conflict of interest • Bribery, arrangements, gifts
Low risk	• Fraud, embezzlement	• Travel/expenses • Human rights abuses • Bullying and harassment

FIGURE 1.1 Ethics cases: Occurrence and risk

Source: Adapted from the diagram in R. Heitzman, 'Values and Ethics: A Canadian Journey', a World Bank presentation, 15 March 2005. McPhee Andrewartha, 2011.

FIGURE 1.2 Drivers of values and ethics performance

Source: Adapted from R. Heitzman, 'Values and Ethics: A Canadian Journey', a World Bank presentation, 15 March 2005.

Heitzman (2005) then provides a neat framework (Figure 1.2), which ties together the drivers for achieving higher levels of ethical performance and the management thereof. This model places management and leadership skills front and centre for achieving high values in the workplace.

The figure identifies two foundation factors—namely, the implementation of clear ethical standards and recourse mechanisms, as well as risk assessment and controls. Ethical standards should be clearly set and communicated, and clear, safe recourse mechanisms must be in place to encourage staff to report breaches of ethical standards and guidelines. Risk assessment involves the continuous identification of those functions and areas within the organisation that are at high risk for ethical breaches, and then ensuring that strong controls and oversight are in place.

Effective control systems include things like:

- clear policies, procedures and controls
- separation of duties and effective oversight
- effective monitoring, audit and reporting
- clear mechanisms for reporting wrongdoing
- effective and transparent action when wrongdoing is discovered
- leadership
- organisational culture
- people management.

The three key management drivers are: leadership, organisational culture and people management.

Ethical vision

This is the foundation of an organisation's positive values and ethics. This requires that all managers:

- establish clear values and ethics standards for the organisation
- personally model the values and ethics
- continuously build and reinforce a strong values and ethics culture
- assess and manage the areas of high risk
- establish effective control and monitoring systems
- act decisively and transparently when values and ethics standards are breached.

Organisational culture

According to the research, the values and ethics culture of an organisation can either deter or promote unethical behaviour. A strong culture means:

- establishing clear standards and expectations for values and ethics behaviour for staff
- creating an environment where staff are comfortable reporting wrongdoing
- regularly measuring staff members' perception of the organisation's values and ethics culture, and the performance of the organisation's leaders and managers
- implementing improvements based on the results of staff surveys.

People management

Research suggests that organisations where staff feel valued, have high job satisfaction, and are committed to the goals of the organisation, have fewer values and ethics problems. This is encouraged by managers who regularly measure employee satisfaction, commitment, and quality of working life, and who respond to employees' priorities for improvement through a systematic organisational development plan.

Not only is the groundwork for ethical performance created and maintained as described above, but also it is relevant in the overview and long term as part of effective strategic planning. McManus (2011: 215) says: 'The notion that strategy and ethics are separate and distinct fields of study does not hold true in a twenty-first century global and digital business economy.' Andrews (1971) identified four components of strategy, one of which was obligations to people and society and not just to shareholder returns.

Ethics, culture and the self

Formulating and following a clear set of ethical values is considered a prerequisite for developing management skills. It is not sufficient to have a commitment to a set of ethical values; it is necessary also to have a level of self-awareness so that you can identify your own unconscious and subtle prejudices and biases in management practice. Two key skills (fundamental skills that begin this book) assist in the maintenance of ethical management: (1) matching, and (2) self-awareness. Matching and observing others continually provides a different perspective on our own behaviour. It creates honesty. Self-awareness increases our understanding of the difference between values and action, between our espoused principles and our actual behaviours—also referred to as the 'knowing–doing gap'.

Self-awareness is a technique improved by independent perspective. Openness to feedback from others, management coaching and 360-degree appraisal are ways in which self-awareness can be enhanced. Like all attributes, these skills need to be in balance: matching enlivened with assertiveness, self-awareness fortified with self-confidence, self-confidence softened with humility.

It was these two qualities—honesty and self-knowledge—that Nobel prize-winning author Toni Morrison argued were the key requisites for living a significant life. Operating with honesty and self-knowledge generates respect, which engenders mutual trust.

> *Treating people with respect cannot occur simply by commanding it should happen. Mutual recognition has to be negotiated ... accepting in others what one does not understand ... grants them their dignity; by granting them their dignity you thereby strengthen your own. (Sennet 2003: 4)*

Employed together, matching and self-awareness skills provide a gap analysis of the self which, when combined with the material in this book and supported by management coaching, will maximise the development of effective management skills. These are the building blocks of 'communicative learning' and 'collective dialogue' that are essential elements of leadership and management (Boudreau, Ramstad & Dowling 2003).

Few managers are deliberately unethical. Most managers consciously espouse ethical principles and yet are unaware of some of the more subtle forms of unethical behaviour. Unconscious prejudicial behaviour damages effective management practices and is hard to change because it is unconscious.

This unconscious unethical behaviour is most strongly evident in the human tendency to feel comfortable with the familiar and uncomfortable with the unfamiliar or different. Between and within cultures we have the propensity to judge negatively people we see as different (DiStefano & Maznevski 2003). What is different, unfamiliar and uncomfortable can be very subtle and quite often outside our awareness.

Mahzarin, Bazerman and Chugh (2003) identify four types of unintentional or unconscious unethical decision making: (1) implicit forms of prejudice; (2) bias that favours one's own group; (3) conflicts of interest; and (4) a tendency to overclaim credit.

Implicit prejudice can strongly affect recruitment and selection of managers, promotion, performance appraisal, task allocation, and growth and development. An example would be a manager's reluctance to appropriately confront a female employee for fear of hurting her feelings, just because she is a female. In-group favouritism can operate where a group excludes members of different gender, age, social standing or ethnic backgrounds. Overrating our own contribution occurs when we make unfavourable judgments of other people with whom we work, and this has an impact on employee commitment and morale. Finally, subtle conflicts of interest can relate to more forms of behaviour than just insider trading.

Some strategies to combat implicit prejudices are developed further in this book, but three strategies from Mahzarin, Bazerman and Chugh (2003) are identified here.

1. *Collect sufficient objective data to reveal unconscious bias.* Actually examining numbers, facts and concrete data, and testing our assumptions against the data, can help reduce such bias.
2. *Shape and develop your work environment.* Examine your work environment. Who do you select for the best tasks? What are the environmental patterns in your workplace? What characteristics form the in-group versus the out-group? These sorts of questions can help you to increase your awareness of this prejudice.
3. *Broaden your decision making.* When considering a new situation, whom do you consult? Review your methods of selection. What objective criteria could you use for selecting and consulting?

Many authors have noted that we do not always mean what we say and we do not always do what we mean (Argyris 1992; Boyatzis, Murphy & Wheeler 2000; Buber 1958). The gap between our conscious intent and our actual behaviour is wide. This gap is a fundamental cause of perceived poor management skills and poor behaviour in the workplace. Cross-culturally, the difference between espoused management behaviours and observed behaviour is consistently identified as poor management practice. Universally, it is identified as a lack of trust (Mobley & Dorfman 2003: 6).

When people feel overlooked and misunderstood, especially when they also perceive that their culture is being dismissed, they feel undervalued and not trusted (Andrewartha 2002). 'Trust' is from the Icelandic, meaning protection or firmness. Trust is a property of relationships. Trust and mistrust are also sociological/cultural phenomena. Trust has its roots in individual characteristics (Mobley & Dorfman 2003: 13).

> *Trust involves one's expectations, assumptions or beliefs about the likelihood that another's future actions will be beneficial, favourable or at least not detrimental to one's interests. (Robinson 1996: 576)*

Reflect on this in relation to your experience of management practice.

Trust increases an organisation's ability to operate efficiently and to adapt more effectively to complex and innovative changes (Mobley & Dorfman 2003: 17). Organisational strategic flexibility—which has never been more in demand in this globalised world—depends upon flexible people and is, of course, enhanced by trust between people. Research identifies that leaders who are honest and open build more trust and more productive social capital. Actual and perceived fairness is essential to the maintenance of trust and the building of effective relationships (Mobley & Dorfman 2003: 19).

Being responsible and thinking in terms of responsibility, rather than right and wrong, praise and blame, engenders trust. In responsibility, both obedience and freedom are achieved. 'Identifying who was at fault and caused the error is both the cause and a consequence of distrust. Identifying what happened and striving to see what we can learn from the experience is the essence of trust' (Bonhoeffer 1955: 15).

Good ethical practice can also be good successful business practice. Evidence abounds to suggest that business ethics benefit productivity.

> *Business is about integrity as well as profits, and the profits mean little if they sacrifice integrity. (In other walks of life, this is called prostitution.) Values have to be translated into action, and that means acting according to our values cannot merely be an abstract obligation. It must be built into our ways of dealing with the world. That is what virtue is, and that is what good business and good business ethics are all about. (Solomon 1999: xix)*

While high-profile or charismatic managers have been promoted in recent times, there has also been much-needed emphasis placed on the unassuming or quiet manager. The three quiet virtues of restraint, modesty and tenacity (Badarucco 2002) have a real resonance for an ethical manager.

Ethical behaviour is the responsibility of each individual, but it is also an organisational responsibility. Managers need to support the development and vitality of an organisational code of conduct and promote and encourage ethical practice from their colleagues. An effective performance management system builds and maintains managerial responsibility and ethical responsibility as well.

With this consideration of ethics, we now outline some of the recent research and thinking about cross-cultural management skills and practice.

Cross-cultural management considerations

It is difficult to use cultural analyses to provide general guidelines for managers, for there are cultures within cultures and individual variations within each culture. Moreover, each culture is itself ever-changing, developing and transforming (Au & Mason 1983; Soderberg & Holden 2002; Tayeb 2001). Despite these limitations, some research provides rich information to assist with the effective development of cross-cultural management skills.

Considerable advances have been made in understanding the appropriateness and effectiveness of Western management theories and techniques in non-Western management settings. The suitability and reliability of many approaches and theories have been identified, and the differences can often be formulated as a continuum rather than a contradiction.

Hofstede's work (2001) identified five cultural dimensions: (1) power distance, (2) collectivism versus individualism, (3) femininity versus masculinity, (4) uncertainty avoidance, and (5) long-term versus short-term orientation. China, Taiwan, Japan and South Korea are at the top of the scale for power distance and long-term orientation, whereas the US, UK, Germany and Australia are near the bottom on these two dimensions. In terms of management skills, Asian managers are more unwilling to express disagreement with their supervisors and tend to take a long-term perspective on organisational matters, in contrast to managers from Western countries.

A recent study examined influence skills, considered to be the building blocks of management and leadership styles, across 12 cultures. Countries included China, India, the Netherlands, Mexico, Thailand, the US, Turkey and France. The researchers found that rational persuasion, consultation, collaboration and appraising were identified as effective tactics in all the countries. Gaining influence by the giving of gifts, socialising, exerting pressure and making informal influence attempts were rated low in effectiveness (Kennedy, Fu & Yukl 2003: 127). The differences between cultures tended to correlate with aspects of the matching process (Hofstede 2001; Parsons 1951; Trompenaars 1998); this is discussed in the next chapter. In any culture,

> *...a manager is more likely to be effective if he or she has a good understanding of the range of available influence tactics and conditions that determine how effective they are likely to be. (Kennedy, Fu & Yukl 2003: 144)*

Another work identifies cultural adaptability as a key feature of cross-cultural management practice. Again, this competency is anchored in the ability to match one's self to others based on self-knowledge and self-awareness. Managers who rated high on cultural adaptability were also identified by their bosses as high performers who displayed emotional stability (Deal et al. 2003: 161).

A study across 53 cultures (Smith 2003) examined the sources of guidance used by managers to assist them in ambiguous management situations. He found that managers from European nations showed stronger reliance on their own experience than many Asian and South American managers, who reported greater reliance on superiors and formal rules. Interestingly, managers in Japan and the United States clustered together in the middle. Smith concludes that cross-cultural conflict has more to do with individual interpretation of values and meanings than it has to do with a fundamental clash in values.

A corporate culture and organisational effectiveness approach provides another unifying perspective on cross-cultural management skills. One model is based on four cultural traits of effective organisations: involvement, consistency, adaptability and mission. Involvement is the capacity of the organisation to develop ownership and commitment in its people. Consistency relates to the organisation's ability to maintain a strong set of core values. Adaptability is the paradoxical quality of maintaining consistency while at the same time reacting flexibly to the changing environment. Organisational mission is the clarity of purpose and direction translated through effective performance management (Denison, Haaland & Goelzer 2003).

DiStefano and Maznevski (2003) provide a model for developing global managers that is similar to the developmental model used in this book. Their 'Map, Bridge, Integrate' approach is based on understanding the differences between cultures, communicating and motivating across the differences, then managing the differences through involvement in resolving conflict.

Hampden-Turner and Trompenaars (1997) have developed a thesis that the creation of values underlies wealth creation. This connects with the discussion of ethics in the previous section. They suggest that different cultures develop particular productivities based on those things that their members most value. They argue that East and West have complementary and varying versions of cooperation and competition.

One of the authors of this volume (Andrewartha & Vast 2003) conducted an assessment of perceptions of the key management skills presented in this book in China, Indonesia, Australia, Singapore and Malaysia. The findings suggest that motivation, communication (especially listening skills), gaining power and influence, and managing change were perceived as the most important leadership qualities identified in all countries. In contrast, managing conflict, creative problem solving and self-awareness consistently produced the least number of responses in all countries, suggesting that these skills were more culturally specific and difficult to develop. In resonance with the previous section, one of the most overwhelming leadership qualities identified by participants across these cultures was fairness. Leadership issues such as favouritism, bias, discrimination, prejudice, hypocrisy and cronyism were among the most dominant negative qualities universally identified. Managers who were autocratic, authoritarian and controlling, as well as those seen as submissive, fearful and unassertive, were also identified as possessing negative qualities.

Whatever cultural background, training and education they have, all managers will, at several points in their career, experience formal assessment of their skills and abilities. This process, often used for selection, is also a management development opportunity.

Management and productivity

Considerable research has identified a direct linkage between effective leadership/management skills and organisational success. Moreover, one fundamental element of these management skills is the ability to effectively match the attributes of the situation and the people involved.

If an organisation provides the learning and organisational support systems people need, then that will set that organisation apart from the rest (Armstrong 2000). Keep (2000) noted that high-performance organisations develop a workplace in which people management systems encourage a partnership, with high trust relations and management skill development. Within such workplaces, work organisation and job design are reconfigured to allow employees greater autonomy and discretion, and to maximise job satisfaction and hence employee commitment.

Pfeffer's (1998) seven factors in improved management skills in organisations (such as selective hiring, extensive training, reduction of status differences and the sharing of information) have been shown to result in superior performance in regard to productivity, innovation, quality and customer satisfaction and, consequently, they achieve greater profits. Easton and Jarrell (1998) found that firms adopting total quality management (TQM) systems improved their accounting and stock performance. The more advanced the management system, the more substantial the advantage.

Davis, Lucas and Marcotte (1998), by implementing an extensive leadership development intervention with measurement criteria to make the link between the intervention and subsequent business results, realised a 21 per cent productivity improvement at the pilot location of their General Motors program. This productivity improvement represented nearly US$4.4 million in savings. Ridlehuber (2006) found the relationship management process increased revenue and customer satisfaction.

Darling and Fischer (1998) explored the relationship between the success of top multinational managers and strong management skills. Evidence suggests that managers with superior management skills were more successful in dealing with economic and social change. Shipper and White (1999), using data gathered for earlier US survey research, concluded that the mastery of managerial behaviours impacts directly on organisational performance and does so more than the frequency of managerial intervention. They recommend the improvement of managerial skills before increasing the frequency of their application.

Hanson (1986) investigated the factors that best accounted for financial success over a five-year span in 40 major manufacturing firms. The question was: 'What explains the financial success of the firms that are highly effective?' The results of statistical analyses revealed that one factor, the ability of managers to manage their people effectively, was three times more powerful than all other factors combined in accounting for a firm's financial success over a five-year period. Good management was more important than all other factors in predicting profitability.

The research establishes that management is a key factor in both the success and failure of a company. When excellent management is present, dramatic and rapid improvements can be effected. Surveys of CEOs, executives and business owners consistently find that the factor most responsible for business failure is 'bad management' and the best way to overcome business failures is to 'provide better management'. This has been dramatically emphasised in the recent business failures referred to in the 'Introduction' section of the book. Of much less importance are factors such as interest rates, foreign competition, taxes, inflation and government regulation. Two answers outnumber all other responses to the question: 'What are the factors that are most important in overcoming business failure?' They are:

- 'Provide better managers.'
- 'Train and educate current managers.'

Matching skills for managers

The fundamental skill underlying this managerial and organisational effectiveness is the ability to match the nature of the person with whom you are communicating so that you are understood and are influential. Communication is understanding.

Principles of understanding

Understanding is defined as 'using verbal and non-verbal communication to convey meaning, in a way that is matched to the other person's view of the world'.

1. We do not respond to what others say; we respond to the way they say it.
2. Learning to see how others say things helps us to hear properly.
3. Saying things the way someone else expects to hear it helps us to be understood.
4. Being understood is essential for success.

(Andrewartha 2002a: 6)

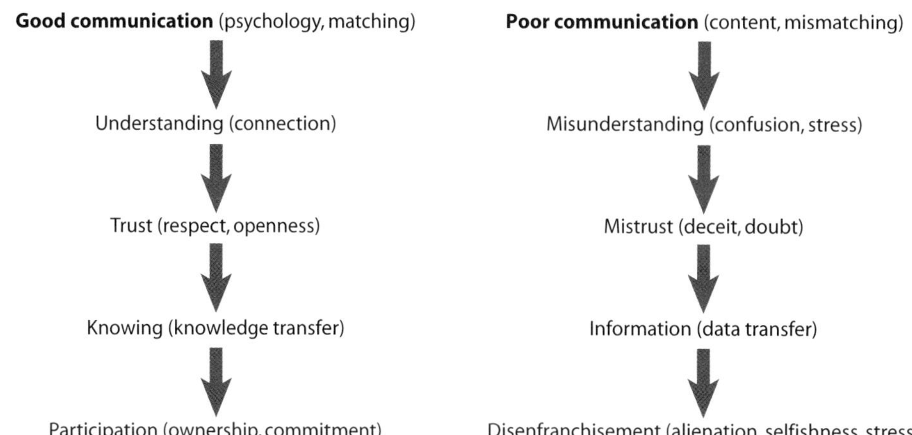

FIGURE 1.3 Flow chart of good and poor communication

Source: Reproduced from G. Andrewartha, 'Creating the learning relationship', *Learning Organization*, 10, November 2002.

Effective matched communication is essential for excellent management skills (see Figure 1.3). Effective communication acknowledges our humanity. It recognises others in a fundamental way, connects people and creates shared understanding. It creates trust.

Matching or respectful imitation is the essential element for understanding the feeling (or the meaning) of the message. Matching creates more understanding. Matching also generates interactive dialogue. There is evidence from animal and human studies that interactive communication (two-way conversation or dialogue) builds understanding between those communicating (Andrewartha 2002a).

Matching may be defined as 'the process of utilising self-awareness and acute observation to match the mood, manner and "culture" of the other person so as to maximise influence and understanding. Information presented in this way is familiar and recognised by the other party'.

To achieve effective matching, practise the following behaviours:

1. Make sure your communication is congruent. Ensure that the three crucial elements of body language, voice tone, and verbal content are all consistent and aligned. (This is discussed in more detail in the following chapter.)
2. Pay a lot more attention to how you present the communication, rather than just the words themselves.
3. When listening and presenting, carefully observe and imitate or match the non-verbal communication of the other person. A good manager attempts to match the body language, meaning, worldview and expectations of the other party.

Given the importance of matching, it is also a major requirement that we skilfully select and develop our managerial talent, a topic to which we now turn.

Management assessment: The start of management skill development

Managerial assessment for selecting, developing and promoting managers is a significant element of developing management skills. Where most management surveys indicate that the interview is the most favoured method of selecting managers, management assessment is a significantly undervalued aspect of management skills development. This is gradually changing as many countries in the region begin to invest in assessment in order to maximise their organisational effectiveness. The fact that the Chinese Centre for Leadership Assessment (CCLA) is currently examining the use and adaptation of Western psychological tests and assessment techniques for the selection of China's senior cadres is a significant confirmation of this trend.

Leadership or management assessment is naturally bonded to the strategic goals of the organisation, and requires continuous development of emotional intelligence and constant support and recognition to maintain and enhance leadership performance.

We now briefly outline four forms of leadership/management assessment:

- the structured interview
- psychological testing
- the assessment centre technique
- 360-degree appraisal.

Whether these forms of management assessment are for selection and appointment or promotion and role allocation, they can be and should be the means by which managers can develop and improve their skills. This presumes the process is transparent to the candidate and that comprehensive and constructive feedback is provided.

The structured interview

A formal interview is one of the least reliable ways of selecting a suitable manager. Consistently, the evidence shows that we select those we like. The effectiveness of the interview improves as it moves along the spectrum from the unstructured interview to the structured interview to the behavioural interview. Effectiveness is enhanced even more when the interview is combined with testing and a structured referee checking process (Rioux & Bernthal 1999; Van Iddekinge et al. 2004).

The art and practice of conducting effective interviews for selection and other purposes is detailed in the supplementary companion website Chapter 12.

Psychological testing

Testing is not new, nor is it predominantly Western. Rudimentary forms of psychological testing were practised in China as long ago as 2200 BC. Psychological testing brings out the most dramatic supporters and detractors of all the management assessment techniques. Advocates claim that it is the only reliable method for accurate selection of people possessing the desired competencies for particular positions, while critics claim that it lacks validity and has a racist and gender bias. Like all arguments of this kind, an effective outcome depends on who administers the tests, in what context the data are applied, and in what manner judgments are made and feedback is provided. Often tests are poorly administered by untrained people, with paper and pencil testing administered by one person and scored separately by the psychologist. The cheapest cost drives expedient and inadequate test selection and administration, and the test findings are not comprehensively discussed with the selection panel or the candidate.

For middle and senior management positions, the most reliable and valid means of assessing managerial ability involves:

- carefully selected tests matched to the job position
- face-to-face testing conducted by an experienced organisational psychologist
- the evaluation of data from several tests
- consideration given only to consistent data that are supported by other evidence, from the interview, referees and the CV
- comprehensive debriefing of the candidate by the psychologist (see Gregory 1999).

One example of a psychological test battery includes the following:

- *Intelligence testing*—because it is important for managers to be intelligent enough to solve problems and understand complex situations (Mant 1999):
  — the Weschler Adult Intelligence Scale or the Ravens Progressive Matrices.
- *Aptitude testing*—because it is important for managers to be technically competent in their position:
  — Watson-Glaser Test of Critical Thinking

  - ACER tests—AL/AQ, BL/BQ
  - computer literacy tests, and so on.
- *Impulse control testing*—because it is crucial for managers to react decisively but also to handle complexity and impulsive reactions:
  - Wisconsin Card Sorting Test. This measure is a good cross-cultural tool and there is anecdotal evidence that it correlates with Goleman's emotional quotient.
- *Personality testing*—because it is important to match personality characteristics with job and task role expectations:
  - OPQ, 16 PF, CPI, the CPM Scale (a Chinese instrument).
- *Emotional intelligence testing*—because it is crucial to have intellectual ability combined with emotional maturity and responsibility:
  - Goleman's EQ instrument.
- *Leadership-style testing*—because it is useful to understand the matching between managers and their team:
  - Myers–Briggs testing instrument (MBTI)
  - Team Management Systems (TMS)
  - Leadership Enhancement Team Style (LETS).

In terms of cross-cultural assessment and development, the Chinese government's CCLA is embracing some Western leadership assessment techniques, combining this with its expectation that leadership assessment should also take moral character into consideration. This factor is also emphasised by advocates of the CPM Scale (Ling & Fang 2003). There is a direct emphasis in the traditional culture for ethical prescription based on the moral standing of individuals in the community. This goes directly to the intrinsic view of the leader and their relationship with subordinates—that is, individual influence is viewed as powerful and therefore requires a leader to display the highest moral behaviour.

The assessment centre technique

This process is a powerful way to assess and develop management skills (see Bray & Grant 1966; Cascio & Silbey 1979; Gaugler et al. 1987; Thornton 1992). In an assessment centre each candidate participates in a series of exercises that simulate actual situations from the target job. The performance of candidates is evaluated by expert assessors (usually psychologists) using reliable and standardised rating systems. In contrast to interviews and written examinations, the reliability and validity of assessment centres are quite high.

Typically, activities are spread over a one-day assessment process and include such things as a specifically designed in-box exercise, a group simulation activity involving all the candidates, a leaderless group activity, a values/problem-solving case study, a 360-degree appraisal and selected psychological testing.

Assessment centres arose out of the need for rapid assessment of officers during the First World War and especially the Second World War. In recent years, assessment centres have been used less for assessment and more for succession planning, development of management skills, management of diversity, and cross-cultural management skills and career transition. Some of the recent global leadership research referred to above supports the benefits of the assessment centre process for assisting managers to develop their leadership and cross-cultural management skills.

Like all such processes, assessment centres are quite effective if customised in design, professionally conducted with an optimum balance of assessors to candidates (8:4) and in the right environment. These conditions mean that assessment centres are expensive and time-consuming.

360-degree appraisal

Several researchers have established the reliability and efficacy, the popularity, range, limitations and usefulness of the 360-degree process (Brutus, Fleenor & London 1998; Carver & Scheier 1982; Coates 1998; Edwards 1996; Edwards & Ewen 1996; Fletcher 1999; London & Smither 1995; Tornow &

London 1998). Current survey research suggests that over 90 per cent of *Fortune* 1000 firms have used 360-degree feedback or some form of multi-source assessment.

Assessment by 360-degree appraisal, or multi-source feedback, is a process by which managers receive ratings on their performance from a range of people around them. This includes ratings from self-assessment, their supervisor, their colleagues, their direct reports and sometimes their customers. The whole process is standardised and packaged so that the feedback is valid and consistent. Customarily, the questionnaire is built around the key managerial leadership capabilities required of senior managers in the organisation. As a management development tool it is used in addition to a formal performance management system rather than as a replacement for it.

Employee attitude surveys, performance appraisal systems and the need for flexibility in rapidly changing organisations have contributed to the use of the 360-degree process. Many systems (either off-the-shelf or customised) are paper and pencil instruments, while others are available online. It is administered once a year or once every two years. It is common to have 10–15 raters per candidate, providing feedback anonymously and confidentially on the standardised questionnaire.

The power of the 360-degree process comes not from the report itself but from the face-to-face comprehensive briefing session about the contents of the report, preferably from an external consultant. Analysing the data and providing powerful, accurate, effective and sometimes confronting feedback requires a skilled professional. The session is used to establish an individualised management development plan based on the feedback. The feedback initiates the goals for improvement in performance. (This goal-directed motivation in the tradition of Latham and Locke (1979) is discussed in more detail in Chapter 8.)

It is beneficial to commence a 12-month management development program with a 360-degree appraisal, using the skills described in this book and supported by ongoing management coaching. Such feedback, combined with goal setting and coaching, achieves greater results than training alone. Because of its developmental and confidential nature, this process should not be connected to bonuses or performance pay (Coates 1998; Ganzel 1998).

Some researchers suggest that the 360-degree process may work differently in different types of organisations, and there seems to be a positive relationship between self- and other-rating agreement and effective managerial performance. Peers tend to be more generous than reports, but there is little evidence of a halo effect from the former or a punitive effect from the latter. One benefit, given the complexities of managerial life, is that different constituents (subordinates, peers, supervisor) may legitimately view the same manager's performance differently. So, feedback from different sources can assist managers in understanding the variable effects of their behaviour, shape their development and improve their performance. Overwhelmingly, researchers attest to the accuracy and the specific detail provided by this process. It is a standardised way of helping managers to see themselves as others see them.

We now identify some of the benefits and limitations of the 360-degree process.

Benefits

- It helps to align senior managers with the agreed leadership capabilities of the organisation.
- It enhances management skills.
- It provides a continuous improvement framework.
- It enables customers to participate directly in their relationship with the organisation.
- It provides comprehensive information for succession planning.
- It offers convincing data for assisting with poor performance.
- It provides information about the senior management group's performance.

Limitations

- It is a relatively costly process.
- It is time-consuming.
- It can be abused if not used confidentially with an external consultant.
- It needs to be 'refreshed' after two or three iterations.

A typical 360-degree questionnaire is about 70 items long, covering seven management capabilities with ten behavioural questions for each capability.

Developing effective ethical management in this way with regular assessments and ongoing development opportunities, and perhaps supported by management coaching for succession planning or for managing changes in the organisation, are effective ways to maintain and extend management skills.

Summary

The development of excellent management skills requires a firm philosophical and principled foundation. Managers are first and foremost human beings with all the complexity and paradox that entails. It is important to have a considered set of values and to choose to work for an organisation that reflects those values. Excellent management is as much about who we are as what we do. In a constantly changing and exciting business environment the requirement is to be multi-talented, highly flexible, and experienced in working with different structures, different people and different conditions.

Management development starts with personal values, is reinforced by ethical frameworks and behaviours and expanded through management assessment and performance management, and is supported and enhanced by expert coaching and continuous development of management skills. In Chapter 2 we explore the nature of the managerial skill of developing self-awareness.

Skill analysis

Case study involving management skills

The best candidate

There is a newly created position in the Chinese Centre for Leadership Assessment (CCLA), a core unit of the Communist Party of China's Organisation Department in Beijing. The position is for manager of the Beijing Assessment Centre. The position calls for 'an excellent understanding of Western leadership assessment practices combined with a need to integrate these techniques appropriately with Chinese assessment procedures'.

You are a manager working with the CCLA. You know that there are many people who are enthusiastic about adopting Western techniques completely. You also know that there are many who are concerned about this, as well as others who believe that the Chinese examination system, based on years of studious development, should not be changed. There is a fairly strict hierarchy of reporting in your organisation and yet you know that your supervisor has often been impressed with Western techniques of leadership assessment. He asks you and your team for a report about the best way to proceed with selecting a candidate for this vacant position.

DISCUSSION QUESTIONS

1. *What ethical considerations are involved in this decision?*
2. *How would you go about collecting information for writing your report?*
3. *How would you go about motivating and involving your team in this project?*
4. *What approaches would be best for this candidate selection?*
5. *What are the key capabilities required for such a position? Why?*
6. *Who should be involved in the selection process? Why?*
7. *What are your key recommendations?*

Skill practice

Exercise in applying management skills

Asian Electronics' in-basket

This exercise gives you a realistic glimpse of the tasks faced regularly by practising managers. It enables you to assess your own strengths and limitations in management skills in an actual managerial work situation. Complete the exercise and then compare your own decisions and actions with those of other classmates.

Asian Electronics designs and develops customised software for businesses. It also integrates this software with the customers' existing systems and provides system maintenance. Asian Electronics has customers in the following industries: airlines, automobile, finance/banking, health/hospital, consumer products, electronics and government. The company has also begun to generate important international clients. These include the Indonesian telecommunications industry and a consortium of banks and financial firms based elsewhere in Asia.

The company has grown rapidly since its inception eight years ago. Its revenue, net income and earnings per share have all been above the industry average for the past several years. However, competition in this technologically sophisticated field has also increased rapidly. Recently, it has become more difficult to compete for major contracts. Although Asian Electronics' revenue and net income continue to grow, the rate of growth declined during the last fiscal year.

Asian Electronics' 250 employees are divided into several operating divisions with employees at four levels: non-management, technical/professional, managerial and executive. Non-management employees take care of the clerical and facilities support functions. The technical/professional staff perform the core technical work for the firm. Most managerial employees are group managers who supervise a team of technical/professional employees working on a project for a particular customer. Staff who work in specialised areas such as finance, accounting, human resources, nursing and law are also considered managerial employees. The executive level comprises the 12 highest-ranking employees at Asian Electronics. The organisation chart in Figure 1.4 illustrates Asian Electronics' structure.

In this exercise you will play the role of Chris Pearson, director of operations for Health and Financial Services. You learned last Wednesday, 13 October, that your predecessor, Michael Grant, had resigned and gone to Universal Business Solutions, in the United States. You were offered his former job and you accepted it. Previously, you were the group manager for a team of 15 software

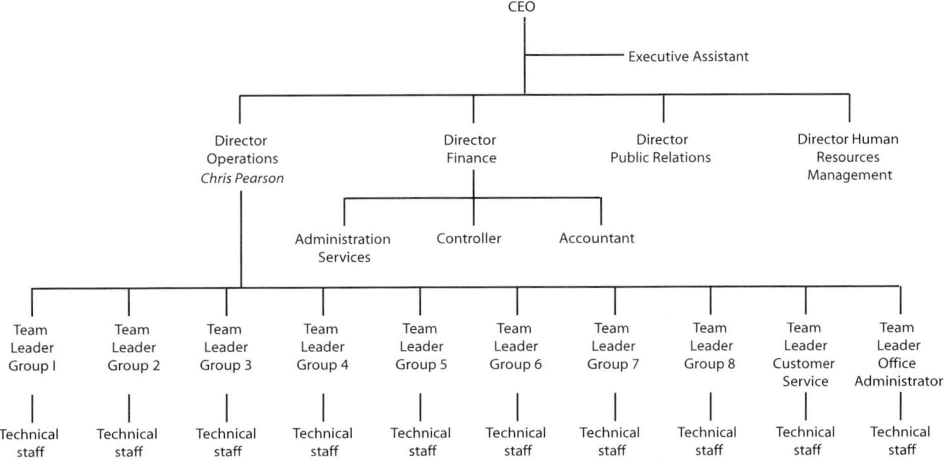

FIGURE 1.4 Organisational chart of operations for Asian Electronics

developers assigned to work on the Indonesian project in the Airline Services Division. You spent all of Thursday, Friday and most of the weekend finishing up parts of the project, briefing your successor and preparing an interim report that you will deliver in Jakarta on 21 October.

It is now 7 am on Monday and you are in your new office. You have arrived at work early so that you can spend the next two hours reviewing the material in your in-basket (including some memos and messages to Michael Grant), as well as your voice mail and email. Your daily planning book indicates that you have no appointments today or tomorrow, but you will have to catch a plane for Jakarta early Wednesday morning. You have a full schedule for the remainder of the week and all of next week.

Assignment

During the next two hours, review all the material in your in-basket, as well as your voice mail and email. Take only two hours. Using the response form below as a model, indicate how you want to respond to each item (that is, via letter/memo, email, phone/voice mail or personal meeting). If you decide not to respond to an item, tick 'no response' on the response form. All your responses must be written on the response forms. Write your precise, detailed response (do not merely jot down a few notes). For example, you might draft a memo or write out a message that you will deliver via phone/voice mail. You may also decide to meet with an individual (or individuals) during the limited time available on your calendar today or tomorrow. If so, prepare an agenda for a personal meeting and list your goals for the meeting. As you read through the items, you may occasionally observe some information that you think is relevant and want to remember (or attend to in the future) but that you decide not to include in any of your responses to employees. Write down such information on a sheet of paper titled 'Note to self'.

Sample response form

RELATES TO:
Memo #__________ Email #__________ Voice mail #__________

RESPONSE FORM:

__________	**Letter/Memo**	__________	**Meet with person (when, where)**
__________	**Email**	__________	**Note to self**
__________	**Phone call/Voice mail**	__________	**No response**

ITEM 1 Memo
TO: All employees
FROM: Robert Choo, Chief Executive Officer
DATE: 10 October

I am pleased to announce that Chris Pearson has been appointed as Director of Operations for Health and Financial Services. Chris will immediately assume responsibility for all operations previously managed by Michael Grant. She will have end-to-end responsibility for the design, development, integration and maintenance of custom software for the health and finance/banking industries. This responsibility includes all technical, financial and staffing issues. Chris will also manage our program of software support and integration for the recently announced merger of three large health maintenance organisations. Chris will be responsible for our recently announced project with a consortium of banks and financial firms operating in Asia. This project represents an exciting opportunity for us, and her background seems ideally suited to the task.

Chris comes to this position with an undergraduate degree in Computer Science and an MBA. She began as a member of our technical/professional staff six years ago and has most recently served for three years as a group manager supporting domestic and international projects for our airlines industry group, including our recent work for the Indonesian project.

I am sure you all join me in offering congratulations to Chris for this promotion.

PRACTICE

ITEM 2 Memo
TO: All Managers
FROM: Sharon Shapiro, Director, Human Resources Management
DATE: 12 October

For your information, the following article appeared on page 3 of Thursday's *Asian Financial Review.*

In a move that may create problems for Asian Electronics, Michael Grant and Janice Ramos have left Asian Electronics and moved to Universal Business Solutions Inc. Industry analysts see the move as another victory for Universal Business Solutions Inc. in its battle with Asian Electronics for a share of the growing software development and integration business. Both Grant and Ramos had been with Asian Electronics for more than seven years. Grant was most recently director of operations for all Asian Electronics' work in two industries: health and hospitals, and finance and banking. Ramos brings to Universal Business Solutions Inc. her special expertise in the growing area of international software development and integration.

Hillary Collins, an industry analyst, said, 'The loss of key staff to a competitor can often create serious problems for a firm such as Asian Electronics. Grant and Ramos have an insider's understanding of Asian Electronics' strategic and technical limitations. It will be interesting to see if they can exploit this knowledge to the advantage of Universal Business Solutions Inc.'

ITEM 3 Memo
TO: Chris Pearson
FROM: Paula Sprague, Executive Assistant to Robert Choo
DATE: 18 October

Chris, I know that in your former position as a group manager in the Airline Services Division, you have probably met most of the group managers in the Health and Financial Services Division but I thought you might like some more personal information about them. These people will be your direct reports on the management team.

Group 1: Janet Meow, 55-year-old, married (Arnold) with two children and three grandchildren. Active in local politics. Well regarded as a 'hands-off' manager heading a high-performing team. Plays golf regularly with Mark McIntyre, John Small and a couple of directors from other divisions.

Group 2: Narida Idris, 38-year-old, partner (Gustav), one school-age child. A fitness 'nut', has run in several marathons. Some experience in Indonesia and Japan. Considered a hard-driving manager with a constant focus on the task at hand. Will be the first person to show up every morning.

Group 3: William Chen, 31-year-old, married (Harriet), two young children from his first marriage. Enjoys tennis and is quite good at it. A rising star in the company, he is highly respected by his peers as a 'man of action' and a good friend.

Group 4: Jeremy Fernandez, 36-year-old, married (Janet) with an infant daughter. Recently returned from paternity leave. Has travelled extensively on projects, since he speaks three languages. Has played squash for the last ten years. Considered a strong manager who gets the most out of his people.

Group 5: Mark McIntyre, 45-year-old, married (Mary Theresa) to an executive in the banking industry. No children. A lot of experience in Germany and Eastern Europe. Has been writing a mystery novel. Has always been a good 'team player', but several members of his technical staff are not well respected and he has not addressed the problem.

Group 6: John Small, 38-year-old, recently divorced. Three children living with his wife. A gregarious individual who likes sports. He spent a lot of time in Mexico and Central America before he came to Asian Electronics. Recently has been doing mostly contract work with the federal government. An average manager, has had some trouble keeping his people on schedule.

Group 7: This position vacant since Janice Ramos left. Robert thinks we ought to fill this position quickly. Get in touch with me if you want information on any in-house candidates for any position.

Group 8: Sivar Kumar, 42-year-old, married (Tamara) with two teenage children. Recently won an award in a local photography contest. Considered a strong manager who gets along with peers and works long hours.
Customer Services: Armand Marke, 38-year-old, divorced. A basketball fan. Previously a group manager. Worked hard to establish the Technical Services Phone Line, but now has pretty much left it alone.
Office Administrator: Michelle Harrison, 41-year-old, single. Grew up in the Australian outback and still rides horses whenever she can. A strict administrator.

There are several good people here, but they don't function well as a management team. I think Michael played favourites, especially with Janice and Jeremy. There are a few cliques in this group and I'm not sure how effectively Michael dealt with them. I expect you will find it a challenge to build a cohesive team.

ITEM 4 Memo
TO: Chris Pearson
FROM: Narida Idris, Group 2 Manager
DATE: 15 October
CONFIDENTIAL AND RESTRICTED

Although I know you are new to your job, I feel it is important that I let you know about some information I just obtained concerning the development work we recently completed for First National Investment. Our project involved the development of asset management software for managing their international funds. This was a very complex project due to the volatile exchange rates and the forecasting tools we needed to develop.

As part of this project, we had to integrate the software and reports with all their existing systems and reporting mechanisms. To do this, we were given access to all their existing software (much of which was developed by Universal Business Solutions Inc.). Of course, we signed an agreement acknowledging that the software to which we were given access was proprietary and that our access was solely for the purpose of our system integration work associated with the project.

Unfortunately, I have learned that some parts of the software we developed actually 'borrow' heavily from complex application programs developed for First National Investment by Universal Business Solutions Inc. It seems obvious to me that one or more of the software developers from Group 5 (Mark McIntyre's group) inappropriately 'borrowed' algorithms developed by Universal Business Solutions Inc. I am sure that doing so saved us significant development time on some aspects of the project. It seems very unlikely that First National Investment or Universal Business Solutions Inc. will ever become aware of this issue.

Finally, First National Investment is successfully using the software we developed and is thrilled with the work we did. We brought the project in on time and under budget. You probably know that they have invited us to bid on several other substantial projects.

I'm sorry to bring this delicate matter to your attention, but I thought you should know about it.

ITEM 5A Memo
TO: Chris Pearson
FROM: Paula Sprague, Executive Assistant to Robert Choo
DATE: 11 October
RE: Letter from CARE Services (copies attached)

Robert asked me to work on this CARE project and obviously wants some fast action. A lot of the staff are already booked solid for the next couple of weeks. I knew that Elise Soto and Chu Hung Woo have the expertise to do this system and when I checked with them, they were relatively free.

I had them pencil in the next two weeks and wanted to let you know. Hopefully, it will take a 'hot potato' out of your hands.

ITEM 5B Copy of fax
CARE
Child and Adolescent Rehabilitative and Educational Services
200 Mailer Street
Singapore 24 8850
DATE: 11 October

Mr Robert Choo, CEO
Asian Electronics
13 Miller Avenue #05–02
Singapore 23 8850

Dear Robert,

This letter is a follow-up to our conversation after last night's board meeting. I appreciated your comments during the board meeting about the need for proper advice in non-profit organisations and I especially appreciate your generous offer of Asian Electronics providing assistance to deal with the immediate problem with our accounting system. Since the board voted to fire the computer consultant, I am very worried about getting our reports done in time to meet the state funding cycle.

Thanks again for your offer of help during this crisis.

Sincerely yours,

Janice Polocizwic

Janice Polocizwic
Executive Director

ITEM 5C Copy of letter
ASIAN ELECTRONICS
13 Miller Avenue #05–02
Singapore 23 8850
DATE: 12 October

Janice Polocizwic
Executive Director, CARE Services
200 Mailer Street
Singapore 24 8550

Dear Janice,

I received your fax of 11 October. I have asked Paula Sprague, my executive assistant, to line up people to work on your accounting system as soon as possible. You can expect to hear from her shortly.

Sincerely,

Robert Choo

Robert Choo
cc: Paula Sprague, Executive Assistant

ITEM 6 Memo
TO: Michael Grant
FROM: Harry Withers, Group 6 Technical Staff
DATE: 12 October
PERSONAL AND CONFIDENTIAL

Our team is having difficulty meeting the submission deadline of 5 November for the Halstrom project. Kim, Fred, Peter, Kyoto, Susan, Mala and I have been working on the project for several weeks, but are experiencing some problems and may need additional time. I hesitate to write this letter, but the main problem is that our group manager, John Small, is involved in a relationship with Mala. Mala gets John's support for her ideas and brings them to the team as required components of the project. Needless to say, this has posed some problems for the group. Mala's background is especially valuable for this project, but Kim and Fred, who have both worked very hard on the project, do not want to work with her. In addition, one member of the team has been unavailable recently because of child-care needs. Commitment to the project and team morale have plummeted. However, we'll do our best to get the project finished as soon as possible. Mala will be on holiday for the next two weeks, so I'm expecting that some of us can complete it in her absence.

ITEM 7 Voice Mail

Hello, Michael. This is Jim Bishop of the Combined Hospitals Group. I wanted to talk to you about the quality assurance project that you are working on for us. When Joe Martin first started talking with us, I was impressed with his friendliness and expertise. But, recently, he doesn't seem to be getting much accomplished and has seemed distant and on edge in conversations. Today, I asked him about the schedule and he seemed very defensive and not entirely in control of his emotions. I am quite concerned about our project. Please give me a call.

ITEM 8 Voice Mail

Hi, Michael. This is Armand. I wanted to talk to you about some issues with the Technical Services Phone Line. I've recently received some complaint letters from Phone Line customers whose complaints have included: long delays while waiting for a technician to answer the phone; technicians who are not knowledgeable enough to solve problems; and, on occasion, rude service. Needless to say, I'm quite concerned about these complaints.

I believe that the overall quality of the Phone Line staff is very good, but we continue to be understaffed, even with the recent hires. The new technicians look strong, but are working on the help-line before being fully trained. Anna, our best tech, often brings her child to work, which is adding to the craziness around here.

I think you should know that we're feeling a lot of stress here. I'll talk with you soon.

ITEM 9 Voice Mail

Hi, Chris, it's Pat. Congratulations on your promotion. They definitely picked the right person. It's great news for me, too. You've been a terrific mentor so far, so I'm expecting to learn a lot from you in your new position. How about lunch next week?

ITEM 10 Voice Mail

Chris, this is Janet Meow. Just thought you'd like to know that John's joke during our planning meeting has disturbed a few of the women in my group. Frankly, I think the thing's being blown out of proportion, especially since we all know this is a good place for both men and women to work. Give me a call if you want to chat about this.

ITEM 11 Voice Mail

Hello. This is Lorraine Adams from Westside Hospital. I read in today's *Fin. Review* that you will be taking over from Michael Grant. We haven't met yet, but your division has recently finished two large projects for Westside. Michael Grant and I had some discussion about a small conversion of a piece of existing software to be compatible with the new systems. The original vendor had said that they would do the work, but has been stalling, and I need to move quickly. Can you see if Harris Wilson, Chu Hung Woo and Elise Soto are available to do this work as soon as possible? They were on the original project and work well with our people. You can call me at 0364 9843.

Um … (long pause) … I guess I should tell you that I got a call from Michael offering to do this work. But I think I should stick with Asian Electronics. Give me a call.

ITEM 12 Voice Mail

Hi, Chris, this is Robert Moore calling. I'm a member of your technical/professional staff. I used to report to Janice Ramos, but since she left the firm, I thought I'd bring my concerns directly to you. I'd like to arrange some time to talk to you about my experiences since returning from leave. Some of my major responsibilities have been turned over to others. I seem to be out of the loop and wonder if my career is at risk. Also, I am afraid that I won't be supported or seriously considered for the opening created by Janice's departure. Frankly, I feel like I'm being screwed for taking my leave. I'd like to talk to you this week.

ITEM 13 Email
TO: Michael Grant
FROM: Joe Martin, Group 1 Technical Staff
DATE: 12 October

I would like to set up a meeting with you as soon as possible. I suspect that you will get a call from Jim Bishop of the Combined Hospitals Group and want to be sure that you hear my side of the story first. I have been working on a customised system design for quality assurance for them using a variation of the J-3 product we developed several years ago. They had a number of special requirements and some quirks in their accounting systems, so I have had to put in especially long hours. I've worked hard to meet their demands, but they keep changing the ground rules. I keep thinking, this is just another J-3 I'm working on, but they have been interfering with an elegant design I have developed. It seems I'm not getting anywhere on this project. Earlier today, I had a difficult discussion with their Controller. He asked for another major change. I've been fighting their deadline and think I am just stretched too thin on this project. Then Mr Bishop asked me if the system was running yet. I was worn out from dealing with the Controller and I made a sarcastic comment to Mr Bishop. He gave me a funny look and just walked out of the room.

I would like to talk to you about this situation at your earliest convenience.

ITEM 14 Email
TO: Chris Pearson
FROM: John Small, Group 6 Manager
DATE: 15 October

Welcome aboard, Chris. I look forward to meeting you. I just wanted to put a bug in your ear about finding a replacement for Janice Ramos. One of my technical staff, Mala Andrews, has the ability and drive to make an excellent group manager. I have encouraged her to apply for the position. I'd be happy to talk with you further about this, at your convenience.

ITEM 15 Email
TO: Chris Pearson
FROM: Paula Sprague, Executive Assistant to Robert Choo
DATE: 15 October

Robert asked me to let you know about the large contract we have won in Asia. It means that a team of four managers will be making a short trip to determine current needs. They will assign their technical staff the tasks of developing a system and software here over the next six months, and then the managers and possibly some team members will be spending about ten months on site to handle the implementation. Robert thought you might want to hold an initial meeting with some of your managers to check on their interest and willingness to take this sort of assignment. Robert would appreciate an email of your thoughts about the issues to be discussed at this meeting, additional considerations about sending people to Asia, and about how you will put together an effective team to work on this project. The 15 October memo I sent to you will provide you with some information you'll need to start making these decisions.

ITEM 16 Email
TO: Chris Pearson
FROM: Sharon Shapiro, Director of Human Resources Management
DATE: 15 October
RE: Upcoming meeting

I want to update you on the ripple effect of John Small's sexist joke at last week's planning meeting. Quite a few women have been very upset and have met informally to talk about it. They have decided to call a meeting of all people concerned about this kind of behaviour throughout the firm. I plan to attend, so I'll keep you posted.

Ethics code

This is an example of a code of ethics.

—Actively work for the common good—

LEADERSHIP

Model MAP's corporate vision, mission and values, as well as these team values.

RESPONSIBILITY and INTEGRITY

Participate—say what you believe.
Work to know who will do what and by when.
Do what you say you're going to do when you say you're going to do it.
Take initiative!

RESPECT

Actively listen and acknowledge my viewpoint.
Recognise the value of my job—ask for my help and realise that I have other priorities.
Be sensitive to my values, my culture—reap the richness of diversity.
Be friendly and thoughtful to all.

TEAMWORK

Recognise others' contributions and successes.
Cooperate with fellow staff members and support their efforts.
Support MAP decisions and strategic objectives.
Don't take ourselves too seriously—have fun!

CREATIVITY

Encourage thinking 'outside the box'.
Encourage discussion around points of disagreement or uncertainty.
Challenge the status quo.
Envision possibilities.
Allow yourself to experiment, fail and try again.

—Respectfully hold people responsible for these team values—

Source: C. McNamara (ed.), *The Management Assistance Program for Nonprofits' Team Values* (St Paul, MN: 1997).

Assignment

Refer to the code of ethics in your organisation and compare it to the one above. Using both codes, write a code of ethics for your organisation that you consider would be essential to guide good management behaviour.

Ethics case studies

Assignment

In your study group discuss the issues represented by these four case studies, referring to the cross-cultural, ethical and other matters discussed in this chapter.

Case one

Your company builds whatsits, whose primary component is the rorem. As long as you can remember, you have bought your rorems from old George, who has come to depend on your business for his very survival. But now a large-scale competitor produces rorems much more efficiently than old George, which is reflected in the price—lower by almost 20 per cent. Is your standing relationship with old George and his dependence on you any consideration whatever? What do you do? Do you have any obligation to old George?

Source: R. Solomon, *It's Good Business* (Boston: Rowman and Littlefield, 1997), p. 13.

Case two

You are in charge of new product development at company A in the midst of a fierce competition for the development of a new and more efficient gizmo. The Research Department has come up with a workable model, and the Engineering Department is just now in the midst of getting the bugs out. One of your main competitors, Company B, has obviously fallen behind and offers you a lucrative position, more than commensurate with your present duties and at almost double the salary. Your current employer insists he cannot possibly match the offer but does give you a 20 per cent raise, 'to show our appreciation'. Should you feel free to accept a competing offer from company B? If you do accept it, should you feel free to develop for company B the gizmo designed by company A?

Source: R. Solomon, *It's Good Business* (Boston: Rowman and Littlefield, 1997), p. 13.

Case three

In 1993 senior managers at Levi Strauss and Co., the world's largest brand-name apparel manufacturer, were deciding whether the company should have a business presence in China, given the human rights and other problems there. The China Policy Group has been asked to use the company's 'principled reasoning approach' to make a recommendation based on the company's ethical values and newly adopted global sourcing guidelines.

Source: J. Katz and L. Paine, Harvard Business School, reference number 9–395–137, 1994.

Case four

Members of the development team for the AES Corporation's power plant project in India must decide what plant technology to specify in their application for techno-economic clearance from the government of India's Central Electric Authority. Their choice is between more expensive technology that would enable the plant to meet demanding US environmental standards and less costly technology that would meet local environmental standards and free up funds for contributions for the needs of communities surrounding the projected plant. At the same time, executives at AES headquarters in Arlington, Virginia, are considering whether the company's traditional focus on meeting its social responsibility through CO_2-offset programs is the best approach to social responsibility as the company expands worldwide.

Source: L. Paine, A. Strimling, C. Nichols III and R. Crawford, Harvard Business School, reference number 9–399–136, 1999.

Skill application

Application plan and evaluation

The aim of this exercise is to help you apply the skills referred to in this chapter in a real-life, out-of-class setting. Unlike a classroom activity, in which feedback is immediate and others can assist you with their evaluations, this skill application activity is one you must accomplish and evaluate on your own.

There are two parts to this activity. Part 1 helps to prepare you to apply the skill. Part 2 helps you to evaluate and improve on your experience. Be sure to write down answers to each item. Do not short-circuit the process by skipping steps.

Part 1: Planning

1. Write down the two or three aspects of ethics that are most important to you. These may be areas of weakness, areas you most want to improve, or areas that are most salient to a problem you face right now. Identify the specific aspects of this skill that you want to apply.
2. Now identify the setting or the situation in which you will apply this skill. Establish a plan for performance by writing down a description of the situation. Who else will be involved? When will you do it? Where will it be done?
   Circumstances
   — Who else?
   — When?
   — Where?
3. Identify the specific behaviours you will engage in to apply this skill. Set action plans for your skill performance.
4. What are the indicators of successful performance? How will you know you have been effective? What will indicate you have performed competently?

Part 2: Evaluation

5. When you have completed your implementation, record the results. What happened? How successful were you? What was the effect on others?
6. How can you improve? What modifications can you make next time? What will you do differently in a similar situation in the future?
7. Looking back on your whole skill practice and application experience, what have you learned? What has been surprising? In what ways might this experience help you in the long term?

Scoring keys and supplementary materials

How ethical are you? (p. 4)

Score:

1. If you scored below 24, you seem to have a good handle on your implicit and the unconscious biases and prejudices.
2. If you scored 24 to 31, you may want to concentrate on your matching and self-awareness development.
3. If you scored 32 to 40, it may be very beneficial for you to engage in some significant coaching and skill development around your unconscious values.

Personal assessment of management skills (p. 4)

SCORING KEY		**ASSESSMENT**	
Skill area	*Items*	*Personal*	*Associates*
Self-awareness	**1–5**	______	______
Self-disclosure and openness	1, 2	______	______
Awareness of self	3–5	______	______
Managing stress	**6–11**	______	______
Eliminating stressors	6, 7	______	______
Developing resiliency	8, 9	______	______
Short-term coping	10, 11	______	______
Solving problems creatively	**12–23**	______	______
Rational problem solving	12–14	______	______
Creative problem solving	15–19	______	______
Fostering innovation	20–23	______	______
Communicating supportively	**24–32**	______	______
Coaching and counselling	24, 25	______	______
Effective negative feedback	26–28	______	______
Communicating supportively	29–32	______	______
Gaining power and influence	**33–40**	______	______
Gaining power	33–37	______	______
Exercising influence	38–40	______	______
Motivating others	**41–49**	______	______
Managing conflict	**50–58**	______	______
Initiating	50–52	______	______
Responding	53–55	______	______
Mediating	56–58	______	______
Empowering and delegating	**59–66**	______	______
Empowering	59–62	______	______
Delegating	63–67	______	______
Building effective teams	**68–72**	______	______
Team leadership	68–72	______	______
	TOTAL SCORE (Sum of bold headings)	☐	☐

Comparison data

Compare your scores with at least four referents:

1. If you asked others to rate you using the associates' version, compare how you rated yourself with how your associates rated you.
2. Compare the ratings you received to those received by other students in the class.
3. Compare the ratings you received to a norm group of 300 business school students (see the information below).
4. Compare your score against the maximum possible (432).

For the survey as a whole, if you scored

293 or above	you are in the top quartile.
274–292	you are in the second quartile.
260–273	you are in the third quartile.
259 or below	you are in the bottom quartile.

Assessment of management skills—associates' version

This instrument uses 'he or she' instead of 'I' in the questions. Give copies to at least three other people who know you well or who have observed you in a managerial situation. They should complete the instrument by rating your behaviour. Bring the completed surveys back to class and compare your own ratings to your associates' ratings, your associates' ratings to the ratings received by others in the class, and the ratings you received to those of a national norm group.

Rating scale
6 Strongly agree
5 Agree
4 Slightly agree
3 Slightly disagree
2 Disagree
1 Strongly disagree

In regard to his or her level of self-knowledge:

______ 1. He or she seeks information about his or her strengths and weaknesses from others as a basis for self-improvement.

______ 2. In order to improve, he or she is willing to share his or her beliefs and feelings with others.

______ 3. He or she is very much aware of his or her preferred style in gathering information and making decisions.

______ 4. He or she has a good sense of how he or she copes with situations that are ambiguous and uncertain.

______ 5. He or she has a well-developed set of personal standards and principles that guide his or her behaviour.

When faced with stressful or time-pressured situations:

______ 6. He or she uses effective time-management methods such as keeping track of his or her time, making to-do lists and setting task priorities.

______ 7. He or she frequently confirms his or her priorities so that less important things do not drive out more important things.

______ 8. He or she maintains a program of regular exercise for fitness.

______ 9. He or she maintains an open, trusting relationship with someone with whom he or she can share his or her frustrations.

______ 10. He or she knows and practises several temporary relaxation techniques such as deep breathing and muscle relaxation.

______ 11. He or she strives to redefine problems as opportunities for improvement.

When he or she approaches a typical, routine problem:

______ 12. He or she always defines clearly and explicitly what the problem is.

______ 13. He or she always generates more than one alternative solution to the problem.

______ 14. He or she keeps problem-solving steps distinct; that is, he or she makes sure that the processes of formulating definitions, generating alternatives and finding solutions are separated.

When faced with a complex or difficult problem that does not have a straightforward solution:

______ 15. He or she tries to be flexible in the way he or she approaches the problem; he or she does not just rely on conventional wisdom or past practice.

______ 16. He or she tries to unfreeze his or her thinking by asking lots of questions about the nature of the problem.

______ 17. He or she frequently uses metaphors or analogies to help analyse the problem and discover what else it is like.

______ 18. He or she strives to look at problems from different perspectives so as to generate multiple definitions.

______ 19. He or she does not evaluate the merits of each alternative solution to the problem until he or she has generated many alternatives.

When trying to foster more creativity and innovation among those with whom he or she works:

______ 20. He or she makes sure there are divergent points of view represented in every problem-solving group.

______ 21. He or she tries to acquire information from customers regarding their preferences and expectations.

______ 22. He or she provides recognition not only to those who are idea champions but also to those who support others' ideas and who provide resources to implement them.

______ 23. He or she encourages informed rule breaking in pursuit of creative solutions.

In situations where he or she has to provide negative feedback or offer corrective advice:

______ 24. He or she helps others recognise and define their own problems when he or she counsels them.

______ 25. He or she understands clearly when it is appropriate to offer advice and direction to others and when it is not.

______ 26. He or she always gives feedback that is focused on problems and solutions, not on personal characteristics.

______ 27. His or her feedback is always specific and to the point, rather than general or vague.

______ 28. He or she is descriptive in giving negative feedback to others. That is, he or she objectively describes events, their consequences and his or her feelings about them.

______ 29. He or she takes responsibility for his or her statements and point of view by using, for example, 'I have decided' instead of 'They have decided'.

______ 30. He or she conveys flexibility and openness to conflicting opinions when presenting his or her point of view, even when he or she feels strongly about it.

______ 31. He or she does not talk down to those who have less power or less information than him or her.

______ 32. He or she does not dominate conversations with others.

In a situation where it is important to obtain more power:

______ 33. He or she always puts forth more effort and takes more initiative than expected in his or her work.

______ 34. He or she is continually upgrading his or her skills and knowledge.

______ 35. He or she strongly supports organisational ceremonial events and activities.
______ 36. He or she forms a broad network of relationships with people at all levels throughout the organisation.
______ 37. In his or her work, he or she consistently strives to generate new ideas, initiate new activities and minimise routine tasks.
______ 38. He or she consistently sends personal notes to others when they accomplish something significant or when passing along important information to them.
______ 39. He or she refuses to bargain with individuals who use high-pressure negotiation tactics.
______ 40. He or she always avoids using threats or demands to impose his or her will on others.

When another person needs to be motivated:

______ 41. He or she always determines if the person has the necessary resources and support to succeed in a task.
______ 42. He or she uses a variety of rewards to reinforce exceptional performances.
______ 43. He or she designs task assignments to make them interesting and challenging.
______ 44. He or she makes sure that the person gets timely feedback from those affected by task performance.
______ 45. He or she always helps the person establish performance goals that are challenging, specific and time-bound.
______ 46. Only as a last resort does he or she attempt to reassign or release a poorly performing individual.
______ 47. He or she consistently disciplines when effort is below expectations and capabilities.
______ 48. He or she makes sure that people feel fairly and equitably treated.
______ 49. He or she provides immediate compliments and other forms of recognition for meaningful accomplishments.

When he or she sees someone doing something that needs correcting:

______ 50. He or she avoids making personal accusations and attributing self-serving motives to the other person.
______ 51. He or she encourages two-way interaction by inviting the respondent to express his or her perspectives and to ask questions.
______ 52. He or she makes a specific request, detailing a more acceptable option.

When someone complains about something he or she has done:

______ 53. He or she shows genuine concern and interest, even when he or she disagrees.
______ 54. He or she seeks additional information by asking questions that provide specific and descriptive information.
______ 55. He or she asks the other person to suggest more acceptable behaviours.

When two people are in conflict and he or she is the mediator:

______ 56. He or she does not take sides but remains neutral.
______ 57. He or she helps the parties generate multiple alternatives.
______ 58. He or she helps the parties find areas on which they agree.

In situations where he or she has an opportunity to empower others:

______ 59. He or she helps people feel competent in their work by recognising and celebrating their small successes.
______ 60. He or she provides regular feedback and needed support.
______ 61. He or she tries to provide all the information that people need to accomplish their tasks.
______ 62. He or she exhibits caring and personal concern for each person with whom he or she has dealings.

When delegating work to others:

______ 63. He or she specifies clearly the results he or she desires.

______ 64. He or she specifies clearly the level of initiative he or she wants others to take (for example, wait for directions, do part of the task and then report, do the whole task and then report, and so forth).

______ 65. He or she allows participation by those accepting assignments regarding when and how the work will be done.

______ 66. He or she avoids upward delegation by asking people to recommend solutions rather than merely asking for advice or answers when a problem is encountered.

______ 67. He or she follows up and maintains accountability for delegated tasks on a regular basis.

When he or she is attempting to build and lead an effective team:

______ 68. He or she helps team members establish a foundation of trust among one another and between themselves and him or her.

______ 69. He or she helps members learn to play roles that assist the team in accomplishing its tasks as well as building strong interpersonal relationships.

______ 70. He or she encourages a win-win philosophy in the team—that is, when one member wins, every member wins.

______ 71. He or she encourages the team to achieve dramatic breakthrough innovations as well as small continuous improvements.

______ 72. He or she manages difficult team members effectively, through supportive communication, collaborative conflict management and empowerment.

Does your organisation have a strong ethical management culture? (p. 8)

Score:

1. If your score is over 48, your organisation appears to have a strong management culture.
2. If your score is between 36 and 47, your organisation appears to have a reasonable management culture.
3. If your score is less than 36, your organisation has a long way to go before it establishes a strong management culture.

Management communication skills (p. 9)

Score:

1. If you scored 50 to 60—congratulations. You are already an excellent management communicator.
2. If you scored 40 to 50—that's not too bad. You will find this book (and especially Chapter 5) very helpful in improving your communication skills.
3. If you scored 30 to 40—your communication will really benefit from some practice and careful planning.
4. If you scored 15 to 30—you have quite a bit of work to do.

References

Andrewartha, G. 2002, *Be Understood or Be Overlooked* (Sydney: Allen & Unwin).

Andrewartha, G. and R. Vast 2003, 'Effective and non-effective management skills across cultures', unpublished paper.

Andrews, K. R. 1971, *The Concept of Corporate Strategy* (Homewood, IL: Irwin).

Argyris, C. 1992, *On Organizational Learning*, 2nd ed. (Cambridge, UK: Blackwell).

Armstrong, G. 2000, 'Foreword', in Chartered Institute of Personnel and Development, *Success through Learning: The Argument for Strengthening Workplace Learning* (London: CIPD).

Au, K. H. P. and J. M. Mason 1983, 'Cultural congruence in classroom participation structures: Achieving a balance of rights', *Discourse Processes*, 6(2), pp. 145–67.
Badarucco, J. 2002, *Leading Quietly* (New York: Harvard Business School Press).
Baik, K. 2003, 'Issue leadership theory and its implications in global settings', in W. H. Mobley and P. W. Dorfman (eds), *Advances in Global Leadership* (Oxford, UK: Elsevier Science Ltd), pp. 37–62.
Bennis, W. G. 1989, *On Becoming a Leader* (Reading, MA: Addison-Wesley).
Bennis, W. G. and J. Goldsmith 1997, *Learning to Lead* (Reading, MA: Addison-Wesley).
Bennis, W. G. and B. Nanus 1985, *Leaders: The Strategies for Taking Charge* (New York: Harper and Row).
Benson, G. 1983, 'On the campus: How well do business schools prepare graduates for the business world?', *Personnel*, 60, pp. 61–65.
Bonhoeffer, D. 1955, *Ethics* (London: SCM Press).
Boudreau, J. W., P. M. Ramstad and P. J. Dowling 2003, 'Global talentship: Toward a decision science connecting talent to global strategic success', in W. H. Mobley and P. W. Dorfman (eds), *Advances in Global Leadership*, vol. 3 (Oxford: Elsevier Science Ltd), pp. 63–100.
Boyatzis, R. E. 1982, *The Competent Manager* (New York: John Wiley & Sons).
Boyatzis, R. E., A. J. Murphy and J. V. Wheeler 2000, 'Philosophy as a missing link between values and behavior', *Psychological Reports*, 86, pp. 47–64.
Bray, D. W. and D. L. Grant 1966, *The Assessment Center in the Measurement of Potential for Business Management*, Psychological Monographs 80 (whole no. 625).
Brutus, S., J. W. Fleenor and M. London 1998, 'Does 360-degree feedback work in different industries?', *Journal of Management Development*, 17(3), pp. 177–90.
Buber, M. 1958, *I and thou* (New York: Charles Scribner).
Cameron, K. and M. Tschirhart 1988, *Managerial Competencies and Organizational Effectiveness.* Working paper, School of Business Administration, University of Michigan.
Cameron, K. S. and D. A. Whetten 1984, 'A model for teaching management skills', *Organizational Behavior Teaching Journal*, 8, pp. 21–27.
Carver, C. S. and M. F. Scheier 1982, 'Control theory: A useful conceptual framework for personality-social, clinical, and health psychology', *Psychological Bulletin*, 92, pp. 111–35.
Cascio, W. F. and V. Silbey 1979, 'Utility of the assessment center as a selection device', *Journal of Applied Psychology*, 64, pp. 107–18.
Coates, D. E. 1998, 'Don't tie 360 degree feedback to pay', *Training*, 35(9), p. 68.
Collins, H. and E. Wray-Bliss 2005, 'Discriminating ethics', *Human Relations*, 58(6), pp. 799–824.
Cortada, J. and J. Woods (eds) 1999, *The Knowledge Management Yearbook 1999–2000* (Woburn, MA: Butterworth Heinemann).
Curtis, D. B., J. L. Winsor and D. Stephens 1989, 'National preferences in business and communication education', *Communication Education*, 38, pp. 6–15.
Darling, J. R and A. K. Fischer 1998, 'Developing the management leadership team in a multinational enterprise', *European Business Review*, 98(2), pp. 100–8.
Davis, S. R., J. H. Lucas and D. R. Marcotte 1998, 'GM links better leaders to better business', *Workforce*, 77(4), April.
Deal, J. J., J. Leslie, M. Dalton and C. Ernst 2003, 'Cultural adaptability and leading across cultures', in W. H. Mobley and P. W. Dorfman (eds), *Advances in Global Leadership*, vol. 3 (Oxford: Elsevier Science Ltd), pp. 149–66.
Deering, A., R. Dilts and J. Russell 2003, 'Leadership cults and cultures', *Leader to Leader*, 28, Spring, pp. 36–43.
Dekker, S. 2011, *Drift into Failure: From Hunting Broken Components to Understanding Complex Systems* (London: Ashgate).
Denison, D. R., S. Haaland and P. Goelzer 2003, 'Corporate culture and organizational effectiveness: Is there a similar pattern around the world?', in W. H. Mobley and P. W. Dorfman (eds), *Advances in Global Leadership*, vol. 3 (Oxford: Elsevier Science Ltd), pp. 205–30.
DiStefano, J. J. and M. L. Maznevski 2003, 'Developing global managers: Integrating theory, behavior, data and performance', in W. H. Mobley and P. W. Dorfman (eds), *Advances in Global Leadership*, vol. 3 (Oxford: Elsevier Science Ltd), pp. 341–72.
Drucker, P. 1954, *The Practice of Management* (New York: Harper & Row).
Drucker, P. 1967, *The Effective Executive* (New York: Heinemann).
Drucker, P. 1998, *Management's New Paradigms* [online]. Forbes.com. Available from <www.forbes.com/premium/archives/purchase.jhtml?storyURL=/forbes/1998/1005/6207152a.htmland_ requestid=468>, accessed 8 January 2004.
Drucker, P. 2001, *Management Challenges for the 21st Century* (New York: HarperCollins).
Easton, G. and S. Jarrell 1998, 'The effects of total quality management on corporate performance: An empirical investigation', *Journal of Business*, 71(2), pp. 253–307.
Edwards, M. R. 1996, 'Improving performance with 360-degree feedback', *Career Development International*, 1(3), pp. 5–8.
Edwards, M. R. and A. J. Ewen 1996, '360-degree feedback: Royal fail or Holy Grail?', *Career Development International*, 1(3), pp. 23–31.
Fletcher, C. 1999, 'The implication of research on gender differences in self-assessment and 360 degree appraisal', *Human Resource Management Journal*, 9(1), p. 39.

Fortune/Hay Group 1999, 'What makes great leaders: Rethinking the route to effective leadership from the executive survey of leadership effectiveness'.

Ganzel, R. 1998, 'What's wrong with pay for performance?' *In Training*, 35(12).

Gaugler, B. B., D. B. Rosenthal, G. C. Thornton and C. Bentson 1987, 'Meta-analysis of assessment center validity', *Journal of Applied Psychology*, 72, pp. 493–511.

Ghiselli, E. E. 1963, 'Managerial talent', *American Psychologist*, 18(10), October, pp. 631–42.

Goleman, D. 1998, *Working with Emotional Intelligence* (New York: Bantam).

Gowdy, L. N. 2010, *Logics Origin of Ethics, Morals, Virtue, and Quality* (self-published).

Gregory, R. J. 1999, *Psychological Testing: History, Principles, and Applications*, 3rd ed. (Boston: Allyn & Bacon).

Hampden-Turner, C. and F. Trompenaars 1997, *Mastering the Infinite Game: How East Asian Values are Transforming Business Practices* (Oxford, UK: Capstone).

Handy, C. 1995, *The Age of Paradox* (Boston: Harvard Business School Press).

Hanson, G. 1986, 'Determinants of firm performance: An integration of economic and organizational factors', Unpublished doctoral dissertation, University of Michigan Business School.

Heitzman, R. 2005, 'Values and Ethics, a Canadian Journey', World Bank presentation, 15 March.

Hofstede, G. 2001, *Culture's Consequences: Comparing Values, Behaviors, Institutions and Organizations across Nations* (Thousand Oaks, CA: Sage).

Hollan, R. 2002, 'Management decision-making and ethics: Practices, skills and preferences', Management decision 40/9 PPS 862 to 870.

Kabacoff, R. 2002, 'Personal motivations and leadership styles in organizational settings', Paper presented at the 110th Annual Convention of the American Psychological Association, Chicago, IL.

Karpin, D. S. 1995, *Enterprising Nation: Report of the Industry Task Force on Leadership and Management Skills* (Canberra: Australian Government Publishing Service).

Kambil, A. 2010, 'Developing the next generation of leaders', *Journal of Business Strategy*, 31(2), pp. 43–45.

Katz, J. and L. Paine 1994, Harvard Business School reference number 9–395–137.

Katz, R. L. 1974, 'Skills of an effective administrator', *Harvard Business Review*, 52(5), pp. 90–102.

Keep, E. 2000, *Upskilling Scotland—A New Horizon Report* (Edinburgh: Centre for Scottish Public Policy).

Kennedy, J. C., P. Fu and G. Yukl 2003, 'Influence tactics across twelve cultures', in W. H. Mobley and P. W. Dorfman (eds), *Advances in Global Leadership*, vol. 3 (Oxford: Elsevier Science Ltd), pp. 127–48.

Koontz, H. 1980, 'The management theory jungle revisited', *Academy of Management Review*, 5 April, pp. 175–87.

Kotter, J. P. 1990, *A Force for Change: How Leadership Differs from Management* (New York: Free Press).

Latham, G. P. and E. A. Locke 1979, 'Goal setting—a motivational technique that works', *Organizational Dynamics*, 8, pp. 68–80.

Leys, S. 1997, *The Analects of Confucius* (New York: W. W. Norton).

Ling, W. and L. Fang 2003, 'The Chinese leadership theory', in W. H. Mobley and P. W. Dorfman (eds), *Advances in Global Leadership*, vol. 3 (Oxford: Elsevier Science Ltd), pp. 183–204.

Livingston, J. S. 1971. 'Myth of the well-educated manager', *Harvard Business Review*, 49, pp. 79–89.

London, M. and J. W. Smither 1995, 'Can multi-source feedback change perceptions of goal accomplishment, self-evaluations, and performance related outcomes? Theory-based applications and directions for research', *Personnel Psychology*, 48, pp. 803–39.

Luthans, F., S. A. Rosenkrantz and H. W. Hennessey 1985, 'What do successful managers really do? An observation study of managerial activities', *Journal of Applied Behavioral Science*, 21, pp. 255–70.

MacDonald, C. 2011, *The Business Ethics Blog*, <http://businessethicsblog.com/2010/03/21/ethics-definition/>.

McManus, J. 2011, 'Revisiting ethics in strategic management', *Corporate Governance*, 11(2), pp. 214–23.

McNamara, C. (ed.) 1997, *The Management Assistance Program for Nonprofits' Team Values* (St Paul, MN: Wiley).

Mahzarin, B., M. Bazerman and D. Chugh 2003, 'How (un)ethical are you?', *Harvard Business Review*, December, pp. 56–65.

Mant, A. 1999, *Leaders We Deserve* (Melbourne: Australian Commission for the Future).

Margerison, C. J and A. Kakabadse 1984, *How American Chief Executives Succeed: Implications for Developing High-potential Employees* (New York: American Management Association).

Mintzberg, H. 1975, 'The manager's job: Folklore and fact', *Harvard Business Review*, 53, pp. 49–71.

Mobley, W. H. and P. W. Dorfman 2003, 'Introduction', in W. H. Mobley and P. W. Dorfman (eds), *Advances in Global Leadership*, vol. 3 (Oxford: Elsevier Science Ltd), p. xiii.

Nahavandi, A. 1997, *The Art and Science of Leadership* (Upper Saddle River, NJ: Prentice Hall).

Ng, L. C. 2011, 'Best management practices', *Journal of Management Development*, 30(1), pp. 93–105.

Paine, L., A. Strimling, C. Nichols, III, and R. Crawford 1999, Harvard Business School Publishing, reference number 9–399–136.

Parsons, H. M. 1974, 'What happened at Hawthorne?', *Science*, 183, pp. 922–32.

Parsons, T. 1951, *The Social System* (New York: The Free Press).

Peters, T. J. and R. H. Waterman 1982, *In Search of Excellence* (New York: Harper & Row).

Pfeffer, J. 1998, *The Human Equation: Building Profits by Putting People First* (Boston: Harvard Business School Press).

Provis, C. 2001, 'Why is trust important?', *Reason in Practice: The Journal of Philosophy of Management*, 1(2), pp. 31–41.

Rawls, J. A. 1971, *Theory of Justice* (Cambridge, MA: Harvard University Press).

Ridlehuber, E. 2006, *Affluent for Life* (Shrewsbury, NJ: Better World Books).
Rioux, S. and P. Bernthal 1999, *Succession Management Practices Report* (Pittsburgh, PA: Development Dimensions International).
Robinson, S. L. 1996, 'Trust and breach of the psychological contract', *Academy of Management Journal*, 41, pp. 574–99.
Saul, J. R. 1993, *Voltaire's Bastards: The Dictatorship of Reason in the West* (London: Penguin).
Schulz, K. 2010, *Being Wrong: Adventures in the Margin of Error* (New York: HarperCollins).
Schwartz, M. 2007, 'The "business ethics" of management theory', *Journal of Management History*, 13(1), pp. 43–54.
Selznick, P. 1957, *Leadership in Administration: A Sociological Interpretation* (Evanston, IL: Row, Peterson).
Senge, P. M. 1990, *The Fifth Discipline: The Art and Practice of the Learning Organization* (New York: Doubleday Books).
Sennett, R. 2003, *Respect: The Formation of Character in an Age of Inequality* (New York: W. W. Norton).
Shipper, F. and C. S. White 1999, 'Mastery frequency, and interaction of managerial behaviors relative to subunit effectiveness', *Human Relations*, 52(1), pp. 49–66.
Shriberg, A., C. Lloyd, D. L. Shriberg and M. L. Williamson 1997, *Practicing Leadership: Principles and Applications* (New York: John Wiley & Sons).
Smith, P. B. 2003, 'Leaders' sources of guidance and the challenge of working across cultures', in W. H. Mobley and P. W. Dorfman (eds), *Advances in Global Leadership*, vol. 3 (Oxford: Elsevier Science Ltd), pp. 167–82.
Soderberg, A. and N. Holden 2002, 'Rethinking cross-cultural management in a globalizing business world', *International Journal of Cross-Cultural Management*, 2(1), pp. 103–21.
Solomon, R. 1997, *It's Good Business* (Boston: Rowman and Littlefield).
Solomon, R. 1999, *The Best Way to Think about Business* (New York: Oxford University Press).
Stogdill, R. M. 1974, *Handbook of Leadership: A Survey of Theory and Research* (New York: The Free Press), p. xvii.
Svensson, G. and G. Wood 2011, 'A conceptual framework of corporate and business ethics across organizations. Structures, processes and performance', *The Learning Organization*, 18(1), pp. 21–35.
Tayeb, M. H., 2001, 'Conducting research across cultures: Overcoming drawbacks and obstacles', *International Journal of Cross-Cultural Management*, 1(1), pp. 113–29.
Taylor, F. W. 1903, *Shop Management* (New York: Harper & Row).
Taylor, F. W. 1911, *Principles of Scientific Management* (New York: Harper & Row).
Taylor, F. W. 1947, *Scientific Management: Comprising Shop Management, the Principles of Scientific Management, Testimony before the Special House Committee* (New York: Harper & Brothers Publishers).
Thornton, G. C. 1992, *Assessment Centers in Human Resource Management* (Reading, MA: Addison-Wesley).
Thornton, G. C. and W. C. Byham 1982, *Assessment Centers and Managerial Performance* (New York: Academic Press).
Tornow, W. and M. London 1998, *Maximizing the Value of 360-degree Feedback: A Tool and Process for Continuous, Self-directed Management Development* (San Francisco: Jossey-Bass).
Trompenaars, F. 1998, *Riding the Waves of Culture: Understanding Diversity in Global Business* (New York: Irwin).
Van Iddekinge, C. H., P. H. Raymark, C. E. Eidson, Jr and W. J. Attenweiler 2004, 'What do structured selection interviews really measure? The Construct Validity of Behavior Description Interviews', *Human Performance*, 17 January, pp. 71–93.
Wee, C. H. 2001, *Inspirations of Tao Zhu-Gong* (Singapore: Prentice-Hall).
Wren, D. A. 1987, *The Evolution of Management Thought* (New York: John Wiley & Sons).
Wren, D. A. 2005, *The History of Management Thought*, 5th ed. (New York: John Wiley & Sons).
Yapko, M. D. 2009, *Depression is Contagious* (New York: The Free Press).
Zaleznik, A. 1977, 'Managers and leaders: Are they different?', *Harvard Business Review*, May–June, pp. 67–78.

CHAPTER 2

DEVELOPING SELF-AWARENESS

OBJECTIVES

Increase personal awareness of your:

- **sensitive line**
- **personal values**
- **attitude towards change**
- **interpersonal style**
- **emotional intelligence**
- **communication and matching skills**

2

CHAPTER OUTLINE

Skill assessment

Evaluative surveys for self-awareness

Self-awareness assessment

Step 1: Before you read the material in this chapter, respond to the following statements by writing a number from the rating scale below in the left-hand column (pre-assessment). Your answers should reflect your attitudes and behaviour as they are now, not as you would like them to be. Be honest. This instrument is designed to help you discover how self-aware you are so that you can tailor your learning to your specific needs. When you have completed the survey, use the scoring key at the end of the chapter to identify the skill areas discussed in this chapter that are most important for you to master.

Step 2: When you have completed the reading and the exercises in this chapter and, ideally, as many of the skill application assignments at the end of the chapter as you can, cover up your first set of answers. Then respond to the same statements again, this time in the right-hand column (post-assessment). When you have completed the survey, use the scoring key at the end of the chapter to measure your progress. If your score remains low in specific skill areas, use the behavioural guidelines at the end of the skill-learning section to guide further practice.

Rating scale

1 Strongly disagree
2 Disagree
3 Slightly disagree
4 Slightly agree
5 Agree
6 Strongly agree

Assessment

Pre-	*Post-*	
______	______	1. I seek information about my strengths and weaknesses from others as a basis for self-improvement.
______	______	2. When I receive negative feedback about myself from others, I do not get angry or defensive.
______	______	3. In order to improve, I am willing to be self-disclosing to others (that is, to share my beliefs and feelings).
______	______	4. I am very much aware of my personal style of gathering information and making decisions.
______	______	5. I am very much aware of my own interpersonal needs when it comes to forming relationships with other people.
______	______	6. I have a good sense of how I cope with situations that are ambiguous and uncertain.
______	______	7. I have a well-developed set of personal standards and principles that guide my behaviour.
______	______	8. I feel very much in charge of what happens to me, good and bad.
______	______	9. I seldom, if ever, feel angry, depressed or anxious without knowing why.
______	______	10. I am conscious of the areas in which conflict and friction most frequently arise in my interactions with others.
______	______	11. I have a close personal relationship with at least one other person with whom I can share personal information and personal feelings.

The scoring key is on page 112.

Leadership Enhancement Team Style (LETS)

The Leadership Enhancement Team Style (LETS) (Andrewartha 2011) is a means of understanding your unique team leadership and communication style. The theory and practice are outlined in subsequent sections of this chapter. Your responses to the questionnaire will help you to identify your individual managerial behaviour as described in the text.

Step 1: To obtain your LETS profile, go online to <www.mcpheeandrewartha.com.au>.
Step 2: Click on the 'Developing management skills ed 5' logo on the home page.
Step 3: Click on the 'Questionnaire' logo.
Step 4: Enter username DMS5 and password ed5 and answer each of the statements as directed.
Step 5: Click 'Submit Answers' and your unique one-page profile will appear for you to print out.
Step 6: Use this profile against the text beginning on page 77 to understand your team leadership style and your matching behaviours in relation to other people.

A guide to interpretation of the LETS data from over 4000 managers is found on page 113.

If you have any problems with the online process, contact 61 8 8357 1800 or send an email to people@mcpheeandrewartha.com.au.

Emotional intelligence assessment

Finish each statement below by selecting the one alternative that is most likely to be your response. Think about the way you usually respond to these kinds of situations, not the way you would like to respond or the way you think you should respond. No correct answers exist for any of the items, and your scores will be most useful if you provide an accurate assessment of your typical behaviour. Mark only one answer per item.

1. When I get really upset, I ...
    a. Analyse why I am so disturbed.
    b. Blow up and let off steam.
    c. Hide it and remain calm.
2. In a situation in which a colleague takes credit in public for my work and my ideas, I would probably ...
    a. Let it slide and do nothing, in order to avoid a confrontation.
    b. Later, in private, indicate that I would appreciate being given credit for my work and ideas.
    c. Thank the person in public for referencing my work and ideas, and then elaborate on my contributions.
3. When I approach another person and try to strike up a conversation but the other person does not respond, I ...
    a. Try to cheer up the person by sharing a funny story.
    b. Ask the person if he or she wants to talk about what is on his or her mind.
    c. Leave the person alone and find someone else to talk to.
4. When I enter a social group, I usually ...
    a. Remain quiet and wait for people to talk to me.
    b. Try to find something complimentary I can tell someone.
    c. Find ways to be the life of the party or the source of energy and fun.
5. On important issues, I usually ...
    a. Make up my own mind and ignore others' opinions.
    b. Weigh both sides, and discuss it with others before making a decision.
    c. Listen to my friends or colleagues and make the same decision they do.
6. When someone that I do not particularly like becomes romantically attracted to me, I usually ...
    a. Tell that person directly that I am not interested.
    b. Respond by being friendly but cool or aloof.
    c. Ignore the person and try to avoid him or her.

7. When I am in the company of two people who have diametrically opposing points of view about an issue (for example, politics, abortion, war) and are arguing about it, I …
   a. Find something about which they can both agree and emphasise it.
   b. Encourage the verbal battle.
   c. Suggest that they stop arguing and calm down.
8. When I am playing a sport and the game comes down to my last-second performance, I …
   a. Get very nervous and hope that I do not choke.
   b. See this as an opportunity to shine.
   c. Stay focused and give it my best effort.
9. In a situation in which I have an important obligation and need to leave work early, but my colleagues ask me to stay to meet a deadline, I would probably …
   a. Cancel my obligation and stay to complete the deadline.
   b. Exaggerate a bit by telling my colleagues that I have an emergency that I cannot miss.
   c. Require some kind of compensation for missing the obligation.
10. In a situation in which another person becomes very angry and begins yelling at me, I …
   a. Get angry in return. I do not take that from anyone.
   b. Walk away. It does not do any good to argue.
   c. Listen first, and then try to discuss the issue.
11. When I encounter someone who has just experienced a major loss or tragedy, I …
   a. Really do not know what to do or say.
   b. Tell the person I feel very sorry and try to provide support.
   c. Share a time when I experienced a similar loss or tragedy.
12. When someone makes a racist joke or tells a crude story about a member of the opposite sex in mixed company, I usually …
   a. Point out that this is inappropriate and not acceptable, and then change the subject.
   b. Ignore it so I do not cause a scene.
   c. Get really upset and tell the person just what I think of what was said.

The scoring key is on page 115.

The Defining Issues Test

This instrument assesses your opinions about controversial social issues. Different people make decisions about these issues in different ways. You should answer the questions for yourself without discussing them with others. You are presented with three stories. Following each story are 12 statements or questions. Your task after reading the story is to rate each statement in terms of its importance in making a decision. After rating each statement, select the four most important statements and rank them from one to four in the spaces provided. Each statement should be ranked in terms of its relative importance in making a decision.

Some statements will raise important issues, but you should ask yourself whether the decision should rest on that issue. Some statements sound high and lofty but are largely gibberish. If you cannot make sense of a statement, or if you do not understand its meaning, mark it 5—'Of no importance'.

For information about interpreting and scoring the Defining Issues Test, refer to the scoring key at the end of the chapter. Use the following rating scale for your response.

Rating scale

1	Of great importance	This statement or question makes a crucial difference in making a decision about the problem.
2	Of much importance	This statement or question is something that would be a major factor (though not always a crucial one) in making a decision.
3	Of some importance	This statement or question involves something you care about, but it is not of great importance in reaching a decision.
4	Of little importance	This statement or question is not very important to consider in this case.

5	Of no importance	This statement or question is completely unimportant in making a decision. You would waste your time thinking about it.

The scoring key is on page 116.

The escaped prisoner

A man had been sentenced to prison for ten years. After one year, however, he escaped, moved to a new area of the country, and took on the name of Ben Thompson. For eight years he worked hard, and gradually he saved enough money to buy his own business. He was fair to his customers, gave his employees top wages, and gave most of his own profits to charity. Then one day, Margaret Jones, an old neighbour, recognised him as the man who had escaped from prison eight years before and for whom the police had been looking.

Should Margaret report Ben Thompson to the police and have him sent back to prison? Write a number from the rating scale on the previous page in the blank beside each statement.

_______ She should report him.
_______ I cannot decide.
_______ She should not report him.

Importance

______ 1. Hasn't Ben Thompson been good enough for such a long time to prove he is not a bad person?
______ 2. Every time someone escapes punishment for a crime, does that not encourage more crime?
______ 3. Wouldn't we be better off without prisons and the oppression of our legal system?
______ 4. Has Ben Thompson really paid his debt to society?
______ 5. Would society be failing if it did not impose the punishment that Ben Thompson should fairly expect?
______ 6. What benefit would prison be, apart from to society, especially for a charitable man?
______ 7. How could anyone be so cruel and heartless as to send Ben Thompson to prison?
______ 8. Would it be fair to prisoners who have to serve out their full sentences if Ben Thompson is let off?
______ 9. Was Margaret Jones a good friend of Ben Thompson?
______ 10. Is it a citizen's duty to report an escaped criminal, regardless of the circumstances?
______ 11. How would the will of the people and the public good best be served?
______ 12. Would going to prison do any good for Ben Thompson or protect anybody?

From the list of questions above, select the four most important:

______ Most important
______ Second most important
______ Third most important
______ Fourth most important

The scoring key is on page 116.

The doctor's dilemma

A woman was dying of incurable cancer and had only about six months to live. She was in terrible pain, but was so weak that a large dose of a painkiller such as morphine would probably kill her. When she was not delirious with pain, she would ask her doctor to give her a fatal dose of morphine. She said she could not stand the pain, and that she was going to die in a few months anyway.

What should the doctor do? (Check one.)

______ He should give the woman an overdose that will cause her to die.
______ I cannot decide.
______ He should not give her the overdose.

Importance

______ 1. Is the woman's family in favour of giving her the overdose?
______ 2. Is the doctor obligated by the same laws as everybody else?
______ 3. Would people be better off without society regimenting their lives and even their deaths?
______ 4. Should the doctor make the woman's death from a drug overdose appear to be an accident?
______ 5. Does the state have the right to force continued existence on those who do not want to live?
______ 6. Regardless of society's perspective on personal values, what is the value of death?
______ 7. Should the doctor have sympathy for the woman's suffering, or should he care more about what society might think?
______ 8. Is helping to end another's life ever a responsible act of cooperation?
______ 9. Can only God decide when a person's life should end?
______ 10. What values has the doctor set for himself in his own personal code of behaviour?
______ 11. Can society afford to let anybody end his or her life whenever he or she desires?
______ 12. Can society allow suicide or mercy killing and still protect the lives of individuals who want to live?

From the list of questions above, select the four most important:
______ Most important
______ Second most important
______ Third most important
______ Fourth most important

The scoring key is on page 116.

The newspaper

Rami, a Year 12 student, wanted to publish a newspaper for students so that he could express his opinions. He wanted to speak out against military build-up and some of the school's rules, such as the rule that forbids boys to wear their hair long.

When Rami started his newspaper, he asked his principal for permission. The principal agreed, on the understanding that, before each issue was published, Rami submitted all his articles for the principal's approval. Rami agreed to this condition and turned in several articles for approval. The principal approved all of them, and Rami published two issues of the paper in the next two weeks.

However, the principal had not expected that Rami's newspaper would receive so much attention. The students were so excited by the paper that they began to organise protests against the government, and the school's hair regulations and other rules. Angry parents objected to Rami's opinions. They phoned the principal telling him that the newspaper was unpatriotic and should not be published. As a result of the rising excitement, the principal wondered if he should order Rami to stop publishing on the grounds that the controversial newspaper articles were disrupting the operation of the school.

What should the principal do? (Check one.)
______ He should instruct Rami to stop publishing the newspaper.
______ I cannot decide.
______ He should not stop publication of the newspaper.

Importance

______ 1. Is the principal more responsible to the students or to the parents?
______ 2. Did the principal give his word that the newspaper could be published for a long time, or did he just promise to approve the newspaper one issue at a time?
______ 3. Would the students start protesting even more if the principal stopped the newspaper?
______ 4. When the welfare of the school is threatened, does the principal have the right to give orders to students?

______ 5. Does the principal have the freedom of speech to say no in this case?
______ 6. If the principal stopped the newspaper, would he be preventing full discussion of important issues?
______ 7. Would the principal's stop order make Rami lose faith in him?
______ 8. Is Rami really loyal to his school and patriotic to his country?
______ 9. What effect would stopping the paper have on the students' education in critical thinking and judgment?
______ 10. Is Rami in any way violating the rights of others in publishing his own opinions?
______ 11. Should the principal be influenced by some angry parents when it is the principal who knows best what is going on in the school?
______ 12. Is Rami using the newspaper to stir up hatred and discontent?

From the list of questions above, select the four most important:

______ Most important
______ Second most important
______ Third most important
______ Fourth most important

Source: Adapted from J. R. Rest, *Revised manual for the Defining Issues Test: An objective test of moral judgment development* (Minneapolis: Minnesota Moral Research Projects, 1979).

The scoring key is on page 117.

Core self-evaluation scale (CSES)

Below are several statements with which you may agree or disagree. Using the response scale below, indicate your level of agreement or disagreement with each statement.

Rating scale

1 Strongly disagree
2 Disagree
3 Neutral
4 Agree
5 Strongly agree

______ 1. I am confident I get the success I deserve in life.
______ 2. Sometimes I feel depressed.
______ 3. When I try, I generally succeed.
______ 4. Sometimes when I fail, I feel worthless.
______ 5. I complete tasks successfully.
______ 6. Sometimes, I do not feel in control of my work.
______ 7. Overall, I am satisfied with myself.
______ 8. I am filled with doubts about my competence.
______ 9. I determine what will happen in my life.
______ 10. I do not feel in control of my success in my career.
______ 11. I am capable of coping with most of my problems.
______ 12. There are times when things look pretty bleak and hopeless to me.

Source: T. A. Judge, A. Erez, J. E. Bobo and C. T. Thoreson, 'The core self-evaluation scale: Development of a measure', *Personnel Psychology*, 56, 2003, pp. 303–31.

The scoring key is on page 117.

The cognitive-style instrument

With this instrument, you should put yourself in the position of someone who must gather and evaluate information. The purpose is to investigate the ways you think about information you encounter. There are no right or wrong answers, and one alternative is just as good as another. Try to indicate the ways you do or would respond, not the ways you think you *should* respond.

For each scenario there are three pairs of alternatives. For each pair, select the alternative that comes closest to the way you would respond. Answer each item. If you are not sure, make your best guess. When you have finished answering all the questions, compare the scoring key on page 118 as a basis for comparing your score with others.

You are the chief executive of a company and have asked division heads to make presentations at the end of the year. Which of the following would be more appealing to you?

______ 1. a. A presentation analysing the details of the data.
b. A presentation focused on the overall perspective.

______ 2. a. A presentation showing how the division contributed to the company as a whole.
b. A presentation showing the unique contributions of the division.

______ 3. a. Details of how the division performed.
b. General summaries of performance data.

You are a scientist with a scientific institute whose job it is to gather information about the moons of Saturn. Which of the following would you be more interested in investigating?

______ 4. a. How the moons are similar to one another.
b. How the moons differ from one another.

______ 5. a. How the whole system of moons operates.
b. The characteristics of each moon.

______ 6. a. How Saturn and its moons differ from Earth and its moon.
b. How Saturn and its moons are similar to Earth and its moon.

You are visiting an African country and you are sending an email home to tell about your trip. Which of the following would be most typical of the email you would write?

______ 7. a. A detailed description of people and events.
b. General impressions and feelings.

______ 8. a. A focus on the similarities of our culture and theirs.
b. A focus on the uniqueness of their culture.

______ 9. a. Overall, general impressions of the experience.
b. Separate, unique impressions of parts of the experience.

You are attending a concert featuring a famous symphony orchestra. Which of the following would you be most likely to do?

______ 10. a. Listen for the parts of individual instruments.
b. Listen for the harmony of all the instruments together.

______ 11. a. Pay attention to the overall mood associated with the music.
b. Pay attention to the separate feelings associated with different parts of the music.

______ 12. a. Focus on the overall style of the conductor.
b. Focus on how the conductor interprets different parts of the score.

You are considering taking a job with a certain organisation. Which of the following would you be more likely to do in deciding whether or not to take the job?

______ 13. a. Systematically collect information about the organisation.
b. Rely on personal intuition or inspiration.

______ 14. a. Consider primarily the fit between you and the job.
b. Consider primarily the politics needed to succeed in the organisation.

______ 15. a. Be methodical in collecting data and making a choice.
b. Mainly consider personal instincts and gut feelings.

You inherit some money and decide to invest it. You learn of a new high-technology firm that has just issued shares. Which of the following is most likely to be true of your decision to purchase the firm's shares?

______ 16. a. You would invest on a hunch.
b. You would invest only after a systematic investigation of the firm.

______ 17. a. You would be somewhat impulsive in deciding to invest.
b. You would follow a pre-set pattern in making your decision.

______ 18. a. You could rationally justify your decision to invest in this firm and not in another.
b. It would be difficult to rationally justify your decision to invest in this firm and not another.

You are being interviewed on TV and you are asked the following questions. Which alternative would you be most likely to select?

______ 19. How are you more likely to cook?
a. With a recipe.
b. Without a recipe.

______ 20. How would you predict the Rugby League winner next year?
a. After systematically researching the personnel and records of the teams.
b. On a hunch or by intuition.

______ 21. Which games do you prefer?
a. Games of chance (like Bingo).
b. Chess, chequers or Scrabble.

You are a manager and need to hire an executive assistant. Which of the following would you be most likely to do in the process?

______ 22. a. Interview each applicant using a set outline of questions.
b. Concentrate on your personal feelings and instincts about each applicant.

______ 23. a. Consider primarily the personality fit between yourself and the candidates.
b. Consider the match between the precise job requirements and the candidates' capabilities.

______ 24. a. Rely on factual and historical data on each candidate in making a choice.
b. Rely on feelings and impressions in making a choice.

The scoring key is on page 118.

Locus of control scale

This questionnaire assesses your opinions about certain issues. Each item consists of a pair of alternatives marked with (a) or (b). Select the alternative with which you most agree. If you believe both alternatives to some extent, select the one with which you most strongly agree. If you do not believe either alternative, mark the one with which you disagree least strongly. Since this is an assessment of opinions, there are no right or wrong answers. When you have finished each item, turn to the scoring key on page 118 for instructions on how to tabulate the results and for comparison data.

This questionnaire is similar, but not identical, to the original locus of control scale developed by Julian Rotter. The comparison data provided at the end of this chapter comes from research using Rotter's scale instead of this one. However, the two instruments assess the same concept, are the same length and their mean scores are similar.

______ 1. a. Leaders are born, not made.
b. Leaders are made, not born.

______ 2. a. People often succeed because they are in the right place at the right time.
b. Success depends mostly on hard work and ability.

______ 3. a. When things go wrong in my life, it is generally because I have made mistakes.
b. Misfortunes occur in my life regardless of what I do.

______ 4. a. Whether there is war or not depends on the actions of certain world leaders.
b. It is inevitable that the world will continue to experience wars.

______ 5. a. Good children are mainly the products of good parents.
b. Some children become delinquents no matter how their parents behave.

______ 6. a. My future success depends mainly on circumstances I cannot control.
b. I am the master of my fate.

______ 7. a. History judges certain people to have been effective leaders mainly because circumstances made them visible and successful.
b. Effective leaders are those who have made decisions or taken actions that resulted in significant contributions.

______ 8. a. Not punishing children guarantees that they will grow up irresponsible.
b. Spanking children is never appropriate.

______ 9. a. I often feel that I have little influence over the direction my life is taking.
b. It is unreasonable to believe that fate or luck plays a crucial part in how my life turns out.

______ 10. a. Some customers will never be satisfied no matter what you do.
b. You can satisfy customers by giving them what they want when they want it.

______ 11. a. Anyone can get good marks in school if they work hard enough.
b. Some people are never going to excel in school no matter how hard they try.

______ 12. a. Good marriages result when both partners continually work on the relationship.
b. Some marriages are going to fail because the partners are just incompatible.

______ 13. a. I am confident that I can improve my basic management skills through learning and practice.
b. It is a waste of time to try to improve management skills in a classroom.

______ 14. a. More management skills courses should be taught in business schools.
b. Less emphasis should be put on skills in business schools.

______ 15. a. When I think back on the good things that happened to me, I believe they happened mainly because of something I did.
b. The bad things that have happened in my life have mainly resulted from circumstances outside my control.

______ 16. a. Many exams I took at school were unconnected to the material I had studied, so studying hard did not help at all.
b. When I prepared well for exams at school, I generally did quite well.

______ 17. a. I am sometimes influenced by what my astrological chart says.
b. No matter how the stars are lined up, I can determine my own destiny.

______ 18. a. Government is so big and bureaucratic that it is very difficult for any one person to have any impact on what happens.
b. Single individuals can have a real influence on politics if they speak up and let their wishes be known.

______ 19. a. People seek responsibility in work.
b. People try to get away with doing as little as they can.

______ 20. a. The most popular people seem to have a special, inherent charisma that attracts people to them.
b. People become popular because of how they behave.

______ 21. a. Things over which I have little control just seem to occur in my life.
b. Most of the time I feel responsible for the outcomes I produce.

______ 22. a. Managers who improve their personal competence will succeed more than those who do not improve.
b. Management success has very little to do with the competence possessed by the individual manager.

______ 23. a. Teams that win championships in most sports are usually the teams that, in the end, have the most luck.
b. More often than not, teams that win championships are those with the most talented players and the best preparation.

______ 24. a. Teamwork in business is a prerequisite to success.
b. Individual effort is the best hope for success.

______ 25. a. Some workers are just lazy and cannot be motivated to work hard no matter what you do.
b. If you are a skilful manager, you can motivate almost any worker to put forth more effort.

______ 26. a. In the long run, people can improve this country's economic strength through responsible action.
b. The economic health of this country is largely beyond the control of individuals.

______ 27. a. I am persuasive when I know I am right.
b. I can persuade most people even when I am not sure I am right.

______ 28. a. I tend to plan ahead and generate steps to accomplish the goals that I have set.
b. I seldom plan ahead because things generally turn out alright anyway.

______ 29. a. Some things are just meant to be.
b. We can change anything in our lives by hard work, persistence and ability.

The scoring key is on page 118.

Skill learning

Key dimensions of self-awareness

For thousands of years, knowledge of the self has been considered to be at the very core of human behaviour. The ancient dictum 'Know thyself' has been variously attributed to Plato, Pythagoras, Thales and Socrates. Plutarch noted that this inscription was carved on the Delphic Oracle, the mystical sanctuary where kings and generals sought advice on matters of greatest importance to them. As early as 42 BC, Publilius Syrus proposed, 'It matters not what you are thought to be, but what you are.' Alfred Lord Tennyson said, 'Self-reverence, self-knowledge, self-control, these three alone lead to sovereign power.' Probably the most oft-quoted passage on the self is Polonius's advice in *Hamlet*: 'To thine own self be true, and it must follow as the night the day, thou canst not then be false to any man.' And Confucius said, 'What the superior man seeks is in himself; what the small man seeks is in others.'

This chapter on self-awareness, together with the material on managing stress in Chapter 3, allows us to construct a hierarchy of self-management skills. As the Chinese philosopher Lao Tzu said over 2000 years ago, 'He is strong who conquers others; he who conquers himself is mighty' (*The Simple Way*, no. 33). Philip Massinger, writing in the 17th century, said in *The Bondman*, 'He that would govern others must first master himself.' Self-management depends first and foremost on self-awareness, but, as illustrated in Figure 2.1, other skills are also closely linked to and build on self-awareness. Setting personal priorities and goals, for example, helps individuals direct their own lives, and time and stress management helps individuals adapt to and organise their environments.

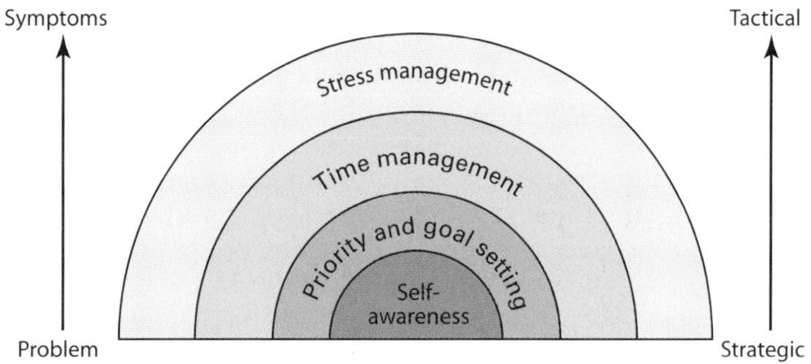

FIGURE 2.1 A hierarchy of personal life-management skills

This chapter focuses on the core aspects of self-management and serves as the foundation for the following chapter on stress and time management. Moreover, as Figure 2.1 illustrates, when problems arise in personal management, the easily recognised symptoms are often time pressures or stress. However, those symptoms are often linked to more fundamental problems with self-awareness and out-of-balance priorities. Developing and maintaining these aspects of self-awareness leads to long-term strategic improvement.

Students of human behaviour have long known that knowledge of oneself—self-awareness, self-insight, self-understanding—is essential to productive personal and interpersonal functioning, and in understanding and empathising with other people. A host of techniques and methods for achieving self-knowledge have been devised. Various therapies, group methods, meditation techniques and exercise programs are available for enhancing insight into the self and bringing inner peace. This chapter does not aim to summarise those procedures and does not espouse any one procedure in particular. Rather, what is discussed here is the importance of self-awareness in managerial behaviour, and several self-assessment instruments that research has shown to relate to managerial success are introduced. The emphasis is on scientifically validated information that links self-awareness to the behaviour of managers. Generalisations that have not been tested in research have been avoided.

Self-understanding and self-management

Erich Fromm was one of the first behavioural scientists to observe the close connection between our self-concept and our feelings about others: 'Hatred against oneself is inseparable from hatred against others' (1939). Carl Rogers (1961) later proposed that self-awareness and self-acceptance are prerequisites for psychological health, personal growth, and the ability to know and accept others. In fact, Rogers suggested that self-regard, which he found to be more powerful in his clinical cases than physiological needs, develops from good self-awareness. Brouwer (1964: 156) asserted:

> *The function of self-examination is to lay the groundwork for insight, without which no growth can occur. Insight is the 'Oh, I see now' feeling that must consciously or unconsciously precede change in behaviour. Insights—real, genuine glimpses of ourselves as we really are—are reached only with difficulty and sometimes with real psychic pain. But they are the building blocks of growth. Thus, self-examination is a preparation for insight, a ground-breaking for the seeds of self-understanding which gradually bloom into changed behaviour.*

A key outcome of increased self-awareness is the appreciation of differences in what managers may be trying to communicate (intent) and how they actually come across (impact).

An overview self-awareness instrument is the core self-evaluation tool. This is a recently developed construct that captures the essential aspects of personality. More than 50 000 studies have been conducted on what has been referred to as 'the Big Five' personality dimensions—neuroticism, extraversion, conscientiousness, agreeableness and openness—but an underlying factor has been found to account for the effects of these personality dimensions. It is referred to as 'core self-evaluation' (Judge et al. 2003), and an instrument is provided in the skill assessment section (page 59) to assess your core self-evaluation. The chapter explains some important research on this construct relating to how scores correlate with success at work and in life. By analysing your scores, you will learn not only about your underlying personality dimensions but also about how they are associated with other important behaviours such as motivation, problem solving, creativity, life satisfaction and work performance.

Core self-evaluation identifies the general personality orientation that guides behaviour. It uncovers levels of self-esteem, self-efficacy, emotional stability and self-control that have important effects on individuals' happiness as well as managerial effectiveness. The core self-evaluation reveals our core self-concept (see Figure 2.2).

Goleman's research (Goleman 1998b) on EQ, or emotional intelligence, which is discussed later in the chapter, adds more evidence to the proposition that the knowledge we possess about ourselves (which makes up our self-concept) is central to improving our management skills. Cervone (1997)

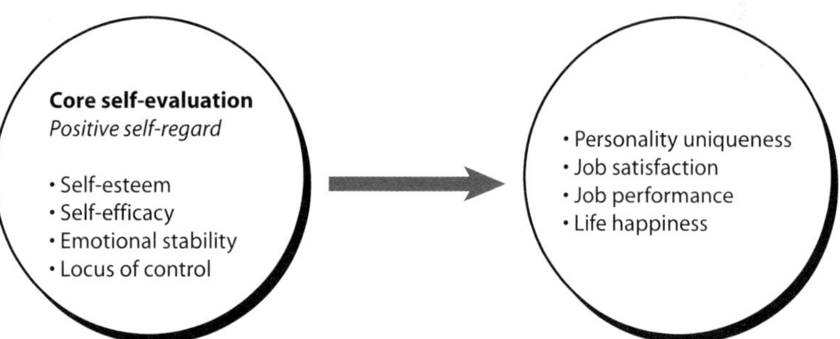

FIGURE 2.2 The effects of core self-evaluation

and Spencer and Spencer (1993) also support the correlation between more self-awareness and good management and leadership skills. We cannot improve ourselves or develop new capabilities until we know what level of capability we currently possess.

However, many of us may resist developing self-awareness. We may avoid acquiring additional information in order to protect our existing self-concept. As Maslow (1962: 57) noted:

> *We tend to be afraid of any knowledge that would cause us to despise ourselves or to make us feel inferior, weak, worthless, evil, shameful. We protect ourselves and our ideal image of ourselves by repression and similar defences, which are essentially techniques by which we avoid becoming conscious of unpleasantness or dangerous truth.*

Thus, avoidance of self-knowledge may occur because we fear finding out that we are not all that we would like to be. How, then, can management skills be developed if the self-knowledge necessary for the development of those skills is resisted? How can we overcome our resistance and alert ourselves to the need for change?

The sensitive line

One answer relies on the concept of the *sensitive line.* This concept refers to the point at which individuals become defensive or protective when encountering information about themselves that is inconsistent with their self-concept or when meeting pressure to alter their behaviour. Most people regularly experience information about themselves that does not quite fit or that is marginally inconsistent. For example, a friend might say, 'You look tired today. Are you feeling okay?' If you are feeling fine, the information is inconsistent with your self-awareness. But because the discrepancy is relatively minor, it would not be likely to offend you or evoke a strong defensive reaction. That is, it would probably not require that you re-examine and change your self-concept.

On the other hand, the more discrepant the information or the more serious its implications for your self-concept, the closer it would be to approaching your sensitive line, generating a need to defend yourself against it. For example, having a co-worker judge you incompetent as a manager may cross your sensitive line, especially if you think you have done a good job as a manager. This would certainly be true if the co-worker was an influential person. Your response would probably be to defend yourself against the information to protect the image you hold of yourself.

This response is known as the *threat–rigidity response* (Staw, Sandelands & Dutton 1981; Weick 1993). When individuals are threatened, when they encounter uncomfortable information or when uncertainty is created, they tend to become rigid. They protect themselves and become risk-averse. Individuals become psychologically and emotionally rigid when they encounter information that is a threat to their self-concept. They tend to redouble their efforts to protect what is comfortable and familiar (Cameron 1994; Cameron, Kim & Whetten 1987; Weick & Sutcliffe 2000). They rely on first-learned or most-reinforced behaviour patterns and emotions. When discrepancies in the self-image are encountered, the validity of the information or its source is denied, or other kinds of defence mechanisms are used to ensure that the self-concept remains stable. Crossing the sensitive line creates rigidity and self-preservation.

Dexter Dunphy (1993: 104–5) believes that:

> *Underlying all defensive behaviour is anxiety and fear. A threat to self-esteem is experienced as a feeling of psychological discomfort, which may be as strong as or stronger than physical pain. If we are able to cope with the threat, the discomfort ceases, we feel successful and our self-esteem is enhanced. As a result, we are more likely to be able to cope with the threat if it recurs. But remaining in a threatening situation and taking realistic, coping action requires courage and time. It usually requires that we endure immediate discomfort for longer-term gain. Consequently, we frequently seize on the opportunity for quick, palliative actions, which remove our immediate discomfort even though they fail to solve the problem.*

In light of this defensiveness, then, how can increased self-knowledge and personal change ever occur? There are at least two answers. One is that information that is verifiable, predictable and controllable is less likely to cross the sensitive line than information without those characteristics. That is, if an individual can test the validity of the discrepant information (for example, if some objective standard exists), if the information is not unexpected or 'out-of-the-blue' (for example, if it is received at regular intervals) and if there is some control over what, when and how much information is received (for example, if it is requested), it is more likely to be heard and accepted. The information you receive about yourself in this chapter possesses those three characteristics. You have already completed several self-assessment instruments that have been used extensively in research. Their reliability and validity have been established. Moreover, they have been found to be associated with managerial success. Therefore, in your analysis of your scores, you can gain important insights that can prove helpful to you.

A second answer to the problem of overcoming resistance to self-examination lies in the role other people can play in helping insights to occur. It is almost impossible to increase skill in self-awareness unless we interact with and disclose ourselves to others. Unless we are willing to open up to others, to discuss aspects of the self that seem ambiguous or unknown, little growth can ever occur. Self-disclosure, therefore, is a key to improvement in self-awareness.

As you engage in the practice exercises in this chapter, you are encouraged to discuss your insights with someone else. A lack of self-disclosure not only inhibits self-awareness but may also affect adversely other aspects of managerial skill development. Several studies have shown that low self-disclosers are less healthy and more self-alienated than high self-disclosers. Highest ratings for interpersonal competence go to high self-disclosers, and individuals who are high self-disclosers are liked best. However, both excessive self-disclosure and insufficient self-disclosure result in less liking and acceptance by others (see, for example, Covey 1989; Goleman 1998b; Jourard 1964). Some of the exercises in this chapter require you to discuss your experiences with others—a critical aspect of your personal growth.

The challenge—and risk—of self-awareness can be managed, then, by exercising some control over when and what kind of information you receive about yourself, and by involving others in your pursuit of self-understanding. The social support individuals receive from others during the process of self-disclosure, besides helping to increase feedback and self-awareness, helps to provide information that contributes to greater self-awareness without crossing the sensitive line.

Understanding and respecting individual differences

Another important reason for focusing on self-awareness is to help you develop the ability to diagnose important differences among others with whom you interact. There is considerable evidence that an individual's effectiveness as a manager is closely related to their ability to recognise, appreciate and ultimately use, key fundamental differences among others. This chapter has two objectives:

1. to help you to understand better your own uniqueness as an individual, in order to become better equipped to manage yourself
2. to help you diagnose, respect and benefit from the differences you find in other people, whether they be from your own culture or a different culture.

Self-knowledge will help you to understand your own taken-for-granted assumptions, trigger points, sensitive line, comfort zone, strengths and weaknesses, and so forth. This knowledge is useful for all of us, because it helps make our interactions with others more effective and insightful. It also helps us gain a more complete understanding of our potential for contributing value in our future career roles and our special strengths relative to others. It is not unusual for many of us to sometimes feel overshadowed, for example, by heroic or luminary figures whose success is attributed to charisma, intelligence or style. We feel we are somehow diminished and less able because of what we see in others. Self-knowledge allows us to recognise our own special gifts and strengths and to capitalise on our talents. The book *Built to Last* by Collins and Porras (2002) provides excellent examples of self-aware, non-charismatic and very successful leaders.

Recognising and accurately diagnosing fundamental differences in others is, similarly, an important part of being an effective manager. Being aware of, and empathetic towards, the different perspectives, needs and inclinations of other people is a key part of emotional intelligence and interpersonal maturity. Most people, however, have a tendency to interact with individuals who are like themselves, to choose similar people to work with them and to exclude others who seem to be different (Berscheid & Walster 1978). The history of human warfare and conflict attests to the fact that differences are often interpreted as frightening or threatening. Although fostering similarity seemingly makes it easier to interact with other people, especially in a work setting, it also reduces creativity, complex problem solving, and the likelihood that working colleagues will challenge the perspective of the authority figure. Research on organisational failure has repeatedly demonstrated that a lack of diversity in the composition of key decision-making bodies makes it difficult for them to recognise changes in their environment and to respond in appropriately new and novel ways (Cameron, Kim & Whetten 1987).

One key to helping individuals feel comfortable discussing ways in which they are different is by sharing a commitment to focus on differences, not distinctions or prejudices. We observe differences; we create distinctions. Differences help us to understand potential sources of misunderstanding between people and give us clues to how we can work together more effectively. Distinctions create social barriers between people for the express purpose of establishing (or reinforcing) advantages and disadvantages. When someone discounts the opinion of a co-worker on the grounds that the person is 'a member of the old boys' club', 'from marketing', 'a woman' or 'doesn't have a university degree', they are creating a distinction that is not only potentially hurtful on a personal basis but also ineffective for the organisation.

The creation of such distinctions destroys trust among people, even if the distinctions refer to individuals who are not present. If you apply distinctions that belittle someone in another group, for example, that action plants a seed of mistrust in the minds of the people present regarding what distinctions you may be privately using to discount *them.* The ladder of inference discussed later in the chapter describes this process in more detail. This is also an outcome of 'mobbing', which is discussed in Chapter 7. Recognising differences is not the same as evaluating distinctions. One is helpful; the other is hurtful. When others feel that self-disclosing information could be used against them—that is, they could be placed on the disadvantaged side of a distinction—they will be reluctant to participate in any self-discovery process, especially one that requires them to share information about their personal characteristics.

Self-awareness and understanding differences cannot occur without self-disclosure, sharing and trusting conversations. Self-knowledge requires an understanding and a valuing of differences, not the creation of distinctions. We encourage you to use the information you discover about yourself and others in a respectful manner, so that both you and the people you interact with can grow and develop.

Five major areas of self-awareness

There are many personal dimensions to explore if we are to develop in-depth self-awareness. This chapter focuses on five major areas of self-awareness that have been found to be important in developing successful management: (1) values, (2) interpersonal style, (3) emotional intelligence, (4) attitude towards change, and (5) cognitive style. These areas represent a limited set of factors, but they have been found to be important predictors of various aspects of effective managerial performance, such as achieving life success, performing effectively in teams, competent decision making, life-long learning and development, creativity, communication competency and self-empowerment (Allan & Waclawski 1999; Atwater & Yammarino 1992; Goleman 1998a, 1998b; Parker & Kram 1993; Sosik & Megerian 1999).

Values are discussed first because they are 'the core of the dynamics of behaviour and play so large a part in unifying personality' (Allport, Gordon & Vernon 1931: 2). That is, all attitudes, orientations and behaviours arise out of individuals' values. Cultural values and personal values drive our ethical behaviour and impact on a person's management skills.

The second area of self-awareness is *interpersonal style*. This concerns how we communicate with, interact with and influence others.

Third is *emotional intelligence*. Goleman's research on emotional intelligence, or EQ, is discussed, along with how it is essential for effective managers to possess emotional maturity.

The fourth area considered is *people's attitude towards change*, which focuses on the methods people use to cope with change in their environment. Everyone, but especially managers, is faced with increasingly fragmented, rapidly changing, tumultuous conditions. It is important that people become aware of their orientation towards adapting to these conditions.

The last area explored is *cognitive style*, which refers to the manner in which individuals gather and process information.

Figure 2.3 summarises these five aspects of self-awareness, together with their functions in defining the self-concept.

Of course, there are many other aspects of self-awareness that could be considered in this chapter, but all these aspects of the self are related fundamentally to the five core concepts selected for review. These are among the most important building blocks upon which other aspects of the self emerge.

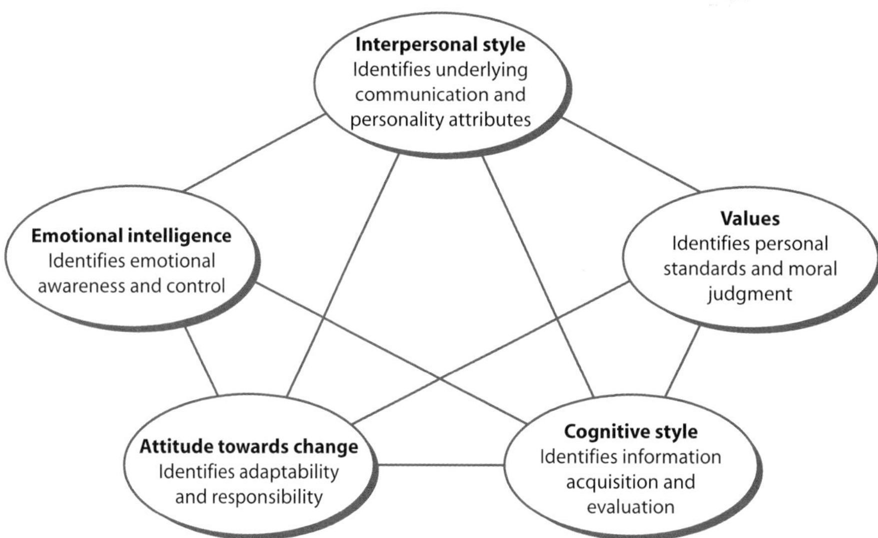

FIGURE 2.3 Five core aspects of self-awareness

Core aspect 1: Values

Values are among the most stable and enduring characteristics of individuals. They are the foundation on which attitudes and personal preferences are formed. They are the basis for crucial decisions, life directions, ethics and personal tastes.

Much of what we are is a product of the basic values we have developed throughout our lives. An organisation, too, has a value system, usually referred to as the 'organisational culture'. Research has found that employees who hold values that are matched with or congruent with their organisation's values are more productive and satisfied (Cable & Judge 1996; Cameron & Quinn 1999; Nwachukwu & Vitell 1997, Posner & Kouzes 1993). Holding values that are mismatched with organisational values, on the other hand, is a major source of frustration, conflict and non-productivity. Being aware of our own priorities and values, therefore, is important if we expect to achieve compatibility at work and in a long-term career. (See Lobel 1992)

Not conforming to our personal values

Simon (1974) and others have suggested that people sometimes lose touch with their own values, behaving in ways that are inconsistent with those values. That is, they pursue lower priorities at the expense of higher priorities, substituting goals with immediate payoffs for those with more long-term, central value. They may pursue an immediate reward or a temporary satisfaction, for example, in place of long-term happiness and inner peace. Not being cognisant of our own value priorities can lead to misdirected decisions and frustration in the longer term.

As in many areas of self-awareness, however, many people feel that they have a clear understanding of their values. Because their values are seldom challenged, they do not think much about the extent to which they hold certain values more highly than others. On the other hand, it is precisely because they are seldom challenged that people tend to forget value priorities and behave in incongruous ways. Until people encounter a contradiction or a threat to their values, they seldom assert them or seek to clarify them.

The values held by each of us are affected by a variety of factors, and a number of ways have been used to measure and describe values. We point out several ways in this chapter, each of which has been widely used in research and in management circles. The first is a framework for describing the broad, general value orientations that characterise large groups, such as nationalities, ethnic groups, industries or organisations. Much research has been done, for example, in identifying the differences in values that arise across cultural groups. The point of this research is to identify ways in which nationalities differ from one another, since almost all managers now face the need to manage across national boundaries or to manage staff from different cultures. It has been discovered that values differ systematically across national cultures, and these differences are a strong influence in predicting the values each of us hold. At least some of our values are affected significantly by the country and culture in which we have been raised.

Cultural values

In Chapter 1 we saw how management is a social theory intricately bound up with the psychology and sociology of people. Parsons (1951), Hofstede (2001), Trompenaars (1996), and Trompenaars and Hampden-Turner (1999) identified cultural factors covering the ways in which human beings form relationships with each other. These social values may be sharply defined between different cultures but they are also subtly present within any culture.

Trompenaars and Hampden–Turner (1999) identified seven value dimensions on which significant differences exist between national cultures. His data are based on 30 000 managers in 55 countries, and he found that certain cultures emphasise some values more than others. Table 2.1 identifies Trompenaars' seven dimensions, and examples are provided of countries that represent each of the value dimensions. No national culture emphasises one of these dimensions to the exclusion of another, but there are clear differences in the amount of emphasis placed on each dimension.

These seven factors are like continua, with the poles at each end of each factor representing opposites. That is, when an individual or group communicates with another, they are significantly matched in their understanding if they are operating from the same end of each continuum. For example, two individuals (or groups) will be on the same wavelength if they are both universalists. Both of them, in discussing a performance contract or setting up a new office, will focus on the right and proper way of doing it, on the established rules for doing these things.

TABLE 2.1 Trompenaars' seven value dimensions

VALUE DIMENSION	EXPLANATION	EXAMPLES OF COUNTRIES WITH DOMINANCE
Universalism	Societal rules and norms are valued.	United States, Switzerland, Norway, Sweden
vs		
Particularism	Individual relationships are valued.	Korea, Venezuela, China, Indonesia
Individualism	Individual contributions are valued.	United States, Nigeria, Denmark, Austria
vs		
Collectivism	Team contributions are valued.	Mexico, Indonesia, Japan, Philippines
Affective	Showing emotions is valued.	Iran, Spain, France, Switzerland
vs		
Neutral	Unemotional responses are valued.	Korea, Ethiopia, China, Japan
Specific	Segregating life's roles is valued.	Holland, Sweden, Denmark, United Kingdom
vs		
Diffuse	Integrating life's role is valued.	China, Nigeria, Singapore, Korea
Achievement	Personal accomplishment is valued.	United States, Norway, Canada, Austria
vs		
Ascription	Inherent attributes are valued.	Egypt, Indonesia, Korea, Czech Republic
Past and Present	Past is tightly connected to future.	France, Japan, United Kingdom
vs		
Future	Future is disconnected but valued.	United States, Holland
Internal	Individual control is valued.	United States, Canada, Austria, United Kingdom
vs		
External	Control comes from outside forces.	Czech Republic, Japan, Egypt, China

Source: F. Trompenaars and C. Hampden-Turner, *Riding the Waves of Culture* (London: McGraw-Hill, 1999). Reproduced with permission of The McGraw-Hill Companies.

They are mismatched if they are coming from opposite ends of these continua. Their understanding and connection will be weakened and may result in serious misunderstandings and even conflict. For example, a universalist communicating with a particularist is likely to present general, agreed principles only to find the other person discussing exceptions and special friends. They may talk their way through this complexity, but it is highly likely that the discomfort caused by their different values and meanings (different worldviews) will lead to a delayed or even a failed outcome.

The first five dimensions of the model refer to how individuals tend to relate to other people.

Universalism/particularism

Some countries (for example, the United States, Norway, Sweden, Switzerland) emphasise a value of universalism, in which other people's behaviour is governed by universal standards and rules (for example, do not lie, do not cheat, do not run a red light even if no one is coming the other way). General societal rules govern behaviour. Other countries (for example, Korea, China, Indonesia, Singapore) hold a value of particularism, in which the relationship with an individual governs behaviour (for example, is the other person a friend, a family member, a relative?). Trompenaars and Hampden-Turner (1999) state:

> *In practice we use both kinds of judgment, and in most situations we encounter they reinforce each other. If a female employee is harassed in the workplace we would disapprove of this because 'harassment is immoral and against company rules' and/or because 'it was a terrible experience for Jennifer and really upset her'. The universalist's chief objection, though, will be the breach of rules; 'women should not have to deal with harassment in the workplace; it is wrong'. The particularist is likely to be more disapproving of the fact that it caused distress to poor Jennifer. (Reproduced with permission of The McGraw-Hill companies.)*

Consider your answer to this question: You are driving in a car with a close friend who hits a pedestrian while doing 60 kilometres an hour in a 40-kilometre-per-hour zone. There are no witnesses and your friend's lawyer says that he will get off if you will testify that he was travelling at only 40 kilometres an hour. Will you lie for him? People in universalistic cultures are more likely to refuse than people in particularistic cultures. For example, 97 per cent of the Swiss and 93 per cent of North Americans (Canada and the United States) would refuse to testify, whereas only 32 per cent of Venezuelans and 37 per cent of South Koreans would refuse.

For each of these cultural dimensions, managerial behavioural tips are provided for how to best engage and achieve more effective outcomes with an individual (or group) from the other polarity of the dimension.

Matching tips (for particularists matching with universalists)

1. Be prepared for black and white, right versus wrong, 'this is the proper way to do it' type of discussions.
2. Realise that the formal, impersonal, rigid and businesslike approach is not intended as rudeness.
3. Follow the lead and be a little more formal, even to the point of checking out formal documents, contracts and so on.

Matching tips (for universalists matching with particularists)

1. Be prepared for personal anecdotes and apparent irrelevancies that do not seem to be going anywhere.
2. Do not dismiss personal, get-to-know-you discussions as small talk. In fact, stretch yourself and engage in some response.
3. Consider that personal connections might not always be improper and that not everything needs to be formally constructed to be correct.

Individualism/collectivism

A second value dimension differentiates cultures that value individualism (an emphasis on the self, or independence and/or uniqueness) over collectivism (an emphasis on the group, the combined unit, and on joining with others). Individualistic values hold the contributions of individuals to be most valued, whereas collectivism values team contributions. In general, individual responsibility dominates much more in Western cultures than in Eastern ones.

Consider your answer to this question: What kind of job is found most frequently in your organisation, one in which everyone works together and you do not get individual credit, or one in which everyone is allowed to work individually and you receive individual recognition? Eastern Europeans (for example, Russia, Czech Republic, Hungary, Poland) average above 80 per cent in agreeing that individual credit is received (the United States' score is 72 per cent.), whereas Asians (for example, Japan, India, Nepal) average below 45 per cent.

Matching tips (for individualists matching with collectivists)

1. Slow down and be more patient with the need for extra consultation and discussion time.
2. Recognise that the focus is on the group relationship and process as much as on the outcome and the goal.
3. In negotiations it may be the case that further consultation and reformulation of options need to occur outside the negotiation situation.

Matching tips (for collectivists matching with individualists)

1. Be prepared for rapid, apparently individualistic decision making and propositions.
2. Remember that their aim is to make a quick deal or to reach a solution as quickly as possible.
3. Try to reflect and access their individual interest in a way that would fit with your group interest.

LEARNING

Affective/neutral

A third value dimension refers to the display of feelings in public. It identifies an affective (emotional display) versus neutral orientation. Cultures with high affective values show emotions openly and deal with problems in emotional ways. Loud laughter, anger and intense passion may all be displayed in the course of a business negotiation. Cultures with neutral values are more controlled and stoic in their approach to problem solving. Instrumental, goal-directed behaviours rather than emotions dominate interactions.

Consider this scenario: If you became very upset at work or in class—say, you felt slighted, offended or angry—how likely would you be to display your feelings openly in public? Managers in Japan, Ethiopia, the United States and Hong Kong, for example, average 64 per cent, 74 per cent, 81 per cent and 43 per cent, respectively, in refusing to show emotions publicly. On the other hand, only 15 per cent of Kuwaiti managers, 18 per cent of Egyptian managers and 19 per cent of Spanish managers would refuse to show emotions publicly.

Matching tips (for neutrals with affectives)

1. While you may be concerned by the reactions and drama, give yourself time out from the intensity of the situation for some breathing space.
2. The probability is that much of the focus is personal, and reactions to you and your manner may seem to outweigh considerations of the object and outcomes.
3. Do not mistake enthusiasm or anger for inflexibility and a closed mind.

Matching tips (for affectives with neutrals)

1. Remember that your energy and enthusiasm can feel like pressure and they may need some time out to consider and reflect before continuing.
2. Do not mistake lack of emotion and energy for lack of commitment or lack of skill and tenacity. Be careful not to underestimate neutrals.
3. Try to minimise your overly expressive and reactive gestures, non-verbal expressions and comments.

Specific/diffuse

A fourth dimension—specific versus diffuse—describes the difference between cultures that segregate the different roles in life so as to maintain privacy and personal autonomy, compared with those cultures that integrate and merge their roles. Cultures with specific values separate work relationships from family relationships, whereas diffuse cultures entangle work and home relationships. People with specific values may seem hard to get to know because they keep a boundary between their personal lives and their work lives. People with diffuse values may seem too forward and too superficial because they seem to share personal information freely. Diffuse cultures have lower turnover rates among employees and higher degrees of loyalty to an employer because work and personal relationships are more intertwined.

To illustrate the difference, how would you respond to this question: Your boss asks you to come to her home to help her paint her house. You are unwilling to do it because you hate painting. Would you refuse? More than 82 per cent of the Dutch, Americans and Swedes would refuse, whereas only 32 per cent of the Chinese and 46 per cent of Nigerians would refuse.

Matching tips (for specific with diffuse)

1. Take a little more time than usual and look for the key issues and pointers contained within the indirect communication.
2. Allow things to meander, occasionally directing and influencing the flow.
3. Spend some time trying to understand the values and worldview of the person or the vision and culture of the organisation.

Matching tips (for diffuse with specific)

1. Plan to be a little more direct and to the point than usual.
2. Do not take offence if they appear to be somewhat abrupt or too focused on specific issues.
3. Set up a modest agenda and work hard to stick within it.

Achievement/ascription

A fifth value dimension differentiates cultures that emphasise an achievement orientation versus an ascription culture. People tend to acquire high status based on their personal accomplishments in some cultures, whereas in other cultures status and prestige are based more on ascribed characteristics such as age, gender, family heritage or ethnic background. Who you know (ascription) versus what you can do (achievement) helps to identify the difference on this value dimension. For example, the following statement serves to highlight achievement versus ascription value differences: 'It is important to act the way you are, to be consistent with your true self, even if you do not accomplish the task at hand.' Only 10 per cent of managers from Uruguay, 12 per cent from Argentina and 13 per cent from Spain disagree with the statement, whereas 77 per cent of Norwegians and 75 per cent of managers from the United States disagree.

Matching tips (for achievers with ascriptives)

1. Be careful to show some respect for status and seniority, despite what you may feel about their competence and knowledge.
2. Include a reference to status in some of your discussions, rather than relying solely on knowledge and ability.
3. Remember that to challenge is to threaten and encourage defensiveness.

Matching tips (for ascriptives with achievers)

1. Show some respect for ability and competence even if you are concerned about their importance or status.
2. Make sure that as well as seniority or status you have enough technical data and solid knowledge behind you.
3. Do not underestimate their need to achieve. Challenge is responded to as motivation.

Past/present/future

A sixth value dimension relates to how people interpret and manage time. It distinguishes the emphasis placed on the past, present and future in various cultures. Some cultures, for example, value the past and traditions more than the future; other cultures place more value on the future than the past. What you have achieved in the past matters more in some cultures than where you are headed in the future. Time differences also exist regarding short versus long time horizons. For example, some people are oriented towards very short time horizons, where they think in terms of minutes and hours (a short time horizon). Other people think in terms of months or years (a long time horizon).

Complete this brief exercise to get a sense of your own time horizon. Using the rating scale, assign a number to each of the following statements:

- My past started _______ ago, and ended _______ ago.
- My present started _______ ago and will end _______ from now.
- My future will start _______ from now and will end _______ from now.

Rating scale: 7 = years, 6 = months, 5 = weeks, 4 = days, 3 = hours, 2 = minutes, 1 = seconds.

By way of comparison, people in the Philippines averaged 3.40 on the scale, Irish managers averaged 3.82, Brazilians averaged 3.85 and the United States averaged 4.30. On the other hand, managers in Hong Kong averaged 5.71, Portugal averaged 5.62 and Pakistan averaged 5.47.

Internal/external control

The seventh and final value dimension focuses on internal and external control. This value dimension is discussed in more detail later in the chapter. It differentiates cultures that presume that individuals are in control of their own destinies from those that presume that nature or external forces control much of what happens. For example, some countries emphasise the value of individuals inventing or creating things themselves (internal control), whereas other countries emphasise the value of taking what already exists or has been created elsewhere and then refining or improving it (external control). Two statements that illustrate this difference are:

1. What happens to me is my own doing.
2. Sometimes I feel that I do not have enough control over the directions my life is taking.

More than 80 per cent of managers from Uruguay, Norway, Israel and the United States agree with the first statement, whereas less than 40 per cent of Venezuelans, Chinese and Nepalese agree.

These seven factors represent cultural differences at both the macro and the micro level. Manifestations of culture are below awareness in the sense that no one needs to verbalise it, yet it forms the roots of action. Culture is made by people, confirmed by others, conventionalised and passed on for younger people or newcomers to learn. It provides people with a meaningful context in which to meet, to think about themselves and to face the outer world. In the language of Clifford Geertz (1973: 60), culture is the means by which people 'communicate, perpetuate, and develop their knowledge about attitudes towards life. Culture is the fabric of meaning in terms of which human beings interpret their experience and guide their action.' This is very true for our contemporary organisational cultures.

Throughout this book, reference will be made to some of the differences that have been discovered among various cultures. It is recommended that you begin using these dimensions to raise your awareness of individual differences around you. Because virtually every manager will be faced with the opportunity to interact with and manage individuals born in other cultures, being aware of value differences, and being able to diagnose and manage those differences, is an important prerequisite for success in the 21st century. Stereotyping people based on their national culture, or overgeneralising based on trends such as those reported here, can be dangerous and misleading. Nobody wants to be pigeonholed on the basis of a general country profile. These dimensions, as you will see, are most useful for increasing sensitivity and helping with diagnosis, rather than for placing people in categories.

Different types of values

Rokeach (1973) argued that the total number of values people possess is relatively small and that all individuals possess the same values but in different degrees. For example, most people value peace, but some make it a higher priority than others. Two general types of values were identified by Rokeach, and independent priority ratings have been found to exist for each type (that is, the two sets of values are largely unrelated). One general type of values is labelled *instrumental*, or means-oriented; the other is *terminal*, or ends-oriented.

Instrumental values prescribe desirable standards of conduct or methods for attaining an end. Two types of instrumental values relate to morality and competence. Violating moral/ethical values (for example, behaving wrongly) causes feelings of guilt, while violating competence values (for example, behaving incapably) brings about feelings of shame.

Terminal values prescribe desirable ends or goals for the individual. There are fewer of them, according to Rokeach, than there are instrumental values, so the sum total for all individuals in all societies can be identified. Terminal values are either personal (for example, peace of mind) or social (for example, world peace). Rokeach has found that an increase in the priority of one personal value tends to increase the priority of other personal values and decrease the priority of social values. Conversely, an increase in the priority of one social value tends to increase the priority of other social values and decrease the value of personal values.

In one study of 567 managers in 12 nations, the instrumental values *broadminded, capable* and *courageous* were held in the highest esteem by managers from all 12 nations, but significant national differences were found on 75 per cent of the values (Bigoness & Blakely 1996). Another study of 658 Egyptians, 132 Americans, 43 Africans and 101 Arabs found significant national differences on both instrumental and terminal values, with Egyptians being least like Americans (Elsayed-Elkhouly & Buda 1997).

Managers' values

Even within the same culture different groups of people tend to differ in the values they hold. For example, in the 1980s North American business school students and professors tended to rate 'ambition', 'capability', 'responsibility' and 'freedom' higher than people in general. They tended to place lower importance than people generally on concern and helpfulness to others, aesthetics and cultural values, and overcoming social injustice (Cavanaugh 1980). In a study that compared highly successful, moderately successful and unsuccessful managers, highly successful managers gave significantly higher scores to values relating to economic values (for example, a comfortable life) and political values (for example, social recognition) than less successful managers (Rokeach 1973).

Paul Chippendale (2004a, 2004b, 2004c) of the Minessence Group has been researching Australian and New Zealand values for close to 20 years. He has seen the change from when managers considered values 'too soft' to be included in any serious approach to management to now, when they have become a central part of mainstream management. He believes this shift in management focus has been brought about through society's increased demands on managers in respect of professional responsibility, quality and customer focus. The world has also become a much more complex and uncertain place. Managers can no longer avoid dealing with human complexity.

Management by values

Figure 2.4 illustrates the shift of focus. In the 1920s it was sufficient to manage by instruction (MBI), as change was not rapid and the way things were done in the past worked well enough to pass on to others. By the 1960s, change was accelerating to the point where more flexibility of action was

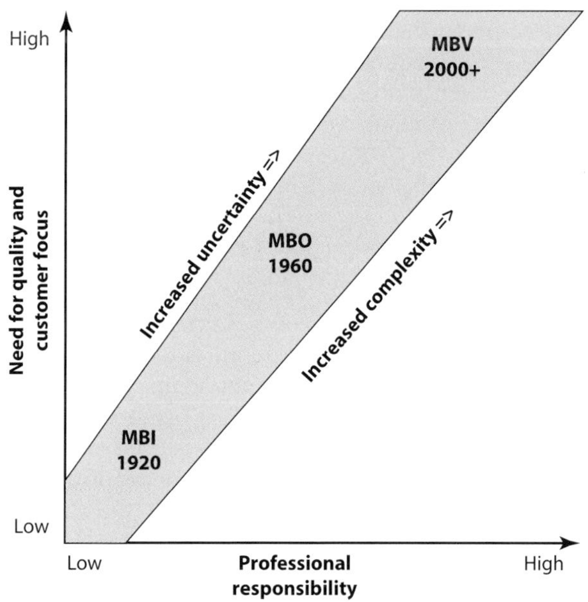

FIGURE 2.4 Shift in management focus

Source: P. Chippendale, *Minessence eZine#19*, 2004. Reproduced with permission of P. Chippendale, Minessence Group.

required by managers. The introduction of management by objectives (MBO) enabled managers to agree on direction and to choose their own strategy. In 1986, Prigogine put forward the notion that an analysis of the value systems of complex living entities was the key to understanding their behaviour (Prigogine 1986). Years of research since has confirmed that value systems are indeed the key to understanding the behaviour of individuals, organisations and society, leading today to the emergence of management by values (MBV).

Implications for managers

Values are people's motivators. For most people they are unconscious motivators. However, in highly successful organisations, each person in the organisation is aware of their personal values and how they relate to the organisation's value system; in the successful organisation, values are conscious motivators. Today, effective managers tap into people's values as a way of motivating them.

Managers who operate in the belief that all people hold the same values will not be effective in motivating their people. The world is in a state of flux and worldviews can change overnight. To function effectively in this turbulent world, today's managers must be able to identify the value systems of their organisation. They must be able to motivate others uniquely and communicate the key role that values play in organisational success. They must also be able to match their organisational structure and processes to the emergent value system. It is the era of MBV (Chippendale 2004b).

Establishing our own set of ethical principles

There is a major values conflict faced over and over again by managers. It is a conflict between maximising the economic performance of the organisation (revenues, costs, profits) or the social performance of the organisation (obligations to customers, employees, suppliers). Most ethical trade-offs are conflicts between these two desirable ends: economic versus social performance (Hosmer 1987). Making these kinds of decisions effectively is not merely a matter of selecting between right and wrong alternatives or between good and bad choices. Most of these choices are between right and right, or between one good and another. Individuals who effectively manage these kinds of ethical trade-offs are those who have a clear sense of their own values and have developed a principled level of moral maturity. They have articulated and clarified their own internal set of universal, comprehensive and consistent principles on which to base their decisions. It is seldom the case, of course, that a manager could choose economic performance goals every time or social performance goals every time—trade-offs are inevitable.

It is not a simple matter, on the other hand, to generate a personal set of universal, comprehensive and consistent principles to guide decision making. Most adults have neither constructed, nor do they follow, a well-developed set of principles in making decisions. One reason is that they have no model or example of what such principles might be. We offer some standards against which to test your own principles for making moral or ethical choices. These standards are neither comprehensive nor absolute, and are not independent of one another. They simply serve as a reference against which to test the principles that you include in your personal values statement.

- *Front page test.* Would I be embarrassed if my decision became a headline in the media or Facebook? Would I feel comfortable describing my actions or decision to a customer or shareholder?
- *Golden rule test.* Would I be willing to be treated in the same manner?
- *Dignity and liberty test.* Are the dignity and liberty of others preserved by this decision? Is the basic humanity of the affected parties enhanced? Are their opportunities expanded or curtailed?
- *Equal treatment test.* Are the rights, welfare and betterment of minorities and lower-status people given full consideration? Does this decision benefit those with privilege but without merit?
- *Personal gain test.* Is an opportunity for personal gain clouding my judgment? Would I make the same decision if the outcome did not benefit me in any way?
- *Congruence test.* Is this decision or action consistent with my espoused personal principles? Does it violate the spirit of any organisational policies or laws?

- *Procedural justice test.* Can the procedures used to make this decision stand up to scrutiny by those affected?
- *Cost–benefit test.* Does a benefit for some cause unacceptable harm to others? How critical is the benefit? Can the harmful effects be mitigated?
- *Good night's sleep test.* Does anyone else know about my action? Will it produce a good night's sleep?

In the skill application section of this chapter, you may want to consider these alternatives when constructing your own set of comprehensive, consistent and universal principles.

The next section considers how people communicate their values directly or indirectly in their interactions with others.

Core aspect 2: Interpersonal style

The second critical area of self-awareness is interpersonal style. The quality and type of our interpersonal activity can vary widely, however, so it is important for you to be aware of your own interpersonal influence patterns in order to maximise the opportunities for building productive working relationships.

This aspect concerns our ability to be aware of our own communication style. Without this we cannot effectively match and manage those we work with. Our interpersonal skill development is a product of our cultural values (discussed above) as well as our own personal communication behaviour.

Leadership Enhancement Team Style (LETS)

© McPhee Andrewartha 2011

We often refuse to accept an idea merely because the tone of voice in which it has been expressed is unsympathetic to us.

Friedrich Nietzsche

Eighty per cent of the people who fail at work do so for one reason: they do not relate well to other people.

Robert Bolton

Leadership (and effective management) is built on subtle influence skills (Kennedy, Fu & Yukl 2003). Effective management and leadership requires a relationship in which people speak and listen in a considered way, and use an attitude about working with others that is thoughtful and strategic.

LETS (Andrewartha 2011) is based on the comprehensive research of Dr Milton Erickson (Rossi 1980) and his colleague Dr Jeff Zeig (1985). As Erickson's foundation work was cross-cultural, this instrument identifies the basic attributes needed for effective influence within organisations and across cultures.

There are two elements on which LETS is constructed:

- Non-verbal behaviours influence performance and communication quite significantly.
- Matching the non-verbal behaviour of others increases the effectiveness of communication and leadership.

Let us examine these two factors in a little more detail.

The power of non-verbal behaviour. Mehrabian (1971) conducted extensive research on trust and respect between people. He analysed verbal and non-verbal behaviour and found that when these two behaviours were congruent the person was trusted or perceived as genuine. When these behaviours were incongruent (for example, a positive statement said with a frown or lack of interest), then the person was distrusted and not well regarded. Moreover, when presented with mismatched verbal and non-verbal behaviours, people always respond to the message contained in the non-verbal part. In fact, Mehrabian's research has shown that 93 per cent of all communication is non-verbal! The details of his work indicated that body language (the way we look, move, and express ourselves in facial expressions and gestures) constitutes 55 per cent of the message. Voice tone (hard, soft, varying, monotonous) contributes 38 per cent of the communication, and the verbal utterance, or the words themselves, conveys only 7 per cent of the message.

These findings raise significant issues about the impact of non-verbal elements on management skills and supportive communication (Chapter 5). Culture also has a direct impact on verbal and non-verbal communication, as does individual family culture (see Black & Porter 1996). The complexity of non-verbal influence has also been described in terms of gender differences in managers (see Tanner 1996). Mismatching of non-verbal behaviours also contributes to the perception of subtle unethical or untrustworthy behaviour, discussed in Chapter 1.

Matching. Erickson and Zeig clearly established that if you match the non-verbal communication of the person with whom you are communicating, then your capacity to motivate, influence and achieve your goals is greatly enhanced. Subtle matching of specific non-verbal dimensions enhances intuition and establishes strong rapport. This work has connections to the organisational relationships described by Argyris (1992), Senge (1990) and Andrewartha (2002) in terms of mental models and influence. Effective learning occurs when there is an agreed connection of meaning. Our internal mental models of the world are based on the unique meanings we attach to things. Predominantly, the essence of our mental models (or meaning) is conveyed non-verbally. By matching non-verbal patterns or responding in a similar manner to an employee's communication, our capacity to demonstrate shared meaning and therefore effective motivation is greatly enhanced.

Matching communication is defined as 'the process of utilising self-awareness and acute observation to match the mood, manner and "culture" of the other person so as to maximise influence and understanding. Information presented in this way is familiar and recognised by the other party' (Andrewartha 2002). This process, often conducted unconsciously, is the background to good management skills. Matching communication builds understanding and connection between people. Recent Israeli research has found that getting along well with fellow workers is not only good for office morale, but also helps you to live longer!

The LETS model discussed below makes this process both conscious and strategic. Behind the obviousness of task determination, goal setting, problem solving and business planning lies this hidden element of management ability: the capacity to communicate in such a way that others are influenced to achieve their tasks and goals. Bekmeier-Feuerhahn and Eichenlaub (2010) show that similarity in language (and, implicitly, body language) creates the perception of 'sameness' which enhances trustworthiness and promotes an understanding and receptive atmosphere. For similar research, see also Ireland et al. (2010). The LETS model is based on this process of similarity by enhancing trust through matching language and style. LETS provides a way of understanding your interpersonal style in the context of your membership in a work team. You may use the information here to explain and expand on your personal LETS profile that was generated from your answers to the online LETS questionnaire you completed on page 55. This will also assist you in communicating supportively (Chapter 5).

LETS Team leadership styles

There are four fundamental team leadership styles: Planner, Analyser, Developer and Creator (see Figure 2.5). The essence of these interpersonal styles is as follows:

1. *Planners* approach team projects by scheduling, planning, designing timelines and managing resources. They supervise/oversee/coordinate tasks and people to achieve a goal. Planners are detail-oriented and like organising people and tasks. They make things happen.
2. *Creators* leap into creative problem solving with any new project or task. They display a passion and energy that can be inspiring or confronting. Creators are less concerned about facts and practicalities, and are more strongly focused on innovation, discovery and feelings. They motivate and engage.

3. *Analysers* approach a project in the 'proper and correct' way. They are 'evidence based,' and examine rules and regulations, policies and procedures against the relevant history, to determine the necessary strategy. Team member relations are of less significance in such evaluations. They strive for quality.
4. *Developers* tend to take on a project and develop it into something bigger than was originally conceived. They are people focused, ensuring that team cohesion is as important as completing the project. They tend to be maintainers and finishers. They strive for continuity.

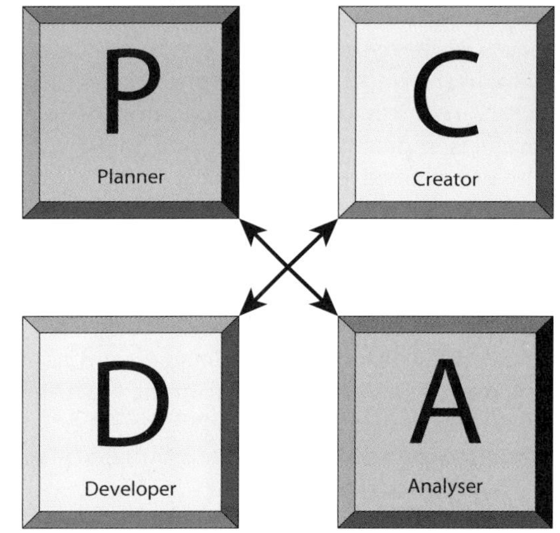

FIGURE 2.5 Leadership Enhancement Team Style

While some people clearly display one dominant team style type, others may combine two team styles: planner/analyser; planner/creator; planner/developer; analyser/creator; analyser/developer; creator/developer. For combined team styles, the interpersonal behaviour is a hybrid/combination of elements from the relevant fundamental team style types embodied.

In terms of matching (discussed earlier), Figure 2.5 shows how Planners and Analysers are matched, or naturally similar in style, as are Creators and Developers. In contrast, there is a mismatch or difference of understanding between the opposite styles. The arrows in the diagram indicate complementary, or matched team styles. For a team to function effectively, a mix of all four team styles is valuable for diversity, creativity, and complex problem solving. For very focused team projects, the team leader should possess the relevant style. For example, a very analytical task (auditing, evaluation) should have an Analyser as the lead; while a Creator as leader would enhance a fun brainstorming project.

We will now examine the four team styles in detail to enable you to appreciate the nature of your contribution to your team's dynamics and function, and to understand your colleagues' varied qualities. As each person is complex and unique, there may well be some aspects from these generalised outlines that differ in some respects from how you may behave in every team context.

While most of us are flexible, easily adapting our innate style to match our colleagues or a specific context, when we are under stress and pressure we tend to revert to our dominant or natural team leader style. As such, the team style descriptions below identify how we are most likely to behave when under pressure, which is invariably when we need to be the most flexible.

For teams, complex problem solving is a common occurrence that tests team members' interpersonal skills. The LETS problem-solving model (see Figure 2.6) demonstrates the most effective methodology for this task and highlights the different skills that are needed at each stage.

- *Step 1* involves carefully analysing the nature and scope of the problem. A clear definition of the issue is vital before attempting to generate solutions.

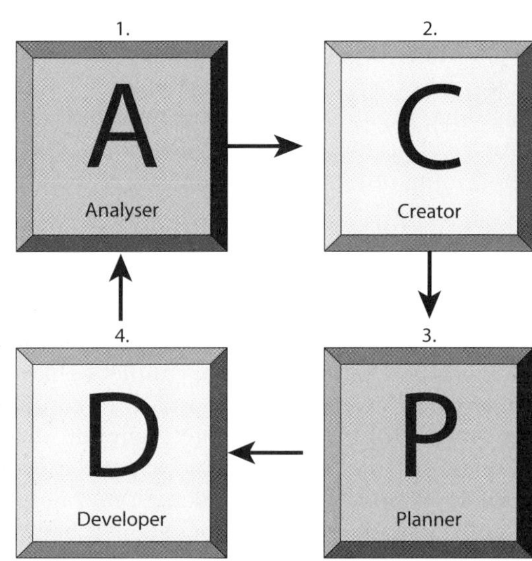

FIGURE 2.6 LETS problem-solving model

- *Step 2* requires solution generation. All creative potential options need to be accessed.
- *Step 3* is where the options need to be organised so as to select the best, most practical option and to plan the implementation process.
- *Step 4* requires the implementation of the plan and suitable follow-through. For complicated projects, repeating this process of analysis, creativity, planning and developing refines and embeds the most effective outcome.

Let us now examine the interpersonal styles of each of the four team leader types in more detail.

Planners

'I think we can. I will organise it so we can.'

Unsurprisingly, Planners like to make (and adhere to) plans both within and outside the workplace. They arrange work schedules, the home environment, shopping, and holidays according to calculated/organised procedures. Planners believe there is a correct place and a right time for most things. They like familiar routines and may be troubled by spontaneous events and reactions. Rituals and agendas can become important.

Planners bring logical analysis and often acute questioning to team problems and projects. They can appear fairly tough-minded because solving the problem becomes an intellectual drive and organising people to this end often takes precedence. Planners may keep moving forward on the issue and not be as empathic or considerate of those people who are not progressing at the same pace. Methodology is important to Planners, and they may often dismiss or overlook more creative options, which may have been very helpful.

Planners naturally like to gain new information in an organised and well-designed way. They prefer the program to follow an agenda, to start and end on time, and to make sense/to be commonsensical. They are less inclined to embrace creative, ambiguous and ill-defined learning experiences without specified goals and learning outcomes. They can enjoy a little fun and lightness in the learning experience as long as it is planned spontaneity.

In terms of the problem-solving model (see Figure 2.6, above), Planners are particularly useful at the third stage by providing concrete and definitive steps and methods that can be followed in order to implement the project or solve the problem. Planners may resist creative suggestions from team members and gradual developmental contributions, as they want to leap into the planned solution and not 'waste' time.

The following are good (matched) tasks for Planners:

- short, quick projects and assignments
- a job where urgency outweighs perfection
- hurrying others along by providing a sense of urgency
- handling rapid multi-tasks (for example, a call-centre service person)
- single issue, straightforward jobs
- motivating others in the team.

Suitable team roles/functions include: organiser, planner, timekeeper and manager.

Given earlier discussions about matching and effective team performance, it is useful to consider how Planners may see themselves in contrast to Creators and Developers. Table 2.2 shows how Planners may see themselves in contrast to other team members.

Managing conflict. In the model of conflict behaviour (see Chapter 7, page 350), Planners tend towards a competing or collaborating approach to conflict resolution. There is a tendency for Planners to see things in terms of black and white; right and wrong. This is reinforced by Planners' inclination to ask many questions in a conflict situation in order to analyse and understand the conflict. As a result, there is sometimes the possibility that a Planner may not spend enough time helping those who are troubled by the conflict to handle their feelings about it before Planners jump into finding solutions. Planners often prefer to solve team problems on their own, or involve very few people in the problem-solving process. Planners are usually comfortable sharing their own feelings (negative and positive) about the conflict.

TABLE 2.2 Planner-perceived behaviours

Planners often see themselves as ...	Creators and Developers may see them as ...
considered	constrained
procedural	inflexible
sequential	dogmatic
organised	bossy
systematic	dramatic
precise	impatient
determined	intolerant
movers and shakers	domineering
organisers	authoritative
planners	derisive
decision makers	tunnel-visioned
consistent	hard-nosed
well prepared	task drivers

Managing change. Planners tend to take a theoretical and abstract position in relation to change and managing the change process. They can become attracted to models and frameworks of change and miss some of the practical human impacts. Planners like change and can underestimate the impact it has upon others. They are naturally very good at planning ahead and taking the appropriate amount of time in regards to the implementation of complex change. They provide detailed steps and processes for handling change, as the novelty of change itself is attractive to them. Planners do access their own feelings and share them with others in the team, but may generalise their own feelings as being equally applicable to the rest of the team.

Matching tips for planners to enhance communication with other team members:

- Purposely take a little longer when managing a situation.
- Use as many statements as questions.
- Observe and listen carefully to others, and try not to interrupt or take charge.
- Continually remind yourself that there may be many different solutions to a matter, and that some seemingly bizarre ideas can actually lead to very effective outcomes.
- Double-check your assumptions and reinvestigate the facts and realities against the models and blueprints.
- Consider sharing your feelings and impressions with more than a few selected colleagues.
- Recognise that even the best plans can become problematic in an instant and that flexibility and adaptability are crucial, particularly in complex change scenarios.

Creators

'I absolutely know we can! Let's try it and see what happens.'

Creators bring a dynamic, enthusiastic or disruptive, fresh and spontaneous approach to team tasks. They are not time conscious and can be sidetracked and act in a manner out of proportion to the importance of the task. Creators bring a risk-taking and innovative approach, which is sometimes exhilarating. They are capable of quickly changing their opinion to passionately embrace a belief that is almost the opposite of one they previously held. They are very good at sharing ideas and motivating others. Creators tend to be open-minded, flexible, and open to unusual and unexpected possibilities.

Creators welcome ambiguous and unusual learning situations. They are delighted to try something without knowing where it might end up. Activities of discovery, 'what if' scenarios, and all unstructured learning environments feel like home to Creators. They like extended learning environments and do not have a concept of wasting time when they are learning. They do not take in information as effectively in highly controlled, overly planned or precisely prescribed contexts. Creators like to try anything and explore everything. They run things spontaneously. Meetings can be set up unexpectedly, comments can occur out of left field, and non sequiturs can flourish. Disagreements and fun may burst out unpredictably and may be forgotten just as quickly.

In terms of the problem-solving model, Creators are best at step 2 where they bring some energy, fun and innovation to the process. They do not watch the clock, as they enjoy the journey. Being at the second stage, Creators often miss some data analysis and engagement with the evidence, but they bring a wealth of lateral thinking and creativity to solution generation. They benefit from the direction of a Planner to limit and channel their creative options into feasible solutions.

Suitable team roles include: motivator, team jester, energy source, enthusiast, drama queen.

Table 2.3 contrasts Creator behaviours with other team members.

TABLE 2.3 Creator-perceived behaviours

Creators often see themselves as ...	Planners and Analysers may see them as ...
exciting	histrionic
dynamic	inconsistent
challenging	illogical
creative	exhausting
inventive	attention-seeking
flexible	time-wasters
resourceful	disorganised
stimulating	emotional
passionate	impetuous
spontaneous	inefficient
energetic	dreamers
experimenters	
engaging	

Managing conflict. In the model of conflict behaviour (page 350), Creators prefer a competing or avoidance approach to conflict resolution. They can work very well with authoritative colleagues, but may dominate if other teammates are not determined and assertive. Creators can introduce valuable humour and spontaneity into serious conflict situations, although it is also possible for them to escalate the drama. They tend to engage everybody in the resolution process. Creators are as concerned about the relationships and feelings of colleagues as they are with addressing the conflict. They can inspire others to take risks and to become more daring or creative in their engagement with the matter at hand. Creators may skip over some of the details and facts that other team members believe to be important in the resolution of such difficulties.

Managing change. Creators like changeable situations because they enjoy unpredictability and ambiguity. Their vitality is healthy and they tend to give lots of recognition and support to others. In direct contrast, they may also overreact to change that threatens them and become overly dramatic. They can escalate a modest change situation into a real crisis. Creators are often valuable in brief change situations, but can become burnt-out or disinterested with complex or drawn-out change scenarios.

Matching tips for creators to enhance communication with other team members:

- Seek out recommendations for change management strategies from your more organised and methodical colleagues.
- Monitor yourself and others in relationship to the risk of burn-out and the timing of activities.
- Check in with team members to see if they need any time out.
- Occasionally tone down some of your comments.
- Remember that some team members prefer 'planned' spontaneity.

Analysers

'We can do it. I need to ensure we do it properly.'

Analysers tend to be perfectionist in character and may be a little tunnel-visioned. This is a great attribute in situations that demand a high level of accuracy. However, where the matter is not that vital and/or time is quite limited, Analysers may need some help in being less precise and accepting of a slightly lower standard of quality.

Analysers make note of important matters, such as key anniversaries and mementos, as well as the core values of individual colleagues, the team, and the organisation. They can keep to themselves in a team and not engage with all team members. Analysers provide suggestions to others, both positive and negative, but they can be perceived as lacking some warmth. The task and resolving the problem is most important to Analysers, and any team building may take second place.

They can be very effective when they are able to monitor the appropriateness of the activities and to assist in keeping things in order and on time. They tend to like gathering and assessing data, and researching and investigating opportunities. They often find it hard to accept compliments. They are very good at team error detection.

Analysers feel most comfortable and learn most effectively in organised and appropriately resourced learning situations. The materials and the facilitators need to be appropriately qualified, supported, and matched to the learning tasks and objectives. They do not respond well to ambiguous, unstructured and experiential learning approaches. They do not like wasting time, both intellectually and in terms of content, but they like to be thorough and work through the material in a methodical and cautious way.

Analysers are matched to the first stage of the problem-solving model. They gravitate towards data analysis, facts and figures, policies and procedures, and the rules. They are evidence-based thinkers who accumulate information upon which the team can assess options. Analysers like to do things in what they consider to be the 'proper and correct' way. They like order and consistency. They can focus on guiding principles rather than responding to what is happening in the here-and-now.

The team roles to which Analysers are best suited include: statistician, data analyser, rule keeper, evidence collector, compliance officer, ethics guardian, critic, monitor, quality evaluator.

Table 2.4 contrasts Analyser behaviours with other team members.

TABLE 2.4 Analyser-perceived behaviours

Analysers often see themselves as ...	Creators and Developers may see them as ...
thoughtful	dogmatic
intellectual	hard
cautious	inflexible
systematic	uninspiring
logical	judgmental
considered	pedantic
principled	unapproachable
correct	cold
objective	critical
precise	understated
consistent	uninteresting
meticulous	reserved
analytical	dry
firm but fair	boring

Managing conflict. In the model of conflict behaviour (page 350), Analysers tend towards a competing approach to conflict resolution. They feel they know the 'answer' and want the team to understand this and get on with the resolution. They like the team to be right, and compromise is not seen as an option. In this way they can persist with a position way past the importance of the matter. Similarly, they may appear to be stubborn and inflexible if others look for solutions that are 'close enough'.

Where the situation demands it, they are unflinching in maintaining the true path.

Managing change. In general, Analysers only accept change that is researched, planned and well laid out in advance. They do not enjoy random change or reactive approaches to situations. They can provide a firm structure or foundation for teams to handle difficult changes and offer effective support and observations about options and approaches.

Matching tips for analysers to enhance communication with other team members:

- Lighten up a little.
- Help team members understand the importance of the rules and values.
- Consider there are often several 'right' answers to a problem.
- 'Out of the box' ideas can sometimes be very valuable.
- Others may take more time to fully understand the challenges of a matter.

Developers

'I hope we can. Let's take our time and ensure that everyone is on board.'

Developers like to take someone's idea and develop it into something quite remarkable. They can extend and embellish on original ideas, options and solutions. They are often supportive, caring, understanding, and considerate of colleagues and friends and even of strangers. They are good listeners, they rarely complain, and they attempt to keep things bubbling along. Developers may not receive due credit as key contributors, yet without them many events and ideas would falter or be less impressive. Developers produce things for others, while sometimes overlooking their own needs.

Developers need gradual, open and adaptable learning environments in which they can absorb ideas, think them through, experience their reactions, and then formulate their understanding of the matter. They do not like being rushed, nor do they appreciate presentations that are fully complete and final. They place much value upon participant support and interaction.

Developers sometimes find it hard to make tough decisions, as they achieve many goals by being supportive. They are therefore more likely to see the emotional side of any matter. Developers are able to clarify and elaborate, involve others, minimise conflict, and provide a way of keeping different parties working together effectively. Developers look at the implementation side of decision making, and may sometimes be more occupied with people's feelings than with the end goal.

Developers excel in the fourth stage of the problem-solving model (see Table 2.5). They are reliant on other team members to assess data, create options, and form a plan so they can fully develop the scope and implementation aspects. They will be uncomfortable with Planners or Analysers if they seem to be rushing to judgment or pushing one outcome against the wishes of other team members.

The following are good (matched) tasks and team roles for Developers:

- Long, involved projects and assignments.
- Complex tasks requiring perfect outcomes.
- Slowing others down.
- Helping to reduce stress and tension.
- Supporting and encouraging people.
- Giving accurate and constructive feedback.
- Tasks that require patience.
- Bringing ideas/tasks to fruition/conclusion.
- Assisting in team cohesion.
- Organising the social and practical elements of home and office.

The best team roles for Developers include: social organiser, listener, the reliable experienced hand, maintenance expert, expander, concluder.

TABLE 2.5 Developer-perceived behaviours

Developers often see themselves as ...	Planners and Analysers may see them as ...
constant	soft
tolerant	slow
strategic	low key
facilitators	understated
expanders	smothering
multi-skilled	unassuming
even-handed	followers
caring	unoriginal
nurturers	not pragmatic
doers	not task-oriented
pragmatic	wishy-washy
low key	
considered	

Managing conflict. In the model of conflict behaviour (see page 350), Developers tend towards a compromising, collaborative or accommodating approach to conflict resolution. They are not naturally forceful; nor are they avoiders. They do need time, however, and have difficulty in those scenarios where conflict needs to be addressed and resolved very quickly. They may spend too much time being supportive and avoid an early intervention. This may lead to the conflict reaching a serious stage before they are fully engaged.

Managing change. Developers appreciate change that is considered and introduced in a consultative manner. Fast, forced change is resisted. They usually focus first on the people impact of change, and on the business or task outcomes second. They require time and information in order to process change most effectively.

Matching tips for developers to enhance communication with other team members:

- Acknowledge the importance of outcomes and facts.
- Contribute some task-focused comments.
- Know when to let go.
- Focus on the present sometimes, as well as the future.
- Allow the possibility that some people are not suited to some tasks and that that is okay.
- Be prepared to discuss things on the spot.

How do I work with someone with a different LETS team leadership style?
When conversing with a *Planner*:

- offer them a plan or a structure
- organise your ideas into some order
- ask them to shape your ideas more logically.

When conversing with a *Creator*:

- let yourself have some fun
- be a little disorganised and haphazard
- be more enthusiastic.

When conversing with an *Analyser*:

- be precise and clear
- pay attention to the rules and expectations
- treat the conversation seriously.

When conversing with a *Developer*:

- take time and go through the points a few times
- ask for their thoughts on how your ideas could be improved
- be aware of their feelings and good relationships.

Six dimensions of LETS communication styles

Having considered your team leadership style, we now turn to the unique communication patterns that are associated with your leadership style. (These are displayed on the bottom half of your profile from the scoring of your online questionnaire.)

There are six dimensions of communication, each of which is on a continuum. Every person generally displays some of the behaviour patterns on each side of the continuum. However, people tend to lean more strongly towards one end or the other. Neither one of the two ends of each dimension is better than the other. They are simply different aspects of interpersonal communication traits. Each dimension therefore identifies unique differences in the way we communicate and shape our own performance style. For example, dimension two involves exaggerator/understator behaviours. From the profile, your style may be identified in one of the following ways:

Exaggerator+	Very strongly down the exaggerator end of the continuum
Exaggerator	Definitely down this end of the continuum
Exaggerator/Understator	Balanced style between both behaviours
Understator	Definitely down this end of the continuum
Understator+	Very strongly down the understator end of the continuum

This scoring process is repeated for each of the other five dimensions—or continued.

Understanding your profile can benefit you in two ways: first, it is a significant part of understanding and developing your own skills as a manager; and second, it provides a framework for enhancing your interpersonal and team skills. That is, the LETS profile has implications for the skills described throughout this book. As a self-awareness tool, it lets you monitor your own mental models and basic assumptions more closely. Using this awareness when talking to team members increases your communication skills and your ability to gain respectful power and influence. It directly creates motivation and streamlines conflict-management situations. Finally, it is most effective for building and maintaining effective teams.

One of the most common problems in organisations is that people tend to get on best with staff who are like themselves. Paradoxically, this often reduces influence and effectiveness in team communication. LETS will help you improve your ability to manage in a diverse range of situations and with all types of people within and across different cultures. It identifies the core competencies needed to flexibly match with others and to effectively communicate by reducing unconscious biases and misunderstandings.

In all communication the non-verbal emphasis given to the expression of the words adds a crucial element to the message.

1. The rapid/gradual continuum. Some managers prefer to evaluate an idea rapidly, or respond quickly to events, while others do better by absorbing the situation gradually over time.

Rapid: 'Let's do it now—as soon as possible.' Rapid managers like to receive all the information at once and are frustrated by delays and constant changes. They tend to be a little impatient and sceptical about change possibilities, but can be committed when all the facts are presented. They can be impatient with fools, or people who present information slowly. As team leaders, these managers do well with major tasks that are full of many elements, and where many things need to be coordinated simultaneously. They tend to get bored with slow-moving tasks with little risk or challenge, seeing them as tedious and mundane. Rapid processors never miss an opportunity, but they may rush headlong into mistakes. The same often occurs with meetings and task delegation.

They are matched (and get on well with) other rapid team members. The timing is in tune, as is what is expected. Occasionally, two rapid processors can fly off at a speedy tangent from the rest of the team and need to be reconnected with the pace of the group. Managers who are rapid usually find gradual people too slow to deal with patiently. This mismatch leads to many misunderstandings and difficulties simply because of differing mental assumptions about timing. In communicating with more gradual colleagues, they could slow down a little and allow more time for thought and preparation.

Gradual: 'Let's take it slowly and carefully.' Gradual managers tend to feel overwhelmed if too much data is presented too quickly. They like to take in each element and digest it thoroughly before absorbing the next. As team leaders, they tend to take things as they come. They have a more accepting and fatalistic optimism about change, expecting it will all work out in the end. This group likes well-defined and well-focused tasks. They tend not to be so good in high-pressure, high-change situations. Gradual processors never make impulsive mistakes, but they can miss out on golden opportunities. Meetings and tasks will be handled well, but not quickly or with much risk taking.

They match well with other gradual staff members, although gradual processors can seem far too slow to the rapid processors. They may need encouragement to move more quickly if the situation demands it. They are mismatched with the rapid group, sometimes seeing them as impetuous or reactive. This simple lack of alignment can easily lead to a bias about another person whose timing is out of kilter with their own.

Rapid: OK, I'm ready to go now.
Gradual: Hang on a minute.
Rapid: For God's sake, hurry up. You're never ready on time.
Gradual: I'm nearly ready now. Anyway, what's your hurry? We'll get there in plenty of time, knowing how you drive.
Rapid: What's wrong with trying to drive efficiently? I get fed up with dithering motorists who clog up the roads. Besides, I arrive safely.
Gradual: You may think you're hot stuff, but it's no fun being your passenger. You take too many risks just to save a few seconds.
Rapid: Are you ready now?
Gradual: Hang on. You know I can't do two things at once. Stop chatting to me and I'll get these clothes put away.
Rapid: Just throw them into the wardrobe, don't fold them up; we haven't got time.
Gradual: There, I'm ready now.
Rapid: Are you sure? About time, too.

2. The exaggerate/understate continuum

Exaggerator: 'Wow! This is unbelievably effective!' Exaggerators tend to exaggerate and to blow things out of proportion. They make mountains out of molehills. They have an enthusiasm, energy and a noticeable reaction to events. When things are extremely good, they are excited and demonstrative. When things are very bad, they react quite strongly and negatively. They tend to be flexible even with bare facts. There is extra emphasis in their body language and voice tone in all their significant communications. They tend to be good motivators, but they are not good with repetitive tasks. They are not so effective where a calm and consistent approach is required. They are often creative managers and ideas people.

They are well matched with other exaggerators and would naturally communicate well with them. They tend to be mismatched with understators and may perceive them as being too low-key to get their attention easily. To be more effective and not overwhelming with understators, it would be useful for them to tone down their presentation a little. Otherwise, from the perspective of an understator, these managers risk being seen as lacking emotional control or as not having a balanced viewpoint.

Understator: 'Yes, this is fairly useful.' Understators play things down. They tend to be more low-key and make molehills out of mountains. It is often hard to tell how things affect them. They provide little body language and minimal voice inflection. They are quiet and shy in their presentations overall. They can be overlooked in a meeting and handle crises quietly. They stick very closely to the facts. They tend to be excellent at repetitive roles, and in situations that require someone who is unflappable and immovable in the face of disruptions and distractions. They are excellent as calm, consolidating managers and team leaders.

They are well matched with others who have a low-key presentation, and are likely to be mismatched with exaggerators. They perceive exaggerators as being 'over the top', too energetic and not always credible. It is possible for exaggerators to discount the ideas of understators and not take them very seriously. In dealing with exaggerators, it would be helpful if understators could put more energy and drama into their presentation in order to gain better attention. Such managers may otherwise risk being seen as less powerful or uncertain in their management style.

Here is an example of an understator manager talking to his exaggerator staff member.

Exaggerator: I don't know why you appointed John to the position. You've made a big mistake. The problems in that area are huge.

Understator: Well, I thought he'd bring a mixture of skills to the job that have been lacking. I don't understand why you think there are 'huge' problems.

Exaggerator: Well, there are big problems with the way it's being done already, and John certainly isn't the answer.

Understator: Oh, I don't think the problems are all that 'big', and what we need is a cool approach to work them out.

Exaggerator: What's needed is a bloody big shake-up and some energy. John's a wimp. There's no way he can fix it. I don't have any faith in him.

Understator: I think that John is a quiet achiever. I believe he'll do it well, without a lot of fuss. I'm sorry you don't agree.

Exaggerator: Well, we need more than quiet achievers. What we need are people with more to offer than John. He'll be a disaster for us all.

Organisations need both exaggerators and understators. Both behavioural traits are valid and vital. However, mutual respect and understanding is a problem when the manager and staff member are mismatched. If matching of this dimension can be achieved, they can make a formidable team.

3. The linear/lateral continuum

The way we store information and analyse it occurs in two distinct ways. This can be described by the linear–lateral thinking continuum.

Linear thinker: 'Let's approach this one step at a time.' As managers and team leaders, linear thinkers are carefully ordered, sequential and one-directional in their thought processes. The first thing leads to the next, and so on to the logical conclusion. Linear thinkers are traditional in the way they approach tasks. When travelling they tend to follow car navigator systems religiously. They like methodical tasks with set routines and clear guidelines. They run a meeting by the book and do not tend to be flexible with changes. They are uncomfortable with unclear guidelines, ambiguous tasks and changeable circumstances.

They respond well to other linear thinkers who analyse in the same methodical and sequential way. They like familiar routines, and can sometimes be inflexible in their approach to some tasks. Linear thinkers sometimes perceive lateral thinkers as scatterbrained, disorganised and illogical. They feel that lateral-thinking people are unable to keep on track. Once again, this bias is not correct but arises out of the difference in this dimension of analysis.

Lateral thinker: 'There are so many ways we can approach this.' Lateral thinkers are more variable in their thinking and planning. They move from one aspect of the problem to another without an obvious connection. They can initiate ideas from anywhere. As managers, they are innovative and creative in their thought processes. Lateral thinkers use navigator systems creatively, if at all, and tend to give creative directions rather than coordinates. They are usually comfortable with handling several different tasks simultaneously. They are not well suited to rigid guidelines and highly structured situations. They can stray in meetings and tasks, and tend not to manage time efficiently. They relate well when ideas are presented in an ambiguous or randomised manner. They tend to have variable routines and may have so much flexibility that it is hard to pin them down.

Lateral managers get on best with like-minded team members, exploring a range of possibilities, often simultaneously. They are not well matched with linear thinkers, whom they often perceive as rigid, inflexible, non-creative and boring.

This difference in management style often causes difficulties in team-based problem solving. For example, some team members may have a very precise, analytical problem-solving style, whereas other people may use undirected random brainstorming. Without understanding these differences it can be difficult to get both groups to work effectively together on the same problem.

Linear thinker: Let's look at this logically. First, we need a marketing plan. Then we need the target to be defined, we need to select the key staff, and finally begin the project.
Lateral thinker: Why don't we buy a new building?
Linear thinker: What are you talking about? What's that got to do with anything?
Lateral thinker: But it's a waste of time to assess the market unless we know where we might be located.
Linear thinker: What a weird connection. They have nothing to do with each other.
Lateral thinker: No, wait. You're missing the point. It's ...
Linear thinker: Oh, forget it. Let's get back to the agenda.
Lateral thinker: But this will save us money. It's ...
Linear thinker: Your idea of planning makes no sense. Now, the marketing plan. Well, first I think we need ...

4. The detail/concept continuum

Any analysis of events in the work situation divides people into those who focus more on the specific details and those who focus more on the bottom line or the overall concept.

Detailer: 'Let me see all the details.' As managers, detailers examine each specific element that is essential to achieving the task. They zoom in and catch the vital elements. They may make lists or identify them on their fingers one at a time. They may resent being diverted from this process to look at the basic issue at stake. Detailers excel at all tasks where complex details are crucial to the achievement of the goal. They are more effective once a new project is already under way. They need to identify the specific details of a task before being totally committed and then may get into too much detail. They are not well matched with the conceptualiser, who to them seems quite uninterested in 'mere details'. They enjoy focusing on all the nitty-gritty details with fellow detailers. There is a sense of rapport with detailers that is missing with conceptualisers.

Conceptualiser: 'What's the bottom line?' Those concerned with the overall concept need to have the overarching purpose of the matter addressed as rapidly as possible before they can be really comfortable with the task. They zoom out and see the bigger view. Details may seem irrelevant to them and better left to others, or they may pick up the details after establishing the bottom line. As managers, conceptualisers tend to make good motivators and marketers. They are initially concerned about the value of the project or task and, until they are satisfied that the basic goal can be achieved, their involvement is tentative. Occasionally, they may overlook an important detail because of their interest in the concept.

They are naturally matched with other 'big picture' people, and tend to work most comfortably with them. In a team, this can easily result in important details being overlooked. Conceptualisers are likely to be mismatched with detailers, whom they see as irrelevant or picky and obsessed with trivia. This difference in perspective can impede many management situations.

Conceptualiser: Okay, we take the sales figures from 100 to 500 in 12 months.
Detailer: Exactly how are we going to do that?
Conceptualiser: What, do you think it's too ambitious?
Detailer: No, but how are we going to do it? What's the budget? When does it start? Are we putting on extra staff?
Conceptualiser: You ask too many questions. It's achievable. Don't you believe it can be done?
Detailer: Well, I suppose if we put on another person or two, and change our marketing strategy, anything is possible, but the details aren't clear.
Conceptualiser: Oh, details, details. Now, that's settled. What's next on the agenda?
Detailer: But how precisely are we going to start?

5. The self/other continuum

In any work situation, things sometimes go wrong. People examine this event and evaluate what happened in quite different ways. The continuum proceeds from self-evaluation at one end to evaluation of others at the other end, and offers some insights into effective management.

Self-evaluator: 'I got that wrong.' When things go wrong, self-evaluators look inside and tend to assess their own contribution and behaviour in a critical or evaluative manner. They tend, at least initially, to overlook others' contributions and behaviour in their assessment. They tend to take too much responsibility for delegated tasks and can become overburdened. As a manager, it is not possible to assist them by disagreeing with their initial reaction. They feel they did wrong, and only by matching their own view and initially agreeing can a manager enable them to shift their focus from their own contribution to look at others' roles. As team leaders, they tend to be very demanding of themselves and take responsibility for the whole team. They often have problems in delegating. They are matched with other evaluators, but can become stuck if their communication does not shift from this complementary position. They tend to be less effective with other staff members who are also self-evaluators, because each person tends to blame his or her own behaviour.

This example shows how two self-evaluators can get nowhere:

Self-evaluator 1: Sorry, Margaret, I didn't realise the problems I had caused. I'll redo the whole thing and get those sales figures right.
Self-evaluator 2: It's disappointing. You're wrong to blame yourself, though. Maybe I messed it up for you by not giving you the full information.
Self-evaluator 1: No, it was all my fault. I feel useless.
Self-evaluator 2: No. No. You can't be blamed for this.
Self-evaluator 1: Yes, it was my job. I'm sorry.
Self-evaluator 2: Of course not. It was my responsibility. Look, don't be so hard on yourself.
Self-evaluator 1: You shouldn't make excuses for me. I'll stay and fix it tonight.
Self-evaluator 2: Oh, I give up!

Other-evaluator: 'You're wrong!' Other-evaluator managers look outside and tend to evaluate other's contribution and, at least initially, to assess or blame them and their behaviour before evaluating their own input. With delegated tasks, they tend to shift responsibility on to others. In staff counselling, it is important to match the tendency of other-evaluators to blame others, before it is possible to have them examine their own role. These managers are naturally matched with people who are also other-evaluators. They can get on well if they are discussing the errors of a third person. They tend, however, to argue if the topic of blame is between the two of them. Other-evaluators tend not to be as stressed as their self-evaluator colleagues, but they can limit their own potential development.

6. The initiate/respond continuum

In any context, we can either initiate or respond to an idea or action.

Initiator: 'Follow me.' Initiators like introducing new concepts and tend to take the lead in most communications. They tend to produce ideas and to assume the dominant position quickly and rapidly. Initiators tend to be good in a team-leadership role but are inclined to be directive. They expect a response to their ideas and automatically tend to give directions or point the way that others should follow. They can easily lead a meeting, and they start off really well with tasks but may have difficulty in finishing them. Initiator managers like to give assistance, ideas and reactions.

They naturally communicate well with responders in a complementary and matched relationship. They may become jammed or get into conflict with another initiator. This is likely to result in a competitive relationship. In this situation, the cause of the conflict between the two people is often not even obvious.

Responder: 'I'm right behind you.' Responders like other people to take the lead. They prefer to understand the setting, the background and the nature of the circumstances before committing themselves. They prefer to respond to others' initiatives and follow their lead. Responders are good managers when clear directions are provided and their tasks are clearly spelt out. They tend to be less comfortable in isolated command and prefer supportive roles. They can be excellent leaders where democratic or participative leadership is required. They are usually good at finishing off and taking things through to a conclusion.

They are usually matched with initiators with whom they have an understanding relationship, even if there is a difference in status between them. The relationship can be less effective when communicating with other responders, as there is a tendency for no one to take the lead.

The following is an example of a matched relationship:

Initiator: I think we can get this contract if we do it right.
Responder: I agree with you. Now, what do you want me to do?
Initiator: It's going to be tough. People won't understand why you're doing it and you'll cop heaps of criticism.
Responder: I don't mind that, as long as I get your support.
Initiator: You've certainly got that. You know how much I rely on you.
Responder: Leave it with me. I'll get the contract for us. Is there anything else? You're the one with the ideas.
Initiator: Yes, but I'll leave it with you for a while. You check out the lie of the land and see how we should respond.
Responder: Okay. That's fine.

Perceptual system: Visual mode, auditory mode, experiential mode

In your LETS profile you may be identified as visual+, visual, auditory+, auditory, experiential+ or experiential. Or some combination of these qualities may be identified according to the way you answered the questionnaire. The following description identifies how your perceptual system can impact on your management communication style.

How we form our concepts, explain our ideas and evaluate things is dramatically influenced by our perception of the world. Our brain is developed to perceive the outside world by visual, auditory and tactile means. We see, hear and touch (or feel) our world. As we learn, we develop our favourite or preferred mode of perception. To a greater or lesser extent, we use this preferred mode more consistently than the other two. As part of our leadership management style, this means we vary in our assessments of people and things according to our perceptual system. Further, it means that our communication is subtly altered by this aspect. Where our dominant perceptual mode matches with another staff member's, we are on the same wavelength. Where there is a mismatch, there may be such misunderstanding that it is almost as if you are speaking another language.

Visual mode

'Looks good.'

Visual people *see* the idea. They are predominantly influenced by a visual perspective and prefer to think in visual images. They may use more visual words, such as 'see', 'clear', 'look', and so on. When choosing a new staff member, it is the visual discrimination that will help them to make the final decision. Their appearance, dress and presentation are very important. In general, they prefer to see it, read it, study the diagram and examine it visually. Visualisers prefer seeing the facts and looking at the other person; they respond best to pictures, images, slides, overheads, taking notes, as well as visual word pictures. As leaders, they often see the direction to follow. Visualisers naturally relate well to others who are also visual. They are less effective with auditory and tactile staff members. In a real sense, they speak a different language.

About 60 per cent of people are visualisers.

Auditory mode

'Sounds good.'

Auditory people *listen* to the concept and prefer to sound out their ideas. They tend to use language with more auditory elements in it. They use words such as 'noise', 'listen', 'hear', 'sounds like', and so on. When making the final choice on a new staff member, they tend to be influenced by the sound of the candidate, the candidate's voice tone and the genuineness of the candidate's pronunciation of words. They like listening to conversations and the sound of their own voice, and respond to discriminations in pitch and intensity. As managers, they talk things through conclusively. In a team, they like to talk it over and sound it out. The tone of voice and sound of things is often quite important. Auditory managers naturally relate well to others who are auditory. They are less effective with visual and tactile people. With auditory people, it may be necessary to talk things through more and use less visual presentation.

About 20 per cent of people are auditory.

Experiential mode

'Feels good.'

Experiential people like to *grasp* the concept and prefer to 'chew it over' and 'get in touch with' their ideas. They use language that includes words like 'grasp', 'connect', 'feel' and 'get in touch'. Their choice of a new staff member is determined more by how they feel about them during the interview. They tend to rely on their intuition. They like being involved and having the experience in a 'hands-on' manner, rather than listening to it or looking at it. They prefer good practical exercises at a seminar, rather than watching and listening. They appreciate participating and are predominantly influenced by how they feel. As managers, they often understand things intuitively without necessarily being able to describe their reasons. This group naturally relates well with others who are experiential. They may be less effective with their visual and auditory staff members. With experiential people, look for examples that describe the concept in concrete terms and help them to have some experience of what is being presented.

About 20 per cent of the population have an experiential perspective.

The LETS instrument can be used for assessing a team or an organisation's overall strengths and limitations. As an illustration, Table 2.6 contrasts a Chinese government senior management group with an Australian marketing company.

The contrasts in occupational role, and also culture differences, are apparent: for example, the dominance of exaggerator/conceptualiser for the Australian marketers, the majority of analysers for the Chinese officials, and the stronger other-evaluator in the Australian culture. Unsurprisingly, the Chinese group wanted to develop their capacity to be more innovative! With only one creator, this was proving a challenge.

Other instruments

You are encouraged to explore other self-awareness instruments as well as the Leadership Enhancement Team Style. You may consider the Herrmann Brain Dominance Instrument, DISC, Strong-Interest Inventory, the 16 PF, the Kolb Learning Style Inventory (LSI) (Kolb 1984; Kolb, Boyatzis & Mainemelis

TABLE 2.6 The LETS cultural group comparisons

Group 1						
Thirty senior Chinese government directors						
Timing:	RAPID	**30**	GRADUAL	**14**		
Emphasis:	EXAGGERATE	**5**	UNDERSTATE	**29**		
Thinking:	LINEAR	**31**	LATERAL	**4**		
Focus:	DETAIL	**21**	CONCEPT	**12**		
Evaluation:	SELF	**24**	OTHER	**7**		
Relationship:	INITIATE	**20**	RESPOND	**17**		
Perceptual system:	VISUAL	**26**	AUDITORY	**18**	EXPERIENTIAL	**10**
Team leadership/learning style:	PLANNER	**13**	DEVELOPER	**5**		
	CREATOR	**1**	ANALYSER	**17**		
Group 2						
Twenty-nine Australian marketing company employees						
Timing:	RAPID	**27**	GRADUAL	**12**		
Emphasis:	EXAGGERATE	**20**	UNDERSTATE	**11**		
Thinking:	LINEAR	**15**	LATERAL	**17**		
Focus:	DETAIL	**11**	CONCEPT	**22**		
Evaluation:	SELF	**13**	OTHER	**17**		
Relationship:	INITIATE	**25**	RESPOND	**18**		
Perceptual system:	VISUAL	**25**	AUDITORY	**9**	EXPERIENTIAL	**20**
Team leadership/learning style:	PLANNER	**6**	DEVELOPER	**14**		
	CREATOR	**12**	ANALYSER	**5**		

Source: © G. Andrewartha, McPhee Andrewartha 2007. Reproduced with permission.

2000; Kolb & Kolb 1999), the Myers–Briggs Type Indicator (MBTI®) and the Honey and Mumford Learning Styles Questionnaire (LSQ). Students wishing to explore the underpinning model of the latter can find a useful description in *Using Your Learning Styles* (Honey & Mumford 1995). Although a number of psychometric limitations of the MBTI have been identified (Boyle 1995), it continues to be used globally and has informed or been incorporated into other well-tested and well-used frameworks such as the Kolb LSI and the more recently developed Margerisson McCann Team Management Index (TMI).

People's interpersonal style is also affected by, and developed from, their emotional development, to which we now turn.

Core aspect 3: Emotional intelligence

Emotional self-awareness is crucial to the development of management skills. The research suggests that emotions are remarkably consistent across cultures (Ekman 2004), are central to successful leadership and effective engagement with others (Goleman 1998a, 1998b, 2001), influence people's decision making and problem solving (Nussbaum 2001; Shiv, Loewenstein & Bechara 2005), and impact on the way people manage conflict (Hartig & Frosch 2006; Zapf 1999).

> *People who make decisions based on emotions are more committed to the decisions, and emotional ability helps distinguish merely making choices from making effective decisions (Shiv et al. 2005). One aspect of EQ awareness is 'mindfulness' which is the individual's awareness of their present experience. Individuals high in mindfulness are more likely to act ethically and uphold ethical standards. (Ruedy & Schweitzer 2011)*

There has been a growing interest in the construct of *emotional intelligence* and its use in helping leaders and managers gain greater awareness of themselves and their relationships with others. A large number of studies have confirmed that everyone has multiple intelligences, the most common of which is IQ, or cognitive intelligence. By and large, cognitive intelligence is beyond a person's control, especially after the first few years of life. It is a product of the gifts with which we were born, or our genetic code. Interestingly, above a certain threshold level the correlation between IQ and success in life (for example, achieving high occupational positions, accumulated wealth, luminary awards, satisfaction with life, and performance ratings by peers and superiors) is essentially zero. Very smart people have no greater likelihood of achieving success in life or of achieving personal happiness than people with average IQ scores (Goleman 1998b; Spencer & Spencer 1993). On the other hand, emotional intelligence has strong positive relationships to success in life and to a reduced degree of encounter stress.

The early emotional intelligence theory was developed during the 1970s and 1980s by the work and writings of psychologist Howard Gardner. Then Salovey and Mayer (1990) went on to propose an ability model (Mayer & Salovey 1997) that defined emotional intelligence as 'intelligence' in the traditional sense—that is, as a set of mental abilities to do with emotions and the processing of emotional information that are part of and contribute to logical thought and intelligence in general.

Bar-On's (1997: 14) model defines emotional intelligence as an array of non-cognitive capabilities, competencies and skills that influence our ability to succeed in coping with everyday environmental and social pressures.

The third and most widely used model was developed by Goleman (2001) and specifically relates to workplace applications.

The term 'emotional intelligence', then, refers to: (1) the ability to diagnose and recognise your own emotions; (2) the ability to control your emotions; (3) the ability to recognise and diagnose the emotions displayed by others; and (4) the ability to respond appropriately to those emotional cues. These abilities are not inherited, but can be developed and improved. Unlike IQ, for example, which remains relatively constant over a lifetime, emotional intelligence can be enhanced with practice. With concerted effort, people can change their levels of emotional intelligence. The instrument you completed in the skill assessment section assesses the four dimensions of EQ.

Emotionally intelligent people are able to get in touch with and accurately diagnose their own internal feelings. Emotionally intelligent people are also able to regulate and control their emotions. They are less likely to blow up and lose control, less likely to experience debilitating depression and anxiety, and more likely to manage their own emotional states than are those with less emotional intelligence. Think of how you behave in a sporting event—for example, when the umpire makes a bad call, when someone gets angry at you and berates you, when you are criticised for something you did, or, alternatively, when you receive special accolades and recognition. Emotionally intelligent people remain in control of their emotions, whereas less emotionally intelligent people lose control. This ability does not mean being bland or even-tempered all the time; emotionally intelligent people may display a wide range of emotions and intensity. Instead, it means that a person can control his or her emotions so that they are not unrestrained.

Emotionally intelligent people are also able to accurately diagnose and empathise with the feelings of others. They are sensitive to what others are experiencing, and they can share in those feelings. 'Empathy' refers to the ability to understand and connect with others' feelings. It does not mean sympathising or adopting the same feelings, and it is not based on a memory of having experienced the same emotions. If someone has experienced a tragedy or loss, for example, emotionally intelligent people can empathise, share in, and understand those feelings even if they have never experienced something similar. They need not be depressed themselves, for example, in order to understand another person's depression.

Emotionally intelligent people also respond appropriately to the emotions of others. Their responses match the intensity of the emotions other people feel, and they support and encourage emotional expressions. That is, if others are excited and happy, they do not remain aloof and withdrawn. They endorse and match the expression of emotions in others, rather than suppressing or censoring those emotions. On the other hand, they are not manipulated in their feelings and responses by the emotions of others. They do not respond merely on the basis of others' feelings. Rather, they remain in personal control of their responses. They advance a sense of caring for, and acceptance of, the other person by means of their emotional responses.

One reason emotional intelligence is so important is that general competency levels seem to have deteriorated over time. Whereas average IQ points have increased almost 25 points over the last 100 years—people tend to be smarter now than 100 years ago—emotional intelligence scores have actually declined (Goleman 1998a). Think, for example, of the amount of litigation, conflict, disrespect and divorce that characterises Western society. Less emphasis is placed on emotional intelligence development now than in the past. This is a problem, because emotional intelligence has strong predictive power regarding success in management and in the work setting—much stronger, in fact, than IQ scores. For example, it is estimated that IQ accounts for only about 10 per cent of the variance in job performance and in life success (Sternberg 1996), but by adding emotional intelligence to the equation, four times more variance can be accounted for.

For example, a study was conducted of 450 boys who grew up in a small town in Massachusetts, in the United States. Two-thirds of the boys lived in welfare families and one-third had IQ scores below 90. The boys were followed over 40 years, and it was found that IQ had almost nothing to do with life success. Emotional intelligence, on the other hand, was the most predictive factor (Snarey & Vaillant 1985). Another study of 80 PhDs in science who attended the University of California at Berkeley in the 1950s found that what accounted for life success 40 years after graduation was mainly the person's emotional intelligence score. Emotional intelligence was four times more important than IQ in determining who had achieved in their careers or were evaluated by experts as being highly successful (Feist & Barron 1996). A study of workers followed over 20 years found that employees who were better at empathising with others—that is, demonstrating a key aspect of emotional intelligence—were more successful in their work, as well as in their social lives (Rosenthal 1977). Emotional intelligence has also been found to be an important predictor of managerial success. In a study of managers on three continents, for example, 74 per cent of successful managers had emotional intelligence as their most salient characteristic, whereas this was the case in only 24 per cent of the failures. A study at PepsiCo found that company units headed by managers with well-developed emotional intelligence skills outperformed yearly revenue targets by 15–20 per cent. Those with underdeveloped skills underperformed their targets by about the same amount (Goleman, Boyatzis & McKee 2002).

A McBer study comparing outstanding managers with average managers found that 90 per cent of the difference was accounted for by emotional intelligence. In a worldwide study of what companies were looking for in hiring new employees, 67 per cent of the most desired attributes were emotional intelligence competencies (Goleman, Boyatzis & McKee 2002). In a study of highly emotionally intelligent partners in a consulting firm, in which they were compared with partners with average emotional intelligence, 41 per cent of the high emotional intelligence group had been promoted after two years, whereas only 10 per cent of the lower emotional intelligence partners had been promoted. More importantly, high emotional intelligence partners contributed more than twice as much revenue to the company as did the lower emotional intelligence partners (Boyatzis 1982). The point should be clear: effective managers have developed high levels of competency in emotional intelligence.

The emotional intelligence assessment instrument that you completed in the skills-assessment section provides an evaluation of your competency in the four general areas of emotional intelligence—emotional awareness, emotional control or balance, emotional diagnosis or empathy, and emotional response. Of course, a fully accurate and valid measure of these factors would require an instrument many times longer than the one included here, so this assessment provides just a glimpse or an incomplete evaluation of your emotional intelligence capability. Your scores should help you to identify areas of strength but also motivate you to pursue the development of your emotional intelligence. This may effectively be done by consciously practising emotional diagnosis, control, and response in yourself and others, but, especially, it may also be significantly enhanced by learning and improving the skills discussed in this book. They are, according to a variety of writers (for example,

Boyatzis, Murphy & Wheeler 2000; Goleman 1998b), critical components of the broad definition of emotional intelligence.

Goleman (2000) expanded these four domains into a framework for developing emotional competence in the workplace (see Table 2.7).

TABLE 2.7 Goleman's emotional competence framework

PERSONAL COMPETENCE		SOCIAL COMPETENCE	
Self-Awareness	**Self-Management**	**Social Awareness**	**Social Skill**
• *Emotional self-awareness:* the ability to read and understand your emotions as well as recognise their impact on work performance, relationships, and the like. • *Accurate self-assessment:* a realistic evaluation of your strengths and limitations. • *Self-confidence:* a strong and positive sense of self-worth.	• *Self-control:* the ability to keep disruptive emotions and impulses under control. • *Trustworthiness:* a consistent display of honesty and integrity. • *Conscientiousness:* the ability to manage yourself and your responsibilities. • *Adaptability:* skill at adjusting to changing situations and overcoming obstacles. • *Achievement orientation:* the drive to meet an internal standard of excellence. • *Initiative:* a readiness to seize opportunities.	• *Empathy:* skill at sensing other people's emotions, understanding their perspective, and taking an active interest in their concerns. • *Organisational awareness:* the ability to read the currents of organisational life, build decision networks, and navigate politics. • *Service orientation:* the ability to recognise and meet customers' needs.	• *Visionary leadership:* the ability to take charge and inspire with a compelling vision. • *Influence:* the ability to wield a range of persuasive tactics. • *Developing others:* the propensity to bolster the abilities of others through feedback and guidance. • *Communication:* skill at listening and at sending clear, convincing, and well-tuned messages. • *Change catalyst:* proficiency in initiating new ideas and leading people in a new direction. • *Conflict management:* the ability to de-escalate disagreements and orchestrate resolutions. • *Building bonds:* proficiency at cultivating and maintaining a web of relationships. • *Teamwork and collaboration:* competence at promoting cooperation and building teams.

Source: D. Goleman, 'Leadership that gets results', *Harvard Business Review*, March–April 2000, p. 6. Reproduced with permission.

Goleman (1998b: 14) defines emotional intelligence as follows:

> *A different way of being smart. It includes knowing your feelings and using them to make good decisions; managing your feelings well; motivating yourself with zeal and persistence; maintaining hope in the face of frustration; exhibiting empathy and compassion; interacting smoothly; and managing your relationships effectively. Those emotional skills matter immensely—in marriage and families, in career and the workplace, for health and contentment.*

His research identified that *67 per cent*—two out of three—of the abilities deemed essential for effective management or leadership performance were emotional competencies (Goleman 1998b: 31). He concluded, 'for star performance in all jobs, in every field, emotional competence is twice as important as purely cognitive abilities' (p. 37).

It is significant that one of Goleman's most important research findings relates directly to the themes of this book. He found that the two most common traits of senior managers who failed were rigidity and poor relationships.

> [Rigidity] *They were unable to adapt their style to changes in the organizational culture, or they were unable to take in or respond to feedback about traits they needed to change or improve. They couldn't listen or learn.*

[Poor relationships] *The single most frequently mentioned factor: being too harshly critical, insensitive, or demanding, so that they alienated those they worked with. (p. 40)*

With these two traits in mind, it is appropriate now to consider one's attitude to change, whether personal, interpersonal or environmental.

Core aspect 4: Attitude towards change

As the environment in which managers operate continues to become more chaotic, more temporary, more complex and more overloaded with information, people's ability to process information and effectively convey it to others is at least partly constrained by their fundamental attitude about change.

Change in today's global and local organisations is now a constant and will increase. The information explosion, including instantaneous mail and voice communication, immediate document retrieval, desktop libraries and the internet, has changed the environment of modern management dramatically. Access to more information in increasing amounts leads to increased turbulence and complexity for managers. They must make decisions ever faster as both the amount and the rapidity of the information encountered increase. It is now possible for competitors in almost any business to emerge on the internet within 24 hours. Thus, it is no longer possible to predict the competitive environment. Customers are no longer geographically constrained, and the standards for servicing them have changed completely. Speed to market and competing against time have begun to dominate the traditional competitive advantages learned in business schools. Rapid decision making, mostly without the benefit of adequate information and careful analysis, is becoming the norm.

In the midst of this chaotic pace of change—what some refer to as 'permanent white water'—being aware of your own orientation towards change is an important prerequisite for successfully coping with it. One dimension of change orientation or attitude that is particularly relevant for managers is 'locus of control'.

Locus of control

Locus of control is one of the most studied aspects of attitude towards change. It refers to the extent to which people believe they are in control of their own destinies. When individuals receive information about the success or failure of their actions, or when something changes in the environment, they differ in how they interpret that information. People receive reinforcements, both positive and negative, as they attempt to make changes around them. If individuals interpret the reinforcement they receive to be contingent upon their own actions, it is called an 'internal locus of control' (that is, 'I was the cause of the success or failure of the change'). If they interpret the reinforcement as being a result of outside forces, it is called an 'external locus of control' (that is, 'Something or someone else caused the success or failure'). Over time, people develop a 'generalised expectancy' about the dominant sources of the reinforcements they receive. Thus, they become largely internally focused or largely externally focused with regard to the source of control they perceive in a changing environment.

It is important to remember that locus of control can shift over time, particularly as a function of the position held at work. Although Western cultures value highly an internal locus of control, it does not assure managerial success, any more than an external locus of control inhibits individuals from attaining positions of power and influence at the top of organisations. Therefore, no matter what your internal–external score is, you can be a successful manager in the right setting, or you can alter your locus of control. More than 1000 studies have been done using the locus of control scale. In general, the research suggests that managers in Australia and North America have a far greater tendency to an internal locus of control than, say, Middle Eastern and Far East Asian managers (Trompenaars 1996). In Japan, an external locus of control has been associated with high levels of stress and violence among teenagers, presumably due to less emphasis on self-control (Tubbs 1994). In Australian and North American culture, internal locus of control is associated with the most successful managers, (For reviews of the literature, see Hendricks 1985; Spector 1982).

People with an internal locus of control are more likely to:

- be attentive to aspects of the environment that provide useful information for the future
- engage in actions to improve their environment
- place greater emphasis on striving for achievement
- be more inclined to develop their own skills
- ask more questions
- remember more information

than are people with an external locus of control (see also Seeman 1982).

On the other hand, research has also found that an internal locus of control is not a panacea for all management problems, nor is it always a positive attribute. For example, individuals with an external locus of control have been found to be more inclined to initiate structure as leaders (to help clarify roles) and to show consideration to people (Durand & Shea 1974). Internals are less likely to comply with leaders' directions and are less accurate in processing feedback about successes and failures than are externals (Cravens & Worchel 1977). Internals also have more difficulty arriving at decisions that entail serious consequences for someone else (Wheeler & Davis 1979).

Research in cultures outside the United States suggests that locus of control is not a measure that can distinguish the successful from the less successful. As Trompenaars and Hampden-Turner (1999) have found:

> *To accept direction from customers, market forces or new technologies can be more advantageous than opposing these with your own preferences. The 'obvious' advantages (to Americans) of being inner-directed may not be obvious at all to managers in Japan or Singapore, and will be at least less obvious in Italy, Sweden or the Netherlands, for example. Outer-directed need not mean God-directed or fate-directed; it may mean directed by the knowledge revolution or by the looming pollution crisis, or by a joint venture partner. The ideal is to fit yourself advantageously to an external force.*
>
> *In the original American concept of internal and external sources of control, the implication is that the outer-directed person is offering an excuse for failure rather than a new wisdom. In other nations it is not seen as personal weakness to acknowledge the strength of external forces or the arbitrariness of events. (Reproduced with permission of The McGraw-Hill Companies.)*

The locus of control scale in the skill assessment section helps you to generate a score showing the extent to which you have an internal or external locus of control. The scoring key and some comparison information are located on page 118.

While substantial research exists associating some positive managerial behaviours with an internal locus of control, this is neither an assurance of success as a manager nor a solution to the problems that managers face. By knowing your score, however, you will be able to choose situations in which you are more likely to feel comfortable, to perform effectively, and to understand the point of view of those whose perspectives differ from yours. Self-understanding is a prerequisite to self-improvement and change.

The last element of the five aspects of self-awareness considers how we acquire and process new information at a cognitive level.

Core aspect 5: Cognitive style

Cognitive style consists of a large number of factors that relate to the way individuals perceive, interpret and respond to information. This chapter considers the two major dimensions of cognitive style discussed in the research literature that have been shown to relate to managerial behaviour:

- the manner in which individuals gather information
- the manner in which individuals evaluate information they receive.

The basic premise is that every individual is faced with an overwhelming amount of information, and only part of it can be given attention and acted upon at any one time. Individuals, therefore, develop strategies for assimilating and interpreting the information they receive. No strategy is inherently good or inherently bad, and not everyone adopts an identifiable, consistent set of strategies that become part of their cognitive style. However, about 80 per cent of individuals do eventually develop (mostly unconsciously) a preferred set of information-processing strategies, and these make up their particular cognitive styles. The cognitive style instrument in the assessment section assesses the two core dimensions of your information-processing preferences.

The two-dimensional cognitive model

The theory of the cognitive style instrument is grounded in the work of Jung (1923). Figure 2.7 illustrates the two cognitive dimensions. The information-gathering dimension distinguishes an intuitive strategy from a sensing strategy, and the information-evaluation dimension distinguishes a thinking strategy from a feeling strategy.

Different strategies for taking in, coding and storing information (information gathering) develop as a result of certain cognitive filters used by individuals to select the information to which they pay attention. An intuitive strategy takes a holistic view and emphasises commonalities and generalisations—that is, the relationships between the various elements of data. Intuitive thinkers often have preconceived notions about what sort of information may be relevant, and they look at the information to find what is consistent with their preconceptions. They tend to be convergent thinkers.

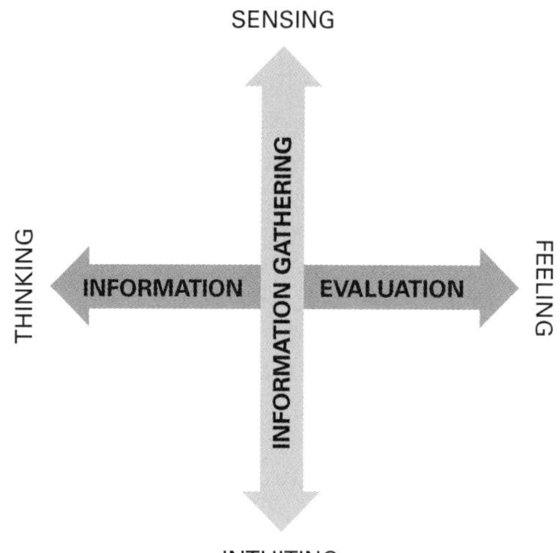

FIGURE 2.7 Model of cognitive style based on two dimensions

The sensing strategy focuses on detail, or on the specific attributes of each element of data, rather than on relationships between the elements. Sensing thinkers are rational and have few preconceptions about what may be relevant, so they insist on a close and thorough examination of the information. They are sensitive to the unique attributes of various parts of the information they encounter and tend to be divergent thinkers.

In simple terms, an intuitive strategy focuses on the whole, whereas a sensing strategy looks at the parts of the whole. An intuitive strategy seeks commonalities and overall categories, while a sensing strategy looks for uniqueness, detail and exceptions to general rules.

The second dimension of Jung's model refers to strategies for interpreting and judging information (information evaluation). These strategies develop from reliance on a particular problem-solving pattern. A thinking strategy evaluates information using a systematic plan with specific sequential steps. There is a focus on appropriate methods and logical progressions. Individuals who use a thinking style generally rely on objective data. Attempts are made to fit problems into a known model or framework. When such people defend their solutions, they emphasise the methods and procedures used to solve the problems.

A feeling strategy, on the other hand, approaches a problem on the basis of 'gut feel', or an internal sense of how to respond. Problems are often defined and redefined, and approaches are based on trial and error rather than on logical procedures. Feeling individuals have a penchant for subjective or impressionistic rather than objective data, and frequently cannot describe their own problem-solving or decision-making processes. Problem solutions are often found through using analogies or seeing unusual relationships between the problem and a past experience.

Evaluation of strategies

These different strategies have important implications for managerial behaviour. Each has advantages and disadvantages. For example, when faced with a large amount of data, sensing managers, because they focus on detail, experience information overload and personal stress more readily than intuitive managers do. When they encounter too much detail, or too much heterogeneity, sensing managers become overloaded because each detail receives attention.

Intuitive managers, on the other hand, focus on the relationships between elements and the whole, and handle additions of detail relatively easily. However, when diversity or ambiguity is encountered in the information, when aberrations from expected relationships occur, or when preformed categories do not fit, intuitive managers are likely to have more difficulty processing the information than sensing managers do. Encountering exceptions or the absence of a clear set of relationships between elements is particularly problematic for intuitive managers. Sensing managers are likely to handle these situations more easily because of their tendency to do 'fine-grained analyses' of problems.

Thinking managers are less likely to be effective when encountering problems requiring creativity and discontinuous thinking, or when encountering highly ambiguous problems that have only partial information available. When no apparent system exists for solving a problem, these individuals are likely to have more difficulty than feeling managers.

On the other hand, when one program or system will solve a variety of problems—that is, when the information suggests a straightforward, computational solution—feeling managers are less effective because of their tendency to try new approaches, to redefine problems, and to reinvent the solution over and over without following past programs. This generally leads to inefficient problem solving or even solving the wrong problem. Thinking managers have less difficulty in such situations.

Research on these cognitive dimensions has found that no matter what type of problem they face, most individuals use their preferred cognitive style to approach it. They prefer, and even seek, decision situations and problem types that are consistent with their own cognitive style (for example, individuals scoring high on thinking prefer problems with a step-by-step method of solution). Another study found that differences in cognitive style led to significantly different decision-making processes in managers (see Chenhall & Morris 1991; Henderson & Nutt 1980; Ruble & Cosier 1990).

Table 2.8 summarises some personal characteristics associated with each of these major cognitive orientations. This is the basis of the Myers–Briggs Type Indicator, or MBTI instrument.

TABLE 2.8 Characteristics of Cognitive Styles

INFORMATION GATHERING	
INTUITIVE TYPES	**SENSING TYPES**
Like solving new problems.	Dislike new problems unless there are standard ways to solve them.
Dislike doing the same thing over and over again.	Like an established routine.
Enjoy learning a new skill more than using it.	Enjoy using skills already learned more than learning new ones.
Work in bursts of energy powered by enthusiasm, with slack periods in between.	Work more steadily, with realistic idea of how long it will take.
Jump to conclusions frequently.	Must usually work all the way through to reach a conclusion.
Patient with complicated situations.	Impatient when the details are complicated.
Impatient with routine details.	Patient with routine details.
Follow inspirations, good or bad.	Rarely trust inspirations, and don't usually feel inspired.
Often tend to make errors of fact.	Seldom make errors of fact.
Dislike taking time for precision.	Tend to be good at precise work.
INFORMATION EVALUATION	
FEELING TYPES	**THINKING TYPES**
Tend to be very aware of other people and their feelings.	Are relatively unemotional and uninterested in people's feelings.
Enjoy pleasing people, even in unimportant things.	May hurt people's feelings without knowing it.
Like harmony. Efficiency may be badly disturbed by office feuds.	Like analysis and putting things into logical order. Can get along without harmony.
Often let decisions be influenced by their own or other people's personal likes and wishes.	Tend to decide impersonally, sometimes ignoring people's wishes.
Need occasional praise.	Need to be treated fairly.
Dislike telling people unpleasant things.	Are able to reprimand people or fire them when necessary.
Relate well to most people.	Tend to relate well only to other thinking types.
Tend to be sympathetic.	May seem hard-hearted.

Ladder of inference

Another model of cognitive processing is worth considering briefly. The ladder of inference was initially developed by Argyris and subsequently appeared in *The Fifth Discipline Fieldbook: The Art and Practice of the Learning Organization* by Senge et al. (1994). The ladder of inference is a model of how people process information (see Figure 2.8).

The ladder of inference starts at the bottom and progresses to the top level of Actions. It demonstrates how in any encounter we begin with actual data and our experience of that observed real data. That is, we see, hear and feel some event or communication. We then (physiologically and psychologically) unconsciously select only some of that data and experience to pay attention to. We affix meaning, develop assumptions and come to conclusions about that selected information based on our values (as discussed in the values section previously), which further develop and reinforce our long-held beliefs or values. Finally, on the basis of all this we take action, which usually creates additional data and experience, and the process sustains itself in a circular fashion (see Figure 2.9).

Consider this example from a real encounter. Jane is conducting a team meeting and she notices Hua and his behaviour (real data and experience). She observes that Hua is frowning and looking away on several occasions (selected data). She thinks that this means he is not interested in what she is saying (affixed meaning). She assumes that he is doing this because he disagrees with her point of view (assumption) and then concludes that he does not agree that she should be the manager of the team (conclusions). This reinforces her vague belief that he wanted her job himself (belief) and she decides to manage his performance more closely (action). This sequence, of course, virtually ensures that the outcome Jane imagined becomes a reality, even if the actual reality was that Hua was preoccupied with his relationship break-up and was not attending to the meeting content at all.

All these steps on the ladder can happen in a few minutes and can really interfere with effective management practice and cause considerable stress and conflict. So, how do we avoid the ladder?

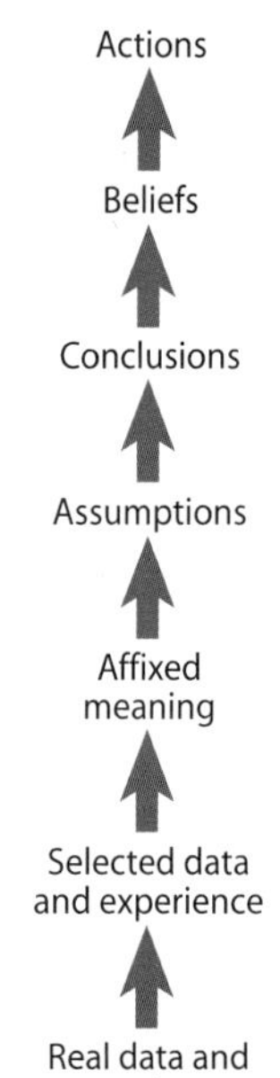

FIGURE 2.8 The ladder of inference

Source: P. Senge et al., *The Fifth Discipline Fieldbook* (New York: Doubleday, 1994), p. 243. Copyright 1994 by Peter M. Senge, Charlotte Roberts, Richard B. Ross, Bryan J. Smith and Art Kleiner. Reproduced with permission of Doubleday, a division of Random House Inc.

Obviously we cannot go through life without making some assumptions, generalising from experience, adding meaning or drawing conclusions. It would be very inefficient and cumbersome. But we can improve our communication and effectiveness through careful understanding of the nature of the ladder of inference. Try these effective management behaviours:

- Increase your level of self-awareness by using the exercises discussed in this chapter.
- Do not assume you are right. So much of human communication looks absolutely evidentiary but often turns out to be something quite different.
- Identify some of your pet assumptions and beliefs that might interfere with your effective understanding, and develop an early warning signal if they are triggered at any time.

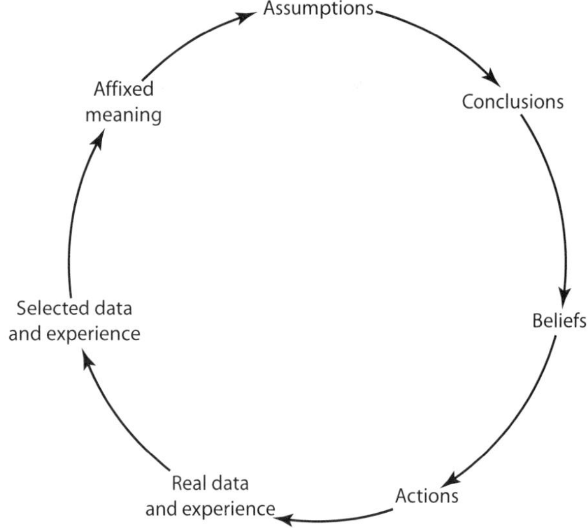

FIGURE 2.9 A circular model of the ladder of inference

Source: G. Bellinger, 'Ladder of inference. Short circuiting reality', <www.systemswiki.org/index.php?title=Ladder_of_Inference:_Short_Circuiting_Reality>

- Whenever you make a negative assumption or conclusion, make your thinking transparent to the other person and check out your perceptions with them.
- Simply ask others, 'How did this incident occur? Let's review how we got to this point.'
- Employ the 'When you do X, Y results and I feel Z' technique (described in Chapter 7).

In the example above, Jane could stop and say, 'Hua, I notice that you are frowning and I wonder if there is any difficulty?' Alternatively, she could ask Hua if he agrees with the matter to hand. She could employ the 'I see, I imagine and I feel' technique. Finally, she could have a private conversation with Hua after the meeting and share her impressions and ask him for his perceptions of the meeting.

Summary

Successful organisations have discovered the power of developing self-awareness in their managers. For example, the Leadership Enhancement Team System has been used by many organisations, including Deakin University, Adelaide University, the University of South Australia, the Singapore Government, the Public Sector Management Course, Telstra, Divisions of General Practitioners and many government agencies. The Myers–Briggs Type Indicator (MBTI) is being used by major Australian organisations such as Qantas, Telstra, the Australian Taxation Office, the Queensland Police Force, Australia Post and major Australian banks. Each year more than two million people around the world take the MBTI.

Developing self-awareness is also important in helping individuals to develop understanding of the differences in others. Most people will regularly encounter individuals who possess different styles, different sets of values and different perspectives. Most workforces are becoming more, not less, diverse. Self-awareness training, as discussed in this chapter, can be a valuable tool in helping individuals to develop empathy and understanding for the expanding diversity they will face in work and university settings. Self-awareness is a key component of emotional intelligence, and a high EQ is a prerequisite for successful management. The relationship between the five critical areas of self-awareness and these management outcomes is summarised in Figure 2.10.

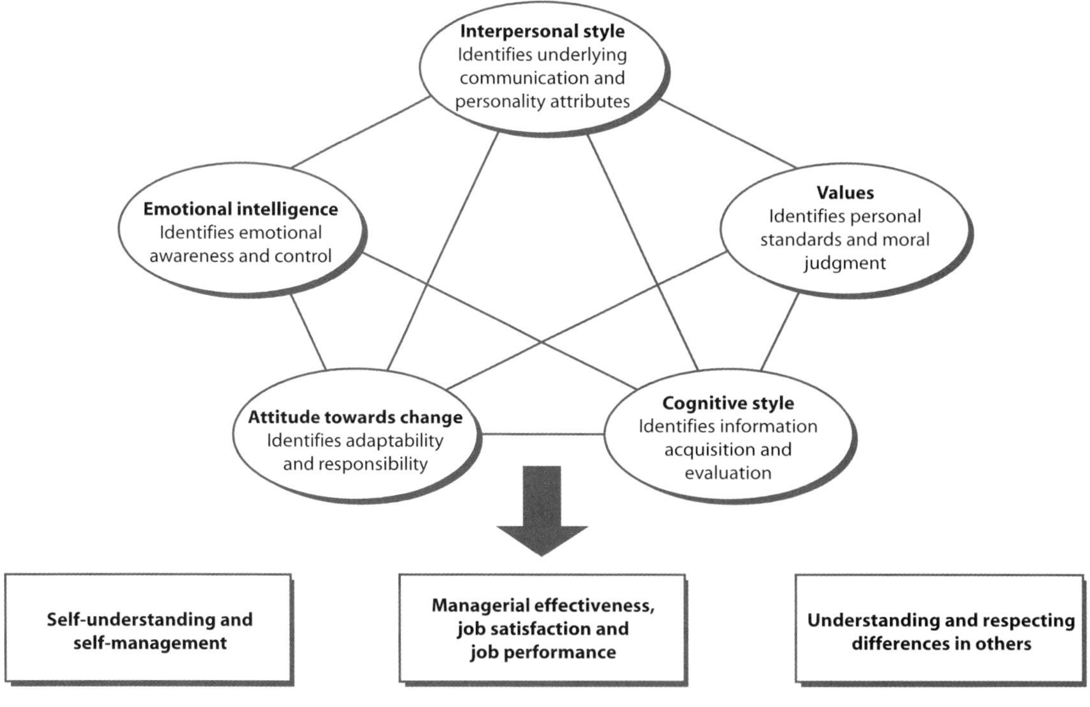

FIGURE 2.10 Five core aspects of self-awareness and managerial implications

Most of the following chapters relate to skills in interpersonal or group interaction, but successful skill development in those areas will occur only if individuals have a firm foundation in self-awareness. In fact, there is an interesting paradox in human behaviour: we can know others only by knowing ourselves, but we can know ourselves only by knowing others. Our knowledge of others, and therefore our ability to manage or interact successfully with them, comes from relating what we see in them to our own experiences. If we are not self-aware, we have no basis for knowing certain things about others. Self-recognition leads to recognition, respect and understanding of others.

Behavioural guidelines

The following is a list of behavioural guidelines relating to the improvement of self-awareness. These guidelines will be helpful to you as you engage in practice and application activities designed to improve your self-awareness.

1. Identify your sensitive line. Determine what information about yourself you are most likely to defend against.
2. Use the seven dimensions of national culture to diagnose differences between your own values orientation and that of individuals from other cultures, age categories or ethnic groups.
3. Identify a comprehensive, consistent and universal set of principles on which you will base your behaviour. Identify the most important values that guide your decisions.
4. Review and use your LETS interpersonal style. Expand your cognitive style and your internal locus of control by increasing your exposure to new information and engaging in different kinds of activities from those you are used to. Seek ways to expand and broaden yourself.
5. Apply principles of communicating supportively (Chapter 5) and managing conflict (Chapter 7) when disagreements do arise.
6. Engage in honest self-disclosure with someone who is close to you and accepting of you. Check out aspects of yourself that you are not sure of.
7. Keep a journal and make time to engage regularly in self-analysis. Balance life's activities with some time for self-renewal.

Skill analysis

Case study involving self-awareness

Decision dilemmas

Read the three scenarios below. What would you choose to do in each situation? List your key considerations.

1. A young manager in a high-technology firm was offered a position by the firm's chief competitor at almost double her current salary. Her firm sought to prevent her from changing jobs, arguing that her knowledge of certain specialised manufacturing processes would give the competitor an unfair advantage. Since she had acquired that knowledge through special training and unique opportunities in her current position, the firm argued that it was unethical for her to accept the competitor's offer.
2. After many profitable years, Hans Ericksson's Advance Australia Toy Company (AATC) was up for sale. Hans had enjoyed the challenges and successes involved in creating and building AATC but the increasing overseas competition was such that Hans believed the optimum time for selling had arrived. Several firms were interested in purchasing the company for the asking price, but

one firm was particularly aggressive. It sponsored several parties and receptions in Hans' honour, a 12-metre yacht was made available for his use during the summer, and several gifts for family members arrived during the holidays. Hans' wife questioned the propriety of these activities. Was it appropriate for Hans to accept the gifts? Should he sell to that firm?

3. Evelyn's company had been battered by competition from New Zealand firms. New Zealand products were not only selling for less money but their quality was substantially higher. By investing in some high-technology equipment and fostering better union–management relations, Evelyn was relatively certain that the quality gap could be overcome. But her overhead costs were more than 40 per cent above that of the competitor firms. She reasoned that the most efficient way to lower costs would be to close one of her older plants, put off the employees and increase production in the newer plants. She knew just which plant would be the one to close. The trouble was, the community depended on that plant as its major employer and had recently invested a great deal of money for highway repairs and street-light construction around the plant. Most of the workforce was made up of older people who had lived in the area most of their lives. It was improbable that they could obtain alternative employment in the same area.

DISCUSSION QUESTIONS

Form a small group and discuss the following questions regarding these three scenarios:

1. *Why did you make the choices you did in each case? Justify each answer.*
2. *What principles or basic values for decision making did you use in each case?*
3. *What additional information would you need in order to be certain about your choices?*
4. *What circumstances might arise to make you change your mind about your decision? Could there be a different answer to each case in a different circumstance?*
5. *What do your answers tell you about your own values, cognitive style, attitude towards change and interpersonal style?*

Hazelwood Hospital

Hazelwood is a recently privatised 1000-bed hospital in Melbourne. Further restructuring of the nursing division is being considered. The nursing divisions are being reduced from four to two, with corresponding reductions in the number of assistant directors of nursing. The positions of clinical nurse consultants (CNCs) and charge nurses are being amalgamated to form a new role of nurse manager, with a loss of eight CNCs. Twenty nursing staff will also be made redundant in the restructure.

You are Jane Telford, director of human resources and chair of the Consultative Committee. On your committee is the current director of nursing, Robert Matzione, a clinical nurse consultant, Carole Cornell (a union representative), the assistant director of nursing, Cathy Turvill, and your assistant, Marcus Woollaroo.

In this role-play you are about to conduct the first meeting of the Consultative Committee since the restructuring was announced. It is important that it is a consultative process that can evolve so that the details are worked out over time. Yet it is crucial for the principle of the restructuring and amalgamation to be accepted as quickly as possible and for the committee to move on to discuss the details of the process, the number of people involved, and so on. For this role-play, people should read only their own role description before the first session is conducted.

Jane Telford, director of human resources

You have been with the hospital through many changes over the last 14 years. You tend to be very calm and like to take things fairly quietly and spend some time mulling them over. When things get too rushed or argumentative you get a little flustered and are certainly concerned about establishing harmony in the group. You have not particularly endorsed or accepted this restructuring proposal, but it has been handed to you by the CEO of the hospital and it is your job to make it happen. You are quite concerned about Carole Cornell, partly because of her union position, which can be quite strident, but also because she tends to shout when people disagree with her. You would like to get Cathy Turvill on side, but she tends to go all over the place when she should be more focused.

With a sigh, you prepare for your opening meeting, having given some consideration to your agenda. You know there are particular matters that should be on the agenda, but some of the critically important issues really need to be understood first. You are hoping to keep things at a low-key level so that the Consultative Committee can achieve its goals peacefully.

Robert Matzione, director of nursing

Like Jane, you have been at the hospital for quite a few years and have seen many changes. Jane is a bit of a lightweight, in your opinion, and typical of the old-style human resources director. In your view, if a job is worth doing it is worth doing well and you work out the requirements and get stuck into it. You have a lot of impatience with people who muck around too much on people stuff, because they waste so much time. This restructuring is yet another disaster typical of the government, put forward without any consideration for efficient service. Nonetheless, while you have some sympathies with the union's position, you have no time for their rat-baggery. If Jane does not chair the meeting firmly, you feel that you may have to step in and get things organised. On further reflection, you probably have a lot more in common with the union representative than with any of the other people on the committee. It is just that the politics of your different positions make it hard to be seen to appear to be too obviously supportive.

Carole Cornell, clinical nurse consultant and representative of the Australian Nursing Federation

You are just bursting for this meeting so that you can get stuck into the administration for violating every principle of efficient service and for undermining staff conditions. You know every code and regulation by heart, every violation and every deviation from prior agreements, and the conditions of effective service in the hospital. You certainly feel angry and can express this anger even though you tend to do this in a fairly precise and considered way. Of the people on the committee, you have a grudging regard for the director of nursing but you would never admit it, quite a bit of disdain for Jane Telford and her wussy assistant Marcus Woollaroo, and almost no time for that 'head in the clouds' Cathy Turvill. Your aim in the Consultative Committee is to ensure that violations and diversions from agreed protocol are identified and that, as far as possible, the amalgamation is stopped and the impact of its consequences is reduced considerably.

Cathy Turvill, assistant director of nursing

You are feeling particularly concerned about this process because you hold one of the four assistant director positions, which will be reduced to two, and you have a strong feeling that you are going to be in the out-group. You have been in the position for only three years. At your age, and given several moves in recent years, you feel you cannot go back to a nurse manager position comfortably. Moving to another hospital is unlikely. Normally you are very cheery and would like looking at the different opportunities and options that such a restructuring and amalgamation could offer. You certainly wonder whether you have the necessary skills to be an effective member of this group, let alone an assistant director of nursing.

Quite a lot of possibilities have occurred to you about the way the clinical nurse consultants could be retrained and how the excess staff could be looked after and offered different positions that could be quite valuable to them. You are hoping that some of your ideas will be heard in the committee meeting, because you believe that many of them have never been considered by the administration. You have a lot of regard for Jane Telford, the director of human resources, and wish that you had more time to discuss some of your ideas with her. In many ways, although you are apprehensive about the process, you are really looking forward to contributing to this committee.

Marcus Woollaroo, assistant to the director of human resources

You have been with the hospital for only 12 months but have naturally hit it off with Jane Telford, your director. It is almost as if you begin sentences and she finishes them, and vice versa. You are very similar in terms of style and ideas about human resources, and approaches to managing people. With her direction and with the task in front of you, you are prepared to ensure that all the outcomes required will be achieved in the fullness of time. This is one of the most important tasks you have had since joining the hospital and you are looking forward to showing your skills to the group.

DISCUSSION QUESTIONS

1. *Identify the probable LETS dimensions for each person.*
2. *Identify the probable learning styles for each person.*
3. *Describe two or three key matching elements for each person.*
4. *Identify and describe mismatching that occurred on ID dimensions during the role-play.*
5. *List some options for how these mismatches might be converted into more effective matching.*
6. *Identify some of Trompenaars and Hampden–Turner's social dimensions that might fit each of these roles.*

Skill practice

Exercises for improving self-awareness through self-disclosure

Through the looking glass

In the 19th century, the concept of 'looking-glass self' was developed to describe the process used by people to develop self-awareness. It means that other people serve as a looking glass for each of us. They mirror back our actions and behaviours. In turn, we form our opinions of ourselves as a result of observing and interpreting this mirroring. The best way to form accurate self-perceptions, therefore, is to share your thoughts, attitudes, feelings, actions and plans with others. This exercise helps you do that by asking you to analyse your own styles and inclinations and then share and discuss them with others. This sharing exercise will provide insights that you have not recognised before.

Assignment

In a group of three or four, share your scores on the skill assessment instruments. Determine what similarities and differences exist among you. Do systematic ethnic or gender differences exist? Now read aloud the ten statements listed below. Each person should complete each statement, but take turns going first. The purpose of your completing the statements aloud is to help you articulate aspects of your self-awareness and to receive reactions to them from others.

1. In taking the assessment instruments, I was surprised by …
2. Some of my dominant characteristics captured by the instruments are …
3. Among my greatest strengths are …
4. Among my greatest weaknesses are …
5. The time I felt most successful was …
6. The time I felt least competent was …
7. My three highest priorities in life are …
8. The way in which I differ most from other people is …
9. I get along best with people who …
10. From what the others in this group have shared, here is an impression I have formed about each:

Diagnosing managerial characteristics

This exercise is designed to give you practice in diagnosing differences in others' styles and inclinations. Being aware of the styles, values and attitudes of others will help you manage them more effectively. Below are brief descriptions of four successful managers. They differ in values, learning styles, orientations toward change, and interpersonal orientation. After reading the scenarios, form small groups to discuss the questions that follow.

Michael Dell

Michael Dell is the kind of guy people either love or hate. He is worth more than $13 billion, loves to go to work each day, and is as likely to tear a computer apart and put it back together again as to read a financial report. More than 15 years after he started assembling computers while he was at university, Michael is still fascinated with the hardware. Despite his billionaire status, 'if anyone believes that he [Michael] is not the chief technologist in this company, they are naive,' says Robert McFarland, vice president of Dell's federal sales group. Although Dell Computer is the quintessential lean-and-mean company, Michael does not play the part of the whipcracker. After recently receiving an award from the Austin, Texas, Chamber of Commerce, for example, Michael and his wife stayed long after the program was over to chat with everyone who wanted to meet him. He has been described as shy and quiet and not inclined towards public hyperbole. 'Michael has a genuine shyness.... He is a genuinely mild-mannered, low-key person who was very focused on reaching his objectives,' says Brian Fawkes, a former Dell employee. Admittedly, Dell has experienced several missteps and losses, but Michael has been unafraid to learn from missteps. 'Michael makes mistakes. He just never makes the same mistake twice,' says Mark Tebbe, president of a firm Dell recently acquired.

Source: Adapted from B. Darrow, 'Michael Dell', *ComputerReseller News*, November 16, 1998, pp. 124–125.

Patrick M. Byrne

As president and chairman of Overstock.com in Salt Lake City, Utah, Byrne was a Marshall Scholar who received his PhD in philosophy from Stanford University. His management style, personality, and core values are illustrated in his interview with *Fast Company*: 'Learning philosophy has been useful in teaching me how to get to the heart of things—to be able to deconstruct what the real issues are. People think we're endless debaters, but what we're really doing is refining concepts in order to reach agreement. With negotiations, instead of trying to fight someone on every one of the issues, most of the time it turns out he cares about a whole bunch of things that you don't care about. Make those trade-offs, and he'll think you're being too generous when in fact you're just giving him the sleeves off your vest. Ultimately, philosophy is about values, and that definitely has its place in business. I consider myself a far outsider to Wall Street. There's a whole lot of obfuscation involved. In August, I spoke out on how the Wall Street system was corrupt and how the financial press was co-opted. Because of it I got called a buffoon and wacky; then a lot of lies came out about my being gay, taking cocaine, and hiring a stripper. That's sort of the fifth-grade level we're operating on. It doesn't bother me. When you decide to stand for things, you have to be prepared to face criticism, mockery, and derision.'

Source: Adapted from Patrick M Byrne and Maurice Blanks, *Fast Company*, 2005.

Maurice Blanks

When Maurice started architecture school, one of the professors said that only 25 per cent of the students would make it. Sure enough, Maurice dropped out in his forties after operating his own office in Chicago. He moved to Minneapolis to devote himself full-time to Blu Dot, a company he helped create. His discussion about architecture reveals a great deal about his personal attributes. 'Architecture is about keeping track of thousands of pieces of information and making sure they're all covered in the design. The implications of failure are pretty high if you don't—people could get hurt. Therefore, you learn that you must be very efficient with information and organisation, which naturally translates to running the day-to-day operations of a company. It's funny how the word "sell" is never used in architecture school, but to me the critiques were kind of informal lessons in sales. For exams, you'd present your work to a jury—professors, peers, local architects, and so on. Their job was to shell you; your job was to defend yourself. It's pretty brutal. Tears are not uncommon. But it taught me how to communicate ideas quickly and tailor information to an audience.'

Source: Adapted from Patrick M Byrne and Maurice Blanks, *Fast Company*, 2005.

Gordon Bethune

Gordon Bethune has been described as the other earthy, exuberant, hard-drinking Texas CEO who turned around an airline that is now famous for good service, happy employees and admirable profitability. Herb Kelleher at Southwest Airlines is the best known, but Gordon Bethune at Continental Airlines is the most successful. A high school drop-out mechanic who spent years in the Navy, Gordon took over a twice-bankrupt airline in 1994 and led it from a US$960 million loss to more than US$600 million profit in five years. Even from his early years as a Navy mechanic, Gordon was known as a superb motivator of people and a network builder. 'He had a web of relationships that enabled him to get whatever he needed,' said a former commanding officer. At Continental, Gordon turned around a culture where morale was in the pits, on-time performance was abysmal, and everything from the planes to the meals were a mess. Part of the turnaround was due to Gordon's personal attention to employees—for example, he attends the graduation ceremonies of every new class of flight attendants, hands out candy canes to employees during the Christmas season, shows up regularly at employee birthday parties, and holds a monthly open house in his office to encourage employee communication. 'Anybody who's worked here longer than two months can recognise Gordon,' says a baggage handler in Newark, New Jersey. When he walks through an airport, employees wave and call out his name. Whereas Gordon is known as an irreverent and wild guy, he demands precision and standardised levels of service in every place in the company. When he discovered slightly larger white coffee cups in a Houston airport lounge, for example, he was told that they were needed to fit the new coffee maker. He demanded that the coffee maker be changed so that the standard blue cups could be used. No exceptions.'

Source: Adapted from B. O'Reilly, 'The mechanic who fixed Continental', *Fortune*, 1999, 140: 176–186.

DISCUSSION QUESTIONS

1. *Rank these individuals from highest to lowest in terms of*
   - *Emotional intelligence*
   - *Values maturity*
   - *Tolerance of ambiguity*
   - *Core self-evaluation*

   Justify your evaluations in a discussion with your colleagues and compare your scores.
2. *What is your prediction about the dominant learning styles of each of these individuals? What data do you use as evidence?*
3. *If you were assigned to hire a senior manager for your organisation and this was your candidate pool, what questions would you ask to identify the*
   - *cognitive styles*
   - *values orientations*
   - *orientation towards change*
   - *core self-evaluation*

   of these individuals? Which one of these people would you hire if you wanted a CEO for your company? Why?
4. *Assume that each of these individuals were members of your team. What would be the greatest strengths and weaknesses of your team? What kinds of attributes would you want to add to your team to ensure that it was optimally heterogeneous?*

An exercise for identifying aspects of personal culture: A learning plan and autobiography

The purpose of this exercise is to assist you in articulating your key goals and aspirations as well as identifying a personal learning plan to facilitate your success. Because continuous learning is so important for you to succeed throughout your life, we want to help you identify some specific ambitions and to develop a set of procedures to help you reach your potential.

This exercise is accomplished in four steps:

- *Step 1: (Aspirations):* Write an autobiographical story that might appear in *Fortune* magazine, *Fast Company* or the *Wall Street Journal* on this date 15 years from now. This story should identify your notable accomplishments and your newsworthy successes. What will you have achieved that will fulfil your dreams? What outcomes would make you ecstatically happy? What legacy do you want to be known for?
- *Step 2: (Characteristics):* Review your scores on the pre-assessment instruments. Using Figure 2.11, identify the extent to which you are satisfied with your scores on these various instruments.

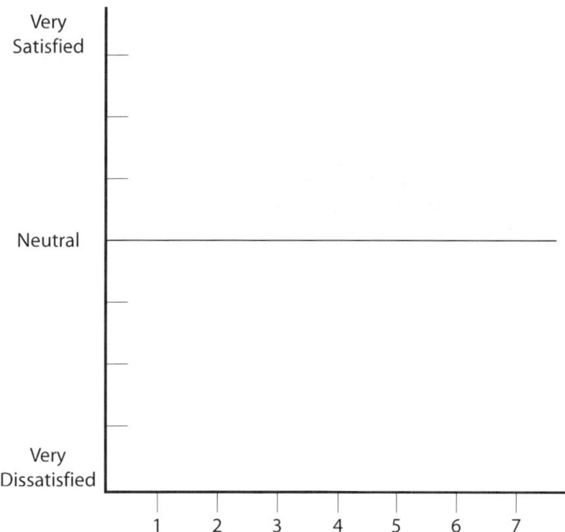

1 – Self-Awareness Assessment (current level of self-awareness)
2 – Emotional Intelligence Assessment (level of emotional intelligence)
3 – The Defining Issues Test (level of values maturity)
4 – The Cognitive Style Indicator (information gathering and evaluation)
5 – Locus of Control Scale (internal versus external locus of control)
6 – Tolerance of Ambiguity Scale (level of intolerance of ambiguity)
7 – Core Self-Evaluation Scale (level of positive self-regard)

FIGURE 2.11 Satisfaction with self-awareness scores

The vertical axis in the figure ranges from Very Satisfied to Very Dissatisfied. The horizontal axis identifies the five areas of self-awareness being assessed in this chapter. For each of the seven instruments, plot your satisfaction level with how you scored. By joining those points together, you will have created a Self-Awareness Satisfaction Profile. This will help you to highlight areas in which you will want to improve.

Based on that plot, identify your distinctive competencies, your strengths and your unique attributes. What are the values, styles and attitudes that will assist you in achieving the aspirations you have identified in step 1?

- *Step 3: (Feedback):* Interview a member of your family or someone who knows you very well. Ask that person to describe what they see as your unique strengths and capabilities. What does he or she see for you in your future? Include the following questions in your interview:
  - Who do you know that you admire a great deal because of their success in life?
  - What capabilities and attributes do they possess?
  - Who do you know that has failed to achieve their potential? What do you see as the most significant causes of their failure?
  - What do you see as the distinctive and notable capabilities that I possess?
  - In what areas do you think I should focus my improvement and development efforts?
  - What do you see me doing in 15 years?
- *Step 4: (Planning):* Now identify the developmental activities in which you will engage if you are to achieve your aspirations. With the insight you have gained from steps 2 and 3, identify the things you must do to help you achieve what you hope to accomplish. Consider the following activities.
  - What courses will you take?
  - What people will you get to know?

PRACTICE

- In what extracurricular or life-balance activities will you engage?
- What will you read?
- What spiritual activities will be most meaningful?

This written product should be handed in to your instructor, or it should be given to a family member for safekeeping. Open and reread this document in five years to determine the extent to which you are on track.

Skill application

Suggested assignments

1. Using the information about Trompenaars and Hampden–Turner's five social dimensions, identify your own likely management style. Consider your significant communications at work, and identify several key colleagues with whom you are matched or mismatched on these five dimensions. What actions do you need to take to improve and develop your matching skills? What actions do you need to take to develop more effective matching with those colleagues with whom you are on opposite poles? Practise some of these new behaviours and review your success.
2. a. Rate three of your colleagues on the LETS scales by using your own understanding of your profile and your relationship with them.
   b. Next consider two dimensions of your communication-style profile that you know often tend to be mismatched with others. That is, select two that often cause you some performance or communication difficulties.
   c. Plan a course of action to alter or change that aspect of your profile to shift your behaviour towards the other end of the continuum. For example, if you tend to be down the exaggerator end of the profile, and if this is a regular area in which you have management or supervisory difficulties, look at steps you could take at work and at home to reduce the level of exaggeration and to down-play some of your responses and reactions.
      i. Do this with two of your dimensions.
      ii. Practise these amendments over the next three weeks. Take note of the outcomes and your experience during this time.
   d. Finally, look back over your work and evaluate the results of the process of adaptation.
3. Put your LETS profile in a place where you can see it—on a filing cabinet or in your diary—and look at it regularly over the next three months. List the number of situations in which you use it automatically. Identify those situations in which you tended not to use it but where it would have been very effective. Consider a process by which you can be more proactive in using the LETS profile in those situations.
4. Consider a situation where you need to introduce a new project to Chay Yee. Chay Yee tends to exaggerate and is very rapid, extremely linear and visual in his approach. Design an interaction with Chay Yee in which you:
   a. Mismatch the words and body language in your presentation and identify the probable outcome of this approach.
   b. Match the words and body language in your presentation and identify the probable outcome of this style.

Matching, self-awareness and cross-cultural management

These case studies are adapted from Smith (2003: 177). Copyright Elsevier 2003.

Case one

In his book *Vikings and Mandarins*, Worm (1996) identified how Nordic managers who were working in a joint venture company with Chinese managers attempted to give face to their Chinese associates by introducing policies in ways that gave respect to age and built trust gradually over time. These attempts were largely successful in developing a positive working relationship and successful outcomes. Nonetheless, the attempts made the Nordic managers feel uncomfortable. They felt they had not spoken as directly and honestly as they should. It was not their normal style and it felt unfamiliar and unsatisfying.

Case two

A manager of a Coca-Cola bottling plant in China was faced with his subordinates' demand to appoint their relatives to positions at the plant. This was clearly against global company policy. However, attempts to argue this position were met with absenteeism and passive resistance. Finally, the manager established a budget for each of his subordinates and told them they could hire whomever they chose, as long as they operated within their allocated budget. This strategy provided an incentive to hire people who would be effective in the jobs even if they were relatives. In this way, the manager saved face for the subordinates but also set the standard for subordinates to evaluate the selection of their relatives for positions.

Case study analysis

Considering the material in Chapters 1 and 2, write a description of each case study that identifies the strategy used, the matching skills according to Trompenaars' social factors and the ethical considerations.

Keeping a journal

1. Keep a journal for at least the remainder of this course. Record significant discoveries, insights, learnings and personal recollections (not daily activities). Write in your journal at least twice a week. Give yourself some feedback.
2. Write down the comprehensive, consistent and universal principles that guide your behaviour under all circumstances. What core principles will you rarely violate?
3. After completing these personal assessment instruments and discussing their implications with someone else, write a statement or an essay responding to the following four questions:
   a. Who am I?
   b. What are my main strengths and weaknesses?
   c. What do I want to achieve in my life?
   d. What legacy do I want to leave?
4. Spend an evening with a close friend or relative discussing your values, cognitive style, attitude towards change and interpersonal orientation. You may want to have that person complete the instruments, giving their impressions of you, so that you can compare and contrast your scores. Discuss implications for your future and your relationship with your friend or relative.
5. Teach someone else the value of self-awareness in managerial success and explain the relevance of values maturity, cognitive style, attitude towards change and interpersonal style. Describe the experience in your journal.

Application plan and evaluation

The intent of this exercise is to help you apply this cluster of skills in a real-life, out-of-class setting. Now that you have become familiar with the behavioural guidelines that form the basis of effective skill performance, you will improve most by trying out those guidelines in an everyday context. Unlike a classroom activity, in which feedback is immediate and others can assist you with their evaluations, this skill application activity is one you must accomplish and evaluate on your own.

There are two parts to this activity. Part 1 helps to prepare you to apply the skill. Part 2 helps you to evaluate and improve on your experience. Be sure to write down answers to each item. Do not short-circuit the process by skipping steps.

Part 1: Planning

1. Write down the two or three aspects of this skill of self-awareness that are most important to you. These may be areas of weakness, areas you most want to improve, or areas that are most salient to a problem you face right now. Identify the specific aspects of this skill that you want to apply.

2. Now identify the setting or the situation in which you will apply this skill. Establish a plan for performance by writing down a description of the situation. Who else will be involved? When will you do it? Where will it be done?
3. Identify the specific behaviours you will engage in to apply this skill. How will you put these behaviours into practice?
4. What are the indicators of successful performance? How will you know you have been effective? What will indicate you have performed competently?

Part 2: Evaluation

5. When you have completed your implementation, record the results. What happened? How successful were you? What was the effect on others?
6. How can you improve? What modifications can you make next time? What will you do differently in a similar situation in the future?
7. Looking back on your whole skill practice and application experience, what have you learned? What has been surprising? In what ways might this experience help you in the long term?

Scoring keys and supplementary materials

Self-awareness (p. 54)

SCORING KEY

Skill area	*Items*	ASSESSMENT *Pre-*	*Post*
Self-disclosure and openness to feedback from others	1, 2, 3, 9, 11	______	______
Awareness of own values, cognitive style and change orientation	4, 5, 6, 7, 8, 10	______	______
	TOTAL SCORE	☐	☐

Comparison data

Compare your scores with three comparison standards:

1. Compare your scores with the maximum possible (66).
2. Compare your scores with the scores of other students in your group.
3. Compare your scores with a norm group consisting of 500 business school students. In comparison to the norm group, if you scored:

55 or above	you are in the top quartile
52–54	you are in the second quartile
48–51	you are in the third quartile
47 or below	you are in the bottom quartile.

Leadership Enhancement Team Style (LETS) (p. 55)

The LETS scoring was conducted online and the profile you printed represents your scores on this instrument. The text in this chapter clarifies the meaning of your profile. The following tables provide data from over 4000 managers.

LETS Guide to Interpretation

Gender Comparisons

Timing

	Percentage		
	Female	Male	Total
Gradual	17.61%	18.42%	18.00%
Rapid/Gradual	44.63%	45.80%	45.19%
Rapid	37.76%	35.78%	36.81%

There is a weak gender effect for Timing, such that males are more likely to be gradual and females more likely to be rapid.

Emphasis

	Percentage		
	Female	Male	Total
Understate	72.62%	74.61%	73.57%
Exaggerate/Understate	9.02%	8.87%	8.94%
Exaggerate	18.36%	16.53%	17.48%

There is a clearly greater likelihood for members of both genders to understate. Nevertheless, there is a weak gender effect for Emphasis, such that males are more likely to understate and females more likely to exaggerate.

Thinking

	Percentage		
	Female	Male	Total
Lateral	19.11%	17.38%	18.29%
Linear/Lateral	9.17%	8.39%	8.80%
Linear	71.72%	74.22%	72.92%

There is a clearly greater likelihood for members of both genders to be linear thinkers. Nevertheless, there is a weak gender effect for Thinking, such that males are more likely to be linear and females more likely to be lateral.

Focus

	Percentage		
	Female	Male	Total
Concept	37.68%	48.13%	42.68%
Detail/Concept	11.91%	11.75%	11.83%
Detail	50.40%	40.12%	45.48%

There is a strong gender effect for Focus, such that males are significantly more likely to be conceptual and females more likely to be detail-focused.

Evaluation

	Percentage		
	Female	Male	Total
Other	26.22%	30.19%	28.12%
Self/Other	7.80%	7.59%	7.70%
Self	65.98%	62.22%	64.18%

There is a greater likelihood for members of both genders to be self-evaluators. Nevertheless, there is a moderate gender effect for Evaluation, such that males are more likely to be other-evaluators and females more likely to be self-evaluators.

Relationship

	Percentage		
	Female	Male	Total
Initiate	26.23%	30.12%	28.09%
Initiate/Respond	30.35%	33.57%	31.89%
Respond	43.42%	36.31%	40.02%

There is a moderate gender effect for Relationship, such that males are more likely to be initiators or initiator/responders and females significantly more likely to be responders.

Perceptual Orientation

	Percentage		
	Female	Male	Total
Visual	56.39%	61.39%	58.98%
Auditory	21.26%	16.47%	18.78%
Experiential	22.35%	22.13%	22.24%

There is a greater likelihood for members of both genders to have a visual perceptual orientation. Nevertheless, there is a moderate gender effect for Perceptual Orientation, such that males are more likely to have a visual orientation and females more likely to have an auditory orientation. Males and females are equally distributed in the experiential orientation.

Leadership

	Percentage		
	Female	Male	Total
Planner	27.54%	29.38%	28.41%
Developer	17.85%	19.75%	18.75%
Creator	9.94%	10.61%	10.26%
Analyser	44.67%	40.25%	42.59%

There is a weak gender effect for Leadership, such that males are slightly more likely to be planners or developers and females more likely to be analysers. In both genders, being an analyser is most common and being a creator is least common.

Age Comparisons

Timing

	Average Age	N	Std. Deviation
Gradual+	31.91	157	11.304
Gradual	34.52	1644	11.281
Rapid/Gradual	34.44	4485	10.550
Rapid	33.54	3091	9.926
Rapid+	32.63	648	9.762

Leaving the small number of very gradual responses aside, there is otherwise a weak trend for younger people to be more rapid (impetuous) and to become more gradual (deliberative) with age.

Emphasis

	Average Age	N	Std. Deviation
Exaggerate+	32.20	76	11.565
Exaggerate	31.36	1752	9.929
Exaggerate/Understate	32.41	920	10.115
Understate	34.80	5985	10.457
Understate+	35.25	1302	10.691

Leaving the small number of very exaggeratory responses aside, there is otherwise a moderate trend for younger people to be more exaggeratory (expressive) and to become more understated (cautious) with age.

Thinking

	Average Age	N	Std. Deviation
Lateral+	36.38	53	11.210
Lateral	36.43	1815	9.946
Linear/Lateral	34.73	907	10.226
Linear	33.64	6337	10.455
Linear+	30.92	908	10.689

There is a strong trend for younger people to be more linear (targeted) and to become more lateral (encompassing) with age.

Focus

	Average Age	N	Std. Deviation
Concept+	37.31	298	10.726
Concept	35.57	3999	10.358
Detail/Concept	31.81	1173	10.372
Detail	33.38	4144	10.357
Detail+	29.52	412	9.689

There is a strong trend for younger people to be more detail-focused (task-aware) and to become more conceptual (context-aware) with age.

Evaluation

	Average Age	N	Std. Deviation
Other+	33.57	164	10.636
Other	34.36	2634	10.138
Self/Other	33.25	812	10.823
Self	34.68	4232	10.569
Self+	32.64	2185	10.404

There is no discernible age-related trend for the Evaluation dimension. It could be inferred from this that evaluation is fixed and does not change with age.

Relationships

	Average Age	N	Std. Deviation
Initiate+	40.12	25	12.693
Initiate	35.18	2765	10.374
Initiate/Respond	35.39	3180	10.235
Respond	32.26	3960	10.440
Respond+	27.49	102	8.759

There is a very strong trend for younger people to be responders (supporting) and to become initiators (confident to lead) with age.

Perceptual Orientation

	Average Age	N	Std. Deviation
Auditory	34.39	398	9.842
Experiential	35.43	486	9.982
Visual	34.64	1247	9.725

There is no discernible age-related trend for the Perceptual Orientation dimension. It could be inferred from this that perceptual orientation is fixed and does not change with age.

Leadership

	Average Age	N	Std. Deviation
Analyser	32.75	3084	10.671
Creator	36.28	790	10.268
Developer	36.66	1393	10.503
Planner	32.71	2129	9.927

There is a strong trend for younger people to be analysers or planners and for older people to be developers or creators with age.

Emotional intelligence assessment (p. 55)

SCORING KEY

The statements below have been reorganised according to the key dimension of emotional intelligence being assessed. The numbers next to each alternative indicate the number of points attached to that alternative. Circle the alternatives you selected, and then add up the points for the 12 items.

Item	Alternative	Points
Emotional awareness		
1	a	10
	b	0
	c	0

EXPLANATION: Only alternative (a) indicates that you are aware of what is going on emotionally inside.

5	a	5
	b	10
	c	0

EXPLANATION: Alternative (a) may be okay if you are clear about your priorities, but alternative (b) indicates that you are aware of possible alternative points of view.

9	a	0
	b	0
	c	10

EXPLANATION: Only alternative (c) indicates that you are aware of your own emotional reactions and will require compensation for the inevitable upset it will create.

Emotional control (balance)

2	a	0
	b	5
	c	10

EXPLANATION: Alternative (c) implies that you are confident enough to handle the situation on the spot. Alternative (b) confronts the issue but not in the presence of those affected.

6	a	10
	b	5
	c	0

EXPLANATION: Alternative (a) is honest if it is done skilfully and avoids being harsh. Alternative (b) relies on the other person getting an indirect hint.

10	a	0
	b	0
	c	10

EXPLANATION: Only alternative (c) demonstrates emotional control.

Emotional diagnosis (empathy)

3	a	5
	b	10
	c	0

EXPLANATION: Alternative (a) may be appropriate in some circumstances, but alternative (b) indicates sensitivity to a possible emotional issue on the part of the other person.

7	a	10
	b	5
	c	0

EXPLANATION: Alternative (a) indicates an ability to recognise different emotions but to not get carried away by them. Alternative (b) acknowledges different emotional perspectives but may engender bad feelings or emotional casualties. Alternative (c) does not acknowledge the different emotional commitments.

11	a	0
	b	10
	c	0

EXPLANATION: Only alternative (b) empathetically acknowledges the other person's feelings.

Emotional response

4	a	0
	b	10
	c	0

EXPLANATION: Alternatives (a) and (c) may indicate that you are not sensitive to the emotional climate of the group, and your behaviour may be inappropriate.

8	a	0
	b	5
	c	10

EXPLANATION: Alternative (b) may be appropriate if it is not a sign of narcissism, but alternative (c) is clearly an indication of emotional control.

12	a	10
	b	0
	c	5

EXPLANATION: Alternative (b) implies losing emotional control, whereas alternative (a) indicates remaining under control.

Total ____________________

Comparison data

Mean score:	70
Top quartile:	86 or higher
Third quartile:	71–85
Second quartile:	55–70
Bottom quartile:	54 or lower

Defining Issues Test (p. 56)

The possibility of misusing and misinterpreting this instrument is high enough that its author, James Rest, maintains control over the scoring procedure associated with its use. Some people may interpret the results of this instrument to be an indication of inherent morality, honesty or personal worth, none of which the instrument is intended to assess. A scoring manual may be obtained from James Rest, Minnesota Moral Research Center, Burton Hall, University of Minnesota, Minneapolis, MN 55455, United States.

Our purpose is to help you become aware of the stage of moral development you rely on most when facing moral dilemmas. To help determine that, the following lists present the stage of moral development each statement associated with each story reflects. By looking at the four statements you selected as most important in deciding what action to take in each situation, you can determine which stage of development you use most often.

After you have done this, you should discuss which action you would take in each situation and why, and why you selected the statements you did as the most important ones to consider.

The escaped prisoner (p. 57)

1. Hasn't Ben Thompson been good enough for such a long time to prove he is not a bad person? (Stage 3)
2. Every time someone escapes punishment for a crime, does that not encourage more crime? (Stage 4)
3. Wouldn't we be better off without prisons and the oppression of our legal system? (Indicates anti-authoritarian attitudes.)
4. Has Ben Thompson really paid his debt to society? (Stage 4)
5. Would society be failing if it did not provide what Ben Thompson should fairly expect? (Stage 6)
6. What benefits would prison be, apart from to society, especially for a charitable man? (Nonsense alternative, designed to identify people picking high-sounding alternatives.)
7. How could anyone be so cruel and heartless as to send Ben Thompson to prison? (Stage 3)
8. Would it be fair to prisoners who have to serve out their full sentences if Ben Thompson is let off? (Stage 4)
9. Was Margaret Jones a good friend of Ben Thompson? (Stage 3)
10. Is it a citizen's duty to report an escaped criminal, regardless of the circumstances? (Stage 4)
11. How would the will of the people and the public good best be served? (Stage 5)
12. Would going to prison do any good for Ben Thompson or protect anybody? (Stage 5)

The doctor's dilemma (p. 57)

1. Whether the woman's family is in favour of giving her an overdose or not. (Stage 3)
2. Is the doctor obligated by the same laws as everybody else if giving her an overdose would be the same as killing her? (Stage 4)
3. Whether people would be much better off without society regimenting their lives and even their deaths. (Indicates anti-authoritarian attitudes.)
4. Whether the doctor could make it appear like an accident. (Stage 2)
5. Does the state have the right to force continued existence on those who do not want to live? (Stage 5)

6. What is the value of death prior to society's perspective on personal values? (Nonsense alternative, designed to identify people picking high-sounding alternatives.)
7. Whether the doctor has sympathy for the woman's suffering or cares more about what society might think. (Stage 3)
8. Is helping to end another's life ever a responsible act of cooperation? (Stage 6)
9. Whether only God should decide when a person's life should end. (Stage 4)
10. What values the doctor has set for himself in his own personal code of behaviour. (Stage 5)
11. Can society afford to let everybody end their lives when they want to? (Stage 4)
12. Can society allow suicides or mercy killing and still protect the lives of individuals who want to live? (Stage 5)

The newspaper (p. 58)

1. Is the principal more responsible to students or to the parents? (Stage 4)
2. Did the principal give his word that the newspaper could be published for a long time, or did he promise to approve the newspaper one issue at a time? (Stage 4)
3. Would the students start protesting even more if the principal stopped the newspaper? (Stage 2)
4. When the welfare of the school is threatened, does the principal have the right to give orders to students? (Stage 4)
5. Does the principal have the freedom of speech to say 'no' in this case? (Nonsense alternative, designed to identify people picking high-sounding alternatives.)
6. If the principal stopped the newspaper, would he be preventing full discussion of important problems? (Stage 5)
7. Whether the principal's order would make Rami lose faith in the principal. (Stage 3)
8. Whether Rami was loyal to his school and patriotic to his country. (Stage 3)
9. What effect would stopping the paper have on the students' education in critical thinking and judgment? (Stage 5)
10. Whether Rami was in any way violating the rights of others in publishing his own opinions. (Stage 5)
11. Whether the principal should be influenced by some angry parents when it is the principal who knows best what is going on in the school. (Stage 4)
12. Whether Rami was using the newspaper to stir up hatred and discontent. (Stage 3)

Core self-evaluation scale (p. 59)

SCORING KEY

Sum your scores for all 12 items, making certain that you reverse your scores for items 2, 4, 6, 8, 10 and 12. That is, for these items a scored 1 becomes 5, 2 becomes 4, 3 equals 3, 4 becomes 2, and 5 becomes 1. Divide the sum by 12 to produce an average CSES score.

1.	_______	I am confident I get the success I deserve in life.
2.	_______	Sometimes I feel depressed. **(reverse)**
3.	_______	When I try, I generally succeed.
4.	_______	Sometimes when I fail, I feel worthless. **(reverse)**
5.	_______	I complete tasks successfully.
6.	_______	Sometimes, I do not feel in control of my work. **(reverse)**
7.	_______	Overall, I am satisfied with myself.
8.	_______	I am filled with doubts about my competence. **(reverse)**
9.	_______	I determine what will happen in my life.
10.	_______	I do not feel in control of my success in my career. **(reverse)**
11.	_______	I am capable of coping with most of my problems.
12.	_______	There are times when things look pretty bleak and hopeless to me. **(reverse)**
Total	_______	
÷12	_______	**(average score)**

Comparison data

(Compared with psychology students, business students, practising managers)

Mean score:	3.88
Top quartile:	4.41 or above
Third quartile:	3.88 and 4.40
Second quartile:	3.35 and 3.87
Bottom quartile:	3.34 or below

The cognitive style instrument (p. 59)

SCORING KEY

To determine your score on the two dimensions of cognitive style, circle the items below that you checked on this instrument. Then count up the number of circled items and put your scores in the spaces below.

GATHERING INFORMATION		EVALUATING INFORMATION	
1b	1a	13a	13b
2a	2b	14b	14a
3b	3a	15a	15b
4a	4b	16b	16a
5a	5b	17b	17a
6b	6a	18a	18b
7b	7a	19a	19b
8a	8b	20a	20b
9a	9b	21b	21a
10b	10a	22a	22b
11a	11b	23b	23a
12a	12b	24a	24b
Intuitive score	Sensing score	Thinking score	Feeling score

Comparison data

Males:	5.98	6.02	6.08	5.20
Females:	6.04	5.96	6.94	5.06

Locus of control scale (p. 61)

SCORING KEY

Count up the number of items you selected of those listed below:

2a	5b	9a	12b	16a	20a	23a	28b
3b	6a	10a	13b	17a	21a	25a	29a
4b	7a	11b	15b	18a	22b	26b	

TOTAL SCORE

Note: The items omitted (1, 8, 14, 19, 24, 27) are filler items only and are not required for scoring.

Comparison data

Corporate business executives' average:	8.29	Sd: 3.57
Elite career military officers' average:	8.28	Sd: 3.86

A score below 8.29 means you have an increasingly internal locus of control.
A score above 8.29 means you have an increasingly external locus of control.

Additional comparisons (from Rotter 1966)

Sample	Mean	S.d.	Source
Ohio State psychology students (N=1180)	8.29	3.97	1966
Connecticut psychology students (N=303)	9.22	3.88	1966
Peace Corps trainees (N=155)	5.95	3.96	1966
National high school students (N=1000)	8.50	3.74	1966
Municipal administrators, Alberta, Canada (N=50)	6.24	3.31	1971
Business executives (N=71)	8.29	3.57	1980
Career military officers (N=261)	8.28	3.86	1980

References

Allan, H. and J. Waclawski 1999, 'Influence behaviors and managerial effectiveness in lateral relations', *Human Resource Development Quarterly*, 10, pp. 3–34.

Allport, G., R. Gordon and P. Vernon 1931, 1960, *The Study of Values Manual* (Boston: Houghton Mifflin Co.).

Andrewartha, G. 1997, *The McPhee Andrewartha Influence Dimensions*, 3rd rev. ed. (Adelaide: McPhee Andrewartha Pty Ltd).

Andrewartha, G. 2002, *Be Understood or Be Overlooked* (Sydney: Allen & Unwin).

Andrewartha, G. 2011, *Leadership Enhancement Team Style (LETS)* (Adelaide: McPhee Andrewartha Pty Ltd).

Argyris, C. 1992, *On Organizational Learning*, 2nd ed. (Cambridge, UK: Blackwell).

Atwater, L. and F. Yammarino 1992, 'Does self-other agreement on leadership perceptions moderate the validity of leadership and performance predictions?', *Personnel Psychology*, 45, pp. 141–64.

Bar-On, R. 1997, *Bar-On Emotional Quotient Inventory: User's Manual* (New York: Multi-Health Systems).

Bekmeier-Feuerhahn, S. and Eichenlaub, A. 2010, 'What makes for trusting relationships in online communication?', *Journal of Communication Management*, 14(4), pp. 337–55.

Bellinger, G. 2004, 'Ladder of inference. Short circuiting reality', <www.systemswiki.org/index.php?title=Ladder_of_Inference:_Short_Circuiting_Reality>

Berscheid, E. and E. H. Walster 1978, *Interpersonal Attraction* (Reading, MA: Addison-Wesley).

Bigoness, W. and G. Blakely 1996, 'A cross-national study of managerial values', *Journal of International Business Studies*, 27, pp. 739–52.

Black, S. and L. Porter 1996, *Management: Meeting the Global Challenges* (Reading, MA: Addison-Wesley Longman).

Boyatzis, R. E. 1982, *The Competent Manager* (New York: John Wiley & Sons).

Boyatzis, R. E., A. J. Murphy and J. V. Wheeler 2000, 'Philosophy as a missing link between values and behavior', *Psychological Reports*, 86(1), February, pp. 47–64.

Boyle, G. 1995, 'Myers–Briggs Type Indicator (MBTI): Some psychometric limitations', *The Australian Psychologist*, 30(1), pp. 71–74.

Brouwer, P. J. 1964, 'The power to see ourselves', *Harvard Business Review*, 42, pp. 156–65.

Budner, S. 1982, 'Intolerance of ambiguity as a personality variable', *Journal of Personality*, 30, pp. 29–50.

Byrne, P. M. and Maurice Blanks 2005, *Fast Company*, <www.fastcompany.com>

Cable, D. and T. A. Judge 1996, 'Person-organization fit, job choice decisions, and organizational entry', *Organizational Behavior and Human Decision Processes*, 67, pp. 294–311.

Cameron, K. S. 1994, 'Strategies for successful organizational downsizing', *Human Resource Management Journal*, 33, pp. 189–212.

Cameron, K. S., M. U. Kim and D. A. Whetten 1987, 'Organizational effects of decline and turbulence', *Administrative Science Quarterly*, 32, pp. 222–40.

Cameron, K. S. and R. E. Quinn 1999, *Diagnosing and Changing Organizational Culture* (Reading, MA: Addison-Wesley Longman).

Cavanaugh, G. F. 1980, *American Business Values in Transition* (Englewood Cliffs, NJ: Prentice-Hall).

Cervone, D. 1997, 'Social-cognitive mechanisms and personality coherence: Self-knowledge, situational beliefs, and cross-situational coherence in perceived self-efficacy', *Psychological Science*, 8, pp. 156–65.

Chenhall, R. and D. Morris 1991, 'The effect of cognitive style and sponsorship bias on the treatment of opportunity costs in resource allocation decisions', *Accounting, Organizations, and Society*, 16, pp. 27–46.

Chippendale, P. 2004a, *Minessence eZine #19*, <www.minessence.net/eZines/eZine19.htm>.

Chippendale, P. 2004b, 'Resources for values-based management', <www.minessence.net/html/articles.htm #satt>.

Chippendale, P. 2004c, 'Values definitions', <www.minessence.net/pdfs/values_definitions.pdf>.

Collins, J. and J. Porras 2002, *Built to Last* (London: Random House).

Covey, S. R. 1989, *The Seven Habits of Highly Effective People* (New York: Simon & Schuster).

Cravens, R. W. and P. Worchel 1977, 'The differential effects of rewarding and coercive leaders on group members differing in locus of control', *Journal of Personality*, 45, pp. 150–68.

Darrow, B. 1998, 'Michael Dell', *Computer Reseller News*, 16 November, pp. 124–125.

Dunphy, D. 1993, *Organisational Change by Choice* (Sydney: McGraw-Hill).

Durand, D. and D. Shea 1974, 'Entrepreneurial activity as a function of achievement motivation and reinforcement control', *Journal of Psychology*, 88, pp. 57–63.

Ekman, P. 2004, *Emotions Revealed* (London: Phoenix Press).

Elsayed-Elkhouly, S. M. and R. Buda 1997, 'A cross-cultural comparison of value systems of Egyptians, Americans, Africans and Arab executives', *International Journal of Commerce and Management*, 7, pp. 102–19.

Feist, G. J. and F. Barron 1996, 'Emotional intelligence and academic intelligence in career and life success', presented at the American Psychological Association meetings, San Francisco.

Fromm, E. 1939, 'Selfishness and self love', *Psychiatry*, 2, pp. 507–23.

Geertz, C. 1973, *The Interpretation of Cultures* (New York: Basic Books).

Goleman, D. 1998a, 'What makes a leader?', *Harvard Business Review*, 76, pp. 92–102.

Goleman, D. 1998b, *Working with Emotional Intelligence* (New York: Bantam).

Goleman, D. 2000, 'Leadership that gets results', *Harvard Business Review*, March–April, pp. 3–17.

Goleman, D. 2001, 'An EI-based theory of performance', in C. Cherniss and D. Goleman (eds), *The Emotionally Intelligent Workplace* (San Francisco: Jossey-Bass).

Goleman, D., R. Boyatzis and A. McKee 2002, *Primal Leadership* (Cambridge, MA: Harvard Business School Press).

Hartig, K. and J. Frosch 2006, 'Workplace mobbing syndrome: The "silent and unseen" occupational hazard', Our Work ... Our Lives: National Conference on Women and Industrial Relations, Queensland Working Women's Service and Griffith Business School, Griffith University, Brisbane, 12–14 July.

Henderson, J. C. and P. C. Nutt 1980, 'The influence of decision style on decision making behavior', *Management Science*, 26, pp. 371–86.

Hendricks, J. A. 1985, 'Locus of control: Implications for managers and accountants', *Cost and Management*, May–June, pp. 25–29.

Hofstede, G. 2001, *Culture's Consequences: Comparing Values, Behaviors, Institutions and Organizations across Nations* (Thousand Oaks, CA: Sage).

Honey, P. and A. Mumford 1995, *Using Your Learning Styles*, Peter Honey, Learning Styles Questionnaire (LSQ) (Maidenhead, UK).

Hosmer, L. T. 1987, *Ethics of Management* (Homewood, IL: Irwin).

Ireland, M., R. Slatcher, P. Eastwick, L. Scissors, E. Finkel and J. Pennebaker 2010, 'Language style matching predicts relationship initiation and stability', *Psychological Science* (online), December.

Jourard, S. M. 1964, *The Transparent Self* (Princeton, NJ: D. Von Nostrand Company).

Judge, T. A., A. Erez, J. E. Bobo and C. T. Thoreson 2003, 'The core self-evaluation scale: Development of a measure', *Personnel Psychology*, 56, pp. 303–31.

Jung, C. 1923, *Psychological Types* (London: Routledge and Kegan Paul).

Kennedy, J., P. Fu and G. Yukl 2003, 'Influence tactics across cultures', in W. H. Mobley and P. W. Dorfman (eds), *Advances in Global Leadership*, vol. 3 (Oxford: Elsevier Science Ltd).

Kolb, A. and D. A. Kolb 1999, *Bibliography of Research on Experiential Learning Theory and the Learning Style Inventory* (Cleveland, OH: Weatherhead School of Management, Case Western Reserve University).

Kolb, D. A. 1984, *Experiential Learning: Experience as the Source of Learning and Development* (Upper Saddle River, NJ: Prentice Hall).

Kolb, D. A., R. E. Boyatzis and C. Mainemelis 2000, 'Experiential learning theory: Previous research and new directions', in R. J. Sternberg and L. F. Zhang (eds), *Perspectives on Cognitive, Learning, and Thinking Styles* (Hillsdale, NJ: Lawrence Erlbaum).

Lobel, S. 1992, 'A value-laden approach to integrating work and family life', *Human Resource Management Journal*, 31, pp. 249–65.

Maslow, A. H. 1962, *Toward a Psychology of Being* (Princeton, NJ: D. Von Nostrand Company).

Mayer, J. D. and P. Salovey 1997, 'What is emotional intelligence?', in P. Salovey and D. J. Sluyter (eds), *Emotional Development and Emotional Intelligence* (New York: Basic Books).

Mehrabian, A. 1971, *Silent Messages* (Oxford, UK: Wadsworth).

Nussbaum, M. C. 2001, *Upheavals of Thought* (Cambridge, UK: Cambridge University Press).

Nwachukwu, S. L. S. and S. J. Vitell 1997, 'The influence of corporate culture on managerial ethical judgments', *Journal of Business Ethics*, 16, pp. 757–76.

O'Reilly, B. 1999, 'The mechanic who fixed Continental', *Fortune, 140*, pp. 176–186.

Parker, V. and K. Kram 1993, 'Women mentoring women', *Business Horizons*, 36, pp. 101–2.

Parsons, T. 1951, *The Social System* (New York: The Free Press).

Posner, B. and J. Kouzes 1993, 'Values congruence and differences between the interplay of personal and organizational values', *Journal of Business Ethics*, 12, pp. 341–7.

Prigogine, I. 1986, 'Science, civilization and democracy: Values, systems, structures and affinities', *Futures*, 18, pp. 493–507.

Rest, J. R. 1979, *Revised manual for the Defining Issues Test: An objective test of moral judgment development* (Minneapolis: Minnesota Moral Research Projects).

Rogers, C. R. 1961, *On Becoming a Person* (Boston: Houghton Mifflin Co.).

Rokeach, M. 1973, *The Nature of Human Values* (New York: The Free Press).

Rosenthal, R. 1977, 'The PONS test: Measuring sensitivity to nonverbal cues', in P. McReynolds (ed.), *Advancement on Psychological Assessment* (San Francisco: Jossey-Bass).

Rossi, E. L. (ed.) 1980, *The Collected Papers of Milton H. Erickson* (New York: Irvington).

Rotter, J. B. 1966, 'Generalized expectancies for internal versus external control of reinforcement', *Psychological Monographs*, 80, pp. 1–28.

Ruble, T. and R. Cosier 1990, 'Effects of cognitive styles and decision settings on performance', *Organizational Behavior and Human Performance*, 46, pp. 283–95.

Ruedy, N. and M. Schweitzer 2011, 'In the moment: The effect of mindfulness on ethical decision making', *Journal of Business Ethics*, 98(4), pp. 73–87.

Salovey, P. and J. D. Mayer 1990, 'Emotional intelligence', *Imagination, Cognition and Personality*, 9, pp. 185–211.

Seeman, M. 1982, 'On the personal consequences of alienation in work', *American Sociological Review*, 32, pp. 273–85.

Senge, P. M. 1990, *The Fifth Discipline: The Art and Practice of the Learning Organization* (New York: Doubleday).

Senge, P., A. Kleiner, C. Roberts, R. Ross and B. Smith 1994, *The Fifth Discipline Fieldbook* (New York: Doubleday).

Shiv, B., G. Loewenstein and A. Bechara 2005, 'The dark side of emotion in decision-making: When individuals with decreased emotional reactions make more advantageous decisions', *Cognitive Brain Research*, 23, April, pp. 85–92.

Simon, H. A. 1974, 'Applying information technology to organization design', *Public Administration Review*, 34, pp. 268–78.

Smith, P. 2003, 'Leaders' sources of guidance and the challenge of working across cultures', in W. H. Mobley and P. W. Dorfman (eds), *Advances in Global Leadership* (Oxford, UK: Elsevier Science Ltd).

Snarey, J. R. and G. E. Vaillant 1985, 'How lower-and working-class youth become middle-class adults', *Child Development*, 56, pp. 899–910.

Sosik, J. and L. E. Megerian 1999, 'Understanding leader emotional intelligence and performance: The role of self–other agreement on transformational leadership perceptions', *Group and Organization Management*, 24, pp. 367–90.

Spector, P. E. 1982, 'Behavior in organizations as a function of employees' locus of control', *Psychological Bulletin*, 47, pp. 487–9.

Spencer, L. M. and S. M. Spencer 1993, *Competence at Work: Models for Superior Performance* (New York: John Wiley & Sons).

Staw, B., L. Sandelands and J. Dutton 1981, 'Threat-rigidity effects in organizational behavior', *Administrative Science Quarterly*, 26, pp. 501–24.

Sternberg, R. J. 1996, *Successful Intelligence* (New York: Simon & Schuster).

Tanner, D. 1996, 'The power of talk', *Harvard Business Review*, September–October, pp. 138–48.

Trompenaars, F. 1996, 'Resolving international conflict: Culture and business strategy', *Business Strategy Review*, 7, pp. 51–68.

Trompenaars, F. and C. Hampden-Turner 1999, *Riding the Waves of Culture* (New York: McGraw-Hill).

Tubbs, W. 1994, 'The roots of stress-death and juvenile delinquency in Japan: Disciplinary ambivalence and perceived locus of control', *Journal of Business Ethics*, 13, pp. 507–22.

Weick, K. E. 1993, 'The collapse of sense-making in organizations', *Administrative Science Quarterly*, 38, pp. 628–52.

Weick, K. E. and K. Sutcliffe 2000, 'High reliability: The power of mindfulness', *Leader to Leader*, 17, pp. 33–38.

Wheeler, R. W. and J. M. Davis 1979, 'Decision making as a function of locus of control and cognitive dissonance', *Psychological Reports*, 44, pp. 499–502.

Worm, V. 1996, *Vikings and Mandarins* (Copenhagen: Copenhagen Business School).

Zapf, D. 1999, 'Organizational, work group related and personal causes of mobbing/bullying at work', *International Journal of Manpower*, 20(1/2), pp. 70–85.

Zeig, J. 1985, 'Diagnostic criteria', unpublished paper.

CHAPTER 3

MANAGING STRESS

OBJECTIVES

- **Develop a healthy workplace**
- **Improve your stress management skills**
- **Enhance your personal stress management**

3

CHAPTER OUTLINE

Skill assessment

Evaluative surveys for managing stress

Stress management

Step 1: Before you read the material in this chapter, respond to the following statements by writing a number from the rating scale below in the left-hand column (pre-assessment). Your answers should reflect your attitudes and behaviour as they are now, not as you would like them to be. Be honest. This instrument is designed to help you discover your level of competency in stress management so that you can tailor your learning to your specific needs. When you have completed the survey, use the scoring key at the end of the chapter to identify the skill areas that are most important for you to master.

Step 2: When you have completed the reading and the exercises in the chapter and, ideally, as many as you can of the skill application assignments at the end of the chapter, cover up your first set of answers. Then respond to the same statements again, this time in the right-hand column (post-assessment). When you have completed the survey, use the scoring key to measure your progress. If your score remains low in specific skill areas, use the behavioural guidelines at the end of the skill learning section to guide further practice.

Rating scale

1 Strongly disagree
2 Disagree
3 Slightly disagree
4 Slightly agree
5 Agree
6 Strongly agree

Assessment

Pre-	*Post-*		*When faced with stressful or time-pressured situations:*
______	______	1.	I use effective time-management methods such as keeping track of my time and drawing up a daily/weekly 'to do' plan that lists my tasks in order of priority (what is important/urgent).
______	______	2.	I maintain a program of regular exercise for fitness.
______	______	3.	I maintain an open, trusting relationship with someone with whom I can share my frustrations.
______	______	4.	I know and practise several temporary relaxation techniques such as deep breathing and muscle relaxation.
______	______	5.	I frequently affirm my priorities and define my critical roles so that less important things do not drive out more important things.
______	______	6.	I maintain balance in my life by pursuing a variety of interests outside work.
______	______	7.	I have a close relationship with someone who serves as my mentor or adviser.
______	______	8.	I effectively use others in accomplishing work assignments.
______	______	9.	I encourage others to generate recommended solutions, not just questions, when they come to me with problems or issues.
______	______	10.	I strive to redefine problems as opportunities for improvement.

The scoring key is on page 173.

Time management

In responding to the following statements, fill in the blanks with the number from the rating scale that indicates the frequency with which you do each activity. Assess your behaviour as it is, not as you would like it to be. How useful this instrument will be to you depends on your ability to accurately assess your own behaviour.

The first section of the instrument can be completed by anyone. The second section applies primarily to individuals currently serving in a managerial position.

Turn to the end of the chapter to find the scoring key and an interpretation of your scores.

Rating scale

0 Never
1 Seldom
2 Sometimes
3 Usually
4 Always

Section I

______ 1. I read selectively, skimming the material until I find what is important, then highlight it.
______ 2. I make a list of tasks to accomplish each day/week.
______ 3. I keep everything in its proper place at work.
______ 4. I organise the tasks I have to do according to their importance and urgency.
______ 5. I concentrate on only one important task at a time, but I do multiple trivial tasks at once (such as signing letters while talking on the phone).
______ 6. I make a list of short five- or ten-minute tasks to do.
______ 7. I divide large projects into smaller, separate stages.
______ 8. I identify which 20 per cent of my tasks will produce 80 per cent of the results.
______ 9. I do the most important tasks at my best time during the day.
______ 10. I have some time during each day when I can work uninterrupted.
______ 11. I don't procrastinate. I do today what needs to be done.
______ 12. I keep track of the use of my time with devices such as a time log or a detailed diary.
______ 13. I set deadlines for myself.
______ 14. I do something productive whenever I am waiting.
______ 15. I do routine work at one set time during the day.
______ 16. I finish at least one thing every day.
______ 17. I schedule some time during the day for personal time alone (for planning, meditation, exercise).
______ 18. I allow myself to worry about things only at one particular time during the day, not all the time.
______ 19. I have clearly defined long-term objectives towards which I am working.
______ 20. I continually try to find little ways to use my time more efficiently.

Section II

______ 21. I hold routine meetings at the end of the day.
______ 22. I hold all short meetings standing up.
______ 23. I set a time limit at the outset of each meeting.
______ 24. I cancel scheduled meetings that are not necessary.
______ 25. I have a written agenda for every meeting.
______ 26. I stick to the agenda and reach closure on each item.
______ 27. I ensure that someone is assigned to take minutes and to watch the time in every meeting.

______ 28. I start all meetings on time.
______ 29. I have minutes of meetings prepared promptly after the meeting and see that follow-up occurs promptly.
______ 30. When staff members come to me with a problem, I ask them to suggest solutions.
______ 31. I meet visitors to my office outside the office or in the doorway.
______ 32. I go to other people's offices when feasible so that I can control when I leave.
______ 33. I leave at least one-quarter of my day free from meetings and appointments I cannot control.
______ 34. I have someone else who can answer my calls and greet visitors at least some of the time.
______ 35. I have one place where I can work uninterrupted.
______ 36. I do something definite with every piece of paper I handle.
______ 37. I keep my workplace clear of all materials except those I am working on.
______ 38. I delegate tasks.
______ 39. I specify the amount of personal initiative I want others to take when I assign them a task.
______ 40. I am willing for others to get the credit for tasks they accomplish.

The scoring key is on page 173.

Social readjustment rating scale

Circle any of the following you have experienced in the past year. Using the weightings at the left, total up your score.

Mean value		*Life event*
87	1	Death of spouse/mate.
79	2	Death of a close family member.
78	3	Major injury/illness to self.
76	4	Detention in gaol or another institution.
72	5	Major injury/illness of a close family member.
71	6	Foreclosure on a loan/mortgage.
71	7	Divorce.
70	8	Being a victim of crime.
69	9	Being a victim of police brutality.
69	10	Infidelity.
69	11	Experiencing domestic violence/sexual abuse.
66	12	Separation or reconciliation with spouse/mate.
64	13	Being fired/laid-off/unemployed.
62	14	Experiencing financial problems/difficulties.
61	15	Death of a close friend.
59	16	Surviving a disaster.
59	17	Becoming a single parent.
56	18	Assuming responsibility for a sick or elderly loved one.
56	19	Loss of or major reduction in health insurance/benefits.
56	20	Self/close family member being arrested for violating the law.
53	21	Major disagreement over child support/custody/visitation.
53	22	Experiencing/involved in a car accident.
53	23	Being disciplined at work/demoted.
51	24	Dealing with an unwanted pregnancy.
50	25	Adult child moving in with parent/parent moving in with adult child.
49	26	Child develops behaviour or learning problem.

48	27	Experiencing employment discrimination/sexual harassment.
47	28	Attempting to modify addictive behaviour of self.
46	29	Discovering/attempting to modify addictive behaviour of a close family member.
45	30	Employer reorganisation/downsizing.
44	31	Dealing with infertility/miscarriage.
43	32	Getting married/remarried.
43	33	Changing employers/careers.
42	34	Failure to obtain/qualify for a mortgage.
41	35	Pregnancy of self/spouse/mate.
39	36	Experiencing discrimination/harassment outside the workplace.
39	37	Release from gaol.
38	38	Spouse/mate begins/ceases work outside the home.
37	39	Major disagreement with boss/co-worker.
35	40	Change in residence.
34	41	Finding appropriate child care/day care.
33	42	Experiencing a large, unexpected monetary gain.
33	43	Changing positions (transfer, promotion).
33	44	Gaining a new family member.
32	45	Changing work responsibilities.
30	46	Child leaving home.
30	47	Obtaining a home mortgage.
30	48	Obtaining a major loan other than home mortgage.
28	49	Retirement.
26	50	Beginning/ceasing formal education.
22	51	Receiving a fine for violating the law.

Total of circled items: _____

Source: C. J. Hobson, J. Kamen, J. Szostek et al., 'Stressful life events: A revision and update of the Social Readjustment Rating Scale', *International Journal of Stress Management*, 5, 1998, pp. 1–23. Reproduced with permission of Springer/The Language of Science.

The scoring key is on page 174.

Skill learning

Stress reactions

The consequences of working in the modern workplace, facing the stressors, hazards and pressures that are commonplace without any healthy responses, are enormous. Stress reactions include industrial accidents, workplace conflicts, physical illness, psychological stress, absenteeism, sabotage, resignations, lowered morale and lowered productivity. In the healthy workplace model, these stress reactions are likely outcomes if healthy responses to counter workplace pressures are not in place.

According to Dahl-Hansen et al. (2005), the UK Health and Safety Executive (HSE) reported that in 2003/04 musculoskeletal disorders and stress were by far the most commonly reported work-related illnesses.

In Asia, studies from Japan and China have found a high prevalence of work-related distress (Liu & Tanaka 2002). In the United States, the National Occupational Research Agenda has chosen the organisation of work to prevent stress as one of five prioritised work environment categories.

In Britain, estimates suggest that stress costs the nation 3.5 per cent of its GNP and 40 million working days a year. In the United States, the National Institute for Occupational Safety and the

American Psychological Association estimate the national cost of stress to be in the order of US$500 billion annually (Whetten & Cameron 1998). Research in Australia is also producing alarming statistics. Comcare Australia found that in 1989/90 stress claims made up 4 per cent of all claims for compensation in the public sector, while costing 16 per cent of all claims. By 1993/94, this figure had risen to 8.3 per cent, reducing to 6.9 per cent for 1994/95 (Peterson 1999). Periods of incapacity caused by stress (7.7 weeks) are longer than periods of incapacity for all other conditions (2.4 weeks), with the resulting stress claims averaging nearly $30 000 each. This amount does not take into consideration costs such as staff replacement and retraining, workflow interference, special supervision, sick leave leading up to the compensation claim and other hidden costs (Toohey 1995). The massive research data on stress reactions can be summarised in Figure 3.1.

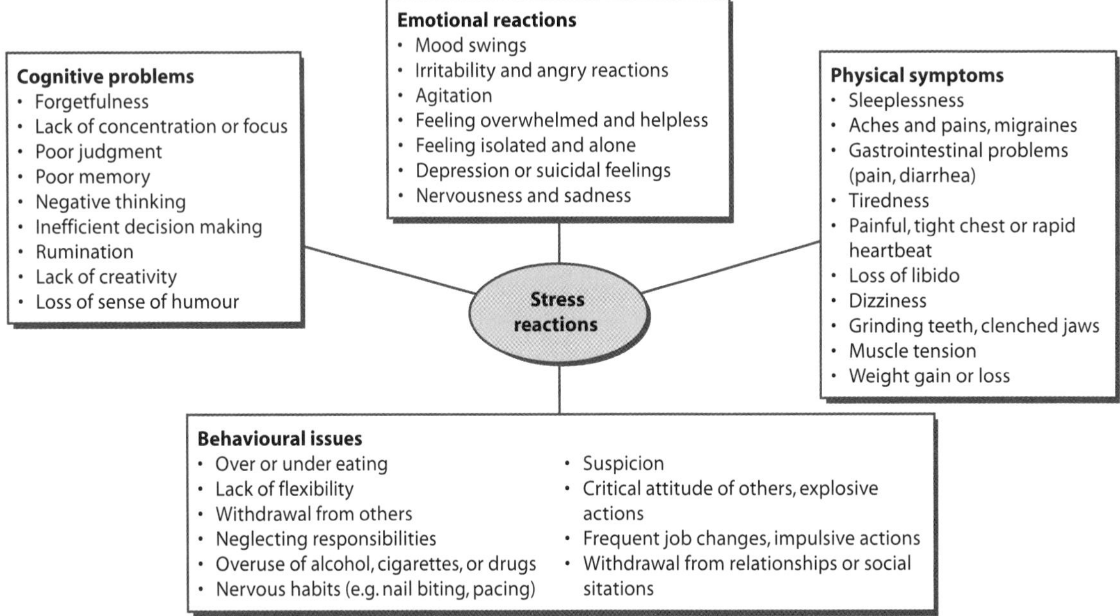

FIGURE 3.1 Some physiological effects of stress

Sources: Adapted from 'Understanding Stress: Symptoms, Signs, Causes and Effects', Helpguide.org, <http://helpguide.org/mental/stress_signs.htm> and 'Stress and Heart Disease', MedicineNet.com, <http://medicinenet.com/stress_and_heart_disease/page2.htm>, accessed 22 November 2011.

Citing National Occupational Health and Safety Commission figures, *Sydney Morning Herald* reporter Guy Allenby wrote that 'mental stress' compensation claims made up 5 per cent of all compensation claims in 2001–2004 (19 February 2004).

Dr Chris Peterson, formerly of the School of Public Health at La Trobe University, Melbourne, also spoke of stress as an (emerging) epidemic in Australia. He saw the problem as a result of job insecurity, work intensification, endemic organisational change, cost-containment pressures and increasing exposure to occupational violence (1999: 174). In a radio interview, he succinctly summed up the problem as 'a loss of control', a point discussed later in this chapter.

Symptoms of stress range from headaches, backache, anxiety and fatigue to major illnesses such as heart attacks, ulcers, high blood pressure and strokes.

Of course, stress produces positive as well as negative effects. In the absence of any stress, people feel completely bored and lack any inclination to act; that is, 'rustout' occurs. Even when high levels of stress are experienced, equilibrium can be quickly restored if there is sufficient resiliency. If there are multiple stressors that overpower the available restraining forces, 'burnout' occurs (see Figure 3.2). However, before reaching such an extreme state, individuals typically progress through three stages of reactions: an alarm stage, a resistance stage and an exhaustion stage.

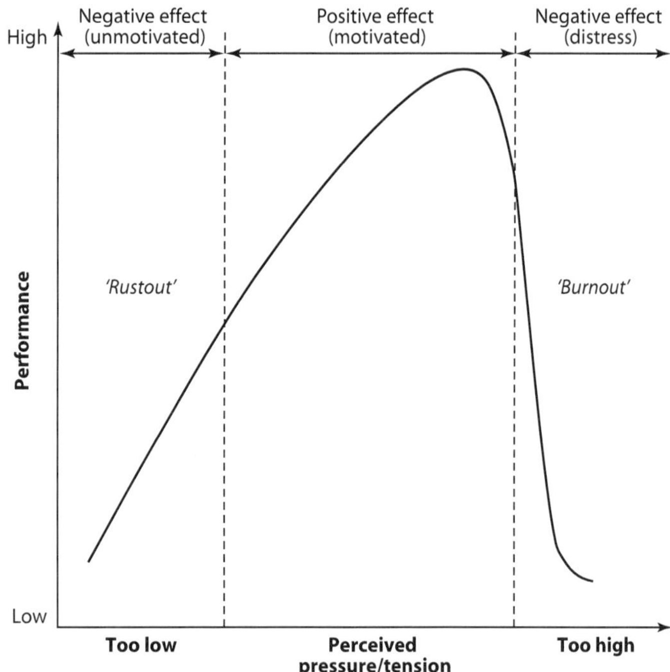

FIGURE 3.2 Common responses to levels of stress

The role of management

Research conducted during the past few years in the Australian workplace—in both the private and the public sector—has revealed that, rather than shorter working hours or higher wages, the Australian worker wants effective leadership from management and better communication flows (Pope & Berry 1995). The high level of frustration identified during this research can be linked closely to the increase in stress-related problems.

In analysing the Comcare research into compensation claims for stress, Toohey (1995: 59–66) emphasised the most important outcome as:

> *... the recognition that most of the problems presenting as occupational stress, either as claims or medical conditions, were primarily associated with human resource management (HRM), rather than illness or injury. Consequently the management of stress-related problems should be mainly based on HRM intervention and not simply on medical referrals. These interventions would include attention to workload; decision-making latitude; organisational support; and knowledge of job requirements.*

A 25-year study conducted in the United States revealed that incompetent management was the largest cause of workplace stress. Three out of four surveys listed employee relationships with immediate supervisors as the worst aspect of the job (Auerbach 1998). See also the research noted in the introduction. Research in psychology has found that stress not only affects workers negatively but also produces less-visible (though equally detrimental) consequences for managers themselves. For example, when managers experience stress, they tend to:

- perceive information selectively and see only what confirms their previous biases
- become very intolerant of ambiguity and demanding of right answers
- fixate on a single approach to a problem
- overestimate how fast time is passing (hence, they often feel rushed)
- adopt a short-term perspective or crisis mentality and cease to consider long-term implications

- have less ability to make fine distinctions in problems, so that complexity and nuances are missed
- consult and listen to others less
- rely on old habits to cope with current situations
- have less ability to generate creative thoughts and unique solutions to problems (Auerbach 1998; Staw, Sandelands & Dutton 1981; Weick 1993).

As well as negatively affecting employees in the workplace, the results of stress also drastically impede effective management behaviours—for example, listening, making good decisions, solving problems effectively, and planning and generating new ideas. Developing the skill of managing stress and pressure, therefore, can have significant pay-offs. The ability to deal appropriately with stress not only enhances individual self-development but can also have an enormous bottom-line impact on entire organisations.

As mentioned in Chapter 2, discrepancy between an organisation's values and an employee's personal values is a major source of frustration, conflict and non-productivity. Attracta Lagan (1995), writing in the *Newsletter of the St James Ethics Centre, Sydney*, put it this way: 'The degree of disparity between a company's formal value system or espoused value system and its informal value system or values in use, which are reflected in its actions, will often indicate the degree of stress its members experience in their work situations.' Quoting from a *Values Survey Report* from the New College Institute for Values Research, Lagan (1995: 1–2) added:

> *A recent survey amongst the management of the top 300 Australian companies found that nearly 40% of respondents 'make decisions which conflict with their personal beliefs or values'. Such a mismatch of values has implications on the level of stress under which these people work. The level of trust that exists within their organisations and the degree of commitment that the company can expect from its employees is also compromised.*

Unfortunately, most of the scientific literature on stress focuses on its consequences. Too little of it examines how to cope effectively with stress, and even less addresses how to prevent stress. The next section presents a framework for developing a healthy workplace culture by understanding stress and learning how to manage it. This model explains the main types of stressors faced by managers, the primary reactions to stress and the reasons some people experience more negative reactions than others. It identifies four healthy responses to combat stress, along with specific examples and behavioural guidelines.

The healthy workplace model

The healthy workplace model is based on the pioneering work conducted by James Reason (Reason 1997). His model has been updated and extended, and more emphasis has been given to prevention rather than defences against stress and hazard events. The essential formula of Reason's model is retained—namely, that stress and pressure in the workplace can cause significant negative and costly stress reactions. In between the cause (pressure events) and the outcome (stress reactions) there are four barriers or healthy response mechanisms that can prevent or minimise a negative outcome. The four response mechanisms are (1) deep responses, (2) individual responses, (3) interpersonal/team responses, and (4) organisational responses. There are several elements that constitute each of these response types. The model proposes that if there are no levels of response or defence against stress and pressure, then stress reactions will follow. If there are strong responses in some or all of the four response levels, then stress outcomes will be minimised or removed entirely. In fact, when all four response barriers to workplace pressure are operating effectively, this enables a healthy workplace. If only one or two response levels are being affected, there is some stress reaction. If none of the response barriers are operating, the result is what is described in the literature as a toxic workplace, where there are no healthy responses to workplace stress and pressures. A healthy workplace is the responsibility of all members of the organisation, not just the senior managers. From this model, the healthiest workplace is obviously one in which all response barriers are operating effectively (see Figure 3.3).

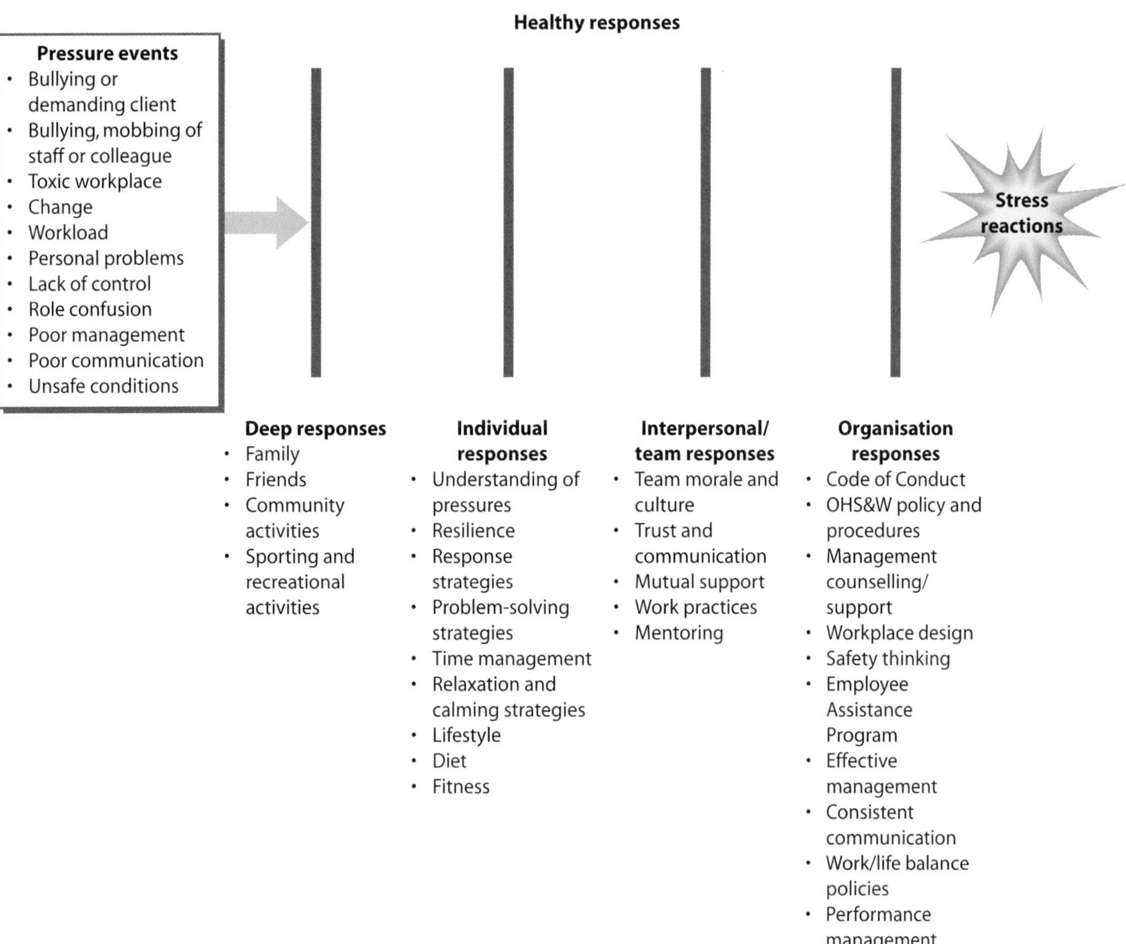

FIGURE 3.3 The healthy workplace model

Source: Adapted from the model developed by James Reason (1997), *Managing the Risks of Organisational Accidents*, and amended by McPhee Andrewartha 2007.

The healthy workplace is:

- conducive to good health
- safe and friendly
- environmentally responsible
- consistently clear about its procedures and policies
- equitable
- a place of good judgment and moral well-being.

In contrast, a toxic workplace is:

- capable of causing injury or death
- capable of causing harm
- detrimental to good health
- injurious to physical or mental health (see Figure 3.4).

This section considers the nature of pressure events and their stress reactions in the workplace. The four different levels of responses or defences against these stressors are then identified. The elements that constitute these different levels of responses are often interconnected and are not necessarily exclusive.

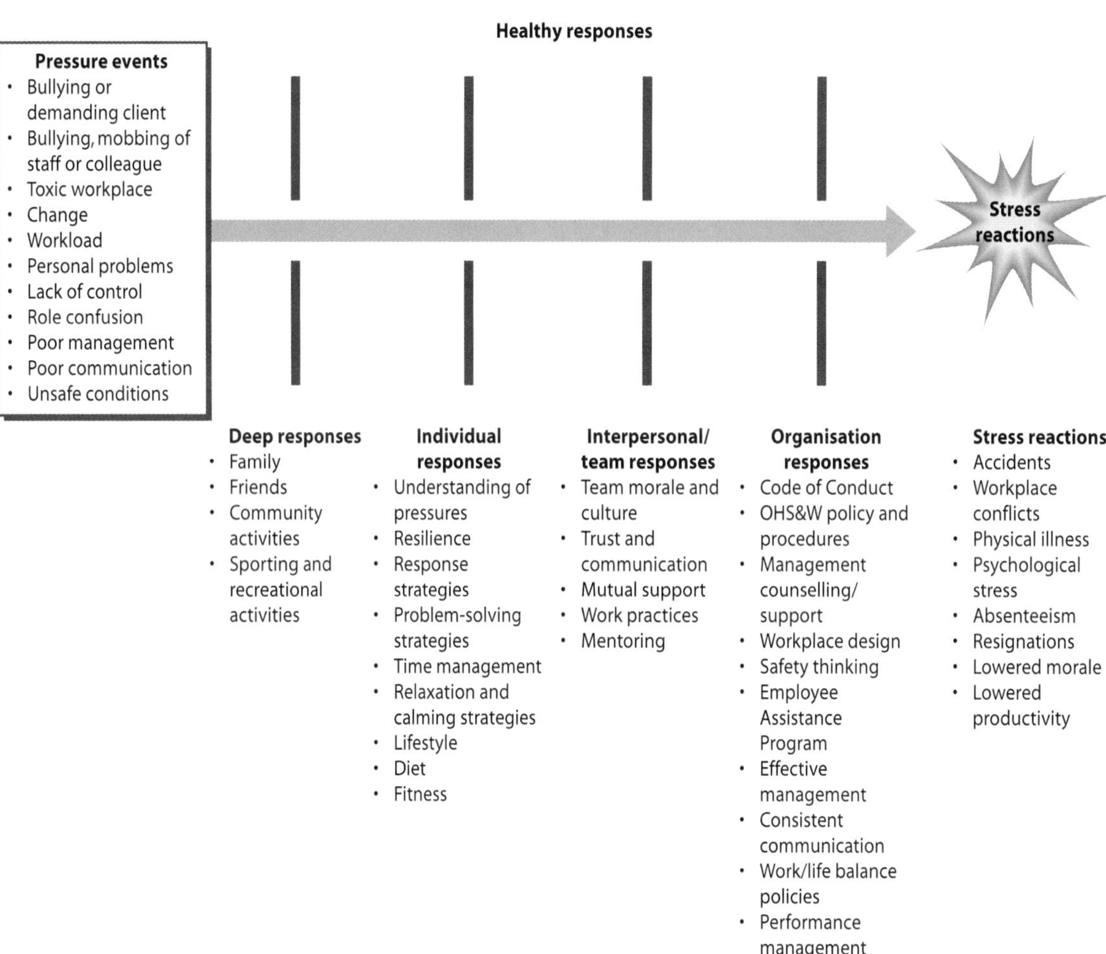

FIGURE 3.4 Toxic workplace (with poor response barriers)

Source: Adapted from the model developed by James Reason (1997), *Managing the Risks of Organisational Accidents*, and amended by McPhee Andrewartha 2007.

Pressure events

In today's globally competitive workplaces, the following are common stressors or pressure events:

- aggressive or demanding clients
- bullying or mobbing staff or colleagues
- hazardous or unsafe conditions
- unplanned change
- unreasonable workload
- personal problems among staff
- lack of control
- role confusion
- poor management
- poor communication.

Where some or all of these stressors are present, the nature of stress in the workplace correspondingly becomes greater and leads directly to the sort of stress reactions discussed above.

Clients and other stakeholders who are demanding or aggressive in their manner can cause significant pressure in the workplace. The organisation is responsible for providing effective protection for staff, and for training staff in how to manage difficult people.

In Western workplaces there has been increasing concern about bullying and aggressive behaviour by various members of staff. Levels of intimidation are also quite high in many Asian cultures, although the demanding behaviour is more systemic and pervasive, rather than individual and aggressive.

In 2002 the Office of the Employee Ombudsman in South Australia produced a booklet, *Bullies Not Wanted*, in which it described bullying as follows:

> *Workplace bullying involves the persistent ill treatment of an individual at work by one or more other persons. To be recognised as bullying the ill-treatment must be continuous and directed against a particular person. Workplace bullying has many features in common with school bullying.*
>
> *It need not involve physical ill-treatment, such as punching, kicking and other ways of inflicting physical pain. In fact the research that has been done on this issue suggests that only around 10% of bullying involves some form of physical assault. Most cases of bullying involve such treatment as verbal abuse, 'nit-picking', threats, sarcasm, ostracism, sabotage of a person's work and so on.*
>
> *Commonly reported forms of workplace bullying include:*
>
> - *Persistent and unjustified criticisms, usually of the nit-picking variety.*
> - *Threats of dismissal or other severe punishment for no reason.*
> - *Giving the victim a much greater proportion of unpleasant work than that given to others.*
> - *Humiliating the victim through sarcasm, criticism and insults, often in front of customers or other employees.*
> - *Constant checking of the victim's work or whereabouts to a much greater extent than with others of the same seniority.*
> - *Denying opportunities for training, promotion or interesting work.*
> - *Deliberately withholding information that is important to the victim.*
> - *Overloading the victim with work or requiring work to be done without there being sufficient time to do it. The victim is then criticised for taking too long over a job or for not doing it properly.*
> - *Abusing the victim loudly, usually when others are present.*
> - *Sabotaging the victim's work, usually by hiding documents or equipment, by not passing on messages, by changing figures and, in other ways, getting him or her into trouble.*
> - *Excluding the victim from workplace social events (including conversations). In extreme cases this can involve the victim not being spoken to at all.*
> - *Spreading gossip or false rumours about the victim.*
> - *Not helping the victim when he or she is in difficulties but pointedly helping others in the same situation. (Source: Bullies Not Wanted, p. 5. Reproduced with permission of the Employee Ombudsman.)*

Such behaviour is totally unacceptable in any workplace and is preventable. The reason this behaviour occurs at all has to do with the nature of personal difficulties and lack of emotional intelligence, poor workplace performance management, confused responsibility and ineffective preventative policies.

Bullies lack the personal awareness that leads to emotional intelligence and mature behaviour, or they fail to develop competencies based on their self-awareness. It also needs to be said that bullies survive only if they are not opposed.

Lack of tolerance is often considered bullying or intimidation, and sometimes effective performance management is inappropriately viewed as intimidation. The following behaviours involve grey areas that are often viewed as leading to or being bullying behaviours:

- sickness or any form of weakness or vulnerability
- differences of opinion or different professional decisions
- confusion of roles and appropriate use of authority
- lack of clarity about how people combine personal life and work life
- managers who only manage rather than participate in the work of the team
- staff judging the performance of other staff they do not manage.

The rules for controlling and eliminating bullying are quite simple. The implementation of the rules is more complex. First and foremost is the setting up of an organisational code of conduct in which every member is trained and expected to subscribe.

Managers have a responsibility to prevent bullying. One of the ways they can do this is to provide consistent and regular performance management for all staff. They also need to accept that they have a duty of care to both the complainant and the respondent, and must ensure that the complainant has raised the complaint with the offending party, offering to be present when this happens if the complainant is too anxious to do it alone. Managers must manage any complaint in an open and equitable manner and provide natural justice to all parties.

An employee who believes that he or she is being bullied has a responsibility to advise the person concerned that the behaviour is offensive and to ask for the behaviour to cease. If this is not done and if the perceived offending behaviour continues, it cannot be classed as bullying. If individuals are suspected of intimidating or harassing behaviour, they need to be told about that behaviour in a way that will afford them the opportunity to change the behaviour if they wish. If the individuals are not fully aware of what specific actions are causing offence, they are not responsible for the offence they are causing. Bullying specifically refers to behaviour that is clearly marked as offensive and intimidating which nonetheless persists after the person is told that the behaviour is offensive. Behaviour committed in ignorance of its impact is not bullying. And it is in this area that much confusion and distress occurs in workplaces. Many people believe that certain behaviours are self-evident as intimidating (see the ladder of inference in the previous chapter), while others are afraid to challenge the behaviour even if support and protection is offered to them.

There has been a strong reaction (some would say an overreaction) to bullying in the workplace, and there is a wealth of literature, programs and directives aimed at preventing it. See also 'mobbing', which is described in Chapter 8 on managing conflict.

Response level 1: Deep responses

These elements constitute our out-of-work strengths and barriers against work stress. They are our private social support team and our diversions or releases from work pressures. They include such things as our family, friends, community activities, holidays, and sporting and recreational activities.

'Work/life balance' is the name that encompasses all these elements. People who have strong balance in all such aspects are more resilient. People vary widely in their ability to cope with stress. Some individuals seem to crumble under pressure, while others appear to thrive. Recent research suggests that 85 per cent of Australians in relationships claimed that their personal relations were in turmoil due to difficulties in maintaining work/life balance (*Human Resources Magazine*, 23 January 2007, p. 22).

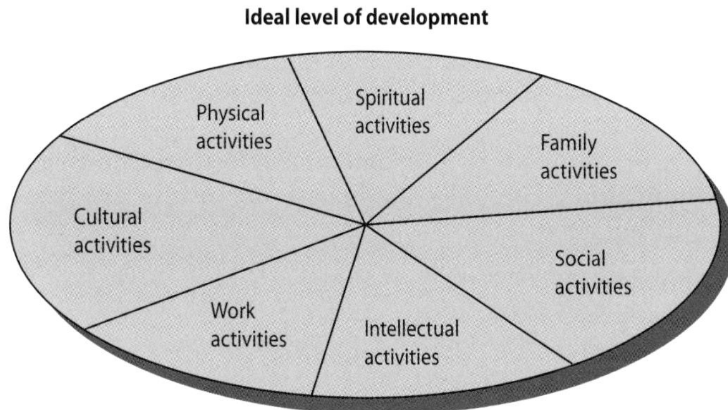

FIGURE 3.5 Balancing life activities

Assume that the wheel in Figure 3.5 represents resiliency development. Each wedge in the figure identifies an important aspect of life that must be developed in order to achieve resiliency. The most resilient individuals are those who have achieved work/life balance. For example, if the centre of the figure represents the zero point of resiliency development and the outside edge of the figure represents maximum development, shading in a portion of the area in each wedge would represent the amount of development achieved in each area. (This exercise is included in the skill practice section.) Individuals who are best able to cope with stress would shade in a majority of each wedge, indicating that not only have they spent time developing a variety of aspects of their lives but also that the overall pattern is relatively balanced. A lopsided pattern is as much an indicator of non-resiliency as not having some segments shaded at all. Overemphasising one or two areas to the exclusion of others often creates more stress than it eliminates. Life balance is the key (Lehrer 1996; Murphy 1996; Rostad & Long 1996).

This is a counter-intuitive prescription. Generally, when we are feeling stress in one area of life, such as work, we respond by devoting more time and attention to it. While this is a natural reaction, it is counterproductive for several reasons. First, the more we concentrate exclusively on work, the more restricted and less creative we become. As will be seen in the discussion of creativity in Chapter 4, many breakthroughs in problem solving come from using analogies and metaphors gathered from unrelated activities. That is why some organisations use adventure learning programs for senior manager retreats that incorporate activities such as mountain climbing, abseiling, bushwalking and white-water rafting. Most organisations also encourage their managers to involve themselves in community activities in an honorary capacity.

Second, refreshed and relaxed minds think better. A bank executive commented recently during an executive development workshop that he has gradually become convinced of the merits of taking the weekend off work. He finds that he gets twice as much accomplished on Monday as his colleagues who have been in their offices all weekend.

Third, the cost of stress-related illness decreases markedly when employees participate in work/lifestyle programs. Research conducted by Dr Christopher Sharpley, and reported in *HR Monthly* (1999), demonstrated that:

> ... *employees who had received effective self-management training to deal with stress at work actually reduced the harmful ways their bodies responded to stress by up to 93% when compared to pre-training data. Additionally, when interviewed 2.5 years later, these employees reported that they still used the strategies we taught them and that these had enabled them to increase their productivity at work and also improve their sporting performance, family relationships and everyday health.*

A major predictor of which individuals cope well with stress and which do not is the amount of resiliency they have developed. Well-developed individuals who give time and attention to cultural, physical, spiritual, family, social and intellectual activities in addition to work are more productive and less stressed than those who are workaholics (Adler & Hillhouse 1996; Hepburn, McLoughlin & Barling 1997). This section, therefore, concentrates on three common areas of resiliency development for managers: physical resiliency, psychological resiliency and social resiliency. Development in each of these areas requires initiative on the part of the individual and takes a moderate amount of time to achieve. These are not activities that can be accomplished by lunchtime or by the weekend. Rather, achieving life balance and resiliency requires ongoing initiative and continuous effort. Components of resiliency are summarised in Box 3.1.

BOX 3.1 Resiliency: Moderating the effects of stress

PHYSIOLOGICAL RESILIENCY
Cardiovascular conditioning
Proper diet

PSYCHOLOGICAL RESILIENCY
Balanced lifestyle
Hardy personality
- High internal control
- Strong personal commitment
- Love of challenge

Small-wins strategy
Deep-relaxation techniques

SOCIAL RESILIENCY
Supportive social relations
Teamwork
Mentors

Physiological resiliency

One of the most crucial aspects of resiliency development involves our physical condition, because physical condition significantly affects the ability to cope with stress. Two aspects of physical condition combine to determine physical resiliency: cardiovascular conditioning and dietary control.

Cardiovascular conditioning

An emphasis on physical conditioning in business has resulted partly from overwhelming evidence that individuals in good physical condition are better able to cope with stressors than those in poor physical condition. Box 3.2 shows the benefits of regular physical exercise.

BOX 3.2 Confirmed benefits of regular vigorous exercise

- Blood pressure is lowered.
- Resting heart rate is lowered; the heart is better able to distribute blood where needed under stress.
- Cardiac output is increased; the heart is better able to distribute blood where needed under stress.
- Number of red blood cells is increased; more oxygen can be carried per litre of blood.
- Elasticity of arteries is increased.
- Triglyceride level is lowered.
- Blood cholesterol level is decreased. High-density cholesterol, which is more protective of blood vessels than low-density cholesterol, is proportionately increased.
- Adrenal secretions in response to emotional stress are lowered.
- Lactic acid is more efficiently eliminated from the muscles. (This has been associated with decreased fatigue and tension.)
- Fibrin, a protein that aids in the formation of blood clots, is decreased.
- Additional routes of blood supply are built up in the heart.

Source: F. G. Rostad and B. C. Long, 'Exercise as a coping strategy for stress: A review', *International Journal of Sport Psychology*, 27, 1996, pp. 197–222.

Three primary purposes exist for a regular exercise program: maintaining optimal weight, increasing psychological well-being and improving the cardiovascular system.

One indirect cause of stress is the sedentary lifestyle adopted by many individuals. An office worker burns up only about 5000 kilojoules (1200 calories) during an eight-hour day—fewer kilojoules than are contained in an only slightly indulgent lunch! The World Health Organization (WHO) has called the worldwide rise in obesity a 'global epidemic' (WHO 2000). Current levels of obesity in Australia mean that we are not immune from this problem. Analysis of the Australian Bureau of Statistics (ABS) 1991 National Health Survey found that, on the basis of self-reported height and weight, around 16 per cent of Australians aged 18 years and over were obese and a further 34 per cent were overweight but not obese. In contrast, data from the 1989/90 National Health Survey showed that 9 per cent of Australians aged 18 years and over were obese and 30 per cent were overweight but not obese. Thus, in only 13 years the proportion of obese Australian adults increased substantially—by almost 80 per cent—and the proportion of overweight but not obese Australian adults increased by 14 per cent (Australian Institute of Health and Welfare 1991).

The hitherto low-fat diets of Asian countries are being influenced by Western tastes and the convenience of 'fast foods'. A survey in Hong Kong in 1994 found that rice consumption had dropped dramatically since a 1961 survey, while the consumption of meat, dairy products and wheat-based foods had soared. A further study completed in 2001 confirmed that an increasingly Westernised diet has worrying implications for Asian countries. Correspondingly, obesity rates are now a serious problem in young people, with children in Hong Kong suffering from the second-highest blood cholesterol in the world (*Sydney Morning Herald*, 19 April 1995). It can be expected that some of these children will be the future managers of our marketplace.

Excess weight places extra strain on both the heart and the self-image, which makes overweight individuals more vulnerable to stress (Wolman 1982). An advantage of regular physical exercise is that it improves mental as well as physical outlook. It increases self-esteem. It gives individuals the energy to be more alert and attentive throughout the day. Episodes of depression are far less frequent. Exercise fosters the necessary energy to cope with the stresses of both unexpected events and dull routine. Physically active individuals are less prone to anxiety, have less illness and miss fewer days of work (Greist et al. 1979; Murphy 1996). Researchers have found a chemical basis for the psychological benefit of exercise: the brain releases endorphins (similar to morphine) during periods of intense physical activity. This substance numbs pain and produces a feeling of well-being, sometimes referred to as the 'jogger's high', which is a euphoric, relaxed feeling reported by long-distance runners (Rostad & Long 1996).

Another vital benefit of exercise is a strengthened cardiovascular system. The best results come from aerobic exercises that do not require more oxygen than a person can take in comfortably (as compared with all-out sprinting or long-distance swimming). This type of exercise includes brisk walking, jogging, riding a bicycle and climbing stairs. However, the cardiovascular system is improved by exercise only when the following two conditions are met:

1. The target heart rate is sustained throughout the exercise. This rate is 60–80 per cent of the heart's maximum. To figure your target rate, subtract your age in years from 220, then take 60–80 per cent of that number. You should begin your exercise program at the 60 per cent level and gradually increase to the 80 per cent rate. To check your heart rate during your exercise, periodically monitor your heartbeat for six seconds and multiply by ten.
2. The exercise occurs for 20 to 30 minutes, three or four days each week. Since cardiovascular endurance decreases after 48 hours, it is important to exercise at least every second day.

Dietary control

The adage that 'You are what you eat' is sobering, considering some of the less salutary habits acquired during the past decade or so. Most people are well informed about healthy foods and eating habits, although the key principles cannot be repeated too often. For example:

- Eat a variety of foods, maintain optimal weight, eat sufficient whole foods, consider vitamin and mineral supplements in times of high stress, and make eating a relaxing time.
- Avoid excessive quantities of fats, sugar, sodium, alcohol and caffeine. (Caffeine is a stimulant that exacerbates stress.)

The National Heart Foundation has a number of useful publications on good eating habits, recipes that specifically lower blood cholesterol, and general recipe books such as *Deliciously Healthy*.

Psychological resiliency

Another important moderator of the effects of stress is an individual's psychological resiliency. Personal hardiness is a key example of this.

Hardiness

Lambert, Lambert and Hiroaki (2003) view psychological hardiness as a personality style consisting of commitment, control and challenge which encourages human survival and the enrichment of life through development. In their book *The Hardy Executive*, Maddi and Kobasa (1984) describe three elements that characterise a hardy, or highly stress-resistant, personality. Hardiness results from:

- feeling in control of one's life, rather than powerless to shape external events
- feeling committed to and involved in what one is doing, rather than alienated from one's work and other individuals
- feeling challenged by new experiences, rather than viewing change as a threat to security and comfort.

According to Maddi and Kobasa, hardy individuals tend to interpret stressful situations positively and optimistically, and respond to stress constructively. As a result, their incidence of illness and emotional dysfunction under stressful conditions is considerably below the norm.

Martin Seligman (2011) proposes that the Master Resilience Training (MRT) program he has developed for the armed forces identifies how to build resilience as a major process for workforce efficiency and happiness. His program has similar features to Reason's model in that it concentrates on building optimism and mental toughness through developing emotional, family, social and spiritual fitness.

Anne Deveson has been a model of resiliency in her personal and work life. She agrees that resilience is strongly connected to emotional maturity or emotional intelligence, which is discussed in Chapter 2. In her book *Resilience* (2003), she says: 'Risk, stress and resilience are intertwined. Without risk we would not be talking about resilience' (p. 48). She later concludes: 'Resilience is learning how to absorb sadness and how to live with it' (p. 177).

It is this feature of resilience in both personal life and organisational life that has attracted the interest of several researchers. Herman and Gioia (2006) have suggested that resilience is a significant trait of successful managers and leaders. They consider that resilience encompasses such qualities as tough-mindedness and the ability to accept criticism. They report that PsyMax Solutions, a human capital assessment firm, recently completed a study of more than 2000 employees. The firm analysed the profiles of district and regional managers, department or unit managers, and supervisors. The middle managers' median tough-minded score was the highest of all groups. By comparison, the company presidents and CEOs ranked lowest for resiliency, followed by the executives, and professional, technical and administrative employees.

'The study suggests that middle managers have the greatest ability to accept criticism,' says PsyMax Solutions CEO, Dr Wayne Nemeroff. 'Perhaps because of the nature of the middle management role they continuously get feedback from all directions, from above, below and sideways.' Those at the centre of the organisational structure demonstrate strength in being able to manage stress and to keep resilient in the face of frustration, disappointment or criticism. According to Nemeroff, resilience is an essential skill for middle managers, who provide leadership to front-line supervisors. Middle managers plan, direct and/or coordinate the day-to-day operations of companies. Sometimes they are owners who head small businesses and require the ability 'to handle frequent criticism or rejection, to work through tough negotiations, and to build credibility by remaining even-tempered'. Problems can result when the resiliency skill is not developed, Nemeroff advises. Some common issues include allowing stress and frustration to show, becoming defensive in response to criticism, and having difficulty rebounding from setbacks.

Nemeroff believes that people who need to develop resilience should readily accept constructive criticism and seek to learn from it. These people should also share their thoughts or reactions, and not hold them in. In fact, too much emotional control sometimes causes others to shut down communication and forget about their listening skills. 'People who want to develop resilience should speak more openly and make themselves more vulnerable' (Herman & Gioia 2006: 11–12).

Feeling in control. Maddi and Kobasa's three concepts that characterise the hardy individual—control, commitment and challenge—are central to the development of a variety of management skills and are crucial for mitigating the harmful effects of stress (Cowley 2000; Kobasa 1982). As discussed in Chapter 2, individuals who score high on internal locus of control feel that they are in charge of their own destinies. They take responsibility for their actions and feel they can neutralise negative external forces. They generally believe that stressors are the result of their personal choices rather than uncontrollable, capricious or even malicious external forces. The belief that we can influence the course of events is central to developing high self-esteem. Self-esteem, in turn, engenders self-confidence and the optimistic view that bad situations can be improved and problems overcome. Confidence in our own efficacy produces low fear of failure, high expectations, a willingness to take risks and persistence under adversity (Anderson 1977; Bandura 1997; Ivancevich & Matteson 1980; Mednick 1982; Sorenson 1998), all of which contribute to resiliency under stress.

Being committed. Commitment implies both selection and dedication. Hardy individuals not only feel that they choose what they do, but they also strongly believe in the importance of what they do. This commitment is both internal (that is, applied to their own activities) and external (that is, applied to a larger community). The feeling of being responsible to others is an important buffer against stress. Whereas self-esteem and a sense of purpose help provide a psychological support system for coping with stressful events, an individual's belief that others are counting on them to succeed and that they belong to a larger community fosters psychological resiliency during stressful periods. Feeling part of a group, feeling cared about and feeling trusted by others engender norms of cooperation and commitment and encourage constructive responses to stress (Bandura 1997).

Welcoming the challenge of change. Hardy people also welcome challenge. They believe that change, rather than stability, is the normal and preferred mode of life. Therefore, much of the disruption associated with a stressful life event is interpreted as an opportunity for personal growth, rather than as a threat to security. This mode of thinking is consistent with the Chinese word for crisis, which has two meanings: 'threat' and 'opportunity'. Individuals who seek challenges search for new and interesting experiences and accept stress as a necessary step towards learning. Because these individuals prefer change to stability, they tend to have a high tolerance for ambiguity and high resiliency under stress (Ivancevich & Ganster 1987; Maddi & Kobasa 1984). See also Chapter 2, 'Developing Self-awareness'.

The three characteristics of hardy personalities—control, commitment and challenge—have been found to be among the most powerful mitigators of the adverse consequences of stress. By contrast, a different complex of personality attributes, the so-called Type A syndrome, is associated with reduced hardiness and higher levels of psychological stress.

Healthy tips for managers

Gordon Livingston published two books, *Never Stop Dancing* (2006) and *Too Soon Old, Too Late Smart* (2004), that offer deep support for a healthy lifestyle and a stress-free existence. A selection of his chapter headings from both books is included below, as they offer a distilled wealth of healthy tips for managers trying to create a healthy workplace when under pressure. They also mirror many of the themes in this book.

- *It is difficult to remove by logic an idea not placed there by logic in the first place*
- *The statute of limitations has expired on most of our childhood traumas*
- *Any relationship is under the control of the person who cares the least*
- *Feelings follow behaviour*
- *The perfect is the enemy of the good*
- *Life's two most important questions are Why? and Why not? The trick is knowing which one to ask*
- *Our greatest strengths are our greatest weaknesses*
- *Only bad things happen quickly*
- *There is nothing more pointless than doing the same things and expecting different results*
- *It's a poor idea to lie to oneself*
- *Nobody likes to be told what to do*
- *We are afraid of the wrong things*
- *Of all forms of courage, the ability to laugh is the most profoundly therapeutic*
- *Forgiveness is a form of letting go, but they are not the same thing*
- *Paradox governs our lives*
- *Much of what we think we know is untrue*
- *Forgiveness is a gift we give ourselves*
- *It is easier to be angry than sad*
- *One of life's most difficult tasks is to see ourselves as others see us*
- *Relinquish dignity last*
- *Attachment is the source of all suffering*
- *You can change who you are without rejecting who you were*
- *The primary difference between intelligence and stupidity is that there are limits to intelligence*
- *We're drowning in information but starved for knowledge*

- *Happiness requires an ability to tolerate uncertainty*
- *Every snowflake in an avalanche pleads not guilty*

Understanding and maintaining these mantras in the face of adverse conditions in any aspect of our life represents our determination and is a measure of our personal resilience.

Response level 2: Individual responses

In our model, healthy individual responses or defences against work pressures include such elements as understanding and recognising risks, pressures and hazardous situations, resilience, effective response strategies, problem-solving strategies, time management, relaxation and calming strategies, and a healthy lifestyle (which includes working reasonable hours during the week, taking regular holidays, and maintaining a healthy diet and appropriate fitness levels).

Individuals vary in the extent to which stressors lead to pathologies and dysfunctions. Some people are labelled 'hot reactors', meaning they have a predisposition to experience extremely negative reactions to stress (Adler & Hillhouse 1996; Elliot & Breo 1984).

Cryer, McCraty and Childre (2003), in an article entitled 'Pull the plug on stress', stated:

> *Accumulated over time negative stress can depress you, burn you out or even kill you. This is because our research shows negative stress (can be) both an emotional and a psychological habit.*

Others experience stress more favourably. Their physical condition, personality characteristics and social support mechanisms mediate the effects of stress and produce resiliency, or the capacity to cope effectively with stress. Resiliency serves as a form of inoculation against the effects of stress. It eliminates exhaustion. This helps explain why some athletes do better in 'the big game', while others do worse. Some managers appear to be brilliant strategists when the stakes are high; others fold under the pressure.

Hierarchy of management strategies

In managing stress, using a particular hierarchy of approaches has been found to be most effective. First, the best way to manage stress is to eliminate or minimise stressors with *enactive strategies*. These strategies create, or enact, a new environment for the individual that does not contain the stressors (Weick 1979). The second most effective approach is for individuals to enhance their overall capacity to handle stress by increasing their personal resiliency. These are called *proactive strategies* and are designed to initiate action that resists the negative effects of stress. Finally, developing short-term techniques for coping with stressors is necessary when an immediate response is required. These are *reactive strategies*—applied as on-the-spot remedies to reduce temporarily the effects of stress.

To understand why this hierarchy of stress management techniques is recommended, consider the following analogy. When the human body experiences a stressor, it reacts like a car engine when the driver steps on the accelerator pedal: it 'revs up'. The body releases chemicals such as adrenaline and cortisol that increase the heart and breathing rates, the blood flow and the energy level. Continual or repetitive revving up of the body's engine can have the same damaging or toxic consequences over time as racing a car's engine without driving it anywhere. Burnout occurs. Individuals are better off if they can eliminate harmful stressors and the potentially negative effects of frequent, potent stress reactions.

However, most individuals do not have complete control over their environment or their circumstances, and can seldom eliminate all harmful stressors. Their next best alternative is to develop a greater capacity to withstand the negative effects of stress and to mobilise the energy generated by stressors. Developing personal resiliency that helps the body return to normal levels of activity more quickly—or directs the 'revved-up engine' in a productive direction—is the next best strategy to eliminating the stressors altogether. Finally, on a temporary basis, individuals can respond to the revved-up state by using constructive strategies such as relaxation techniques and mind control. These techniques are designed to help the 'engine' return to idle more quickly, at least for a short time.

Anticipatory stressors

Anticipatory stressors include potentially disagreeable events that threaten to occur—unpleasant things that have not happened yet, but might happen. Stress results from anticipation or fear of the event.

Anticipatory stressors need not be highly unpleasant or severe, however, to produce stress. Schachter (1959), Milgram (1963) and others induced high levels of stress by telling individuals that they would experience a loud noise or a mild shock, or that someone else might become uncomfortable because of their actions. Fear of failure or fear of embarrassment in front of peers is a common anticipatory stressor; consider, for example, the anticipatory stress that some people experience before giving a major speech or making an important presentation. Anxieties about retirement and losing vitality during middle age are common stress producers as well.

Common coping strategies

Unfortunately, most people reverse the order of coping strategies presented—that is, they rely first on temporary reactive methods to cope with stress because these actions can be implemented immediately. But reactive strategies have to be repeated whenever stressors are encountered, because their effects are short-lived. Moreover, some common reactive strategies, such as drinking, taking sleeping pills or letting off steam through anger, can become habit-forming and harmful in themselves. Without more long-term strategies, relying on repetitive reactive strategies can create a vicious circle.

It takes more effort to develop proactive resiliency strategies, but the effects are more long-lasting. However, resiliency strategies can take time to implement; hence, the pay-off, while substantial, is not immediate. The best and most permanent strategies are those that eliminate stressors altogether. They require the longest time to implement and they may involve complex arrangements. But, because stress is purged, the pay-off is enduring.

Time stressors

Time stressors generally result from having too much to do in too little time. These are the most common and most pervasive sources of stress faced by managers in business firms. The emphasis on time is evidenced by the many ways we have of talking about time. We have time, keep time, buy time, save time, mark time, spend time, sell time, waste time, kill time, pass time, give time, take time and make time.

This preoccupation with time makes it an important source of stress. A variety of researchers have studied the relationships between role overload and chronic time pressures, on the one hand, and psychological and physiological dysfunction on the other (Fisher & Gitelson 1983; French & Caplan 1972; Kahn et al. 1964; Singh 1993, 1998). They found significant relationships between the presence of time stressors and job dissatisfaction, tension, perceived threat, heart rate, cholesterol levels, skin resistance and other factors.

When experienced on a daily basis, time stressors can be highly detrimental. The presence of temporary time stressors may serve as motivators for getting work done, and some individuals accomplish much more when faced with an immediate deadline than when left to work at their own pace. However, a constant state of time pressure—having too much to do and not enough time to do it—is usually harmful.

As mentioned in Chapter 2, time stressors are experienced differently in different national cultures (Trompenaars 1996; Trompenaars & Hampden-Turner 1999). Some cultures have an orientation towards a short time horizon in which time stressors are more prevalent (for example, the Philippines, the United States, Ireland, Brazil, India, Australia). In cultures with a longer time horizon (for example, Hong Kong, Czech Republic, Austria, Sweden, Portugal), the immediacy of time demands is less prevalent. Long-term planning and extended time horizons make time stressors very different. Americans are more inclined to pack a day full of short-term activities, each of which has a completion point. Japanese or Polynesian people, on the other hand, may have busy days, but their orientation is less towards immediate task completion than a long-term wholeness.

Effective time management

With the explosion of time management books, organisers, consultants, efficiency enhancers and technological time savers, you would expect most of us to be pretty good at managing our time. Laptops, iPads, smart phones, email and internet communications have greatly speeded up our data and information capture and sharing, and have also speeded up our response expectancy time. As a consequence, faster and easier means more pressure. Just look around you. Who do you know who is a busy manager, who is not overloaded or who does not complain about being stressed because of time? Which of your acquaintances is not increasingly stressed by a perceived absence of time? It is no surprise that time stress is escalating, given the rapidity of change and the overwhelming amounts of information that people encounter in the 21st century. Most people are moving pretty fast just to keep up, and most people feel inadequate because they find it impossible to keep up completely. The Hilton Time Value Survey found that 77 per cent of people identified their top goal in the coming decade as 'spending more time with family and friends'. Two-thirds of respondents indicated a desire to put more emphasis on 'having free time' (Davidson 1995). The trouble is, another study showed that the average manager was required to engage in between 237 and 1073 separate incidents a day. More than one-third of managers indicated that they did not accomplish what they set out to do each day. This section reviews some time management principles that can enable you to gain control over your time and organise your fragmented, chaotic environment.

Two different sets of skills are important for managing time effectively and eliminating time stressors. One set focuses on using time efficiently each day. The other set focuses on using time effectively over the long term. Because the effectiveness approach to time management serves as the foundation for the efficiency approach, it is explained first. Then the tools and techniques for achieving efficiency in time use are reviewed.

As pointed out, overload and lack of control are the greatest sources of time stress for managers. Actually, you do not have to be a manager to feel overloaded and out of control. Almost everyone suffers now and then from a pervasive feeling of time stress. Somehow, no matter how much time is available, it seems to get filled up and squeezed out. Probably the most commonly prescribed solutions for attacking problems of time stress are to use calendars and planners, to generate 'to do' lists and to learn to say 'no'. Although almost everyone has tried such tactics, almost everyone still claims to be under enormous time stress. This is not to say that calendars, lists and saying 'no' are never useful, but they are examples of an *efficiency* approach to time management rather than an *effectiveness* approach. In eliminating time stressors, efficiency without effectiveness is fruitless.

Defining the effective approach

Managing time with an effectiveness approach means that:

- individuals spend their time on important matters, not just urgent matters
- people are able to distinguish clearly between what they view as important and what they view as urgent
- results, rather than methods, are the focus of time management strategies
- people have a reason not to feel guilty when they must say 'no'.

A number of time management specialists have pointed out the usefulness of a 'time management matrix' in which activities are categorised in terms of their relative importance and urgency (Covey 1989; Lakein 1989). Important activities are those that produce a desired result. They accomplish a valued end, or they achieve a meaningful purpose. Urgent activities are those that demand immediate attention. They are associated with a need expressed by someone else, or they relate to an uncomfortable problem or situation that requires a solution as soon as possible. Figure 3.6 outlines this matrix and provides examples of types of activities that fit in each quadrant.

Activities such as handling employee crises or customer complaints are both urgent and important (cell 1). A ringing telephone, the arrival of the mail or unscheduled interruptions might be examples of urgent but potentially unimportant activities (cell 2). Important but non-urgent activities include

IMPORTANCE \ URGENCY	High	Low
High	1 Crises Customer complaints	3 Developmental opportunities Innovating Planning
Low	2 Mail Ringing telephone Unscheduled interruptions	4 Escapes Routines Arguments

FIGURE 3.6 Types of activities that determine time use

developmental opportunities, innovating, planning and so on (cell 3). Unimportant and non-urgent activities are escapes and routines that people may pursue but which produce little valuable pay-off—for example, small talk, daydreaming, shuffling paper and arguing (cell 4).

Activities in the important/urgent quadrant (cell 1) usually dominate the lives of managers. They are seen as 'have to' activities that demand immediate attention. Attending a meeting, responding to a call or request, interacting with a customer or completing a report might all legitimately be defined as important/urgent activities. The trouble with spending all our time on activities in this quadrant, however, is that they all require the manager to react. They are usually controlled by someone else and they may or may not lead to a result the manager wants to achieve.

The problem is even worse in the unimportant/urgent quadrant (cell 2). Demands by others that may meet their needs but serve only as deflections or interruptions to the manager's agenda only escalate a sense of time stress. Because they may not achieve results that are meaningful, purposeful and valued—that is, important—feelings of time stress will never be overcome. Experiencing overload and loss of control can be guaranteed. Managers are simply reactive.

Moreover, when these time stressors are experienced over an extended period of time, people generally try to escape into unimportant/non-urgent activities (cell 4) to relieve the stress. They escape, shut out the world or put everything on hold. But although feelings of stress may be temporarily relieved, no long-term solutions are implemented, so time stress is never permanently reduced. This means that lives are spent battling crises 95 per cent of the time and escaping 5 per cent of the time.

Sorting out our priorities

A better alternative is to focus on activities in the important/non-urgent quadrant (cell 3). Activities that are important/non-urgent might be labelled 'opportunities' instead of 'problems'. They are oriented towards accomplishing high-priority results. They prevent problems from occurring or build systems that eliminate problems rather than just coping with them. Preparation, relationships, alliances, preventive maintenance, planning, networking, building resiliency and organising are all 'non-have-to' activities that are crucial for long-term success. Because they are not urgent, however, they often get driven out of managers' time schedules.

Important/non-urgent activities should be the top priority on the time management agenda. By ensuring that these kinds of activities get priority, the urgent problems being encountered can be reduced. Time stressors can be eliminated.

How to establish what is really important

One of the most difficult, yet crucially important, decisions that we must make in managing time effectively is determining what is important and what is urgent. There are no automatic rules of thumb that divide all activities, demands or opportunities into those neat categories. Problems do not come with an 'important/non-urgent' tag attached. In fact, for some, every problem or time demand may hold some degree of importance. But if managers let others determine what is and what is not important, they will never effectively manage their time.

Many successful CEOs decide what activities they want to accomplish, then allocate specific blocks of time to work on those activities. Only after they have made these determinations do they make their diaries available to their assistants to schedule other appointments.

The question still remains, however: how can people make certain that they focus on activities that are important, not just urgent? The answer is to identify clear and specific personal priorities. In Chapter 2, it was pointed out how important it is for people to be aware of their own core values and to establish a set of basic principles to guide their behaviour. In order to determine what is important in time management, those core values, basic principles and personal priorities must be clearly identified. Otherwise, individuals are at the mercy of the unremitting demands that others place upon them. (The congruence of individuals' personal values with the values held by their organisation, also touched on in Chapter 2, can be seen to have important implications for effective time management.)

Staying in control of your own time

Basing time management on core principles to judge the importance of activities is also the key to being able to say 'no' without feeling guilty. When you have decided what it is that you care about passionately, what it is you most want to accomplish and what legacy you want to leave, you can more easily say 'no' to activities that are not congruent with those principles. Everyone is always saying 'no' to something anyway, but usually they are saying 'no' to important/non-urgent activities (cell 3) that are most congruent with their personal missions. People who experience the most time stress are those who allow others to generate their personal mission statement for them through their demands for time. Making personal core principles precise and public not only helps make them more powerful but also provides a basis for saying 'no' without feeling guilty. You can opt for prevention, planning, personal development and continuous improvement, knowing that these important/non-urgent activities will help eliminate and prevent the problems that create time stress.

Effectiveness in time management, then, means that you accomplish what you want to accomplish with your time. How you achieve those accomplishments relates to efficiency of time use, to which we now turn.

Efficient time management to eliminate stressors

'I love deadlines. I like the whooshing sound they make as they fly by.'

—Douglas Adams of 'Dilbert' fame

In addition to approaching time management from the point of view of effectiveness (that is, aligning time use with core personal principles), it is also important to adopt the efficiency point of view (that is, accomplishing more during a day by not wasting time). Many tools and systems are now available to help managers use more efficiently the time they have each day.

For example, the same PDAs mentioned earlier can also assist in efficient time management. They can upload or download information relating to daily, weekly and yearly appointments, and client telephone and email addresses. In addition, there are many sophisticated software systems available to assist managers and their colleagues schedule time and activities, and to keep track of progress across multiple projects and programs.

Identifying how we use time

One way to enhance efficient time use is to be alert to your own tendencies to use time inefficiently. The propositions in Box 3.3 show general patterns of behaviour for most individuals in their use of

BOX 3.3 Typical patterns of time use

We do what we like to do before we do what we do not like to do.
We do the things we know how to do faster than the things we do not know how to do.
We do the things that are easiest before things that are difficult.
We do things that require a little time before things that require a lot of time.
We do things for which the resources are available.
We do things that are scheduled (for example, meetings) before non-scheduled things.
We sometimes do things that are planned before things that are unplanned.
We respond to demands from others before demands from ourselves.
We do things that are urgent before things that are important.
We readily respond to crises and to emergencies.
We do interesting things before uninteresting things.
We do things that advance our personal objectives or that are politically expedient.
We wait until a deadline before we really get moving.
We do things that provide the most immediate closure.
We respond on the basis of who wants it.
We respond on the basis of the consequences to us of doing or not doing something.
We tackle small jobs before large jobs.
We work on things in the order of their arrival.
We work on the basis of the squeaky-wheel principle (the squeaky wheel gets the grease).
We work on the basis of consequences to the group.

time. In many situations these tendencies may represent appropriate responses. But in others they can get in the way of efficient time management and increase time stressors unless individuals are aware of them and their possible consequences.

For example, if we do things that are planned before things that are unplanned, some important tasks may never get done unless they are consciously scheduled. Because many people have a tendency to do things that are urgent before things that are important, they may find themselves saying 'no' to important things in order to attend to urgent things, thereby perpetuating feelings of overload. If we do the things that are easiest before the things that are difficult, our time may be taken up dealing with mundane and easy-to-resolve issues while difficult but important problems go unresolved.

It is because time is such a universal stressor, and time management is such an effective means of coping with it, that an instrument to help you diagnose your own time management competency—the time management survey—has been included in the assessment section at the start of the chapter. The first section of that survey applies to everyone in their daily life. The second section is most applicable to individuals who have managed or worked in an organisation. The scoring information at the end of the chapter (page 173) will show you how well you manage your time compared with others. The numbered techniques correspond to the item numbers in the assessment survey.

The time management survey lists techniques that have been derived from research on the management of time. Although one kind of time stressor is having too much time available (that is, boredom), that is not usually the one facing managers and students. These particular rules, therefore, relate to the opposite problem—that is, having too little time available due to an overloaded schedule.

Of course, no individual can or should implement all these time management techniques at once. The amount of time spent trying to implement all the techniques would be so overwhelming that time stressors would only increase. It is best to incorporate a few of these techniques at a time into everyday life. Implement first those hints that will lead to the most improvement in your use of time. Saving just 10 per cent more time or using an extra 30 minutes a day more wisely can produce astounding results over months and years. Effective time management, then, not only helps a person accomplish more in a typical workday but also helps to eliminate feelings of stress and overload that are so detrimental to personal accomplishment and satisfaction.

As Koch (2007) identifies, the most important part of 'to do' lists is not the planned list but a good understanding of the time it takes to do the task.

Time management checklist

What follows is a brief discussion of 20 time management techniques that are applicable to anyone in all aspects of life. The next section discusses 20 other techniques that relate more directly to managers and the management role.

Rule 1: Read selectively. This applies mainly to individuals who find themselves with too much material to read, such as mail, emails, magazines, newspapers, books, brochures, instructions and so on. Except when you read for relaxation or pleasure, most reading should be done the way you read a newspaper: that is, skim most of it, but stop to read what seems most important. Even the most important articles do not need a thorough reading, since important points generally occur at the beginning of paragraphs or sections. If you underline or highlight what you find important, you can review it quickly when needed.

Rule 2: Make a list of key roles, and things to perform within each of these roles, on a weekly as well as a daily basis. This is a commonsense rule that implies that you need to do some advance planning each workday and not rely solely on your memory. (It is best to have only one list, not multiple lists on multiple scraps of paper.)

Rule 3: Have a place for everything and keep everything in its place. Letting things get out of place robs you of time in two ways: you need more time to find something when you need it; and you are tempted to interrupt the task you are doing to do something else. For example, if material for several projects is scattered on top of your desk, you will be continually tempted to switch from one project to another as you shift your eyes or move the papers. This also applies to computer 'desktops', where effective filing systems can help reduce search time and avoid 'distractions'.

Rule 4: Deal with your tasks in order of priority. Each day, focus first on the important tasks and then deal with the urgent tasks. During the Second World War, General Dwight D. Eisenhower, who had an overwhelming number of tasks to perform, successfully managed his time by following rule 4 strictly. He focused his attention rigorously on important matters that only he could resolve, leaving urgent but less important matters to be dealt with by subordinates.

Rule 5: Do one important thing at a time but several trivial things simultaneously. You can accomplish a lot by doing more than one thing at a time when tasks are routine, trivial or require little thought. This rule allows managers to get rid of multiple trivial tasks in less time (for example, signing letters while talking on the phone).

Rule 6: Make a list of some five- or ten-minute discretionary tasks. This makes use of the small bits of time that almost everyone has during the day (waiting for something to begin, between meetings or events, while talking on the telephone). Beware, however, of spending all your time doing small discretionary tasks while letting high-priority items go unattended.

Rule 7: Divide up large projects. This helps you avoid feeling overwhelmed by large, important, urgent tasks. Feeling that a task is too big to accomplish contributes to a feeling of overload and leads to procrastination.

Rule 8: Determine the critical 20 per cent of your tasks. Pareto's law states that only 20 per cent of the work produces 80 per cent of the results, so it is important to analyse which tasks make up the most important 20 per cent and spend the bulk of your time on those.

Rule 9: Save your best time for important matters. Time spent on trivial tasks should not be your 'best time'. Do routine work when your energy level is low, your mind is not sharp or you are not on top of things. Reserve your high-energy time for accomplishing the most important and urgent tasks. Managers are often like puppets whose strings are being pulled by a crowd of unknown and unorganised people. Do not let others interrupt your best time with unwanted demands. You, not others, should control your time.

Rule 10: Reserve some time during the day when others do not have access to you. Use this time to accomplish important/non-urgent tasks, or spend it just thinking. This might be the time before others in the household get up, after everyone else is in bed or at a location where no one else comes. The point is to avoid being in the line of fire all day, every day, without personal control over your time.

Rule 11: Do not procrastinate. If you do certain tasks promptly, they will require less time and effort than if you put them off. Of course, you must guard against spending all your time on trivial, immediate concerns that crowd out more important tasks. The line between procrastination and time wasting is a fine one, but if you keep in mind the rules in Box 3.4 you can avoid both procrastination and being overburdened by trivia.

BOX 3.4 Criteria for analysing time commitments

ANALYSE EACH ACTIVITY BASED ON THE FOLLOWING FOUR CRITERIA:

1. **Importance**—how important is this activity?
   a. Very important: it must be done.
   b. Important: it should be done.
   c. Not so important: it may be useful, but it is not necessary.
   d. Unimportant: it does not accomplish anything.
2. **Urgency**—how urgent is this activity?
   Very urgent: it must be done now.
   Urgent: it should be done now.
   Not urgent: it can be done later.
   Time is not a relevant factor.
3. **Delegation**—do I have to do it?
   a. I am the only one who can do this.
   b. I can delegate it to someone who reports directly to me and whom I trust implicitly.
   c. I can delegate it to someone not close to me (staff) whom I assume can be trusted.
   d. I can delegate it to anyone.
4. **Involvement**—how often must others be involved?
   a. I must interact with others very frequently and consistently.
   b. I need to interact with others quite frequently.
   c. I should interact with others sometime.
   d. I do not need to involve anyone else at all.

Rule 12: Keep track of time use. This is one of the best time management strategies. It is impossible to improve your management of time or decrease time stressors unless you know how you spend your time. You should keep time logs in short enough intervals to capture the essential activities, but not so short that they create a recording burden (for example, 30-minute periods). Parts of the skill practice and skill application sections suggest that you keep a time log for at least two weeks. One way to analyse a time log after it has been recorded is to use the rating scales in Box 3.4. Eliminate those activities that consistently receive Cs and Ds.

Rule 13: Set deadlines. This helps to improve your efficient use of time. Work always expands to fill the available time, so if you do not specify a termination time tasks tend to continue longer than they need to.

Rule 14: Do something productive while waiting. It has been estimated that up to 20 per cent of an average person's time is spent in waiting. During such time, try reading, planning, preparing, rehearsing, reviewing, outlining or doing other things that help you accomplish your work.

Rule 15: Do routine work at one set time during the day. Because it is natural to let simple tasks drive out difficult tasks, specify a certain period of time for doing routine work. Refusing to answer mail or read the newspaper until a specified time, for example, can help ensure that those activities do not supersede priority time.

Rule 16: Reach closure on at least one thing every day. Reaching the end of a day with nothing completely finished (even a ten-minute task) serves to increase a sense of overload and time stress. Finishing a task, on the other hand, produces a sense of relief and releases stress.

Rule 17: Schedule some personal time. You need some time when no interruptions will occur, when you can get off the 'fast track' for a while and be alone. This time should be used to plan, establish priorities, take stock, meditate or just relax. Among other advantages, personal time also helps to maintain self-awareness.

Rule 18: Don't worry about anything continuously. Allow yourself to worry only at a specified time and avoid dwelling on a worrisome issue at other times. This keeps your mind free and your energy focused on the task at hand. It may seem difficult, but controlling your worry time will do wonders to make your time use more efficient and relieve your stress.

Rule 19: Write down long-term objectives. This helps you to maintain consistency in activities and tasks. You can be efficient and organised but still accomplish nothing unless you have a clear direction in mind. Writing down your long-term objectives helps to make them real, and they will constantly serve as reminders.

Rule 20: Be on the alert for ways to improve your management of time. Read a list of time management hints periodically. All of us need reminding, and it will help to make continuous improvement in your time use a part of your lifestyle.

Efficient time management for managers

The second list of rules encompasses the main activities in which managers engage at work. The first nine rules deal with conducting meetings, since some managers report that approximately 70 per cent of their time is spent in meetings.

Rule 1: Hold routine meetings at the end of the day. Energy and creativity levels are highest early in the day and should not be wasted on trivial matters. Furthermore, an automatic deadline—quitting time—will set a time limit on the meeting.

Rule 2: Hold short meetings standing up. This guarantees that meetings will be kept short. Getting comfortable helps to prolong meetings.

Rule 3: Set a time limit. This establishes an expectation of when the meeting should end and creates pressure to conform to a time boundary. Set such limits at the beginning of every meeting and appointment.

Rule 4: Cancel unnecessary meetings. Meetings should be held only if they are needed. Thus, meetings that are held are more productive and more time-efficient.

Rules 5, 6 and 7: Have agendas; stick to them; and keep track of time. These rules help people prepare for a meeting, stick to the subject and remain work-oriented. Many things will be handled outside meetings if they have to appear on a formal agenda to be discussed. Managers can set a verbal agenda at the beginning of even impromptu meetings. Keeping a record of the meeting ensures that assignments are not forgotten, that follow-up and accountability occur, and that everyone is clear about expectations. Keeping track of the time motivates people to be efficient and conscious of finishing on time.

Rule 8: Start meetings on time. This helps to guarantee that people will arrive on time. (Some managers set meetings for odd times, such as 10.13 am, to make attendees minute-conscious.) Starting on time rewards the people who arrive on time, not the laggards.

Rule 9: Prepare minutes promptly and follow up. This practice keeps items from appearing again in a meeting without having been resolved. It also creates the expectation that most work should be done outside the meeting. Commitments and expectations made public through minutes are more likely to be fulfilled.

Rule 10: Insist that staff members suggest solutions to problems. This rule is discussed in Chapter 10. Its purpose is to eliminate the tendency towards upward delegation: that is, for staff members to delegate difficult problems back to managers by asking for their ideas and solutions. It is more efficient for managers to choose between alternatives devised by staff members than to generate their own.

Rule 11: Meet visitors in the doorway. This helps managers to maintain control of their time by controlling the use of their office space. It is easier to keep a meeting short if you are standing in the doorway rather than sitting in your office.

Rule 12: Go to colleagues' offices. The advantage is that it helps managers control the length of a meeting by being free to leave. Of course, if managers spend a great deal of time travelling between staff members' offices, the rule is not practical.

Rule 13: Do not over-schedule the day. Effective managers stay in control of at least some of their time. Others' meetings and demands can undermine managers' personal control of their schedules unless they make an effort to maintain control. This does not mean that the day can be free of all appointments or meetings, but the manager initiates, rather than responds to, schedule requirements.

Rule 14: Have someone else answer calls and scan emails. This provides managers with a buffer from interruptions for at least some part of the day and eliminates the time wasted on unwanted/unimportant emails.

Rule 15: Have a place to work uninterrupted. This helps to guarantee that, when a deadline is near, the manager can concentrate on the task at hand. Trying to get one's mind focused once more on a task or project after interruptions wastes a lot of time. Mental 'gearing up' is wasteful if done repeatedly.

Rule 16: Do something definite with every piece of paperwork handled. This keeps managers from shuffling the same items over and over. Not infrequently 'doing something definite' with a piece of paper means throwing it away.

Rule 17: Keep the workplace clean. This minimises distractions and reduces the time it takes to find things.

Rules 18, 19 and 20. These all relate to effective delegation, a key time management technique. These last three rules are discussed in Chapter 8, 'Empowering and Delegating'.

A workload management approach

Another approach to time management is for managers to take a workload management approach to managing, delegating and completing tasks in the workplace on time and, where applicable, within budget (Correll 2005). The four elements of the workload management approach are:

- task acceptance
- task scheduling
- capacity to complete
- task closure.

Task acceptance

- Clarify the output and the time required. This includes a checking process:
  — Is this a regular or an ad hoc task?
  — Is it a discretionary or a non-discretionary task?
- Manage acceptance of the task to a delegate.
- Include the task in a list of work to complete for the delegate.
- Prioritise the task against other tasks.
- Ensure you anticipate, communicate and support teamwork.

Task scheduling

- Schedule the task into the workflow.
- Delegate and/or work as a team.
- Group like tasks.
- Ensure you account for the impact of travel.

Capacity to complete

- Check there is enough time available.
- Allow for the skill level of staff. Are they proficient or learning?
- Review and monitor the impact on efficiency of process.
- Get started.
- Keep going.

Task closure

- Manage delivery of the task.
- For staged tasks, ensure they are handed on appropriately.
- Review blocks and interruptions.
- Sign-off: who needs to know?

As can be seen, this approach is based on *project* management, rather than *time* management. With this change of focus, you will be able to ensure that you better use the time you have available.

Remember that these techniques for managing time are a means to an end, not the end itself. If trying to implement rules creates more rather than less stress, they should not be applied. However, research has indicated that managers who use these kinds of techniques have better control of their time, accomplish more, have better relations with staff and colleagues, and eliminate many of the time stressors most managers ordinarily encounter. Therefore, you will find that as you select a few of these hints to apply in your own life, the efficiency of your time use will improve and your time stress will decrease. Remember that saving just 30 minutes a day amounts to one full year of free time during your working lifetime. That is 8760 hours of free time!

Most time management techniques involve single individuals changing their own work habits or behaviours by themselves. Greater effectiveness and efficiency in time use occurs because individuals decide to institute personal changes; the behaviour of other people is not involved. However, effective time management must often take into account the behaviour of others, because that behaviour may tend to inhibit or enhance effective time use. For this reason, effective time management sometimes requires the application of other skills discussed in this book. Chapter 8 provides principles for efficient time management by involving other people in task accomplishment. Chapter 6, 'Motivating Others', explains how to help others be more effective and efficient in their own work. Chapter 5, 'Communicating Supportively', identifies ways in which interpersonal relationships can be strengthened, thus relieving stressors resulting from interpersonal conflicts.

Eliminating anticipatory stressors by establishing priorities, goal setting and small wins

Redesigning work can help to structure an environment in which stressors are minimised, but it is much more difficult to eliminate entirely the anticipatory stressors experienced by individuals. Stress associated with anticipating an event is more a product of psychological anxiety than current work circumstances. To eliminate that source of stress requires a change in thought processes, priorities and plans.

Chapter 2 discusses the central place of cognitive style (thought processes), values (priorities) and moral maturity (personal principles) for effective management. Earlier in this chapter, the central importance of establishing clear personal priorities was discussed, such as identifying what is to be accomplished in the long term, what cannot be compromised or sacrificed and what lasting legacy you desire. Establishing this core value set, or statement of basic personal principles, helps to eliminate not only time stressors but also anticipatory stress by providing clarity of direction. When travelling on an unknown road for the first time, having a road map or GPS device reduces anticipatory stress. You do not have to figure out where to go or where you are by trying to diagnose unknown landmarks along the roadside. In the same way, a personal mission statement acts as a map or guide. It makes clear where you will eventually end up. Fear of the unknown, or anticipatory stress, is thus eliminated.

Goal setting

Establishing short-term plans also helps to eliminate anticipatory stressors by focusing attention on immediate goal accomplishment, rather than a fearful future. Short-term planning, however, implies more than just specifying a desired outcome. Several action steps are needed if short-term plans are to be achieved (Locke & Latham 1990). The model in Figure 3.7 outlines the four-step process associated with successful short-term planning.

FIGURE 3.7 A model for short-term planning and goal setting

Step 1: Identify the desired goal. Most goal-setting or management-by-objectives (MBO) programs specify this step, but most also stop at that point. Unfortunately, the first step alone is not likely to lead to goal achievement or stress elimination. Merely establishing a goal, while helpful, is not sufficient. Steps 2, 3 and 4 are also essential.

Step 2: Identify actions. These are specific activities and behaviours that will lead towards accomplishing the goal. The more difficult the goal is to accomplish, the more rigorous, numerous and specific the behaviours and activities should be.

Take, for example, a heavy smoker. She is concerned for her health and aware of the social disadvantages of smoking. She would like to stop smoking but her past attempts at 'going cold turkey' have failed dismally. Setting herself an achievable goal could involve a time-frame of, say, three months. As stopping smoking can be a difficult goal, she could approach it by identifying a dozen or so specific behaviours and guidelines to help her—for example, removing cigarettes and ashtrays from the office and home, requesting friends not to smoke in her presence, having a supply of low-kilojoule snack foods available at all times, beginning an exercise program with friends to increase fitness and awareness of physical well-being, developing a hobby that occupies her hands (such as woodworking, knitting, lead-lighting), noting associated activities and times when she smokes most and avoiding those activities as much as possible, and putting money saved on cigarettes into a bank account and giving herself a special treat with the proceeds. All these behaviours would have a direct effect on the ultimate goal of giving up smoking.

(Our example is not a real-life case; rather, it is a demonstration of the accumulative benefit of small wins. However, as approximately three million Australians were smokers in 2001, according to Australian Bureau of Statistics figures, many of whom would have tried to give up smoking, the scenario is real. For those smokers who would like to stop, the Centre for Education and Information on Drugs and Alcohol (Ceida) in Rozelle, Sydney, has information on Quit Smoking programs throughout New South Wales. Similar organisations operate throughout Australia.)

Step 3: Establish accountability and reporting mechanisms. The principle at the centre of this step is to make it more difficult to stay the same than to change. This is done by involving others in ensuring adherence to the plan, establishing a social support network to obtain encouragement from others and instituting penalties for non-conformance. In the smoking example, in addition to announcing to friends and colleagues that she wishes to give up smoking, the smoker could instruct her doctor to book her into a spartan, although expensive, $500-a-day health retreat if at the end of three months she had not achieved the goal on her own. It would clearly be more uncomfortable and costly not to succeed than to accomplish the goal.

Step 4: Establish an evaluation and reward system. What evidence will there be that the goal has been accomplished? In the case of stopping smoking, the goal is self-evident. But for improving management skills, becoming a better friend, developing more patience or establishing more effective leadership, the criteria of success are not so easily identified. That is why this step is crucial. 'I'll know it when I see it' is not good enough. Specific indicators of success, or specific changes that will have been produced when the goal is achieved, must be identified. Carefully outlining these criteria serves as a motivation towards goal accomplishment by making the goal more observable and measurable.

The purpose of this short-term planning model is to eliminate anticipatory stress by establishing a focus and direction for activity. The anxiety associated with uncertainty and potentially negative events is dissipated when mental and physical energy are concentrated on purposeful activity.

Small wins

Another principle related to eliminating anticipatory stressors is the small-wins strategy. A 'small win' means a tiny but definite change made in a desired direction. You begin by changing something that is relatively easy to change. Then another 'easy change' is added, and so on. Although each individual success may be relatively modest when considered in isolation, the multiple small gains eventually mount up, generating a sense of momentum that creates the impression of substantial movement towards a desired goal. This momentum helps to convince us, as well as others, of our ability to accomplish our objective. The fear associated with anticipatory change is eliminated as we build self-confidence through small wins. We also gain the support of others as they see progress being made.

In the case of our cigarette-addicted person, one key was to begin changing what she could change, a little at a time. Tackling the task of giving up smoking immediately had proved too overwhelming in the past. But she could make the suggested changes in order to reduce the number of cigarettes smoked. Each successful change would generate more and more momentum, allowing her eventually to give up cigarettes for one day, then two days at a time, and so on. When combined, these successful changes would lead to the larger change that she desired. Her ultimate success was a product of multiple small wins.

In summary, the rules for instituting small wins are simple:

1. Identify something that is under your control.
2. Change it in a way that leads towards your desired goal.
3. Find some other small thing to change and change it.
4. Keep track of the changes you are making.
5. Maintain the small gains you have made.

Anticipatory stressors are eliminated because the fearful unknowns are replaced by a focus on immediate successes.

Having examined some of the ways we can boost our individual responses to avoid or minimise stress, it is now time to consider the encounter stressors that require interpersonal/team responses.

Response level 3: Interpersonal/team responses

The aspects that compose this level of defence are all focused around how we manage our relationships with other people in our workgroups and teams. It involves team morale and culture, trust and communication, mutual support, mentoring and teamwork practices.

Encounter stressors result from interpersonal interactions. Most people have experienced the debilitating effects of a quarrel with a friend, flatmate or partner; of trying to work with an employee or supervisor with whom there has been an interpersonal conflict; or of trying to accomplish a task in a group that is divided by lack of trust and cohesion. Each of these stressors results from some kind of interpersonal conflict. Encounter stressors are especially common for managers. They generally arise from three types of conflict: (1) *role conflicts*, in which roles performed by group members are incompatible; (2) *issue conflicts*, in which disagreement exists over how to define or solve a problem; and (3) *interaction conflicts*, in which individuals fail to get along well because of mutual antagonism (Balzer, Doherty & O'Connor 1989; Cordes & Dougherty 1993; Fisher & Gitelson 1983; Singh 1998).

Research shows that encounter stressors in organisations have significant negative effects on productivity and satisfaction (Cameron 1994; Cameron & Whetten 1987) and lie at the very heart of most organisational dysfunction (Peters 1988; Pfeffer 1998; Thoits 1995). Not surprisingly, encounter stressors more frequently affect managers with responsibility for people rather than equipment. The highest levels of encounter stress exist among managers who interact frequently with other people and have responsibility for individuals in the workplace (French & Caplan 1972; Singh 1998). Poor relationships with others cause particularly high levels of stress. Mishra (1993) reviewed the literature on interpersonal trust, for example, and reported that lack of trust among individuals not only blocks quality communication, information sharing, decision competence and problem-solving capabilities but also results in high levels of personal stress.

Differences have also been discovered between national cultures with regards to encounter stressors (Trompenaars & Hampton-Turner 1999). Cultures that are *egalitarian*, for example, and emphasise interpersonal relationships as a way to accomplish work (such as the United States, Norway, Ireland and Finland) face more encounter stress as a general rule than countries with a *hierarchical* or position-based orientation (for example, South Korea, India, Spain and Israel). Similarly, country cultures that emphasise *affectivity* (for example, Iran and Mexico) as opposed to *neutrality* (for example, China and Japan) also have a tendency towards more encounter stress due to the outward expression of emotions. Reacting personally or emotionally to issues tends to increase encounter stress in the workplace. The point to keep in mind in managing stress is that some people will experience certain kinds of stress more than others. National culture is one predictive factor. Thus, whereas encounter stress is a key for everyone, it will be more typical of some people than others.

In a survey of American workers by the insurance company Northwest National Life (1992), encounter stressors were cited as a major cause of burnout. Table 3.1 summarises the results of that study. When workers reported not feeling free to interact socially, experienced workplace conflict, did not talk openly to managers, felt unsupported by fellow employees, were stifled by red tape and did not feel recognised, burnout was significantly higher than when those encounter stressors were not present. Of the ten most significant stressors associated with burnout, seven were encounter stressors.

TABLE 3.1 Causes of burnout

WORKSITE CHARACTERISTICS	PERCENTAGE OF EMPLOYEES REPORTING BURNOUT
Employees are not free to talk with one another	48
Employees are free to talk with one another	28
Personal conflicts on the job are common	46
Personal conflicts on the job are rare	22
Employees are given too little control	46
Employees are given enough control	25
Staffing or expense budgets are inadequate	45
Staffing or expense budgets are adequate	21
Management and employees do not talk openly	44
Management and employees talk openly	20
Management is unsupportive of employees	44
Management is supportive of employees	20
Sick and vacation benefits are below average	44
Sick and vacation benefits are average or better	26
Employee benefits have been reduced	42
Employee benefits have been maintained	24
Dealing with red tape is common	40
Dealing with red tape is rare	22
Employees are not recognised and rewarded	39
Employees are recognised and rewarded	20

Source: ReliaStar Life Insurance Company (formerly Northwestern National Life Insurance Company), *Employee Burnout: Causes and Cures* (Minneapolis, MN: 1992), p. 6. Copyright 1993 by Northwestern National Life Insurance Company.

Eliminating encounter stressors through collaboration and interpersonal competence

As mentioned earlier, dissatisfying relationships with others, particularly with a direct manager or supervisor, are prime causes of job stress among workers. These encounter stressors result directly from abrasive, unfulfilling relationships. Even if work is going smoothly, when encounter stress is present everything else seems wrong. It is difficult to maintain positive energy when you are fighting or at odds with someone, or when feelings of acceptance and amiability are not typical of your important relationships at work.

Collaboration

One important factor that helps eliminate encounter stress is membership of a stable, closely knit group or community. When people feel part of a group, or accepted by someone else, stress is relieved. For example, it was discovered some years ago by Dr Stewart Wolf that in the town of Roseto, Pennsylvania, residents were completely free from heart disease and other stress-related illnesses. He suspected that their protection sprang from the town's uncommon social cohesion and stability. The town's population consisted entirely of descendants of Italians who had moved there 100 years before from Roseto, Italy. Few married outside the community; the first born of each family was always named after a grandparent; conspicuous consumption and displays of superiority were avoided; and social support among community members was a way of life.

Wolf predicted that residents would begin to display the same level of stress-related illnesses as the rest of the country if the modern world intruded. It did, and they did. By the time the residents in Roseto had Cadillacs, ranch-style homes, mixed marriages, new names and competition with one another, they also had a rate of coronary disease the same as any other town's (Farnham 1991). They had ceased to be a cohesive, collaborative clan and instead had become a community of selfishness. Self-centredness, it was discovered, was dangerous to health.

Developing supportive relationships

The number one psychological discovery resulting from the American experience of the Vietnam War and the first Persian Gulf War was the strength associated with the small, primary workgroup. In Vietnam, unlike the Persian Gulf, teams of soldiers did not stay together and did not form the strong bonds that occurred during the 1991 Persian Gulf War. The constant injection of new personnel into squadrons, and the constant transfer of soldiers from one location to another, made soldiers feel isolated, without loyalty and vulnerable to stress-related illnesses. In the Persian Gulf War, by contrast, soldiers were kept in the same unit throughout the campaign, they were brought home together and were given a lot of time to debrief together after the battle. Using a closely knit group to provide interpretation of, and social support for, behaviours was found to be the most powerful deterrent to post-battle trauma. David Marlowe, chief of psychiatry at the Walter Reed Army Institute of Research in the United States, explained that 'Squad members are encouraged to use travel time en route home from a war zone to talk about their battlefield experience. It helps them detoxify. That's why we brought them back in groups from Desert Storm. Epistemologically, we know it works' (Farnham 1991).

Building emotional bank accounts

Developing collaborative relationships with others is a powerful deterrent to encounter stress. One way of developing this kind of relationship is by applying a concept introduced by Stephen Covey (1989) in describing the habits of highly effective people. Covey used the metaphor of an emotional bank account to describe the trust or feeling of security that one person has towards another. The more 'deposits' made in an emotional bank account, the stronger and more resilient the relationship becomes. Conversely, too many 'withdrawals' from the account weaken relationships by destroying trust, security and confidence. 'Deposits' are made by treating people with kindness, courtesy, honesty and consistency. The emotional bank account grows when people feel they are receiving love, respect and caring. 'Withdrawals' are made by not keeping promises, not listening, not clarifying expectations or not allowing choice. Because disrespect and autocratic rule devalue people and destroy their sense of self-worth, relationships are ruined because the account becomes overdrawn.

The more people interact, the more deposits must be made in the emotional bank account. When you see an old friend after years of absence, you can often pick up right where you left off, because the emotional bank account has not been touched. But when you interact with someone frequently, the relationship is constantly being fed or depleted. Cues from everyday interactions are interpreted as either deposits or withdrawals. When the emotional account is well stocked, mistakes, disappointments and minor abrasions are easily forgiven and ignored. But when no reserve exists, those incidents may become creators of distrust and contention.

The commonsense prescription, therefore, is to base relationships with others on mutual trust, respect, honesty and kindness. Make deposits into the emotional bank accounts of others. Collaborative, cohesive communities are, in the end, a product of the one-on-one relationships that people develop with each other. As Dag Hammarskjöld, former Secretary-General of the United Nations, stated: 'It is more noble to give yourself completely to one individual than to labour diligently for the salvation of the masses.' That is because building a strong, cohesive relationship with an individual is more powerful, and more difficult, than the leadership of the masses. Feeling trusted, respected and loved is, in the end, what most people desire as individuals. People want to experience those feelings personally, not just as a member of a group. Therefore, because encounter stressors are almost always the product of abrasive individual relationships, they are best eliminated by building strong emotional bank accounts with others.

Interpersonal competence

In addition to one-on-one relationship building, a second major category of encounter stress eliminators is developing interpersonal competence. The skilful management of groups and interpersonal interactions is also an effective way of eliminating encounter stressors. For example, the ability to resolve conflict, to build and manage high-performing teams, to conduct efficient meetings, to coach and counsel employees needing support, to provide negative feedback in constructive ways, to influence others' opinions, to motivate and energise employees and to empower individuals on the job all help eliminate the stress associated with abrasive, uncomfortable relationships. The survey summarised in Table 3.1 (on page 154) established that employees who rated their manager as supportive and interpersonally competent had lower rates of burnout, lower stress levels, lower incidence of stress-related illnesses, higher productivity, more loyalty to their organisation and more efficiency in work than employees with unsupportive and interpersonally incompetent managers.

Interpersonal competence is at considerable risk in this electronic age, when we can find ourselves sending an email to a colleague ten metres away. In *Turning Point*, Hugh Mackay (1999) emphasises the importance of recognising the difference between data transfer and communication. He believes it is our failure to recognise this difference that explains why so many employees complain that, in the organisations for which they work, 'there are too many messages but not enough communication' (p. 102).

A third category of factors that can eliminate encounter stressors is the development of emotional intelligence (see Chapter 2). Goleman (1995, 1998) cites a number of studies which suggest that emotional intelligence can be taught and influenced positively. That is, people can achieve higher levels of emotional intelligence with careful teaching and training.

In a study at Stanford University, four-year-old children were involved in activities that tested aspects of their emotional intelligence. (For example, a marshmallow was placed in front of them and they were given two choices: eat it now, or wait until the adult supervisor returned from running an errand, when the child would get two marshmallows.) A follow-up study with these children 14 years later, upon graduation from high school, found that students who demonstrated more emotional intelligence (that is, postponed gratification in the marshmallow task) were less likely to fall apart under stress, became less irritated and less stressed by interpersonally abrasive people, were more likely to accomplish their goals and scored an average of 210 points higher on the SAT college entrance exam (Goleman 1998). The IQ scores of the students did not differ significantly, but the emotional intelligence scores were considerably different. Consistent with other studies, emotional intelligence predicted success in life as well as the ability to handle encounter stress for these students.

The skills this book can help you develop are among the most important of those that comprise emotional intelligence. By improving your abilities in the management skills covered in this book—for example, self-awareness, problem solving, supportive communication, motivating self and others, managing conflict, empowering others—your emotional competence scores will increase.

The remaining chapters in this book address these topics in detail. They provide techniques and behavioural guidelines designed to assist you in improving your interpersonal competence. After completing the book, including the practice and application exercises, you will have improved several skills related to interpersonal competence and, therefore, your ability to eliminate many forms of encounter stress.

Mentor support

Most individuals, with the possible exception of the most senior managers, can profit from a mentoring relationship. (Senior managers may need to seek mentors outside their organisation.) The research is clear that career success, work satisfaction and resiliency to stress are enhanced by a mentoring relationship (Appelbaum, Ritchie & Shapiro 1994; Bell 1998; Hendricks 1996; Kram 1985). Investigations by Christopher Conway of Ashridge Management Research Group have affirmed the benefits of mentoring. As a result of research workshops, organisational case studies and extensive literature review, Conway (1995: 28) found the following:

- Mentoring is a sophisticated and adaptable tool that gives the best results when tailored to an individual organisation's needs.
- Mentoring is not a universal panacea.
- Mentoring is a relationship, not an activity or product.
- Being a mentor is not exclusively about the 'older manager' and the new entrant to the organisation. Many busy managers in the 40-plus age group actively mentor in their organisations, which contradicts much of what has been written in the literature. Being a mentor is certainly not a 'parental' (but rather a collegial) role.
- 'Boundary management' between the person being mentored, the person's boss and the mentor is essential to avoid building in potential conflict by turning the mentoring relationship into a reporting one.
- As organisations slim down and hierarchies flatten, reporting relationships and structures often disappear. Mentoring may be able to fill the gap by providing support for people who find themselves more isolated in organisations than before.
- The matching of both parties to the relationship is crucial, as is the training or orienting of the managers who are to be mentors.

Individuals need someone else in the organisation who can provide a role model, from whom they can learn, and from whom they can receive personal attention and a reinforcement of self-worth, especially under uncertain, crucial and stressful situations.

Some organisations formally prescribe a mentoring system by assigning a senior manager to shepherd a junior manager when he or she enters the organisation. With rare exceptions, when the contact is one-way—that is, from the top down—these relationships do not work out (Kram 1985). The junior manager must actively seek and foster the mentoring relationship as well. The junior manager can do this, not by demonstrating over-dependence or over-ingratiation, but by expressing a desire to use the senior person as a mentor and then by making certain that the relationship does not become a one-way street. The junior staff member can pass along important information and resources to the potential mentor, while both will share in working out solutions to problems.

The remaining level of healthy responses to pressures at work involves the contribution of the organisation itself.

Response level 4: Organisational responses

This last level of healthy responses to workplace stress involves one of the key contributors of stress and pressure in the workplace: the organisation itself. The organisation is therefore also a key foundation in providing and enabling healthy responses to hazardous and stressful situations.

The types of organisational responses include having an effective code of conduct, strong occupational health and safety and welfare policies and procedures, effective management counselling and support, thoughtful workplace design, continuous safety thinking, a strong employee assistance program, good management skills, consistent communication, appropriate work/life balance policies and an effective performance management system. All of these organisational elements contribute to a healthy workplace.

One of the most common forms of situational stress is unfavourable working conditions, including a lack of resources and back-up support. For many managers, such stressors can cause a highly tense and pressured work environment, often characterised by crises, long hours, continual organisational restructuring and subsequent fear of retrenchment.

One of the most well-researched links between situational stressors and negative consequences involves rapid change, particularly the effects of changes in life events (Hobson et al. 1998; Holmes & Rahe 1970; Wolff, Wolf & Hare 1950). The Social Readjustment Rating Scale (SRRS) was introduced in 1967 to track the number of changes individuals had experienced over the previous 12 months. Since changes in some events were thought to be more stressful than others, a scaling method was used to assign weights to each life event. More than 3100 studies have been published just since 1995, covering a variety of cultures, age groups and occupations, using the SRRS instrument.

Recently, Hobson et al. (1998) revised the SRRS and updated the weightings of individual items. The instrument was expanded from the original 43 items in the Holmes and Rahe work to 51 items. Confirmation of the item weights was produced by 3122 adults of various cultural, ethnic, socioeconomic and gender backgrounds. The weightings are similar and consistent across the various groups. (Females have slightly higher stress scores than males, for example, but the differences are so small as not to be meaningful.) In other words, we can have some confidence that the revised instrument matches the situational stress experienced by most people in the 21st century (also see Adler & Hillhouse 1996; Rahe, Ryman & Ward 1980). You completed this instrument in the assessment section.

Unexpected and imposed structural and systems changes can also be a major source of anxiety and pain for people working in organisations, especially when the reasons for change are not clearly understood. Frost and Robinson (1999) also identify 'toxic' managers as stressors, especially when they leave staff 'hanging, confused and paralysed' during times of large-scale change.

Eliminating organisational stressors through work redesign

Most of us would never declare that we feel less stress now than a year ago, that we have less pressure or that we are less overloaded. We all report feeling more stress than ever, at least partly because it is expected to be stressed. 'I'm busier than you are' is a common theme in social conversations. However, these feelings are not without substance for many people. Repeated downsizings have introduced new threats in the workplace, roads are increasingly congested, financial pressures are escalating, crime is pervasive and workers' compensation claims for stress-related illness are ballooning. Unfortunately, in medical treatment and time lost, stress-related illnesses are almost twice as expensive as workplace injuries because of longer recovery times, the need for psychological therapy and so on (Farnham 1991). Situational stressors, in other words, are costly—and they are escalating.

For decades, researchers in the area of occupational health have examined the relationship between job strain and stress-related behavioural, psychological and physiological outcomes. Studies have focused on various components of job strain, including levels of task demand (for example, the pressure to work quickly or excessively), the level of individual control (say, the freedom to vary the work pace) and the level of intellectual challenge.

Research in this area has challenged the common myth that job strain occurs most frequently in the executive suite (Karasek et al. 1988). Writing on stress in *Management Today*, Peter Kelleher (1999) quoted a British study conducted on 7000 women and men in the British Civil Service. The study investigated how the level of influence in the workplace could affect the risk of coronary heart disease (CHD). The study found that those in lower clerical and office-support grades were more likely to develop CHD than those in higher administrative positions and management. The greatest contributor to CHD frequency was low control at work. In Australia, there are well-documented cases of greater participation in decision making leading to reduced stress and greater job satisfaction. Absenteeism (often a behavioural manifestation of stress) has been researched at Ford's Victorian manufacturing plants. Peter Roberts (1995) reported:

> *Ford (surveyed) 600 staff and found that absenteeism was correlated with low job involvement, low organisational commitment and an acceptance of an absence culture. Other factors included poor opportunities to participate in decision making and low satisfaction with supervisors.*
>
> *The company's 500 work teams are one of the main mechanisms for tackling absenteeism. As teams have become more entrenched at Ford, there are greater opportunities to participate in decision making and to build awareness of the benefits of working together as a group.*

The steps Ford took to solve the absenteeism problem, including giving employees time off (made up at a later date) to attend to family and other important matters, produced a reduction in absenteeism from 8.7 per cent to 4.4 per cent. As a 1 per cent reduction saves Ford more that $2 million each year, the benefits extended far beyond the individual workers.

Unplanned absences often require extra staffing, disrupt production, threaten lower quality and poison staff–management relations, and thus produce stressful situations. Job redesign to solve the problem, as exemplified by Ford, has proved effective in reducing stress and increasing satisfaction and productivity.

The following points are guidelines for eliminating situational stressors at work.

1. *Combine tasks.* When individuals are able to work on a whole project and perform a variety of related tasks (for example, programming all components of a computer software package), rather than being restricted to working on a single repetitive task or subcomponent of a larger task, they are more satisfied and committed. In such cases, they are able to use more skills and feel a pride of ownership in their job.
2. *Form identifiable work units.* Building on the first step, individuals feel more integrated, productivity improves and the strain associated with repetitive work is diminished when teams of individuals performing related tasks are formed. When these groups combine and coordinate their tasks, and decide internally how to complete the work, stress decreases dramatically. This formation of natural work units has received a great deal of attention in Japanese car plants in the United States, where workers have combined in teams to assemble an entire car from start to finish, rather than do separate tasks on an assembly line. Workers learn one another's jobs, rotate assignments and experience a sense of completion in their work.
3. *Establish customer relationships.* One of the most enjoyable parts of a job is seeing the consequences of one's labour. In most organisations, producers are buffered from consumers by intermediaries such as customer relations departments and sales personnel. Eliminating those buffers allows workers to obtain first-hand information concerning customer satisfaction as well as the needs and expectations of potential customers. Stress resulting from filtered communication is also eliminated.
4. *Increase decision-making authority.* Managers who increase the autonomy of staff members to make important work decisions eliminate a major source of job stress for their staff. Being able to influence the what, when and how of work increases an individual's feelings of control. Cameron, Freeman and Mishra (1990) found a significant decrease in experienced stress in firms that were downsizing when workers were given the authority to make decisions about how and when they did the extra work required of them.
5. *Open feedback channels.* A major source of stress is not knowing what is expected and how task performance is being evaluated. As managers communicate their expectations more clearly and give timely and accurate feedback, staff members' satisfaction and performance improve. A related form of feedback in production tasks is quality control. Firms that allow the individuals who assemble a product to test its quality, instead of shipping it off to a separate quality assurance group, find that quality increases substantially and that conflicts between production and quality control personnel are eliminated.

Classification of stress-reduction strategies

Three common themes for stress management emerge from a survey of the current literature. As indicated above, these themes can be summarised as management of self, management of support systems, and management of the organisation. Stress management can also be categorised as to the time at which the intervention of stress management strategies should occur: that is, before, concurrent with, or after the stressful event. These concepts of theme and time can be integrated into a model for managerial stress management.

Themes

Management of self encompasses an individual's efforts to take control of his or her own body, activities and personal organisation. Management of the support system is an individual's attempt to manage personal relationships both inside and outside the organisation. Management of the organisation involves the effective use of strategies to cope with one's work environment. These three themes and the strategies associated with each are illustrated in Table 3.2.

TABLE 3.2 Model for interaction between strategies and stress management themes

	Stress management themes		
Strategies	**Management of self**	**Management of support system**	**Management of organisation**
Diet and nutrition	X		
Sleep	X		
Exercise	X		
Recreation/leisure	X	X	
Relaxation technique	X		
Biofeedback	X		
Autogenic training	X		
Meditation	X		
Stress plan	X		
Goal setting	X	X	X
Time management	X	X	X
Self-assessment measures	X		
Creative problem solving and decision making	X	X	X
Supportive relationships	X	X	X
Psychoanalysis	X	X	
Stress counselling	X	X	X
Development programs	X	X	X
Behaviour change techniques	X	X	X
Systematic desensitisation	X		
Dynamic psychotherapy	X		
Avoidance of negative strategies	X		
Assertiveness training	X	X	X
Delegation	X		X
Choice of work environment	X	X	X
Conflict management	X	X	X
Job restructuring	X	X	X

Source: H. R. Sailer, J. Schlacter and M. R. Edwards, 'Stress: Causes, consequences, and coping strategies', *Personnel*, July–August 1982.

Time

The time dimension for strategy intervention consists of three phases. The first, prevention, occurs before the stressful event. Once the event is in progress, the second phase is in operation, and the manager or executive is called upon to use a variety of strategies to gain the strength and ability to cope effectively with the event. The third phase of stress management comes into play after the stressful event has occurred, when the person may or may not still be feeling stressed by it. However, the possibility that the event will occur again or trigger other stressful events can lead the person to seek treatment.

Coordination of the three themes of stress management with the time dimensions permits the development of an integrative model of the relationships. Some strategies, because of their nature, are included under several themes and time dimensions. This overlap may point to the added significance of these strategies as essential to a person's coping-skill repertoire.

Table 3.3 presents an integration of the theme and time-dimension exhibits. This model provides a classification of stress management strategies along the two dimensions of theme and time. Using the three themes and three time dimensions previously identified, the model seeks to organise the strategies within these dimensions in order to highlight which particular strategies would be useful

TABLE 3.3 Classification of stress management strategies: Interaction between themes and time dimensions

	Stress management themes		
Time dimensions	**Management of self**	**Management of support system**	**Management of the organisation**
Before stressful event	Diet and nutrition, sleep, exercise, recreation/leisure, biofeedback, autogenic training, meditation, stress plan, goal setting, time management, self-assessment measurement, supportive relationships, assertiveness training, avoidance of negative strategies, creative problem solving and decision making, behaviour-change techniques, psychoanalysis, stress counselling, development programs, relaxation techniques	Recreation/leisure, time management, supportive relationships, development programs, assertiveness training, choice of work environment, creative problem solving and decision making, psychoanalysis, stress counselling, goal setting, behaviour-change techniques	Development programs, choice of work environment, assertiveness training, creative problem solving and decision making, stress counselling, behaviour-change techniques, delegation, goal setting, time management, job restructuring
During stressful event	Creative problem solving and decision making, avoidance of negative strategies, relaxation techniques, autogenic training, supportive relationships, diet and nutrition, meditation, sleep, exercise	Creative problem solving and decision making, supportive relationships, conflict management	Delegation, conflict management, creative problem solving and decision making, supportive relationships
After stressful event	Diet and nutrition, sleep, exercise, recreation/leisure, relaxation techniques, biofeedback, autogenic training, stress plan, goal setting, time management, self-assessment measurements, avoidance of negative strategies, assertiveness training, creative problem solving and decision making, systematic desensitisation, dynamic psychotherapy, meditation, behaviour-change techniques, stress counselling, psychoanalysis, development programs, supportive relationships	Recreation/leisure, time management, creative problem solving and decision making, supportive relationships, psychoanalysis, development programs, stress counselling, assertiveness training, choice of work environment, conflict management, job restructuring, stress counselling, goal setting, behaviour-change techniques	Goal setting, time management, creative problem solving and decision making, supportive relationships, stress counselling, development programs, choice of work environment, conflict management, behaviour-change techniques, delegation, job restructuring, assertiveness training

Source: H. R. Sailer, J. Schlacter and M. R. Edwards, 'Stress: Causes, consequences, and coping strategies', *Personnel*, July–August 1982.

under a given set of conditions. Different strategies come into play depending upon the theme (self, others or the organisation) and the time dimension (before, during or after the stressful event) involved. Such an approach can help a person decide which skills or strategies can be used and when they ought to be called into action.

Temporary stress-reduction techniques

Thus far, the emphasis has been on eliminating sources of stress and developing resiliency to stress. These are the most desirable stress management strategies, as they can have a long-term effect on well-being. However, even under ideal circumstances, it may be impossible to eliminate all stressors and individuals must use temporary reactive mechanisms to maintain equilibrium. Although increased resilience can buffer the harmful effects of stress, people must sometimes take immediate action in the short term to cope with stress. Implementing short-term strategies reduces stress temporarily so that longer-term stress elimination or resiliency strategies can operate. Short-term strategies are largely reactive and must be repeated whenever stressors are encountered because, unlike other strategies, their effects are only temporary. On the other hand, they are especially useful for immediately calming feelings of anxiety or apprehension. Individuals can use them when they are asked a question they cannot answer, when they become embarrassed by an unexpected event, when they are faced with a presentation or an important meeting, or almost any time they are suddenly stressed and must respond quickly.

Some brief relaxation tips are provided, and then five of the best known and easiest to learn temporary stress-reduction techniques are discussed.

Quick and convenient relaxation techniques

- Gain control of your breathing.
- Repeat a helpful quote or word.
- Visualise yourself in a tranquil place.
- Have a brain-to-brain talk.
- Use progressive relaxation.
- Get away from the noise.
- Use good scents.
- Lose the coffee.
- Laugh.

With more time and on a regular basis

- Exercise.
- Meditate.
- Get a massage.
- Practise yoga or tai chi.
- Take a brain power nap.
- Use guided imagery tapes.
- Take an aromatherapy bath.
- Listen to Mozart or other music.
- Use biofeedback or hypnotherapy.
- Take time-out: a short walk or a long holiday.
- Take a news fast: stop being a receptacle for the world's problems.

Muscle relaxation

Muscle relaxation involves easing the tension in successive muscle groups. Each muscle group is tightened for five to ten seconds and then completely relaxed. Starting with the feet and progressing to the calves, thighs, stomach, and on to the neck and face, this can relieve tension throughout the entire body. All parts of the body can be included in the exercise. One variation is to roll the head around on the neck several times, shrug the shoulders, stretch the arms up towards the ceiling for five to ten seconds, then release the position and relax the muscles. The result is a state of temporary relaxation that helps to eliminate tension and refocus energy.

Deep breathing

A variation of muscle relaxation involves deep breathing. This is done by taking several successive, slow, deep breaths, holding them for five seconds, then exhaling completely. You should focus on the act of breathing itself, so that the mind becomes cleared for a brief time while the body relaxes. After each deep breath, muscles in the body should consciously be relaxed.

Guided imagery

Another technique uses imagery and fantasy to eliminate stress temporarily by changing the focus of our thoughts. Imagery involves visualising an event, using 'mind pictures'. An increasingly common practice for athletes is to visualise a successful performance or to imagine themselves achieving their goal. Research has confirmed the stress-reduction advantages of this technique as well as the performance enhancement benefits (for example, Deepak 1995).

In addition to visualisation, imagery can also include recollections of sounds, smells and textures. Focus the mind on a pleasant experience from the past (for example, a fishing trip, a family holiday, a visit with relatives, a day at the beach) that can be recalled vividly. Fantasies, on the other hand, are not past memories but make-believe events or images. It is especially well known, for example, that children often construct imaginary friends, make-believe occurrences or special wishes that are comforting to them when they encounter stress. Adults also use daydreams or other fantasy experiences to get them through stressful situations. The purpose of this technique is to relieve anxiety or pressure temporarily by focusing on something pleasant. Other, more productive stress-reducing strategies can be developed over the long term.

Rehearsal

Using the rehearsal technique, people work themselves through potentially stressful situations, trying out different scenarios and alternative reactions. Appropriate reactions are rehearsed, either in a safe environment before stress occurs, or 'off-line', in private, in the midst of a stressful situation. Removing yourself temporarily from a stressful circumstance and working through dialogue or reactions, as though rehearsing for a play, can help you regain control and reduce the immediacy of the stressor.

Reframing

Reframing involves temporarily reducing stress by optimistically redefining a situation as manageable. Reframing serves as a key to developing hardiness and emotional intelligence. Although reframing is difficult in the midst of a stressful situation, it can be facilitated by silently reminding yourself:

- 'I understand this situation.'
- 'I've solved similar problems before.'
- 'Other people are available to help me get through this situation.'
- 'Others have faced similar situations and made it through.'
- 'In the long run, this really isn't so critical.'
- 'I can learn something from this situation.'
- 'There are several good alternatives available to me.'

With a strategy that engages both the physiological and psychological processes, Cryer, McCraty and Childre (2003) propose a 'freeze frame' process for breaking out of negative stress chain reactions. This process has five steps:

1. Recognise and disengage.
2. Breathe through your heart.
3. Involve a positive feeling.

4. Ask yourself if there is a better alternative.
5. Note the change in perspective.

Cryer et al. believe this 'freeze frame' process to be particularly useful for managers who become 'stress carriers', making everyone around them anxious and on edge.

Summary

Many kinds of stressors cause negative physiological, psychological and social reactions in individuals. These reactions are moderated by four levels of healthy responses to stress. A primary capacity is the resiliency that individuals have developed for coping with stress. The best way to manage stress and develop a healthy work culture is through healthy living, maintaining a positive work/life balance, time management, delegation, collaboration, interpersonal competence, work redesign, establishing priorities, goal setting and small wins. A major effective stress management strategy involves improving our resiliency. Physiological resiliency is strengthened through increased cardiovascular conditioning and improved diet. Psychological resiliency and hardiness is improved by practising small-wins strategies and deep relaxation. Social resiliency is increased by fostering teamwork among co-workers and mentoring relationships. These strategies produce long-term benefits, but they also take quite a long time to implement and maintain.

When circumstances make it impossible to apply longer-term strategies for reducing stress, short-term relaxation techniques can temporarily alleviate the symptoms of stress. These strategies have short-term consequences, but they can be applied immediately and repeated over and over again.

Behavioural guidelines

Following are some specific behavioural guidelines for improving your stress management skills.

1. Use effective time management practices. Make sure that you use time effectively as well as efficiently by generating your own personal mission statement. Ensure that low-priority tasks do not drive out time to work on high-priority activities. Make better use of your time by using the guidelines in the time management survey in the assessment section.
2. Build collaborative relationships with individuals based on mutual trust, respect, honesty and kindness. Make 'deposits' into the 'emotional bank accounts' of other people. Form close, stable communities among those with whom you work.
3. Consciously work to improve your emotional intelligence or interpersonal competency by learning and practising the principles discussed in other chapters of this book (for example, communicating supportively, managing conflict, empowering and delegating).
4. Redesign your work to increase its skill variety, importance, task identity (comprehensiveness), autonomy and feedback. Make the work itself stress-reducing, rather than stress-inducing.
5. Reaffirm priorities and short-term plans that provide direction and focus to activities. Give important activities priority over urgent ones.
6. Increase your general resiliency by leading a balanced life and consciously developing yourself in physical, intellectual, cultural, social, family and spiritual areas, as well as in your work.
7. Increase your physical resiliency by engaging in a regular program of exercise, as well as eating properly.
8. Increase your psychological resiliency and hardiness by implementing a small-wins strategy. Identify and celebrate the small successes that you and others achieve.
9. Learn at least one deep-relaxation technique and practise it regularly.
10. Establish a teamwork relationship with those with whom you work or study by identifying shared tasks and structuring coordinated action among team members.
11. Increase social resiliency by forming an open, trusting, sharing relationship with at least one other person. Facilitate a mentoring relationship with someone who can affirm your worth as a person and provide support during periods of stress.
12. Learn at least two short-term relaxation techniques and practise them consistently.

Skill analysis

Case study involving stress management

The day at the beach

Not long ago I came to one of those bleak periods that many of us encounter from time to time, a sudden drastic dip in the graph of living when everything goes stale and flat, energy wanes, enthusiasm dies. The effect on my work was frightening. Every morning I would clench my teeth and mutter: 'Today life will take on some of its old meaning. You've got to break through this thing. You've got to!'

But the barren days went by, and the paralysis grew worse. The time came when I knew I had to get help.

The man I turned to was a doctor. Not a psychiatrist, just a doctor. He was older than I, and under his surface gruffness lay great wisdom and compassion. 'I don't know what's wrong,' I told him despairingly, 'but I just seem to have come to a dead end. Can you help me?'

'I don't know,' he said slowly. He made a tent with his fingers and gazed at me thoughtfully for a long while. Then, abruptly, he asked, 'Where were you happiest as a child?'

'As a child?' I echoed. 'Why, at the beach, I suppose. We had a weekender there. We all loved it.'

He looked out of the window and watched the autumn leaves drifting down. 'Are you capable of following instructions for a single day?'

'I think so,' I said, ready to try anything.

'All right. Here's what I want you to do.'

He told me to drive to the beach alone the following morning, arriving not later than nine o'clock. I could take some lunch, but I was not to read, write, listen to the radio or talk to anyone. 'In addition,' he said, 'I'll give you a prescription to be taken every three hours.'

He then tore off four prescription blanks, wrote a few words on each, folded them, numbered them and handed them to me. 'Take these at nine, twelve, three and six.'

'Are you serious?' I asked.

He gave a short bark of laughter. 'You won't think I'm joking when you get my bill!'

The next morning, with little faith, I drove to the beach. It was lonely, all right. A southerly was blowing; the sea looked grey and angry. I sat in the car, the whole day stretching emptily before me. Then I took out the first of the folded slips of paper. On it was written: '**Listen carefully**.'

I stared at the two words. 'The man must be mad,' I thought. He had ruled out music and newscasts and human conversation. What else was there?

I raised my head and I did listen. There were no sounds but the steady roar of the sea, the creaking cry of a seagull, the drone of some aircraft high overhead. All these sounds were familiar. I got out of the car. A gust of wind slammed the door with a sudden clap of sound. 'Was I supposed to listen carefully to things like that?' I asked myself.

I climbed a sandhill and looked out over the deserted beach. Here the sea bellowed so loudly that all other sounds were lost. And yet, I thought suddenly, there must be sounds beneath sounds—the soft rasp of drifting sand, the tiny wind-whisperings in the beach grasses—if the listener got close enough to hear them.

On an impulse I ducked down and, feeling fairly ridiculous, thrust my head into a clump of seaweed. Here I made a discovery: if you listen intently, there is a fractional moment in which everything seems to pause, wait. In that instant of stillness, the racing thoughts halt. For a moment, when you truly listen for something outside yourself, you have to silence the clamorous voices within. The mind rests.

I went back to the car and slid behind the wheel. **Listen carefully**. As I listened again to the deep growl of the sea, I found myself thinking about the white-fanged fury of its storms.

I thought of the lessons it had taught us as children. A certain amount of patience: you can't hurry the tides. A great deal of respect: the sea does not suffer fools gladly. An awareness of the vast and

ANALYSIS

mysterious interdependence of things: wind and tide and current, calm and squall and hurricane, all combining to determine the paths of the birds above and the fish below. And the cleanness of it all, with every beach swept twice a day by the great broom of the sea.

Sitting there, I realised I was thinking of things bigger than myself—and there was relief in that.

Even so, the morning passed slowly. The habit of hurling myself at a problem was so strong that I felt lost without it. Once, when I was wistfully eyeing the car radio, a phrase from Carlyle jumped into my head: 'Silence is the element in which great things fashion themselves.'

By noon the wind had polished the clouds out of the sky and the sea had a hard, merry sparkle. I unfolded the second 'prescription'. And again I sat there, half-amused and half-exasperated. Three words this time: '**Try reaching back**.'

Back to what? To the past, obviously. But why, when all my worries concerned the present or the future?

I left the car and started tramping reflectively on the firm sand. The doctor had sent me to the beach because it was a place of happy memories. Maybe that was what I was supposed to reach for: the wealth of happiness that lay half-forgotten behind me.

I decided to experiment: to work on these vague impressions as a painter would, retouching the colours, strengthening the outlines. I would choose specific incidents and recapture as many details as possible. I would visualise people complete with dress and gestures. I would listen (carefully) for the exact sound of their voices, the echo of their laughter.

The tide was going out now, but there was still thunder in the surf. So I chose to go back 20 years to the last fishing trip I made with my younger brother, who had died some years ago. I found that if I closed my eyes and really tried, I could see him with amazing vividness, even the humour and eagerness in his eyes that far-off morning.

In fact, I could see it all: the ivory scimitar of beach where we were fishing; the eastern sky smeared with sunrise; the great rollers creaming in, stately and slow. I could feel the backwash swirl warm around my knees, see the sudden arc of my brother's rod as he struck a fish, hear his exultant yell. Piece by piece I rebuilt it, clear and unchanged under the transparent varnish of time. Then it was gone.

I sat up slowly. **Try reaching back**. Happy people were usually assured, confident people. If, then, you deliberately reached back and touched happiness, might there not be released little flashes of power, tiny sources of strength?

This second period of the day went more quickly. As the sun began its long slant down the sky, my mind ranged eagerly through the past, reliving some episodes, uncovering others that had been completely forgotten. For example, when I was around 13 and my brother 10, our father had promised to take us to the circus. But at lunch there was a phone call: some urgent business required his attention at the office. We braced ourselves for disappointment. Then we heard him say, 'No, I won't be in. It'll have to wait.'

When he came back to the table, our mother smiled. 'The circus keeps coming back, you know.'

'I know,' said Dad. 'But childhood doesn't.'

Across all the years I remembered this and knew from the sudden glow of warmth that no kindness is ever wasted or ever completely lost.

By three o'clock the tide was out and the sound of the waves was only a rhythmic whisper, like a giant breathing. I stayed in my sandy nest, feeling relaxed and content—and a little complacent. The doctor's prescriptions, I thought, were not too hard to take.

But I was not prepared for the next one. This time the three words were not a gentle suggestion. They sounded more like a command. '**Re-examine your motives**.'

My first reaction was purely defensive. 'There's nothing wrong with my motives,' I said to myself. 'I want to be successful—who doesn't? I want to have a certain amount of recognition—but so does everybody. I want more security than I've got—and why not?'

'Maybe,' said a small voice somewhere inside my head, 'those motives aren't good enough. Maybe that's the reason the wheels have stopped going round.'

I picked up a handful of sand and let it stream between my fingers. In the past, whenever my work went well there had always been something spontaneous about it, something uncontrived, something free. Lately it had been calculated, competent—and dead. Why? Because I had been looking past the job itself to the rewards I hoped it would bring. The work had ceased to be an end in itself; it had been merely a means to make money, pay bills. The sense of giving something, of helping people, of making a contribution, had been lost in a frantic clutch at security.

In a flash of certainty I saw that if one's motives are wrong, nothing can be right. It makes no difference whether you are a postman, a hairdresser, an insurance salesperson, a housewife—whatever. As long as you feel you are serving others, you do the job well. When you are concerned only with helping yourself, you do it less well. There is a law as inexorable as gravity.

For a long time I sat there. Far out on the bar I heard the murmur of the surf change to a hollow roar as the tide turned. Behind me the spears of light were almost horizontal. My time at the beach had almost run out, and I felt a grudging admiration for the doctor and the 'prescriptions' he had so casually and cunningly devised. I saw, now, that in them was a therapeutic progression that might well be of value to anyone facing any difficulty.

Listen carefully—to calm a frantic mind, slow it down, shift the focus from inner problems to outer things.

Try reaching back—since the human mind can hold but one idea at a time, you blot out present worry when you touch the happiness of the past.

Re-examine your motives—this was the hard core of the 'treatment', this challenge to reappraise, to bring one's motives into alignment with one's capabilities and conscience. But the mind must be clear and receptive to do this—hence the six hours of quiet that went before.

The western sky was a blaze of crimson as I took out the last slip of paper. Six words this time. I walked slowly out on the beach. A few yards below the high-water mark I stopped and read the words again: '**Write your troubles on the sand**.'

I let the paper blow into the sea, reached down and picked up a fragment of shell. Kneeling there under the vault of the sky, I wrote several words on the sand, one above the other. Then I walked away, and I did not look back. I had written my troubles on the sand. And the tide was coming in.

Source: A. Gordon, 'A day at the beach', *Reader's Digest*, 1959. Reprinted by permission of Pamela McGuire Gordon.

DISCUSSION QUESTIONS

1. *What is effective about these strategies for coping with stress? Why did they work? On what principles are they based?*
2. *Which of these techniques can be used on a temporary basis without going to the beach?*
3. *Are these prescriptions effective coping strategies or merely escapes?*
4. *What other prescriptions could the author take besides the four mentioned here? Generate your own list based on your experience of stress.*

Skill practice

Exercises for managing stress

This section provides some short exercises to help you practise good stress management. We strongly urge you to complete the exercises with a partner who can give you feedback and who will monitor your progress in improving your skill. Because managing stress is a personal skill, most of your practice will be done in private. But having a partner who is aware of your commitment will help foster substantial improvement.

The small-wins strategy

An ancient Chinese proverb says that long journeys are always made up of small steps. In Japan, the feeling of obligation to make small, incremental improvements in one's work is known as '*kaizen*'. In this chapter, the notion of small wins was explained as a way to break apart large problems and identify small successes in coping with them. Each of these approaches represents the same basic philosophy—to recognise incremental successes—and each helps individuals to build up their psychological resiliency to stress.

Assignment

Answer the following questions. An example is given to help clarify each question, but your response need not relate to the example.

1. What major stressor do you currently face? What creates anxiety or discomfort for you? (For example, 'I have too much to do.')
2. What are the major attributes or components of the situation? Divide the major problem into smaller parts or sub-problems. (For example,'I have said "yes" to too many things. I have deadlines approaching. I don't have all the resources I need to complete all my commitments right now.')
3. What are the sub-components of each of those sub-problems? Divide them into yet smaller parts. (For example, 'I have the following deadlines approaching: a report due, a large amount of reading to do, a family obligation, an important presentation, a need to spend some personal time with someone I care about, a committee meeting that requires preparation.')
   Attribute 1:
   Attribute 2:
   Attribute 3:
   And so on:
4. What actions can I take that will affect any of these sub-components? (For example, 'I can engage the person I care about in helping me prepare for the presentation. I can write a shorter report than I originally intended. I can carry the reading material with me wherever I go.')
5. What actions have I taken in the past that have helped me cope successfully with similar stressful circumstances? (For example, 'I have found someone else to share some of my tasks. I have done some reading while waiting, travelling and eating. I have prepared only key elements for the committee meeting.')
6. What small thing should I feel good about as I think about how I have coped or will cope with this major stressor? (For example, 'I have accomplished a lot when the pressure has been on in the past. I have been able to use what I had time to prepare to its best advantage.')

Repeat this process each time you face major stressors. The six specific questions may not be as important to you as:

- breaking the problem down into incremental parts and then breaking those parts down again
- identifying actions that can be done, and have been done in the past, that have been successful in coping with components of the stressor.

Work/life balance analysis

The prescription to maintain a balanced life seems both intuitive and counter-intuitive. On the one hand, it makes sense that life should have variety and that each of us should develop multiple aspects of ourselves. Narrowness and rigidity are not highly valued by anyone. On the other hand, the demands of work, study or family, for example, can be so overwhelming that we do not have time to do much except respond to those demands. Work could take all of our time. So could study. So could family. The temptation for most of us, then, is to focus on the few areas of our lives that place a great deal of pressure on us and leave the other areas undeveloped. This exercise helps you discover which areas need more attention.

Assignment

Use Figure 3.5 (on page 134) to complete this exercise. In responding to the seven segments that make up the figure, think of the amount of time you spend in each area, the amount of experience and development you have had in the past in each area, and the extent to which development in each area is important to you.

1. In Figure 3.5, shade in the portion of each segment that represents the extent to which that aspect of your life has been well developed. How satisfied are you that each aspect is adequately cultivated?
2. Now write down at least one thing you can start doing to improve your development in the areas that need it. For example, you might do more general reading to develop culturally, invite a foreign visitor to your home to develop socially, enrol in a management course to develop career opportunities, begin a regular exercise program, and so on.
3. Because the intent of this exercise is not to add more pressure and stress to your life but to increase your resiliency through life balance, identify the things you will stop doing that will make it possible to achieve better life balance.
4. To make this a practice exercise and not just a planning exercise, do something today that you have on your list for items 2 and 3 above. Write down specifically what you will do and when. Do not let the rest of the week go by without implementing something you have written.

Deep relaxation

To engage in deep relaxation, you need to reserve time that can be spent concentrating on relaxing. Cognitive control and physiological control are involved. By focusing your mind, you can positively affect both your mental and your physical state. This exercise describes one technique that is easily learned and practised.

The deep-relaxation technique presented below combines key elements of several well-known formulas. It is recommended that this technique be practised for 20 minutes a day, three times a week. Reserve at least 30 minutes to engage in this exercise for the first time.

Find a quiet spot with a partner. (You may want to do this in the classroom itself the first time.) Have that person read the instructions below. Do not rush through the instructions. Allow time between each step to complete it unrushed. When you have finished, switch roles. (Since you will be practising this exercise later in a different setting, you may want to make a recording of these instructions. Alternatively, agree to do the exercise regularly with a friend or partner.)

Assignment

Step 1 *Assume a comfortable position.* You may want to lie down. Loosen any tight clothing. Close your eyes and be quiet.

Step 2 *Assume a passive attitude.* Focus on your body and on relaxing specific muscles. Tune out all other thoughts.

Step 3 *Tense and relax each of your muscle groups for five to ten seconds,* in the following order:

Forehead: wrinkle your forehead. Try to make your eyebrows touch your hairline for five seconds, then relax.

Eyes and nose: close your eyes as tightly as you can for five seconds, then relax.

Lips, cheeks and jaw: draw the corners of your mouth back and grimace for five seconds, then relax.

Hands: extend your arms in front of you, clench your fists tightly for five seconds, then relax.

Forearms: extend your arms out against an invisible wall and push forward for five seconds, then relax.

Upper arms: bend your elbows and tense your biceps for five seconds, then relax.

Shoulders: shrug your shoulders up to your ears for five seconds, then relax.

Back: arch your back off the floor for five seconds, then relax.

Stomach: tighten your stomach muscles by lifting your legs off the ground about five centimetres for five seconds, then relax.

Hips and buttocks: tighten your hip and buttock muscles for five seconds, then relax.

Thighs: tighten your thigh muscles by pressing your legs together as tightly as you can for five seconds, then relax.

Feet: bend your ankles towards your body as far as you can for five seconds, then point your toes for five seconds, then relax.

Toes: curl your toes as tightly as you can for five seconds, then relax.

Step 4 *Focus on any muscles that are still tense.* Repeat the exercise for that muscle group three or four times until it relaxes.

Step 5 *Now focus on your breathing.* Do not alter it artificially, but focus on taking long, slow breaths. Concentrate exclusively on the rhythm of your breathing until you have taken at least 45 breaths.

Step 6 *Now focus on the heaviness and warmth of your body.* Let all the energy in your body seep away. Let go of your normal tendency to control your body and mobilise it towards activity.

Step 7 *With your body completely relaxed, relax your mind.* Picture a plain object such as a glass ball, an empty white vase, the moon or a favourite thing. Do not analyse it; do not examine it; just picture it. Concentrate fully on the object for at least three minutes without letting any other thoughts enter your mind. Begin now.

Step 8 *Now open your eyes, slowly get up, and return to your hectic, stressful, anxiety-ridden Type A environment, better prepared to cope with it effectively.*

(Guided relaxation audiotapes are available from a number of retail outlets, including the Australian Institute of Management's bookshop.)

Monitoring and managing time

Time management is the main problem identified most often by managers and business school students. Most people feel overwhelmed at least part of the time with having too much to accomplish in too little time. It is interesting, however, that even though people may be extremely busy, if they feel that their time is discretionary—that is, it can be used in any way that they choose, such as in recreation, playing with friends or family, or by themselves—they feel less stress. Increasing discretionary time, therefore, is a key to effective time management. This exercise helps you to identify and better manage your discretionary time. It takes one full week to complete. It requires that you record how you spend your time for the next seven days. Virtually every executive who is a good time manager has completed this exercise and, in fact, regularly repeats it.

Assignment

Complete the following five steps, then use a partner or close friend to get feedback and ideas for improving and refining your plans.

Step 1 Beginning today, keep a time log for a whole week. Record how you spend each 30-minute block in the next seven 24-hour periods. Using the following format, record the log in your own notebook, diary or journal. Simply write down what you did during each 30-minute period. If you did a number of things, record them one above the other.

Time	Activity	Required/Discretionary	Productive/Unproductive
1.00–1.30			
1.30–2.00			
2.00–2.30			
.			
.			
.			
23.00–23.30			
23.30–24.00			

PRACTICE

Step 2 Beneath the heading 'Required/Discretionary', write whether the time spent in each 30-minute block was required by someone or something else (R) or was discretionary (D). That is, to what extent did you have a choice about whether or not you would engage in this activity? You do not have a choice about a certain amount of sleep, for example, or attending class. But you do have a choice about watching TV or spending time socialising.

Step 3 Beneath the heading 'Productive/Unproductive', rate the extent to which each activity was productive. That is, identify the extent to which the activity achieved what it was intended to achieve. To what extent did the activity accomplish your own goals or lead to improvements of some kind? Use the following scale for your rating:

4 Used productively
3 Used somewhat productively
2 Used somewhat unproductively
1 Used unproductively

Step 4 Draw up a plan for increasing the amount of discretionary time you have during the week. Refer to the time management survey in the assessment section for suggestions. Write down the things you will stop doing and start doing.

Step 5 Identify ways in which you can use your discretionary time more productively, especially any blocks of time you rated 1 or 2 in step 3. What will you do to make sure the time you control is used for more long-term benefit? What will you stop doing that impedes your effective use of time?

Skill application

Suggested assignments

1. Do a systematic analysis of the stressors you face in your job, family, university and social life. List the types of stressors you face and identify strategies to eliminate or sharply reduce them. Record this analysis in your journal.
2. Find someone you know well who is experiencing a great deal of stress. Teach them how to manage that stress better by applying the concepts, principles, techniques and exercises in this chapter. Describe what you taught the person and record the results in your journal.
3. Implement at least three of the time-management techniques suggested in the time-management survey or elsewhere that you are not currently using but think you might find helpful. In your time log, keep track of the amount of time these techniques save you over a one-month period. Be sure to use that extra time productively.
4. With a co-worker or colleague, identify ways in which your work at university, office or home can be redesigned to reduce stress and increase productivity. Use the hints provided in the chapter to guide your redesign.
5. Write a personal mission statement. Specify precisely: your core principles; those things you consider to be central to your life and your sense of self-worth; and the legacy you want to leave. Identify at least one action you can take in order to accomplish that mission statement. Begin working on it today.
6. Identify the most important roles you perform at work, at home and in the community.
7. Establish a short-term goal or plan that you wish to accomplish this year. Make it compatible with the top priorities in your life. Specify the behavioural action steps, the reporting and accounting mechanisms, and the criteria of success and rewards, as outlined in Figure 3.6. Share this plan with others you know so that you have an incentive to pursue it even after you finish this class.

8. Get a physical examination, then outline and implement a regular physical fitness and diet program. Even if it is just regular walking, do some kind of physical exercise at least three times a week. Preferably, institute a regular, vigorous cardiovascular fitness program. Record your progress in your journal.
9. Pick at least one long-term deep-relaxation technique. Learn it and practise it on a regular basis. Record your progress in your journal.
10. Establish a mentoring relationship with someone with whom you work or go to university. Your mentor may be a professor, a senior manager or someone who has been around longer than you have. Make certain that the relationship is reciprocal and that it will help you cope with the stresses you face at work or university.

Application plan and evaluation

The intent of this exercise is to help you apply this cluster of skills in a real-life, out-of-class setting. Now that you have become familiar with the behavioural guidelines that form the basis of effective skill performance, you will improve most by trying out those guidelines in an everyday context. Unlike a classroom activity, in which feedback is immediate and others can assist you with their evaluations, this skill application activity is one you must accomplish and evaluate on your own. There are two parts to the activity. Part 1 helps to prepare you to apply the skill. Part 2 helps you to evaluate and improve on your experience. Be sure to write down answers to each item. Do not short-circuit the process by skipping steps.

Part 1: Planning

1. Having chosen an assignment from the above options, write down the two or three aspects of the particular skill you are developing. These aspects may be areas of weakness, areas you most want to improve, or areas that are most salient to a problem you are facing right now. Identify the specific aspects of this skill that you want to apply.
2. Now identify the setting or the situation in which you will apply this skill. Establish a plan for performance by writing down a description of the situation. Who else will be involved? When will you do it? Where will it be done?
3. Identify the specific behaviours you will engage in to apply this skill. How will you put these behaviours into operation?
4. What are the indicators of successful performance? How will you know you have been effective? What will indicate that you have performed competently?

Part 2: Evaluation

5. When you have completed your implementation, record the results. What happened? How successful were you? What was the effect on others?
6. How can you improve? What modifications can you make next time? What will you do differently in a similar situation in the future?
7. Looking back on your whole skill practice and application experience, what have you learned? What has been surprising? In what ways might this experience help you in the long term?

Scoring keys and supplementary materials

Stress management (p. 124)

SCORING KEY

Skill area	*Items*	ASSESSMENT *Pre-*	*Post*
Eliminating stressors	1, 5, 8, 9	________	________
Developing resiliency	2, 3, 6, 7	________	________
Short-term coping	4, 10	________	________
	TOTAL SCORE	☐	☐

Comparison data

Compare your scores with three comparison standards:

1. Compare your score against the maximum possible (72).
2. Compare your scores with the scores of other students in your class.
3. Compare your scores with a norm group consisting of 500 business school students. In comparison with the norm group, if you scored:

50 or above	you are in the top quartile
45–49	you are in the second quartile
40–44	you are in the third quartile
39 or below	you are in the bottom quartile.

Time management (p. 125)

SCORING KEY

To determine how effective you are as a manager of your time, give yourself the following number of points for the boxes you ticked:

POINTS	FREQUENCY
0	Never
1	Seldom
2	Sometimes
3	Usually
4	Always

If you completed only Section I of the instrument, double the scores for each category.

Add up your total points for the 40 items. If you scored 120 or above, you are an excellent manager of your time, both personally and at work. If you scored between 100 and 120, you are doing a good job of managing your time, and making a few refinements or implementing a few hints will help you achieve excellence. If you scored between 80 and 100, you should consider improving your time management skills. If you scored below 80, training in time management will considerably enhance your efficiency.

Note: Sometimes people have markedly different scores in the two sections of this instrument. That is, they are better time managers at the office than in their personal lives, or vice versa. You may want to calculate your scores for each section of the instrument and compare them.

Social readjustment rating scale (p. 126)

Holmes and Rahe consider a score of less than 150 to be minor stress. Those who score 150–199 are experiencing mild stress, those who score 200–299 are experiencing moderate stress, and a score over 300 is someone experiencing major stress. It is estimated that 35 per cent of those with a score below 150 will experience an illness or accident within two years, those with a score between 150 and 300 have a 51 per cent chance of experiencing an illness or accident within two years, and those with a score of over 300 have an 80 per cent chance of having a significant illness oraccident.

You might not be able to control the stressful events in your life, but you do have control over your response to them and the effect that they have on your life. The negative effects of stress can be reduced by such things as getting enough rest, exercise, good nutrition, and taking some time for yourself.

References

Adler, C. M. and J. J. Hillhouse 1996, 'Stress, health, and immunity: A review of literature', in T. W. Miller (ed.), *Theory and Assessment of Stressful Life Events* (Madison, CT: International University Press).

Anderson, C. R. 1977, 'Locus of control, coping behaviors and performance in a stress setting: A longitudinal study', *Journal of Applied Psychology*, 62, pp. 446–51.

Appelbaum, S. H., S. Ritchie and B. T. Shapiro 1994, 'Mentoring revisited: An organizational behaviour construct', *Journal of Management Development*, 13(4), pp. 62–72.

Auerbach, S. M. 1998, *Stress Management: Psychological Foundations* (Upper Saddle River, NJ: Prentice Hall).

Australian Institute of Health and Welfare 1991, *National Health Survey 1989–90: Summary of Results* (Canberra: ABS).

Balzer, W. K., M. E. Doherty and R. O'Connor 1989, 'Effects of cognitive feedback on performance', *Psychological Bulletin*, 106, pp. 410–33.

Bandura, A. 1997, *Self-efficacy: The Exercise of Control* (New York: W. H. Freeman).

Bell, C. R. 1998, *Managers as Mentors* (San Francisco: Barrett Koehler).

Cameron, K. S. 1994, 'Strategies for successful organizational downsizing', *Human Resource Management Journal*, 33, pp. 189–212.

Cameron, K. S. and D. A. Whetten 1987, 'Organizational dysfunctions of decline', *Academy of Management Journal*, 30, pp. 126–38.

Cameron, K. S., S. Freeman and A. K. Mishra 1990, 'Effective organizational downsizing: Paradoxical processes and best practices', *Academy of Management Executive*, 5, pp. 57–73.

Conway, C. 1995, 'Mentoring in the mainstream', *Management Development Review*, 8(4), pp. 27–29.

Cordes, C. L. and T. W. Dougherty 1993, 'Review and an integration of research on job burnout', *Academy of Management Review*, 18, pp. 621–56.

Correll, M. 2005, 'Workload management', unpublished paper.

Covey, S. 1989, *Seven Habits of Highly Effective People* (New York: Wiley).

Cowley, J. 2000, 'Stress-busters: What works', *Newsweek*, 14 June, p. 60.

Cryer, B., R. McCraty and D. Childre 2003, 'Managing yourself: Pull the plug on stress', *Harvard Business Review*, July, pp. 102–7. ,

Dahl-Hansen E., R. Treeby, N. Al-Masker, R. Doig, R. Keulemans and S. Lerman 2005, *Managing Workplace Stress* (London: OGP-IPIECA Health Committee).

Davidson, J. 1995, *Managing Your Time* (Indianapolis, IN: Alpha Books).

Deepak, M. D. 1995, *Creating Health: How to Wake Up the Body's Intelligence* (New York: Houghton Mifflin).

Deveson, A. 2003, *Resilience* (Sydney: Allen & Unwin).

Elliot, R. S. and D. L. Breo 1984, *Is it Worth Dying for?* (New York: Bantam Books).

Farnham, A. 1991, 'Who beats stress and how?', *Fortune*, October, pp. 771–86.

Fisher, C. and R. Gitelson 1983, 'A meta-analysis of the correlates of role conflict and role ambiguity', *Journal of Applied Psychology*, 68, pp. 320–33.

French, J. R. P. and R. D. Caplan 1972, 'Organizational stress and individual strain', in J. Marrow (ed.), *The Failure of Success* (New York: AMACOM).

Frost, P. and S. Robinson 1999, 'The toxic handler: Organizational hero—and casualty', *Harvard Business Review*, July–August, pp. 97–106.

Goleman, D. 1995, *Emotional Intelligence* (New York: Bantam).

Goleman, D. 1998, *Working with Emotional Intelligence* (New York: Bantam Books).

Greist, J. H., M. H. Klein, R. R. Eischens, J. Faris, A. S. Gurman and W. P. Morgan 1979, 'Running as treatment for depression', *Comparative Psychiatry*, 20(1), January–February, pp. 41–54.

Helpguide.org, 'Understanding Stress: Symptoms, Signs, Causes and Effects', <http://helpguide.org/mental/stress_signs.htm>, accessed 22 November 2011.
Hendricks, W. 1996, *Coaching, Mentoring, and Managing* (Franklin Lakes, NJ: Career Press).
Hepburn, G. C., C. A. McLoughlin and J. Barling 1997, 'Coping with chronic work stress', in H. Gottlieb (ed.), *Coping with Chronic Stress* (New York: Plenum).
Herman, R. and J. Gioia 2006, 'Skills for future success', *Herman Trend Alert*, 26 January.
Hobson, C., J. Kamen, J. Szostek, C. Nethercut, J. Tiedmann and S. Wojnarowicz 1998, 'Stressful life events: A revision and update of the Social Readjustment Rating Scale', *International Journal of Stress Management*, 5(1), pp. 1–23.
Holmes, T. H. and R. H. Rahe 1970, 'The social readjustment rating scale', *Journal of Psychosomatic Research*, 14, pp. 121–32.
Ivancevich, J. and D. Ganster 1987, *Job Stress: From Theory to Suggestions* (New York: Haworth).
Ivancevich, J. M. and M. T. Matteson 1980, *Stress and Work: A Managerial Perspective* (Glenview, IL: Scott Foresman).
Kahn, R., D. Wolf, R. Quinn, J. Snoek and R. Rosenthal 1964, *Organizational Stress: Studies in Role Conflict and Ambiguity* (New York: Wiley).
Karasek, R. A., T. Theorell, J. E. Schwartz, P. L. Schnall, C. F. Pieper and J. L. Michela 1988, 'Job characteristics in relation to the prevalence of myocardial infarction in the US Health Examination Survey and the Health and Nutrition Examination Survey', *American Journal of Public Health*, 78, pp. 910–18.
Kelleher, P. 1999, 'Let me stress', *Management Today*, August, pp. 15–19.
Kobasa, S. 1982, 'Commitment and coping in stress resistance among lawyers', *Journal of Personality and Social Psychology*, 42, pp. 707–17.
Koch, B. 2007, 'Zen and the art of time management', *Professional Services Journal*, 20 February.
Kram, K. 1985, *Mentoring at Work* (Glenview, IL: Scott Foresman).
Lagan, A. 1995, 'Managing through values', *City Ethics*, 20 (St James Ethics Centre, Sydney).
Lakein, D. 1989, *How to Get Control of Your Time and Your Life* (New York: McKay).
Lambert, V., C. E. Lambert and Y. Hiroaki 2003, 'Psychological hardiness, workplace stress and related stress reduction strategies', *Nursing & Health Sciences*, 5(2), pp. 181–4.
Lehrer, P. M. 1996, *The Hatherleigh Guide to Issues in Modern Therapy* (New York: Hatherleigh Press).
Liu, Y. and H. Tanaka 2002, 'Overtime work, insufficient sleep, and risk of non-fatal acute myocardial infarction in Japanese men', *Journal of Occupational and Environmental Medicine*, 59, pp. 447–51.
Livingston, G. 2004, *Too Soon Old, Too Late Smart* (New York: Avalon Publishing Group).
Livingston, G. 2006, *Never Stop Dancing* (New York: Avalon Publishing Group).
Locke, E. and G. Latham 1990, *A Theory of Goal Setting and Task Performance* (Upper Saddle River, NJ: Prentice Hall).
Mackay, H. 1999, *Turning Point* (Sydney: Macmillan).
Maddi, S. and S. C. Kobasa 1984, *The Hardy Executive: Health under Stress* (Homewood, IL: Dow Jones-Irwin).
McPhee Andrewartha 2007, amended 'Healthy and Toxic Workplace' models by James Reason (1997).
MedicineNet.com, 'Stress and Heart Disease', <http://medicinenet.com/stress_and_heart_disease/page2.htm>, accessed 22 November 2011.
Mednick, M. T. 1982, 'Woman and the psychology of achievement: Implications for personal and social change', in H. J. Bernardin (ed.), *Women in the Workforce* (New York: Praeger).
Milgram, S. 1963, 'Behavioral study of obedience', *Journal of Abnormal and Social Psychology*, 63, pp. 371–8.
Mishra, A. K. 1993, 'Organizational responses to crisis', unpublished doctoral dissertation, University of Michigan.
Murphy, L. R. 1996, 'Stress management in work settings: A critical review of health effects', *American Journal of Health Promotion*, 11, pp. 112–35.
Office of the Employee Ombudsman 2002, *Bullies Not Wanted: Recognising and Eliminating Bullying in the Workplace* (Adelaide: AP Printing Group).
Peters, T. 1988, *Thriving on Chaos* (New York: Knopf).
Peterson, C. I. 1999, 'Perspectives in occupational health and safety', in C. Mayhew and C. L. Peterson (eds), *Occupational Health and Safety in Australia: Industry, Public Sector and Small Business* (Sydney: Allen & Unwin).
Pfeffer, J. 1998, *The Human Equation: Building Profits by Putting People First* (Boston: Harvard Business School Press).
Pope, N. and P. Berry 1995, 'Australia: Top down approach works', *Australian Financial Review*, 11 July.
Rahe, R. H., D. H. Ryman and H. W. Ward 1980, 'Simplified scaling for life change events', *Journal of Human Stress*, 6, pp. 22–27.
Reason, J. 1997, *Managing the Risks of Organisational Accidents* (Aldershot, UK: Ashgate Publishing Limited).
ReliaStar Life Insurance Company 1992, *Employee Burnout: Causes and Cures* (Minneapolis, MN: Northwestern National Life Insurance Company).
Roberts, P. 1995, 'The steps Ford took to solve the absenteeism problem', *Australian Financial Review*, August.
Rostad, F. G. and B. C. Long 1996, 'Exercise as a coping strategy for stress: A review', *International Journal of Sport Psychology*, 27, pp. 197–222.
Sailer, H. R., J. Schlacter and M. R. Edwards 1982, 'Stress: Causes, consequences, and coping strategies', *Personnel*, July–August.
Schachter, S. 1959, *The Psychology of Affiliation: Experimental Studies of the Sources of Gregariousness* (Stanford, CA: Stanford University Press).
Seligman, M. 2011, 'Building resilience', *Harvard Business Review*, April.

Sharpley, C. 1999, 'The hidden cost of stress', *HR Monthly*, August, p. 36.
Singh, J. 1993, 'Boundary role ambiguity: Facts, determinants, and impacts', *Journal of Marketing*, 57, pp. 11–30.
Singh, J. 1998, 'Striking balance in boundary-spanning positions: An investigation of some unconventional influences of role stressors and job characteristics on job outcomes or salespeople', *Journal of Marketing*, 62, pp. 69–86.
Sorenson, M. J. 1998, *Breaking the Chain of Low Self-esteem* (Portland, OR: Wolf Publications).
Staw, B. M., L. Sandelands and J. Dutton 1981, 'Threat-rigidity effects in organizational behavior', *Administrative Science Quarterly*, 26, pp. 501–24.
Thoits, P. A. 1995, 'Stress, coping, and social support processes: Where are we? What next?', *Journal of Health and Social Behavior*, 36, pp. 53–79.
Toohey, J. 1995, 'Managing the stress phenomenon at work', in *Psychological Health in the Workplace: Understanding and Managing Occupational Stress* (Melbourne: Australian Psychological Society), pp. 59–66.
Trompenaars, F. 1996, 'Resolving international conflict: Culture and business strategy', *Business Strategy Review*, 7, pp. 51–68.
Trompenaars, F. and C. Hampden-Turner 1999, *Riding the Waves of Culture*, 2nd ed. (New York: McGraw-Hill).
Weick, K. 1979, *The Social Psychology of Organizing* (Reading, MA: Addison-Wesley).
Weick, K. E. 1993, 'The collapse of sensemaking in organizations', *Administrative Science Quarterly*, 38, pp. 628–52.
Whetten, D. and K. Cameron 1998, *Developing Management Skills*, 4th ed. (Reading, MA: Addison-Wesley).
Wolff, H. G., S. G. Wolf and C. C. Hare (eds) 1950, *Life Stress and Bodily Disease* (Baltimore, MD: Williams and Wilkins).
Wolman, B. B. 1982, *Psychological Aspects of Obesity: A Handbook* (New York: Von Nostrand Reinhold).
World Health Organization 2000, *World Health Report 2000* (Geneva: WHO).

CHAPTER 4

SOLVING PROBLEMS ANALYTICALLY AND CREATIVELY

OBJECTIVES

- **Increase proficiency in analytical problem solving**
- **Recognise personal conceptual blocks**
- **Enhance creativity by overcoming conceptual blocks**
- **Foster innovation among others**

4

CHAPTER OUTLINE

Skill assessment

Evaluative surveys for creative problem solving

- Problem solving, creativity and innovation
- How creative are you?
- Innovative attitude scale

Skill learning

Problem solving, creativity and innovation

Steps in rational problem solving

Limitations of the analytical problem-solving model

Impediments to creative problem solving

Conceptual blocks

Conceptual blockbusting

Cultural considerations

Hints for applying problem-solving techniques

Fostering innovation

Summary

Behavioural guidelines

Skill analysis

Case study involving problem solving

- Creativity at Apple

Skill practice

Exercises for applying conceptual blockbusting

- Individual assignment: Analytical problem solving
- Team assignment: Creative problem solving
- Scenario 1: Moving up in the rankings
- Scenario 2: Preserving our heritage

Skill application

- Suggested assignments
- Application plan and evaluation

Scoring keys and supplementary materials

References

Skill assessment

Evaluative surveys for creative problem solving

Problem solving, creativity and innovation

Step 1: Before you read the material in this chapter, respond to the following statements by writing a number from the rating scale below in the left-hand column (pre-assessment). Your answers should reflect your attitudes and behaviour as they are now, not as you would like them to be. Be honest. This instrument is designed to help you discover your level of competency in problem solving and creativity so that you can tailor your learning to your specific needs. When you have completed the survey, use the scoring key at the end of the chapter to identify the skill areas that are most important for you to master.

Step 2: After you have completed the reading and the exercises in the chapter and, ideally, as many as you can of the skill application assignments at the end of the chapter, cover up your first set of answers. Then respond to the same statements again, this time in the right-hand column (post-assessment). When you have completed the survey, use the scoring key to measure your progress. If your score remains low in specific skill areas, use the behavioural guidelines at the end of the skill learning section to guide further practice.

Rating scale

1 Strongly disagree
2 Disagree
3 Slightly disagree
4 Slightly agree
5 Agree
6 Strongly agree

Assessment
Pre- *Post-*
When I encounter a routine problem:

______ ______ 1. I state clearly and explicitly what the problem is. I avoid trying to solve it until I have defined it.

______ ______ 2. I always generate more than one alternative solution to the problem, instead of identifying only one obvious solution.

______ ______ 3. I keep in mind both long-term and short-term consequences as I evaluate various alternative solutions.

______ ______ 4. I gather as much information as I can about what the problem is before trying to solve it.

______ ______ 5. I keep steps in the problem-solving process distinct; that is, I define the problem before proposing alternative solutions, and I generate alternatives before selecting a single solution.

When faced with an ambiguous or difficult problem that does not have an easy solution:

______ ______ 6. I try out several definitions of the problem. I do not limit myself to just one way of defining it.

______ ______ 7. I try to be flexible in the way I approach the problem by trying out several alternative methods rather than relying on the same approach every time.

______ ______ 8. I try to find underlying patterns among elements in the problem so that I can uncover underlying dimensions or principles that help me to understand the problem.

______ ______ 9. I try to unfreeze my thinking by asking lots of questions about the nature of the problem before considering ways to solve it.

______ ______ 10. I try to think about the problem from both the left (logical) side of my brain and the right (intuitive) side of my brain.

______ ______ 11. To help me understand the problem and generate alternative solutions, I use analogies and metaphors that help me to identify what else this problem is like.

______ ______ 12. I sometimes reverse my initial definition of the problem to consider whether or not the exact opposite is also true.

______ ______ 13. I do not evaluate the merits of an alternative solution to the problem before I have generated a list of alternatives. That is, I avoid selecting one solution until I have developed several possible solutions.

______ ______ 14. I often break down the problem into smaller components and analyse each one separately.

______ ______ 15. I have some specific techniques that I use to help develop creative and innovative solutions to problems.

When trying to foster more creativity and innovation among those with whom I work:

______ ______ 16. I help to arrange opportunities for individuals to work on their ideas outside the constraints of their normal job assignments.

______ ______ 17. I make sure there are divergent points of view represented or expressed in every complex problem-solving situation.

______ ______ 18. I sometimes make outrageous suggestions to stimulate people to find new ways of approaching problems.

______ ______ 19. I try to acquire information from individuals outside the problem-solving group who will be affected by the decision, mainly to determine their preferences and expectations.

______ ______ 20. I sometimes involve outsiders (for example, customers or recognised experts) in problem-solving discussions.

______ ______ 21. I try to provide recognition not only to those who come up with creative ideas (the idea champions) but also to those who support others' ideas (supporters) and who provide resources to implement them (orchestrators).

______ ______ 22. I encourage informed rule breaking in pursuit of creative solutions.

The scoring key is on page 222.

How creative are you?

The following test helps you determine if you have the personality traits, attitudes, values, motivations and interests that characterise creativity. It is based on several years' study of attributes possessed by men and women in a variety of fields and occupations who think and act creatively.

For each statement, write in the appropriate letter:

A Agree
B Undecided or do not know
C Disagree

Be as frank as possible. Try not to second-guess how a creative person might respond. Turn to the end of the chapter (page 222) to find the answer key and an interpretation of your scores.

______ 1. I always work with a great deal of certainty that I am following the correct procedure for solving a particular problem.

______ 2. It would be a waste of time for me to ask questions if I had no hope of obtaining answers.

______ 3. I concentrate harder on whatever interests me than do most people.

______ 4. I feel that a logical step-by-step method is best for solving problems.

______ 5. In groups I occasionally voice opinions that seem to turn some people off.

______ 6. I spend a great deal of time thinking about what others think of me.
______ 7. It is more important for me to do what I believe to be right than to try to win the approval of others.
______ 8. People who seem uncertain about things lose my respect.
______ 9. More than other people, I need to have things interesting and exciting.
______ 10. I know how to keep my inner impulses in check.
______ 11. I am able to stick with difficult problems over extended periods of time.
______ 12. On occasion I get overly enthusiastic.
______ 13. I often get my best ideas when doing nothing in particular.
______ 14. I rely on intuitive hunches and the feeling of 'rightness' or 'wrongness' when moving towards the solution of a problem.
______ 15. When problem solving, I work faster when analysing the problem and slower when synthesising the information I have gathered.
______ 16. I sometimes get a kick out of breaking the rules and doing things I am not supposed to do.
______ 17. I like hobbies that involve collecting things.
______ 18. Daydreaming has provided the impetus for many of my more important projects.
______ 19. I like people who are objective and rational.
______ 20. If I had to choose from two occupations other than the one I now have, I would rather be a doctor than an explorer.
______ 21. I can get along more easily with people if they belong to about the same social and business class as myself.
______ 22. I have a high degree of aesthetic sensitivity.
______ 23. I am driven to achieve high status and power in life.
______ 24. I like people who are sure of their conclusions.
______ 25. Inspiration has nothing to do with the successful solution of problems.
______ 26. When I am in an argument, my greatest pleasure would be for the person who disagrees with me to become a friend, even at the price of sacrificing my point of view.
______ 27. I am much more interested in coming up with new ideas than in trying to sell them to others.
______ 28. I would enjoy spending an entire day alone, just 'chewing the mental cud'.
______ 29. I tend to avoid situations in which I might feel inferior.
______ 30. In evaluating information, the source is more important to me than the content.
______ 31. I resent things being uncertain and unpredictable.
______ 32. I like people who follow the rule 'business before pleasure'.
______ 33. Self-respect is much more important to me than the respect of others.
______ 34. I feel that people who strive for perfection are unwise.
______ 35. I prefer to work with others in a team effort, rather than solo.
______ 36. I like work in which I must influence others.
______ 37. Many problems that I encounter in life cannot be resolved in terms of right or wrong solutions.
______ 38. It is important for me to have a place for everything and everything in its place.
______ 39. Writers who use strange and unusual words merely want to show off.
______ 40. Below is a list of terms that describe people. Choose ten words that best characterise you.

energetic	persuasive	observant
fashionable	self-confident	persevering
original	cautious	habit-bound
resourceful	egotistical	independent
stern	predictable	formal
informal	dedicated	forward-looking
factual	open-minded	tactful
inhibited	enthusiastic	innovative

poised	acquisitive	practical
alert	curious	organised
unemotional	clear-thinking	understanding
dynamic	self-demanding	polished
courageous	efficient	helpful
perceptive	quick	good-natured
thorough	impulsive	determined
realistic	modest	involved
absent-minded	flexible	sociable
well-liked	restless	retiring

Source: Excerpted from E. Raudsepp, *How Creative Are You?* (New York: Perigee Books, 1981). Copyright 1981 by Eugene Raudsepp. Reproduced with permission. Published by Perigee Books/G. P. Putnam's Sons, Inc.

The scoring key is on page 222.

Innovative attitude scale

Indicate the extent to which each of the following statements is true of either your actual behaviour or your intentions at work. That is, describe the way you are or the way you intend to be on the job. Use the scale for your responses.

Rating scale

5 Almost always true
4 Often true
3 Not applicable
2 Seldom true
1 Almost never true

______ 1. I openly discuss with my fellow students and colleagues how to get ahead.
______ 2. I try new ideas and approaches to problems.
______ 3. I take things or situations apart to find out how they work.
______ 4. I welcome uncertainty and unusual circumstances related to my tasks.
______ 5. I maintain an open dialogue with others who disagree with me.
______ 6. I can be counted on to find a new use for existing methods or equipment.
______ 7. I will usually be the first to try out a new idea or method among my colleagues or fellow students.
______ 8. I take the opportunity to incorporate ideas from other fields or disciplines in my work.
______ 9. I demonstrate originality in my work.
______ 10. I will willingly work on a problem that has caused others great difficulty.
______ 11. I provide important input regarding new solutions when working in a group.
______ 12. I avoid jumping to conclusions about others' proposed ideas.
______ 13. I develop contacts with experts outside my area of interest or specialty.
______ 14. I use personal contacts to expand my options for new jobs or assignments.
______ 15. I make time to pursue my own pet ideas or projects.
______ 16. I set aside resources for pursuing a risky project that interests me.
______ 17. I tolerate people who depart from organisational routine.
______ 18. I speak out in class and in meetings.
______ 19. I am good at working in teams to solve complex problems.
______ 20. If my fellow students or colleagues are asked, they will say I am a wit.

Source: Adapted from J. E. Ettlie and R. D. O'Keefe, 'Innovative attitudes, values, and intentions in organisations', *Journal of Management Studies*, 19, 1982, pp. 163–82.

The scoring key is on page 223.

Skill learning

Problem solving, creativity and innovation

Problem solving is a skill that is required of every person in almost every aspect of life. Seldom does an hour go by without people at all levels of organisations being faced with the need to creatively solve some kind of problem (cf. Bilton 2007; Friedrich et al. 2010; Sauber 2006). From change leadership (Kelly 2011), to new-product development in the telecommunications industry (Le Mesurier 2006a), to the development by IAG (Insurance Australia Group) of Risk Radar, a web-based risk-assessment tool designed to help reduce the risk of accidents in the workplace (Le Mesurier 2006b), to improving the productivity of the Australian beef industry (Way 2006) or increasing retail sales (Carter 2006), the manager's job is inherently a problem-solving one. If there were no problems in organisations, there would be no need for managers. Therefore, it is hard to conceive of an incompetent problem solver succeeding as a manager.

This chapter offers specific guidelines and techniques for improving problem-solving skills. Both kinds of problem solving—analytical and creative—are addressed. Effective managers are able to solve problems using both processes, even though different skills are required for each type of problem. First, analytical problem solving is discussed—the kind of problem solving that managers use many times a day. Then creative problem solving is the focus, a kind of problem solving that occurs less frequently. Yet this creative problem-solving ability often separates career successes from career failures, the high-flyers from the rank-and-file and the achievers from the derailed executives. It can also have a dramatic impact on organisational effectiveness. A great deal of research highlights the positive relationship between creative problem solving and successful organisations (cf. Godin 2005; Russo 2006; Sternberg 1999). This chapter provides guidelines for becoming a more effective problem solver and concludes with a brief discussion of how managers can foster creative problem solving and innovation among the people with whom they work.

Both methods of problem solving can assist organisations in becoming more effective, efficient and competitive, with the ability to produce more and/or diverse products and better services in response to a market need. Australians have been clever innovators, but our ability to nurture ideas to a viably commercial end has often let us down. As the Karpin Report (1995) identified, Australian managers/leaders need to think more creatively and with regard to the longer term. They also need to foster creative problem solving and innovation among their co-workers. This is discussed in more detail at the end of the chapter.

Steps in rational problem solving

Most people, including managers, do not particularly like problems. Problems are time-consuming, they create stress and they never seem to go away. In fact, most people try to get rid of problems as soon as they can. Their natural tendency is to select the first reasonable solution that comes to mind. Unfortunately, that first solution is often not the best one. In typical problem solving, most people implement a marginally acceptable or merely satisfactory solution, rather than the optimal or ideal one. In fact, many observers have attributed the extensive failures of internet and dot-com firms—as well as more established companies—to the abandonment of correct problem-solving principles by managers. Shortcuts in analytical problem solving by managers and entrepreneurs, they argue, have had a major negative effect on company survival (Goll & Rasheed 1997). Effective problem solving comes from a rational or logical perspective, rather than from a 'seat of the pants', 'she'll be right' approach. It involves at least four steps, which are now explained.

The most widely accepted model of analytical problem solving is summarised in Table 4.1. This method is well known and lies at the heart of the quality improvement movement. To improve quality as individuals and as organisations, an essential step is to learn and apply this analytical method of problem solving (see Ichikawa 1986; Juran 1988; Riley 1998). Many large organisations (for example, Hewlett-Packard, Ford Motor Company, General Electric) spend millions of dollars to teach their managers this type of problem solving as part of their quality improvement process. Variations on this four-step approach have been implemented in several firms (for example, Ford uses an eight-step approach), but all the steps are merely derivations of the standard model discussed here. It is important to remember, however, that these problem-solving steps are useful mainly when the problems faced are straightforward, when alternatives are readily definable, when relevant information is available, and when a clear standard exists against which to judge the correctness of a solution.

TABLE 4.1 A model of problem solving

STEP	CHARACTERISTICS
1. Define the problem.	• Differentiate fact from opinion. • Specify underlying causes. • Tap everyone involved for information. • State the problem explicitly. • Identify what standard is violated. • Determine whose problem it is and who resolves the problem. • Avoid stating the problem as a disguised solution.
2. Generate alternative solutions.	• Postpone evaluating alternatives. • Be sure all involved individuals generate alternatives. • Specify alternatives that are consistent with goals. • Specify both short-term and long-term alternatives. • Build on others' ideas. • Specify alternatives that solve the problem.
3. Evaluate and select an alternative.	• Evaluate relative to an optimal standard. • Evaluate systematically. • Evaluate relative to goals. • Evaluate main effects and side effects. • State the selected alternative explicitly.
4. Implement and follow up on the solution.	• Implement at the proper time and in the right sequence. • Use a 'small-wins' strategy to engender support. • Provide opportunities for feedback. • Engender acceptance of those who are affected. • Establish an ongoing monitoring system. • Evaluate the success of the solution.

Defining the problem

The first step is to define the problem. This involves diagnosing a situation so that the focus is on the real causes of the problem, not just its symptoms. For example, suppose you must deal with an employee who consistently fails to get her work done on time. Slow work might be the root cause, or it might be only a symptom of another underlying problem such as poor health, low morale, lack of training or inadequate rewards. Defining the problem, therefore, requires a wide search for information that can help to pinpoint underlying causes. The more information that is acquired, the more likely it is that the problem will be defined accurately. As Charles Kettering put it: 'It ain't the things you don't know that'll get you in trouble, but the things you know for sure that ain't so.'

The following are some attributes of good problem definition:

1. Factual information is differentiated from opinion or speculation. Objective data are separated from perceptions and suppositions.

2. A wide range of people are asked for information. Broad participation is encouraged to get as many different perspectives as possible and engender group acceptance.
3. The problem is stated explicitly. For example, writing a statement describing the problem or constructing a cause-and-effect analysis diagram often helps to point out ambiguities in the definition (see Figure 4.1).
4. The problem definition clearly identifies what standard or expectation has been violated (the negative effect). Problems, by their very nature, involve the violation of some standard or expectation.
5. The problem definition needs also to address the question: 'Who needs to take responsibility for resolving the problem?'
6. The definition is not simply a disguised solution. Saying 'The problem is that we need to motivate slow employees' is inappropriate, because the problem is stated as a solution.

Managers often propose a solution before an adequate definition of a problem has been given. This may lead to solving the 'wrong' problem. The definition step in problem solving, therefore, is extremely important.

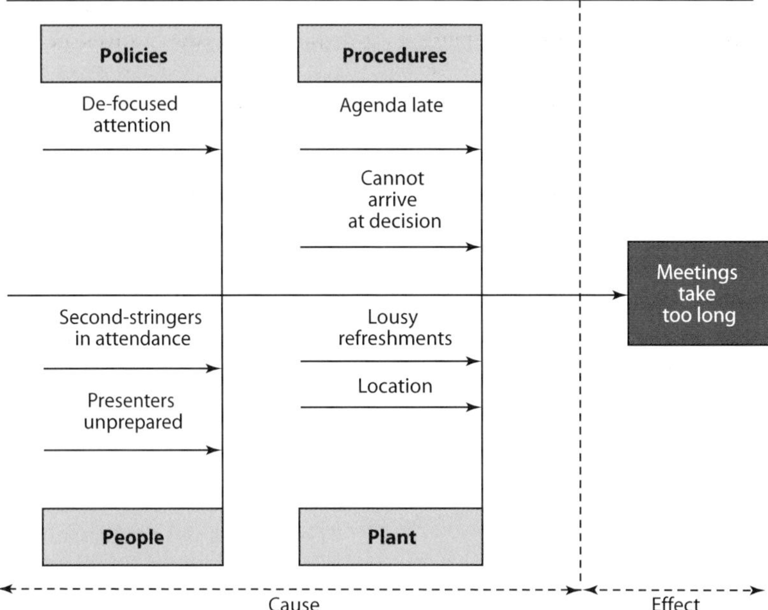

FIGURE 4.1 Cause-and-effect diagram

Source: J. Jablonski, *Implementing TQM* (Albuquerque, NM: Technical Management Consortium, Inc., 1992), p. 167. Reproduced with permission of the author, Joseph R. Jablonski.

Generating alternatives

The second step is to generate alternative solutions. This requires postponing the selection of any one solution until several alternatives have been proposed. We have known for many years that the quality of solutions can be significantly enhanced by considering multiple alternatives (Godin 2005; Kelley 2005; Osborn 1953; Russo 2006). Rather than rushing into judgment too quickly, judgment and evaluation must be delayed so that the first acceptable solution suggested is not necessarily the one immediately selected. Too early an evaluation could eliminate even better ideas that are simply not thought of at the time.

Many alternative solutions should be generated before any of them are evaluated. A common problem in managerial decision making is that alternatives are evaluated as they are proposed, so the first acceptable (although frequently not optimal) one is chosen.

Some attributes of good alternative generation are:

1. The evaluation of each proposed alternative is postponed. All alternatives should be proposed before evaluation is allowed.
2. Alternatives are proposed by all individuals involved in the problem. Broad participation in proposing alternatives improves solution quality and group acceptance.
3. Alternative solutions are consistent with organisational goals or policies. Subversion and criticism are detrimental to both the organisation and the alternative generation process.
4. Alternatives take into consideration both short-term and long-term consequences.
5. Alternatives build on one another. Bad ideas may become good ones if they are combined with or modified by other ideas.
6. Alternatives solve the problem that has been defined. Another problem may also be important, but it should be ignored if it does not directly affect the problem being considered.

Evaluating alternatives

The third problem-solving step is to evaluate and select an alternative. This step involves careful weighing of the advantages and disadvantages of the proposed alternatives before making a final selection. In selecting the best alternative, skilled problem solvers make sure that alternatives are judged in terms of the extent to which they will solve the problem without causing other unanticipated problems, the extent to which all individuals involved will accept the alternative, the extent to which implementation of the alternative is likely, and the extent to which the alternative fits within organisational constraints (is consistent with policies, norms and budget limitations). Care is taken not to short-circuit these considerations by choosing the most conspicuous alternative without considering others. The classic description of the problem with problem solving made almost 50 years ago still remains a core principle in problem solving (March & Simon 1958):

> *Most human decision making, whether individual or organizational, is concerned with the discovery and selection of satisfactory alternatives; only in exceptional cases is it concerned with the discovery and selection of optimal alternatives. To optimize requires processes several orders of magnitude more complex than those required to satisfy. An example is the difference between searching a haystack to find the sharpest needle in it and searching the haystack to find a needle sharp enough to sew with.*

Given the natural tendency to select the first satisfactory solution proposed, this step deserves particular attention in problem solving.

Some attributes of good evaluation are:

1. Alternatives are evaluated relative to an optimal, rather than a satisfactory, standard.
2. Evaluation of alternatives occurs systematically so that each alternative is given due consideration. Short-circuiting evaluation inhibits the selection of optimal alternatives.
3. Alternatives are evaluated in terms of the goals of the organisation and the individuals involved. Organisational goals should be met, but individual preferences should also be considered.
4. Alternatives are evaluated in terms of their probable effects. Both side effects and direct effects on the problem are considered.
5. The alternative ultimately selected is stated explicitly. This helps to uncover latent ambiguities.

Implementing the solution

The final step is to implement and follow up on the solution. A surprising number of times, people faced with a problem will try to jump to step 4 before going through steps 1 to 3. That is, they react to a problem by trying to implement a solution before they have defined it, analysed it, or generated and evaluated alternative solutions. It is important to remember, therefore, that 'getting rid of the problem' by solving it will most likely not occur successfully without the first three steps in the model.

Implementing any solution requires sensitivity to possible resistance from those who will be affected by it. Almost any change engenders some resistance. Therefore, the best problem solvers are careful to select a strategy that maximises the probability that the solution will be accepted and fully implemented. This may involve ordering that the solution be implemented by others, 'selling' the solution to others or involving others in the implementation. Several authors (for example, Carlopio 1998, 2003; Dutton & Ashford 1993; Miller, Hickson & Wilson 1996) have provided models, tools and guidelines for managers to determine which of these implementation behaviours is most appropriate under which circumstances. Generally speaking, participation by others in the implementation of a solution will increase its acceptance and decrease resistance (cf. Black & Gregersen 1997; Farnham & Horton 2003).

Implementation is often effective when it is accomplished in small steps or increments. Weick (1984) introduced the idea of 'small wins' in which solutions to problems are implemented little by little. The idea is to implement a part of the solution that is easy to accomplish, then publicise it. Follow that up by implementing another part of the solution that is easy to accomplish, and publicise it again. Continue implementing incrementally to achieve small wins. This strategy decreases resistance (small changes are usually not worth fighting over), creates support as others observe progress (a bandwagon effect occurs) and reduces costs (failure is not career-ending, and large allocations of resources are not required before success is assured). It also helps to ensure persistence and perseverance in implementation.

Effective implementation also requires follow-up to prevent negative side effects and to ensure the solution of the problem. Follow-up not only helps to ensure effective implementation but also serves a feedback function by providing information that can be used to improve future problem solving.

As Drucker (1974: 480) has emphasised:

> *Feedback has to be built into the decision to provide continuous testing, against actual events, of the expectations that underlie the decision. Few decisions work out the way they are intended to. Even the best decision usually runs into snags, unexpected obstacles, and all kinds of surprises. Even the most effective decision eventually becomes obsolete. Unless there is feedback from the results of the decision, it is unlikely to produce the desired results.*

Some attributes of effective implementation and follow-up are these:

1. Implementation occurs at the right time and in the proper sequence. It does not ignore constraining factors, and it does not come before steps 1, 2 and 3 in the problem-solving process.
2. Implementation occurs using a small-wins strategy in order to discourage resistance and engender support.
3. The implementation process includes opportunities for feedback. How well the selected solution works needs to be communicated.
4. Participation by individuals affected by the problem solution is facilitated in order to create support and commitment.
5. An ongoing monitoring system is set up for the implemented solution. Long-term as well as short-term effects are assessed.
6. Evaluation of success is based on problem solution, not on side benefits. Although the solution may provide some positive outcomes, it is unsuccessful unless it solves the problem being considered.

Limitations of the analytical problem-solving model

Most experienced problem solvers are familiar with the preceding steps in rational problem solving, which are based on empirical research results and sound rationale (March 1999; Miller, Hickson & Wilson 1996; Mitroff 1998; Zeita 1999). Unfortunately, managers do not always practise these steps. The demands of their jobs often pressure managers into circumventing some steps, and problem solving suffers as a result. When these four steps (defining the problem, generating alternatives, evaluating alternatives and implementing the solution) are followed, however, effective problem solving is markedly enhanced, as long as the problems faced are straightforward, alternatives are readily definable, relevant information is available, and standards exist against which to judge the correctness of a solution. Of course, many managerial problems do not fit this description. Definitions, information, alternatives and standards are seldom unambiguous or readily available. Hence, knowing the steps in problem solving and being able to implement them are not necessarily the same thing.

Complex problems such as discovering why staff morale is so low, determining how to implement downsizing without antagonising employees, developing a new process that will double productivity and improve customer satisfaction, designing a new strategy or identifying ways to overcome resistance to change are common and are faced by many managers. These 'wicked problems' (Conklin 2006; Rittel & Webber 1973) do not always have an easily identifiable definition or set of alternative solutions available. It may not be clear how much information is needed, what the complete set of alternatives is, or how one knows if the information being obtained is accurate. Analytical problem solving may not always help with these types of problems and something more is often needed to address them successfully. Well-known management author and commentator Tom Peters said, in characterising the modern world faced by managers: 'If you're not confused, you're not paying attention.'

Table 4.2 summarises some reasons why analytical problem solving is not always effective in day-to-day managerial situations. Constraints exist on each of these four steps and stem from other individuals or from organisational processes that make it difficult to follow the prescribed model.

TABLE 4.2 Some constraints on the analytical problem-solving model

STEPS	CONSTRAINTS
1. Define the problem.	• There is seldom consensus as to the definition of the problem. • There is often uncertainty as to whose definition will be accepted. • Problems are usually defined in terms of the solutions already possessed. • Symptoms get confused with the real problem. • Confusing information inhibits problem identification.
2. Generate alternative solutions.	• Solution alternatives are usually evaluated one at a time as they are proposed. • Usually, few of the possible alternatives are known. • The first acceptable solution is usually accepted. • Alternatives are based on what was successful in the past.
3. Evaluate and select an alternative.	• Usually, only limited information about each alternative is available. • Search for information occurs close to home, in easily accessible places. • The type of information available is constrained by factors such as primacy versus recency, extremity versus centrality, expected versus surprising, and correlation versus causation. • Gathering information on each alternative is costly. • Preferences of which is the best alternative are not always known. • Satisfactory solutions, not optimal ones, are usually accepted. • Solutions are often selected by oversight or default. • Solutions are often implemented before the problem is defined.
4. Implement and follow up on the solution.	• Acceptance by others of the solution is not always forthcoming. • Resistance to change is a universal phenomenon. • It is not always clear what part of the solution should be monitored or measured in the follow-up. • Political and organisational processes must be managed in any implementation effort. • It may take a long time to implement a solution.

Another reason why the rational problem-solving model is not always effective for managers is that some problems are not amenable to systematic or rational analysis. Sufficient and accurate information may not be available, outcomes may not be predictable, or means–ends connections may not be evident. In order to solve such problems, a new way of thinking may be required, multiple or conflicting definitions may be needed, and unprecedented alternatives may have to be generated. In short, creative problem solving must be used.

Impediments to creative problem solving

As mentioned at the beginning of the chapter, analytical problem solving is focused on getting rid of problems. Creative problem solving is focused on generating something new (Covey 1998). The trouble is that many people find it difficult to solve problems creatively. They have developed certain conceptual blocks in their problem-solving activities of which they are not even aware. These blocks inhibit them from solving certain problems effectively. The blocks are largely personal, as opposed to interpersonal or organisational, so skill development is required to overcome them.

Conceptual blocks are mental obstacles that constrain the way problems are defined and limit the number of alternative solutions thought to be relevant (Allen 1986). Every individual has conceptual blocks, but some people have more numerous and more intense ones. These blocks are largely unrecognised, or unconscious, so the only way individuals can be made aware of them is to be confronted with problems that are unsolvable because of them. Conceptual blocks result largely from the thinking processes that problem solvers use when facing problems. Everyone develops some conceptual blocks over time. In fact, we need some of them to cope with everyday life. Here is why.

At every moment, each of us is bombarded with far more information than we can possibly absorb. For example, you are probably not conscious right now of the temperature of the room, the colour of your skin, the level of illumination overhead or how your toes feel in your shoes. All this information is available to you and is being processed by your brain, but you have tuned out some things and focused on others. Over time, you must develop the habit of mentally filtering out some of the information to which you are exposed; otherwise, information overload would drive you crazy. These filtering habits eventually become conceptual blocks. Though you are not conscious of them, they inhibit you from registering some kinds of information and therefore from solving certain kinds of problems.

Paradoxically, the more formal education individuals have, and the more experience they have in a job, the less able they are to solve problems in creative ways. It has been estimated that most adults over 40 display less than 2 per cent of the creative problem-solving ability of a child under five years old. That's because formal education often prescribes 'right' answers, analytic rules or thinking boundaries. Experience in a job leads to accepted ways of doing things, specialised knowledge and rigid expectation of appropriate actions. Individuals lose the ability to experiment, improvise or take mental detours. Consider the following example.

> *If you place in a bottle half a dozen bees and the same number of flies, and lie the bottle down horizontally, with its base to the window, you will find that the bees will persist, until they die of exhaustion or hunger, in their endeavour to discover a way through the glass, while the flies, in less than two minutes, will all have sallied forth through the neck on the opposite side.... It is [the bees'] love of light, it is their very 'intelligence', that is their undoing in this experiment. They evidently imagine that the way out of every prison must be from the direction the light shines; and they act in accordance, and persist in too logical an action. To them glass is a supernatural mystery they have never met in nature; they have had no experience of this suddenly impenetrable atmosphere; and the greater their 'intelligence', the more inadmissible, more incomprehensible, will the strange obstacle appear. Whereas the feather-brained flies, as careless of logic as of the enigma of crystal, disregarding the call of the light, flutter wildly, hither and thither, meeting here the good fortune that often waits on the simple, who find salvation where the wiser will perish, necessarily end by discovering the friendly opening that restores their liberty to them.*

This illustration identifies a paradox inherent in learning to solve problems creatively. On the one hand, more education and experience may inhibit creative problem solving and reinforce conceptual blocks. Like the bees in the story, individuals may not find solutions because the problem requires less 'educated', more 'playful' approaches. On the other hand, as several researchers have found, training directed towards improving thinking significantly enhances creative problem-solving abilities and managerial effectiveness (de Bono 1985).

For many years Edward de Bono has been teaching Australian managers to think creatively to solve problems, and a number of Australia's leading organisations have enrolled managers in his seminars to assist in their further development. Training in problem solving has also occurred as part of the drive for quality and service embraced by many well-known organisations. The use of problem-solving techniques has contributed to the development of such products as the bionic ear, the Super Sopper (Australia's answer to rain-soaked sporting grounds), the portable solar generator and the plastic banknote.

So, resolving the paradox is not just a matter of more exposure to information or education. Rather, we must master the process of thinking about certain problems in a creative way. As Csikszentmihalyi (1996: 11) observed:

> *Each of us is born with two contradictory sets of instructions: a conservative tendency, made up of instincts for self-preservation, self-aggrandizement, and saving energy, and an expansive tendency made up of instincts for exploring, for enjoying novelty and risk—the curiosity that leads to creativity belongs to this set. We need both of these programs. But whereas the first tendency requires little encouragement or support from the outside to motivate behavior, the second can wilt if it is not cultivated. If too few opportunities for curiosity are available, if too many obstacles are placed in the way of risk and exploration, the motivation to engage in creative behavior is easily extinguished. (Reproduced with permission of Mihaly Csikszentmihalyi.)*

The next section focuses on problems that require creative rather than analytical solutions. These are problems for which no acceptable alternative seems to be available, all reasonable solutions seem to be blocked, or no obvious best answer is accessible. This situation may exist because conceptual blocks inhibit the implementation of rational problem solving. Our focus, therefore, must be on tools and techniques that help overcome conceptual blocks and unlock problem-solving creativity.

Two examples help to illustrate the kinds of problems that require creative problem-solving skills. They also illustrate several conceptual blocks that inhibit problem solving, and several techniques and tools you can use to overcome such blocks.

Percy Spencer's magnetron

During the Second World War, the British developed one of the best-kept military secrets of the war, a special radar detector based on a device called the magnetron. This radar was credited with turning the tide of battle in the war between Britain and Germany and helping the British withstand Hitler's Blitzkrieg. In 1940, Raytheon was one of several US firms invited to produce magnetrons for the war effort.

The workings of magnetrons were not well understood, even by sophisticated physicists. Even among the firms that made magnetrons, few understood what made them work. A magnetron was tested, in those early days, by holding a neon tube next to it. If the neon tube got bright enough, the magnetron tube passed the test. In the process of conducting the test, the hands of the scientist holding the neon tube were warmed. It was this phenomenon that led to a major creative breakthrough that eventually transformed lifestyles throughout the world.

At the end of the war, the market for radar essentially dried up and most firms stopped producing magnetrons. At Raytheon, however, a scientist named Percy Spencer had been fooling around with magnetrons, trying to think of alternative uses for the device. He was convinced that magnetrons could be used to cook food by using the heat produced in the neon tube. But Raytheon was in the defence business. Next to its two prize products—the Hawk and Sparrow missiles—cooking devices seemed odd and out of place. Percy Spencer was convinced that Raytheon should continue to produce magnetrons, even though production costs were prohibitively high. But Raytheon had lost money on the devices and now there was no market for them. The consumer product Spencer had in mind did not fit within the bounds of Raytheon's business.

As it turned out, Percy Spencer's solution to Raytheon's problem produced the microwave oven and a revolution in cooking methods throughout the world. Later in this chapter, several problem-solving techniques illustrated by Spencer's creative triumph are analysed.

Spence Silver's glue

A second example of creative problem solving began with Spence Silver's assignment to work on a temporary project team within the 3M company. The team was searching for new adhesives, so Silver obtained some material from AMD Inc., which had potential for a new polymer-based adhesive. He described one of his experiments in this way: 'In the course of this exploration, I tried an experiment with one of the monomers in which I wanted to see what would happen if I put a lot of it into the reaction mixture. Before, we had used amounts that would correspond to conventional wisdom' (Nayak & Ketteringham 1986). The result was a substance that failed all the conventional 3M tests for adhesives. It did not stick. It preferred its own molecules to the molecules of any other substance. It was more cohesive than adhesive. It sort of 'hung around without making a commitment'. It was a 'now-it-works, now-it-doesn't' kind of glue.

For five years, Silver went from department to department within the company trying to find someone interested in using his newly found substance in a product. Silver had found a solution; he just could not find a problem to solve with it. Predictably, 3M showed little interest. The company's mission was to make adhesives that adhered ever more tightly. The ultimate adhesive was one that formed an unbreakable bond, not one that formed a temporary bond.

After four years the task force was disbanded and team members were assigned to other projects. But Silver was still convinced that his substance was good for something. He just did not know what. As it turned out, Silver's solution has become the prototype for innovation in American firms, and it has spawned half a billion dollars in annual revenues for 3M—in a unique product called 'Post-it notes'.

These two examples are positive illustrations of how solving a problem in a unique way can lead to phenomenal business success. Creative problem solving can have remarkable effects on individuals' careers and on business success. To understand how to solve problems creatively, however, we must first consider the blocks that inhibit creativity.

Conceptual blocks

Table 4.3 summarises four types of conceptual blocks that inhibit creative problem solving. Each is discussed and illustrated with problems or exercises. You are encouraged to complete the exercises and solve the problems as you read the chapter, because doing so will help you become aware of your own conceptual blocks. Later, how you can overcome those blocks is discussed in more detail.

TABLE 4.3 Conceptual blocks that inhibit creative problem solving

1. Constancy	
Vertical thinking	Defining a problem in only one way without considering alternative views.
One thinking language	Not using more than one language to define and assess the problem.
2. Misplaced commitment	
Stereotyping based on past experience	Present problems are seen only as variations of past problems.
Ignoring commonalities	Failing to perceive commonalities among elements that initially appear to be different.
3. Compression	
Distinguishing figure from ground	Not filtering out irrelevant information or finding needed information.
Artificial constraints	Defining the boundaries of a problem too narrowly.
4. Complacency	
Non-inquisitiveness	Not asking questions.
Non-thinking	A bias toward activity in place of mental work.

Constancy

Constancy, in the present context, means that an individual becomes wedded to one way of looking at a problem or to using one approach to define, describe or solve it. It is easy to see why constancy is common in problem solving. Being constant, or consistent, is a highly valued attribute for most people. Everyone likes to appear at least moderately consistent in their approach to life, and constancy is often associated with maturity, honesty and even intelligence. Several prominent psychologists theorise, in fact, that a need for constancy is the primary motivator of human behaviour. Many psychological studies have shown that once individuals take a stand or employ a particular approach to a problem, they are highly likely to pursue that same course without deviation in the future (see Cialdini 1993 for multiple examples).

On the other hand, constancy can inhibit the solution of some kinds of problems. Consistency sometimes drives out creativity. Two illustrations of the constancy block are vertical thinking and using only one thinking language.

Vertical thinking

The term 'vertical thinking' was coined by Edward de Bono (1968, 2000). It refers to defining a problem in a single way and then pursuing that definition without deviation until a solution is reached. No alternative definitions are considered. All information gathered and all alternatives generated are consistent with the original definition. In a search for oil, for example, vertical thinkers determine a spot for the hole and drill the hole deeper and deeper until they strike oil. Lateral thinkers, on the other hand, generate alternative ways of viewing a problem and produce multiple definitions. Instead of drilling one hole deeper and deeper, lateral thinkers drill a number of holes in different places in search of oil. The vertical-thinking conceptual block arises from not being able to view the problem from multiple perspectives—to drill several holes—or to think laterally as well as vertically in problem solving. Problem definition is restricted.

There are plenty of examples of creative solutions that occurred because an individual refused to get stuck with a single problem definition. Alexander Graham Bell was trying to devise a hearing aid when he shifted definitions and invented the telephone. Karl Jansky was studying telephone static when he shifted definitions, discovered radio waves from the Milky Way galaxy and developed the science of radio astronomy.

In the development of the microwave industry described earlier, Percy Spencer shifted the definition of the problem from 'How can we save our military radar business at the end of the war?' to 'What other applications can be made for the magnetron?'. Other problem definitions followed, such as: 'How can we make magnetrons cheaper?', 'How can we mass-produce magnetrons?', 'How can we convince someone besides the military to buy magnetrons?', 'How can we enter a consumer products market?', 'How can we make microwave ovens practical and safe?', and so on. Each new problem definition led to new ways of thinking about the problem, new alternative approaches and, eventually, a new microwave oven industry.

Spence Silver at 3M is another example of someone who changed problem definitions. He began with 'How can I get an adhesive that has a stronger bond?' but switched to: 'How can I find an application for an adhesive that doesn't stick firmly?' Eventually, other problem definitions followed: 'How can we get this new glue to stick to one surface but not another (for example, to notepaper but not normal paper)?', 'How can we replace staples and paperclips in the workplace?', 'How can we manufacture and package a product that uses non-adhesive glue?', 'How can we get anyone to pay $2 a pad for scratch paper?', and so on.

Shifting definitions is not easy, of course, because it is not natural. It requires us to deflect our tendency towards constancy. Later, some hints and tools are discussed that can help overcome the constancy block while avoiding the negative consequences of inconsistency.

A single thinking language

A second manifestation of the constancy block is the use of only one thinking language. Most people think in words—that is, they think about a problem and its solution in terms of verbal language.

Analytical problem solving reinforces this approach. Some writers, in fact, have argued that thinking cannot even occur without words. Other thought languages are available, however, such as non-verbal or symbolic languages (for example, mathematics), sensory imagery (smelling or tactile sensation), feelings and emotions (happiness, fear or anger) and visual imagery (mental pictures). You will recall the Influence Dimensions, especially the visual, auditory and tactile dimensions, detailed in Chapter 2. The more languages available to problem solvers, the better and more creative will be their solutions. As Koestler (1967) puts it: '[Verbal] language can become a screen which stands between the thinker and reality. This is the reason that true creativity often starts where [verbal] language ends.'

Percy Spencer at Raytheon is a prime example of a visual thinker:

> *One day, while Spencer was lunching with Dr Ivan Getting and several other Raytheon scientists, a mathematical question arose. Several men, in a familiar reflex, pulled out their slide rules, but before any could complete the equation, Spencer gave the answer. Dr Getting was astonished. 'How did you do that?' he asked. 'The root,' said Spencer shortly. 'I learned cube roots and squares by using blocks as a boy. Since then, all I have to do is visualise them placed together.' (Scott 1974: 287. Reprinted with permission of Scribner, an imprint of Simon & Schuster Adult Publishing Group, from* The Creative Ordeal: The Story of Raytheon *by Otto J. Scott © 1974 by Otto J. Scott. All rights reserved.)*

The microwave oven depended on Spencer's command of multiple thinking languages. In fact, the new oven would never have got off the ground without a critical incident that illustrates the power of visual thinking. By 1965, Raytheon was just about to give up on any consumer application of the magnetron when a meeting was held with George Foerstner, president of the recently acquired Amana Refrigeration Company. In the meeting, costs, applications, manufacturing obstacles and so on were discussed. Foerstner galvanised the entire microwave oven effort with the following statement, as reported by a Raytheon executive:

> *George says, 'It's no problem. It's about the same size as an air conditioner. It weighs about the same. It should sell for the same. So we'll price it at $499.' Now you think that's silly, but you stop and think about it. Here's a man who really didn't understand the technologies. But there is about the same amount of copper involved, the same amount of steel as an air conditioner. And these are basic raw materials. It didn't make a lot of difference how you fit them together to make them work. They're both boxes; they're both made out of sheet metal; and they both require some sort of trim. (Nayak & Ketteringham 1986: 181. Reprinted by kind permission of Ranganath Nayak.)*

In several short sentences, Foerstner had taken one of the most complicated military secrets of the Second World War and translated it into something no more complex than a room air conditioner. He had painted a picture of an application that no one else had been able to capture by describing a magnetron visually, as a familiar object, not as a set of calculations, formulas or blueprints.

A similar occurrence in the Post-it note chronology also led to a breakthrough. Spence Silver had been trying for years to get someone in 3M to adopt his un-sticky glue. Art Fry, another scientist with 3M, had heard Silver's presentations before. One day, while singing in the North Presbyterian Church in St Paul, Minnesota, Fry was fumbling around with the slips of paper that marked the various hymns in his book. Suddenly, a visual image popped into his mind.

> *I thought, 'Gee, if I had a little adhesive on these bookmarks, that would be just the ticket.' So I decided to check into that idea the next week at work. What I had in mind was Silver's adhesive. ... I knew I had a much bigger discovery than that. I also now realized that the primary application for Silver's adhesive was not to put it on a fixed surface like bulletin boards. That was a secondary application. The primary application concerned paper to paper. I realized that immediately. (Nayak & Ketteringham 1986: 63–64. Reprinted by kind permission of Ranganath Nayak.)*

Years of verbal descriptions had not led to any applications for Silver's glue. Nor had tactile thinking (handling the glue) produced many ideas. However, thinking about the product in visual terms, as applied to what Fry initially called 'a better bookmark', led to the breakthrough that was needed.

This emphasis on using alternative thinking languages, especially visual thinking, is now becoming the new frontier in scientific research. With the advent of the digital revolution, scientists are working more and more with pictures and simulated images rather than with numerical data:

> *Scientists who are using the new computer graphics say that by viewing images instead of numbers, a fundamental change in the way researchers think and work is occurring. People have a lot easier time getting an intuition from pictures than they do from numbers and tables or formulas. In most physics experiments, the answer used to be a number or a string of numbers. In the last few years the answer has increasingly become a picture.* (Markoff 1988: D3)

To illustrate the differences between thinking languages, consider the following simple problems:

1. Below is the Roman numeral 9. By adding only a single line, turn it into a 6.

IX

2. Figure 4.2 shows seven matchsticks. By moving only one matchstick, make the figure into a true equality (that is, the value on one side equals the value on the other side). Before looking up the answers on pages 224–225, try defining the problems differently, using different thinking languages. How many answers can you find?

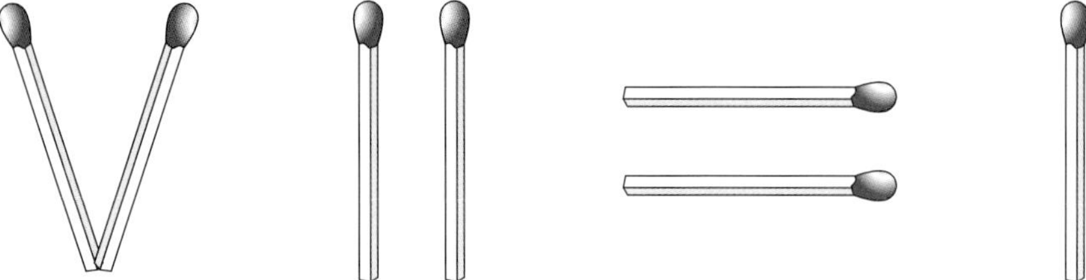

FIGURE 4.2 The matchstick configuration

3. Assume that the numbers in Figure 4.3 are on a scoreboard. Shade in six segments of the numbers and place a mathematical sign in the circle to create a correct calculation.

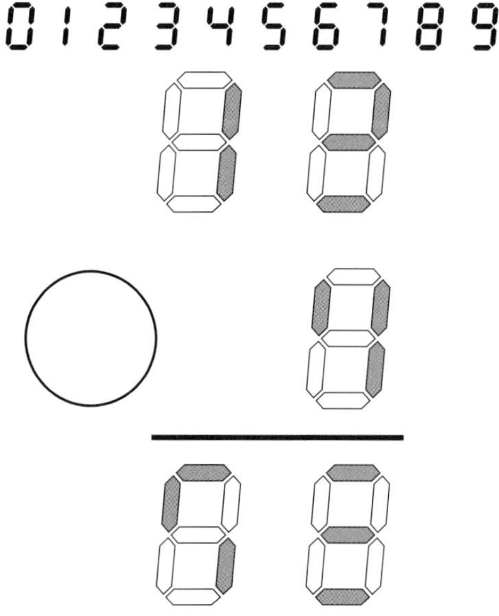

FIGURE 4.3 A numeric calculation

Source: D. J. Bodycombe, *The Mammoth Puzzle Carnival* (New York: Robinson Publishing, 1997). Reproduced with permission of Robinson Publishing, an imprint of Constable & Robinson Ltd.

Misplaced commitment

Commitment can also serve as a conceptual block to creative problem solving. Like constancy, commitment is a highly valued attribute in our society. However, once individuals become totally committed to a particular point of view, definition or solution, it is likely that they will follow through without considering changing needs or circumstances. Thus, misplaced commitment can lead to dysfunctional or foolish decisions, rigidly defended. Two forms of misplaced commitment that produce conceptual blocks are stereotyping based on past experiences and ignoring commonalities.

Stereotyping based on past experiences

A major obstacle to innovative problem solving is that individuals tend to define present problems in terms of problems they have faced in the past (March 1999) or solutions that have worked in the past (cf. Carlopio

2010). Current problems are usually seen as variations on some past situation, so the alternatives proposed to solve the current problem are those that have proved successful in the past. Both problem definitions and proposed solutions are therefore restricted by past experience. This restriction is referred to as perceptual stereotyping (Allen 1986); that is, certain preconceptions formed on the basis of past experience determine how an individual defines a situation.

When individuals receive an initial cue regarding the definition of a problem, all subsequent problems are frequently framed in terms of the initial cue. Of course, this is not all bad, because perceptual stereotyping helps to organise problems on the basis of a limited amount of data, and the need to consciously analyse every problem encountered is eliminated. On the other hand, perceptual stereotyping prevents individuals from viewing a problem in novel ways.

The creation of microwave ovens and Post-it notes provides examples of overcoming stereotyping based on past experiences. Scott (1974) described the first meeting of John D. Cockcroft, technical leader of the British radar system that invented magnetrons, and Percy Spencer of Raytheon.

> *Cockcroft liked Spencer at once. He showed him the magnetron, and the American regarded it thoughtfully. He asked questions—very intelligent ones—about how it was produced and the Briton answered at length. Later Spencer wrote, 'The technique of making these tubes, as described to us, was awkward and impractical.' Awkward and impractical! Nobody else dared draw such a judgment about a product of undoubted scientific brilliance, produced and displayed by the leaders of British science.*
>
> *Despite his admiration for Cockcroft and the magnificent magnetron, Spencer refused to abandon his curious and inquisitive stance. Rather than adopting the position of other scientists and assuming that since the British invented it and were using it, they surely knew how to produce a magnetron, Spencer broke out of the stereotypes and pushed for improvements. (Reprinted with permission of Scribner, an imprint of Simon & Schuster Adult Publishing Group, from* The Creative Ordeal: The Story of Raytheon *by Otto J. Scott © 1974 by Otto J. Scott. All rights reserved.)*

Similarly, Spence Silver at 3M described his invention in terms of breaking stereotypes based on experience.

> *The key to the Post-It adhesive was doing the experiment. If I had sat down and factored it out beforehand, and thought about it, I wouldn't have done the experiment. If I had really seriously cracked the books and gone through the literature, I would have stopped. The literature was full of examples that said you can't do this. (Nayak & Ketteringham 1986: 57. Reprinted by kind permission of Ranganath Nayak.)*

This is not to say that we should avoid learning from past experience, or that failing to learn the mistakes of history does not doom us to repeat them. Rather, it is to say that commitment to a course of action based on past experience can sometimes inhibit us from viewing problems in new ways and even prevent us from solving some problems at all. Consider the following problem as an example.

FIGURE 4.4 The Shakespeare riddle

Source: E. Raudsepp and G. Hough, *Creative Growth Games*. © 1977 Eugene Raudsepp & George P. Hough Jr. Reproduced with permission of Berkley Publishing Group, a division of Penguin Group (USA) Inc.

There are four volumes of Shakespeare on the shelf (see Figure 4.4). The pages of each volume are exactly 50 mm thick. The covers are each 5 mm thick. A bookworm started eating at page 1 of Volume I and ate straight through to the last page of Volume IV. What distance did the worm cover? (See page 225 for the answer.) Solving this problem is relatively simple, but it requires you to overcome a stereotyping block to get the correct answer.

Ignoring commonalities

A second form of the commitment block is failure to identify similarities among seemingly disparate pieces of data. This is among the most commonly identified blocks to creativity. It means that a person becomes committed to a particular point of view and to the fact that elements are different and, consequently, becomes unable to make connections, identify themes or perceive commonalities.

The ability to find one definition or solution for two seemingly dissimilar problems is a characteristic of creative individuals (see Sternberg 1999). The inability to do this can overload a problem solver by requiring that every problem encountered be solved individually. The discovery of penicillin by Sir Alexander Fleming resulted from his seeing a common theme among seemingly unrelated events. Fleming was working with some cultures of staphylococci that had accidentally become contaminated. The contamination, a growth of fungi and isolated clusters of dead staphylococci, led Fleming to see a relationship no one else had ever seen and thus to discover a wonder drug. The famous chemist Friedrich Kekule saw a relationship between his dream of a snake swallowing its own tail and the chemical structure of organic compounds. This creative insight led him to the discovery that organic compounds such as benzene have closed rings rather than open structures.

For Percy Spencer at Raytheon, seeing a connection between the heat of a neon tube and the heat required to cook food was the creative connection that led to his breakthrough in the microwave industry. One of Spencer's colleagues recalled: 'In the process of testing a bulb [with a magnetron], your hands got hot. I don't know when Percy really came up with the thought of microwave ovens, but he knew at that time—and that was 1942. He [remarked] frequently that this would be a good device for cooking food.' Another colleague described Spencer in this way: 'The way Percy Spencer's mind worked is an interesting thing. He had a mind that allowed him to hold an extraordinary array of associations on phenomena and relate them to one another' (Nayak & Ketteringham 1986: 184, 205).

To test your own ability to see commonalities, answer the following three questions:

1. What are some common terms that apply to both water and finance?
2. What is humorous about the following story?

   Descartes, the philosopher, walked into a university class. Recognising him, the instructor asked if he would like to lecture. Descartes replied 'I think not' and promptly disappeared.

3. What does the single piece of wood look like that will pass through each hole in the block in Figure 4.5 and perfectly fill each hole as it passes through?

   (Answers are at the end of the chapter on page 225.)

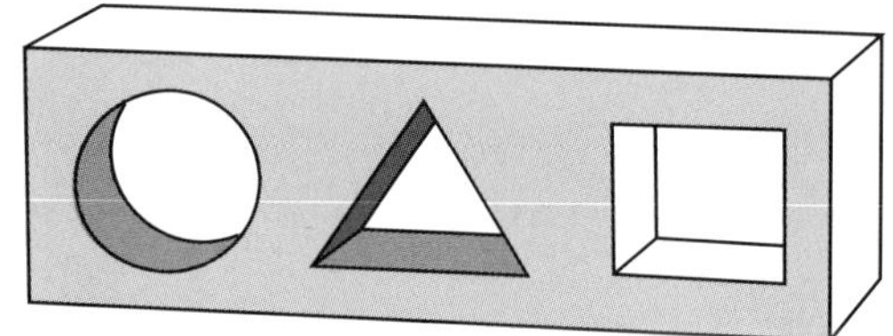

FIGURE 4.5 A block problem

Source: R. H. McKim, *Thinking Visually: A Strategy Manual for Problem Solving* (1980). © 1980 by Pearson Education Inc., publishing as Dale Seymour Publications, an imprint of Pearson Learning Group. Reproduced with permission.

Compression

Conceptual blocks also occur as a result of compression of ideas. Looking too narrowly at a problem, screening out too much relevant data and making assumptions that inhibit problem solution are common examples. Two especially cogent examples of compression are artificially constraining problems and not distinguishing figure from ground.

Artificial constraints

Sometimes people place boundaries around problems, or constrain their approach to them, in such a way that the problems become impossible to solve. Such constraints arise from hidden assumptions people make about problems they encounter. People assume that some problem definitions or alternative solutions are off limits, so they ignore them. For an illustration of this conceptual block, look at Figure 4.6. Without lifting your pencil from the paper, draw four straight lines that pass through all nine eggs. Complete the task before reading further.

FIGURE 4.6 The nine-egg problem

Source: Adapted from 'Christopher Columbus' Egg Puzzle' illustration by Sam Loyd, 1912.

By thinking of the figure as more constrained than it actually is, the problem becomes impossible to solve. Try to break out of your own limiting assumptions about the problem. (One four-line answer is presented on page 226.) Now that you have been cued, can you do the same task with only three lines? Work on this problem for a minute. If you are successful, try to do the task with only one line. Can you determine how to put a single straight line through all nine eggs without lifting your pencil from the paper? The solutions are on page 226.

Artificially constraining problems means that the problem definition and the possible alternatives are limited more than the problem requires. Creative problem solving requires that individuals become adept at recognising their hidden assumptions and expanding the alternatives they consider.

LEARNING

Separating figure from ground

Another illustration of the compression block is the reverse of artificial constraints. It is the inability to constrain problems sufficiently so that they can be solved. Problems almost never come clearly specified, so problem solvers must determine what the real problem is. They must filter out inaccurate, misleading or irrelevant information in order to define the problem correctly and generate appropriate alternative solutions. The inability to separate the important from the unimportant, and to compress problems appropriately, serves as a conceptual block because it exaggerates the complexity of a problem and inhibits a simple definition.

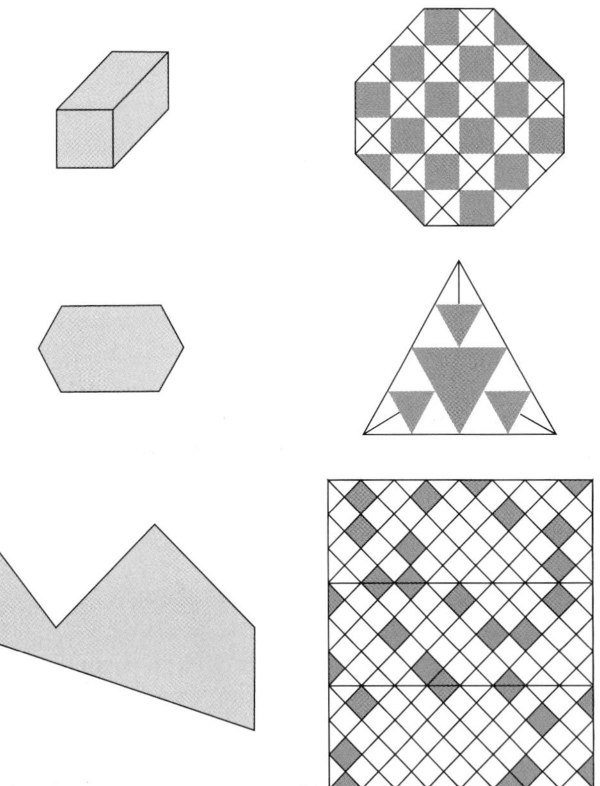

FIGURE 4.7 Embedded patterns

How well do you filter out irrelevant information? Consider Figure 4.7. For each pair, find the pattern on the left that is embedded in the more complex pattern on the right. On the complex pattern, outline the embedded pattern. Now try to find at least two figures in each pattern. (See page 226 for a solution.)

This compression block—separating figure from ground and artificially constraining problems—played an important role in the microwave oven and Post-it note breakthroughs. George Foerstner's contribution to the development and manufacture of the microwave oven was to compress the problem—that is, to separate out all the irrelevant complexity that constrained others. Whereas the magnetron was a device so complicated that few people understood it, Foerstner focused on its basic raw materials, its size and its functionality. By comparing it to an air conditioner, he eliminated much of the complexity and mystery and, as described by two analysts, 'He had seen what all the researchers had failed to see, and they knew he was right' (Nayak & Ketteringham 1986: 181).

On the other hand, Spence Silver had to add complexity, to overcome compression, in order to find an application for his product. Because the glue had failed every traditional 3M test for adhesives, it was categorised as a useless configuration of chemicals. The potential for the product was artificially constrained by traditional assumptions about adhesives—more stickiness, stronger bonding is best—until Art Fry visualised some unconventional applications: a better bookmark, a bulletin board, scratch paper and, paradoxically, a replacement for 3M's main product, tape.

Complacency

Some conceptual blocks occur not because of poor thinking habits or because of inappropriate assumptions but because of fear, ignorance, insecurity or just plain mental laziness. Two especially prevalent examples of the complacency block are a lack of questioning (non-inquisitiveness) and a bias against thinking.

Non-inquisitiveness

Sometimes the inability to solve problems results from a lack of willingness to ask questions, obtain information or search for data. Individuals may think they will appear naive or ignorant if they question something or attempt to redefine a problem. Asking questions puts them at risk of exposing their ignorance. It may also be threatening to others because it implies that what they accept may not be correct. This may create resistance, conflict or even ridicule by others.

Creative problem solving is thus inherently risky because, potentially, it involves interpersonal conflict. It is also risky because it is fraught with mistakes. As Linus Pauling, the Nobel laureate, said: 'If you want to have a good idea, have a lot of them, because most of them will be bad ones.' Years of unsupportive socialisation, however, block the adventuresome and inquisitive stance in most people. When, for example, did you last ask three 'why' questions in a row?

David Feldman (1999) authored a book in which he asks and answers more than 100 such questions, including:

Why are people immune to their own body odour?
Why are there 21 guns in a 21-gun salute?
What happens to the tread that wears off tyres?
Why doesn't sugar spoil or get mouldy?
Why is a telephone keypad arranged differently from that of a calculator?
Why is Jack the nickname for John?
How do they print 'M' on every M&M chocolate-coated peanut?
—and so on.

Many of us are a little too complacent even to ask such questions, let alone find out the answers! We often stop being inquisitive as we get older because we learn that it is good to be intelligent and being intelligent is interpreted as already knowing the answers, instead of asking good questions. Consequently, some of us tend to limit our learning as adults, take fewer risks, avoid asking why, and function in the world without trying to understand it. Creative problem solvers, on the other hand, are frequently engaged in inquisitive and experimental behaviour. Spence Silver at 3M described his attitude about the complacency block this way:

> *People like myself get excited about looking for new properties in materials. I find that very satisfying, to disturb the structure slightly and just see what happens. I have a hard time talking people into doing that—people who are more highly trained. It's been my experience that people are reluctant just to try, to experiment—just to see what will happen. (Nayak & Ketteringham 1986: 58. Reprinted by kind permission of Ranganath Nayak.)*

Bias against thinking

A second manifestation of the complacency block is the inclination to avoid non-active 'thinking'. This block, like most of the others, is partly a cultural bias as well as a personal one. For example, assume that you passed by a colleague's office one day and noticed him leaning back in his chair, staring out of the window. A half-hour later, as you passed by again, he had his feet up on the desk and was still staring out of the window. Twenty minutes later, you noticed that his demeanour had not changed much. What would be your conclusion? Most of us would assume that the fellow was not doing any work. We would assume that, unless we saw action, he was not being productive.

When was the last time you heard someone say, 'I'm sorry. I can't go to the football (or concert, dance, party or movie) because I have to think'? Or, 'I'll do the dishes tonight. I know you need to catch up on your thinking'? The fact that these statements sound humorous illustrates the bias most people develop towards action rather than thought, or against putting their feet up, rocking back in their chair, gazing off into space and engaging in solitary cognitive activity. This does not mean daydreaming or fantasising, but thinking.

There is a particular conceptual block in Western culture against the kind of thinking that uses the right hemisphere of the brain. Left-hemisphere thinking, for most people, is concerned with logical, analytical, linear or sequential tasks. Thinking using the left hemisphere is apt to be organised, planned and precise. Language and mathematics are left-hemisphere activities. Right-hemisphere thinking, on the other hand, is concerned with intuition, synthesis, playfulness and qualitative judgment. It tends to be more spontaneous, imaginative and emotional than left-hemisphere thinking. The emphasis in most formal education is towards left-hemisphere thought development—even more so in Eastern cultures than in Western cultures. Problem solving on the basis of reason, logic and utility is generally rewarded, while problem solving based on sentiment, intuition or pleasure is frequently considered tenuous and inferior.

A number of researchers have found that the most creative problem solvers are ambidextrous in their thinking. That is, they use both left- and right-hemisphere thinking and easily switch from one to the other (Hermann 1981; Hudspith 1985; Martindale 1999). Creative ideas arise most frequently in the right hemisphere but must be processed and interpreted by the left, so creative problem solvers use both hemispheres equally well.

BOX 4.1 Exercise to test ambidextrous thinking

LIST 1	LIST 2
decline	sunset
very	perfume
ambiguous	brick
resources	monkey
term	castle
conceptual	guitar
about	pencil
appendix	computer
determine	umbrella
forget	radar
quantity	blister
survey	chessboard

Try the exercise in Box 4.1. It illustrates this ambidextrous principle. There are two lists of words. Take a minute or two to memorise the first list. Then, on a piece of paper, write down as many words as you can remember. Now take a minute or two and memorise the words in the second list. Repeat the process of writing down as many words as you can remember.

Most people remember more words from the second list than from the first. This is because the second list contains words that relate to visual perceptions. They connect with right-brain activity as well as left-brain activity. People can draw mental pictures or fantasise about them. The same is true for creative ideas. The more both sides of the brain are used, the more creative the ideas.

Review of conceptual blocks

So far, we have suggested that certain conceptual blocks prevent individuals from solving problems creatively. These blocks, summarised in Table 4.3 (on page 192), narrow the scope of problem definition, limit the consideration of alternative solutions and constrain the selection of an optimal solution. Unfortunately, many of these conceptual blocks are unconscious and it is only by being confronted with problems that are unsolvable because of conceptual blocks that individuals become aware that they exist. Attempting to solve problems (like the ones in this chapter) that require you to overcome these mental barriers should help you to become aware of your own conceptual blocks.

These conceptual blocks are not all bad, of course; not all problems can be addressed by creative problem solving. But research has shown that individuals who have developed creative problem-solving skills are far more effective with complex problems that require a search for alternative solutions than others who are conceptually blocked (Basadur 1979; Collins & Amabile 1999; Sternberg 1999; Williams & Yang 1999).

The next section provides some techniques and tools that help to overcome these blocks and improve creative problem-solving skills.

Conceptual blockbusting

Conceptual blocks cannot be overcome all at once, because most blocks are a product of years of habit-forming thought processes. Overcoming them requires practice in thinking in different ways over a long period of time. You will not become a skilled creative problem solver just by reading this chapter. On the other hand, by becoming aware of your conceptual blocks and practising the following techniques you can enhance your creative problem-solving skills.

Stages in creative thought

A first step in overcoming conceptual blocks is recognising that creative problem solving is a skill that can be developed. Being a creative problem solver is not an inherent ability that some people naturally have and others lack. Jacob Rainbow, an employee of the US Patent Office who has more than 200 patents by himself, described the creative process as follows:

> *So you need three things to be an original thinker. First, you have to have a tremendous amount of information—a big data base if you like to be fancy. ... Then you have to be willing to pull the ideas, because you're interested. Now, some people could do it, but they don't bother. They're interested in doing something else. ... It's fun to come up with an idea, and if nobody wants it, I don't give a damn. It's just fun to come up with something strange and different. ... And then you must have the ability to get rid of the trash which you think of. You cannot only think of good ideas. ... (Csikszentmihalyi 1996: 48. Reproduced with permission of Mihaly Csikszentmihalyi.)*

Researchers generally agree that creative problem solving involves four stages: preparation, incubation, illumination and verification. The *preparation* stage includes gathering data, defining the problem, generating alternatives and consciously examining all available information. The primary difference between skilful creative problem solving and rational problem solving is in how this first step is approached. Creative problem solvers are more flexible and fluent in data gathering, problem definition, alternative generation and examination of options. In fact, it is in this stage that training in creative problem solving can significantly improve effectiveness because the other three steps are not amenable to conscious cognitive effort. The following discussion, therefore, is limited primarily to improving functioning in this first stage. Second, the *incubation* stage involves mostly unconscious mental activity in which the mind combines unrelated thoughts in pursuit of a solution. Conscious effort is not involved. *Illumination*, the third stage, occurs when an insight is recognised and a creative solution is articulated. *Verification* is the final stage, which involves evaluating the creative solution relative to some standard of acceptability.

In the preparation stage, two types of techniques are available for improving creative problem-solving abilities. One technique helps people to think about and define problems more creatively; the other helps individuals to gather information and generate more alternative solutions to problems.

One major difference between effective creative problem solvers and other people is that creative problem solvers are less constrained. They allow themselves to be more flexible in the definitions they impose on problems and the number of solutions they identify. They develop a large repertoire of approaches to problem solving. In short, they engage in what Csikszentmihalyi (1996) described as 'playfulness and childishness'. They try more things and worry less about their false starts or failures. As Interaction Associates (1971: 15) explained:

Flexibility in thinking is critical to good problem solving. A problem solver should be able to conceptually dance around the problem like a good boxer, jabbing and poking, without getting caught in one place or 'fixated'. At any given moment, a good problem solver should be able to apply a large number of strategies [for generating alternative definitions and solutions]. Moreover, a good problem solver is a person who has developed, through his understanding of strategies and experiences in problem solving, a sense of appropriateness of what is likely to be the most useful strategy at any particular time.

As a perusal through any bookstore will show, the number of books suggesting ways to enhance creative problem solving is enormous. The next sections present a few tools and hints that are especially effective and relatively simple for business executives and students to apply. Although some of them may seem game-like or playful, a sober pedagogical rationale underlies all of them. They help to unfreeze you from your normal sceptical, analytical approach to problems and increase your playfulness.

Improving problem definition

Problem definition, as with analytical problem solving, is probably the most critical step in creative problem solving. Once a problem is properly defined, solving it is often relatively simple.

Many individuals tend to define problems in terms with which they are familiar. When a problem that is strange or does not appear to have a solution is faced, it either remains undefined or is redefined in terms of something familiar. Unfortunately, new problems may not be the same as old problems, so relying on past definitions may impede the process of solving current problems or may lead to solving the 'wrong' problem. Consider the following story (Dunphy 1993).

The problem consultant

The manager of a high-rise office building was bothered by complaints from his tenants. 'The elevators are too slow!' they complained. So he called in two engineering firms to suggest solutions. After extensive investigation the first firm proposed installing two new and faster elevators in the existing shafts. The second firm proposed adding, at one end of the building, a new shaft, with a high-speed elevator. Both proposals cost hundreds of thousands of dollars and resulted in average gains of less than half a minute's waiting time per floor.

The manager decided to try to find an alternative. Flipping through the pages of the telephone directory, he found a consultant advertising as a 'problem consultant'. 'Perhaps that's what I need,' he thought, and so he called him in.

The problem consultant spent a couple of days wandering about the building rather casually, observing the situation and chatting with the tenants. Then he turned up in the manager's office.

'Well,' he began, 'you told me that your problem was slow elevators, which suggested that your solution to tenant complaints was faster elevators. But that really was not your problem. Your real problem is that people are bored stiff while waiting for the elevators.'

So, for about $1000, mirrors were installed beside the elevators on each floor. People adjusted their ties, patted their hair and admired themselves happily as they waited. And there were no more complaints.

Applying hints for creative problem definition can help people to see problems in alternative ways so that their definitions are less narrowly constrained. Three such hints for improving and expanding the definition process are discussed below.

Make the strange familiar and the familiar strange

By putting something you do not know in terms of something you do know, and vice versa, and by analysing what you know and applying it to what you do not know, you can develop new insights and perspectives.

First, you form a definition of a problem (make the strange familiar). Then you try to make that definition out-of-focus, distorted or changed in some way (make the familiar strange). Use analogies and metaphors to create this distortion. Postpone the original definition of the problem while you analyse the analogy or metaphor. Then impose the analysis on the original problem to see what new insights you can uncover.

For example, suppose you have defined a problem as low morale among members of your team. You may form an analogy or metaphor by answering questions such as the following about the problem:

What does this remind me of? What does this make me feel like? What is this similar to? What is it not similar to? (Your answers might be: This problem reminds me of trying to turn a rusty bolt. It makes me feel like I do when visiting a hospital ward. This is similar to the loser's change room after a football game. And so on.) Metaphors and analogies should connect what you are less sure about (the original problem) to what you are more sure about (the metaphor). By analysing the metaphor or analogy, you may identify attributes of the problem that were not evident before. New insights can occur.

Many creative solutions have been generated by such a technique. For example, William Harvey was the first to apply the 'pump' analogy to the heart, which led to the discovery of the body's circulatory system. Niels Bohr compared the atom to the solar system and supplanted Rutherford's prevailing 'raisin pudding' model of matter's building blocks. Creativity consultant Roger von Oech (1986) helped turn around a struggling computer company by applying a restaurant analogy to the company's operations. The real problems emerged when the restaurant, rather than the company, was analysed.

Gareth Morgan sees the metaphor as a valuable tool in analysing the often complex, ambiguous and paradoxical nature of organisations. Of the wide-ranging efficacy of the metaphor, he says (1986: 17):

> *By building on the use of metaphor—which is basic to our way of thinking generally—we have a means of enhancing our capacity for creative yet disciplined thought, in a way that allows us to grasp and deal with the many-sided character of organizational life. And in doing so, I believe that we can find new ways of organizing and new ways of approaching and solving organizational problems.*

Major contributions in the field of organisational behaviour have occurred by applying analogies to other types of organisation, such as machines, cybernetic or open systems, force fields, clans and so on. Here are some hints to keep in mind when constructing analogies.

1. Include action or motion in the analogy (for example, driving a car, cooking a meal, attending a funeral).
2. Include things that can be visualised or pictured in the analogy (for example, stars, football games, crowded shopping malls).
3. Pick familiar events or situations (for example, families, kissing, bedtime).
4. Try to relate things that are not obviously similar (for example, saying an organisation is like a crowd is not nearly so rich a simile as saying an organisation is like a psychic prison or a poker game).

Four types of analogies are:

1. *Personal analogies*, where individuals try to identify themselves as the problem ('If I were the problem, how would I feel, what would I like, what could satisfy me?').
2. *Direct analogies*, where people apply facts, technology and common experiences to the problem (for example, Brunel solved the problem of underwater construction by watching a shipworm tunnelling into a tube).
3. *Symbolic analogies*, where symbols or images are imposed on the problem (for example, modelling the problem mathematically or diagramming the logic flow).
4. *Fantasy analogies*, where individuals ask the question: 'In my wildest dreams, how would I wish the problem to be resolved?' (for example, 'I wish all employees would work with no supervision').

Elaborate on the definition

There is a variety of ways to enlarge, alter or replace a problem definition once it has been specified. One way is to force yourself to generate at least two alternative hypotheses for every problem definition. That is, specify at least two plausible definitions of the problem in addition to the one originally accepted. Think in plural rather than singular terms. Instead of asking: 'What is the problem?', 'What is the meaning of this?', 'What is the result?', ask instead such questions as: 'What are the problems?', 'What are the meanings of this?', 'What are the results?'.

As an example, look at Figure 4.8. Select the shape that is different from all the others. A majority of people select B first. If you did, you are right. It is the only figure that has all straight lines. On the other hand, quite a few people pick A. If you are one of them, you are also right. It is the only figure with a continuous line and no points of discontinuity. Alternatively, C can also be right, with the rationale that it is the only figure with two straight and two curved lines. Similarly, D is the only one with one curved and one straight line, and E is the only figure that is non-symmetrical or partial. The point is, there can often be more than one problem definition, more than one right answer, and more than one perspective from which to view a problem.

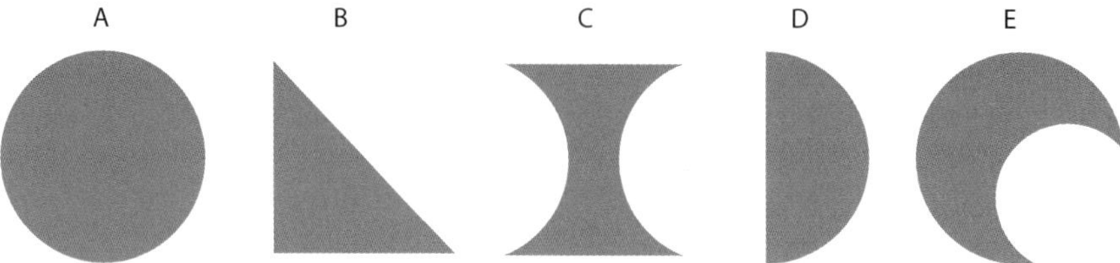

FIGURE 4.8 The five-figure problem

Another way to elaborate definitions is to use a question checklist. This is a series of questions designed to help individuals think of alternatives to their accepted definitions. Several creative managers have shared with us some of their most fruitful questions:

1. Is there anything else?
2. Is the reverse true?
3. Is this a symptom of a more general problem?
4. Can it be stated differently?
5. Who sees it differently?
6. What past experience is this like?

As an exercise, take a minute now to think of a problem you are currently experiencing. Write it down so it is formally specified. Now manipulate that definition by answering the six questions in the checklist. If you cannot think of a problem, try the exercise with this one: 'I am not as attractive/intelligent/creative as I would like to be.'

Reverse the definition

A third tool for improving and expanding problem definition is to reverse the definition of the problem. That is, turn the problem upside down, inside out or back to front. Reverse the way in which you think of the problem. For example, consider the following problem.

> *A concrete tank manufacturer had overproduced a particular range of large concrete tanks. In searching for alternative markets, no solutions were found until the logic of a tank being a structure to keep water in was reversed to focus on keeping water out. This reversal of definition led the tank manufacturer to identify the potential of the unsold tanks as short-term grain silos. Consequently, the outer surface of the tank was waterproofed and the 'tanks', now marketed as stockfeed silos, can be found in a number of rural areas in Australia.*

This reversal is similar to what Rothenberg (1979, 1991) refers to as 'Janusian thinking'. Janus was the Roman god with two faces that looked in opposite directions. Janusian thinking means thinking contradictory thoughts at the same time: that is, conceiving two opposing ideas to be true concurrently. Rothenberg claimed, after studying 54 highly creative artists and scientists (for example, Nobel Prize winners), that most major scientific breakthroughs and artistic masterpieces are products of Janusian thinking. Creative people who actively formulate antithetical ideas and then resolve them produce the most valuable contributions to the scientific and artistic worlds. Quantum leaps in knowledge often occur.

An example is Einstein's account (1919: 1) of having 'the happiest thought of my life'. He developed the following concept:

> *For an observer in free fall from the roof of a house, there exists, during his fall, no gravitational field … in his immediate vicinity. If the observer releases any objects, they will remain, relative to him, in a state of rest. The [falling] observer is therefore justified in considering his state as one of rest.*

Einstein concluded, in other words, that two seemingly contradictory states could be present simultaneously: motion and rest. This realisation led to the development of his revolutionary general theory of relativity.

In another study of creative potential, Rothenberg and Hausman (2000) found that when individuals were presented with a stimulus word and asked to respond with the word that first came to mind, highly creative students, Nobel Prize-winning scientists and prize-winning artists responded with antonyms significantly more often than did individuals with average creativity. The authors argued, based on these results, that creative people think in terms of opposites more often than do other people.

For our purposes, the whole point is to reverse or contradict the currently accepted definition in order to expand the number of perspectives considered. For instance, a problem might be that morale is too high instead of (or in addition to) too low in our team, or that employees need less motivation instead of more motivation to increase productivity. Opposites and looking backwards often enhance creativity.

These three techniques for improving creative problem definition are summarised in Box 4.2. Their purpose is not to help you generate alternative definitions just for the sake of alternatives, but to broaden your perspectives, to help you overcome conceptual blocks and to produce more elegant solutions.

BOX 4.2 Techniques for improving problem definition

- Make the strange familiar and the familiar strange.
- Elaborate on the definition.
- Reverse the definition.

Generating more alternatives

A common tendency is to define problems in terms of available solutions (that is, the problem is defined as a solution already possessed or the first acceptable alternative). This tendency leads to consideration of a minimal number and narrow range of alternatives in problem solving. However, most experts agree that the primary characteristics of effective creative problem solvers are their fluency and flexibility of thought. *Fluency* refers to the number of ideas or concepts produced in a given length of time. *Flexibility* refers to the diversity of ideas or concepts generated. While most problem solvers consider a few homogeneous alternatives, creative problem solvers consider many heterogeneous alternatives. The following techniques are designed to help you improve your ability to generate many varied alternatives when faced with problems. They are summarised in Box 4.3.

BOX 4.3 Techniques for generating more alternatives

- Defer judgment.
- Expand current alternatives.
- Combine unrelated attributes.

Defer judgment

Probably the most common method of generating alternatives is the technique of brainstorming, originally developed by Osborn (1953). This tool is powerful because most people make quick judgments about each piece of information or each alternative solution they encounter. This technique is designed to help people generate alternatives for problem solving without prematurely evaluating, and hence discarding, them. Four main rules govern brainstorming:

1. No evaluation of any kind is permitted as alternatives are being generated. Individual energy is spent on generating ideas, not on defending them.
2. The wildest and most divergent ideas are encouraged. It is easier to tighten up alternatives than to loosen them.
3. The quantity of ideas takes precedence over the quality. Emphasising quality engenders judgment and evaluation.
4. Participants should build on or modify the ideas of others. Poor ideas that are added to or altered often become good ideas.

Brainstorming techniques are best used in a group setting so that individuals can stimulate ideas in one another. Recent research has found, however, that brainstorming in a group may be less efficient than alternative forms of brainstorming (due to free riders, unwitting evaluations, production blocking, and so on). One widely used brainstorming technique is to have individual group members generate ideas on their own, then submit them to the group for exploration and evaluation (Fink, Ward & Smith 1992). Alternatively, electronic brainstorming, where either an 'electronic' or a human facilitator is used, provides the advantage of transcending space and time constraints, allowing anonymity and potentially increasing the quantity and quality of ideas (Sian 1997). What is clear from the research is that generating alternatives using a group in the process produces more and better ideas than can be produced alone.

Another caution about brainstorming should be noted. Often, after a rush of alternatives is produced at the outset of a brainstorming session, the quantity of ideas rapidly subsides. But to stop at that point is an ineffective use of brainstorming. When easily identifiable solutions have been exhausted, that is when truly creative alternatives are often produced in brainstorming groups. So, keep working!

The best way to get a feel for the power of brainstorming groups is to participate in one. Try the following exercise based on an actual problem faced by a group of students and university lecturers. Spend at least ten minutes in a small group, brainstorming ideas.

> *A request has been made for a faculty member to design an executive education program for mid-level managers at a major car manufacturing company. It is to focus on enhancing creativity and innovation among managers. The trouble is that the top human resource executive has indicated that she does not want to approach the subject with brain teasers or games. Instead, she wants other approaches that would help these managers become more creative personally and more effective at fostering innovation among others.*

What ideas can you come up with for teaching this subject of creative problem solving to mid-level managers in an organisation? How could you help them learn to be more creative? Generate as many ideas as you can following the rules of brainstorming. After at least ten minutes, assess the fluency and flexibility of the ideas generated.

Expand current alternatives

Sometimes, brainstorming in a group is not possible or is too costly in terms of the number of people involved and the hours required. Managers pursuing a hectic organisational life can sometimes find brainstorming to be too inefficient. Moreover, people sometimes need an external stimulus or blockbuster to help them generate new ideas. One useful and readily available technique for expanding alternatives is subdivision, or dividing a problem into smaller parts. Subdivision improves problem solving by increasing the speed with which alternatives can be generated and selected. Action can proceed simultaneously on several aspects of the problem. The more detailed the subdivision of the problem, the more simultaneous activity is possible and hence the greater the speed of problem solving.

To see how subdivision helps to develop more alternatives and speeds the process of problem solving, consider the problem, common in the creativity literature, of listing alternative uses for a familiar object. For example, in one minute how many uses can you list for a ping-pong ball? The more uses you identify, the greater your fluency in thinking. The more variety in the list, the greater your flexibility in thinking. You might include the following in your list: bob for a fishing line, Christmas ornament, toy for a cat, gearshift knob, model for a molecular structure, wind gauge when hung from a string, head for a finger puppet, miniature basketball. Your list will be much longer.

After you generate your list, apply the technique of subdivision by identifying the specific characteristics of a ping-pong ball—that is, dividing it into its component attributes. For example, weight, colour, texture, shape, porosity, strength, hardness, chemical properties and conduction potential are all attributes of ping-pong balls that help to expand the uses you might think of. By dividing an object mentally into more specific attributes, you can arrive at many more alternative uses (for example, reflector, holder when cut in half, bug bed, ball for lottery drawing, and so on).

One exercise that has been used with students and executives to illustrate this technique is to have them write down as many of their managerial strengths as they can think of. Most people list a dozen or so attributes relatively easily. Then the various dimensions of the manager's role, the activities that managers engage in, the challenges that most managers face from inside and outside the organisation and so on are analysed. These same people are then asked to write down another list of their strengths as managers. The list is almost always twice as long, or more. By identifying the sub-components of any problem, far more alternatives can be generated than by considering the problem as a whole.

As one final illustration, assume that someone stole one-quarter of the cake shown in Figure 4.9. Four hungry athletes want equal pieces of what remains. Divide the cake into four pieces equal in size, shape and area. Try to do it in a minute or less. The problem is easy if you use subdivision. It is more difficult if you do not. Two answers to the problem can be found on page 226.

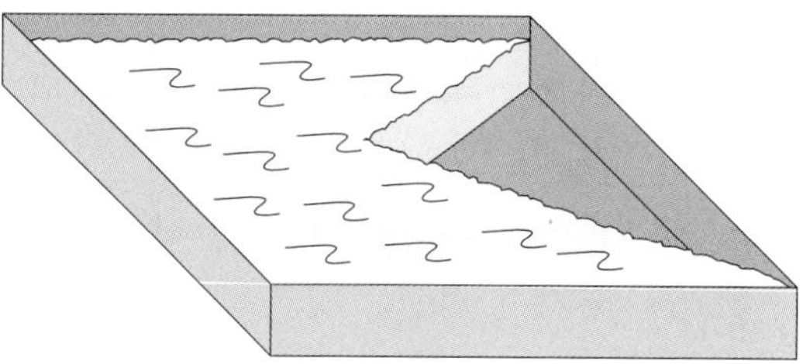

FIGURE 4.9 A slice of cake

Combine unrelated attributes

A third technique focuses on helping problem solvers expand alternatives by forcing the integration of seemingly unrelated elements. Research into creative problem solving has shown that an ability to see common relationships among disparate factors is a major feature differentiating creative from non-creative individuals (Feldman 1999). Two ways to do this are through morphological synthesis (Koberg & Bagnall 1974) and the relational algorithm (Crovitz 1970). (For literature reviews, see Fink, Ward & Smith 1992 and Starko 1995.)

With *morphological synthesis*, a four-step procedure is involved. First, the problem is written down. Second, attributes of the problem are listed. Then alternatives to each attribute are listed, and, finally, different alternatives from the attributes list are combined.

To illustrate this procedure, suppose you are faced with the problem of a personal assistant who takes an extended lunch break almost every day despite your reminders to be back on time. Think of alternative ways to solve this problem. The first solution that comes to mind for most people is to sit down and have a talk with (or threaten) the assistant. If that does not work, most of us would just fire or transfer the person. However, look at what other alternatives can be generated by using morphological synthesis (see Box 4.4).

The primary value of this process is to expand the range of alternatives that can be considered when seeking a solution to the problem. You can see how many more alternatives come to mind when you force together attributes that are not obviously connected. The matrix of attributes can create

LEARNING

BOX 4.4 Morphological synthesis

Step 1 Problem statement: The operator takes extended lunch breaks every day with friends in the cafeteria.

Step 2 Major attributes of the problem:

AMOUNT OF TIME	START TIME	PLACE	WITH WHOM	FREQUENCY
More than 1 hour	12 noon	Cafeteria	Friends	Daily

Step 3 Alternative attributes:

AMOUNT OF TIME	START TIME	PLACE	WITH WHOM	FREQUENCY
30 minutes	11.00	Office	Co-workers	Weekly
90 minutes	11.30	Conference room	Boss	Twice a week
45 minutes	12.30	Restaurant	Management team	Alternate days

Step 4 Combining attributes:

- A 30-minute lunch beginning at 12.30 in the conference room with the boss once a week.
- A 90-minute lunch beginning at 11.30 in the conference room with co-workers twice a week.
- A 45-minute lunch beginning at 11.00 in the cafeteria with the management team every other day.
- A 30-minute lunch beginning at 12.00 alone in the office on alternate days.

a very long list of possible solutions. In more complicated problems—for example, how to improve quality, how to serve customers better, how to improve the reward system—the potential number of alternatives is even greater and hence more creativity is required to analyse them.

The second technique for combining unrelated attributes in problem solving, the *relational algorithm*, involves applying connecting words that force a relationship between two elements in a problem. For example, the following is a list of some relational words:

about	among	because	by	if	now
across	and	before	down	in	of
after	as	between	for	near	off
against	at	but	from	under	on
opposite	over	so	through	until	where
or	round	then	to	up	while
out	still	though	not	when	with

To illustrate the use of this technique, suppose you are faced with the following problem. Our customers are dissatisfied with our service. The two major elements in this problem are customers and service. They are connected by the phrase 'are dissatisfied with'. With the relational algorithm technique, the relational words in the problem statement are removed and replaced with other relational words to see if new ideas for alternative solutions can be identified. For example, consider the following connections where new relational words are used:

- Customers among service (for example, customers interact with service personnel).
- Customers as service (for example, customers deliver service to other customers).
- Customers and service (for example, customers and service personnel work collaboratively together).
- Customers for service (for example, customer focus groups can help improve our service).
- Service near customers (for example, change the location of the service to be near customers).
- Service before customers (for example, prepare personalised service before the customer arrives).
- Service through customers (for example, use customers to provide additional service).
- Service when customers (for example, provide timely service when customers want it).

By connecting the two elements of the problem in different ways, new possibilities for problem solution can be formulated.

Cultural considerations

The perspective taken in this chapter has a clear bias towards Western culture. It focuses on analytical and creative problem solving as methods for addressing specific issues. Enhancing creativity has a specific purpose, and that is to solve certain kinds of problems more effectively. Creativity in Eastern cultures, on the other hand, is often defined differently. Creativity is focused less on creating solutions, originality/novelty and final products/outcomes than on usefulness or uncovering enlightenment, one's true self, or the achievement of wholeness, self-actualisation, skill and process (Chu 1970; Kozbelt & Durmysheva 2007; Kuo 1996; Morris & Leung 2010). It is aimed at getting in touch with the unconscious (Maduro 1976). In both the East and the West, however, creativity is viewed positively. Gods of creativity are worshipped in West African cultures (Olokun) and among Hindus (Vishvakarma), for example (see Ben-Amos 1986; Wonder & Blake 1992), and creativity is often viewed in mystical or religious terms rather than managerial or practical terms.

In fostering creative problem solving in international settings or with individuals from different countries, Trompenaars' (1996), Trompenaars and Hampden–Turner's (1999) model is useful for understanding the differences that must be kept in mind. Countries differ, for example, in their orientation towards internal control (Australia, New Zealand, Canada, the United States, the United Kingdom) versus external control (Japan, China, Singapore, the Czech Republic). In internal cultures, the environment is assumed to be changeable, so creativity focuses on attacking problems directly. In external cultures, because individuals assume less control of the environment, creativity focuses less on problem resolution and more on achieving insight or oneness with nature. Changing the environment is not the usual objective.

Similarly, cultures emphasising a specific orientation (Sweden, Denmark, the United Kingdom, France) are more likely to challenge the status quo and seek new ways to address problems than cultures emphasising a diffuse culture (China, India, Indonesia, South Korea, Singapore) in which loyalty, wholeness and long-term relationships are more likely to inhibit individual creative effort. This is similar to the differences that are likely in countries emphasising universalism (South Korea, Venezuela, China, India) as opposed to particularism (Switzerland, the United States, Sweden, United Kingdom, Germany). Cultures emphasising universalism tend to focus on generalisable outcomes and consistent rules or procedures. Particularistic cultures are more inclined to search for unique aberrations from the norm, thus having more of a tendency towards creative solution finding. Managers encouraging conceptual blockbusting and creative problem solving, in other words, will find some individuals more inclined towards the rule-oriented procedures of analytical problem solving and less inclined towards the playfulness and experimentation associated with creative problem solving than others.

Hints for applying problem-solving techniques

Not every problem is amenable to these techniques and tools for conceptual blockbusting, of course. Our intent in presenting these six suggestions is to help you expand the number of options available to you for defining problems and generating additional potential solutions. They are most useful with problems that are not straightforward, but are complex, ambiguous or imprecise in definition. All of us have enormous creative potential, but the stresses and pressures of daily life, coupled with the inertia of conceptual habits, tend to submerge that potential. These hints are ways to help unlock it again.

Reading about techniques or having a desire to be creative is not, by itself, enough to make you a skilful creative problem solver, of course. Although research has confirmed the effectiveness of these techniques for improving creative problem solving, they depend on application and practice, as well as an environment that is conducive to creativity. Here are six practical hints that will help facilitate your own ability to apply these techniques effectively and improve your creative problem-solving ability.

1. *Give yourself some relaxation time.* The more intense your work, the more your need for complete breaks. Break out of your routine sometimes. This frees your mind and gives room for new thoughts.

2. *Find a place (physical space) where you can think.* It should be a place where interruptions are eliminated, at least for a time. Reserve your best time for thinking.
3. *Talk to other people about ideas.* Isolation produces far fewer ideas than does conversation. Make a list of people who stimulate you to think. Spend some time with them.
4. *Ask other people for their ideas about your problems.* Find out what others think about them. Do not be embarrassed to share your problems, but do not become dependent on others to solve them for you.
5. *Read a lot.* Read at least one thing regularly that is outside your field of expertise. Keep track of new thoughts from your reading.
6. *Protect yourself from idea-killers.* Do not spend time with 'black holes'—that is, people who absorb all your energy and light but give nothing in return. Do not let yourself or others negatively evaluate your ideas too soon.

You will find these hints useful not only for enhancing creative problem solving but for analytical problem solving as well. Figure 4.10 summarises the two problem-solving processes—analytical and creative—and the factors you should consider when determining how to approach each type of problem.

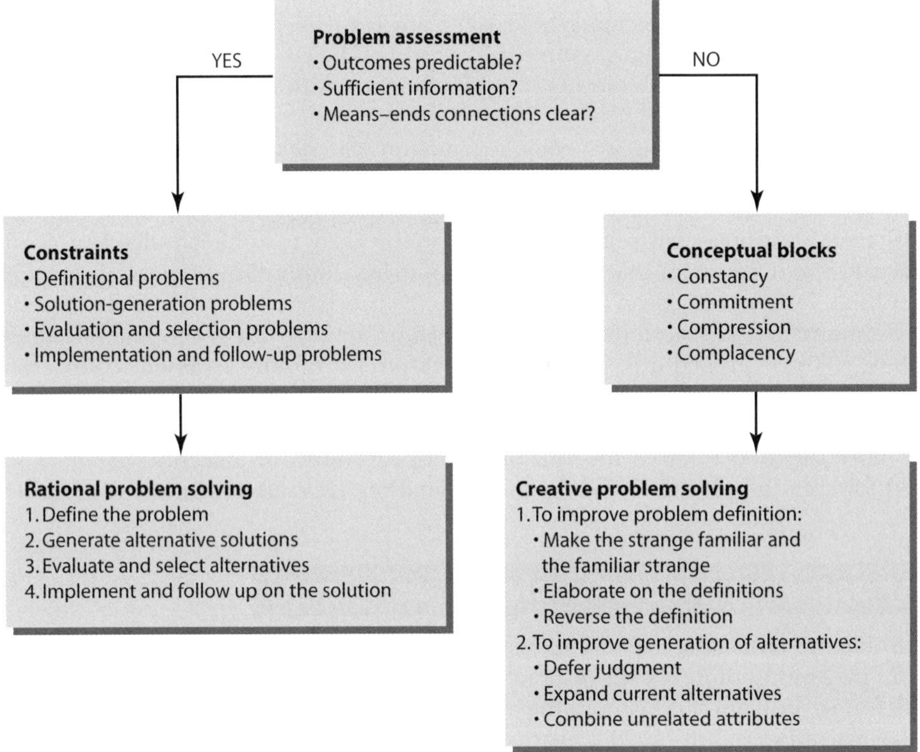

FIGURE 4.10 A model of analytical and creative problem solving

Fostering innovation

Unlocking your own creative potential is not enough, of course, to make you a successful manager. A major challenge is to help unlock it in other people as well. Fostering innovation and creativity among those with whom you work is at least as great a challenge as increasing your own creativity. This last section of the chapter briefly discusses some principles that will help you to accomplish the task of fostering innovation more effectively.

Neither Percy Spencer nor Spence Silver could have succeeded in their creative ideas had there not been a managerial support system present that fostered creative problem solving and the pursuit of innovation. In each case, certain characteristics were present in their organisations, fostered by managers around them, that made their innovations possible. This section does not discuss the macro-organisational issues associated with innovation (for example, organisation design, strategic orientation and human resource systems). Excellent discussions of these factors are reviewed in sources such as McMillan (1985), Tichy (1983), Tushman and Anderson (1997), Van de Ven (1997) and Amabile (1988). Instead, the focus is on activities that individual managers can engage in that foster innovation. Table 4.4 summarises three management principles that help to engender innovativeness and creative problem solving.

TABLE 4.4 Three principles for fostering innovativeness

PRINCIPLE	EXAMPLES
1. Separate people; put people together.	• Let individuals work alone as well as with teams and task forces. • Encourage minority reports and legitimise 'devil's advocate' roles. • Encourage heterogeneous membership in teams. • Separate competing groups or subgroups.
2. Monitor and prod.	• Talk to customers. • Identify customer expectations both in advance and after the sale. • Hold people accountable. • Use 'sharp-pointed' prods.
3. Reward multiple roles.	• Idea champion. • Sponsor and mentor. • Orchestrator and facilitator. • Rule breaker.

Separating people; putting people together

Percy Spencer's magnetron project involved a consumer product closeted away from Raytheon's main-line business of missiles and other defence-contract work. Spence Silver's new glue resulted when a polymer adhesive task force was separated from 3M's normal activities. The Macintosh computer was developed by a task force taken outside the company and given space and time to work on an innovative computer. Many new ideas come from individuals who are given time and resources and allowed to work apart from the normal activities of the organisation. Establishing separately located research and development centres, innovation and problem-solving task forces, organising brainstorming 'retreats' or future search workshops are all good ways to foster innovation. Because most businesses are designed to produce the 10 000th part correctly or to service the 10 000th customer efficiently, they do not function well at producing the first part. That is why separating people and locating them in a different and specific environment is often necessary to foster innovation and creativity.

On the other hand, forming teams (putting people together) is almost always more productive than having people work by themselves. Such teams should be characterised by certain attributes, though. Nemeth (1986: 25) found that creativity increased markedly when minority influences were present in the team—for example, when 'devil's advocate' roles were legitimised, a formal minority report was always included in the final recommendations, and individuals assigned to work on a team had divergent backgrounds or views.

> *Those exposed to minority views are stimulated to attend to more aspects of the situation, they think in more divergent ways, and they are more likely to detect novel solutions or come to new decisions.*

Nemeth found that those positive benefits occur in groups even when the divergent or minority views are wrong. Similarly, Janis (1971) found that narrow-mindedness in groups (dubbed 'groupthink') was best overcome by establishing competing groups working on the same problem, participation in groups by outsiders, assigning a role of critical evaluator in the group, having groups made up of cross-functional participants, and so on. James (1992) believes that, although the dynamics of groupthink have been known for many years, there is anecdotal evidence to suggest that organisations are still getting trapped by this phenomenon. He believes that the most productive groups are those characterised by fluid roles, lots of interaction among members and outside stakeholders, and flat power structures.

Innovativeness can be fostered when individuals are placed in teams and when they are at least temporarily separated from the normal pressures of organisational life. Teams, however, are most effective at generating innovative ideas when they are characterised by attributes of minority influence, competition, heterogeneity and interaction. You can help to foster innovation among people you manage, therefore, by giving people time out in a new environment in order to explore new methods as well as putting people together (for example, on a team).

Monitor and motivate

Percy Spencer was not allowed to work on his project without accountability, and neither was Spence Silver. Both eventually had to report on the results they accomplished with their experimentation and imagination. At 3M, for example, people are expected to allocate 15 per cent of their time away from company business to work on new, creative ideas. They can even appropriate company materials and resources to work on them. However, individuals are always held accountable for their decisions. They need to show results for their 'play time'.

Holding people accountable for outcomes, in fact, is an important motivator for improved performance. Two innovators in the entertainment industry captured this principle with these remarks:

> *The ultimate inspiration is the deadline. That's when you have to do what needs to be done. The fact that twice a year the creative talent of this country is working until midnight to get something ready for a trade show is very good for the economy. Without this kind of pressure, things would turn to mashed potatoes. (von Oech 1986: 119)*

Organisations have various ways of holding people accountable for innovation. Some require employees to submit one or two suggestions for improvement each month, with a certain percentage of the ideas being implemented. Some companies pay for ideas submitted, with an extra payment made if the idea is used. Other organisations have teams working on a similar basis.

In addition to accountability, innovativeness is stimulated by what has been termed 'sharp-pointed prods'—in other words, demanding innovations that require creative solutions. *Australia II*'s winged keel is one such example.

Winning the America's Cup requires more than a fast boat, an expert crew and a skipper as determined as the 1983 challenger, John Bertrand. Australian Ben Lexcen was commissioned to design a 12-metre yacht to win the contest. The boat he designed was not, as it happens, the fastest boat to race at Newport that year. However, having a champion sailor and an outstanding leader to skipper it, a world-class sailmaker to provide its 'engines', and a superb crew who were the ultimate team to sail it made up for the deficiencies of the boat. The leading edge was supplied by the revolutionary winged keel that Lexcen devised, although not quite as folklore would have it.

When optimal conditions prevailed off Newport, *Australia II*'s winged keel performed brilliantly. John Bertrand was to discover that these conditions occurred only two or three times over a period of many months (Bertrand & Robinson 1985: 194). It was not the winged keel as such that gave the Australian boat its leading edge; rather, it was the myth of invincibility, focused on the keel, that gave *Australia II* that extra edge.

The mysterious winged keel was not seen publicly until after the America's Cup had been won. When out of the water, the keel was heavily shrouded and its attributes became a worldwide fascination. At one point an underwater photographer was seized as he tried to photograph the keel. The New York Yacht Club tried to have the Australian boat disqualified because of a keel it had never seen. The aura surrounding the keel provided an amazingly powerful and very creative psychological advantage to the Australians.

Australia II was not, in fact, invincible—it lost a number of races. However, skipper John Bertrand made sure that every loss was accredited to skipper error, sail problems or experimentation of some sort, and the perception of the wonder-boat and its keel was rarely questioned. The lie of invincibility became an accepted truth and the battle for the America's Cup was won by a challenger for the first time.

One of the best methods of generating useful prods is to regularly monitor customers' preferences, expectations and evaluations. Many of the most creative ideas have come from customers, the recipients of goods and services. Identifying their preferences in advance and monitoring their evaluations of products or services later are good ways to get ideas for innovation and to be prodded to make improvements. All employees should be in regular contact with their customers, asking questions and monitoring performance.

'Customers' does not mean just the end-users of a business product or service. In fact, all of us have customers, whether we are students at university, members of a family, or players on a basketball team. Customers are simply those for whom we are trying to produce something or those whom we serve. Students, for example, can count their instructors, fellow class members and potential employers as customers whom they serve. Before and after monitoring of their expectations and evaluations is an important way of helping to foster new ideas for problem solving. This monitoring is best done through one-on-one meetings, but it can also be done through follow-up calls, surveys, customer complaint cards, suggestion systems and so on.

In summary, you can foster innovation by holding people accountable for new ideas and by stimulating them with periodic prods. The most useful prods generally come from customers.

Reward multiple roles

The success of the sticky yellow notes at 3M is more than a story of the creativity of Spence Silver. It also illustrates the necessity of people playing multiple roles in innovation and the importance of recognising and rewarding those who play such roles. Without a number of people playing multiple roles, Spence Silver's glue would probably still be on a shelf somewhere.

Four crucial roles in the innovative process are the idea champion (the person who comes up with innovative solutions to problems), the sponsor or mentor (the person who helps provide the resources, environment and encouragement for the idea champion to work on his or her idea), the orchestrator or facilitator (the person who brings together cross-functional groups and the necessary political support to facilitate implementation of creative ideas) and the rule breaker (the person who goes beyond organisational boundaries and barriers to ensure success of the innovation). Each of these roles is present in most important innovations in organisations and all are illustrated by the Post-it note example.

This story has four main parts.

1. Spence Silver, while fooling around with chemical configurations that the academic literature indicated would not work, invented a glue that would not stick. Silver spent years giving presentations to any audience at 3M that would listen, trying to pawn off his glue on some division that could find a practical application for it. But no one was interested.
2. Henry Courtney and Roger Merrill developed a coating substance that allowed the glue to stick to one surface but not to others. This made it possible to produce a permanently temporary glue—that is, one that would peel off easily when pulled but would otherwise hang on forever.

3. Art Fry found a problem that fitted Spence Silver's solution. He found an application for the glue as a 'better bookmark' and as a note pad. No equipment existed at 3M to coat only a part of a piece of paper with the glue. Fry therefore carried 3M equipment and tools home to his own basement, where he designed and made his own machine to manufacture the forerunner of Post-it notes. Because the working machine became too large to remove from his basement, he blasted a hole in the wall to get the equipment back to 3M. He then brought together engineers, designers, production managers and machinists to demonstrate the prototype machine and generate enthusiasm for manufacturing the product.
4. Geoffrey Nicholson and Joseph Ramsey began marketing the product inside 3M. They also submitted it to the standard 3M market tests. The product failed miserably. No one wanted to pay even a dollar for a pad of scratch paper. But when Nicholson and Ramsey broke 3M rules by personally visiting test market sites and giving away free samples, the consuming public became addicted to the product.

In this scenario, Spence Silver was both a rule breaker and an idea champion. Art Fry was also an idea champion but, more importantly, he orchestrated the coming together of the various groups needed to get the innovation off the ground. Henry Courtney and Roger Merrill helped to sponsor Silver's innovation by providing him with the coating substance that would allow his idea to work. And Geoff Nicholson and Joe Ramsey were both rule breakers and sponsors in their bid to get the product accepted by the public. In each case, not only did all these people play unique roles, but they did so with tremendous enthusiasm and zeal. They were confident of their ideas and willing to put their time and resources on the line as advocates. They fostered support among a variety of constituencies, both within their own areas of expertise and among outside groups. Most organisations are inclined to give in to those who are sure of themselves, persistent in their efforts and motivated enough to make converts of others.

Not everyone can be an idea champion. But when managers reward and recognise those who sponsor and orchestrate the ideas of others, innovation increases in organisations. Teams form, supporters replace competitors and creativity thrives. Facilitating multiple role development is the job of the innovative manager.

EMERGING ISSUES

Dunphy, Griffiths and Benn (2003), along with many others (cf. Tim Flannery 2006, *The Weather Makers*, Atlantic Monthly Press; the special issue of *Issues*, September 2006, <www.issues.com> ; and see Al Gore's documentary *An Inconvenient Truth*), believe that the sustainability of business and our society, both economically and ecologically, is one of this century's central debates. They argue that one of the key challenges ahead for many corporations is how to devise creative solutions for emerging problems, not only in terms of resource use and pollution but also in the critical areas of social and community sustainability. In fact, a Lowy Institute poll revealed that global warming rated ahead of international terrorism as the primary threat to Australia's vital interest (Collis 2006).

Dunphy, Griffiths and Benn (2003: 14) propose a *sustainability phase model* with the following six phases:

- rejection
- non-responsiveness
- compliance
- efficiency
- strategic proactivity
- the sustaining corporation.

This phase model describes how organisations typically approach the need for sustainable development, moving from outright rejection to being absolutely committed to 'the emergence of a society that supports the ecological viability of the planet and its species and contributes to just, equitable social practices and human fulfilment'.

Dunphy et al. believe that 'progress' along the pathway described by the phase model can be facilitated by the actions of key organisational change agents. They cite self-leadership (including self-awareness and self-management) and creative problem-solving skills as two vital attributes of this type of sustainable change agent.

As an example of proactive problem solving at the efficiency and strategic phases, Fuji Xerox Australia has achieved spectacular results in a number of areas. Since Fuji Xerox leases its photocopiers, printers and fax machines to customers and is itself responsible for disposal, it was in the company's interests to reduce the volume of discarded parts and machinery to landfill. Instead of wholesale disposal, the company began to dismantle its machines to identify exactly where problems had occurred and why. This product information was then used to redesign components to extend their life. For example, the redesign of a small roller spring, worth only five cents, has led to millions of dollars of savings worldwide by extending the life of each roller. In 2002, the remanufacture of components alone saved over $20 million at the Sydney factory and led to the employment of 130 new people. Fuji Xerox's aim is eventually to manufacture 'waste-free products in waste-free factories' and thereby totally eliminate the original problem of unsustainable waste disposal costs.

Clearly, both rational and creative problem-solving processes are going to be needed to meet the challenges of sustainability in the 21st century.

Summary

Innovation and invention are difficult and risky, as out of every ten R&D projects, five fail, three are abandoned and only two ultimately become commercially successful (Rizova 2006). Australia and its neighbours have had their fair share of successes, however. As early as the 1850s, Australian James Harrison developed the first form of refrigeration. The Hill's Hoist, the Victa mower and the Holden car are well-known examples of Australian imagination and innovation. It is less well known that Australian inventors also gave the world the pop-top can, the torpedo, ready-mix concrete, the castor wheel, self-erecting cranes, the flight recorder and a host of other inventions. In recent times, Australian inventiveness has produced an aircraft landing system (Interscan) and another CSIRO success, the technology called Gene Shears. In New Zealand, this spirit of creative problem solving and resourcefulness is referred to as 'number 8 thinking' (Anonymous 2005; Wadey 2007). The term comes from the well-known 'brand of fencing wire that, with a bit of creative thinking, could be plied into everything from a replacement radio aerial to a car exhaust support' (Anonymous 2005).

In the past, many Australian inventions became the property of overseas organisations. Now, for a variety of reasons, production rights are still often sold to foreign companies, and new industries, wealth and employment opportunities are lost to Australia. When looking for an Australian company to develop the gene-shearing technology, the CSIRO and the Australian government had to admit defeat. The eventual joint venture between the CSIRO and the French company Group Limagrain, committing each organisation to $22.5 million over five years, was described by *The Age*'s Graeme O'Neill as 'perhaps the lowest point in Australia's sorry history of investment in new technology' (1989).

Peter Roberts in the *Australian Financial Review* lamented the loss of a fledgling business producing plastic bike wheels cheap enough to compete with steel. The wheels will now be made in the Philippines and shipped back to Australia, 'where they will no doubt turn up on good old Aussie (imported) brands such as Repco and Malvern Star' (1995: 28). Catherine Livingstone, however, chair of CSIRO and a board member of Telstra and Macquarie Bank, thinks that this issue of the commercialisation of inventions and scientific discoveries is not simple and is certainly not just a matter of telling scientists and researchers to be more commercial. 'CSIRO is now exploring different industry engagement models, that maximise the impact of its research in industry while also securing enough of a return flow of resources to make the business of research sustainable' (Collis 2006: 6).

Livingstone also thinks that Australia is perfectly placed to creatively work on solving some of our world's greatest problems and 'unearth a wealth of knowledge and industry potential. The world is looking for solutions and technologies. ... It is an area in which Australia could take the lead, with enormous economic rewards if we are able to make it our knowledge and technologies that are sought out. It would produce an innovation yield the likes of which we have never seen before' (Collis 2006: 6).

A well-developed model exists for solving problems. It consists of four separate, sequential stages: defining the problem, generating alternative solutions, evaluating and selecting the best solution, and implementing the chosen solution. This model, however, is mainly useful for solving straightforward problems. Many problems faced by managers are not of this type and managers are often called on to exercise creative problem-solving skills. That is, they must broaden their perspective of the problem and develop alternative solutions that are not immediately obvious.

There are eight main conceptual blocks (summarised in Table 4.3) that inhibit people's creative problem-solving abilities. Overcoming these conceptual blocks is a matter of skill development and practice in thinking, not a matter of innate ability. Everyone can become a skilled creative problem solver with practice. Becoming aware of these thinking inhibiters helps us to overcome them. Three main principles for improving creative problem definition are making the strange familiar and the familiar strange, elaborating the definition and reversing the definition. Techniques for improving the creative generation of alternative solutions include deferring judgment, expanding current alternatives and combining unrelated attributes. Several processes are described to help implement these six techniques.

Creativity and innovativeness must also be fostered among other people. Becoming an effective problem solver yourself is important, but effective managers must also enhance this activity among their colleagues.

Behavioural guidelines

Below are specific behavioural guidelines to help your skill practice in problem solving, creativity and fostering innovation.

1. Follow the four-step procedure outlined in Table 4.1 (on page 185) when solving straightforward problems. Keep the steps separate and do not take shortcuts.
2. When approaching a difficult problem, try to overcome your conceptual blocks by consciously doing the following mental activities:
   - Use lateral thinking in addition to vertical thinking.
   - Use several thought languages instead of just one.
   - Challenge stereotypes based on past experiences.
   - Identify underlying themes and commonalities in seemingly unrelated factors.
   - Delete superfluous information and fill in important missing information when studying the problem.
   - Avoid artificially constraining problem boundaries.
   - Overcome any unwillingness to be inquisitive.
   - Use both right- and left-brain thinking.
3. When defining a problem, make the strange familiar and the familiar strange by using metaphors and analogies, first to focus the definition and then to distort and refocus it.
4. Elaborate definitions of problems by developing at least two alternative (opposite) definitions and by applying a checklist.
5. Reverse definitions of problems by beginning with end results and working backwards.
6. In generating potential solutions to problems, defer any judgment until many solutions have been proposed. Use the four rules of brainstorming:
   - Do not evaluate alternatives as they are suggested.
   - Encourage wild or unusual ideas.
   - Encourage quantity over quality of ideas.
   - Build on others' ideas.
7. Expand the list of current alternative solutions by subdividing the problem into its attributes.
8. Increase the number of possible solutions by combining unrelated problem attributes. Morphological synthesis and relational algorithms may be helpful.
9. Foster innovativeness among those with whom you work by doing the following:
   - Find a 'practice field' where individuals can experiment and try out ideas, and assign them responsibility for fostering innovation.
   - Put people holding different perspectives in teams to work on problems.
   - Hold people accountable for innovation.
   - Use sharp-pointed prods to stimulate new thinking.
   - Recognise, reward and encourage the participation of multiple roles in the innovation process, including idea champions, sponsors, orchestrators and rule breakers.

Skill analysis

Case study involving problem solving

Creativity at Apple

In his annual speech in Paris in 2003, Steven Jobs, the lionised CEO of Apple Computer, Inc., proudly described Apple in these terms: 'Innovate. That's what we do.' And innovate they have. Jobs and his colleagues, Steve Wozniak and Mike Markkula, invented the personal computer market in 1977 with the introduction of the Apple II. In 1980, Apple was the number one vendor of personal computers in the world. Apple's success, in fact, helped spawn what became known as Silicon Valley in California, the mother lode of high-technology invention and production for the next three decades.

Apple has always been a trailblazing company whose innovative products are almost universally acknowledged as easier to use, more powerful and more elegant than those of its rivals. During one ten-year period, Apple was granted 1300 patents, half as many as Microsoft, a company 145 times the size of Apple. Dell Computer, by contrast, was granted half as many patents as Apple. Apple clearly out-innovates its much larger rivals. Apple has invented, moreover, more businesses than just the personal computer. In 1984, Apple created the first computer network with its Macintosh machines, whereas Windows-based PC's did not network until the mid-1990s. A decade ago, Apple introduced the first hand-held, pen-based computing device known as the Newton, and followed that up with a wireless mouse, ambient-lit keyboards for working in the dark, and the fastest computer on the market in 2003. In 2003, Apple also introduced the first legal, digital music store for downloading songs—iTunes—along with its compatible technology, iPods. In other words, Apple has been at the forefront of product and technological innovation for almost 30 years. Apple has been, hands down, the most innovative company in its industry and one of the most innovative companies on the planet.

Here is the problem. By the mid-2000s, Apple commanded just 2 per cent of the US$180 billion worldwide market for PCs. Apple's rivals followed its creative leads and snatched profits and market share from Apple with astonishing effectiveness. From its number one position two decades ago, Apple by the mid-2000s ranked as the 15th-largest IT firm—behind name-brand firms such as IBM, Hewlett-Packard and Dell (the top three), and, embarrassingly, also behind less well-known firms such as Ingram Micro and Computer Sciences.

Moreover, whereas Apple was once among the most profitable companies in the PC industry, its operating profits shrank from 20 per cent in 1981 to 0.4 per cent in 2004, one-tenth the industry average. Its chief competitor in software—Microsoft—sold US$2.6 billion in software during one quarter in the early 2000s compared with US$177 million for Apple.

Today, however, it seems Apple's innovation and creativity efforts have finally started to pay off. For example, according to Shah (2011):

> *Apple was the world's third-largest PC vendor during the fourth quarter last year if iPad shipments are included, research firm Canalys said in a study released Wednesday. With iPads included, Apple's worldwide PC shipments grew 241 percent, which put the company in third place behind Hewlett-Packard and Acer, Canalys said. Apple held a 10.8 percent PC market share with 11.5 million PC units shipped and was neck-and-neck with Dell, which also held a 10.8 percent market share with 11.4 million units shipped.*

Why did it take Apple so long to regain its former levels of success? If one takes seriously the messages being declared loudly and prominently in the business press and in the broader global society today, innovation and creativity are the keys to success. 'Change or die.' 'Innovate or get passed over.' 'Be creative to be successful.' A key tenet on which progressive, market-based, capitalistic societies are based is the idea of creative destruction. That is, without creativity and innovation, individuals and organisations become casualties of the second law of thermodynamics—they disintegrate, wither, disorganise and die. New products are needed to keep consumers happy. Obsolescence is ubiquitous.

Innovation and creativity, consequently, are touted as being at the very heart of success. For more evidence, just skim over the more than 45 000 book titles when you log on to Amazon that use the word 'innovation'.

On the other hand, consider some of the most innovative companies in recent history. Xerox Corporation's famed Palo Alto Research Center, in the United States, gave the world laser printing, the Ethernet, Windows-type software, graphical user interfacing and the mouse, yet it is notorious for having made no money at all. Polaroid introduced the idea of instant images, yet it filed for bankruptcy in 2001. The internet boom in the late 1990s was an explosion in what is now considered to be worthless innovation. And Enron may have been the most innovative financial company ever.

On the other hand, Amazon, Southwest Airlines, eBay, Walmart and Dell are examples of incredibly successful companies, but without inventing any new products or technologies. They are acknowledged as innovative and creative companies, although they do not hold a candle to Apple. Rather than new products, they have invented new processes, new ways to deliver products, new distribution channels and new marketing approaches. It is well-known that Henry Ford did not invent the motor car. He simply invented a new way to assemble a car at a cost affordable to his own workers. The person who invented the motor car hardly made a cent.

One problem is that creativity as applied to business processes—manufacturing methods, sales and marketing, employee incentive systems, or leadership development—is often seen as humdrum, nitty-gritty, uncool, plodding, unimaginative and boring. Creative people, and creative companies, that capture the headlines are usually those that come up with great new product ideas or splashy features. Decide for yourself which is the driver of economic growth: good innovation, good management or some combination of both?

Source: Some information in this case was adapted from Carleen Hawn, 'If he's so smart …', *Fast Company*, January 2004, pp. 68–74.

DISCUSSION QUESTIONS

1. *Consider the four approaches to creativity. What approach(es) has Apple relied upon? What alternatives have other firms in the industry pursued? What other alternatives could Apple implement?*
2. *Assume you are a consultant to the CEO at Apple. What advice would you give on how Apple could continue to capitalise on its creativity? What would you say? How can Apple make money based on its own inclination to pursue creativity in certain ways?*
3. *What are the main obstacles and conceptual blocks that Apple has faced in the past and faces right now? What do employees need to watch out for?*
4. *What tools for fostering creative problem solving are applicable to Apple, and which would not be workable? Which ones do you think the company uses the most?*

Skill practice

Exercises for applying conceptual blockbusting

The purpose of these exercises is to practise problem solving, both analytical and creative. Two scenarios are provided below, presenting real problems faced by real managers. Your purpose in each case is to identify a solution to the problem. You will approach the problem in two ways: first, using analytical problem-solving techniques; and, second, using creative problem-solving techniques. The first approach—analytical problem solving—you should accomplish alone. The second approach—creative problem solving—you should accomplish in a team. Your task is to apply the principles of problem solving to come up with realistic, cost-efficient and effective solutions to these problems. Consider each scenario separately. You should take no more than five minutes to complete the analytical problem-solving assignment. Then take 15 minutes to complete the creative problem-solving assignment. Complete both individual and team assignments (including the judging component) for the first scenario before moving on to the second scenario. At the end of these practice exercises you will have completed four assignments—two in rational problem solving and two in creative problem solving.

Individual assignment: Analytical problem solving (5 minutes)

1. After reading the first scenario, write down a specific problem definition. What precisely worded problem are you going to solve? Complete this sentence: 'The problem I am going to solve is…'
2. Identify at least four or five alternative solutions. What ideas do you have for resolving this problem? Complete this sentence: 'Possible ways to resolve this problem are …'
3. Evaluate the alternatives you have proposed. Make sure you do not evaluate each alternative before proposing your complete set. Evaluate your set of alternatives on the basis of these criteria: Will this alternative solve the problem I have defined? Is this alternative realistic in terms of being cost-effective? Can this solution be implemented in a short time-frame?
4. Write down your proposed solution to the problem. Be specific about what should be done and when. Be prepared to share your solution with other class members.

Team assignment: Creative problem solving (15 minutes)

1. Form a team of four or five people. Each team member should share his or her own definition of the problem. It is unlikely that all definitions will be the same, so make sure you keep track of them. Now add at least three more plausible definitions of the problem. In doing so, use at least two of the techniques for expanding problem definition discussed in the text. Each problem definition should differ from the others in what the problem is, not just a statement of different causes of the problem.
2. Now examine each of the definitions you have proposed. Select one that the entire team can agree on. Since it is unlikely that you can solve multiple problems at once, select just one problem definition that you will work on.
3. Share the four or five proposed solutions that you generated on your own, even if they do not relate to the specific problem your team has defined. Keep track of all the different alternatives proposed by team members. After all team members have shared their alternatives, generate at least five additional alternative solutions to the problem you have agreed on. Use at least two of the techniques for expanding alternatives in the text.
4. Of all the alternatives your team proposes, select the five that you consider to be the most creative and having the highest probability of success.
5. Select one team member from each team to serve as a judging panel. This panel is charged with selecting the team with the most creative and potentially successful alternatives to the problem. Team members cannot vote for their own team.
6. Each team now shares their five alternatives with the class. The judging panel selects the winner.

Scenario 1: Moving up in the rankings

Business schools are operating in an increasingly competitive environment and, while an accreditation process does exist, public perception of the quality and effectiveness of business schools is largely driven by business publications and the various ranking procedures adopted in the popular press.

Each publication relies on slightly different criteria in its rankings, but a substantial portion of each ranking rests on name recognition, visibility or public acclaim. In some polls, more than 50 per cent of the weighting relies on reputation or notoriety of the school. This is problematic, of course, because reputation can be deceiving. A recent poll in the United States, for example, rated the Harvard and Stanford undergraduate business programs among the top three in the country, even though neither school has an undergraduate business program! While numerous other criteria are considered, name recognition appears to be the single most crucial factor in the ranking process.

Many business schools have responded to this pressure to become better known by creating advertising programs, circulating internal publications to other business schools and media outlets, and hiring additional staff to market the school.

As part of a strategy to increase visibility, one business school hired world-renowned architect Frank O. Gehry to design a new business school building. Photographs of models of the building are reproduced below. It is a US$70 million building that houses all the educational activities of the school. Currently, this particular school does not appear in the top 20 on the major rankings lists. However, like about 75 other business schools in the world, it would very much like to reach that level. That is, the school would like to displace another school currently listed in the top 20.One problem with this new landmark building is that it is so unusual, so avant-garde, that it is not even recognised as a building. When looking at a photograph of it for the first time, some people do not even know what they are looking at. On the other hand, it presents an opportunity to leapfrog other schools listed higher in the rankings if the institution is creative in its approach. The challenge, of course, is that no one is exactly sure how to make this happen.

Scenario 2: Preserving our heritage

Our libraries are charged with the responsibility of preserving the accumulated wisdom of the past and gathering information in the present. They serve as sources of information and resources, adjuncts to schools, and places of exploration and discovery. No one would question the value of libraries to societies and cultures. But consider the following problem.

In libraries throughout the world, hundreds of thousands of books printed around the late 19th century and into the 20th century are steadily being eaten away by natural acids, and the preservation of these endangered books has been a major concern. To date, the problem has not been high on the priority list of most governments and, as the conservation of a book costs about $200 on average, current efforts have not kept pace with the growing problem.

With the rapid growth of technology, libraries now have alternatives. Rather than keeping large quantities of books with the associated problems of space and maintenance, digital reformatting is better able in many ways to preserve and disseminate information.

With surrogate forms available, is it necessary to preserve printed material? Perhaps some books could be destroyed and some preserved. If so, who would make the choice? While such questions remain unanswered, the problem of endangered books remains and continues to worsen.

Skill application

Suggested assignments

1. Teach someone else how to solve problems creatively. Explain the guidelines and give examples from your own experience. Record your experience in your journal.
2. Think of a problem that is important to you right now for which there is no obvious solution. It may relate to your family, your classroom experiences, your work situation or some interpersonal relationship. Use the principles and techniques discussed in the chapter to work out a creative solution to that problem. Spend the time it takes to do a good job, even if several days are required. Describe the experience in your journal.
3. Help to direct a group (your family, flatmates, social club, and so on) in a creative or analytical problem-solving exercise using techniques discussed in the chapter. Record your experience in your journal.
4. Write a letter to your Member of Parliament, Vice-Chancellor or CEO identifying several alternative solutions to some perplexing problem facing his or her organisation, community or state. Write about an issue that you care about. Be sure to offer suggested solutions. This will require you to apply in advance the principles of problem solving discussed in the chapter.

Application plan and evaluation

The intention of this exercise is to help you apply this cluster of skills in a real-life, out-of-class setting. Now that you have become familiar with the behavioural guidelines that form the basis of effective skill performance, you will improve most by trying out those guidelines in an everyday context. Unlike a classroom activity, in which feedback is immediate and others can assist you with their evaluations, this skill application activity is one you must accomplish and evaluate on your own. There are two parts to this activity. Part 1 helps to prepare you to apply the skill. Part 2 helps you to evaluate and improve on your experience. Be sure to write down answers to each item. Do not short-circuit the process by skipping steps.

Part 1: Planning

1. Write down the two or three aspects of this skill that are most important to you. These may be areas of weakness, areas you most want to improve, or areas that are most salient to a problem you face right now. Identify the specific aspects of this skill that you want to apply.
2. Now identify the setting or the situation in which you will apply this skill. Establish a plan for performance by writing down a description of the situation. Who else will be involved? When will you do it? Where will it be done?
3. Identify the specific behaviours you will engage in to apply this skill. How will you put these behaviours into practice?
4. What are the indicators of successful performance? How will you know you have been effective? What will indicate that you have performed competently?

Part 2: Evaluation

5. After you have completed your implementation, record the results. What happened? How successful were you? What was the effect on others?
6. How can you improve? What modifications can you make next time? What will you do differently in a similar situation in the future?
7. Looking back on your whole skill practice and application experience, what have you learned? What has been surprising? In what ways might this experience help you in the long term?

Scoring keys and supplementary materials

Problem solving, creativity and innovation (p. 180)

SCORING KEY

Skill area	*Items*	*Pre-*	*Post*
Analytical problem solving	1, 2, 3, 4, 5	______	______
Creative problem solving	6, 7, 8, 9, 10, 11, 12, 13, 14, 15	______	______
Fostering creativity	16, 17, 18, 19, 20, 21, 22	______	______

Comparison data

Compare your scores with three comparison standards:

1. Compare your score against the maximum possible (132).
2. Compare your scores with the scores of other students in the class.
3. Compare your scores with the norm data from more than 1000 business school students. In comparison with the norm group, if you scored:

105 or above	you are in the top quartile
94–104	you are in the third quartile
83–93	you are in the second quartile
82 or below	you are in the bottom quartile.

How creative are you? (p. 181)

SCORING KEY

Circle and add up the values assigned to each item below.

Item	*A* *Agree*	*B* *Undecided or don't know*	*C* *Disagree*	*Item*	*A* *Agree*	*B* *Undecided or don't know*	*C* *Disagree*
1	0	1	2	21	0	1	2
2	0	1	2	22	3	0	−1
3	4	1	0	23	0	1	2
4	−2	0	3	24	−1	0	2
5	2	1	0	25	0	1	3
6	−1	0	3	26	−1	0	2
7	3	0	−1	27	2	1	0
8	0	1	2	28	2	0	−1
9	3	0	−1	29	0	1	2
10	1	0	3	30	−2	0	3
11	4	1	0	31	0	1	2
12	3	0	−1	32	0	1	2
13	2	1	0	33	3	0	−1
14	4	0	−2	34	−1	0	2
15	−1	0	2	35	0	1	2
16	2	1	0	36	1	2	3
17	0	1	2	37	2	1	0
18	3	0	−1	38	0	1	2
19	0	1	2	39	−1	0	2
20	0	1	2				

40 The following have values of 2:

energetic	dynamic	perceptive	dedicated
resourceful	flexible	innovative	courageous
original	observant	self-demanding	curious
enthusiastic	independent	persevering	involved

The following have values of 1:

self-confident	determined	informal	forward-looking
thorough	restless	alert	open-minded

The rest have values of 0.

TOTAL SCORE ☐

Comparison data

Exceptionally creative	95–116
Very creative	65–94
Above average	40–64
Average	20–39
Below average	10–19
Non-creative	Below 10

Innovative attitude scale (p. 183)

SCORING KEY

Add up the numbers associated with your responses to the 20 items. When you have done so, compare your scores with the norm group of graduate and undergraduate business school students, all of whom were employed full-time. The percentile indicates the percentage of people who are expected to score below you.

Score	*Percentile*
39	5
53	16
62	33
71	50
80	68
89	86
97	95

Applying conceptual blockbusting

Observer's feedback form

After the group has completed its problem-solving task, take the time to give the group feedback on its performance. Also provide feedback to each individual group member, either by means of written notes or verbal comments.

Group observation

1. Was the problem defined explicitly?
   a. To what extent was information sought from all group members?
   b. Did the group avoid defining the problem as a disguised solution?
   c. What techniques were used to expand or alter the definitions of the problem?

2. Were alternatives proposed before any solution was evaluated?
   a. Did all group members help generate alternative solutions without judging them one at a time?
   b. Did people build on the alternatives proposed by others?
   c. What techniques were used to generate more creative alternatives for solving the problem?
3. Was the optimal solution selected?
   a. Were alternatives evaluated systematically?
   b. Was consideration given to the realistic long-term effects of each alternative?
4. Was consideration given to how and when the solution could be implemented?
   a. Were obstacles to implementation discussed?
   b. Was the solution accepted because it solved the problem under consideration, or for some other reason?
5. How creative was the group in defining and solving the problem?
6. What techniques of conceptual blockbusting did the group use?

Individual observation

1. What violations of the rational problem-solving process did you observe in this person?
2. What conceptual blocks were evident in this person?
3. What conceptual blockbusting efforts did this person make?
4. What was especially effective about the problem-solving attempts of this person?
5. What could this individual do to improve his or her problem-solving skills?

Answers and solutions to the creativity problems

Solution to the Roman numeral problem (p. 195)

‘S’IX

Solution to the matchstick problem (in Figure 4.2 on p. 195)

By moving the second of the two vertical matchsticks, we create the mathematical equation representing the phrase ‘the square root of one equals one’.

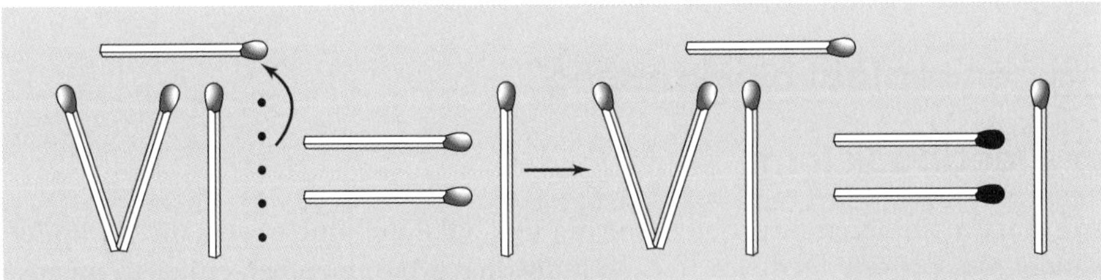

Answer to scoreboard calculation problem (in Figure 4.3 on p. 195)

13 × 4 = 52

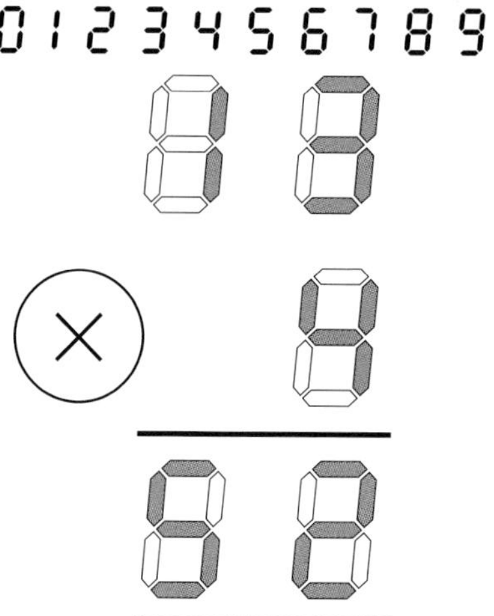

Answer to the Shakespeare riddle (in Figure 4.4 on p. 196)

130 mm (be careful to note where page 1 of Volume 1 is and where the last page of Volume 4 is).

Common terms applying to both water and finance (p. 197)

banks
currency
cash flow
washed up
deposits
frozen assets
float a loan
underwater pricing
capital drain
sinking fund
liquid assets
slush fund

Answer to the Descartes story (p. 197)

The foundation of Descartes' philosophy was the statement: 'I think, therefore I am.'

Solution to the block of wood problem (in Figure 4.5 on p. 197)

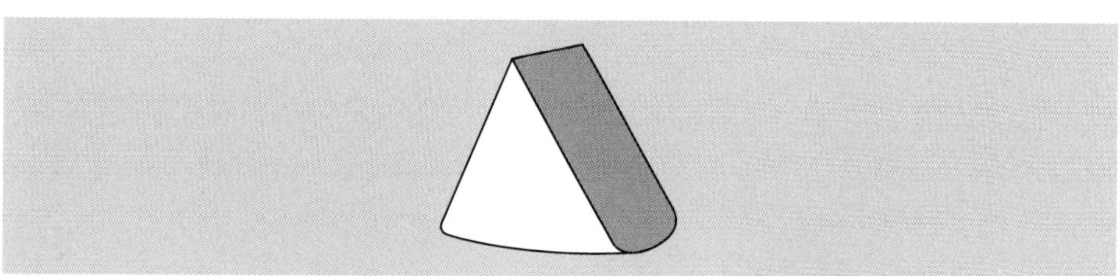

Solutions to the nine-egg problem (in Figure 4.6 on p. 198)

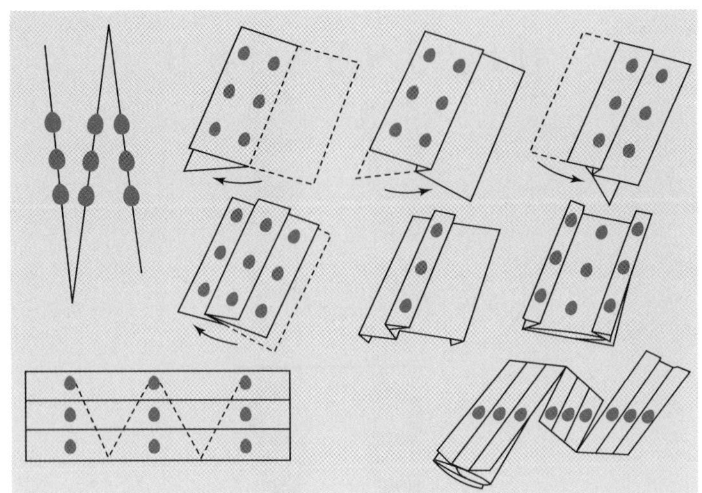

Solutions to embedded-patterns problem (in Figure 4.7 on p. 198)

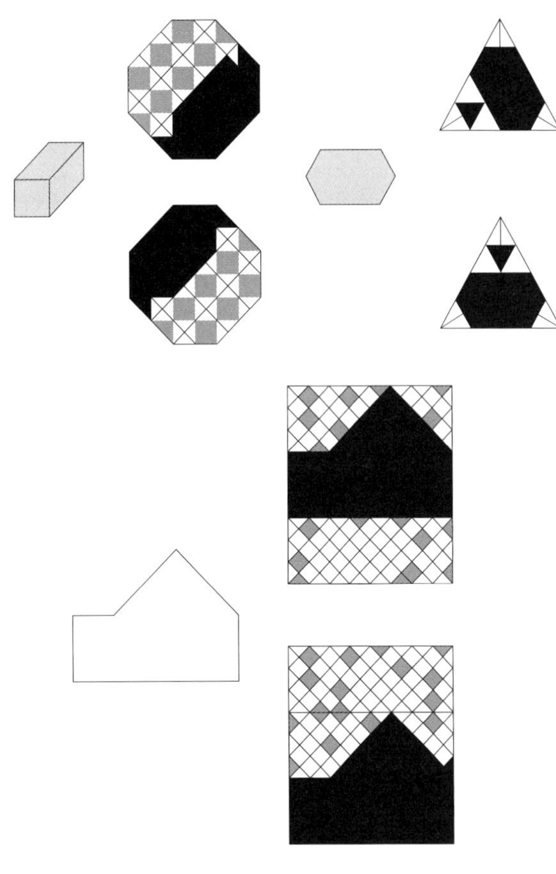

Solution to the slice of cake problem (in Figure 4.9 on p. 207)

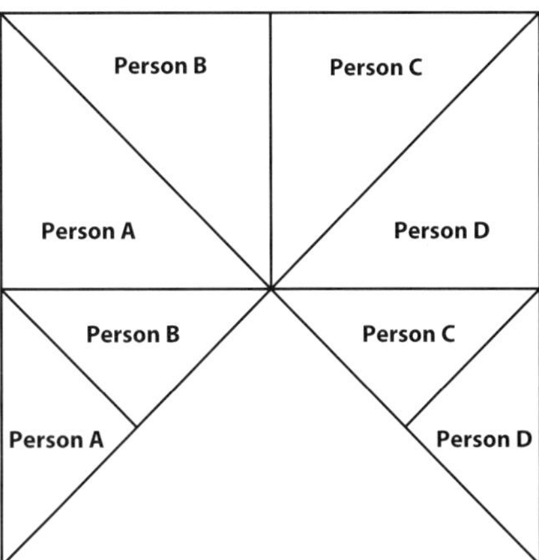

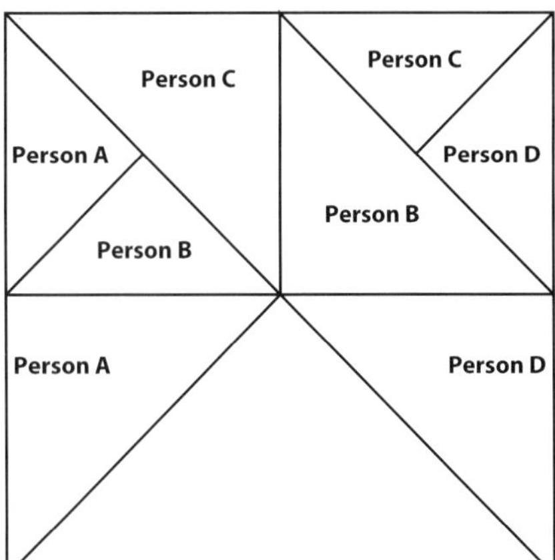

References

Allen, J. L. 1986, *Conceptual Blockbusting: A Guide to Better Ideas* (Reading, MA: Addison-Wesley).

Amabile, T. M. 1988, 'A model of creativity and innovation in organizations', in L. L. Cummings and B. M. Staw (eds), *Research in Organizational Behavior*, vol. 10, pp. 123–67.

Anonymous 2005, 'NZ SMS adopts the "power of 8"', *Precision Marketing*, 17(30), p. 9.

Basadur, M. S. 1979, 'Training in creative problem solving: Effects of deferred judgment and problem finding and solving in an industrial research organization', unpublished doctoral dissertation, University of Cincinnati.

Ben-Amos, P. 1986, 'Artistic creativity in Benin Kingdom', *African Arts*, 19, pp. 60–63.

Bertrand, J. and P. Robinson 1985, *Born to Win* (Sydney: Corgi and Bantam Australia).

Bilton, C. 2007, *Management and Creativity: From Creative Industries to Creative Management* (Chichester, UK: Wiley-Blackwell).

Black, J. S. and H. B. Gregersen 1997, 'Participative decision making: An integration of multiple dimensions', *Human Relations*, 50, pp. 859–78.

Bodycombe, D. J. 1997, *The Mammoth Puzzle Carnival* (New York: Carroll and Graf).

Carlopio, J. 1998, *Implementation: Making Workplace Innovation and Technical Change Happen* (Sydney: McGraw-Hill).

Carlopio, J. 2003, *Changing Gears: The Strategic Implementation of New Technology* (London: Palgrave Macmillan).

Carlopio, J. 2010, *Strategy by Design* (New York: Palgrave Macmillan).

Carter, F. 2006, 'Creativity provides retail some therapy', *Business & Technology Weekly*, 56(2560), pp. 14–16.

Chu, Y-K. 1970, 'Oriented views of creativity', in A. Angloff and B. Shapiro (eds), *Psi Factors in Creativity* (New York: Parapsychology Foundation), pp. 35–50.

Cialdini, R. B. 1993, *Influence: Science and Practice* (Glenview, IL: Scott, Foresman).

Collins, M. A. and T. M. Amabile 1999, 'Motivation and creativity', in R. J. Sternberg (ed.), *Handbook of Creativity* (Cambridge, UK: Cambridge University Press).

Collis, B. 2006, 'Time to unleash the power of science', *SOLVE*, 9, November, pp. 6–9.

Conklin, J. 2006, *The Dialogue Mapping: Building Shared Understanding of Wicked Problems* (Chichester, UK: Wiley).

Covey, S. R. 1998, 'Creative orientation', *Executive Excellence*, 1, pp. 13–14.

Crovitz, H. F. 1970, *Galton's Walk* (New York: Harper and Row).

Csikszentmihalyi, M. 1996, *Creativity: Flow and the Psychology of Discovery and Invention* (New York: HarperCollins).

de Bono, E. 1968, *New Think* (New York: Basic Books).

de Bono, E. 1985, *Conflicts: A Better Way to Solve Them* (London: Harrap Limited).

de Bono, E. 2000, *New Thinking for the New Millennium* (New York: Millennium Press).

Drucker, P. F. 1974, *Management* (New York: Harper and Row).

Dunphy, D. 1993, *Organisational Change by Choice* (Sydney: McGraw-Hill).

Dunphy, D., A. Griffiths and S. Benn 2003, *Organisational Change for Corporate Sustainability* (London: Routledge).

Dutton, J. E. and S. J. Ashford 1993, 'Selling issues to top management', *Academy of Management Review*, 18, pp. 397–421.

Einstein, A. C. 1919, 'Fundamental ideas and methods of relativity theory, presented in their development', unpublished manuscript, G. Holton.

Farnham, D. and S. Horton 2003, 'Organisational change and staff participation and involvement in Britain's public services', *International Journal of Public Sector Management*, 16(6), pp. 434–48.

Feldman, D. H. 1999, 'The development of creativity', in R. J. Sternberg (ed.), *Handbook of Creativity* (Cambridge, UK: Cambridge University Press).

Fink, R. A., T. B. Ward and S. M. Smith 1992, *Creative Cognition: Theory, Research, and Applications* (Cambridge, MA: MIT Press).

Friedrich, T., M. Mumford, B. Vessey, C. Beeler and D. Eubanks 2010, 'Leading for innovation', *International Studies of Management and Organization*, 40(2), July, pp. 6–29.

Godin, S. 2005, *The Big Moo: Stop Trying to be Perfect and Start Being Remarkable* (New York: Penguin).

Goll, I. and A. M. A. Rasheed 1997, 'Rational decision making and firm performance: The moderating role of environment', *Strategic Management Journal*, 18, pp. 583–91.

Hermann, N. 1981, 'The creative brain', *Training and Development Journal*, 35, pp. 11–16.

Hudspith, S. 1985, 'The neurological correlates of creative thought', unpublished PhD dissertation, University of Southern California.

Ichikawa, A. 1986, *Practical Strategic TQM for Middle Management* (Tokyo: Diamond).

Interaction Associates 1971, *Tools for Change* (San Francisco: Interaction Associates).

James, D. 1992, 'Why companies become trapped by group-think', *Business Review Weekly*, 9 October.

Janis, I. L. 1971, *Groupthink* (New York: Free Press).

Juran, J. 1988, *Juran on Planning for Management* (New York: Free Press).

Karpin, D. S. 1995, *Enterprising Nation: Report of the Industry Task Force on Leadership and Management Skills* (Canberra: Australian Government Publishing Service).

Kelley, T. 2005, *The Ten Faces of Innovation* (New Yortk: Doubleday).

Kelly, R. 2011, 'Using creativity to lead change', *Student Affairs Leader*, 39(2), 15 January, pp. 4–7.

Koberg, D. and J. Bagnall 1974, *The Universal Traveler: A Soft-system Guidebook to Creativity, Problem Solving, and the Process of Design* (Los Altos, CA: William Kaufmann).

Koestler, A. 1967, *The Act of Creation* (New York: Dell).

Kozbelt, A. and Y. Durmysheva 2007, 'Lifespan creativity in a non-Western artistic tradition: A study of Japanese Ukiyo-e printmakers', *International Journal of Aging and Human Development*, 65(1), pp. 23–51.

Kuo, Y-Y. 1996, 'Taoistic psychology of creativity', *Journal of Creative Behavior*, 30, pp. 197–212.
Le Mesurier, K. 2006a, 'A big call', *Business Review Weekly*, 28(23), p. 45.
Le Mesurier, K. 2006b, 'Creative safety', *Business Review Weekly*, 28(23), p. 52.
McKim, R. H. 1980, *Thinking Visually: A Strategy Manual for Problem Solving* (Dale Seymour Publications, an imprint of Pearson Learning Group).
McMillan, I. 1985, 'Progress in research on corporate venturing', working paper, Center for Entrepreneurial Studies, New York University.
Maduro, R. 1976, *Artistic Creativity in a Brahmin Painter Community*, Monograph 14 (Berkeley, CA: University of California Center for South and Southeast Asia Cultures).
March, J. G. (ed.) 1999, *The Pursuit of Organizational Intelligence* (New York: Blackwell).
March, J. G. and H. A. Simon 1958, *Organizations* (New York: Wiley).
Markoff, J. 1988, 'For scientists using supercomputers, visual imagery speeds discoveries', New York Times News Service, *Ann Arbor News*, 2 November, p. D3.
Martindale, C. 1999, 'Biological bases of creativity', in R. J. Sternberg (ed.), *Handbook of Creativity* (Cambridge, UK: Cambridge University Press).
Miller, S. J., D. J. Hickson and D. C. Wilson 1996, 'Decision making in organizations', in S. R. Clegg and C. Hardy (eds), *Handbook of Organizational Studies* (London: Sage), pp. 293–312.
Mitroff, I. I. 1998, *Smart Thinking for Crazy Times: The Art of Solving the Right Problems* (San Francisco: Barrett Koehler).
Morgan, G. 1986, *Images of Organization* (San Francisco: Sage Publications).
Morris, M. and K. Leung, 2010, 'Creativity East and West: Perspectives and parallels', *Management & Organization Review*, 6(3), pp. 313–27.
Nayak, P. R. and J. M. Ketteringham 1986, *Breakthroughs!* (New York: Rawson Associates).
Nemeth, C. J. 1986, 'Differential contributions of majority and minority influence', *Psychological Review*, 93, pp. 23–32.
O'Neill, G. 1989, *The Age* (Melbourne), 19 July.
Osborn, A. 1953, *Applied Imagination* (New York: Scribner).
Raudsepp, E. and G. Hough 1977, *Creative Growth Game* (New York: Jove Publications).
Riley, S. 1998, *Critical Thinking and Problem Solving* (Upper Saddle River, NJ: Prentice Hall).
Rittel, H. and M. Webber 1973, 'The dilemmas in a general theory of planning', *Policy Sciences*, 4(2), pp. 155–69.
Rizova, P. 2006, 'Are you networked for successful innovation?', *MIT Sloan Management Review*, 47(3), Spring, pp. 49–55.
Roberts, P. 1995, 'No office and less officious—the new executive', *Australian Financial Review*, 9 September.
Rothenburg, A. 1979, *The Emerging Goddess* (Chicago: University of Chicago Press).
Rothenberg, A. 1991, 'Creativity, health and alcoholism', *Creativity Research Journal*, 3, pp. 179–269.
Rothenberg, A. and C. Hausman 2000, 'Metaphor and creativity', in M. A. Runco (ed.), *Creativity Research Handbook*, vol. 2 (Creskill, NJ: Hampton).
Russo, F. 2006, 'The hidden secrets of the creative mind', *Time*, 167(3), pp. 89–90.
Sauber, T. 2006, *Structured Creativity: Formulating an Innovation Strategy* (London: Palgrave Macmillan).
Scott, O. J. 1974, *The Creative Ordeal: The Story of Raytheon* (New York: Atheneum).
Shah, A. 2011, 'Research firm: iPad makes Apple third-largest PC maker', *IDG News Service*, 27 January, <www.macworld.com>.
Sian, K. L. 1997, 'Electronic brainstorming', *Innovative Leader*, 6(4).
Starko, A. J. 1995, *Creativity in the Classroom: Schools of Curious Delight* (New York: Longman).
Sternberg, R. J. (ed.) 1999, *Handbook of Creativity* (Cambridge, UK: Cambridge University Press).
Tichy, N. 1983, *Strategic Human Resource Management* (New York: Wiley).
Trompenaars, F. 1996, 'Resolving international conflict: Culture and business strategy', *Business Strategy Review*, 7, pp. 51–68.
Trompenaars, F. and C. Hampden-Turner 1999, *Riding the Waves of Culture* (New York: McGraw-Hill).
Tushman, M. L. and P. Anderson 1997, *Managing Strategic Innovation and Change* (New York: Oxford University Press).
Van de Ven, A. 1997, 'Technological innovation, learning, and leadership', in R. Garud, P. R. Nayyar and Z. B. Shapira (eds), *Technological Innovation: Oversights and Foresights* (Cambridge, UK: Cambridge University Press).
von Oech, R. 1986, *A Kick in the Seat of the Pants* (New York: Harper and Row).
Wadey, C. 2007, 'Breaking down creativity barriers', *NZ Business*, 20(11), p. 20.
Way, N. 2006, 'Farmers take stock', *Business Review Weekly*, 28(23), pp. 54–55.
Weick, K. E. 1984, 'Small wins', *American Psychologist*, 39, pp. 40–49.
Williams, W. M. and L. T. Yang 1999, 'Organizational creativity', in R. J. Sternberg (ed.), *Handbook of Creativity* (Cambridge, UK: Cambridge University Press).
Wonder, J. and J. Blake 1992, 'Creativity East and West: Intuition versus logic', *Journal of Creative Behavior*, 26, pp. 172–85.
Zeita, P. 1999, *The Art and Craft of Problem Solving* (New York: Wiley).

PART 2

INTERPERSONAL SKILLS

CHAPTER 5

COMMUNICATING SUPPORTIVELY

OBJECTIVES

- **Differentiate between coaching and counselling problems**
- **Apply principles of supportive communication to avoid defensiveness and disconfirmation, and to allow the healthy expression of emotions**
- **Improve work relationships by using personal management interviews**

5

CHAPTER OUTLINE

Skill assessment

Evaluative surveys for supportive communication

Communicating supportively

Step 1: Before you read the material in this chapter, respond to the following statements by writing a number from the rating scale that follows in the left-hand column (pre-assessment). Your answers should reflect your attitudes and behaviour as they are now, not as you would like them to be. Be honest. This instrument is designed to help you discover your level of competency in communicating supportively so that you can tailor your learning to your specific needs. When you have completed the survey, use the scoring key at the end of the chapter to identify the skill areas discussed in this chapter that are most important for you to master.

Step 2: When you have completed the reading and the exercises in this chapter and, ideally, as many as you can of the skill application assignments at the end of the chapter, cover up your first set of answers. Then respond to the same statements again, this time in the right-hand column (post-assessment). When you have completed the survey, use the scoring key at the end of the chapter to measure your progress. If your score remains low in specific skill areas, use the behavioural guidelines at the end of the skill learning section to guide your further practice.

Rating scale

1 Strongly disagree
2 Disagree
3 Slightly disagree
4 Slightly agree
5 Agree
6 Strongly agree

Assessment

Pre- *Post-*

In situations in which I have to provide negative feedback or offer corrective advice:

______ ______ 1. I am clear about when I should coach someone and when I should provide counselling instead.

______ ______ 2. I am able to help others recognise and define their own problems when I counsel them.

______ ______ 3. I am able to be completely honest in the feedback that I give to others, even when it is negative.

______ ______ 4. When I give feedback to others, I avoid referring to personal characteristics and focus on problems or solutions instead.

______ ______ 5. I always link negative feedback to a standard or expectation that has been violated.

______ ______ 6. When I try to correct someone's behaviour, our relationship is almost always strengthened.

______ ______ 7. I am descriptive in giving negative feedback to others. That is, I objectively describe events, their consequences and my feelings about them.

______ ______ 8. I always suggest specific alternatives to individuals whose behaviour I am trying to correct.

______ ______ 9. I reinforce other people's sense of self-worth and self-esteem in my communication with them.

______ ______ 10. I convey genuine interest in the other person's point of view, even when I disagree with it.

______ ______ 11. I do not talk down to those who have less power or less information than I have.

______ ______ 12. Even when I feel strongly about my point of view, I convey to others that I am flexible and open to new information.

______ ______ 13. I strive to identify some area of agreement in a discussion with someone who has a different point of view.

______ ______ 14. My feedback is always specific and to the point, rather than general or vague.

______ ______ 15. I do not dominate conversations with others.

______ ______ 16. I take ownership of my statements and point of view by using personal words such as 'I think', rather than impersonal words like 'they think'.

______ ______ 17. When discussing someone's problem, I usually respond with a reply that indicates understanding rather than advice.

______ ______ 18. When asking questions of others in order to understand their viewpoints better, I generally ask 'what' questions rather than 'why' questions.

______ ______ 19. I hold regular private meetings with people with whom I work and with whom I live.

______ ______ 20. I understand clearly when it is appropriate to offer advice and direction to others and when it is not.

The scoring key is on page 268.

Communication styles

This assessment instrument is divided into two parts. In Part 1, four people complain about problems they face in their jobs. Following each complaint are five possible responses. Rank three of the responses you would be most likely to make, with 3 being your first choice, 2 being your second choice and 1 your third choice.

Part 2 of the assessment describes a particular situation. Several pairs of statements follow. Place a check mark next to the statement in each pair that you would most probably use in responding to that situation. Do not identify your preference. Instead, mark the alternatives that are most like your current behaviour.

To score this communication styles instrument, turn to page 268 to find the scoring key and an interpretation of your scores.

Part 1

1. I've been in this job now for six months and I hardly know anyone at all in the organisation. I just can't seem to make friends or be accepted by other people. Most people are extremely busy and don't take time to socialise. I feel isolated and excluded from what's going on.

   ______ a. Don't be concerned about not making friends yet. Things will get better the longer you are with the organisation, you'll see.

   ______ b. When you first meet people, what do you say? Are you the one to be friendly first?

   ______ c. Because organisation members are so busy, probably no one has time to get close socially. You shouldn't expect too much.

   ______ d. So, you're feeling that people haven't accepted you in the organisation?

   ______ e. When I first joined the organisation, it took me more than six months to get adjusted. I still don't know some of the people in several departments.

2. I can't stand my boss. He is the most autocratic, demanding person you can imagine. I've never worked around anyone who cared less for his employees than he does. His complete insensitivity and lack of humanity have made this a miserable place to work.

   ______ a. You sound as if you're having difficulty dealing with rigid control and authority.

   ______ b. I know how you feel, because last year we had a woman in our department who would drive *anybody* crazy. She was the ultimate domineering boss.

_______ c. You're going to have problems unless you work this out. I think you should go to him and tell him how you feel.
_______ d. You really are having a hard time adjusting to your boss, aren't you?
_______ e. Why do you feel so strongly about him?

3. What I want to know is, what happened with that last promotion decision? I thought I was in line for it. I'm sure no one else in the department has my experience, and the rumour I heard indicated the job was mine for the asking. I'm really disappointed that you brought in someone from the outside over me. I don't think it's fair. What does it take to get promoted around here, anyway?
_______ a. What was it that made you think this promotion was yours? Are you aware of the requirements of the job and what kind of person we were looking for?
_______ b. Don't be discouraged. Your work is good and if you're patient I'm sure other chances will come along. I'll try to help you be ready the next time around.
_______ c. I think you have the wrong impression about this. The criteria were very clear for the new position and the other person was just a better fit.
_______ d. In other words, you feel kind of puzzled about where you stand with the company?
_______ e. Are you interpreting this decision as a challenge to your technical competence?

4. Hey, what's the idea of not approving my request for a new personal computer? I really need it in the office. We've got far more work to do than one machine can handle and we're doing things manually that ought to be done on a spreadsheet. And don't give me that old story about tight company resources again. I've been in line for new equipment for a long time now.
_______ a. I understand that you are really upset about not getting your request approved.
_______ b. Why do you need a new computer? Can you borrow one during the times you really feel the crunch?
_______ c. You know, others are facing the same problem. We're having a terrible time trying to get the necessary work accomplished with the existing machines.
_______ d. If you'll be patient, I'm sure I can work out a solution to your problem.
_______ e. We turned you down because resources are really tight. You'll just have to make do.

The scoring key is on page 269.

Part 2

You are the manager of Carole Schulte, a 60-year-old supervisor who has been with the company for 21 years. She will retire at age 65, the first year she is eligible for a full pension. The trouble is, her performance is sliding, she is not inclined to put in extra time when required, and occasionally her work is below standard. Several colleagues and customers have complained that she has treated them rather abruptly and without much sensitivity, even though superior customer service is a hallmark of your organisation. She does not do anything bad enough to be fired, but she is just not performing at the levels you expect. Assume that you are having your monthly one-on-one meeting with her in your office. Which of the statements in each pair would you be most likely to use?

_______ 1. a. I've received complaints from some of your customers that you haven't followed company standards in being responsive to their requests.
b. You don't seem to be motivated to do a good job anymore, Carole.

_______ 2. a. I know that you have been doing a great job as supervisor, but there is just one small thing I want to raise with you about a customer complaint, probably not too serious.
b. I have some concerns about several aspects of your performance on the job and I would like to discuss them with you.

_______ 3. a. When one of your subordinates called the other day to complain that you had criticised his work in public, I became concerned. I suggest that you sit down with that subordinate to work through any hard feelings that might still exist.
b. You know, of course, that you were wrong to criticise your subordinate's work in public. That's a sure way to create antagonism and lower morale.

_______ 4. a. I would like to see the following changes in your performance: (1), (2) and (3).
b. I have some ideas for helping you to improve; but first, what do you suggest?

_______ 5. a. I must tell you that I'm disappointed in your performance.
b. Several of our employees seem to be unhappy with how you have been performing lately.

The scoring key is on page 269.

Skill learning

The importance of effective communication

Many people are afraid of change, new technology or job loss, and communication helps to ease their fears and helps innovation and change happen in a variety of ways (Anynomous 2006; Carlopio 1996; Cudney 2007; Moss Kanter 2003; Schultz, Utz & Goritz 2011). When leading change processes, leadership equals communication. Information is the life-blood of an organisation (Wheatley 1999). Every time two people who don't usually talk to each other do so, it creates new possibilities within the organisation. When you want to stimulate change, you want information flowing freely through your organisation. Communication has been referred to as the very essence of a social system or organisation.

Communication is essential because the structure, effectiveness and scope of organisations are determined almost entirely by communication. Great companies practise great communication (Pomeroy 2006) as, for example, organisational communication has been shown to impact both job satisfaction and performance (Giri & Kumar 2010). If we take away communication, we wouldn't have an organisation. Innovation and change mean increased uncertainty and a lack of order, predictability and stability. Information and communication mean decreased uncertainty. Therefore, the more change there is, the more communication is necessary to counter the uncertainty.

Research shows consistently that the ability to communicate effectively is critical in many ways. It has been shown to lead to the success of open source software teams (Yuan & Keng 2007) and information system development (Fowler & Horan 2007), and is the characteristic judged by managers to be most critical in determining promotability and success (Brownell 1990; Bryan et al. 2006; Morley 2002; Randle 1956). Research also suggests that the culprit in 85 per cent of IT project failures is lack of communication (Scott 2007). Recent research illustrates that communication positively impacts technological proactivity, organisational learning and organisational innovation (García-Morales, Matías-Reche & Verdú-Jover 2011).

It is not just managers, however, that have for years been aware of the importance of communication and relationships. Neil Pope and Peter Berry, in the *Australian Financial Review* (1995: 17), addressed the questions: 'What do most Australian workers believe would improve their workplace more than anything else? Higher wages? More perks? Shorter working hours?' According to Pope and Berry, the answer that emerged loud and clear from research conducted with thousands of employees across more than 80 Australian organisations is that people want effective leadership and good communication with management. More recent Australian research, outlined by Horin (2003), similarly suggests that the main differences between excellent workplaces that produce superb business results and merely good ones is the quality of relationships—how people relate to each other as friends, colleagues and co-workers.

Communicating may involve a broad array of activities, from writing to public speaking and body language. While skill in all these activities is important, for many managers it is face-to-face, one-on-one communication that dominates all other types, and predicts managerial success (Crocker 1978; Rosen 1998). It is not surprising, therefore, that serious attention has been given to the topic of interpersonal communication. Scholars and researchers have written extensively on the topic. Most universities have academic departments dedicated to the field, and many organisations have public communication departments and intra-organisational communication specialists such as newsletter editors and speechwriters. Even with all this available information about the communication process and the dedicated resources in many organisations for fostering better communication, many managers consistently indicate that poor communication is one of their biggest problems and that communication skills are critical for organisational success (Maes, Weldy & Icenogle 1997; Schnake et al. 1990; Subramanian 2006).

In a classic study of major manufacturing organisations undergoing large-scale changes, Cameron (1994a, 1994b) asked two key questions:

1. What is your major problem in trying to get organisational changes implemented?
2. What is the key factor that explains your past success in effectively managing organisational change?

To both questions, a large majority of managers gave the same answer: communication. All of them agreed that more communication is better than less communication. Most thought that over-communicating with employees was more a virtue than a vice. It would seem surprising, then, that in light of this agreement by managers about the importance of communication, it remains a major problem for them. Why might this be?

One reason is that most people feel that they, personally, are very effective communicators. They feel that communication problems are a product of others' weaknesses, not their own (Brownell 1990; Carrell & Willmington 1996; Golen 1990). Most people readily admit that their organisation is fraught with faulty communication, but it is almost always 'those other people' who are responsible. Thus, while most agree that proficiency in interpersonal communication is critical to managerial success, many people do not seem to feel a strong need to improve their own skill level (Spitzberg 1994).

It is also important to keep in mind that cultural differences sometimes call for a modification of the skills discussed in this chapter. For example, Asian managers are sometimes less inclined to be open in the initial stages of a conversation, and they consider managers from Australia, New Zealand or the United States to be rather brash and aggressive when they become too personal too soon. Similarly, certain types of response patterns may differ between cultures—for example, deflecting responses are more typical of Eastern than Western cultures. Language patterns and structures across cultures can be dramatically different; considerable evidence exists that individuals are most effective interpersonally, and display the greatest amount of emotional intelligence, when they recognise, appreciate and capitalise on these differences.

While stylistic differences may exist among individuals and across cultures, certain core principles of effective communication remain critical (cf. Peng-Hsiang & Hsin 2007). Research on interpersonal communication among various cultures and nationalities confirms that the eight attributes of supportive communication discussed later in this chapter are effective across all cultures and nationalities (Gudykunst, Ting-Toomey & Nishida 1996; Triandis 1994). These eight factors have almost universal applicability in solving interpersonal problems.

We use Trompenaars' (1996), Trompenaars and Hampden–Turner's (1999) model of cultural diversity to identify key differences between people raised in different cultural contexts. Differences exist on an *affectivity orientation* versus a *neutral orientation*. Affective cultures (for example, the Middle East, Southern Europe, the South Pacific) are more inclined to be expressive and personal in their responses than neutral cultures (for example, East Asia, Scandinavia). Sharing personal data and engaging quickly in sensitive topics may be comfortable for people in some cultures but very uncomfortable in others. Thus, timing and pace of communication will vary across different cultures. Similarly, *particularistic* cultures (such as Korea, China, Indonesia) are more likely to allow individuals to work out issues in their own way than *universalistic* cultures (such as Norway, Sweden, the United States), where a common pattern or approach is preferred. This implies that reflective responses may be more common in particularistic cultures and advising responses more typical of universalistic cultures. When people are assumed to have a great deal of individual autonomy, for example, coaching responses (directing, advising, correcting) are less common than counselling responses (empathising, probing, reflecting) in interpersonal problem solving. Research by Trompenaars (1996), Gudykunst and Ting-Toomey (1988) and others clearly points out, however, that the differences across cultures are not great enough to negate or dramatically modify the principles outlined in this chapter.

The focus on accuracy

Much of the writing on interpersonal communication focuses on the accuracy of the information being communicated. The emphasis is generally on making certain that messages are transmitted and received with little variation from the original intent. Even the legal profession is taking heed. In New Zealand, if one of Chapman Tripp's lawyers started a sentence with something like 'Notwithstanding prognostications to the contrary, as well as what has been stated, we heretofore express our considered opinion that subject to further qualification …', he or she would have to deal with the firm's manager for breach of good English. 'Project Clarity' is a program designed to get the lawyers to write material the rest of us can understand (Parker 1999).

The communication skill of most concern is the ability to transmit clear, precise messages. The incident described below illustrates the problems that can result from inaccurate communication.

> *A motorist was driving on the M5 south of Sydney when the engine stalled. She quickly determined that the battery was dead and managed to stop another driver who consented to push her car to get it started.*
>
> *'You'll have to get me up to 40 or 50 kays and then back off. I'll engage the clutch and be on my way. Thank you.'*
>
> *The second motorist nodded and walked back to his car. The first motorist climbed into her car and waited for the good Samaritan to pull up behind. She waited and waited. Finally, she turned round to see what was wrong.*
>
> *There was the good Samaritan coming up behind her car at about 50 kilometres an hour! The insurance adjuster had a hard time believing this story. (Adapted from Haney 1979: 285)*

The following story illustrates the more subtle and complex side of interpersonal communication problems.

> *Melburn McBroom was a domineering boss, with a temper that intimidated those who worked with him. This fact might have passed unremarked had McBroom worked in an office or a factory. But McBroom was an airline pilot.*
>
> *One day in 1978 McBroom's plane was approaching Portland, Oregon, when he noticed a problem with the landing gear. So McBroom went into a holding pattern, circling the field at a high altitude while he fiddled with the mechanism.*
>
> *As McBroom obsessed about the landing gear, the plane's fuel gauges steadily approached the empty level. But his co-pilots were so fearful of McBroom's wrath that they said nothing, even as disaster loomed. The plane crashed, killing ten people. (Goleman 1995: 148)*

When accuracy is the primary consideration, attempts to improve communication generally centre on improving the mechanics: transmitters and receivers, encoding and decoding, sources and destinations, and noise. When communication is inhibited, distorted or dysfunctional, we frequently have an even more complex, interpersonal situation on our hands.

Much progress has been made recently in improving the transmission of accurate messages—that is, in improving their clarity and precision. Mainly through the development of sophisticated information-based technology, major strides have been taken to enhance communication speed and accuracy in organisations. However, comparable progress has not occurred in the interpersonal aspects of communication. People still become offended with one another, make insulting statements and communicate clumsily. The interpersonal aspects of communication involve the nature of the relationship between the communicators. Who says what to whom, what is said, why it is said and how it is said all have an effect on the relationships between people. This has important implications for the effectiveness of the communication, quite apart from the accuracy of the statement. A statement made more than 80 years ago illustrates this point:

LEARNING

The government are very keen on amassing statistics. They collect them, add them, raise them to the nth power, take the cube root and prepare wonderful diagrams. But you must never forget that every one of these figures comes in the first instance from the village watchman, who just puts down what he damn pleases.

People still communicate very much as they please—often in abrasive, insensitive and unproductive ways. And more often than not, it is the interpersonal aspect of communication that stands in the way of effective message delivery rather than the inability to deliver accurate information (Golen 1990).

Ineffective communication may lead people to dislike each other, be offended by each other, lose confidence in each other, refuse to listen to each other and disagree with each other, as well as cause a host of other interpersonal problems. Interpersonal problems, in turn, lead to restricted communication flow, inaccurate messages and misinterpretation of meanings. Figure 5.1 summarises this process.

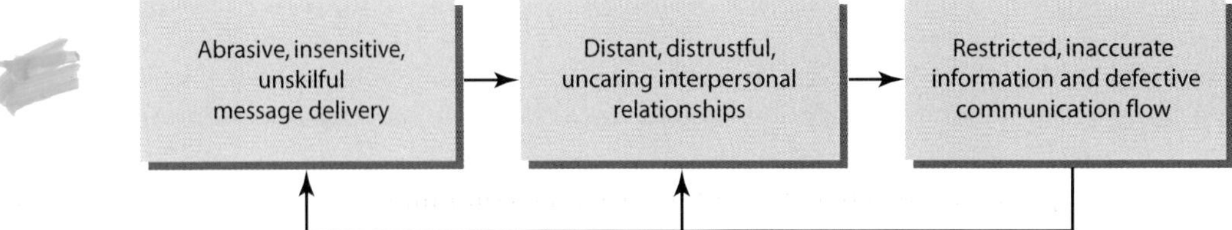

FIGURE 5.1 Links between unskilful communication and interpersonal relationships

To illustrate, consider the following situation. Col is introducing his new goal-setting program to the organisation as a way of overcoming some productivity problems. After Col's carefully prepared presentation in the management council meeting, Clara raises her hand. 'In my opinion, this is a naïve approach to solving our productivity issues. The considerations are much more complex than Col seems to realise. I don't think we should waste our time by pursuing this plan any further.'

Clara's opinion may be justified, but the manner in which she delivered the message would probably eliminate any hope of its being dealt with objectively. Instead, Col would probably hear a message such as 'You're naïve', 'You're stupid' or 'You're incompetent'. It wouldn't be surprising if Col's response was defensive or even hostile. Any good feelings between the two would probably have been jeopardised and their future communication will probably be reduced to self-image protection. The merits of the proposal would have been smothered by personal defensiveness. Future communication between the two will probably be minimal.

It is important to remember that successful interpersonal communication requires us to attend to both the *content* of the message we are sending and the *process* of how we send the information. As the example illustrates, there is little value in sending excellent content to someone in an ineffective manner. The process of how we say what we say is a critical component of good communication.

What is supportive communication?

This chapter focuses on a kind of interpersonal communication that helps managers to communicate accurately and honestly without jeopardising interpersonal relationships—namely, supportive communication (Cole 1999). Not only is a message delivered accurately when supportive communication is used, but the relationship between the two communicating parties is supported, even enhanced, by the interchange. Positive interpersonal relationships result. However, the goal of supportive communication isn't merely to be liked by other people or to be judged a nice person. Nor is it used merely to produce social acceptance. Positive interpersonal relationships have practical, instrumental value in organisations. Researchers have found, for example, that organisations fostering these kinds of relationships enjoy higher productivity, faster problem solving, higher-quality outputs and fewer conflicts, while individuals benefit from greater career success and higher earnings (Bishop 2006; Chang 2003; Holt & Jones 2005; Jay 2003; Levinson 2003; Tomer 2003). Supportive communication, therefore, isn't just a 'nice-person technique' but a proven competitive advantage for both individuals and organisations. Moreover, delivering outstanding customer service is almost impossible without supportive communication. Customer complaints and misunderstandings frequently require supportive communication skills to resolve. Not only must managers be competent in using this kind of communication; they must help their employees to develop this competency as well.

Relationship skills and interpersonal communication skills form part of a type of emotional intelligence that has been shown to be:

> *... significantly more important than cognitive ability and technical expertise combined. In fact, some studies indicate that EQ is more than twice as important as standard IQ abilities. Further, evidence increasingly shows that the higher one goes in an organisation, the more important EQ can be. For those in leadership positions, emotional intelligence skills account for close to 90 per cent of what distinguishes outstanding leaders from those judged as average.* (Kemper 1999: 15)

Coaching and counselling

The principles of supportive communication discussed in this chapter are best understood and most useful when they are applied to the challenging interpersonal communication tasks of coaching and counselling. They also apply to a broader array of activities, of course, such as handling customer complaints, passing critical or negative information upwards, handling conflicts between other parties, negotiating for a certain position and so on. However, coaching and counselling are almost universal managerial activities and they are used here to illustrate and explain the behavioural principles involved.

Later in this chapter the differences between coaching and counselling are explored in more detail, and when each is more appropriate. For now, let us consider that coaching applies to ability problems where the manager's approach is: 'I can help you do this better.' The coaching manager then provides information and focuses on the task and task performance. Counselling applies to attitude problems where the manager's approach is: 'I can help you recognise that a problem exists.' The counselling manager is concerned more with attitudes, personality and emotions.

Skilful coaching and counselling are especially important in the following situations:

- rewarding positive performance
- correcting problem behaviours or attitudes.

Research indicates that, through these types of mentoring relationship, both the mentor and the protégé can experience job-related benefits (Fine & Pullins 1998; Grensing-Pophal 2007).

Both activities are discussed in more detail in Chapter 8 where the content of rewarding and correcting behaviour (that is, what to do) is dealt with. The discussion here focuses on the processes used by effective managers to coach and counsel employees (that is, how to do it). Coaching and counselling are more difficult to carry out effectively when employees are not performing up to expectations, when their attitudes are negative, when their behaviour is disruptive, or when their personalities clash with others in the organisation. Whenever managers have to help employees change their attitudes or behaviours, coaching or counselling is required. In these situations, managers are faced with the responsibility of providing negative feedback to employees or getting them to recognise problems that they do not want to acknowledge. Managers often need to provide negative feedback and correct performance problems, but this needs to be done in a way that preserves relationships and facilitates positive work outcomes.

What makes coaching and counselling so challenging is the risk of offending or alienating others, or of coaching when counselling is necessary, and vice versa. This can happen easily if managers ignore the feelings and reactions of employees and take a directive, hard-nosed, 'shape-up-or-ship-out' approach to correcting behaviour or attitudes, when what is needed is listening and helping people to reach their own conclusions. Other managers may soft-pedal, avoiding confrontations for fear of hurting feelings and destroying relationships. They adopt the 'don't worry, be happy' approach, when what is needed is a realistic assessment of skills and abilities and some appropriate information and skills development. The principles described in this chapter not only facilitate accurate message delivery in sensitive situations, but also their effective use can produce higher levels of motivation, increased productivity and better interpersonal relationships.

Coaching and counselling skills are also required when negative feedback is not involved, such as when someone asks for advice, needs someone to listen to their problems or wants to register a complaint. Sometimes just listening is the most effective form of coaching or counselling. Although the risk of damaged relationships, defensiveness or hurt feelings is not as great as when negative feedback is given, these situations still require competent communication skills. Guidelines for how to implement supportive communication effectively in both negative and positive coaching and counselling situations are discussed in the rest of this chapter.

Consider these two scenarios:

Tom Nielson is the manager of the division sales force in your firm, which makes and sells components for the aerospace industry. He reports directly to you. Tom's division consistently misses its sales projections, its revenues per salesperson are below the firm's average, and Tom's monthly reports are almost always late. You make another appointment to visit Tom after getting the latest sales figures, but he is not in his office when you arrive. His secretary tells you that one of Tom's sales managers dropped by a few minutes ago to complain that some employees are coming in late for work in the morning and taking extra-long coffee breaks. Tom had immediately gone with the manager to his sales department to give the salespeople a 'pep talk' and to remind them of performance expectations. You wait for 15 minutes until he returns.

Erika Christensen has an MBA from a prestigious university and has recently joined your firm in the financial planning group. She came with great recommendations and credentials. However, she seems to be trying to enhance her own reputation at the expense of others in her group. You have heard increasing complaints lately that she acts arrogantly, is self-promotional and is openly critical of other group members' work. In your first conversation with her about her performance in the group, she denied there was a problem. She said that, if anything, she was having a positive impact on the group by raising its standards. You schedule another meeting with Erika after the latest set of complaints from her co-workers.

What are the basic problems in these two cases? How would you approach them so that the problems get solved and, at the same time, your relationships with your employees are strengthened? What would you say, and how would you say it, so that the best possible outcomes result? This chapter can help you to improve your skill in handling such situations effectively.

Coaching and counselling problems

First, let's distinguish two basic kinds of interpersonal communication problems faced by managers. The two cases above help to identify these two kinds of problems. In the case of Tom Nielson, the basic need is for coaching. Coaching situations are those in which managers must pass along advice and information, or set standards for performance. Employees must be advised on how to do their jobs better and coached to better performance. Coaching problems are usually caused by lack of ability, insufficient information or understanding, and/or incompetence on the part of employees. In these cases, the accuracy of the information passed along by managers is important. The employee must understand clearly what the problem is and how to overcome it.

In the Tom Nielson case, Tom is accepting upwards delegation from his employees and not allowing them to solve their own problems. Upwards delegation is one of the main causes of ineffective time management. By not insisting that his employees bring recommendations for solutions to him rather than problems, and by intervening directly in the problems of his direct report's employees, Tom becomes overloaded himself. He does not allow his people to do their jobs. Productivity almost always suffers in cases where one person is trying to resolve all the problems and run the whole show. Tom needs to be coached on how to avoid upwards delegation and how to delegate responsibility, as well as authority, effectively.

The Erika Christensen case illustrates a counselling problem. Managers need to counsel employees, rather than coach them, when the problem stems from attitudes, personality clashes, defensiveness or other factors tied to emotions. Erika's competency or skill is not a problem, but her unwillingness to recognise that a problem exists or that a change is needed on her part requires counselling by the manager. Erika is highly qualified for her position, so coaching or giving advice would not be a useful approach. Instead, an important goal of counselling is to help her recognise that a problem exists and to identify ways in which that problem might be addressed.

Many problems involve both coaching and counselling. Managers frequently have to give direction and advice (coaching) as well as help to facilitate understanding and a willingness to change (counselling). It is important to recognise the difference between these two types of problems, because a mismatch of problem with communication approach can aggravate, rather than resolve, a problem. Giving direction or advice (coaching) in a counselling situation often increases defensiveness or resistance to change. For example, advising Erika about how to do her job or about the things she should not be doing (such as criticising others' work) would probably only magnify her defensiveness because she does not perceive that she has a problem. Similarly, counselling in a situation that calls for coaching simply side-steps the problem and does not resolve it. Tom Nielson knows that a problem exists, but he does not know how to resolve it. Coaching, not problem recognition, is needed.

The questions that remain are: 'How do I effectively coach or counsel another person? What behavioural guidelines help me to perform effectively in these situations?' Coaching and counselling rely on the same set of key supportive communication principles; these are summarised in Table 5.1 and discussed throughout the chapter.

TABLE 5.1 Eight attributes of supportive communication

Supportive		Not supportive
1. *Problem-oriented, not person-oriented* 'How can we solve this problem?'	*Not*	'Because of you there is a problem.'
2. *Congruent, not incongruent* 'Your behaviour really upset me.'	*Not*	'Do I seem upset? No, everything's fine.'
3. *Descriptive, not evaluative* 'Here is what happened; here is my reaction; here is what I suggest would be more acceptable to me.'	*Not*	'You are wrong for doing what you did.'
4. *Validating, not invalidating* 'I have some ideas, but do you have any suggestions?'	*Not*	'You wouldn't understand, so we'll do it my way.'
5. *Specific, not global* 'You interrupted me three times during the meeting.'	*Not*	'You're always trying to get attention.'
6. *Conjunctive, not disjunctive* 'Relating to what you just said, I'd like to discuss this.'	*Not*	'I want to discuss this (regardless of what you want to discuss).'
7. *Owned, not disowned* 'I've decided to turn down your request because ...'	*Not*	'You have a pretty good idea, but they just wouldn't approve it.'
8. *Supportive listening, not one-way listening* 'What do you think are the obstacles standing in the way of improvement?'	*Not*	'As I said before, you make too many mistakes. You're just not doing the job.'

Defensiveness and disconfirmation

If principles of supportive communication aren't followed when coaching or counselling, two major problems result that lead to a variety of negative outcomes (Brownell 1986; Cupach & Spitzberg 1994; Gibb 1961; Sieburg 1978; Steil, Barker & Watson 1983). These problems are summarised in Box 5.1.

One barrier is the presence of *defensiveness* in one of the communicating parties. If an individual feels threatened or punished by the communication, both the message and the interpersonal relationship are blocked. Self-protection becomes paramount, and the focus is more on self-defence

BOX 5.1 Two major obstacles to effective interpersonal communication

Supportive communication engenders feelings of support, understanding and helpfulness. It helps overcome the two main problems resulting from poor interpersonal communication.

DEFENSIVENESS

- One individual feels threatened or attacked as a result of the communication.
- Self-protection becomes paramount.
- Energy is spent on constructing a defence, rather than on listening.
- Aggression, anger, competitiveness and/or avoidance are common reactions.

DISCONFIRMATION

- One individual feels incompetent, unworthy or insignificant as a result of the communication.
- Attempts to re-establish self-worth take precedence.
- Energy is spent on trying to portray self-importance, rather than on listening.
- Showing off, self-centred behaviour, withdrawal and/or loss of motivation are common reactions.

than on listening. Having our behaviour criticised is often perceived as a threat or an attack. Common reactions are anger, aggression, competitiveness and avoidance.

The second barrier is *disconfirmation*. This occurs when one of the communicating parties feels put down, ineffectual or insignificant because of the communication. Recipients of the communication feel that their self-worth is being questioned, so they focus more on building themselves up rather than listening. Reactions are often self-aggrandising or show-off behaviours, loss of motivation, withdrawal, and loss of respect for the offending communicator.

In order to overcome these two major problems while helping others to change their attitudes or behaviours, eight principles of supportive communication are explained and illustrated in the following pages. These principles serve as behavioural guidelines and should be learned and practised to improve interpersonal communication.

Principles of supportive communication

1. Supportive communication is problem-oriented, not person-oriented

Person-oriented communication focuses on the characteristics of the individual, not the event, and it communicates the impression that the individual is inadequate. One problem with person-oriented communication is that, while most people can change their behaviour, few can change their basic personalities. Because nothing can generally be done to accommodate person-oriented communication, it leads to a deterioration in the relationship, rather than to problem solving. Person-oriented messages often try to persuade the other individual that 'this is how you should feel' or 'this is the kind of person you are' (for example, 'You are an incompetent manager/a lazy employee/an insensitive office mate'). Most individuals react to person-oriented communication by defending themselves against it or rejecting it outright. Even when communication is positive (for example, 'You are a wonderful person'), it may not be viewed as trustworthy if it is not tied to a behaviour or an accomplishment. The *absence of a meaningful referent* is the key weakness in person-oriented communication.

Problem-oriented communication focuses on problems and solutions rather than on personal traits. It separates the person from the behaviour. It is useful even when performance appraisals are called for, since it focuses on behaviours and events rather than on personality. For example, statements such as 'You are an autocrat' and 'You are insensitive' are person-oriented, while 'I seldom meet with you to help make decisions' and 'Our relationship is deteriorating' are more descriptive of problems. Assigning motives to an individual's behaviour is person-oriented (for example, 'It's because you want to control other people'), whereas expressing concern about observable behaviours is problem-oriented (for example, 'You made several comments that seemed sarcastic to me in the meeting today').

In coaching and counselling, problem-oriented communication should also be linked to accepted standards or expectations rather than to personal opinions. Personal opinions are more likely to be interpreted as person-oriented and arouse defensiveness than statements that compare the behaviour to an accepted standard. For example, the statement 'I don't like the way you dress' is an expression of a personal opinion and will probably create resistance, especially if the listener does not feel that the communicator's opinions are any more legitimate than his or her own. On the other hand, 'Your dress isn't in keeping with the company dress code' or 'Males are expected to wear a tie to work' are comparisons with external standards that have some legitimacy. Feelings of defensiveness are less likely to arise, since the problem, not the person, is being addressed. In addition, other people are more likely to support a statement based on a common standard.

Effective supportive communicators need not avoid expressing personal opinions or feelings about the behaviour or attitudes of others. But, when doing so, they should keep in mind the additional principles that follow.

2. Supportive communication is based on congruence, not incongruence

For many years, research has consistently illustrated that the best interpersonal communications, and the best interpersonal relationships, are based on congruence. In other words, when what is communicated, verbally and non-verbally, matches exactly what the individual is thinking and feeling, communication and relations work better (Dyer 1972; Hyman 1989; Knapp & Vangelisti 1996; Rogers 1961; Schnake et al. 1990).

Two kinds of incongruence are possible. One is a mismatch between what we are experiencing and what we are aware of. For example, we may not even be aware that we are experiencing anger towards another person, even though the anger is present. Therapists must frequently help individuals to reach greater congruence between experience and awareness. A second kind of incongruence, and the one more closely related to supportive communication, is a mismatch between what we feel and what we communicate. For example, we may be aware of the fact that we feel angry, but we do not explicitly express the feeling. This can create a 'mixed message', as the words are saying one thing but our tone and non-verbal communication are shouting another.

When coaching and counselling, genuine, honest statements are always better than artificial or dishonest statements. Managers who hold back their true feelings or opinions, or who do not express what is really on their minds, create the impression that a hidden agenda exists. People sense that there is something else not being said. They trust the communicator less and focus on trying to figure out what the hidden message is, not on listening or trying to improve. False impressions and miscommunication occur, resulting in superficial relationships and a lack of trust.

The well-known psychologist and counsellor Carl Rogers (1961: 344–5) suggests that congruence in communication lies at the heart of a general law of interpersonal relationships:

> *The greater the congruence of experience, awareness and communication on the part of one individual, the more the ensuing relationship will involve a tendency toward reciprocal communication with increasing congruence; a tendency toward more mutually accurate understanding of the communications; improved psychological adjustment and functioning in both parties; mutual satisfaction in the relationship.*
>
> *Conversely, the greater the communicated incongruence of experience and awareness, the more the ensuing relationship will involve further communication with the same quality; disintegration of accurate understanding; less adequate psychological adjustment and functioning in both parties; and mutual dissatisfaction in the relationship.*

Striving for congruence, of course, does not mean that we should explode immediately on getting upset, or that we should not repress certain feelings (for example, anger, disappointment, aggression) until a more appropriate time for their expression. Other principles of supportive communication must also be practised, and achieving congruence at the expense of all other considerations is not productive. On the other hand, in problematic interactions, when reactive feedback must be given, we are more likely to express too little congruence than too much. This is because many people are afraid to respond in a completely honest way or are not sure how to communicate congruently without being offensive. Saying exactly what we feel sometimes offends the other person.

Consider the problem of someone who is not performing up to expectations and displays a nonchalant attitude when given hints that the division's rating is being negatively affected. What could the manager say that would strengthen the relationship with the individual and still resolve the problem? How can we express honest feelings and opinions and still remain problem-focused, not person-focused? How can we be completely honest without offending another person? Other principles of supportive communication provide some guidelines.

3. Supportive communication is descriptive, not evaluative

When people use evaluative communication, they make a judgment or place a label on other individuals or on their behaviour: 'You are bad', 'You are doing it wrong', 'You are incompetent'. This evaluation generally makes the other person feel under attack and the response is defensive. Probable responses are: 'No, I'm not bad', 'I'm not doing it wrong' or 'I am as competent as you are'. Arguments, bad feelings and a weakening of the interpersonal relationship result.

The tendency to evaluate others is strongest when the issue is charged with emotion or when someone feels personally threatened. When people have strong feelings about an issue or they experience threat as a result of a situation, they tend to make a negative evaluation of others' behaviour. Sometimes, they try to resolve their own bad feelings or reduce their own anxiety by placing a label on others: 'You are bad, and that implies I am good. Therefore, I feel better.' At other times, they have such strong feelings that they want to punish the other person for violating their expectations or standards: 'What you've done deserves to be punished. You deserve what's coming to you.'

The problem with this approach is that evaluative communication is likely to be self-perpetuating. Placing a label on another generally leads that person to respond by placing a label on you, which makes you defensive in return. The accuracy of the communication as well as the strength of the relationship deteriorates, rather than improves. Arguments ensue.

An alternative to evaluation is the use of descriptive communication. Because it is difficult to avoid evaluating other people without some alternative strategy, the use of descriptive communication helps to eliminate the tendency to evaluate or perpetuate a defensive interaction. Descriptive communication involves three steps, summarised in Box 5.2.

BOX 5.2 Descriptive communication

Step 1

- Describe as objectively as possible the event, behaviour or circumstances.
- Avoid accusations.
- Present data or evidence, if needed.

Step 2

- Describe your own reactions to or feelings about the event, behaviour or circumstances.
- Describe the objective consequences that have resulted or that are likely to result.
- Focus on the behaviour and on your own reaction, not on the other person or their personal attributes.

Step 3

- Suggest a more acceptable alternative.
- Be prepared to discuss additional alternatives.
- Focus on the alternative solutions, not on who is right or wrong.

First, describe as objectively as possible the event that occurred or the behaviour that needs to be modified. This description should be objective in the sense that it relies on elements of the behaviour that could be confirmed by another person. Behaviour, as mentioned before, should be compared with accepted standards rather than with personal opinions or preferences. Subjective impressions or attributions to the motives of another person are not helpful in describing the event. The description 'You have finished fewer projects this month than anyone else in the division' can be confirmed (an objective record can be made available) and relates strictly to the behaviour and to an objective standard, not to the motives or personal characteristics of the individual. It is less likely that the person will feel threatened, since no evaluative label is placed on the behaviour and no attack is being made on the person. Describing a behaviour, as opposed to evaluating a behaviour, is relatively neutral.

Second, describe reactions to the behaviour or its consequences. Rather than projecting on to another person the cause of the problem, the focus should be on the reactions or consequences the behaviour has produced. This requires communicators to be aware of their own reactions and to be able to describe them. Using one-word descriptions for feelings is often the best method: 'I'm concerned about our productivity', 'Your level of accomplishment frustrates me'. Similarly, the consequences of the behaviour can be pointed out: 'Profits are off this month', 'Department quality ratings are down', or 'Two customers have called in to express dissatisfaction'. Describing feelings or consequences also lessens the likelihood of defensiveness since the problem is framed in the context of the communicator's feelings or objective consequences, not the attributes of the person. If those feelings or consequences are not described in an accusing way, the major energies of the communicators can be focused on problem solving rather than on defending against evaluations.

Third, suggest a more acceptable alternative. This helps the other person save face and feel valued by separating the individual from the behaviour. Their self-esteem is preserved; it is just the behaviour that should be modified. Care should be taken not to give the message, 'I don't like the way things are, so what are you going to do about it?' The change need not be the responsibility of only one of the communicating parties. The emphasis should be on finding a solution that is acceptable to both, not on deciding who is right and who is wrong or who should change and who should not: 'I'd like to suggest that we meet regularly to help you complete six more projects than last month', or 'I would like to help you identify the things that are standing in the way of higher performance'.

One concern that is sometimes expressed about descriptive communication is that these steps may not work unless the other person knows the rules, too. For example, the other person might say, 'I don't care how you feel' or 'I have an excuse for what happened, so it's not my fault' or 'It's too bad if this annoys you, as I'm not going to change'. Any such lack of concern or a defensive stance now becomes the priority problem, because the problem of low performance will be very difficult to address as long as the more important interpersonal problem between the manager and the employee is blocking progress. If the manager and the employee cannot work on the problem together, no amount of communication about the consequences of poor performance will be productive. Instead, the focus of the communication should be shifted to the obstacles that inhibit working together to improve performance.

Effective managers never abandon the three steps listed so far. They simply switch the focus. They might respond: 'I'm surprised to hear you say that you don't care how I feel about this problem (step 1). Your response concerns me and I think it might have important implications for the productivity of our team (step 2). I suggest we spend some time trying to identify the obstacles you feel might be inhibiting our ability to work together on this problem (step 3).'

It is important to keep in mind, however, that the steps of descriptive communication do not imply that one person should do all the changing. Frequently, a middle ground must be reached on which both individuals are satisfied. Also, when it is necessary to make evaluative statements, the evaluations should be made in terms of established criteria (for example, 'Your behaviour doesn't meet the prescribed standard'), probable outcomes (for example, 'Continuation of your behaviour will lead to worse consequences') or less appropriate behaviour by the same individual (for example, 'This behaviour isn't as good as your past behaviour'). The important point is to avoid disconfirming the other person or arousing defensiveness.

4. Supportive communication validates, rather than invalidates, individuals

Communication that is invalidating arouses negative feelings about self-worth, identity and relatedness to others. It denies the presence, uniqueness and importance of other individuals. Especially destructive are communications that invalidate people by conveying superiority, rigidity or indifference (Cupach & Spitzberg 1994).

Barnlund (1968: 618) observed:

> *People do not take time, do not listen, do not try to understand, but interrupt, anticipate, criticise, or disregard what is said; in their own remarks they are frequently vague, inconsistent, verbose, insincere or dogmatic. As a result, people often conclude conversations feeling more inadequate, more misunderstood and more alienated than when they started.*

Communication that is superiority-oriented gives the impression that the communicator is informed while others are ignorant, adequate while others are inadequate, competent while others are incompetent, or powerful while others are impotent. It creates a barrier between the communicator and those to whom the message is sent.

Superiority-oriented communication can take the form of put-downs, in which others are made to look bad so that the communicator looks good. Or it can take the form of 'one-upmanship', where communicators try to elevate themselves in the esteem of others. One common form of superiority-oriented communication is the use of jargon, acronyms or words in such a way as to exclude others or to create barriers in a relationship. Doctors, lawyers, government employees and many other professionals are well known for their use of jargon or acronyms to exclude others or to elevate themselves rather than to clarify a message. Speaking a foreign language in the presence of people who do not understand it may also be done to create the impression of superiority. In most circumstances, using words or language that a listener cannot understand is bad manners because it invalidates the other person.

Rigidity in communication is the second main type of invalidation: the communication is portrayed as absolute, unequivocal or unquestionable. No other opinion or point of view could possibly be considered. Individuals who communicate in dogmatic, know-it-all ways often do so in order to minimise others' contributions or to invalidate others' perspectives. It is possible to communicate rigidity, however, in ways other than just being dogmatic. Rigidity is communicated, for example, by:

- never expressing agreement with anyone else or, when agreement is expressed, expressing it in terms of 'they agree with me' rather than 'I agree with them'
- reinterpreting all other viewpoints to conform to one's own
- never saying 'I don't know', but having an answer for everything
- not expressing openness to others' opinions or information
- using evaluative and invalidating statements, instead of communicating understanding and validation for others
- appearing unwilling to tolerate criticisms or alternative points of view
- reducing complex issues to simplistic definitions
- using all-encompassing and overgeneralised statements (that is, communicating the impression that everything worthwhile that can be said about the subject has just been said)
- merging definitions of problems with solutions so that alternatives are not considered
- placing exclamation points after statements so the impression is created that the statement is final, complete or unqualified.

Indifference is communicated when the other person's existence or importance is not acknowledged. A person may do this, within most Western cultures, by using silence, by making no verbal response to the other's statements, by avoiding eye contact or any facial expression, by interrupting the other person frequently, by using impersonal words ('one should not' instead of 'you should not') or by engaging in unrelated activity during a conversation. The communicator appears not to care about the other person and gives the impression of being impervious to the other person's feelings or perspectives.

Imperviousness means that the communicator does not acknowledge the feelings or opinions of the other person. The feelings or opinions are either labelled illegitimate ('You shouldn't feel that way' or 'Your opinion is incorrect') or the person is labelled as naïve ('You don't understand', 'You've been misinformed' or, even worse, 'Your opinion is uninformed').

Communication is invalidating when it denies the other person an opportunity to establish a mutually satisfying relationship or when contributions cannot be made by both parties. When one person does not allow the other to finish a sentence, adopts a competitive, win-or-lose stance, sends confusing messages, or disqualifies the other person from making a contribution, communication is invalidating and therefore dysfunctional for effective problem solving.

Invalidating communication, then, 'reflects unawareness of others, misperceptions of them, rejection of their attempt to communicate, denial of their self-experience or disaffiliation with them' (Sieburg 1978: 146). Invalidation is even more destructive in coaching and counselling than criticism or disagreement, because criticism and disagreement validate the other person by recognising that what was said or done is worthy of correction, response or at least notice.

Validating communication, on the other hand, helps people feel recognised, understood, accepted and valued. It has four attributes:

1. It is egalitarian.
2. It is flexible.
3. It is two-way.
4. It is based on agreement.

Egalitarian communication (the opposite of superiority-oriented communication) is especially important when coaching or counselling. When a hierarchical distinction exists between coaches/counsellors and employees, it is easy for employees to feel invalidated, since they have access to less power and information than their manager. Supportive communicators, however, help people feel that they have a stake in identifying problems and resolving them by communicating an egalitarian stance. They treat employees as worthwhile, competent and insightful, and emphasise joint problem solving rather than projecting a superior position. One way they do this is by using flexible (rather than rigid) statements.

Flexibility in communication is the willingness of the coach or counsellor to accept the fact that additional data and other alternatives may exist, and other individuals may be able to make significant contributions to both the problem solution and the relationship. It means communicating genuine humility—not self-abasement or weakness—and openness to new insights. As Bertrand Russell, the respected British philosopher, logician and social critic, stated: 'One's certainty varies inversely with one's knowledge.' Benjamin Disraeli, one of Britain's greatest political leaders and British prime minister in the late 19th century, noted: 'To be conscious that you are ignorant is a first great step toward knowledge.'

Perceptions and opinions are not presented as facts in flexible communication, but are stated provisionally. That is, a distinction is made between facts and opinions, between evidence and assumptions, and no claim is made for the truthfulness of opinions or assumptions. Rather, they are identified as being changeable if more data should become available. Flexible communication conveys a willingness to enter into joint problem solving, rather than a desire to control the other person or to assume a master–teacher role. Being flexible is not the same as being wishy-washy. 'Gee, I can't make up my mind' is wishy-washy; whereas 'I have my own opinions, but what do you think?' suggests flexibility.

Two-way communication is an implied result of egalitarianism and flexibility. Individuals feel validated when they are asked questions, given 'air time' to express their opinions, and encouraged to participate actively in the coaching and counselling process. Two-way interchange communicates the message that employees are valued by the manager and that coaching and counselling are best accomplished in an atmosphere of teamwork.

Finally, the manager's communication validates the individual when it identifies areas of mutual agreement and joint commitment. One way to express validation based on agreement is to identify positive behaviours and positive attitudes, as well as negative ones, during the process of coaching or counselling. The manager should point out important points made by the employee before commenting on trivial ones, areas of agreement before areas of disagreement, advantages of the employee's statements before disadvantages, compliments before criticisms, and positive next steps before past mistakes. The point is, validating other people helps to create feelings of self-worth and self-confidence that can translate into self-motivation and improved performance. Invalidation, on the other hand, seldom produces positive outcomes, yet it is a common form of management response to employees.

5. Supportive communication is specific (useful), not global (not useful)

The more specific a statement is, the more useful it is. For example, the statement 'You're a poor time manager' is too general to be useful, whereas 'You spent an hour scheduling meetings today when that could have been done by your assistant' provides specific information that can serve as a basis for behavioural change. 'You are a poor communicator' is not nearly as useful as the more specific 'In this role-play, you used evaluative statements 60 per cent of the time and descriptive statements 10 per cent of the time.'

Specific statements avoid extremes and absolutes. The following are extreme statements that lead to defensiveness or disconfirmation:

A: You never ask for my advice.
B: Yes, I do. I always consult you before making a decision.

A: You have no consideration for others' feelings.
B: I do so. I am completely considerate.

A: This job stinks.
B: You're wrong. It's a great job.

Another common type of global communication is the either–or statement: 'Either you do what I say or you will have to find another job'; 'Life is either a daring adventure or nothing' (Helen Keller); 'If Australia doesn't reduce its trade deficit, our children will never sustain the standard of living we enjoy today.'

The problem with extreme and either–or statements is that they deny any alternatives. The possible responses of the recipient of the communication are severely constrained. About the only response to such a statement is to contradict or deny it, and this simply leads to defensiveness and arguments. A statement by Adolf Hitler in 1933 illustrates the point: 'Everyone in Germany is a National Socialist—the few outside the party are either lunatics or idiots.'

Specific statements are more useful in coaching and counselling because they focus on behavioural events and indicate gradations in positions. More useful forms of the examples above are the following:

A: You made that decision yesterday without asking for my advice.
B: Yes, I did. While I generally like to get your opinion, I didn't think it was necessary in this case.

A: By using sarcasm in your response to my request, you gave me the impression you don't care about my feelings.
B: I'm sorry. I know I am often sarcastic without thinking how it affects others.

A: The readings in this class are hard to understand.
B: That may be so, but I find the instructor's illustrations very helpful.

As these examples point out, the use of qualifier words such as 'generally', 'frequently', 'appears to be', 'may be', 'about', 'seldom', 'quite' and 'very' help to avoid global connotations, as does linking the statement to a specific event. To illustrate this point, list a word of opposite meaning to each of the following words:

good ______________________ light ______________________
happy ______________________ hot ______________________

You probably found that quite simple. Now take the same words and provide some gradations between the two extremes. The middle words will be more specific than the words on the ends of the continuum.

good ________________	________________ bad
happy ________________	________________ sad
light ________________	________________ dark
hot ________________	________________ cold

Not all specific statements are useful just because they refer to a behaviour or are qualified in some way. Specific statements may not be useful if they focus on things over which another person has no control. 'I hate it when it rains', for example, may relieve some personal frustration, but the referent of the statement is something about which little can be done. The communication is not useful. Similarly, communicating the message (even implicitly) 'I don't like people of your background' or 'Your personality bothers me' only proves frustrating for the interacting individuals. Such statements are usually interpreted as personal attacks. Specific communication is useful to the extent that it focuses on an identifiable problem or behaviour about which something can be done (for example, 'It bothers me that you checked up on me four times today').

6. Supportive communication is conjunctive, not disjunctive

Conjunctive communication is joined to previous messages in some way. It flows smoothly. Disjunctive communication is disconnected from what was stated before.

Communication can appear disjunctive in at least three ways. First, there can be a lack of equal opportunity to speak. When one person interrupts another, when someone dominates by controlling 'air time', or when two or more people try to speak at the same time, the communication is disjunctive. The transitions between speeches don't flow smoothly. Second, extended pauses are disjunctive. When speakers pause for long periods in the middle of their speech, or when there are long pauses before responses, the communication is disjunctive. Pauses need not be total silence; the space may be filled with 'umm', 'aaah' or a repetition of something stated earlier, but the communication does not progress. Third, topic control can be disjointed. When one person decides unilaterally what the topic of conversation will be (as opposed to having it decided bilaterally), the communication is disjunctive. Individuals may switch topics, for example, with no reference to what was just said, or they may control the other person's communication topic by directing what should be responded to.

These three factors—taking turns speaking, management of timing and topic control—contribute to what Wiemann (1977) calls 'interaction management'. They have been found to be critical to effective supportive communication. In a now classic empirical study of perceived communication mastery, Wiemann (1977: 104) found that 'the smoother the management of the interaction [of the three factors above], the more competent the communicator was perceived to be'. In fact, interaction management was concluded to be the most powerful determinant of perceived communication mastery in his experimental study. People who used conjunctive communication were rated as being significantly more competent in interpersonal communication than those whose communication was disjunctive. By using conjunctive communication, they confirm the worth of the other person's statements, thereby helping to foster joint problem solving and teamwork.

Skilled coaches and counsellors use several kinds of behaviours in managing communication situations so that they are conjunctive rather than disjunctive. For example, they foster conjunctive communication in an interaction by asking questions that are based directly on the individual's previous statement, by waiting for a sentence to be completed before beginning a response (for example, not finishing a sentence for someone else) and by saying only two or three sentences at a time before pausing to give the other person a chance to add input. In addition, they avoid long pauses, their statements refer to what has been said before, and they take turns speaking. Figure 5.2 illustrates that a continuum may exist for conjunctive statements.

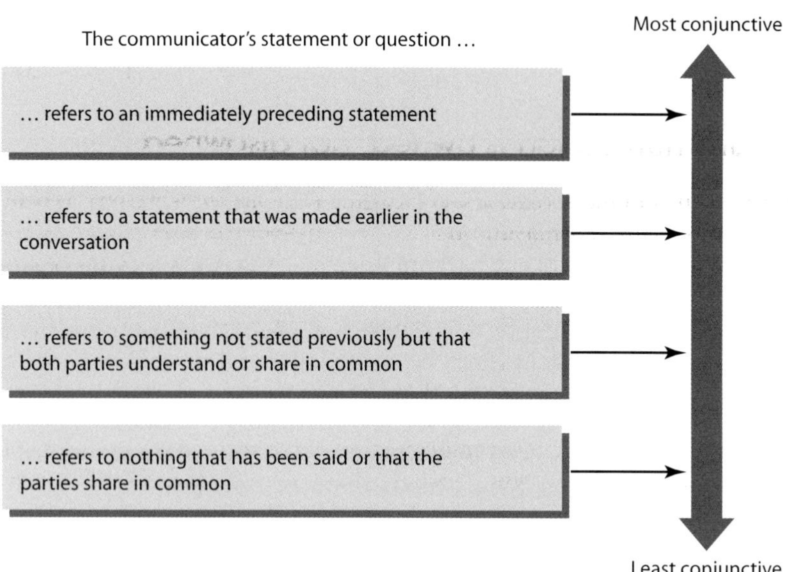
The communicator's statement or question ...
Most conjunctive
... refers to an immediately preceding statement
... refers to a statement that was made earlier in the conversation
... refers to something not stated previously but that both parties understand or share in common
... refers to nothing that has been said or that the parties share in common
Least conjunctive

FIGURE 5.2 A continuum of conjunctive statements

For example, statements that relate to the immediately preceding statement are most conjunctive; statements that relate to something that occurred earlier in the conversation are somewhat less so; statements that relate to something that both parties share in common are less conjunctive still; and statements that relate to none of these factors are the least conjunctive.

A fourth type of disjunctive communication has to do with our use of the words 'but' and 'and'. There is a subtle and powerful difference between these two conjunctions. We frequently use the word 'but' as a connector in our speaking and writing. Unfortunately, the word 'but' is really a disconnecting word that makes a lie out of what came before it. Whatever we say before the word 'but' gets negated by it: 'You did a good job, but ...'; 'I really don't want to let you go, but ...'. We all know the real meaning.

Let us examine this more closely by revisiting the following phrase from the previous paragraph: 'a subtle and powerful difference between the two'. How is this different from saying 'a subtle but powerful difference between the two'? In the first instance we are saying that the difference is both subtle and powerful at the same time. In the second instance we are saying that there is some inherent contradiction in that the difference is somehow powerful even though it is subtle. This may seem somewhat trivial to some of you. Others may think it is totally unimportant 'semantics'. Hold on to those potentially valid criticisms and put them aside for a moment. Let's first agree that there is a difference, even if you are not yet convinced of its utility or importance.

Now let's take a more relevant example. Your course instructor tells you: 'You're doing well so far in this course, but you are having some problems in terms of....' What is this communication saying? Is it different in any non-trivial way from saying, 'You're doing well so far in this course, and you are having some problems in terms of ...'? Using the word 'but' in the first case turns the 'You are doing well' part into a lie; it totally negates it. In all probability you will not hear the 'good' part but will totally concentrate on, and attend to, the negative information that follows. In the second case, using the word 'and' as a connector allows you to hear more fully the fact that 'You're doing well so far in this course' and, at the same time, 'you are having some problems in terms of ...'. This language enables you to hear both messages more clearly.

For the next few hours or days, or for however long you can attend to it, listen for the word 'but' in your own and others' conversations. Whenever you hear a 'but', replace it with an 'and'. If you are speaking, try to make the change and see what the differences are. If you hear someone else saying 'but', mentally repeat the sentence at an appropriate time and replace 'but' with 'and' and note the differences, or explain this game to them and do it together. Many people have noted that 'and' makes a significant positive difference, but do not take their word for it. (We hope you caught that 'but'.)

7. Supportive communication is owned, not disowned

Taking responsibility for our statements and acknowledging that our ideas are our own and not those of another person or group is *owning* communication. Using first-person words, such as 'I', 'me', 'mine', indicates owning communication. Disowning communication is suggested by the use of third-person or first-person-plural words: 'We think', 'They said' or 'One might say'. Disowned communication is attributed to an unknown person or group, or to some external source (for example, 'Lots of people think'). The communicator avoids taking responsibility for the message and therefore avoids investing in the interaction. This conveys the message that the communicator is aloof or uncaring about the receiver, or does not have enough confidence in the ideas expressed to take responsibility for them.

This happens more frequently than you might realise. Take some time to think about how many times you use the word 'you' (the 'royal "you"') when what you really mean is 'I'. For example:

'It's not easy to admit that you are wrong.'
'When you are really tired after a night out you always ...'
'When you take an exam, you are always nervous.'

When we make these and other statements like them, we usually mean:

'It's not easy to admit that I was wrong.'
'When I am really tired after a night out I always ...'
'When I take an exam, I am always nervous.'

Take some time over the next few hours to 'watch' and 'listen' to yourself as you talk to your family or co-workers. Most people seem to be more comfortable using the 'royal "you"' and not taking direct responsibility and ownership for what they think, feel and do. How about you?

Glasser (1965, 2000) actually based his approach to mental health—reality therapy—on the concept of taking responsibility for, or owning, communication and behaviour. According to Glasser, individuals are mentally healthy if they accept responsibility for their statements and behaviours. They are ill if they avoid taking responsibility. According to this theory, taking responsibility for our communication builds self-confidence and a sense of self-worth in the communicator. It also builds confidence in the receiver of the communication by confirming that his or her worth is valued.

One result of disowning communication is that the listener is never sure whose point of view the message represents and is apt to misinterpret it: 'How can I respond if I don't know to whom I am responding?', 'If I don't understand the message, who can I ask?' Moreover, an implicit message associated with disowned communication is: 'I want to keep distance between you and me.' The speaker communicates as a representative rather than a person, as a message conveyer rather than an interested individual. Owning communication, on the other hand, indicates a willingness to invest oneself in a relationship and to act as a colleague or helper.

8. Supportive communication requires listening, not one-way message delivery

The previous seven attributes of supportive communication all focus on message delivery, where a message is initiated by the coach or counsellor. Another aspect of supportive communication—that is, listening and responding effectively to someone else's statements—is at least as important as delivering supportive messages. Unfortunately, as Hugh Mackay, the noted Australian social researcher and commentator, highlights: 'Our reluctance to listen is legendary, and there are many physical and psychological reasons why that is so' (1994: 143). In conversation, managers, salespeople and customer service staff who do not listen end up with less information on which to base their decisions—and they learn very little about the other person. Many of us would benefit by considering ourselves professional listeners, rather than professional speakers.

Haas and Arnold (1995) found that, in the workplace, about one-third of the characteristics that people use to judge communication competence have to do with listening. Kramer (1997) found that good listening skills accounted for 40 per cent of the variance in effective leadership. In short, good listeners are more likely to be seen as skilful communicators. In fact, people who are judged to be the most 'wise', or to possess the attribute of wisdom—and, therefore, are the most sought-after people with whom to interact—are also the best listeners (Kramer 2000; Sternberg 1990).

Despite its importance in managerial success, most people have underdeveloped listening skills. Tests have shown, for example, that individuals are usually about 25 per cent effective in listening (Huseman, Lahiff & Hatfield 1976); that is, they listen to and understand only about a quarter of what is being communicated. When asked to rate the extent to which they are skilled listeners, 85 per cent of all individuals rate themselves as average or worse. Only 5 per cent rate themselves as highly skilled (Steil 1980). It is particularly unfortunate that listening skills are often poorest when people interact with those closest to them, such as family members and co-workers. They interrupt and jump to conclusions (that is, they stop listening) more frequently with people who are close to them.

When individuals are preoccupied with meeting their own needs (for example, saving face, persuading someone else, winning a point, avoiding getting involved), when they have already made a prior judgment, or when they hold negative attitudes towards the communicator or the message, they cannot listen effectively. Because people listen at the rate of 500 words a minute but speak at a normal rate of only 125 to 250 words a minute, the listener's mind can dwell on other things half the time. Therefore, being a good listener is neither easy nor automatic. It requires developing the ability to hear and understand the message sent by another person, while at the same time helping to strengthen the relationship between the interacting parties.

The importance of listening

Decision makers who do not listen have less information for making sound decisions (cf. Hernandez 2006; Ohren 2007). The process of listening involves receiving information with your ears and eyes, giving meaning to that information, and deciding what you think and feel about that information. If you take a moment to identify the people in your life who really seem to care about you, who are interested in what you have to say and who seem to be really good communicators, you might find that these people have excellent listening skills.

At work, there are dozens of situations in which listening is critical, yet we typically think of talking when we think of relating to people and communication. When we are at meetings, briefings and seminars, most of us spend the vast majority of our time listening. When we are coaching, counselling, giving and/or receiving instructions or feedback, it is critical that we hear, listen and understand the speaker. When we are involved in a sale, or when we are servicing or helping clients and customers, we will be more successful and effective if we begin to consider ourselves professional listeners rather than professional speakers.

Most of us never take the time to seriously consider the topic of listening. We know quite a bit about the way we listen. Humans tend to be selective listeners. We sometimes choose to listen and at other times we do not. If we think that the message is important and/or we are interested in the topic for some reason, we will listen. On other occasions, we just 'turn off' or 'tune out'. Consider the last time you were on an aeroplane. How carefully did you listen to the information on safety and what to do in an emergency? Would you have listened differently if you had received that same information after being told that the aircraft was about to crash?

Another thing we may not be aware of is that our emotions affect our ability and willingness to listen. If we hear something and react emotionally by getting angry, frustrated, hurt or sad, this will affect our ability and willingness to listen. The same is true for more positive emotions. If we get good news, we may become so excited and preoccupied with our own feelings and thoughts that we 'tune out' for a while. Another important thing to remember about listening is that we sometimes hear what we expect to hear and may filter out information that is not consistent with our existing feelings, attitudes and beliefs. For example, if we have prejudged someone, we may discount things they say that are contrary to that preconception.

Good listening can help make you a better manager and a better partner, parent or spouse. It can lead to any number of more positive outcomes in your work-life and your life in general. There are many different skills involved in good listening. A good listener does the following:

- *Stops talking*. If you are talking, you are not listening.
- *Makes eye contact*. This shows interest and attention. It also allows you to 'hear' and 'see' what the person is saying. The eyes and face are very expressive. You can learn to listen with your eyes as well as your ears.
- *Exhibits appropriate body language (for example, head nods)*. This encourages the speaker and shows you are following the conversation and are attentive.
- *Avoids distracting actions and gestures that suggest boredom*. Show the talker that you want to listen. If you read your mail while someone is talking, they have good reason to think that you are not fully listening to them.
- *Asks questions*. This encourages a talker and is evidence that you are really listening and thinking about what they have said.
- *Paraphrases*. Restate what has been said to ensure understanding. Listen to understand, rather than to oppose, what is said.
- *Avoids interrupting*. If you are interrupted, you may think and feel that the other person does not want to listen to what you have to say.
- *Makes smooth transitions between the role of speaker and listener*. Good listeners do not rush into speaking after another has stopped.
- *Does not over-talk*. If you are talking, you are not listening.

In addition to these skills, good listening also takes courage, generosity and patience (Mackay 1994). It takes courage to really listen and to seriously entertain the ideas of another. It means we may have to admit some new information and change our minds. The good news is that 'people are more likely to listen to us if we listen to them' (Mackay 1994: 157). Effective listening takes generosity, as we are offering the other the gifts of understanding, acceptance (even if we do not fully agree) and of being taken seriously. Listening also requires patience, as we need to hold back our judgments and our statements in order to fully hear the other out.

Listening to how others are listening

By listening to what someone says in response to you, you can get a sense of *how* they are listening to you. This will help you to determine if they have really heard you or not, and if they are understanding your message. If someone says something totally unexpected, something that really does not make any sense to you, given what you have just said and your current train of thought, it is very easy, and hugely ineffective, to let it pass with a nod or a chuckle. This happens more frequently than you may think.

People do not know they are being listened to unless the listener makes some type of response. Competent managers who must coach and counsel select carefully from a repertoire of response alternatives that affirm to the listener that he or she has been heard, that clarify the communication and strengthen the interpersonal relationship. One of the skills of a supportive listener is the ability to select appropriate responses to others' statements.

The appropriateness of a response depends largely on whether the focus of the interaction is primarily coaching or counselling. Of course, seldom can these two activities be separated from one another completely—effective coaching often involves counselling, and effective counselling sometimes involves coaching—and attentive listening involves the use of a variety of responses. But some responses are more appropriate under certain circumstances than others.

Figure 5.3 shows four main response types arranged on a continuum from most directive and closed to most non-directive and open.

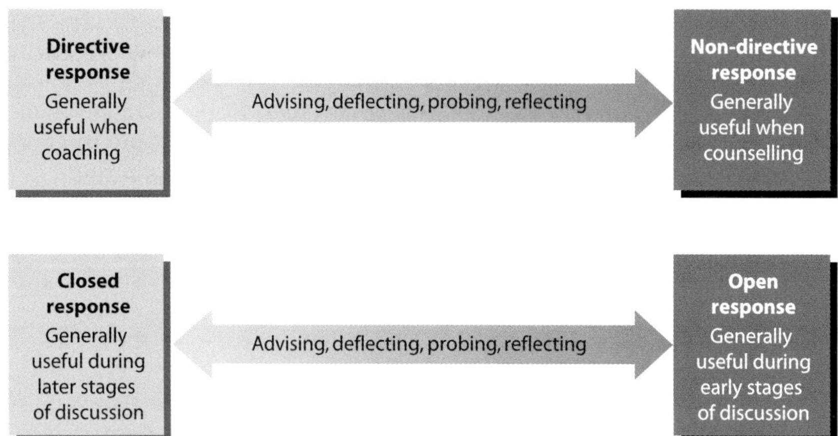

FIGURE 5.3 Types of response in supportive listening

Most people get into the habit of relying heavily on one or two response types, using them regardless of the circumstances; and most people have been found to rely first and foremost on evaluative or judgmental responses (Rogers 1961). That is, when they encounter another person's statements, most people tend to agree or disagree, pass judgment, or immediately form a personal opinion about the legitimacy or veracity of the statement. On average, about 80 per cent of most people's responses have been found to be evaluative. Supportive listening, however, avoids evaluation and judgment as a first response. Instead, it relies on flexibility in the type of response and the appropriate matching of responses to circumstances.

The four response types—advising, deflecting, probing, reflecting—are discussed next.

Advising

An advising response provides direction, evaluation, personal opinion or instructions. Such a response imposes on the communicator the point of view of the listener and creates listener control over the topic of conversation. The advantages of an advising response are that it helps the communicator understand something that may have been unclear before, it helps to identify a solution to a problem, and it can provide clarity about how the communicator should feel or act in the future. It is most appropriate when the listener has expertise that the communicator does not possess or when the communicator is in need of direction. Supportive listening sometimes means that the listener does the talking, but this is usually appropriate only when advice or direction is specifically requested. Most listeners have a tendency to offer much more advice and direction than is appropriate.

One problem with advising is that it can produce dependence. People get used to someone else generating answers, directions or clarifications. They are not permitted to figure out issues and solutions for themselves. A second problem is that advising also creates the impression that the communicator is not being understood by the listener. Rogers (1961) found that most people, even when they seem to be asking for advice, mainly desire understanding and acceptance, not advice. They want the listener to share in the communication but not take charge of it. The problem with advising is that it removes from the communicator control of the conversation; it focuses attention on the advice itself rather than on the communicator's problem.

A third problem with advising is that it shifts the focus from the communicator's message to the listener's advice. When listeners feel advising is appropriate, they concentrate more on the legitimacy of the advice, or on the generation of alternatives and solutions, than on simply listening attentively. When listeners are expected to provide advice and direction, they may focus more on their own experience than on the communicator's. A fourth potential problem with advising is that it can imply that communicators do not have sufficient understanding, expertise, insight or maturity and that they need help because of their incompetence.

One way to help overcome the disadvantages of advising is to avoid giving advice as a first response in coaching and counselling. It should follow other responses that allow communicators to have control over the topics of conversation, that show understanding and acceptance, and that encourage self-reliance on the part of communicators. In addition, advice that is given should either be connected to an accepted standard or should be equivocal. An accepted standard means that communicators and listeners both acknowledge that the advice will lead to a desired outcome and that it is inherently good, right or appropriate. When this is impossible, the advice should be communicated as the listener's opinion or feeling, and as only one option (that is, with flexibility), not as the only option. This permits communicators to accept or reject the advice without feeling that the adviser is being invalidated or rejected if the advice is not accepted.

Deflecting

A deflecting response switches the focus from the communicator's problem to one selected by the listener. The listener changes the subject. Listeners may substitute their own experience for that of the communicator (for example, 'Let me tell you something similar that happened to me') or introduce an entirely new topic (for example, 'That reminds me of [something else]'). The listener may think the current problem is unclear to the communicator and that the use of examples or analogies will help. Or the listener may feel that the communicator needs to be reassured that others have experienced the same problem and that support and understanding are available.

Deflecting responses are most appropriate when a comparison or reassurance is needed. They can provide empathy and support by communicating the message, 'I understand because of what happened to me (or someone else).' They can also convey the assurance that 'Things will be fine. Others have also had this experience.' Deflection is also often used to avoid embarrassing either the communicator or the listener. Changing the subject when either party gets uncomfortable and answering a question other than the one asked are common examples.

The disadvantages of deflecting responses, however, are that they can imply that the communicator's message is not important or that the experience of the listener is more significant than that of the communicator. It may produce competitiveness or feelings of being outwitted by the listener. Deflection can be interpreted as: 'My experience is more worthy of discussion than yours.' Or it may simply change the subject from something that is important and central to the communicator to a topic that is not important.

Deflecting responses are most effective when they are conjunctive—that is, when they are clearly connected to what the communicator has just said, when the listener's response leads directly back to the communicator's concerns, and when the reason for the deflection is made clear. That is, deflecting can produce desirable outcomes in coaching and counselling if the communicator feels supported and understood, not invalidated, by the change in topic focus.

Probing

A probing response asks a question about what the communicator just said or about a topic selected by the listener. The intent of a probe is to acquire additional information, to help the communicator say more about the topic, or to help the listener foster more appropriate responses. For example, an effective way to avoid being evaluative and judgmental, and to avoid triggering defensive reactions, is to continue to ask questions. Questioning helps the listener adopt the communicator's frame of reference so that in coaching situations suggestions can be specific (not global) and in counselling situations statements can be descriptive (not evaluative). Questions tend to be more neutral in tone than direct statements.

Questioning, however, can sometimes have the unwelcome effect of switching the focus of attention from the communicator's statement to the reasons behind it. The question 'Why do you think that?', for example, might force the communicator to justify a feeling or a perception, rather than just report it. Similarly, probing responses can serve as a mechanism for escaping discussion of a topic or for manoeuvring the topic around to one the listener wants to discuss (for example, 'Instead of discussing your feelings about your job, tell me why you didn't respond to my memo'). Probing responses can also allow the communicator to lose control of the conversation, especially when difficult subjects need to be addressed (for example, 'I'll talk about only those things you ask me').

Two important hints should be kept in mind to make probing responses more effective. One is that 'why' questions are seldom as effective as 'what' questions. 'Why' questions lead to topic changes, escape and speculation more often than to valid information. For example, the question 'Why do you feel that way?' can lead to statements such as 'Because my id is not sufficiently controlled by my ego' or 'Because my father was an alcoholic and my mother beat me'. These are extreme examples, but they illustrate how ineffective 'why' questions can be. 'What do you mean by that?' is likely to be more fruitful.

A second hint is to tailor the probes to fit the situation. For example, Chapter 12 (a companion website chapter) summarises four types of probes that are useful in interviewing. When the communicator's statement does not contain enough information, or part of the message is not understood, an *elaboration probe* should be used (for example, 'Can you tell me more about that?'). When the message is ambiguous, a *clarification probe* is best (for example, 'What do you mean by that?'). A *repetition probe* works best when the communicator is avoiding a topic or has not answered a previous question (for example, 'Once again, what do you think about that?'). A *reflective probe* is most effective when the communicator is being encouraged to keep pursuing the same topic in greater depth (for example, 'You say you are discouraged?').

Probing responses are especially effective in turning hostile or conflictual conversations into supportive conversations. Asking questions can often turn attacks into consensus, evaluations into descriptions, general statements into specific statements, or person-focused declarations into problem-focused declarations. In other words, probes can often be used to help others use supportive communication when they have not been trained in advance to do so.

Reflecting

The primary purpose of the reflecting response is to mirror back to the communicator the message that was heard and to communicate understanding and acceptance. Reflective responding involves paraphrasing and clarifying the message. Instead of simply mimicking the communication, supportive listeners contribute meaning, understanding and acceptance to the conversation, while still allowing communicators to pursue topics of their choosing. Athos and Gabarro (1978), Brownell (1986), Steil, Barker and Watson (1983) and others argue that this response should be used most of the time in coaching and counselling, since it leads to the clearest communication and the most supportive relationships.

A potential disadvantage of reflective responses is that communicators may get the opposite impression from the one intended. That is, they can get the feeling that they are not being understood or listened to carefully. If they keep hearing reflections of what they have just said, their response might be: 'I just said that. Aren't you listening to me?' Reflective responses, in other words, can be perceived as an artificial 'technique' or a superficial response to a message.

The most effective listeners keep the following rules in mind when using reflective responses:

- Avoid repeating the same response, such as: 'You feel that ...', 'Are you saying that ...?' or 'What I heard you say was ...'.
- Avoid an exchange in which listeners do not contribute equally to the conversation, but serve only as mimics. (You can use understanding/reflective responses while still taking equal responsibility for the depth and meaning of the communication.)
- Respond to the personal, rather than the impersonal. For example, to a complaint by an individual about close supervision and feelings of incompetence and annoyance, an understanding/reflective response would focus on personal feelings, rather than on supervision style.
- Respond to expressed feelings before responding to content. When expressed, feelings are the most important part of the message to the person and may stand in the way of their ability to communicate clearly.

- Respond with empathy and acceptance. Avoid the extremes of complete objectivity, detachment or distance on the one hand or over-identification (accepting the feelings as your own) on the other.
- Avoid expressing agreement or disagreement with the statements.

The expression of emotions

It is important to address feelings and emotions at work, especially when adopting the counselling role. If we do not, we are neglecting an important part of our being, of our humanity. By addressing grief, fears, anger or the sense of something missing, the wholeness of human expression is acknowledged. Emotional flow leads to emotional, physical and mental health for individuals and organisations. When people are afraid of feelings and emotions, or when emotional expression is seen as a problem, it is often because emotions have been cut off for so long and are so far out of balance that when they do come up and out, they are coming from a state of 'out-of-balance'. This imbalance is what leads to problems.

Unbalanced emotion comes out as inappropriate decisions and rude behaviour towards clients and customers. When emotions are felt and expressed from a place of balance—that is, when they are tempered and balanced with rational thought and careful consideration—they are appropriate and not a problem. Balanced emotion comes out as thoughtful, legitimate expressions of joy or fear that actually enhance the performance of the people in the situation. It is important to provide positive emotional support to employees, especially during times of stress and anxiety. We know that negative emotional arousal (for example, stress, fear, anxiety) can lower self-efficacy expectations. We also know that mastery is enhanced when positive emotional support and a trusting atmosphere are provided.

Henry Mintzberg, a noted organisational scholar and theoretician from Harvard University, was interviewed regarding strategy and intuition in organisations. The conversation focused on the two distinct sides of people and of organisations: the rational, analytical side and the non-rational, synthesising side. Mintzberg continually alluded to the importance of both sides in an organisation. 'I am not saying that analysis is bad or unnecessary. There is the danger, though, that you can preclude synthesis with too much analysis' (Campbell 1991: 109). Mintzberg suggested that expression of the intuitive, feeling and non-rational side of human beings is discouraged in many companies, and that there are a great many forces in our society that drive it out. Many of us, according to Mintzberg, just switch off the right side of our brain every morning. He concluded that great organisations encourage and use both sides of human nature and they get the right mix of analysis and intuition.

The personal management interview

Not only are the eight attributes of supportive communication effective in normal discourse and problem-solving situations, but they can be most effectively applied when specific interactions with employees are planned and conducted frequently. One important difference between effective and ineffective managers is the extent to which they provide their employees with opportunities to receive regular feedback, to feel supported and bolstered, and to be coached and counselled. Providing these opportunities is difficult, however, because of the tremendous time demands most managers face. Many managers want to coach, counsel and train employees, but they simply never find the time. Therefore, one important mechanism for applying supportive communication and for providing employees with development and feedback opportunities is to implement a personal management interview program.

A personal management interview program is a regularly scheduled, one-on-one meeting between managers and their employees. In a study of the performance of departments and teams in a variety of organisations, Boss (1983) found that effectiveness increased significantly when managers conducted regular, private meetings with employees on a biweekly or monthly basis. These meetings were referred to as 'personal management interviews'. Figure 5.4 compares the performance effectiveness of teams and departments that implemented the program versus those that did not.

LEARNING

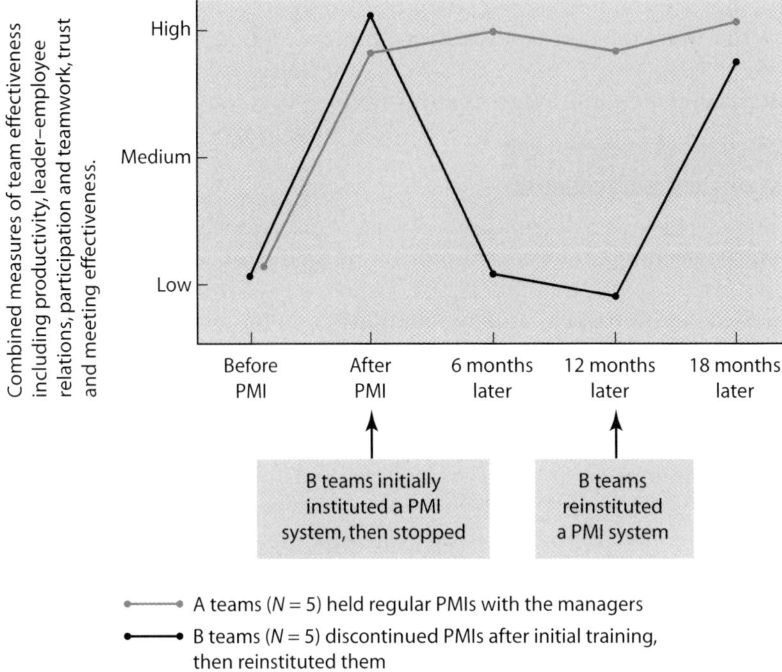

FIGURE 5.4 Effects of an ongoing personal management interview program

Instituting a personal management interview program consists of two steps. First, a role-negotiation session is held in which expectations, responsibilities, standards of evaluation, reporting relationships and so on are clarified. Unless such a meeting is held, most employees do not have a clear idea of exactly what is expected of them or on what basis they will be evaluated. Few managers and executives express confidence that they know precisely what is expected of them or how they are being evaluated in their jobs. In a role-negotiation session, that uncertainty is overcome; the manager and employee negotiate all job-related issues that are not prescribed by policy or by mandate. A written record should be made of the agreements and responsibilities resulting from the meeting to serve as an informal contract between manager and employee. The goal of a role-negotiation session is to ensure clarity between the parties regarding what each expects from the other. Because this role negotiation is not adversarial, but rather focuses on supportiveness and team building, the eight supportive communication principles should characterise the interaction.

The second (and most important) step in a personal management interview plan is a program of ongoing, one-on-one meetings of the manager with each employee. These meetings are held regularly (not just when a mistake is made or a crisis arises) and are private (not overheard by others). The meeting provides managers with the opportunity to coach and counsel employees and help them improve their skills and job performance. Each meeting should last from 45 minutes to an hour and focus on such items as the following:

- managerial and organisational problems
- information sharing
- interpersonal issues
- obstacles to improvement
- training in management skills
- individual needs
- feedback on job performance
- personal concerns or problems.

The meeting always leads towards action items to be accomplished before the next meeting, some by the employee and others by the manager. Both parties prepare for the meeting, and both bring items to be discussed. It is not a formal appraisal session called by the manager, but a development and improvement session in which both manager and employee have a stake. It is a chance for employees to have personal time with the manager to work out issues and report information; consequently, it helps to eliminate unscheduled interruptions and long, inefficient group meetings. At each subsequent meeting, action items are reviewed from previous meetings, so that continuous improvement is encouraged. Box 5.3 summarises the characteristics of the personal management interview program.

BOX 5.3 Characteristics of a personal management interview program

1. The interview is regular and private.
2. The main intent of the meeting is continuous improvement in personal, interpersonal and organisational performance, so the meeting is action-oriented.
3. Both manager and employee prepare agenda items for the meeting. It is a meeting for both of them, not just for the manager.
4. Sufficient time is allowed for the interaction, usually about an hour.
5. Supportive communication is used so that joint problem solving and continuous improvement result (in both task accomplishment and interpersonal relationships).
6. The first agenda item is a follow-up on the action items generated by the previous meeting.
7. Major agenda items for the meeting might include:
   - managerial and organisational problems
   - organisational values and vision
   - information sharing
   - interpersonal issues
   - obstacles to improvement
   - training in management skills
   - individual needs
   - feedback on job performance
   - personal concerns and problems.
8. Praise and encouragement are intermingled with problem solving.
9. A review of action items generated by the meeting occurs at the end of the interview.

Boss's research found that a variety of benefits were evident in teams that instituted this program. It not only increased their effectiveness but also improved individual accountability, department meeting efficiency and communication flows. Managers actually found more discretionary time available because the program reduced interruptions and unscheduled meetings. Participants defined it as a successful experience in itself. When correction or negative feedback had to be communicated, and when coaching or counselling was called for (which is typical of almost every manager–employee relationship at some point), supportive communication helped to strengthen the interpersonal relationship at the same time that problems were solved and performance improved. In summary, setting aside time for formal, structured interaction between managers and their employees in which supportive communication played a part produced markedly improved bottom-line results in those organisations that implemented the program.

Summary

The most important barriers to effective communication in organisations are interpersonal. Much progress has been made in the last two decades in improving the accuracy of message delivery in organisations. Communication problems, however, still persist between managers and their employees and peers. A major reason for these problems is that the kind of communication used frequently does not support a positive interpersonal relationship. Memos and email, for example, are efficient. However, instead of building rapport and trust between the individuals communicating—because of factors such as a lack of social cues, de-individuation and depersonalisation—memos and email can sometimes engender distrust, hostility, defensiveness, and feelings of incompetence and low self-esteem (Spears & Lea 1992). Hugh Mackay (1993: 264) reached a similar conclusion:

> *In corporate life, information technology has become so sophisticated that data transfer is often confused with communication, and personal relationships within organisations have suffered directly as a result. Sending and receiving disembodied information is increasingly allowed to occupy time which used to be spent in keeping closely in touch with each other.*

Dysfunctional communication is seldom associated with situations in which compliments are given, congratulations are made, a bonus is awarded or other positive interactions occur. Most people have little trouble communicating effectively in such situations. Instead, potentially harmful communication patterns are most likely to emerge when we are giving feedback on poor performance, saying 'no' to a proposal or request, resolving a difference of opinion between two employees, correcting problem behaviours, receiving criticism from others or facing other negative interactions. These situations also arise frequently in the context of coaching and counselling employees. Handling these situations in a way that fosters interpersonal growth and a strengthening of relationships is one mark of an effective manager.

Effective communicators adhere to the principles of supportive communication, thus ensuring greater clarity and understanding of messages while making other people feel accepted, valued and supported. Of course, it is possible to become overly concerned with technique in trying to incorporate these principles and thereby defeat the goal of being supportive. Managers may become artificial, or incongruent, by focusing on technique alone, rather than on honest, caring communication. If the principles are practised and consciously implemented in everyday interactions, however, they can be important tools for improving communication and relationships. What is needed is summed up nicely by Daniel Goleman in his book on emotional intelligence. Goleman (1995: 34) suggests that what is needed in the workplace, and in life more generally, are 'abilities such as being able to motivate oneself and persist in the face of frustrations; to control impulse and delay gratification; to regulate one's moods and keep distress from swamping the ability to think; to empathise and to hope'. These are the skills and abilities that have been explored in this chapter.

Behavioural guidelines

The following behavioural guidelines will help you practise supportive communication.

1. Differentiate between coaching situations, which require giving advice and direction to help foster behaviour change, and counselling situations, in which understanding and problem recognition are the desired outcomes.
2. Use problem-oriented statements, rather than person-oriented statements—that is, behavioural referents or characteristics of events, not attributes of the person.
3. Communicate congruently by acknowledging your true feelings without acting them out in destructive ways.
4. Use descriptive, not evaluative, statements. Describe objectively what occurred; describe your reactions to events and their objective consequences; and suggest acceptable alternatives.
5. Use validating statements that acknowledge the other person's importance and uniqueness; communicate an investment in the relationship by demonstrating your egalitarianism and flexibility in statements; foster two-way exchanges; and identify areas of agreement or positive characteristics before pointing out areas of disagreement or negative characteristics.
6. Use specific rather than global (either/or, black-or-white) statements; use qualifier words that allow for finer gradations and focus on things that can be controlled.

7. Use conjunctive statements that flow smoothly from what was said previously; ensure equal speaking opportunities for all; do not cause long pauses; do not completely control the topic; and acknowledge what was said before.
8. Own your statements: use personal words ('I') rather than impersonal words ('you' or 'they').
9. Demonstrate supportive listening: use a variety of responses to others' statements, depending on whether you are coaching or counselling, but with a bias towards reflecting responses.
10. Implement a personal management interview program characterised by supportive communication, in order to coach, counsel and foster personal development among employees.

Skill analysis

Case studies involving coaching and counselling

Find somebody else

Rita Dubrovsky, the relatively new general manager of the machine tooling group at Parker Manufacturing, was visiting one of the plants. She scheduled a meeting with Mike Singh, a plant manager who reported to her.

Rita: Mike, I've scheduled this meeting with you because I've been reviewing performance data, and I wanted to give you some feedback. I know we haven't talked face-to-face before, but I think it's time we reviewed how you're doing. I'm afraid that some of the things I have to say aren't very favourable.

Mike: Well, since you're the new boss, I guess I'll have to listen. I've had meetings like this before with new people who come into my plant and think they know what's going on.

Rita: Look, Mike, I want this to be a two-way exchange. I'm not here to read a verdict to you, and I'm not here to tell you how to do your job. There are just some areas for improvement I want to review.

Mike: Okay, sure, I've heard that before. But you called the meeting. Go ahead and lower the boom.

Rita: Well, Mike, I don't think this is lowering the boom. But there are several things you need to hear. One is what I noticed during the plant tour. I think you're too chummy with some of your female personnel. You know, one of them might take offence and level a sexual harassment suit against you.

Mike: Oh, come on. You haven't been around this plant before, and you don't know the informal, friendly relationships we have. The office staff and the women on the floor are flattered by a little attention now and then.

Rita: That may be so, but you need to be more careful. You may not be sensitive to what's really going on with them. But that raises another thing I noticed—the appearance of your shop. You know how important it is in Parker to have a neat and clean shop. As I walked through this morning, I noticed that it was not as orderly and neat as I would like to see it. Having things in disarray reflects poorly on you, Mike.

Mike: I'll stack my plant up against any in Parker for neatness. You may have seen a few tools out of place because someone was just using them, but we take a lot of pride in our neatness. I don't see how you can say that things are in disarray. You've got no experience around here, so who are you to judge?

Rita: Well, I'm glad you're sensitive to the neatness issue. I just think you need to pay attention to it, that's all. But regarding neatness, I notice that you don't dress like a plant manager. I think you're creating a substandard impression by not wearing a tie, for example. Casualness in dress

ANALYSIS

can be used as an excuse for employees to come to work in really grubby attire. That may not be safe.

Mike: Look, I don't agree with making a big separation between the managers and the employees. By dressing like people out on the shop floor, I think we eliminate a lot of barriers. Besides, I don't have the money to buy clothes that might get oil on them every day. That seems pretty picky to me.

Rita: I don't want to seem picky, Mike. But I do feel strongly about the issues I've mentioned. There are some other things, though, that need to get corrected. One is the appearance of the reports you send in to division headquarters. There are often mistakes, misspellings and, I suspect, some wrong numbers. I wonder if you are paying attention to these reports. You seem to be reviewing them superficially.

Mike: If there is one thing we have too much of, it's reports. I could spend three-quarters of my time filling our report forms and generating data for some bean counter in headquarters. We have reports coming out of our ears. Why don't you give us a chance to get our work done and eliminate all this paperwork?

Rita: You know as well as I do, Mike, that we need to carefully monitor our productivity, quality and costs. You just need to get more serious about taking care of that part of your responsibility.

Mike: Okay. I'm not going to fight about that. It's a losing battle for me. No one at headquarters will ever decrease their demand for reports. But, listen, Rita, I also have one question for you.

Rita: Okay. What's that?

Mike: Why don't you go find somebody else to pick on? I need to get back to work.

ANALYSIS

DISCUSSION QUESTIONS

1. *What principles of supportive communication and supportive listening are violated in this case?*
2. *How could the interaction have been changed to produce a better outcome?*
3. *Categorise each of the statements by naming the rule of supportive communication that is either illustrated or violated.*
4. *What should Rita do in her follow-up meeting with Mike?*

Rejected plans

The following dialogue occurred between two employees in a large firm. The conversation illustrates several characteristics of supportive communication.

Athena: How did your meeting go with Luke Peterson yesterday?

Tony: Well, uh, it went … aaah … it was no big deal.

Athena: It looks as if you're pretty upset about it.

Tony: Yes, I am. It was a totally frustrating experience. I, uh, well, let's just say I would like to forget the whole thing.

Athena: Things must not have gone as well as you hoped they would.

Tony: I'll say! That guy was impossible. I thought the plans I submitted were very clear and well thought out. Then he rejected the entire package.

Athena: You mean he didn't accept any of them?

Tony: You got it.

Athena: I've seen your work before, Tony. You've always done a first-rate job. It's hard for me to figure out why your plans were rejected by Peterson. What did he say about them?

Tony: He said they were unrealistic and too difficult to implement, and.…

Athena: Really?

Tony: Yes, and when he said that I felt he was attacking me personally. But, on the other hand, I was also angry because I thought my plans were very good and, you know, I paid close attention to every detail in those plans.

Athena: I'm certain that you did.

Tony: It really gets to me.

Athena: I'll bet it does. I would be upset, too.

Tony: Peterson must have something against me.

Athena: After all the effort you put into those plans, you still couldn't figure out whether Peterson was rejecting you or your plans, right?

Tony: Yes. Right. How could you tell?

Athena: I can really understand your confusion and uncertainty when you felt Peterson's actions were unreasonable.

Tony: I just don't understand why he did what he did.

Athena: Sure. If he said your plans were unrealistic, what does that mean? How can you deal with a rationale like that? It's just too general—meaningless, even. Did he mention anything specific? Did you ask him to point out some problems or explain the reasons for his rejection more clearly?

Tony: Good point, but, uh, you know ... I was so disappointed at the rejection that I was kind of in outer space. You know what I mean?

Athena: Yes. It's an incapacitating experience. You have so much invested personally that you try to divest as fast as you can to save what little self-respect is left.

Tony: That's it, all right. I just wanted to get out of there before I said something I would regret.

Athena: Yet, in the back of your mind, you probably figured that Peterson wouldn't risk the company's future just because he didn't like you personally. But then, well ... the plans were good! It's hard to deal with that contradiction on the spot, isn't it?

Tony: Exactly. I knew I should have pushed him for more information, but, uh, I just stood there like a dummy. But what can you do about it now? It's spilled milk.

Athena: I don't think it's a total loss, Tony. From what you have told me—what he said and what you said—I don't think that a conclusion can be reached. Maybe he doesn't understand the plans, or maybe it was just his off-day. Who knows, it could be a lot of things. What would you think about pinning Peterson down by asking for his objections, point by point? Do you think it would help to talk to him again?

Tony: Well, I would sure know a lot more than I know now. As it is, I wouldn't know where to begin revising or modifying the plans. And you're right, I really don't know what Peterson thinks about me or my work. Sometimes I just react and interpret with little or no evidence.

Athena: Maybe, uh ... maybe another meeting would be a good thing, then.

Tony: Well, I guess I should get off my duff and schedule an appointment with him. I am curious to find out what the problem is—with the plans, or me. (Pause) Thanks, Athena, for helping me work through this thing.

DISCUSSION QUESTIONS

1. *Categorise each statement in the case according to the supportive communication characteristic or type of response it represents. For example, the first statement by Tony is obviously not very congruent, but the second one is much more so.*
2. *Which statements in the conversation were most helpful? Which do you think would produce defensiveness or close off the conversation?*
3. *What are the potential disadvantages of giving outright advice for solving Tony's problem? Why doesn't Athena just tell Tony what he ought to do? Is it incongruent to ask Tony what he thinks is the best solution?*

Skill practice

Exercises for diagnosing communication problems and fostering understanding

United Mining Pty Ltd

The role of manager encompasses not only one-on-one coaching and counselling with an employee but also frequently entails helping other people understand coaching and counselling principles for themselves. Sometimes, it means refereeing interactions and, by example, helping other people learn the correct principles of supportive communication. This is part of the task in this exercise. In a group setting, coaching and counselling become more difficult because multiple messages, driven by multiple motives, interact. Skilled supportive communicators, however, help each group member to feel supported and understood in the interaction, even though the solution to an issue may not always be the one they would have preferred.

Assignment

In this exercise you should apply the principles of supportive communication you have read about in the chapter. First, form groups of four people. Next, read the case and assign the following roles in your group: Bob, Sue, Damiano and an observer. Assume that a meeting is being held with Bob, Sue and Damiano immediately after the end of the incidents in the following case. Play the roles you have been assigned and try to resolve the problems. The observer should provide feedback to the three players at the end of the exercise. An observer's form to assist in providing feedback can be found at the end of the chapter (page 269). Remember to use the principles of supportive communication during your group discussion and debriefing.

United Mining Pty Ltd is a large producer and distributor of precious metals (copper, zinc, silver, gold), with several sites in Western Australia and Queensland. The main site in West Perth is not only a producing mine but also the company's administrative, research and engineering centre.

The engineering group consists of eight male engineers and their supervisor, Bob Kane. The group has worked together steadily for a number of years and good relationships have developed among all the members. When the workload began to increase, Bob hired a new engineer, Sue Davis, a recent master's degree graduate from one of the foremost engineering schools in the country. Sue was assigned to a project that was intended to expand the capacity and yield of one of the existing sites. Three other engineers were assigned to the project along with Sue: Damiano Keller (age 38, 15 years with the company), Steve Sims (age 40, ten years with the company) and Doug Madson (age 32, eight years with the company).

As a new employee, Sue was very enthusiastic about the opportunity to work at United. She liked her work very much because it was challenging and offered her a chance to apply much of the knowledge she had gained in her university studies. On the job, Sue kept mostly to herself and her work. Her relations with fellow project members were friendly, but she did not go out of her way to have informal conversations with them during or after working hours.

Sue was a diligent employee who took her work seriously. On occasions, when a difficult problem arose, she would stay after hours in order to come up with a solution. Because of her persistence, coupled with her more current education, Sue usually completed her portion of the various project stages several days ahead of her colleagues. This was somewhat irritating to her because on these occasions she had to go to Bob to ask for additional work to keep her busy until her fellow employees caught up to her. Initially, she had offered to help Damiano, Steve and Doug with their assignments, but each time she was abruptly turned down.

About five months after Sue had joined the design group, Damiano asked to see Bob about a problem the group was having. The conversation between Bob and Damiano went as follows:

PRACTICE

Bob: Damiano, I understand you want to discuss a problem with me.

Damiano: Yes, Bob. I don't want to waste your time, but some of the other engineers want me to discuss Sue with you. She is irritating everyone with her know-it-all, pompous attitude. She's just not the kind of person we want to work with.

Bob: I can't understand that, Damiano. She's an excellent worker, and her work is always well done and usually flawless. She's doing everything the company wants her to do.

Damiano: The company never asked her to disrupt the morale of the group or to tell us how to do our work. The animosity in our group could eventually result in lower-quality work for the whole unit.

Bob: I'll tell you what I'll do. Sue has a meeting with me next week to discuss her six-month performance. I'll keep your thoughts in mind, but I can't promise an improvement in what you and the others believe is a pompous attitude.

Damiano: Immediate improvement in her behaviour isn't the problem. It's her coaching others when she has no right to. She publicly shows others what to do. You'd think she was lecturing an advanced class in design with all her high-powered, useless equations and formulas. She'd better back off soon or some of us will quit or transfer.

During the next week, Bob thought carefully about his meeting with Damiano. He knew that Damiano was the informal leader of the design engineers and generally spoke for the other group members. On Thursday of the following week, Bob called Sue into his office for her mid-year review. One portion of the conversation went as follows:

Bob: There is one other aspect I'd like to discuss with you about your performance. As I just related to you, your technical performance has been excellent; however, there are some questions about your relationships with the other employees.

Sue: I don't understand. What questions are you talking about?

Bob: Well, to be specific, certain members of the design group have complained about your apparent 'know-it-all attitude' and the manner in which you try to tell them how to do their job. You're going to have to be patient with them and not publicly call them out about their performance. This is a good group of engineers and their work over the years has been more than acceptable. I don't want any problems that will cause the group to produce less effectively.

Sue: Let me make a few comments. First of all, I have never publicly criticised their performance to them or to you. Initially, when I finished ahead of them, I offered to help them with their work but was bluntly told to mind my own business. I took the hint and concentrated only on my part of the work. What you don't understand is that after five months of working in this group I have come to the conclusion that what is going on is a rip-off of the company. The other engineers are gold-bricking; they're setting a work pace much slower than they're capable of. They're more interested in the music from Steve's radio, the football team and the pub. I'm sorry, but this is just not the way I was raised or trained. And finally, they've never looked on me as a qualified engineer, but as a woman who has broken their professional barrier.

Byron versus Thomas

Effective one-on-one coaching and counselling are skills that are required in many settings in life, not just in management. It is hard to imagine a parent, flatmate, coach or good friend who would not benefit from training in supportive communication. Because there are so many aspects of supportive communication, however, it is sometimes difficult to remember them all. That is why practice, with observation and feedback, is so important. These attributes of supportive communication can become a natural part of your interaction approach as you conscientiously practise and receive feedback from a colleague.

Assignment

In the following exercise, one individual should take the role of Hal Byron and another should take the role of Judy Thomas. To make the role-play realistic, do not read each other's role descriptions. When you have finished reading, role-play a meeting between Hal Byron and Judy Thomas. A third person should serve as the observer. An observer's form to assist in providing feedback can be found at the end of the chapter (on page 269).

Hal Byron, department head

You are Hal Byron, head of the operations group—the 'back room'—in a large bank. This is your second year on the job and you have moved up rather quickly in the bank. You enjoy working for this firm, which has a reputation for being one of the finest in the region. One reason is that outside opportunities for management development and training are funded by the bank. In addition, each employee is given an opportunity for a personal management interview each month and these sessions are usually both productive and developmental.

One of the department's members, Judy Thomas, has been in this department for 19 years, 15 of them in the same job. She is reasonably good at what she does, and she is always punctual and efficient. She tends to get to work earlier than most employees in order to peruse the *Financial Review* and news magazines. You can almost set your watch by the time Judy visits the restroom during the day and by the time she makes her phone call to her daughter every afternoon.

Your feeling about Judy is that, although she is a good worker, she lacks imagination and initiative. This has been indicated by her lack of merit increases over the last five years and by the fact that she has had the same job for so many years. She is content to do just what is assigned, nothing more. Your predecessor must have given hints to Judy that she might be in line for a promotion, however, because Judy has raised this with you more than once. Because she has been in her job so long she is at the top of her pay range, and without a promotion she cannot receive a salary adjustment above the basic cost-of-living increase.

The one thing Judy does beyond the basic minimum job requirements is to help train young people who come into the department. She is patient and methodical with them and she seems to take pride in helping them learn the ropes. She has not been hesitant in pointing out this contribution to you. Unfortunately, this activity does not qualify Judy for a promotion and she could not be transferred into the training and development department. On one occasion you suggested that she take a few courses at university, paid for by the bank, but she said in a matter-of-fact manner that she was too old to start studying. You surmise that she might feel intimidated because she doesn't have a university degree.

As much as you would like to promote Judy, there just does not seem to be any way to do that in good conscience. You have tried putting additional work under her control, but she seems to be slowing down in her productivity rather than speeding up. The work needs to be done, and expanding her role puts you behind schedule.

This approaching interview is probably the time to level with Judy about her performance and her potential. You certainly do not want to lose her as an employee, but there will not be a change in job assignment for a long time unless she improves her performance dramatically.

Judy Thomas, department member

You are a member of the operations group in a large banking corporation. You have been with the bank now for 19 years, 15 of them in the same job. You enjoy the company because of its friendly atmosphere and its prestigious image in the region. It is nice to be known as an employee of this firm. However, lately you have become dissatisfied as you have seen person after person come into the bank and get promoted ahead of you. Your own boss, Hal Byron, is almost 20 years your junior. Another woman who joined the bank at the same time as you is now a senior executive. You cannot understand why you have been neglected. You are efficient and accurate in your work, you have a near-perfect attendance record and you consider yourself to be a good employee. You have gone out of your way on many occasions to help train and orient young people joining the bank. Several of them have written letters later telling you how important your help was in getting them promoted. A lot of good that does you!

The only thing you can figure out is that there is a bias against you because you haven't graduated from university. On the other hand, others have moved up without a degree. You have not taken advantage of any university courses paid for by the bank, as after a long day at work you are not inclined to go to class for another three hours. Besides, you do not want to take time away from your family in the evenings. It does not take a university degree to do your job, anyway.

Your monthly personal management interview is coming up with your department head, Hal Byron, and you have decided the time has come to get a few answers. Several things need explaining. Not only have you not been promoted, but you have not even received a merit increase for five years. You are not getting any credit for the extra contributions you make with new employees, or for your steady, reliable work. Could anyone blame you for being a little bitter?

Skill application

Suggested assignments

1. Tape-record an interview with someone such as a co-worker, friend or spouse. Focus on the issues or challenges faced now by that person. Try to serve as a coach or counsellor. Categorise your statements in the interview on the basis of the supportive communication principles in this chapter. (The rejected plans case on page 262 is an example of such an interview.)
2. Teach someone you know the concepts of supportive communication and supportive listening. Provide your own explanations and illustrations so the person understands what you are talking about. Describe your experience in your journal.
3. Think of an interpersonal problem you share with someone, such as a flatmate, parent, friend or instructor. Discuss the problem with that person, using supportive communication. Write up the experience in as much detail as possible. Concentrate on the extent to which you and the other person used the eight principles of supportive communication. Record and describe areas in which you need to improve.
4. Write two mini case studies. One should recount an effective coaching or counselling situation. The other should detail an ineffective coaching or counselling situation. The cases should be based on a real event, either from your own personal experience or from the experience of someone you know well. Use all the principles of supportive communication and listening in your cases.

Application plan and evaluation

The intent of this exercise is to help you apply this cluster of skills in a real-life, out-of-class setting. Now that you have become familiar with the behavioural guidelines that form the basis of effective skill performance, you will improve most by trying out those guidelines in an everyday context. Unlike a classroom activity, in which feedback is immediate and others can assist you with their evaluations, this skill application activity is one you must accomplish and evaluate on your own. There are two parts to this activity. Part 1 helps to prepare you to apply the skill. Part 2 helps you to evaluate and improve on your experience. Be sure to write down answers to each item. Do not short-circuit the process by skipping steps.

Part 1: Planning

1. Write down the two or three aspects of this skill that are most important to you. These may be areas of weakness, areas you most want to improve, or areas that are most salient to a problem you face right now. Identify the specific aspects of this skill that you want to apply.
2. Now identify the setting or the situation in which you will apply this skill. Establish a plan for performance by writing down a description of the situation. Who else will be involved? When will you do it? Where will it be done?
3. Identify the specific behaviours you will engage in to apply this skill. Operationalise your skill performance.

4. What are the indicators of successful performance? How will you know you have been effective? What will indicate that you have performed competently?

Part 2: Evaluation

5. When you have completed your implementation, record the results. What happened? How successful were you? What was the effect on others?
6. How can you improve? What modifications can you make next time? What would you do differently in a similar situation in the future?
7. Looking back on your whole skill practice and application experience, what have you learned? What has been surprising? In what ways might this experience help you in the long term?

Scoring keys and supplementary materials

Communicating supportively (p. 232)

SCORING KEY

Skill area	*Items*	ASSESSMENT *Pre-*	*Post*
Knowledge of coaching and counselling	1, 2, 20	______	______
Provide effective negative feedback	3, 4, 5, 6, 7, 8	______	______
Communicating supportively	9, 10, 11, 12, 13, 14, 15, 16, 17, 18, 19	______	______
	TOTAL SCORE	[ ]	[ ]

Comparison data

Compare your scores with three comparison standards:

1. Compare your score against the maximum possible (120).
2. Compare your own scores with the scores of the other students in your class.
3. Compare your scores with a norm group consisting of 500 business school students. In comparison to the norm group, if you scored:

99 or above	you are in the top quartile
93–98	you are in the second quartile
87–92	you are in the third quartile
86 or below	you are in the bottom quartile.

Communication styles (p. 233)

SCORING KEY

Part 1: Identify the type of response pattern that you rely on most when required to be a coach or a counsellor by adding the numbers you gave to the response alternatives in Part 1. The chapter discusses the advantages and disadvantages of each of these response types. The most skilled supportive communicators score 9 or above on reflecting responses and 6 or more on probing responses. They score 2 or less on advising responses and 4 or less on deflecting responses.

Part 2: Circle the alternative that you chose. The most skilled communicators select alternatives 1a, 2b, 3a, 4b and 5a.

Part 1

1. a. Deflecting response
   b. Probing response
   c. Advising response
   d. Reflecting response
   e. Deflecting response
2. a. Reflecting response
   b. Deflecting response
   c. Deflecting response
   d. Reflecting response
   e. Probing response
3. a. Probing response
   b. Deflecting response
   c. Advising response
   d. Reflecting response
   e. Probing response
4. a. Reflecting response
   b. Probing response
   c. Deflecting response
   d. Deflecting response
   e. Advising response

Part 2

1. a. Problem-oriented statement
   b. Person-oriented statement
2. a. Incongruent statement
   b. Congruent statement
3. a. Descriptive statement
   b. Evaluative statement
4. a. Invalidating statement
   b. Validating statement
5. a. Owned statement
   b. Disowned statement

Diagnosing communication problems and fostering understanding (p. 264)

United Mining Pty Ltd (p. 264) and Byron versus Thomas (p. 265)

Observer's feedback form

As the observer, rate the extent to which the role-players performed the following behaviours effectively. Place the initials of each individual beside the number on the scale that best represents his or her performance. Identify specific things that each person can do to improve his or her performance.

Rating *Action*

1 = Low
5 = High

_______ 1 Used problem-oriented communication.
_______ 2 Communicated congruently.
_______ 3 Used descriptive communication.
_______ 4 Used validating communication.
_______ 5 Used specific and qualified communication.
_______ 6 Used conjunctive communication.
_______ 7 Owned statements and used personal words.
_______ 8 Listened attentively.
_______ 9 Used a variety of response alternatives.

Comments: ________________________________

References

Anynomous 2006, 'Talking loud and clear: Turning ideas into innovation', *Strategic Direction*, 22(11), pp. 28–31.
Athos, A. and J. Gabarro 1978, *Interpersonal Behavior*, (Englewood Cliffs, NJ: Prentice Hall).
Barnlund, D. C. 1968, *Interpersonal Communication: Survey and Studies* (Boston: Houghton Mifflin).

Bishop, B. 2006, 'Theory and practice converge: A proposed set of corporate communication principles', *Corporate Communications*, 11(3), p. 214.
Boss, R. 1983, *Journal of Applied Behavioural Science*, 19, pp. 1, 67.
Brownell, J. 1986, *Building Active Listening Skills* (Englewood Cliffs, NJ: Prentice Hall).
Brownell, J. 1990, 'Perceptions of effective listeners: A management study', *Journal of Business Communication*, 27, pp. 401–15.
Bryan, S., K. Pickrell, M. Burton and S. Parsons 2006, 'How do I get there? Making the step up to management', *The Safety & Health Practitioner*, 24(12), p. 76.
Cameron, K. S. 1994a, 'Investigating organizational downsizing: Fundamental issues', *Human Resource Management Journal*, 33, pp. 183–8.
Cameron, K. S. 1994b, 'Strategies for successful organizational downsizing', *Human Resource Management Journal*, 33, pp. 89–122.
Campbell, A. 1991, 'Brief case: Strategy and intuition—a conversation with Harry Mintzberg', *Long Range Planning*, 24, pp. 108–10.
Carlopio, J. 1996, *Implementation: Making Workplace Innovation and Technical Change Happen* (Sydney: McGraw-Hill).
Carrell, L. J. and S. C. Willmington 1996, 'A comparison of self-report and performance data in assessing speaking and listening competence', *Communication Reports*, 9, pp. 185–91.
Chang, J. 2003, 'Born to sell?', *Sales and Marketing Management*, 155(7), p. 34.
Cole, M. 1999, 'Become the leader followers want to follow', *Supervision*, 60(12), pp. 9–11.
Crocker, J. 1978, 'Speech communication instruction based on employers' perceptions of the importance of selected communication skills for employees on the job', paper presented at the Speech Communication Association meeting, Minneapolis, Minn.
Cudney, B. 2007, 'Ask the expert', *Industrial Engineer*, 39(2), pp. 54–55.
Cupach, W. R. and B. H. Spitzberg (eds) 1994, *The Dark Side of Interpersonal Communication* (Hillsdale, NJ: Erlbaum).
Dyer, W. G. 1972, 'Congruence', in *The Sensitive Manipulator* (Provo, UT: Brigham Young University Press).
Fine, L. M. and E. B. Pullins 1998, 'Peer mentoring in the industrial sales force: An exploratory investigation of men and women in developmental relationships', *Journal of Personal Selling and Sales Management*, 18(4), pp. 89–103.
Fowler, J. and P. Horan 2007, 'Are information systems' success and failure factors related? An exploratory study', *Journal of Organizational and End User Computing*, 19(2), pp. 1–22.
García-Morales, V., F. Matías-Reche and A. Verdú-Jover 2011, 'Influence of internal communication on technological proactivity, organizational learning, and organizational innovation in the pharmaceutical sector', *Journal of Communication*, 61(1), pp. 150–77.
Gibb, J. R. 1961, 'Defensive communication', *Journal of Communication*, 11, pp. 141–8.
Giri, V. and P. Kumar 2010, 'Assessing the impact of organizational communication on job satisfaction and job performance', *Psychological Studies*, 55(2), pp. 137–43.
Glasser, W. 1965, *Reality Therapy: A New Approach to Psychiatry* (New York: Harper and Row).
Glasser, W. 2000, *Reality Therapy in Action* (New York: HarperCollins).
Goleman, D. 1995, *Emotional Intelligence* (Sydney: Bantam Books).
Golen, S. 1990, 'A factor analysis of barriers to effective listening', *Journal of Business Communication*, 27, pp. 25–35.
Grensing-Pophal, L. 2007, 'Coaching HR', *HRMagazine*, 52(2), pp. 95–99.
Gudykunst, W. B. and S. Ting-Toomey 1988, *Culture and Interpersonal Communication* (Newbury Park, CA: Sage).
Gudykunst, W. B., S. Ting-Toomey and T. Nishida 1996, *Communication in Personal Relationships across Cultures* (Thousand Oaks, CA: Sage).
Haas, J. W. and C. L. Arnold 1995, 'An examination of the role of listening in judgements of communication competence in co-workers', *Journal of Business Communication*, 32, pp. 123–39.
Haney, W. V. 1979, *Communication and Interpersonal Relations* (Homewood, IL: Irwin).
Hernandez, T. 2006, 'Listening to opinions of young people pays off', *Planning*, 1680, August, p. 23.
Holt, S. and S. Jones 2005, 'Emotional intelligence and organizational performance: Implications for performance consultants and educators', *Performance Improvement*, 44(10), pp. 15–21.
Horin, A. 2003, 'Discovering what works on the shop floor', *Sydney Morning Herald*, 26 December.
Huseman, R. C., J. M. Lahiff and J. D. Hatfield 1976, *Interpersonal Communication in Organizations* (Boston: Holbrook Press).
Hyman, R. 1989, 'The psychology of deception', *Annual Review of Psychology*, 40, pp. 133–54.
Jay, M. 2003, 'Understanding how to leverage executive coaching', *Organization Development Journal*, 21(2), p. 6.
Kemper, C. L. 1999, 'EQ vs IQ', *Communications World*, 16(9), pp. 15–19.
Knapp, M.L. and A. L. Vangelisti 1996, *Interpersonal Communication and Relationships* (Boston: Allyn & Bacon).
Kramer, D. A. 2000, 'Wisdom as a classical source of human strength', *Journal of Social and Clinical Psychology*, 19, pp. 83–101.
Kramer, R., 1997, 'Leading by listening', Dissertation Abstracts International Section A: Humanities and Social Sciences 58.
Levinson, M. 2003, 'Are you the strong sensitive type? CIOs who cultivate a sensitivity to others' needs are better managers and lead more effective organizations', *CIO*, 16(10), p. 1.
Mackay, H. 1993, *Re-inventing Australia: The Mind and Mood of Australia in the 90s* (Sydney: Angus & Robertson).

Mackay, H. 1994, *Why Don't People Listen?* (Sydney: Pan).
Maes, J., T. Weldy and M. Icenogle 1997, 'A managerial perspective: Oral communications competency is most important for business students in the workplace', *Journal of Business Communication*, 34(1), pp. 67–80.
Morley, K. 2002, 'Public sector leadership: Qualities for success', *Mt Elisa Business Review*, 4, p. 2.
Moss Kanter, R. 2003, 'Leadership and the psychology of turnarounds', *Harvard Business Review*, 81(6), pp. 58–67.
Ohren, J. 2007, 'Improving local government decision making: Insights from local government officials', *Public Management*, 89(1), pp. 18–23.
Parker, S. 1999, 'Rendering the complex clear', *New Zealand Herald*, 1 December.
Peng-Hsiang, K and K. Hsin 2007, 'Taiwanese executives' leadership styles and their preferred decision-making models used in mainland China', *Journal of American Academy of Business*, 10(2), pp. 71–79.
Pomeroy, A. 2006, 'Great communicators, great communication', *HRMagazine*, 51(7), pp. 44–49.
Pope, N. and P. Berry 1995, 'Top down approach works', *Australian Financial Review*, 11 July.
Randle, C. W. 1956, 'How to identify promotable executives', *Harvard Business Review*, 34, p. 122.
Rogers, C. W. 1961, *On Becoming a Person* (Boston: Houghton Mifflin).
Rosen, S. 1998, 'A lump of clay', *Communication World*, 15(7), August/September, p. 58.
Schnake, M. E., M. P. Dumler, D. S. Cochran and T. R. Barnett 1990, 'Effects of differences in superior and subordinate perceptions of superiors' communication practices', *Journal of Business Communication*, 27, pp. 37–50.
Schultz, F., S. Utz and A. Goritz 2011, 'Is the medium the message? Perceptions of and reactions to crisis communication via Twitter, blogs and traditional media', *Public Relations Review*, 37(1), pp. 20–27.
Scott, R. 2007, 'Silence is deadly', *Computerworld*, 41(6), p. 28.
Sieburg, E. 1978, 'Confirming and disconfirming organizational communication', working paper, University of Denver.
Spears, R. and M. Lea 1992, 'Social influence and the influence of the "social" in computer-mediated communication', in M. Lea (ed.), *Context of Computer-mediated Communication*, (Sydney: Harvester), pp. 30–55.
Spitzberg, B. H. 1994, 'The dark side of (in)competence', in W. R. Cupach and B. H. Spitzberg (eds), *The Dark Side of Interpersonal Communication* (Hillsdale, NJ: Erlbaum).
Steil, L. K. 1980, *Your Listening Profile* (Minneapolis, MN: Sperry Corporation).
Steil, L., L. Barker and K. Watson 1983, *Effective Listening: Key to Your Success* (New York: Addison-Wesley).
Sternberg, R. J. 1990, *Wisdom* (Cambridge, UK: Cambridge University Press).
Subramanian, S. 2006, 'An "open eye and ear" approach to managerial communication', *Vision*, 10(2), pp. 1–10.
Tomer, J. F. 2003, 'Personal capital and EI', *Eastern Economic Journal*, 29(3), p. 453.
Triandis, H. C. 1994, *Culture and Social Behavior* (New York: McGraw-Hill).
Trompenaars, F. 1996, 'Resolving international conflict: Culture and business strategy', *Business Strategy Review*, 7, pp. 51–68.
Trompenaars, F. and C. Hampden-Turner 1999, *Riding the Waves of Culture* (New York: McGraw-Hill).
Wheatley, M. J. 1999, *Leadership and the New Science: Discovering Order in a Chaotic World* (San Francisco: Berrett-Koehler).
Wiemann, J. M. 1977, 'Explanation and test of a model of communicative competence', *Human Communication Research*, 3, pp. 145–213.
Yuan, L. and S. Keng 2007, 'Social network structures in open source software development teams', *Journal of Database Management*, 18(2), pp. 25–39.

CHAPTER 6

MOTIVATING OTHERS

OBJECTIVES

- **Foster a high-performance workplace**
- **Assess and develop work performance and motivation**
- **Motivate performance across generations**
- **Enhance individuals' performance**
- **Improve poor performance**

6

CHAPTER OUTLINE

Skill assessment

Evaluative surveys for motivating others

Assessing performance and enhancing motivation

Step 1: Before you read the material in this chapter, respond to the following statements by writing a number from the rating scale below in the left-hand column (pre-assessment). Your answers should reflect your attitudes and behaviour as they are now, not as you would like them to be. Be honest. This instrument is designed to help you discover your level of experience in motivating others so that you can tailor your learning to your specific needs. When you have completed the survey, use the scoring key at the end of the chapter to identify the skill areas discussed in this chapter that are most important for you to master.

Step 2: When you have completed the reading and the exercises in this chapter and the skill application assignments at the end of the chapter, cover up your first set of answers, then respond to the same statements again, this time in the right-hand column (post-assessment). When you have completed the survey, use the scoring key at the end of the chapter (on page 323) to measure your progress. If your score remains low in specific skill areas, use the behavioural guidelines at the end of the skill learning section to guide further practice.

Rating scale

1 Strongly disagree
2 Disagree
3 Slightly disagree
4 Slightly agree
5 Agree
6 Strongly agree

Assessment

Pre-	*Post-*	*When another person needs to be motivated:*
______	______	1. I always approach a performance problem by first establishing whether it is caused by a lack of motivation or ability.
______	______	2. I always establish a clear standard of expected performance.
______	______	3. I always offer to provide training and information, without offering to do tasks myself.
______	______	4. I am honest and straightforward in providing feedback on performance and assessing advancement opportunities.
______	______	5. I use a variety of rewards to reinforce exceptional performance.
______	______	6. When discipline is required, I give specific suggestions for improvement.
______	______	7. I design task assignments to make them interesting and challenging.
______	______	8. I strive to provide the rewards that each person values.
______	______	9. I make sure that people feel fairly and equitably treated.
______	______	10. I make sure that people get timely feedback from those affected by task performance.
______	______	11. I carefully evaluate the causes of poor performance before taking any remedial or disciplinary action.
______	______	12. I always help people establish performance goals that are challenging, specific and time-bound.

______ ______ 13. Only as a last resort do I attempt to reassign or release a poorly performing individual.
______ ______ 14. Whenever possible, I make sure valued rewards are linked to high performance.
______ ______ 15. I consistently discipline when effort is below expectations and below capabilities.
______ ______ 16. I try to combine or rotate assignments so that people can use a variety of skills.
______ ______ 17. I try to arrange for an individual to work with others in a team, for the mutual support of all.
______ ______ 18. I make sure that people use realistic standards for measuring fairness.
______ ______ 19. I provide immediate compliments and other forms of recognition for meaningful accomplishments.
______ ______ 20. I always determine if a person has the necessary resources and support to succeed in a task.

The scoring key is on page 323.

Work performance assessment

Respond to the following statements based on your current (or recent) work situation. Then turn to the end of the chapter for the scoring key.

Rating scale

1 Strongly disagree
2 Disagree
3 Neutral
4 Agree
5 Strongly agree

______ 1. My supervisor and I agree on the quality of my performance.
______ 2. I feel I have adequate training to perform my current job assignments.
______ 3. I believe that my natural skills and abilities are matched very well with my job responsibilities.
______ 4. I believe that I have adequate resources and supplies to do my job well.
______ 5. I understand my boss's expectations and generally feel they are realistic.
______ 6. I believe that rewards are distributed fairly, on the basis of performance.
______ 7. The rewards and opportunities available to me if I perform well are attractive to me personally.
______ 8. My supervisor indicates that I am not performing as well as I should, but I disagree.
______ 9. I could do a much better job if I had more training.
______ 10. I believe that my job is too difficult for my ability level.
______ 11. I believe that my job performance is hindered by a lack of supplies and resources.
______ 12. I believe my boss's expectations are unclear and unrealistic.
______ 13. I believe my boss plays favourites in allocating rewards.
______ 14. I do not find the rewards and opportunities available to high performers very appealing.

The scoring key is on page 324.

The Ray-Lynn Short Form Achievement Motivation Scale

Please answer the following 14 questions by circling 'YES' if you agree with the statement, '?' if you are undecided, and 'NO' if you disagree with the statement.

The scoring key is on page 324.

1.	Is being comfortable more important to you than getting ahead? R	YES .... ? .... NO
2.	Are you satisfied to be no better than most other people at your job? R	YES .... ? .... NO
3.	Do you like to make improvements to the way the organisation you belong to functions?	YES .... ? .... NO
4.	Do you take trouble to cultivate people who may be useful to you in your career?	YES .... ? .... NO
5.	Do you get restless and annoyed when you feel you are wasting time?	YES .... ? .... NO
6.	Have you always worked hard in order to be among the best in your own line? (school, organisation, profession).	YES .... ? .... NO
7.	Would you prefer to work with a congenial but incompetent partner rather than with a difficult but highly competent one? R	YES .... ? .... NO
8.	Do you tend to plan ahead for your job or career?	YES .... ? .... NO
9.	Is 'getting on in life' important to you?	YES .... ? .... NO
10.	Are you an ambitious person?	YES .... ? .... NO
11.	Are you inclined to read of the successes of others rather than do the work of making yourself a success? R	YES .... ? .... NO
12.	Would you describe yourself as being lazy? R	YES .... ? .... NO
13.	Will days often go by without your having done a thing? R	YES .... ? .... NO
14.	Are you inclined to take life as it comes without much planning? R	YES .... ? .... NO

Source: Ray, J.J. (1979). 'A quick measure of achievement motivation—Validated in Australia and reliable in Britain and South Africa', *Australian Psychologist, 14(3)*, 337–44. Reproduced with permission.

LEARNING

Skill learning

Theories of motivation and performance

Motivation is fundamental to human behaviour. In a sense, organisations do not exist; organisations do not perform or make money or change. It is really *people* who perform, make money and change in the name of the social collective we refer to as an organisation. This conceptual distinction is nowhere more important than when considering the topic of motivation. Organisational performance, therefore, depends on the manner in which managers' and organisational systems and processes stimulate individual performance, which in turn depends on individuals' ability and motivation. An effective organisational performance management process is required to achieve this.

> *Management must focus on the results and performance of the organization. Indeed, the first task of management is to define what results and performance are in a given organization—and this, as anyone who has worked on it can testify, is in itself one of the most difficult, one of the most controversial, but also one of the most important tasks. (Drucker 2001: 39)*

Managing motivation is an individualised continuous improvement task. Motivation has been viewed as the essence of organisational and individual performance and success across a vast range of time, tasks, cultures and contexts (cf. Ashton & Roberts 2011; Dysvik & Kuvaas 2011; Eisenberg & Thompson 2011; Friedlander 1966; Galbraith 1967; Logan, Medford & Hughes 2011; Mir et al. 2011; Penningroth, Scott & Freuen 2011; Weston, Greenlees & Thelwell 2011). It is a complex combination of individual personality, management skills, organisational goals and the work environment.

Motivation is an inducement or an influence; it is a reason for moving or acting. It provides purpose and drive. The workplace, like many other contexts in life, is a social environment that depends for its success on the motivation and commitment of its members (cf. Andrewartha 1995). The value to the individuals and the organisation lies in the manager's ability to marshal the unique motivation of each employee towards a shared goal. This is reflected in the definition of management given in the Introduction.

Bartol and Martin (1998) define motivation as the force that energises and gives direction to behaviour, and underlies the tendency to persist. Similarly, Greenberg and Baron (1997) define motivation as 'the set of processes that arouse, direct, and maintain human behavior towards attaining some goal'. While theorists propose different (sometimes contradictory) theories of motivation, it is nonetheless something that is obviously recognisable. A workplace with highly motivated staff is alive, energetic, cooperative, productive, flexible and fun to work in. A demotivating workplace is immediately experienced as sullen and apathetic, is full of conflict, is characterised by absenteeism and lowered productivity, and is unpleasant to work in.

Many areas of this book relate and contribute to developing motivation as a responsibility of the individual and of management (see Chapters 1, 2, 5 and 8). Especially relevant is the concept of matching (Chapter 2). Let us now examine a few theories of motivation. Thirteen of the most accepted academic theories about motivation are briefly summarised below. You are referred to the excellent website <http://changingminds.org/index.htm> or to the original authors for more detailed exploration of these theories.

Self-discrepancy theory (Higgins 1989). People are strongly motivated to maintain a sense of consistency among their various beliefs and self-perceptions and are demotivated when the beliefs and self-perceptions conflict. For example, in Chapter 2 the power of aligning personal and organisational values was discussed. Inconsistency causes cognitive dissonance and stress (see Chapter 3). The best way of motivating people, then, is to attempt to align their values and beliefs with the actions you want them to take.

Cognitive dissonance (Festinger & Carlsmith 1959). This is the feeling of uncomfortable tension that comes from holding two conflicting thoughts at the same time. For example, if I am an honest person but I am asked to engage in a dishonest act by someone I feel obligated to, then I will experience cognitive dissonance. Cognitive dissonance is present in virtually all evaluations and decision making. Dissonance increases with the importance and impact of the decision, along with the difficulty of reversing it. According to this theory, we are motivated to reduce our experiences of cognitive dissonance.

Attribution theory (Roesch & Amirkham 1997). We all make attributions about the causes of events around us. This gives us a greater sense of control. (See the locus of control and the LETS self/other evaluator dimension in Chapter 2.) When someone makes a mistake, we often make an internal attribution, judging the mistake to be the result of internal personality factors, for example. When *we* make a mistake, however, we may use an external attribution, attributing the mistake to situational factors outside of ourselves rather than blaming ourselves. Motivation can be diminished by blaming others (that is, making internal attributions about them). Similarly, making excuses for your own errors (external attributions) is demotivating.

Intrinsic motivation (Deci & Ryan 1985). Intrinsic motivation relates to internal factors. It is values-based and suggests that people do things best when their actions are derived from their internal or intrinsic beliefs or personal interests. Intrinsic motivation is often a stronger motivator than extrinsic motivation (such as pay). Motivationally, the goal is to identify a person's values and attempt to align them with what you want them to do. Reducing the power of extrinsic motivation (see below), such as providing market-level pay, also enhances intrinsic rewards.

Extrinsic motivation (Petri 1981). This motivator is based on external tangible rewards such as high pay, the best corner office, a prestigious car, and so on. It is the most accepted and obvious motivator. However, it is entirely contingent upon the reward itself, with no internal driver. Better pay being offered by another organisation, for example, may motivate someone to take a new job.

Goal-setting theory (Locke & Latham 1990). This is a similar model to one applied later in the chapter. We are more motivated when we set ourselves goals that are clear and understandable, challenging and achievable. When other people (for example, our manager) set goals for us, we are more likely to be motivated if the goals are set with our input and agreement.

Acquired needs theory (McClelland 1976). Three needs are postulated. Achievers want to excel and be recognised. Affiliation seekers want to form harmonious relationships with other people. Power seekers want power. Recognising and using these needs is motivational.

ERG theory (Alderfer 1977). 'ERG' stands for Existence, Relatedness and Growth. At the existence level, we have the need to be alive and feel safe. Relatedness concerns our social needs and our relationships with other people. It gives us a sense of identity and belonging. Growth is the highest level, where we feel a sense of achievement and fulfilment. Providing a work environment so that people can meet these needs is motivating.

Expectancy theory (Vroom 1964). People are motivated if they believe something is desirable, that the way of achieving it is clear, and that they can achieve it. Motivation is seen as a product of:

- *Valence:* the value of the perceived outcome. (What's in it for me?)
- *Instrumentality:* understanding that certain clear actions will achieve the outcome.
- *Expectancy:* the belief that I am capable of engaging in the actions.

Control theory (Glasser 1998). People like to be in control of their lives. However, it is an endless, fruitless and tiring task to attempt to control everything and everyone around us. The motivational alternative is to encourage people to regard the world as a series of choices and to offer such choices in the workplace.

Maslow's hierarchy of needs theory (Baird, Post & Mahon 1990). Maslow argues that people are motivated to satisfy all five levels of need roughly in turn, from the lowest to the highest. As each need is satisfied, it decreases in importance and the next highest need increases in importance. The five levels of needs are: physiological needs (which include the need for food, air, water, sex, rest and other bodily needs); safety needs (which include the need for security and protection from physical and emotional harm); social needs (which include the need for friendship, love, affection and acceptance by others); esteem needs (which include internal esteem factors such as self-respect, autonomy and achievement, and external esteem factors such as status, recognition and attention); and self-actualisation (which includes the need for self-fulfilment, realisation of full potential, self-expression, accomplishment and growth; it is the drive to become what we are capable of becoming).

Herzberg's two-factor (motivator–hygiene) theory (Herzberg 1968). The two-factor theory states that there are certain factors in the workplace that cause job satisfaction (motivators), while a separate set of factors cause dissatisfaction (hygiene factors). The theory postulates that there are 'motivators' (challenging work, recognition, responsibility), which give positive satisfaction, and 'hygiene' factors (status, job security, salary and fringe benefits), which do not directly provide positive satisfaction, but dissatisfaction results from their absence. Hygiene factors are needed to ensure that an employee is not dissatisfied.

Motivation factors are needed in order to motivate an employee to higher performance. One of the significant implications of this theory is that a higher salary or better conditions may not necessarily increase motivation. Table 6.1 shows this clearly.

Temporal motivational theory (TMT). Steel and König (2005, 2007) have made an ambitious and multidisciplinary attempt to present a broad, unified theory of motivation. They attempt to simplify the field of motivation considerably and their approach allows findings from one theory to be translated into terms of another.

They integrate four closely related motivational theories—picoeconomics (Ainslie 1992), expectancy theory (Vroom 1964), cumulative prospect theory (Tversky & Kahneman 1992) and need theory (Dollard & Miller 1950). The theory's name comes from its emphasis on time as a key motivational factor.

> *We … show that TMT is corroborated with the major findings from Psychobiology and demonstrate how it can account for the findings from another motivational theory altogether, Goal Theory (Locke & Latham 1990). We also use Temporal Motivational Theory to explain procrastination, a prototypical performance problem. As a general theory of human behavior, the applications of Temporal Motivational Theory are numerous. (Steel & König 2005: 5)*

TABLE 6.1 What motivates managers?

MOTIVATING ELEMENT	IMPORTANT OR VERY IMPORTANT %
Challenging work	97
My opinion matters when decisions are made	96
Recognition when I've done a job well	91
Pay clearly tied to my performance	89
Working for a company I can be proud of	87
Good, fair performance measures	85
Autonomy on the job	82
Competitive salary	81
Clear performance goals	78
Opportunity to learn on the job	76
Clear career opportunities	74
Harmonious relationships with my co-workers	71
Job security	59
Generous benefit program	54
Special incentives (merchandise, travel)	9

Source: Towers Watson, US Survey, 1987. (Updated research, post the global financial crisis, shows salary has become more important.)

In considering all the theories outlined above, and the exact mechanisms involved in motivation, as a manager it is important to note some key commonalities of motivation:

- Everyone is different and needs to be motivated in a different way.
- Individual perception determines what is satisfying.
- Rewarding performance skilfully is difficult.
- Motivators vary over time and context.
- Simple recognition and acknowledgment are important.

Fostering a high-performance workplace

The first component of employee performance is motivation. This is a constant challenge for managers given complex workplaces with several generations of employees from different cultures and differing levels of ability and motivation. While it is important to see to the training and support needs of employees, and to be actively involved in the hiring and job-matching processes to ensure adequate aptitude, the influence of a manager's actions on the day-to-day motivation of employees is equally vital. Effective managers devote considerable time to gauging and strengthening their employees' motivation, as reflected in their effort and concern. As Peter Senge (1990: 56) has observed (and as we have known for decades, see Rosenthal & Jacobson 1968), managers' own expectations affect the performance of their employees.

Considerable research provides a strong link between various motivating elements and approaches and a high-performing workplace.

> *The organisation sets resources and goals to achieve compliance. However commitment is a voluntary response that can only occur as an outcome of the relationships that create a shared purpose. This cannot be demanded or directed. The manager can only create an environment in which individuals will respond in a motivated way. (Rabey 2001: 26)*

Again, this reflects our definition of management skills in Chapter 1 (see page 17).

Rabey identifies the core elements from a large body of research into motivation in the workplace, which closely follows the themes in this book. The motivational elements are:

- doing something worthwhile—a goal
- doing one's share—participation

- counting for something—recognition
- knowing what is going on—communication
- getting a decent living—fair wages
- preparing for the future—learning
- doing things together—teamwork
- being challenged—innovation.

Ilies, Judge and Wagner (2006) proposed a mechanism by which leaders can help develop motivation in their employees by inducing positive emotional experiences through the manner of their normal managerial communication. Mendelson, Turner and Barling (2011) tested five high-performance work system models. Measures of eight high-performance work practices (that is, employment security, selective hiring, extensive training, contingent compensation, teams and decentralised decision making, information sharing, reduced status distinctions, and transformational leadership) were used. They found that employees' commitment and job satisfaction were correlated with these measures. A study by Jawahar (2006: 16) showed that performance feedback provided in a manner which satisfied the employee was positively related to organisational commitment, job satisfaction and commitment towards the manager, and was negatively related to turnover intentions.

Ariely (2008) has engaged in a series of tests to establish a strong link between identity and the need to find meaning in work. Providing meaning for work activities is motivating. If a manager pays considered attention to what employees are engaged in and recognises their outputs, it makes them more efficient and effective. Thaler and Sunstein (2008) propose six methods for managers to motivate staff: (1) individual incentives, (2) understanding context, (3) procedures, (4) giving feedback, (5) expecting errors, and (6) organising complex choices.

In *Drive*, Daniel Pink (2009) proposes three elements of true motivation—autonomy, mastery and purpose. Managers need to give staff autonomy over what they are doing and how they do it, an opportunity to master it, and a sense of purpose in doing it in the first place. Practical examples of this include: Best Buy's ROWE ('results oriented work environment') program, where employees have no schedules and are measured only by what they get done; Google's famous 20 per cent program, where engineers are allowed to use 20 per cent of their time to work on projects that interest them; and Australian tech company Atlassian, where engineers are given a full day each quarter to work on any software problem they wish. Ivengar (2010) focuses on choice as a motivator. Those who are enabled to make choices at work are generally more satisfied in their working environment. When choice making was constrained by managers, employee performance and work satisfaction diminished. Another benefit of strong motivation is that executives at high-performing organisations are less likely to move than their colleagues at poor-performing companies (Hamori 2010).

Managers' expectations of their employees depend a lot on how they view their employees. Douglas McGregor (1960), in one of the seminal contributions to management thought, considered that there are two ways managers could view their employees. He labelled the first, which focused on the incompetence of employees, 'Theory X'. The basic assumption of this theory is that people really do not want to work hard or assume responsibility. Therefore, in order to get the job done, managers must coerce, intimidate, manipulate and closely supervise their employees. In contrast, McGregor espoused a second option, the 'Theory Y' view of employees. This view held that employees basically want to do a good job and assume more responsibility. Therefore, management's role is to assist employees to reach their potential by productively channelling their motivation to succeed. McGregor believed that, unfortunately, most managers subscribe to Theory X assumptions about employees' motives.

The alleged prevalence of the Theory X view brings up an interesting series of questions about motivation. What is the purpose of teaching motivation skills to managers? Should managers learn these skills so that they can help employees reach their potential? Or are managers being taught these skills so that they can more effectively manipulate their employees' behaviour? These questions naturally lead to a broader set of issues regarding employee–management relations. Assuming that a manager is responsible for maintaining a given level of productivity, is it also possible to be concerned about the needs and desires of employees? In other words, are concerns about employee morale and company productivity compatible, or are they mutually exclusive?

A good manager or leader motivates staff to achieve organisational goals by providing a clear path for them to follow (House 1971). As indicated in earlier chapters, they do this by adjusting their style to the circumstances and the staff member they are dealing with. A recent study (Silverthorne 2001) found cross-cultural supporting evidence for this motivational model in Taiwanese organisations. Performance-related pay is a popular approach to motivation in the workplace. Milne (2007) suggested that reward and recognition programs can positively affect motivation, performance and interest within an organisation. Team-based incentives, if designed appropriately, can also encourage and support a range of positive outcomes. However, Frey and Osterloh (2002) conclude that stock options and larger rewards do not necessarily lead to more valuable performance. They often have an unintentional negative impact, such as allowing or even encouraging managers to act in a selfish manner (see also Ariely et al. 2009).

One of the most important elements of any workplace motivational system is recognition. The next section examines in detail the potency of basic recognition.

Recognition and motivation

A Towers Watson report in 2010 strongly linked the power of recognition used by managers to employee engagement and improved motivation. Wayne et al. (2002) also found that manager-delivered recognition of employee performance boosts engagement. The research revealed how recognition from the immediate manager can give a powerful lift. 'Recognition, engagement and performance form a self-reinforcing system' (2002: 3). They suggest that motivating recognition requires the manager to engage in three actions: (1) engaging in candid conversations; (2) defining clear and relevant performance goals; and (3) holding people accountable for their results.

> *When an employee has met the defined criteria for recognition, the moment of recognition is expected—appreciated but not unpredictable. But when a manager surprises an employee—and her peers—with unanticipated recognition, the emotional power increases significantly. This contributes to innovative thinking and creative problem solving, both important contributors to high performance. High performance, in turn, produces the next round of reward and recognition, which gives rise to engagement and innovative solutions to problems, and the circle continues. (Wayne et al. 2002: 3)*

The recognition grid (Andrewartha 1996), which is derived from the original work of Skinner (1969), provides further weight to the value of recognition as a motivator. It succinctly displays the potency of the four kinds of recognition or feedback.

As shown in Table 6.2, the nature of feedback provided by a manager to a staff member, or a leader to a team member, has a dramatic effect on their level of motivation and therefore their productivity. This feedback may be provided verbally or non-verbally and needs to be genuine.

TABLE 6.2 Four kinds of recognition or feedback

	Motivation
1. Generalised positive	+100
2. Specific positive	+50
3. Specific negative	–200
4. Generalised negative	–1000

1. A *generalised positive* is a comment like 'You're good to work with' or 'I appreciate you'. It applies to the actual person and is not specifically connected to any behaviour. A non-verbal display of unconditional support (a pat on the back, a warm smile) is also a general positive.
2. A *specific positive* is a comment like 'Thanks for helping me with that job yesterday' or 'I'm glad you got that to me so quickly'. It applies directly to a good task or action the person has done and is only half as potent as a general positive.
3. A *specific negative* is feedback like 'You sure didn't help much yesterday!' or 'This isn't done properly!'. In this case the performance is poor and being clearly pointed out. This feedback is clearly a demotivation.

4. The final type of recognition is the *generalised negative*. This includes expressions like 'You're hopeless!' or 'You're impossible to work with', or non-verbal actions such as ignoring the person altogether. This is directed at the whole person and is not limited to a particular behaviour or action. As such, it causes the most serious level of demotivating force.

It is clear from this model that negatives are always more potent and are remembered far longer than positives. Also, because of this, it is easy to build up a negative motivating economy, or lowered morale, simply because of a lack of attention to the nature of feedback you provide. Type 1 (generalised positive) is necessary for self-esteem, self-confidence and creativity. This form of recognition encourages innovation and risk taking. Type 2 (specific positive) and Type 3 (specific negative) are needed for training people in new tasks. Type 3 is often easier to provide yet is quite demotivating, whereas Type 2 is more rewarding but usually requires more patience and tolerance. Type 4 (generalised negative) usually scares people into short-term performance improvement but it quickly causes demoralisation and reduced productivity. This type of feedback damages self-esteem and confidence.

This simple process makes us aware of how easy it is to motivate or demotivate people, and also clarifies why many organisational change programs fail when they look as if they should work quite successfully. They fail so often because the workforce is already demotivated or because there is a perceived gap between the positives that are promised and people's current experience of recognition.

To be good motivators, managers also need to be models of motivation. One vital feature of this motivational power is the manager's own motivation or drive to be a manager in the first place. 'Motivation to manage has been shown to be a major cause of managerial effectiveness and success' (Ebrahimi1997: 401). Ebrahimi's recent Hong Kong study convincingly demonstrated the truth of this proposition. Alan Fish (1999) further elaborated on the need for a more sophisticated motivational mindset for transnational managers.

Motivation and productivity

A wealth of studies have established a connection between employee motivation and increased organisational productivity (Accor study 2009; Armstrong & Ward 2006; Brown & Reilly 2008; Macey & Schneider 2008; Mercer 2007; and Saks 2006). Deming (1982), one of the pioneers in this area, emphasised the need to examine organisational processes with a view to maintaining and enhancing quality and the removal of impediments to workers' pride in their work. This was, in his view, the foundation of high productivity.

Hatcher (2009) found that when employees are highly engaged, companies achieve 26 per cent higher productivity, 20 per cent lower turnover and 13 per cent higher returns to shareholders. Findings suggest that managers can take specific actions to increase engagement motivation and productivity. Some of these actions are:

- Capitalise on 'engageable moments'.
- Demonstrate strong leadership and clear direction.
- Manage organisational change with effective communication.
- Emphasise customer focus.
- Institute and communicate a system of equitable rewards.
- Invest in the core staff.

Another study in the United Kingdom, by MacLeod and Clarke (2009), provided evidence that organisations that truly inspire their employees, produce world-class levels of innovation, productivity and performance. Halkos and Dimitrios (2010) found increased stress leads to reduced productivity and increased satisfaction leads to increased productivity. Quality work is more related to conscientiousness and personal satisfaction than workload. Managers who develop energetic and active individuals affect productivity positively. In keeping with Pink's thesis, Westover and Taylor in an international study of job satisfaction (2010) found that for all countries, intrinsic rewards explain the most variance in employees' job satisfaction, followed by work relations with management. Additionally, these determinants of job satisfaction varied by country and, apart from age, which is found to be a significant antecedent of job satisfaction for 1989, 1997 and 2005 generational waves, the significance of the personal factors tends to vary with each wave. Another study by Pais (2010) in the automotive industry found that using self-directed teams, who know the needs of external customers and to whom a high level of participation in operational decisions was given, can generate a substantial increase in efficiency and job satisfaction.

		EMPHASIS ON PERFORMANCE	
		Low	High
EMPHASIS ON SATISFACTION	High	Indulging	Integrating
	Low	Ignoring	Imposing

FIGURE 6.1 Relationship between satisfaction and performance

Other research (Steers, Porter & Bigley 1996), as well as the experience of highly acclaimed organisational motivation programs (Greene 1972; Levering, Moskovitz & Katz 1984), supports the position that developing morale and performance improvement need to be connected. As Figure 6.1 shows, effective motivational programs must focus on increasing both satisfaction and productivity. A high emphasis on satisfaction with a low emphasis on performance represents an irresponsible view of the role of management. Managers are hired to look after the company's interests. This entails, among other things, holding employees accountable for producing satisfactory results. Managers who emphasise satisfaction to the exclusion of performance will be seen as nice people, but their indulging or soft management style undermines the respect of their employees. It is easy to imagine an organisational climate that is so satisfaction-oriented that management becomes overly responsive to employees' requests and the resulting country-club-like atmosphere hinders good performance.

A strong emphasis on performance to the exclusion of satisfaction is equally ineffective. Instead of indulging, the manager is imposing. In this situation, managers have little concern for how employees feel about their jobs. The boss issues orders and the employees must follow them. Exploited employees are unhappy employees, and unhappy employees may seek employment with the competition. Thus, while exploitation may increase productivity in the short run, its long-term effects generally decrease productivity through increased absenteeism, employee turnover and, in some cases, even sabotage and violence.

When managers emphasise neither satisfaction nor performance, they are ignoring their responsibilities and their employees. The resulting neglect reflects a lack of management. There is no real leadership, as employees receive neither priorities nor direction. The resulting neglect, if allowed to continue, may ultimately lead to the failure of the work unit.

The integrating motivation strategy emphasises performance and satisfaction equally. (See also the collaborative negotiation style in Chapter 7.) Effective managers are able to combine these forces into integrative, synergistic programs. However, this does not mean that both objectives can be fully satisfied in every specific case. Some trade-offs occur naturally in ongoing work situations. However, in the long run, both objectives should be given equal consideration. The integrative view of motivation proposes that, while the importance of employees feeling good about what they are doing and how they are being treated cannot be downplayed, this concern should not overshadow management's responsibility to hold people accountable for results. Managers should avoid the twin traps of working to engender high employee morale for its own sake and pushing for short-term results at the expense of long-term commitment. This is the purpose of the Balanced Scorecard system discussed later in the chapter. The best managers have productive people under them who are also satisfied with their work environment (Jordan 1986; Kotter 1996; Nadler & Lawler 1977).

Elements of an integrated motivation program

What follows is a six-step approach to creating an integrated motivational program grounded in the belief that employees can simultaneously be high performers and personally satisfied. The six elements are:

1. Establish performance goals.
2. Remove obstacles.
3. Recognise and correct appropriately.
4. Individualise the recognition.
5. Reward equitably.
6. Provide effective feedback.

Box 6.1 shows the basic components of a motivational program that integrates performance and satisfaction.

BOX 6.1 Six elements of an integrative motivation program

MOTIVATION → PERFORMANCE

1. Establish moderately difficult goals that are understood and accepted.
   Ask: 'Do employees understand and accept my performance expectations?'
2. Remove personal and organisational obstacles to performance.
   Ask: 'Do employees feel it is possible to achieve this goal or expectation?'

PERFORMANCE → OUTCOMES

3. Use rewards and discipline appropriately to extinguish unacceptable behaviour and encourage exceptional performance.
   Ask: 'Do employees feel that being a high performer is more rewarding than being a low or average performer?'

OUTCOMES → SATISFACTION

4. Provide salient internal and external incentives.
   Ask: 'Do employees feel the rewards used to encourage high performance are worth the effort?'
5. Distribute rewards equitably.
   Ask: 'Do employees feel that work-related benefits are being distributed fairly?'
6. Provide timely rewards and specific, accurate and honest feedback on performance.
   Ask: 'Are we getting the most out of our rewards by administering them on a timely basis as part of the feedback process?'
   Ask: 'Do employees know where they stand in terms of current performance and long-term opportunities?'

The key assumptions underlying the six elements are:

- Employees start out motivated. Therefore, a lack of motivation is a learned response, often fostered by misunderstood or unrealistic expectations.
- The role of management is to create a supportive, problem-solving work environment in which necessary resources to perform a task are provided.
- Rewards should encourage high personal performance that is consistent with management objectives.
- Motivation works best when it is self-generated.
- Individuals should be treated fairly.
- Individuals deserve timely, honest feedback on work performance.

1. Establish performance goals linked to organisation goals

Managers should provide continuous assessment of the motivational climate of their work environment by asking, 'Do employees understand and agree with the performance expectations?' This needs to be a collaborative dialogue that matches the organisation's expectations with the employee's. The foundation of an effective motivation program is proper goal setting (Locke & Latham 1990).

Goal setting

Across many studies of high-performing work teams it was shown that the average performance of groups that set goals was significantly higher than that of groups that did not set goals. Goal-setting theory suggests that goals are associated with enhanced performance because they mobilise effort, direct attention, and encourage persistence and strategy development (O'Leary-Kelly, Martocchio & Frink 1994). The importance of goal setting is so well recognised that it has been incorporated in several formal management tools, such as management by objectives (MBO). It is the foundation feature of the Balanced Scorecard performance system discussed later. Effective goal setting has three critical components: (1) goal-setting process, (2) goal characteristics, and (3) feedback.

A common theme in this book is: 'The way you do things is often more important than what you do.' Applied to the goal-setting process, this means that the manner in which goals are established must be considered carefully. The basic maxim is that goals must be both understood and accepted if they are to be effective. To that end, research has shown that employees are more likely to 'buy into' goals if they are included in the goal-setting process. It has been well documented that the performance of work groups is higher when they choose their goals rather than have them assigned (O'Leary-Kelly, Martocchio & Frink 1994). This is especially important if the work environment is unfavourable for goal accomplishment (Latham, Erez & Locke 1988). For example, a goal might be inconsistent with accepted practice, require new skills or exacerbate poor management–employee relations. To be sure, if working conditions are highly conducive to goal accomplishment, employees may be willing to commit themselves to the achievement of goals in whose formulation they did not participate. However, such acceptance usually occurs only when management demonstrates an overall attitude of understanding and support (Latham & Locke 1979). When management does not exhibit a supportive attitude, the imposed goals or task assignments are likely to be viewed as unwelcome demands. As a result, employees will question the premises underlying the goals or assignments and will comply only reluctantly with the demands.

Sometimes it is difficult to implement these process guidelines. A manager is often given directions regarding new tasks or assignment deadlines that must be passed on. However, if employees believe that management is committed to involving them in all discretionary aspects of the management of their work unit, they are more willing to accept directions regarding the non-discretionary aspects of work assignments. For example, a computer programming unit may not have any say in which application programs are assigned to the group or what priority is assigned each incoming assignment. However, the manager can still involve unit members in deciding how much time to allocate to each assignment ('What is a realistic goal for completing this task?') or who should receive which job assignment ('Which type of programs would you find challenging?').

Goal characteristics

Shifting from process to content, research has shown that goal characteristics significantly affect the likelihood that the goal will be accomplished (Locke & Latham 1990). What we do know is that effective performance goals, objectives or key performance indicators (KPIs) have these SMART features (Rudman 1997: 291): specific, measurable, agreed, realistic and time-framed.

- *Specific.* Goals should be specific rather than vague: 'increase sales by 10 per cent' rather than 'try to improve sales'. They should also deal with outcomes rather than inputs: 'increase sales by 10 per cent' describes the desired result, whereas 'try to improve sales' deals only with the effort expected of the employee. Specific goals are unambiguous and behavioural. Specific goals reduce misunderstanding about what behaviours will be rewarded. Admonitions such as 'be dependable', 'work hard', 'take the initiative' or 'do your best' are too general and too difficult to measure and are therefore of limited motivational value.
- *Measurable.* So that the nature and extent of the achievement can be assessed, goals should incorporate an agreed measure or standard. These may be *quantitative,* as in 'increase sales by 10 per cent', or *qualitative,* using a standard or statement agreed on by the manager and employee. Often, qualitative goals can be expressed in quantitative terms, as in 'improve customer satisfaction so that service complaints do not exceed one per week on average'. There is no job in which the desired performance or results cannot be measured in some way. Being bothered to take

the time to thoughtfully define the measure at the beginning is a key to effective motivation and performance.

- *Agreed.* Getting the job holder's commitment is a key to setting effective targets. Employees should participate fully in the setting of the objectives for their own jobs, and have an appropriate opportunity to contribute to planning the objectives of the workgroup, the department and the organisation as a whole. But people should not be left to set their own targets: each person's objectives must fit in with, and derive from, those of the wider workgroup or workplace. It is lazy management to send the employee off to set his or her own KPIs. At the very least, managers should ensure that the person responsible for achieving a particular objective understands and accepts it. The motivation is increased significantly when these goals are defined by the entire work team and not just the manager or team leader.
- *Realistic.* Goals should be challenging, but not beyond the reach of the employee. If accepted, difficult goals lead to better performance than easy goals (Wood, Mento & Locke 1987). Simply stated, hard goals are more motivating than easy goals. One explanation for this is called 'achievement motivation' (Atkinson & Raynor 1974). According to this perspective, employees size up new tasks in terms of their chances for success and the significance of the anticipated accomplishment. But employees will simply not accept goals which they perceive to be unreasonable or unreachable. In addition, they get no sense of achievement from pursuing goals they can never reach. Similarly, objectives that are set too low will not challenge people's capabilities and will have no motivating effect.

  Although there is no single standard of difficulty that fits all people, it is important to keep in mind that high expectations generally foster high performance. As one experienced manager said, 'We get about what we expect.' Warren Bennis (1984), author of *The Unconscious Conspiracy: Why Leaders Can't Lead*, agrees: 'In a study of school teachers, it turned out that when they held high expectations of their students, that alone was enough to cause an increase of twenty-five points in the students' IQ scores.' (See also Manzoni & Barsoux 1998.) The potency of such an expectant attitude is described in Chapter 7 on managing conflict.

  Goals are also realistic if they are consistent with the organisation's plans and objectives, and are within the scope of the individual's responsibilities, and within his or her skills and abilities. Some care is needed to discourage individuals or groups from taking on objectives that are beyond their capabilities or are incapable of achievement with the resources available. Goals that are inconsistent in the sense that they are logically impossible to accomplish simultaneously, or incompatible in the sense that each goal requires so much effort that they cannot be accomplished at the same time, create frustration and alienation. When employees complain that goals are incompatible or inconsistent, managers should be flexible enough to reconsider their expectations.
- *Time-framed.* Just as goals should be specific rather than vague, they should also have a time-frame or time limit: for example, 'increase sales by 10 per cent by the end of this year'. If a number of goals are being set, it is important that their time spans or completion dates are staggered through the period. For many people, goals will have only limited effect if their target dates are, say, 12 months away. Similarly, people will feel unduly pressured if all their goals fall due at the same time. Target dates must be realistic: managers frequently underestimate how long it will take to complete certain activities, especially if the individual has a number of objectives to be achieved within a particular period of time.

SMART goals are the cornerstone of the Balanced Scorecard system discussed later.

Feedback and recognition

In addition to selecting the right type of goal, an effective goal program must also include feedback (Fellner & Sulzer-Azaroff 1984). Feedback provides opportunities for clarifying expectations, adjusting goal difficulty, gaining recognition and improving performance. As seen earlier, recognition is very powerful as a motivator and a measure for improvement. Therefore, it is important to provide benchmark opportunities for individuals to determine how they are doing. These 'along-the-way progress reports' are particularly critical when the time required to complete an assignment or reach a goal is very long. For example, feedback is very useful for projects such as writing a complex computer program or raising a million dollars for a local charity. In these cases, feedback should be linked to accomplishing intermediate stages or completing specific components. (This is discussed later in the chapter.)

2. Remove obstacles

The next key ingredient of an effective goal program is a supportive work environment. After setting goals, the manager should shift focus to facilitating successful accomplishment. This can be done by asking, 'Do employees feel it is possible to achieve this goal?' Help from management must come in many forms, including making sure the person has the required abilities for the job, providing the necessary training, securing needed resources and encouraging cooperation and support from other work units. It is the manager's job to make the paths leading towards the targeted goals easier for the employee to travel.

However, as with all general management guidelines, effective results follow from sensitive, informed implementation tailored to specific circumstances. In this case, the manner in which this enabling, facilitative role should be implemented varies considerably among individuals, organisational settings and tasks. When employees believe that strong management support is needed, leaders who are not aware of the obstacles to performance, or not assertive enough to remove them, will probably be perceived as part of the employees' problem, rather than the source of solutions. By the same token, when management intervention is not needed or expected, managers who are constantly involved in the details of employees' job performance will be viewed as meddling and unwilling to trust. This view of management is incorporated in the 'path–goal' theory of leadership (House & Mitchell 1974), shown in Figure 6.2.

The key question the theory addresses is: 'How much help should a manager provide?' In response, the model proposes that the level of involvement should vary according to how much employees need to perform a specific task; how much they expect; and how much support is available to them from other organisational sources.

The key task characteristics of the path–goal model are structure and difficulty. A task that is highly structured, as reflected in the degree of built-in order and direction, and relatively easy to

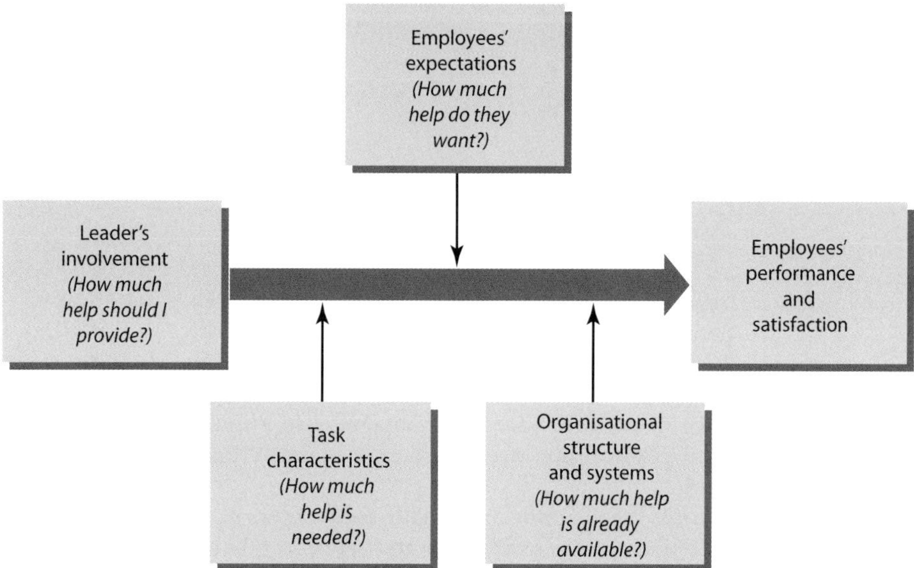

FIGURE 6.2 Modified path–goal model of leadership

Source: Adapted from R. J. House and T. R. Mitchell, 'Path-goal theory of leadership', *Journal of Contemporary Business*, 3, 1974, pp. 81–97.

perform does not require extensive management direction. If managers offer too much advice, they will come across as controlling, bossy or nagging, because from the nature of the task itself it is already clear to the employees what they should do. On the other hand, for an unstructured and difficult task, management's direction and strong involvement in problem-solving activities will be seen as constructive and satisfying.

The second factor that influences the appropriate degree of management involvement is the expectations of the employees. Three distinct characteristics influence expectations: the desire for autonomy, experience and ability. Employees who prize their autonomy and independence prefer managers with a highly participative, unobtrusive leadership style because it gives them more latitude for controlling what they do. In contrast, people who prefer the assistance of others in making decisions, establishing priorities and solving problems prefer greater management involvement.

The connection between a staff member's ability and experience levels and preferred management style is straightforward. Capable and experienced employees feel they need less assistance from their managers because they are adequately trained, know how to obtain the necessary resources and can handle political entanglements with their counterparts in other units. They appreciate managers who 'give them their head' but periodically check to see if further assistance is required. On the other hand, it is frustrating for relatively new employees, or those with marginal skills, to feel that their manager has neither the time nor the interest to listen to basic questions. An important concept in the path–goal approach to leadership is that management involvement should complement, rather than duplicate, organisational sources of support. Specifically, managers should provide more 'shepherding' in situations where workgroup norms governing performance are not clear, organisational rewards for performance are insufficient and organisational controls governing performance are inadequate.

One of the important lessons from this discussion of the path–goal model is that managers must tailor their management style to each individual and the specific conditions, such as those shown in Table 6.3.

TABLE 6.3 Factors influencing management involvement

CONTINGENCIES	CONDITIONS APPROPRIATE FOR *MAXIMUM* MANAGEMENT INVOLVEMENT	CONDITIONS APPROPRIATE FOR *MINIMUM* MANAGEMENT INVOLVEMENT
Task structure	Low	High
Task mastery	Low	High
Employees' desire for autonomy	Low	High
Employees' experience	Low	High
Employees' ability	Low	High
Strength of group norms	Low	High
Effectiveness of organisation's controls and rewards	Low	High

Source: Adapted from R. J. House and T. R. Mitchell, 'Path-goal theory of leadership', *Journal of Contemporary Business*, 3, 1974, pp. 81–97.

Although managers should focus on facilitating task accomplishment, their level of direct involvement should be calibrated to the nature of the work, the availability of organisational support, and the ability and experience of the individuals. If managers are insensitive to these contingencies, they will probably be perceived by some employees as interfering with their desire to explore their own way, while others will feel lost.

This conclusion underscores how important it is for managers to understand and match the needs and expectations of their employees. Effective managers regularly ask their employees three simple questions: 'How is your work going?', 'What do you enjoy the most/least?' and 'How can I help you succeed?' Asking these questions communicates a supportive style; hearing the answers allows managers to fine-tune their facilitative actions.

This dialogue is a good example:

Manager: How's it going, Geoff?
Employee: Fine really, Maria, except for getting the deliveries changed. [Maria knows that Geoff is experienced and able, with an independent spirit. This argues for low intervention on her part. The task structure in this case (the deliveries) is not clear, suggesting stronger involvement.]
Manager: Great. If you need any assistance with the deliveries, please let me know.
Employee: Sure, I'll try it some more myself and call if I can't get anywhere by tomorrow.
Manager: Sounds like you have it under control.
Employee: Yep. It's good. Don't like dealing with Henry, though.
Manager: Yeah, he can be a bit slow. Keep up the good schedule, Geoff, and call if you want.

3. Recognise and correct appropriately

Once clear goals have been established and management has cleared the path to goal completion, the next step in an effective motivational program is to encourage goal accomplishment by linking performance to positive outcomes. The discussion of this important element of an effective motivational program is based on three related principles:

1. Managers should help to create a motivating environment.
2. Managers should link recognition and rewards to performance, rather than to seniority or membership.
3. Managers should use rewards and recognition with high-performance behaviours and use corrective feedback with counterproductive behaviours.

Technological constraints sometimes make it difficult to link rewards and individual performance perfectly. For example, people working on a car assembly line or chemists working on a group research project may not have much control over their personal productivity. In these situations, rewards linked to the performance of the workgroup will foster group cohesion and collaboration and partially satisfy the individual members' concerns about fairness (Lawler 1988). When it is not possible to assess the performance of a workgroup (work shift, organisational department), it is advisable to consider an organisation-wide performance bonus. While the merits and technical details of various group and organisational reward systems are beyond the scope of this chapter, managers should link valued rewards and good performance at the most appropriate level of group size (Lawler 1988).

Effects of managers' responses

An effective motivational program goes beyond the design of the organisational reward system. As seen in the first five chapters, managers' daily interactions with employees constitute powerful individual motivators or demotivators. It is difficult for even highly sensitive and aware managers to understand fully the impact of their actions on the behaviour and attitudes of employees. Unfortunately, some managers do not even try to monitor these effects. The danger of this lack of awareness is that it may lead to managerial actions that actually encourage ineffective behaviours in their employees. This has been called 'the folly of rewarding A while hoping for B' (Kerr 1995).

For example, a director of a research group with a low tolerance for conflict and uncertainty may unwittingly undermine the company's avowed objective of developing highly creative products by punishing workgroups who do not exhibit unity or a clear, consistent set of priorities. Further, while avowing the virtue of risk, the manager may punish failure; while stressing creativity, he or she may kill the spirit of the idea champion (see also Argyris 1992). These actions will encourage a workgroup to avoid challenging projects, suppress debate and cause task performance to become routine.

A common lament among managers is: 'I can't get my people to take enough initiative. They have a very narrow view of their responsibilities, and they are hesitant to exceed those self-imposed boundaries. Why are these individuals unwilling to do more than the bare minimum?' The answer is clear. Managers are, to a large extent, responsible for their employees' actions. A common reaction might be: if an employee did not follow through on something they were supposed to do, then the employee is 'lazy'. A more effective response might be to ask ourselves if the employee was given the proper information and support. It is extremely important that the manager knows that the other person is truly receptive to what is being said. If not, then the manager will become the cause of the error if something goes wrong, not the employee.

The 'dos and don'ts' for encouraging employees to assume more initiative, shown in Box 6.2, demonstrate the power of managers' actions in shaping behaviour.

BOX 6.2 Guidelines for fostering employee initiative

DO	DON'T
• Ask, 'How are we going to do this?', 'What can I contribute to this effort?', 'How will we use this result?', thus implying your joint stake in the work and results.	• Imply that the task is the employees' total responsibility, that they hang alone if they fail. Individual failure means organisational failure.
• Use an interested, exploring manner, asking questions designed to bring out factual information.	• Play the part of an interrogator, firing questions as rapidly as they can be answered. Ask questions that require only 'yes' or 'no' replies.
• Keep the analysis and evaluation as much in the employees' hands as possible by asking for their best judgment on various issues.	• React to their presentations on an emotional basis.
• Present facts about organisation needs, commitments, strategy and so on, which permit them to improve and interest them in improving what they propose to do.	• Demand a change or improvement in a peremptory tone of voice or on what appears to be an arbitrary basis.
• Ask them to investigate or analyse further if you feel that they have overlooked some points or overemphasised others. Ask them to return with their plans after factoring these items in.	• Take their planning papers and cross out, change dates or mark 'no good' next to certain activities.
	• Redo their plans for them unless their repeated efforts show no improvement.

Source: M. S. Kellogg, *Talking with Employees: A Guide for Managers* (Houston, TX: Gulf Publishing Co., 1979), p. 121.

As the recognition grid showed, actions and reactions that might appear insignificant to the boss often have strong positive or negative effects on employees. Hence the truism, 'Managers get what they reward, not what they want', and its companion, 'People do what is inspected'. Indeed, the motivating potential of managers' reactions to employees' behaviours is so strong that it has been argued that 'The best way to change an individual's behavior in a work setting is to change his or her manager's behavior' (Thompson 1978: 52). Given the considerable leverage that managers have over their employees' motivation to reach optimal performance, it is important that they learn how to use positive and negative recognition effectively to produce positive, intended results consistently.

Although there is a lot to be said for managers having a positive attitude and giving poor performers the benefit of the doubt, their failure to reflect and redirect inappropriate behaviours leads to two undesirable outcomes: (1) the work unit's morale is seriously threatened; and (2) the poor performer's behaviours are not improved.

Just as some managers find it unpleasant to give direct feedback for poor performance, other managers have difficulty praising exceptional performance. As a result, employees complain that nothing ever satisfies the manager. This second misapplication of the negative-response behaviour-shaping strategy is just as dysfunctional as the indiscriminate use of praise. These managers mistakenly believe that the best way to motivate people is by always keeping expectations a little higher than their employees' best performance and then chiding them for their imperfection. In the process, they run the risk of burning out their staff or inadvertently encouraging lower performance ('We'll get chewed out anyway, so why try so hard?'). The irony is that this method creates a competitive, self-defeating situation in which employees look forward to the boss making mistakes—the bigger the better!

Unfortunately, many managers genuinely believe that this is the best way to manage in all situations. This negative, desultory style of management creates a demoralising work environment and does not foster exceptional performance. Instead, people are motivated to stay out of the boss's way and to avoid doing anything unusual or untried. Innovation and involvement are extinguished and mundane performance becomes not only acceptable, but desirable.

Having looked at the issues of recognition and feedback, the attention now turns to the proper use of performance behaviour-shaping techniques.

Improving behaviours

The mark of exceptional managers is their ability to foster exceptional behaviour in their employees. This is best accomplished by using a nine-step behaviour improvement process, which can be applied to the full range of employee behaviours. This approach can be used to change unacceptable behaviours to acceptable ones, or to transform acceptable behaviours into exceptional ones. It is designed to avoid the harmful effects typically associated with the improper use of discipline, discussed in the next section (Hamner 1974; Luthans & Kreitner 1975; Maier 1973). It also ensures the appropriate use of rewards and recognition (Latham, Erez & Locke 1988). This process is greatly strengthened by using the non-verbal matching skills of Chapter 2, the communication and feedback skills of Chapter 5, and the recognition grid in the previous section of this chapter.

Box 6.3 shows the nine steps for improving behaviours, organised into three broad initiatives: recognise, reflect and redirect. Steps 1–3 (recognise) are used to reward, motivate and encourage self-confidence. Steps 4–9 (reflect and redirect) are used to clarify, counsel and correct unacceptable behaviours into exceptional behaviours.

BOX 6.3 Guidelines for improving behaviours

RECOGNISE

1. Identify recognition and rewards that are unique to the individual.
2. Link the attainment of desirable outcomes with incremental, continuous improvement.
3. Reward (including using praise) all improvements in performance in a timely and honest manner.

REFLECT

4. Describe the behaviours or standards you expect. Make sure the individual understands and agrees that these are reasonable.
5. Ask if the individual is in agreement.
6. Be appropriately supportive. For example, praise other aspects of the individual's work, identify personal and group benefits of compliance, and make sure there are no work-related problems standing in the way of meeting your expectations.

REDIRECT

7. Identify the specific inappropriate behaviour. Give examples. Indicate that the action must stop.
8. Point out the impact of the problem on the performance of others, on the unit's mission and so forth.
9. Ask questions about causes and explore remedies.

An important principle to keep in mind regarding the use of negative feedback is that it should closely follow the poor behaviour and focus exclusively on the specific problem. This is not an appropriate time to dredge up old concerns or make general, unsubstantiated accusations. The focus of the discussion should be on eliminating a problem behaviour, not on making the employee feel bad. This approach increases the likelihood that the employee will associate the negative response with a specific act, rather than viewing it as a generalised negative evaluation. (See Table 6.2 earlier in this chapter and also the guidelines for initiating a complaint in Chapter 7 for more information on this topic.)

Second, inappropriate behaviours should be redirected into appropriate channels. It is important that people receiving negative feedback understand how they can receive recognition in the future. The process of redirection reduces the despair that occurs when people feel they are likely to be at fault no matter what they do. If expected behaviours are not made clear, then employees may stop the inappropriate behaviour but feel lost, not knowing how to improve. Keep in mind that the primary goal of any negative feedback is to transform inappropriate behaviours into appropriate behaviours. The lingering negative effects of a specific negative will quickly wear off if the manager is able to reward desirable behaviours shortly thereafter. This goal can be achieved only if employees know how they can receive positive outcomes.

Experienced managers know that it is just as difficult to transform acceptable behaviours into exceptional ones. Helping an 'okay, but uninspired' employee catch the vision of moving up to a higher level of desire and commitment can be very challenging. The goal of skilled managers is to avoid having to administer any negative responses and especially to avoid trial-and-error learning among new employees. This is done by clearly expressing what is expected and collaboratively establishing work objectives. In addition, it is a good idea to provide an experienced mentor, known for exceptional performance, as a sounding board and role model.

4. Individualise the recognition

Having established a link between performance and outcomes (through recognition and feedback) as part of an integrative motivational program, it is now important to focus on the relevance, or personal value, of various outcomes. (To simplify the discussion, the focus here is only on rewards.) It stands to reason that performance will be enhanced only to the extent that the recipient personally values the rewards attached to it. The evaluative question then is: 'Do employees feel the rewards used to encourage high performance are worth the effort?'

The broad tendency for managers to miscalculate employees' reward preferences usually takes two forms: (1) assuming that all employees value the same outcomes; and (2) assuming that employees share the manager's reward preferences.

One of the biggest mistakes that can be made in implementing a reward system is assuming that managers understand their employees' preferences. The manager's lament, 'What does Jo expect, anyway? I gave her a bonus and she's still complaining to other members of the accounting department that I don't appreciate her superior performance', indicates an apparent miscalculation of what Jo really values.

Personal needs and personal motivation

One of the most enduring theories of motivation is based on our scientific understanding of human needs. Probably the best-known example of a hierarchical needs model was proposed by Abraham Maslow (1970) (discussed earlier in the chapter).

An alternative perspective to the hierarchy of needs models can be found in Henry Murray's manifest needs model (McClelland 1971: 13). Murray proposed that individuals can be classified according to the strengths of their various needs. In contrast to hierarchical models, in which needs are categorised based on their inherent strength (hunger is a stronger need than self-actualisation), Murray posited that people have divergent and often conflicting needs. Murray proposed about two dozen needs, but later studies have suggested that only three or four of them are relevant to the workplace, including the needs for achievement, affiliation and power. Another important distinction of Murray's conception is his belief that these needs are primarily learned, rather than inherited, and that they are activated by cues from the environment. That is, if a person has a high need for achievement it will become manifest, or an active motivational force, only if the environment cues achievement-oriented behaviour.

The need for achievement is defined as 'behaviour toward competition with a standard of excellence' (McClelland et al. 1953: 111). This suggests that individuals with a high need for achievement would be characterised by: (1) a tendency to set moderately difficult goals; (2) a strong desire to assume personal responsibility for work activities; (3) a single-minded focus on accomplishing a task; and (4) a strong desire for detailed feedback on task performance. The level of a person's need for achievement (high to low) has been shown to be a good predictor of job performance. In addition, it is highly correlated with a person's preference for an enriched job with greater responsibility and autonomy.

The second of Murray's needs, the need for affiliation, involves attractions to other individuals in order to feel reassured and acceptable (Birch & Veroff 1966: 65). It has been suggested that people with a high need for affiliation are characterised by: (1) a sincere interest in the feelings of others; (2) a tendency to conform to the expectations of others, especially those whose affiliation they value: and (3) a strong desire for reassurance and approval from others. One would expect individuals with a high need for achievement to gravitate towards jobs that provide a high degree of interpersonal contact. It is useful to point out that, in contrast to the need for achievement, the need for affiliation does not seem to be correlated with job performance.

Rounding out Murray's model is the need for power, which represents a desire to influence others and control the environment. Individuals with a high need for power seek leadership positions and tend to influence others in a fairly open, direct manner. McClelland (1976) suggests that there are two manifestations of the general need for power. Individuals with a high need for personal power tend to seek power and influence for its own sake. To them, control, dominance and conquest are important indicators of personal efficacy. These leaders inspire their employees to perform heroic feats, but for the sake of the leader, not the organisation. In contrast, individuals with high institutional power needs are more oriented towards using their influence to advance the goals of the group or organisation. These individuals are described by McClelland as follows: (1) they are organisation-minded, feeling personally responsible for advancing the purposes of the organisation; (2) they enjoy work and accomplishing tasks in an orderly fashion; (3) they are often willing to sacrifice their own self-interests for the good of the organisation; (4) they have a strong sense of justice and equity; and (5) they seek expert advice and are not defensive when their ideas are criticised.

A knowledge of need theory helps managers to understand whether organisational rewards are significant reinforcers for specific individuals. If a reward satisfies an activated personal need, it can be used to reinforce desired individual behaviours. The difficulty many managers have in predicting what rewards will be most attractive to their employees is illustrated in Table 6.4.

TABLE 6.4 Order of importance of various job factors

JOB FACTORS	SURVEY OF EMPLOYEES	SURVEY OF BOSSES
Full appreciation of work done	1	8
Feeling of being in on things	2	10
Sympathetic help on personal problems	3	9
Job security	4	2
Good wages	5	1
Interesting work	6	5
Promotional growth in organisation	7	3
Personal loyalty to employees	8	6
Good working conditions	9	4
Tactful disciplining	10	7

Source: A. L. LeDue, Jr, 'Motivation of programmers', *ACM Database*, Quarterly Publication of SIGBOP, 11(4), Summer, 1980, pp. 4–12.

Table 6.4 shows the results of a study consisting of two phases: first, data-processing analysts were asked to rank-order various rewards in terms of their perceived personal value; second, the analysts' managers were asked to estimate the order in which the employees would rank the rewards. Their responses indicate a very low correlation between employees' actual priorities and the priorities attributed to them by their bosses. It is especially interesting to note that the employees surveyed tended to focus primarily on rewards controlled by their immediate supervisors, while the managers assumed that their employees were motivated by organisationally mediated outcomes. (See Larkin & Larkin 1992 for more detail.)

Individual recognition is crucial cross-culturally as well as within a culture. Recognising the diversity of most workgroups, many organisations are experimenting with 'cafeteria-style' incentive systems (Lawler 1987). Employees receive a certain number of work credits based on performance, seniority or task difficulty, and they are allowed to trade them in for a variety of benefits, including upgraded insurance packages, financial planning services, disability income plans, extended vacation benefits, and tuition reimbursement for educational programs. By giving employees an opportunity to select from a benefits menu, these organisations are maximising the motivational value of these outcomes to each individual employee.

A flexible reward system helps managers to avoid the second common motivational mistake: projecting their own preferences on to employees. Ineffective managers do not spend enough quality time with their workers to understand their personal needs and goals. Under these circumstances, it is natural for managers to assume that their employees share their views regarding the attractiveness of various job outcomes.

This error is reflected in the case of an accountant who was promoted to office manager because upper management in the home office felt he was 'the most qualified and most deserving'. Unfortunately, they failed to ask him if he wanted the promotion. They assumed that because they enjoyed their management positions, all their employees shared similar views. Two weeks after receiving his 'reward' for good performance, the accountant-turned-manager was in the hospital with a bleeding ulcer.

It is particularly important for managers to accurately assess the needs of a highly diverse workforce. If you are designing reward systems for a large group, it is important to consider more than the dominant demographic profile. Instead, you should look for subpopulations whose particular needs and interests might not be adequately represented in the overall profile. For example, some research suggests that Chinese, Indonesian and other Asian managers tend to be more inclined towards an institutional power orientation, whereas managers from Australia, the United States and Europe are more prone to demonstrate a personal power orientation (Hofstede 1991; McClelland 1976; Trompenaars 1996). All the cultural matching factors outlined in Chapters 1 and 2 are appropriate in terms of individualising recognition.

Going a step further, if your objective is to understand what motivates a particular individual in your immediate workgroup, it is important to go beyond that person's demographic profile (for example, she is a married Malaysian female without a university degree who is about to retire) and understand what makes that person unique. Effective managers accomplish this through frequent, personal and supportive discussions with their employees. Such informal exchanges might focus on career opportunities, life goals or personal priorities. An information-gathering technique used by some managers is to discuss with employees recent significant changes in the careers of common acquaintances. Employees' responses to changing circumstances affecting others' responsibilities, including their pay, personal time, time away from home, opportunities for collaboration and so forth, often provide useful insights into their own personal preferences.

Managers, in general, vastly underestimate their potential for directly influencing the behaviour of employees (see Senge 1990, and the expectant attitude in Chapter 7).

Figure 6.3 remains the benchmark of motivation research. It clearly identifies precisely what motivates and demotivates employees, although this is influenced by generational and cultural factors (see below).

Managers should be particularly sensitive to the dynamic quality of human needs.

Internal job characteristics

All the outcomes shown in Table 6.4, except for 'interesting work', are called *external motivators*, because someone other than the employee, typically the immediate supervisor, controls them. The supervisor can show appreciation for a job well done, offer job security, show personal loyalty to employees and provide good working conditions. It is a slightly different story for interesting work. Although managers control the components of a job, they have no direct control over whether a specific employee finds a job interesting. The outcomes associated with an interesting job come from *internal motivators,* which are factors inherent in the job itself, not from any particular actions of the manager.

Effective motivators understand that the person–job interface has a strong impact on how employees perform their job. No matter how many externally controlled rewards managers use, if their employees find their jobs uninteresting and unfulfilling, performance will suffer. Attention to internal motivators is particularly critical in situations where managers have relatively little control over the organisational incentive system. In these cases it is often possible to compensate for lack of control over external factors by fine-tuning the person–job fit.

Job design is the process of matching job characteristics and employees' skills and interests. Ward et al. (2000) present a view of the ultimate use of technology integrated with job design to achieve worker satisfaction and maximise productivity. They suggest that increasingly people should be matched to occupations or job categories rather than specific jobs. Kuo et al. (2010) argue that a combination of work redesign and empowerment can generate a significant impact on commitment.

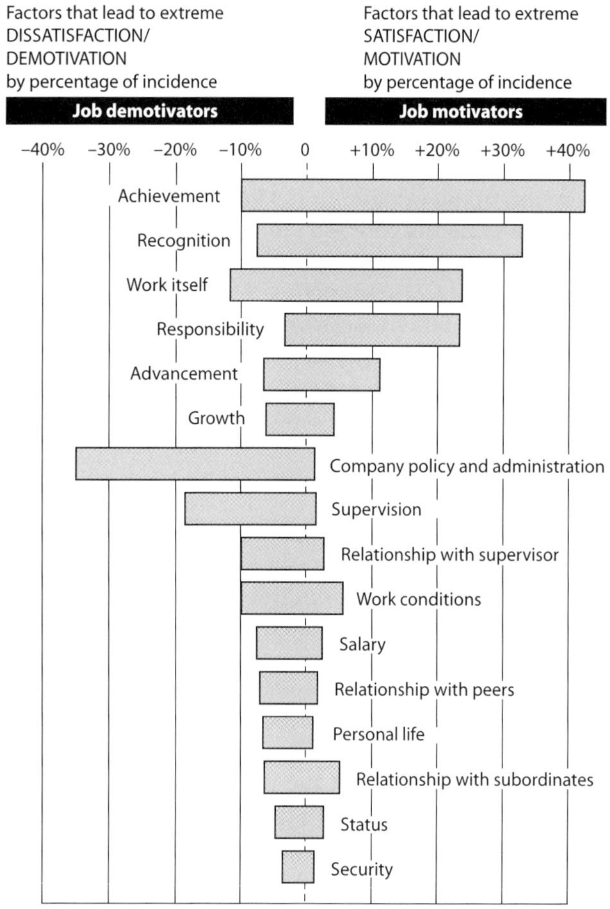

FIGURE 6.3 Benchmark of motivation research

Source: F. Herzberg, 'One more time: How do you motivate employees?', *Harvard Business Review*, 46(1), 1968, pp. 53–62.

Hallowell (2011) has made a compelling case for ensuring excellent job fit. He argues that poor job fit creates many performance problems in the workplace. His book details significant job analysis from the incumbent's perspective, examining issues such as: What talent do you have that you have not developed? Which of your skills are you most proud of? What have you got better at? The investment of this effort can lead to a better understanding of the employee's skill sets, which may well be best matched to another role in the organisation.

A variety of empirical research has found that the five core job dimensions—skill variety, task identity, task significance, autonomy and feedback—are positively related to job satisfaction (Loher et al. 1985).

In general, the greater the variety of skills a person can use in performing their work, the more he or she will perceive the task as being meaningful or worthwhile. Similarly, the more an individual can perform a complete job from beginning to end (task identity), and the greater the direct effect of the work on the work or lives of other people (task significance), the more the employee will view the job as being meaningful. On the other hand, when the work requires few skills, only part of a task is performed or there seems to be little effect on others' jobs, work is experienced as being less meaningful.

The more autonomy in the work (freedom to choose how and when to do particular jobs), the more responsibility employees feel for their successes and failures. Increased responsibility results in increased commitment to the work. Autonomy can be increased by instituting flexible work schedules, decentralising decision making, or selectively removing formalised controls, such as the ringing of a bell to indicate the beginning and end of a work-shift.

Finally, the more feedback individuals receive about how well their jobs are being performed, the more knowledge of results they have. Knowledge of results permits employees to understand the benefits of the jobs they perform. Employees' knowledge of results may be enhanced by increasing their direct contact with clients or by giving them feedback on how their jobs fit in and contribute to the overall operation of the organisation. Many organisations have achieved good results from these approaches.

Enhancing the core job dimensions and increasing critical psychological states increase employees' job fulfilment. Job fulfilment (high internal work motivation) is associated with other outcomes valued by management. These include high-quality work performance, high employee satisfaction with their jobs, and low absenteeism and turnover. Employees who have well-designed jobs enjoy doing them because they are intrinsically satisfying.

Five ways to better jobs

This discussion of job design suggests five managerial action guidelines that can help increase desirable personal and work outcomes.

1. *Combine tasks.* A combination of tasks is by definition a more challenging and complex work assignment. It requires employees to use a wider variety of skills, which makes the work seem more challenging and meaningful.
2. *Create work teams.* A related managerial principle is to form identifiable work teams so that task identity and task significance can be increased. Clerical work in a large insurance firm was handled by 80 employees organised by functional task (for example, opening the mail, entering information into the computer, sending out statements). Work was assigned, based on current workload, by a supervisor over each functional area. To create higher levels of task identity and task significance, the firm reorganised the clerical staff into eight self-contained groups. Each group handled all business associated with specific clients.
3. *Establish client connections.* The third guideline for enhancing jobs is establishing client relationships (Greenberg & Ornstein 1984). A client relationship involves an ongoing personal relationship between an employee (the producer) and the client (the consumer). The establishment of this relationship can increase autonomy, task identity and feedback. Take, for example, research and design employees. While they may be the ones who design a product, feedback on customer satisfaction is generally provided through their managers or a separate customer-relations unit. Job enrichment occurs when members of a research and design group are assigned to make regular contacts with their major clients directly.
4. *Devolve accountability.* 'Devolved empowerment' refers to granting more authority for making job-related decisions to employees. This refers to the distribution of power between an employee and a boss. As supervisors delegate more authority and responsibility, their employees' perceived autonomy, accountability and task identity increase. Historically, employees on car assembly lines have had little decision-making authority. However, in conjunction with increased emphasis on quality, best practice and team-based units, many factories now encourage team members to adjust their equipment, reject faulty materials, and even shut down the line if a major problem is evident. This is being accomplished through the process of self-managing teams (see Chapters 8 and 9).
5. *Encourage open feedback.* The final managerial suggestion is to open feedback channels. People need to know how well or how poorly they are performing their jobs if any kind of improvement is expected. Thus, it is imperative that they receive timely and consistent feedback, which allows them to make appropriate adjustments in their behaviour so they can receive the appropriate rewards and recognition.

Although this management tool, like others, involves trade-offs, the record of job redesign interventions is impressive. Depending on the approach taken, firms typically report a substantial increase in productivity, work quality and employee satisfaction (reflected in lower rates of absenteeism).

This section on external and internal rewards contains two important lessons for managers. First, managers should ensure that there are enough reward and recognition options available for employees so they can personally select their own outcomes. The motivational potential of an effective goal-setting process and a supportive, obstacle-removing management style is dissipated if employees feel that high performance will not lead to personally attractive outcomes. This should be established as part of the organisational culture, such that the rituals and ceremonies of work-life are as varied and available as possible.

Second, managers should recognise that both external and internal outcomes are necessary ingredients of effective motivational programs. In particular, ignoring internal outcomes can significantly undermine a manager's efforts to motivate. Most people desire interesting and challenging work activities. Good wages and job security will do little to overcome the negative effects of individuals' feeling that their abilities are being underused.

A different approach to job design focuses on matching individuals' 'deeply embedded life interests' with the task characteristics of their work (Butler & Waldroop 1999). The proponents of this approach argue that for too long people have been advised to select careers based on what they are good at, rather than what they enjoy. The assumption behind this advice is that individuals who excel at their work are satisfied with their jobs. However, critics of this perspective argue that many professionals are so well educated and achievement-oriented that they could succeed in virtually any job. This suggests that people stay in jobs because they become involved in activities that are consistent with their long-held, emotionally driven passions, intricately entwined with their personality. Hence, we see the value of self-awareness and tools like the LETS and MBTI.

Advocates of this perspective have identified eight such interests for people who are attracted to business careers. Most of the people studied reported that they were drawn to one to three of the following interests:

- application of technology
- quantitative analysis
- theory development and conceptual thinking
- creative production
- counselling and mentoring
- managing people and relationships
- enterprise control
- influence through language and ideas.

Setting aside the differences between the various approaches to matching workers and their work, the overall record of job redesign interventions is impressive. Firms typically report a substantial increase in productivity, work quality and worker satisfaction (reflected in lower rates of absenteeism). For example, the US Social Security Administration increased productivity 23.5 per cent among a group of 50 employees; General Electric realised a 50 per cent increase in product quality as a result of a job-redesign program; and the absenteeism rate among data-processing operators at Travelers Insurance decreased 24 per cent (Kopelman 1985).

In summary, managers should recognise that both extrinsic and intrinsic outcomes are necessary ingredients of effective motivational programs. In addition, recognising that individual preferences for outcomes vary, managers should not assume that a narrow-gauged, outcomes-contingent, performance-reinforcing motivation program will satisfy the needs and interests of a broad group of individuals.

5. Reward equitably

Once appropriate rewards have been determined for each employee, managers must then consider how to distribute those rewards (Greenberg 1990). This brings us to concerns about equity. Any positive benefits of relevant rewards will be negated if employees feel they are not receiving their fair share. The relevant evaluative question here is: 'Do employees feel that work-related benefits are distributed fairly?' (As in the previous section, the focus here is only on rewards. However, the same principles apply to the equitable use of positive and negative feedback.) The concepts discussed in Chapters 1 and 2 on cross-cultural factors, and skilfully matching those elements, are once again particularly relevant here.

'Equity' refers to people's perceptions of the fairness of rewards. Evaluations of equity are based on a social comparison process in which employees individually compare what they are getting out of the work relationship (outcomes) with what they are putting into the work relationship (inputs) (Adams 1963). Outcomes include such items as pay, fringe benefits, increased responsibility and prestige, while inputs might include hours worked and work quality, as well as education and experience. The ratio of outcomes to inputs is then compared with corresponding ratios of other individuals, judged to be an appropriate comparison group. The outcome of this comparison, and making it available to all employees, is the basis for beliefs about fairness.

If employees experience feelings of inequity, they will behaviourally or cognitively adjust their own, or fellow employees', inputs and/or outputs. In some cases, this may lead to a decrease in motivation and performance. For example, if employees believe that they are underpaid, they have a number of options. Cognitively, they may rationalise that they are not really working as hard as they thought they were; thus, they reduce the perceived value of their own inputs. Alternatively, they might convince themselves that co-employees are actually working harder than they thought they were. Behaviourally, employees can request a pay raise (increase their outcomes), or they can decrease their inputs by leaving a few minutes early each day, decreasing their effort, deciding not to complete an optional training program or finding excuses not to accept difficult assignments.

The significance of this aspect of motivation underscores the need for managers to talk regularly to their employees and monitor closely their perceptions of equity. This becomes even more important with increasing diversity in the workforce. In some cases, these conversations may uncover faulty comparison processes. For example, employees might misunderstand the value placed on various inputs, such as experience versus expertise, or quantity versus quality; or they might have unrealistic views of their own or others' performance. A recent survey reported that 75 per cent of respondents felt that their performance was better than that of 75 per cent of the population.

However, just as often these discussions uncover real inequities. For example, the hourly rate of an employee may not be keeping up with recent skill upgrades or increased job responsibilities. The act of identifying and correcting legitimate inequities generates enormous commitment and loyalty.

The important thing to keep in mind about equity and fairness is that we are dealing with perceptions. Remember the power of non-verbal messages in shaping perceptions, described in Chapter 2. Consequently, whether they are accurate or distorted, legitimate or ill founded, they are both accurate and legitimate in the mind of the perceiver until proved otherwise. A basic principle of social psychology states: 'That which is perceived as being real is real in its consequences.' Therefore, effective managers should constantly perform 'reality checks' on their employees' perceptions of equity, using such questions as: 'What criteria for promotions, pay increases and so on do you feel management should be placing more/less emphasis on?', 'Relative to others similar to you in this organisation, do you feel your job assignments, promotions and so on are appropriate?' and 'Why do you think Alice was recently promoted over John?'

6. Provide effective feedback

This leads us to the final element in an integrated motivation program: minimising the time-lag between behaviours and feedback, and providing accurate feedback. The last assessment question contains two parts. The first is: Are we getting the most out of our rewards and recognition by administering them on a timely basis as part of the feedback process?

Up to this point, it has been emphasised that employees need to understand and agree on performance standards; they should feel that management is working hard to help them reach their performance goals; they should feel that available internal and external rewards are personally attractive and attractive to their team; they should believe that recognition (positive and negative) is distributed fairly; and they should feel that these outcomes are administered primarily on the basis of performance. All these elements are necessary for an effective motivational program, but they alone are not sufficient. Recognition and rewards, even highly valued ones, lose their motivating potential unless they are given at the correct time. It is the timing of acknowledgment that lets employees know that the recognition is genuine and indicates which behaviours are being encouraged. Giving a reward at the wrong time can inadvertently send a mixed message and increase an undesirable behaviour.

Although timing is a critical aspect of feedback and recognition, it is frequently ignored in everyday management practice. The formal administrative apparatus of many organisations often delays for months the feedback on the consequences of employee performance. It is customary practice to restrict in-depth discussions of job performance to formally designated review interviews, which generally take place every six or 12 months. ('I'll have to review this matter officially later, so why do it twice?') Delay between performance and feedback dilutes the effectiveness of any rewards or discipline dispensed as a result of the evaluation process.

Content and intent of feedback

Before concluding this discussion of feedback, a note about the message itself is warranted. The second question related to feedback is: 'Do employees know where they stand in terms of current performance and long-term opportunities?' In addition to the timing of feedback, the content of that feedback and the motivation guiding the feedback process can have a powerful impact on the target individual's willingness and ability to improve. If the content is inaccurate, improvement is frustratingly difficult. If the message is masked in subterfuge and obscured by mixed signals, the credibility of the entire motivational system is undermined.

It is important to be honest and open with employees about their current performance and future opportunities. Avoid the time-worn excuses of 'We don't want to run the risk of discouraging marginal performers' and 'We shouldn't tell people their future promotion opportunities are in jeopardy because upper management doesn't like their style'; these excuses usually constitute efforts to cloak managers' feelings of discomfort under the guise of doing what is best for the employee.

When managers are reluctant to share unflattering or unhopeful feedback, it is often because they are unwilling to spend sufficient time with the individuals who are receiving the negative feedback to help them thoroughly understand their shortcomings, put them in perspective, consider options and explore possible remedies. It is sometimes easier to pass on an employee with a poor performance record or unrealistic expectations to the next supervisor than it is to confront the problem directly, provide honest and constructive feedback, and help the individual respond appropriately. (Incidentally, this is an example of the subtle unethical behaviour discussed in Chapter 1.) Many managers feel that supportive communication of negative performance is the management skill that is most difficult to master and therefore the one most highly prized.

Following the six steps of this integrated motivation program with employees from the moment of their starting in the organisation leads to a positive progression of empowerment (see also Chapter 8).

Figure 6.4 illustrates the progression of motivation management from induction, where the employee is strongly guided and seeks clarification from the manager and the organisation, to a stage at which motivation is largely self-managed. This connects with the levels of management involvement discussed in an earlier section of this chapter.

During induction it is important to maximise the performance potential of new employees by clarifying what their job and person specifications mean in relation to performance expectations. In the first instance, the manager will probably suggest the key result areas and spend most of the performance session clarifying what is expected of the employees. As employees become engaged in their work duties, performance management is likely to be based more on their need to gain recognition and confirmation that they are performing to expectations.

As employees increase in confidence, as a result of feedback from the manager that their performance is perceived as appropriate and producing the agreed results, it is important to encourage

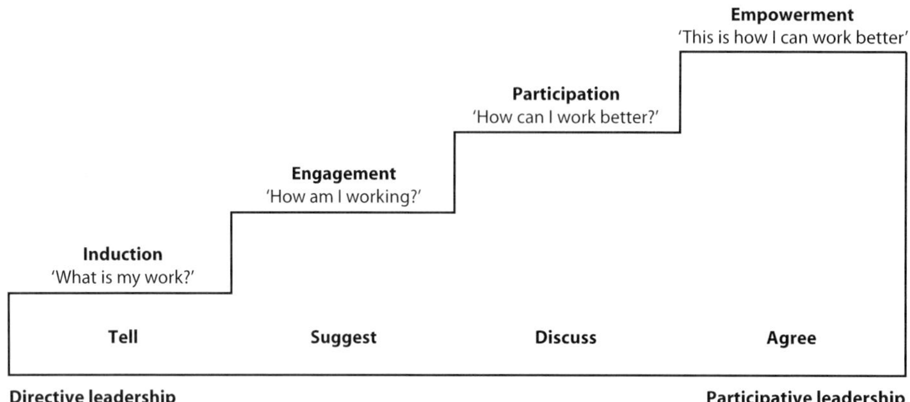

FIGURE 6.4 Four steps to motivational self-management

Source: Michael Correll, *Four Steps to Motivational Self-Management* (McPhee Andrewartha Pty Ltd, 1999). Reproduced with permission.

the employees to question how they might be more efficient and productive in their duties. At this point the manager or team may still be assisting the new employee to come up with possible areas for improvement. To reach the final stage of self-management, employees need to be challenged to consider how their work can be more efficient and productive, and they also need to be coming up with solutions and suggestions that result in performance gains. Employees at this stage will be empowered to negotiate with others to allow them to make changes that may affect other colleagues' work practices or may require investment in new technology or some form of training.

Cross-generational motivation

There is range of studies examining the nature of motivation and generations (Rodriguez, Green & Ree 2003; Ruch 2000; Zemke, Raines & Filipczak 2000). We are at a unique point in history where at least four generations of employees are in the workplace: (1) Traditionalists: those born before 1947; (2) Baby Boomers: those born between 1947 and 1964; (3) Generation X: those born between 1965 and 1980; and (4) Generation Y/Millennials: those born after 1980 (Lunsford 2010).

Managers now face working with groups of employees from these different generational groupings with markedly different needs, goals and motivational interests. Older employees are remaining in the workforce longer and later, while younger employees have different expectations, training needs and loyalties. The pressure for effective motivational management and change management has never been greater. As Table 6.5 shows, the contribution from each of these generational groups is quite different and, correspondingly, the management behaviours for enhancing motivation vary considerably.

When asked about the most important goal in their job (that is, what motivates them), employees across the generations on average identified self-fulfilment and 'feeling good about what I do'. This response was most pronounced for Traditionalists (45 per cent), many of whom are nearing retirement age and likely are at least content—if not satisfied—with their careers just as they are. The second most frequent response was a tie, with 'flexibility in my schedule' selected by 37 per cent of Baby Boomers and 'advancement in my career/profession/company' selected by 37 per cent of Generation Y/Millennials. It is interesting to note that 'flexibility' ranked high by Traditionalists and Generation Xers as well, although only 10 per cent of Generation Y/Millennials see it as their most important motivation. Surprisingly, 'more money/better benefits' did not turn up as a large motivator across the generations as a whole. It was ranked highest by Generation Xers, 16 per cent of whom selected it as their most important motivation (see Figure 6.5).

TABLE 6.5 Contribution and management

	TRADITIONALISTS	BABY BOOMERS	GENERATION X	MILLENNIAL
THESE EMPLOYEES WILL HELP YOU ...	• Help craft case studies to reinforce their perception of the good being done by the organisation and their role in it • Co-facilitate training sessions as SMEs • Be personally exposed to the external business realities that are necessitating change	• Look for easy to identify process improvements that will save time for individuals and the organisation • Play devil's advocate to test new ideas • Participate in scheduled formal 1:1 meetings with their leaders for feedback (in person, if possible)	• Help rewrite job descriptions to define desirable career options • Participate in coach-the-coach development • Define the organisation's employee value proposition • Help interview new-hire candidates • Participate in cross-functional task forces	• Jointly develop personalised learning paths with their leaders • Hone leadership skills by chairing community service projects • Use technology platforms to share knowledge gained in self-study exercises • Lead 'after action reviews' at the completion of key projects to formalise on-the-job learning
AND AVOID THESE COMMON MISTAKES ...	• Send them to training 'cold', without a pre-assessment to identify skill/ knowledge gaps	• Ask them to mentor a new hire without giving them training on how to mentor	• Assume they can innately lead both younger and older generations	• Provide constructive feedback without context

Source: S. Lunsford, 'Survey analysis: Employee motivation by generation factors', *Training Magazine*, April 2010, <www.TrainingMag.com>

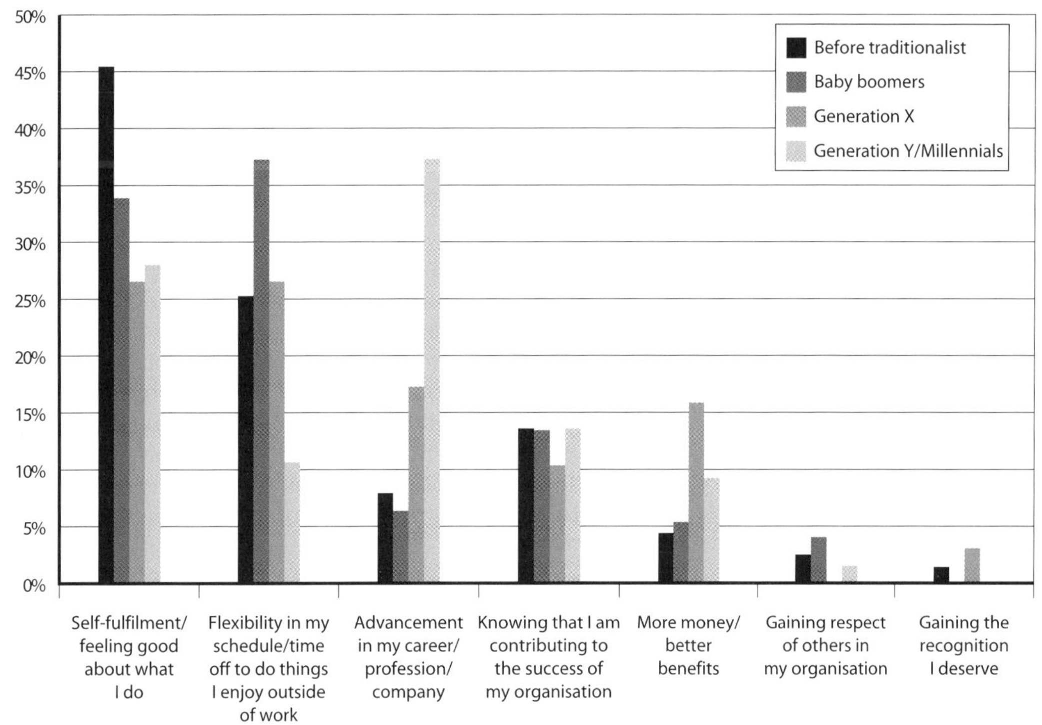

FIGURE 6.5 Most important goals by generation

Source: S. Lunsford, 'Survey analysis: Employee motivation by generation factors', *Training Magazine*, April 2010, <www.TrainingMag.com>

Barbuto (2006) produced similar findings. He examined five sources of work motivation (Motivation Sources Inventory) and found that internal goals were a higher motivator for Baby Boomers compared to Generation Xers, who preferred instrumental goals (specific external rewards such as pay) as a motivator. Lunsford's survey identified what the different generations expected from their managers in terms of assisting them to achieve the goals noted above (see Figure 6.6).

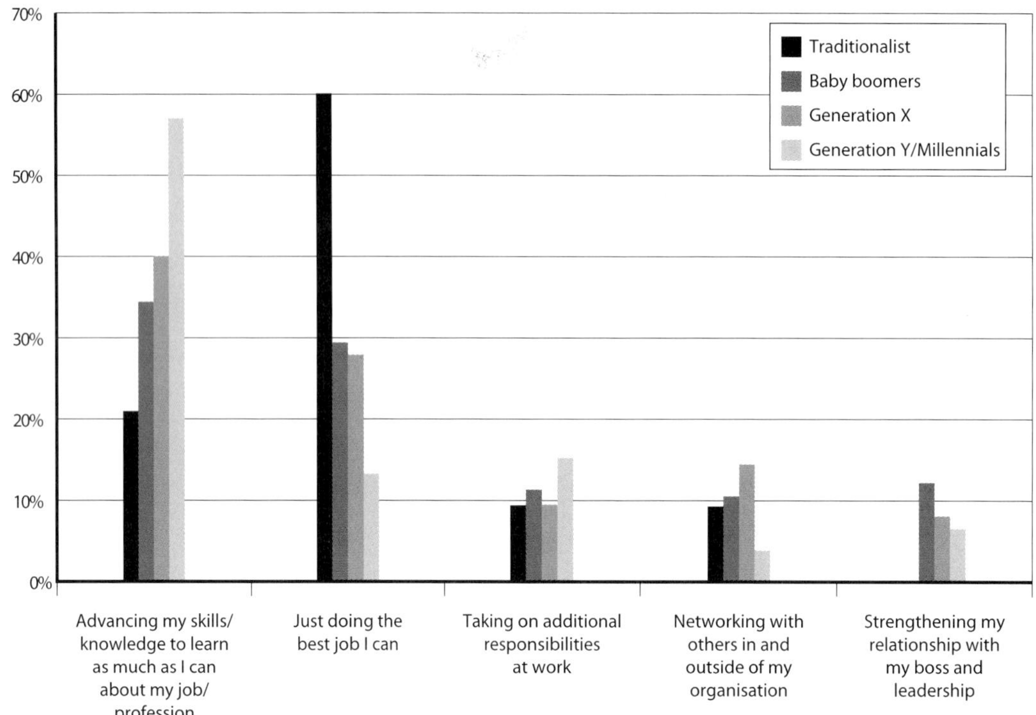

FIGURE 6.6 Methods for achieving goals by generation

Source: S. Lunsford, 'Survey analysis: Employee motivation by generation factors', *Training Magazine*, April 2010, <www.TrainingMag.com>

Jeffries and Hunte (2004) adapt Locke's motivational model used in this book to illustrate how generational differences affect motivation and explain how managers can develop attraction, motivation and retention strategies for various generations of workers. Pink (2009) identifies the motivational challenge for Generation Y/Millennials. They are used to instant feedback and recognition where doing something (games, texting) produces a result immediately. They are not prepared for the once-a-year performance feedback from an uncomfortable manager. Michaelson (2010) found that staff motivation to experience meaningful work crosses generations; older employees are looking for work that is fulfilling even if less financially rewarding, while younger employees are looking for a variety of meanings, giving them a more flexible attitude to work. Montana and Fordham (2008) suggest that Generation Y differ from the other generations, as they ranked 'Getting along well with others' as more important than other generations. They consider that this factor crosses motivation and maintenance needs. Gray (2008) suggests that Generation X employees are very mobile and move from one company to the next seeking financial advantage. This is caused by Baby Boomers refusing to retire, but also by the Millennials jumping ahead of the queue. There are three approaches that managers could take to handle this generational problem: (1) conduct detailed and generational-focused workforce analysis; (2) carefully assess the capability and management training needed by younger staff; and (3) provide cross-generational training and support for employees.

Culture and generations

When cultural diversity is combined with generational differences the motivational challenges increase even more. Di Cesare and Sadri (2003) use Hofstede's model (see Chapter 1) in conjunction with the motivational theories of Maslow, Herzberg and Vroom to contrast Japanese and American workers in terms of motivation. Using Maslow's hierarchy of needs, they have shown that individuals across the world are motivated by essentially the same fundamental human needs. However, improving themselves and their own positions drives American employees (an individualistic approach), whereas Japanese employees are motivated by the success of the group as a whole (a collectivistic approach). They conclude that self-actualisation is likely to mean different things to employees from individualistic cultures than it does to employees from collectivistic cultures. Taormina and Lao (2007) also included psychological factors in the cultural and generational mix as an added motivational complication.

These and many other studies on different generational motivations indicate that managers will be under increasing pressure to sophisticate their skills in regards to motivating their employees.

Motivating others is intricately connected to individual and organisational performance. The foundation for effective motivation is for the manager to operate within the framework of a comprehensive organisation-wide performance management process. Such a program effectively links the organisation's strategic and business plan with organisational and individual performance. It identifies goal expectations, monitors performance against those expectations, promotes excellent performance, provides regular recognition, manages work problems and poor performance, and provides a framework for people's contribution to the organisational goals.

An ideal performance management process is one that is introduced slowly over several years after a comprehensive review, involves extensive training and is matched to the organisation's culture. It includes the following features:

- It is provided for all staff.
- It involves four formal sessions in a 12-month cycle, including a planning session, two review sessions and a concluding session.
- It is a conjoint process between manager and staff member.
- It is a very simple and practical process.
- It focuses on a few agreed key result areas with specific performance indicators.
- It is integrated with the organisation's human resource management practices.
- It establishes accountability for all managers.
- It encourages recognition and professional development.
- It is reviewed and evaluated on a regular basis.

As with all the chapters of this book, the focus is on management skill development. This invariably intersects with, and requires, well-designed organisational systems. The best way to achieve successful performance is to have a strong organisational performance system that guides and integrates with the individual performance process. One excellent example of this integration is the Balanced Scorecard approach.

The Balanced Scorecard: Aligning organisational and individual performance

The Balance Scorecard (BSC) methodology (see Figure 6.7) was developed in 1992 by two Harvard economists, R. S. Kaplan and D. P. Norton. (See also Malina & Selto 2001; Ittner, Larcker & Meyer 2003; Niven 2003; and Irala 2007 for studies on the effectiveness and implementation of the BSC.)

The BSC aims to achieve a balance between the short-term and long-term objectives of the organisation and includes other indicators of performance than purely financial ones. Significantly, it aligns strategic organisational performance to departmental and individual performance, measures results regularly, and holds people accountable for their outcomes. The key business or result areas

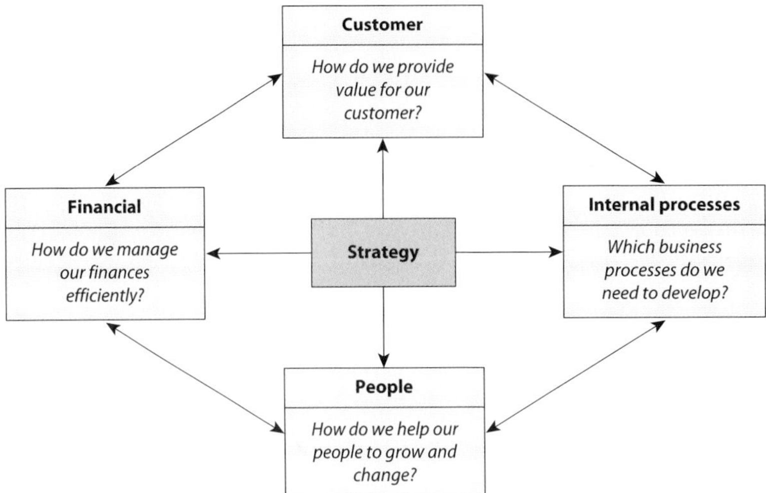

FIGURE 6.7 The Balanced Scorecard

Source: Based on 'The Balanced Scorecard—Measures that Drive Performance', R.S. Kaplan and D.P. Norton, *Harvard Business Review*, January-Febuary 1992.

(KRAs) cascade down the organisation to each level, and key performance targets (KPIs) following the SMART goals principles described earlier are set at the beginning and reviewed regularly.

As mentioned in Chapter 3, the consistent and close alignment between people and organisational goals is a feature of a healthy workplace.

Four Perspectives of the Balance Scorecard

There are four perspectives of the Balanced Scorecard that should represent the essential elements of any manager's performance considerations. They are: (1) customer focus, (2) internal processes, (3) people and growth, and (4) financial focus. Together they form a comprehensive way of measuring successful performance. They are considered here from a manager's point of view.

Customer perspective

This perspective places attention on how well our customers and key stakeholders are served. It requires people to be clear about precisely who are their customers, both internal and external. There are five core measures—namely, customer satisfaction, customer acquisition, market share (or account share), customer retention and customer profitability (profit contribution from customers). Customer value elements such as loyalty, which forms the burgeoning area of client management, may also be considered.

Internal business process perspective

To achieve the organisation's goals, a manager needs to understand and effectively orchestrate the internal support mechanisms that are required to sell the products or provide the services of the organisation. Particularly with new initiatives, the management of the IT system, communication processes, and supply and delivery systems, for example, need to be effectively incorporated into the manager's performance.

Learning and growth perspective

A good manager knows that good organisational performance requires a genuine investment in developing staff skills. This perspective encompasses three intangible assets: (1) human capital (knowledge, skills and capabilities), (2) information capital, and (3) organisation capital (team spirit, leadership and organisational culture). Paying attention to developing these assets in order to achieve excellent performance is often overlooked or underrated by managers.

Financial perspective

The most easily measurable perspective is the financial. Has the manager generated expected returns on invested time and money? Has the manager kept within budget? Is the manager financially prudent, and do his or her risks pay off? Managers need to monitor whether they are delivering their services in a cost-effective manner. Table 6.6 shows the common elements that make up each of these perspectives.

TABLE 6.6 Sample of elements in each of the BSC perspectives

CUSTOMER	INTERNAL PROCESSES	PEOPLE	FINANCE
• Customer retention • Customer complaints • Customer satisfaction • Response rates • Website hits • Customer numbers • Time/return per customer • Positive media stories • Referrals	• Effectiveness of systems and processes • Quality system • Standard operating procedures • Risk management • OH&S processes • Planning mechanisms • Performance management system • Hiring and firing processes	• Staff culture survey • Retention • Absenteeism • Staff development • Performance management usage • Ethics compliance • Diversity measures • Communication processes • Team development • Leadership • Selection	• Financial efficiency and effectiveness • Profit/costs per employee • Cash flow • Return on investment • Balanced budget

The Balanced Scorecard is a strategic organisational performance management and communication tool, as well as an individual performance management process. Using the BSC in this way provides a consistent and motivating performance process to guide managers in supervising their staff.

Managers can develop their own BSC and by sharing this with their staff can cascade the performance map down to each level below them. The planning session at the start of the year sets the SMART goals and expectations for each individual's BSC. Quarterly review sessions then support and measure progress against these targets. Using the skills identified in this chapter, managers ensure effective performance from their staff. A model for these review sessions is described below.

A performance review model

Effective managers use the formal performance evaluation process to discuss long-term trends in performance, solve problems inhibiting performance and set performance goals. But they do not expect these formal discussions to provide all the motivation. They understand the importance of immediate, spontaneous rewards, and therefore they also rely on brief, frequent, highly visible performance feedback. At least once a week they seek some opportunity to praise their employees' desirable work habits. Such mini-reviews are developmental.

The formal reviews also shape and reinforce good performance outcomes. A model for this kind of performance motivating system (Andrewartha 1995: 720) is as follows. During the meeting, the supervising manager or team leader might say to the employee:

- What have you liked about your work in the last month?
- What difficulties have you experienced?
- What I've liked about your work is …
- How are you performing in relation to the agreed goals and objectives?
- What has contributed to you exceeding/meeting/falling behind in achieving the agreed goals?

- What I've noticed is …
- What suggestions do you have:
  a. to continue to do well?
  b. to improve against the objectives?
  c. for training or other support?
  d. to change the targets or goals?
- In what ways have I helped you to achieve the goals?
- In what ways have I hindered you in achieving the goals?

This model ensures timeliness, can be very brief, and yet enables the manager to be sensitive to varying perceptions that can be explored in more detail. This performance-motivating process enables regular recognition and performance development on a natural, ongoing basis. This topic is explored further in Chapter 12, a companion website chapter, 'Conducting Interviews'.

Evaluating and managing work performance problems

Much of this chapter has focused on developing and managing good performance outcomes. Equally as important, but as the last step, is to manage poor performance. Within a positive and consistent organisational performance management culture, this can be as effective and successful as the approaches described in the earlier part of this chapter. At a personal level (except for a few bullies), no one enjoys addressing and managing poor performers. It is a significantly uncomfortable and unpleasant task. Yet it is the crucial test of good management skills. Good managers with strong emotional intelligence take the responsibility and make it successful. The process can be genuinely supportive and instructive for the poor performer. Too often the management of bad performance is avoided, managed superficially, denied for too long, engaged with too late, and handled incompetently. Further, this is very costly to the individual, the team and the organisation. One estimate suggests that poor management of poor performance can cost a minimum of $40 000 per individual (Andrewartha 2002). Moreover, the same review identified that most poor performers were relieved (even if the relief was delayed) to be properly and respectfully confronted with, and counselled about, their poor performance behaviours.

This section examines how to identify correctly the underlying causes of performance problems. A Chinese proverb states: 'For every hundred men hacking away at the leaves of a diseased tree, only one man stoops to inspect the roots.' A good manager needs to have a model to guide the inquiry process. Vroom (1964) (see also Steers, Porter & Bigley 1996) has summarised the determinants of task performance as follows:

Performance = Ability × Motivation (Effort)

where

Ability = Aptitude × Training × Resources
Motivation = Desire × Commitment

According to these formulas, performance is the product of ability (competence) multiplied by motivation, ability is the product of aptitude multiplied by training and resources, and motivation is the product of desire and commitment. The multiplication function in these formulas suggests that all elements are essential. For example, employees who have 100 per cent of the motivation, and 75 per cent of the ability, required to perform a task can perform at an above-average rate. However, if these individuals have only 10 per cent of the ability required, no amount of motivation will enable them to perform satisfactorily.

Ability

The definition of ability used here is broader than most. The focus is on the ability to perform, as well as on the performer's ability. Therefore, the definition includes a third, situational component:

adequate resources. Frequently, highly capable and well-trained people are placed in situations that inhibit job performance. Specifically, they are not given the resources (technical, personnel, political) to perform assigned tasks effectively.

Ability should be assessed during the job-matching process by screening applicants against the skill requirements of the job. If an applicant has minor gaps in skill aptitude but many other desirable characteristics, an intensive training program can be used to increase the applicant's qualifications to perform the job (Wanous 1980).

Aptitude

'Aptitude' refers to the natural skills and abilities a person brings to a job. These involve physical and mental capabilities but, for many people-oriented jobs, they also include personality characteristics such as those discussed in Chapters 2 and 3. Most people's inherent abilities can be enhanced by education and training. Indeed, much of what we call 'natural ability' in adults can be traced to previous skill-enhancement experiences, such as incorporating the social skills of parents or older siblings. Nevertheless, it is useful to consider training as a separate component of ability, since it represents an important mechanism for improving employee performance.

Motivation

This aspect of performance has been discussed in some detail earlier in this chapter. Very briefly motivation represents an employee's desire and commitment and is manifested as effort. Some people want to complete a task but are easily distracted or discouraged. They have high desire but low commitment. Others plod along with impressive persistence, but their work is uninspired. These people have high commitment but low desire.

Performance problems: Ability or motivation?

The first question that should be asked by the manager of a poor performer is whether the person's performance difficulties stem from lack of ability or lack of motivation. Managers need four pieces of information in order to answer this question (Michener, Fleishman & Vaske 1976):

- the difficulty of the tasks assigned to the individual
- the known ability of the employee
- the extent to which the employee seems to be trying to perform well
- the degree to which the employee's performance improves.

Low ability is generally associated with very difficult tasks, overall low individual ability, and evidence of strong effort and lack of improvement over time.

The answer to the question 'Is this an ability or a motivation problem?' has far-reaching ramifications for manager–employee relations. Research on this topic has shown that managers tend to apply more pressure to a person if they feel that the person is deliberately not performing up to expectations, rather than not performing effectively due to external, uncontrollable forces. Managers justify their choice of a forceful influence strategy on the grounds that the employee has a poor attitude, is hostile to authority or lacks dedication (Kipnis 1976). To label an employee before carefully assessing the entire situation is often a manager's first response. Unfortunately, if the manager's assessment is incorrect and poor performance is related to lack of ability rather than lack of motivation, the response of increased pressure will worsen the problem. If employees feel that management is insensitive to their problems—that they lack resources, adequate training or realistic time schedules—they may respond counterproductively to tactics aimed at increasing their effort. They are likely to develop a motivational problem; that is, their desire and commitment will decrease in response to management's insensitive, 'iron-fisted' actions. Seeing this response, management will feel that their original diagnosis has been confirmed and will use even stronger forms of influence to force compliance. The resulting vicious cycle is extremely difficult to break and underscores the high stakes involved in accurately evaluating performance problems. (See also Senge 1990; Manzoni & Barsoux 1998; and the conflict triangle described in Chapter 7.)

There are several reasons why a person's lack of ability might inhibit good performance. Ability may have been assessed inaccurately during the screening process prior to employment, the technical requirements of a job may have been radically upgraded, or a person who performed very well in one position may have been promoted into a higher-level position that is too demanding. (This so-called Peter Principle states that people are typically promoted one position above their level of competence.) In addition, human and material resource support may have been reduced because of organisational restructuring and change.

Three signs of lowered ability

Managers should be alert for individuals who show signs of a decrease in their ability. The following are three danger signals for managers (and employees) (Quick 1977: 41, 43):

1. *Taking refuge in a specialty.* Managers show signs of insufficient ability when they respond to situations not by managing but by retreating to their technical specialty. This often occurs when general managers who feel insecure address problems outside their area of expertise and experience.
2. *Focusing on past performance.* Another danger sign is when the individual measures their value to the organisation in terms of past performance or on the basis of former standards.
3. *Exaggerating aspects of the leadership role.* Managers who have lost confidence in their ability tend to be defensive. This often leads them to exaggerate one aspect of their managerial role. Such managers might delegate most of their responsibilities because they no longer feel competent to perform them well. Or they might become nuts-and-bolts administrators who scrutinise every detail to an extent far beyond its practical value.

Remedies for lack-of-ability problems

Five principal tools are available for overcoming poor performance problems due to lack of ability: resupply, retrain, refit, reassign and release. These tools are discussed in the order in which a manager should consider them.

First, a sensitive management counselling session is required. (See further details in the companion website chapter, Chapter 12, 'Conducting Interviews', and all the techniques in this book.) Once a manager has ascertained that lack of ability is the primary cause of someone's poor performance, a performance review should be undertaken to explore these options, beginning with resupplying and retraining. Unless the manager has overwhelming evidence that the problem stems from low aptitude, it is wise to assume initially that it is due to a lack of resources or training. This gives the employee the benefit of the doubt and reduces the likely defensive reaction to an assessment of inadequate aptitude.

The *resupply* option focuses on the support needs of the job, including personnel, budget and political clout. Asking 'Do you have what you need to perform this job satisfactorily?' allows an employee to express frustration related to inadequate support. As discussed earlier, Hallowell (2011) has suggested that poor job fit causes many performance problems in the workplace. A significant resupply approach is therefore to examine whether there is a good job fit. However, it should be noted that poorly performing employees typically blame external causes (Snyder, Stephen & Rosenfield 1978; Staw, McKechnie & Puffer 1983). Therefore, managers should explore the employee's complaints about lack of support in detail to determine their validity. But even if employees exaggerate their claims, starting a discussion of poor performance in this manner signals a willingness on the part of the manager to help employees solve the problem from their perspective rather than to find fault from the manager's perspective.

The next least threatening option is to *retrain*. Technology and organisations' requirements are changing so quickly that employees' skills can soon become obsolete. It has been said that 25-year-old engineering graduates will need to be re-educated eight times within their 40-year careers

(Lusterman 1985). Second, employees will typically fill a number of different positions throughout their careers, each position demanding different proficiencies. Finally, demographic changes in our society will lead to an increasingly older workforce (Bove 1987). In order for companies to remain competitive, more and more of them must retrain their older employees.

Training programs can take a variety of forms. For example, many firms are using computer technology more in education. This can involve interactive technical instruction and business games that simulate problems likely to be experienced by managers in the organisation.

In many cases, resupplying and retraining are insufficient remedies for poor performance. When this happens, the next step should be to explore *refitting* poor performers to their task assignments. While the employees remain on the job, the components of their work are analysed and different combinations of tasks and abilities that accomplish organisational objectives and provide meaningful and rewarding work are explored. For example, an assistant may be brought in to handle many of the technical details of a first-line supervisor's position, freeing up more time for the supervisor to focus on people development or to develop a long-term plan to present to upper management.

If a revised job description is unworkable or inadequate, the fourth alternative is to *reassign* the poor performer, either to a position of less responsibility or to one requiring less technical knowledge or interpersonal skills. For example, a medical specialist in a hospital who finds it increasingly difficult to keep abreast of new medical procedures but has demonstrated management skills might be shifted to a full-time administrative position.

The last option is to *release*. If retraining and creative redefinition of task assignments have not worked and if there are no opportunities for reassignment in the organisation, the manager should consider releasing the employee from the organisation. This option is generally constrained by enterprise agreements, company policies, seniority considerations and government regulations. Frequently, however, chronically poor performers are not released because management chooses to sidestep a potentially unpleasant task. Instead, the decision is made to set these individuals 'on the shelf', out of the mainstream of activities, where they cannot cause any problems. Even when this action is motivated by humanitarian concerns ('I don't think he could cope with being retrenched'), it often produces the opposite effect. Actions taken to protect an unproductive employee from the embarrassment of termination just substitute the humiliation of being ignored. It is also organisationally irresponsible.

Obviously, retrenchment is a drastic action that should not be taken lightly. However, the consequences for the unproductive individuals and their co-employees of allowing them to remain after the previous four actions have proved unsuccessful should be weighed carefully when considering this option. The impact of these options for employees is tremendous. Time and patience are needed to help the employee make the transition as smoothly as possible. This is important for the employee and the rest of the organisation. In this situation a comprehensive outplacement program and career transition is a valuable extra support that should be provided by the organisation.

Summary

The discussion on enhancing work performance and achieving a high-performing workplace focused on specific analytical and behavioural management skills within the context of the formal organisational performance management system. The topic of motivation was introduced by stressing the need for placing equal emphasis on concerns for satisfaction and performance. Motivation was considered in terms of motivational theory, and the impact of generational cohorts and diversity. The six elements of an integrated approach to motivation and enhanced performance were outlined.

The fundamental distinction between ability and motivation was discussed and several assessment questions for determining whether poor performance was due to insufficient ability were provided. A five-step process for handling ability problems (resupply, retrain, refit, reassign and release) was outlined.

The summary model shown in Figure 6.8 and its 'assessment' version in Figure 6.9 (on pages 310 and 312) encompass the discussions of ability and motivation.

The flow-chart depiction in Figure 6.8 of the factors affecting performance and satisfaction underscores the interdependence among the various components. Skilled managers incorporate all

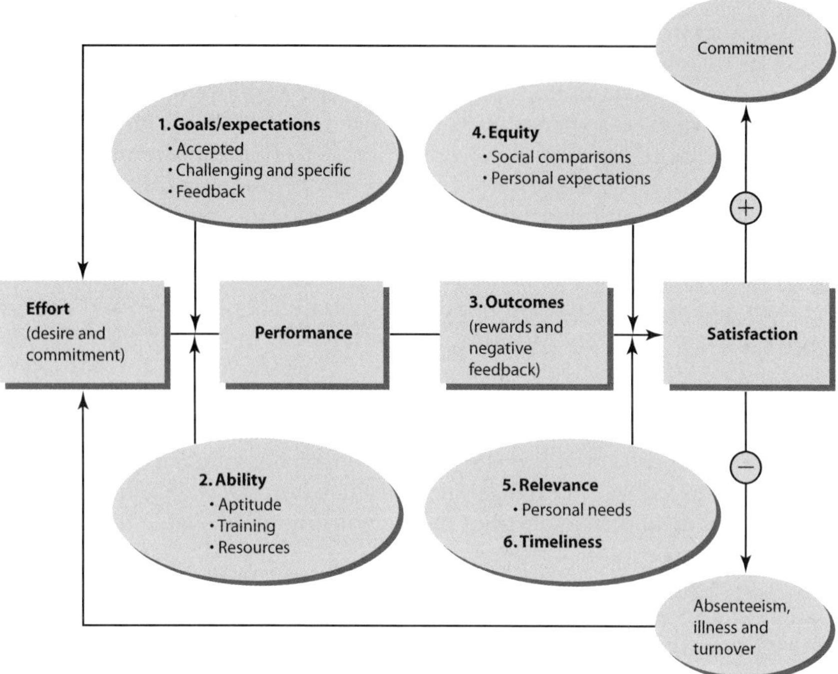

FIGURE 6.8 Model of motivation enhancement

components of this model into their motivational efforts rather than concentrating only on a favourite subset. There are no shortcuts to effective management. All elements of the motivation process must be included in a total, integrated program for improving performance and satisfaction.

Figure 6.8 shows *effort* as the beginning point for the model. Recall that motivation is manifested as work effort and that effort consists of desire and commitment. Motivated employees have the desire to initiate a task and the commitment to do their best. Whether their motivation is sustained over time depends on the remaining elements of the model, which are organised into two major segments:

- the effort → performance link
- the outcomes → satisfaction link.

These two crucial links in the motivational process can best be summarised as questions pondered by individuals asked to work harder, change their work routine or strive for a higher level of quality: first, 'If I put forth more effort, am I likely to be able to perform up to expectations?' and, second, 'Am I likely to find being a high performer personally rewarding?'

Beginning on the left side of Figure 6.8, it can be seen that the combination of goals and ability determines the extent to which effort is successfully transformed into performance. In the path–goal theory of leadership, the importance of fitting the right job to the right person and providing the necessary resources and training is emphasised. These factors must be combined with effective goal setting (understanding and accepting moderately difficult goals) if increased effort is to result in increased performance.

Proceeding to the outcomes' satisfaction segment of the model, the importance of perceived equity and reward relevance stands out. Individuals must believe that the rewards offered are appropriate, not only for their personal performance level but also in comparison to the rewards achieved by 'similar' others. The subjective value that individuals attach to incentives for performance reflects their personal relevance. Rewards with little personal value have low motivational potential. These subjective factors combine with the timeliness and accuracy of feedback to determine the overall motivational potential of rewards.

Based on their perceptions of outcomes, employees will experience varying degrees of satisfaction or dissatisfaction. Satisfaction creates a positive feedback loop, increasing the individual's motivation, as manifested by increased effort. Dissatisfaction, on the other hand, results in decreased effort and therefore lower performance and rewards. If uncorrected, this pattern may ultimately result in absenteeism, illness or turnover.

Behavioural guidelines

This discussion is organised around key assessment models and questions that serve as the basis for enhancing the following skills:

1. strengthening the motivational aspects of the work environment
2. properly evaluating work performance and motivation
3. initiating actions to enhance individuals' abilities.

Box 6.3 on page 291 summarises the process for improving performance. A decision-tree approach to evaluating performance problems is shown in Figure 6.9. The guidelines for thoroughly *investigating work performance* are:

1. Separate ability from motivational problems.
2. Agree on a program for improving performance.
3. Release a poor performer only as a last resort.

The key guidelines for *enhancing ability and creating a highly motivating work environment* are:

1. Clearly define an acceptable level of overall performance or specific behavioural objective:
   - Make sure the individual understands what is necessary to satisfy your expectations.
   - Formulate goals and expectations collaboratively, if possible.
   - Make goals as challenging and specific as possible.
2. Help remove all obstacles to reaching the objective:
   - Make sure the individual has adequate technical resources, personnel and political support.
   - If a lack of ability appears to be hindering performance, use the resupply, retrain, refit, reassign or release series of remedies.
3. Make recognition (positive and negative feedback) contingent on high performance or drawing nearer to the behavioural objective:
   - Carefully examine the behavioural consequences of your non-responses. (Ignoring a behaviour is rarely interpreted as a neutral response.)
   - Consistently provide specific negative feedback to individuals whose effort is below your expectations and their capabilities.
4. When negative feedback is required, treat it as a learning experience for the individual:
   - Specifically identify the problem and explain how it should be corrected.
   - Use the redirect and reflect guidelines in Box 6.3.
5. Transform acceptable into exceptional behaviours:
   - Recognise each level of improvement.
   - Use the 'reflect and recognise' guidelines in Box 6.3.
6. Use recognition and rewards that appeal to the individual:
   - Allow flexibility in individual selection of rewards and recognition.
   - Provide appealing external rewards as well as satisfying and rewarding work (intrinsic satisfaction).
   - To maintain relevance, do not overuse rewards.
7. Periodically check employees' perceptions regarding the equity of reward allocations:
   - Correct misperceptions related to equity comparisons.
8. Minimise the time lag between behaviours and feedback on performance, including the use of recognition or redirection (genuine spontaneous feedback is best):
   - Provide honest and accurate assessments of current performance and long-range opportunities.

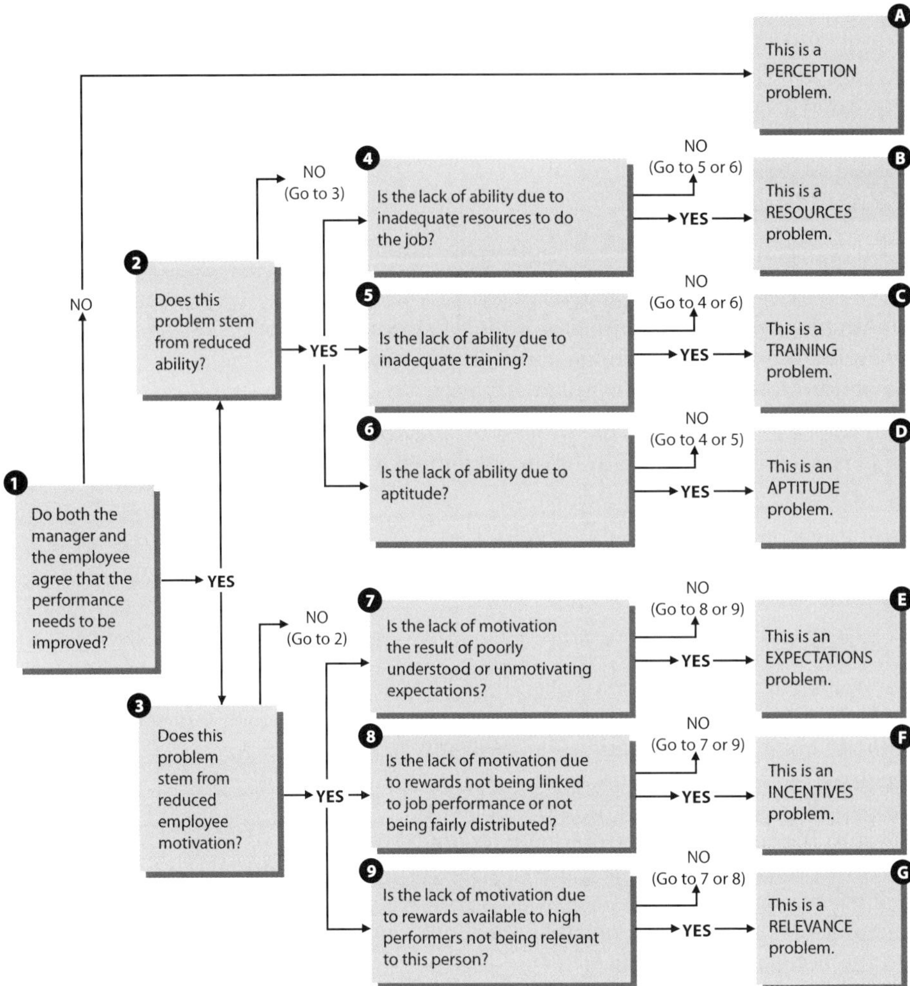

FIGURE 6.9 Performance assessment model

ANALYSIS

Skill analysis

Case study involving motivation problems

Hong Kong Avionics

Hong Kong Avionics (HKA) is a small research and development firm. Its primary mission is to perform basic research on, and development of, a new technology called 'Very Fast, Very Accurate' (VFVA). Founded four years ago by Steve Morgan, an electrical engineering lecturer and inventor of the technology, HKA is primarily funded by government contracts, although it plans to market VFVA technology and devices to non-governmental organisations within the year.

The government is very interested in VFVA, as it will enhance radar technology, robotics and a number of other important defence applications. HKA recently received the largest small-business contract ever awarded by the government to research and develop this technology. Phase I of the contract has just been completed, and the government has agreed to Phase II contracting as well.

The organisational chart of HKA is shown in Figure 6.10. Current staffing of HKA is 75, with roughly 88 per cent in engineering. The hierarchy of engineering titles and the requirements for each are listed in Table 6.7.

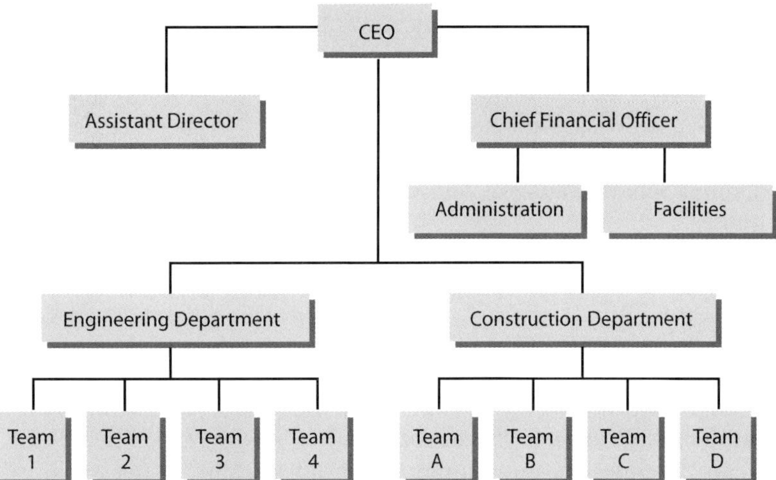

FIGURE 6.10 Hong Kong Avionics organisational chart

TABLE 6.7 Engineering titles and requirements

Title	Requirement
Member of technical staff	Undergraduate science degree
Senior member of technical staff	PhD, MSc with two years' industrial experience
	BSc with five years' industrial experience
Research engineer	PhD with two years' industrial experience
	BSc or MSc with seven years' industrial experience
Research scientist	PhD with appropriate experience in research
Senior research scientist	PhD with appropriate industrial and research experience

Heads of staff are supposedly appointed based on their knowledge of VFVA technology and their ability to manage people. In practice, the CEO of HKA hand-picks these people based on what some might call arbitrary guidelines: most of the staff leaders were or are the CEO's graduate students. There is no predetermined time-frame for advancement up the hierarchy. Salary increases are, however, directly related to performance review evaluations.

Working directly with the engineers are the technicians. These people generally have a technical degree, although some also have university degrees. They are trained on the job, and some have gone through a local community college's program on microtechnology fabrication. The technicians perform the mundane tasks of the engineering department: running tests, building circuit boards, manufacturing VFVA chips and so on. Most are full-time hourly employees.

The administrative staff consists of the staff head (with a degree from a good university), accountants, HR director, graphic artists, purchasing agent, project controller, technical writers/editors and personal assistants. Most of the administrative staff are women. All are hourly employees except the staff head, the HR director and the project controller. The graphic artists and technical writer/editor are part-time employees.

ANALYSIS

The facilities staff consists of the staff head and maintenance personnel. HKA is housed in three different buildings, and the primary responsibility of the facilities staff is to ensure that the facilities of each building are in good working order. Additionally, the facilities staff members are often called upon to remodel parts of the buildings as the number of staff continues to grow.

HKA anticipates a major recruiting campaign to enhance the overall staff. In particular, it is looking for more technicians and engineers. Prior to this recruiting campaign, however, the CEO of HKA hired an outside consultant to assess employee needs as well as the morale and overall effectiveness of the firm. The consultant has been observing HKA for about three weeks and has written some notes on her impressions and observations of the company.

Consultant's notes from observations of Hong Kong Avionics

- *Facilities.* HKA is housed in three different buildings. Two are converted houses and one is an old school building. Senior managers and engineers are in the school and others are scattered between the houses.
- *Meetings.* Weekly staff meetings in the main building are held to discuss objectives and to formulate and review key result areas.
- *Social interaction.* A core group of employees interact frequently on a social basis—for example, for after-work drinks. Members of the administration staff celebrate birthdays at work. The CEO occasionally attends.
- *Work allocation.* Engineers request various tasks from the support staff, which consists of technicians and administrative unit personnel. There is obviously some discretion used by the staff in assigning priorities to the work requests, based on rapport and desirability of the work.
- *Turnover.* The highest turnover is among administration personnel and technicians. Exit interviews indicate that they leave because of the company's crisis-management style, better opportunities for career advancement and security in overseas organisations, and overall frustration with HKA's 'pecking order'. Engineers with the most responsibility and authority tend to leave.
- *Salary and benefits.* In general, wages at HKA are not high by national standards. A small group of scientists and engineers do make substantial salaries and have very attractive benefits packages, including share options. Salaries and benefits for new engineers tend to be linked to the perceived level of their expertise.
- *Offices and facilities.* Only HKA's CEO, assistant director and chief financial officer have their own offices. Engineers are grouped together in 'open space areas' by project assignment. There is very little privacy in these work areas and the noise from the shared printer is distracting. The head of administration shares an area with the personnel director, the facilities head and the project controller. One to three personal assistants per building are located in or near the reception areas. The large building has an employee lounge with three vending machines. There is also a coffee and tea station. The smaller buildings have only a drinks machine in the reception area.

Consultant's interviews with employees

After making these observations, the consultant requested interviews with a cross-section of the staff for the purpose of developing a survey to be taken of all employees. Presented on the following pages are excerpts from those interviews.

Pat Klee, senior member of technical staff

Consultant: What is it about HKA that gives you the most satisfaction?

Pat: I really enjoy the work. I mean, I've always liked to do research, and working on VFVA is an incredible opportunity. Just getting to work with Steve [HKA's CEO and VFVA's inventor] again is exciting. I was his graduate student about six years ago, you know. He really likes to work closely with his people—perhaps sometimes too closely. There have been times when I could have done with a little less supervision.

Consultant: What's the least satisfying aspect of your work?

Pat: Probably the fact that I'm never quite sure that we'll be funded next month, given the defence budget problems and the tentativeness of our research. I've got a family to consider, and this place isn't the most stable in terms of its financial situation. Maybe it'll change once we get more into commercial production. Who knows?

Consultant: You've offered some general positives and negatives about HKA. Can you be more specific about day-to-day dealings? What's good and bad about working here on a daily basis?

Pat: You're sure this isn't going to get back to anyone? Okay. Well, in general I'm not satisfied with the fact that too often we end up changing horses in the middle of the stream, if you know what I mean. In the past seven months, three of my engineers and four of my techs have been pulled off my project and put on to projects whose deadlines were nearer than mine. Now I'm faced with a deadline and I'm supposed to be getting more staff. But I'll have to spend so much time briefing them that it might make more sense for me just to finish the project myself. On the other hand, Steve keeps telling me that we have to be concerned with HKA's overall goals, not just our individual concerns—you know, we have to be 'team players', 'good members of the family'. It's kind of hard to deal with that, though, when deadlines are bearing down and you know your head's on the block, team player or not. But if you go along with this kind of stuff and don't complain, the higher-ups treat you well. Still, it seems to me there's got to be a better way to manage these projects.

Consultant: What are the positive aspects of your daily work?

Pat: Well, the people here are all great to work with. They know their stuff or can learn quickly. I tend to be a social person and I really like socialising with these people. I've got some good friends here, which helps get my work orders filled quickly, if you know what I mean.

Sarah Wu, member of the technical staff

Consultant: You said earlier that Steve was your adviser for your Masters degree. So, you've known him a long time?

Sarah: Yes, that's right. I've known Steve for about eight years. I had him for a few undergraduate classes; then he was my adviser for my two-year Masters program, and now I've worked at HKA for two years.

Consultant: It seems as if you enjoy working with Steve.

Sarah: Oh, yeah. But I really don't get to work directly with him anymore. I'll see him at meetings and such, but that's about it.

Consultant: So, he's not your immediate supervisor?

Sarah: No, but for the amount of time I spend with my supervisor, Steve might as well be. My boss and I meet maybe once every three weeks for about an hour to see if all is well. And that's it. The rest of the time, I'm on my own. I used to talk to Steve when I had questions, but he's so busy now that it's hard to see him—you need to make an appointment a few days in advance.

Consultant: Do you think your supervisor treats all his staff this way?

Sarah: To be honest, I have heard some complaints. In fact, about six months ago the situation was so bad that some other people and I had a meeting with him. He promised that he would be more available to us and he was, for about a month. Then we got involved in a new proposal, so he made himself scarce again. So nothing's really changed. We're coming up to finalising the proposal now and it's important that I see him, ask him questions. The last few drafts I've submitted to him, he's returned, rewritten in his own way, and with no explanation of the changes. Sometimes I think he treats me like somebody who doesn't know anything, as if I had no training whatsoever. I realise his neck is on the line with this project, but sometimes it seems that he uses being busy to avoid talking to me.

Chris Chen, research scientist

Consultant: What kind of characteristics should a person have if they want to work as a research scientist at HKA?

Chris: Well, certainly technical knowledge is important. When I've interviewed recent uni students for entry-level positions, I am always concerned with their ability. I like to see straight-As, if possible. But for experienced research scientists, technical knowledge shows up in their publication records, mostly. So, I'll read their papers. I also think a research scientist has to be highly self-motivated, not look to others for praise and such. Particularly here. If you want someone to tell you you've done a good job, you'll be waiting a long time. It's not clear to me that research scientists really get the support we need from the rest of the staff here. Work orders are often lost or put off for one reason or another. Senior members seem to get more techs than scientists do, and they certainly get more attention from Steve. The rumour is that these guys also get higher raises than the scientists; allegedly, this is to keep pay at an equitable rate—you know, they're supposedly more valuable to the company. Of course, everybody knows that most of the senior members are Steve's old graduate students, and so he takes care of them really well. One of the things that really galls me is that I need to keep up my publication record to maintain my career options. But publishing is frowned on here because it takes time away from your work. I've even been told that my work can't be published because of proprietary rights or that the defence department considers the information classified. However, if somebody important is working with me and needs the publication, then it's full steam ahead.

Consultant: You sound pretty disgruntled with your work.

Chris: It's not my work so much. I'm really very happy doing this work—it's cutting edge, after all. The problem is that I'm never quite sure where the work is going. I do my part of a project, and unless I go out of my way to talk to other people I never find out the final results of the total project. That's just something you learn to live with around here—being part of a system that's not particularly open.

Meg Conroy, assistant to the head of administration

Consultant: You've been here only a short time, is that correct?

Meg: That's right—just a little over a year.

Consultant: Why did you take the job?

Meg: Well, I was in my last year of uni and was looking for a job, like most uni students. A friend was already working for HKA and found out there was an opening. So, I applied.

Consultant: Do you like your job?

Meg: It has a lot to offer. I get paid pretty well for what I'm doing. And I'm learning a lot. I just wish the company would let me take some courses in administration, like accounting. The auditors ask some pretty tough questions. Steve says we should hire that expertise, but I'd still be responsible for supervising the people.

Consultant: Is there any particular aspect of your job that you really find satisfying?

Meg: I guess I like the fact that I get to do a lot of different tasks, so things don't get so boring. I would hate to have to do the same thing, day in and day out. A lot of times I go to the library to do research on different things, and that's nice because it gets me out of the office.

Consultant: What don't you like about your job?

Meg: Well, I often get the feeling that administration isn't taken seriously. You know, the engineers could get along without us quite nicely, or so they seem to think. The whole structure of the department shows that we're the catch-all department: if you don't fit anywhere else, they put you in here. Sometimes it's hard to work with the engineers because they treat you like you don't know anything, and they always want things to be done their way. Clearly, the engineers get the money and consideration and yet, well, we do contribute quite a lot to the whole team, as Steve would say. But words of praise just aren't as impressive as actions. Sure, we get our birthday parties, but that still seems to be a little patronising. We rarely get to see what's going on in the research area. I've asked a number of engineers specific questions and they just kind of look at me with a blank stare and give me some really simplified answer. It seems to me if you want to build a team, like the CEO says, you can't treat administration like a bad relation.

Paul Ginelli, technician

Consultant: I gather you've just been through your performance review. How did it go?

Paul: Like I expected. No surprises.

Consultant: Do you find these reviews useful?

Paul: Sure. I get to find out what he thinks of my work.

Consultant: Is that all?

Paul: Well, I suppose it's a nice opportunity to understand what my supervisor wants. Sometimes he's not so clear during the rest of the year. I suppose he's been given specific goals from higher-ups before he talks with me, so he's clear and then I'm clear.

Consultant: Do you like what you're doing?

Paul: Oh yeah. The best part is that I'm not in the main building and so I don't have to put up with the 'important' people, you know? I've heard from other techs that those guys can be a real pain—trying to be nice and all, but really just being a bother. I mean, how can you get your stuff done when the CEO's looking over your shoulder all the time? On the other hand, if the CEO knows your name, I suppose that's a good thing when it comes to raises and promotions. But my boss sticks up for his techs; we get a fair deal from him.

Consultant: Do you think you'll be able to get ahead at HKA?

Paul: Get ahead? You mean become an engineer or something? No, and I really don't want to do that. Everyone around here keeps pushing me to move up. I'm afraid to tell people how I really feel for fear they'll decide I don't fit into this high-tech environment. I don't want to be the 'black sheep of the family'. I like where I am, and if the raises keep coming, I'll keep liking it. One of my kids is starting uni next year and I need the money to help her out. I get a lot of overtime, particularly when contract deadlines are near. I suppose the rush towards the end of contracts gives some people big headaches, but I don't mind. The work is pretty slow otherwise, and so at least I'm working all the time and then some. But my family wishes my schedule was more predictable.

Consultant: Do you think you'll continue working for HKA?

Paul: I'm not sure. Let's just say that my ratings on the performance review were good and I expect to see an improvement in my pay. I'll stay for that.

Sandra Milton, technician

Consultant: In general, what are your feelings about the work you do for HKA?

Sandra: Well, I feel my work is quite good, but I also feel that I perform rather boring, tedious tasks. From what my supervisor says, the kinds of things I do are what electrical engineering students do in their last year of classes. I gather their final project is to make a circuit board, and that's what I do, day in and day out.

Consultant: What is it that you would like to do?

Sandra: Well, it would be nice to be able to offer some input into some of the designs of these boards. I know I don't have a PhD or anything, but I do have lots of experience. But because I'm a tech, the engineers don't really feel I've got much to offer, even though I build the boards and can tell from the design which one will do what the designer wants it to do. I also would like to maybe supervise other technicians in my department. You know, some kind of advancement would be nice. As it is, lots of techs ask me how to do things and of course I help, but then they get the credit. Around here, you have to have a piece of paper that says you're educated before they let you officially help other people.

DISCUSSION QUESTIONS

1. *Using the behavioural guidelines, the recognition grid and Figure 6.7 as aids, what are the strengths and weaknesses of HKA from a motivational perspective?*
2. *What are the high-priority action items you would include in a consulting report to Steve Morgan, CEO of HKA? Focus on specific actions that he could initiate that would use the abilities of the staff more effectively and foster a more motivating work environment.*

Skill practice

Exercises for assessing work performance problems

Proper assessment is a critical aspect of effective motivation management. Often managers become frustrated because they do not understand the causes of observed performance problems. They might experiment with various 'cures', but the inefficiency of this trial-and-error process often increases their frustration level. In addition, the accompanying misunderstanding adds extra strain to the manager–employee relationship. This generally makes the performance problem even more pronounced, which in turn prompts the manager to resort to more drastic responses, and a vicious downward spiral ensues.

The performance assessment model in Figure 6.9 offers a systematic way for managers and employees to pinpoint collaboratively the causes of dissatisfaction and performance problems. It assumes that employees will work hard and be good performers if the work environment encourages these actions. Consequently, rather than allowing managers to jump to conclusions about poor performance stemming from deficiencies in personality traits or a bad attitude, this process helps managers to focus their attention on improving the selection, job design, performance evaluation and reward-allocation systems. In this manner, the specific steps necessary to accomplish work goals and management's expectations are examined to pinpoint why an employee's performance is falling short.

The manager and low-performing employee should follow the logical discovery process in the model, step by step. They should begin by examining current perceptions of performance as well as the understanding of performance expectations and then proceed through the model until the performance problems have been identified. The model focuses on seven of these problems.

1. *Perception problem.* 'Do you agree your performance is below expectations?' A perception problem suggests that the manager and employee have different views of the employee's current performance level. Unless this disagreement is resolved, it is futile to continue the assessment process. The entire problem-solving process is based on the premise that both parties recognise the existence of a problem and are interested in solving it. If agreement does not exist, the manager should focus on resolving the discrepancy in perceptions, including clarifying current expectations (Problem E).
2. *Resources problem.* 'Do you have the resources necessary to do the job well?' Ability has three components, and these should be explored in the order shown in the model. This order encourages collaboration and reduces an employee's defensive reactions. Poor performance may stem from a lack of resource support. Resources include material and human resources support, as well as cooperation from interdependent workgroups.
3. *Training problem.* 'Is a lack of training interfering with your job performance?' Individuals may be asked to perform tasks that exceed their current skill or knowledge level. Typically, this problem can be overcome through additional training or education.
4. *Aptitude problem.* 'Do you feel this is the right job/blend of work assignments for you?' This is the most difficult of the three ability problems to resolve because it is the most basic. If the resupply (providing additional resources) and retraining solutions have been explored without success, then more drastic measures may be required. These include refitting the person's current job requirements, reassigning them to another position or, finally, releasing the employee from the organisation.
5. *Expectations problem.* 'What are your performance expectations for this position? What do you think my expectations are?' This problem results from poor communication about job goals or job requirements. In some cases, the stated goals may be different from the desired goals. In other words, the employee is working towards one goal while the supervisor desires another. This often occurs when employees are not sufficiently involved in the goal- or standard-setting process. When this results in unrealistic, imposed expectations, motivation suffers.

6. *Incentive problem.* 'Do you believe rewards are linked to your performance in this position?' Either the individual does not believe that 'performance makes a difference', or insufficient performance feedback and recognition have been given. The manager should also ask, 'Do you feel rewards are being distributed equitably?' This provides an opportunity to discuss employees' criteria for judging fairness. Often, unrealistic standards are being used.
7. *Relevance problem.* 'Are the performance incentives attractive to you?' Relevance refers to the importance an individual attaches to available rewards. Often, the incentives offered to encourage high performance are not highly valued by a particular individual. Managers need to be creative in generating a broad range of rewards and flexible in allowing employees to choose among rewards.

Assignment option 1

Read the case 'Jeremy Fernandez' and privately use the assessment model (see Figure 6.9) to pinpoint plausible performance problems. Next, discuss in small groups your individual assessments and list specific questions you would ask Jeremy to identify, accurately, from his point of view, the obstacles to his high performance. Finally, brainstorm ideas for plausible solutions. Prepare to represent your group in role-playing a problem-solving interview with Jeremy.

Jeremy Fernandez

Jeremy Fernandez joined your architectural firm two years ago as a draftsperson. He is 35 years old and has been a draftsperson since graduating from a two-year TAFE course straight after high school. He is married and has four children. He has worked for four architectural firms in 16 years.

Jeremy came with mediocre recommendations from his previous employer, but you hired him anyway because you needed help desperately. Your firm's workload has been extremely high due to a local construction boom. The result is that a lot of the practices that contribute to a supportive, well-managed work environment have been overlooked. For instance, you cannot remember the last time you conducted a formal performance review or did any career counselling. And the tradition of closing the office early on Friday for a social hour was dropped long ago.

Unfortunately, the tension in the office runs pretty high some days due to unbearable time pressures and the lack of adequate staff. Night and weekend work has become the norm rather than the exception.

Overall, you have been pleasantly surprised by Jeremy's performance. Until recently, he worked hard and consistently produced high-quality work. Also, he frequently volunteered for special projects, made lots of suggestions for improving the work environment, and has demonstrated an in-depth practical knowledge of architecture and the construction business. However, during the past few months he has definitely slackened off. He does not seem as excited about his work, and several times you have found him daydreaming at his desk. In addition, he has been in several heated arguments with architects about the specifications and proper design procedures for recent projects.

After one of these disagreements, you overheard Jeremy complaining to a colleague: 'No one around here respects my opinion. I'm just a lowly draftsperson. I know as much as these hotshot architects, but because I don't have the degree they ignore my input and I'm stuck doing the boring work. And I must be the lowest-paid person in this firm.'

In response to a question from a fellow employee about why he did not pursue a degree in architecture, Jeremy said: 'Do you have any idea how hard it is to put bread on the table, pay a mortgage, work overtime, be a reasonably good father and husband, plus study part-time? Come on, be realistic!'

Assignment option 2

Administer the following work performance assessment survey to several employees. Using the scoring key at the end of the chapter, categorise the obstacles to high performance and satisfaction reported by the respondents. Then get together in small groups, with each group assuming the role of a management taskforce charged with the responsibility of analysing this employee survey data. Discuss the patterns in the data, as well as possible remedies for these problems, using the behavioural guidelines and motivational models in the chapter as guides. Prepare a report on your analysis and recommendations for specific changes.

Work performance assessment

Respond to the following statements, based on your current work situation.

Rating scale

1 Strongly disagree
2 Disagree
3 Neutral
4 Agree
5 Strongly agree

______ 1. My supervisor and I agree on the quality of my performance.
______ 2. I feel I have adequate training to perform my current job assignments.
______ 3. I believe that my native skills and abilities are matched very well with my job responsibilities.
______ 4. I believe that I have adequate resources and supplies to do my job well.
______ 5. I understand my boss's expectations and generally feel they are realistic.
______ 6. I believe that rewards are distributed fairly, on the basis of performance.
______ 7. The rewards and opportunities available to me if I perform well are attractive to me personally.
______ 8. My supervisor indicates that I am not performing as well as I should, but I disagree.
______ 9. I could do a much better job if I had more training.
______ 10. I believe that my job is too difficult for my ability level.
______ 11. I believe that my job performance is hindered by a lack of supplies and resources.
______ 12. I believe my boss's expectations are unclear and unrealistic.
______ 13. I believe my boss plays favourites in allocating rewards.
______ 14. I do not find the rewards and opportunities available to high performers very appealing.

The scoring key is on page 324.

Exercise for changing unacceptable behaviours

PRACTICE

One of the most challenging aspects of management is transforming inappropriate behaviours into appropriate behaviours. Managers commonly take insufficient action to transform negative actions into positive ones. Some of these insufficient responses include: (1) assuming that ignoring an employee's shortcomings will make them go away; (2) praising positive aspects of an individual's performance in the hope that this will encourage the individual to rechannel unproductive energies; (3) discussing problems in vague, general terms in a group meeting, in the hope that the unproductive person will 'take the hint' and change; and (4) getting upset with an individual and demanding that he or she 'shapes up'.

Assignment

Assume the role of Andrea Tate in the following case. After reading the case, review the applicable behavioural guidelines shown on the observer's feedback form at the end of the chapter (p. 325). In small groups, discuss how you would resolve this problem. Prepare to role-play your discussion with Kevin Mason. After the discussion, assigned observers will provide feedback on your performance, using the observer's form as a guide. Unless you are assigned to play Kevin's role, do not read the role instructions for him prior to the interview.

Andrea Tate, manager

Kevin has been a member of your staff for only three months. You do not know much about him other than that he is a single parent who has recently returned to work. He is often 10–20 minutes late for work in the morning. You are the manager of a very hectic customer relations office for a gas company. The phones start ringing promptly at eight o'clock. When he is late for work, you have to answer his phone and this interrupts your work schedule. This morning, you are particularly annoyed. He is 25 minutes late and the phones are ringing like crazy. Because you have been forced to answer them, it will be difficult for you to complete an important assignment by the noon deadline. You are getting more upset by the minute.

While you are in the middle of a particularly unpleasant phone conversation with an irate customer, you look out your window and see Kevin bounding up the steps to the building. You think to yourself, 'This is ridiculous. I've got to put a stop to his lateness. Maybe I should just threaten to fire him unless he shapes up.' On further reflection, you realise that would be impractical, especially during this period. Given the rumours about a possible hiring freeze, you know it may be difficult to refill any vacancies.

Also, Kevin is actually a pretty good employee when he is there. He is conscientious and has a real knack with cranky callers. Unfortunately, it has taken him much longer than expected to learn the computer program for retrieving information on customer accounts. He frequently has to put callers on hold while he asks for help. These interruptions have tended to increase an already tense relationship with the rest of the office staff. He has had some difficulty fitting in socially; the others are much younger and have worked together for several years. Kevin is the first new hire in a long time, so the others are not used to breaking someone in. Three of your staff have complained to you about Kevin's constant interruptions. They feel their productivity is going down as a result. And besides, he seems to expect them to drop whatever they are doing every time he has a question. They had expected their workload to be lighter when a new person was hired, but now they are having second thoughts. (In the past, you have had enough time to train new recruits, but your boss has had you tied up on a major project for almost a year.)

Kevin enters the office, obviously flustered and dishevelled. He has 'I'm sorry' written all over his face. You motion for him to pick up the blinking phone line and then scribble a note on a pad while you complete your call: 'See me in my office at 12 sharp!' It's time you got to the bottom of Kevin's disruptive influence on an otherwise smooth-flowing operation.

Kevin Mason, staff member

Boy, what a morning! Your babysitter's father died during the night and she called you from the airport at 6.30 am, saying she would be out of town for three or four days. You tried three usually available back-ups before you finally found someone who could take Emily, your three-year-old. Then Sharon went through five outfits before she was satisfied that she had just the right look for her first school photo. It's a miracle that Peter, your eldest, was able to pull himself out of bed after getting only five hours of sleep. On top of football and drama, he has now joined the chess team, and they had their first tournament last night. Why did it have to fall on the night before his physics exam? This morning you wished you had his knack for juggling so many activities. By the time you got the kids delivered, you were already ten minutes behind schedule. Then there was this accident on the highway that slowed traffic to a crawl.

As you finally pull off the exit ramp, you notice you are almost 20 minutes late for work. 'My kingdom for a mobile phone!' you groan. 'Although by now I probably couldn't get an open line into the office, anyway.' As you desperately scan the side streets for a parking space, you begin to panic. 'How am I going to explain this to Andrea? She'll be furious. I'm sure she's upset about my chronic lateness. On top of that, she's obviously disappointed with my lack of computer skills and I'm sure the other staff complain to her about having to train a newcomer.' You're sure that one of the reasons you got the job was that you had completed a computer class at the local TAFE. Unfortunately, there hadn't been much carryover to the incredibly complex computer program you use at work. (It seems to defy every convention of logic.)

'What am I going to tell her about my being late for work so often?' Unfortunately, there is no easy answer. 'Maybe it will get better as the kids and I get used to this new routine. It's just very difficult to get the kids to the bus stop and the sitter, travel 20 minutes and arrive precisely at 8.00 am. I wonder if she would allow me to come in at 8.30 and take only a half-hour lunch? Staying late wouldn't work because they close down the computers at 5.00, unless there was some paperwork I could do for half an hour.'

And then what about the problems with the computer and the other employees? 'Sooner or later she's going to get on my case about those things. Is it my fault I don't think like a computer? Some people might be able to sit down and figure this program out in a couple of hours, but not me. So is that my fault or should someone be giving me more training? I wish the others weren't so cliquish and unwilling to help me out. I wonder why that's the case? It's like they're afraid I'll become as good as they are if they share their experience with me. I wish Andrea had more time to help me learn the ropes, but she seems to always be in meetings.'

'Well, I'm probably going to catch it this morning. I've never been this late. Maybe I'll be back home full-time sooner than I expected.'

Skill application

Suggested assignments

1. Identify a situation in which you have some responsibility for another person whose performance is significantly below your expectation. Using the work performance assessment survey included in the skill practice section, collect information on the person's perceptions of the situation. Use the assessment model (decision tree) on page 312 to specifically identify the perceived performance problems. Compare these results with your own views of the situation. Conduct an interview with the person and discuss the results, highlighting areas of disagreement. Based on this discussion, formulate a plan of action that both parties accept. If inadequate ability is a problem, follow the resupply, retrain, refill, reassign and release remedial steps. If insufficient effort is a problem, use the steps for recognising, reflecting and redirecting, discussed in the chapter, as a resource for this discussion. Implement this plan for a period of time and then report on the results.
2. Focus on some aspect of your own work in which you feel your performance is below your (or others') expectations. Using the LETS profile from Chapter 2, identify the specific dimensions you consider are obstacles to improved performance. Then formulate a plan for overcoming these obstacles. What steps could you take to alter your style in those areas? Discuss your plan with the people affected by it and arrive at a set of actions all parties accept. Implement the plan for a period of time and report on your results. How successful were you in making the changes? Did your performance improve as expected? Based on this experience, identify other aspects of your work that you could improve in a similar fashion.
3. Identify four or five situations in which you are typically provoked to use negative behaviour. These might involve friends, family members or work associates. Examine these situations and identify one where negative feedback is not working. Using the guidelines for recognising, reflecting and redirecting, design a specific plan for shaping the other person's behaviours so that you can begin rewarding positive actions. Report on your results. Based on this experience, consider how you might be able to use this strategy in similar situations.
4. Using the six-step model for creating a motivating work environment (see Box 6.1), design a specific plan for managing a new relationship (for example, a new employee) or a new phase in an old relationship (for example, friend, family member or employee about to begin work on a new project). Write down specific directions for yourself for implementing each of the six steps. Discuss your plan with this individual and ask for suggestions for improvement. Make sure your perceptions of the key aspects of the plan are consistent with theirs. Implement your plan for a period of time and then report on the consequences. Based on this experience, identify changes that would be appropriate in similar settings.

Application plan and evaluation

The intent of this exercise is to help you apply this cluster of skills in a real-life, out-of-class setting. Now that you have become familiar with the behavioural guidelines that form the basis of effective skill performance, you will improve most by trying out those guidelines in an everyday context. Unlike a classroom activity, in which feedback is immediate and others can assist you with their evaluations, this skill application activity is one you must accomplish and evaluate on your own. There are two parts to this activity. Part 1 helps to prepare you to apply the skill. Part 2 helps you to evaluate and improve on your experience. Be sure to write down answers to each item.

Part 1: Planning

1. Write down the two or three aspects of this skill that are most important to you. These may be areas of weakness, areas you most want to improve, or areas that are most salient to a problem you face right now. Identify the specific aspects of this skill that you want to apply.
2. Now identify the setting or the situation in which you will apply this skill. Establish a plan for performance by actually writing down a description of the situation. Who else will be involved? When will you do it? Where will it be done?
3. Identify the specific behaviours you will engage in to apply this skill. Set action plans for your skill performance.
4. What are the indicators of successful performance? How will you know that you have been effective? What will indicate you have performed competently?

Part 2: Evaluation

5. When you have completed your implementation, record the results. What happened? How successful were you? What was the effect on others?
6. How can you improve? What modifications can you make next time? What will you do differently in a similar situation in the future?
7. Looking back on your whole skill practice and application experience, what have you learned? What has been surprising? In what ways might this experience help you in the long term?

Scoring keys and supplementary materials

Assessing performance and enhancing motivation (p. 274)

SCORING KEY

Skill area	*Items*	**ASSESSMENT** *Pre-*	*Post*
Diagnosing performance problems	1	______	______
	11	______	______
Establishing expectations and settings goals	2	______	______
	12	______	______
Facilitating performance (enhancing ability)	3	______	______
	13	______	______
	20	______	______
Linking performance to rewards and discipline	5	______	______
	14	______	______
	6	______	______
	15	______	______
Using salient internal and external incentives	7	______	______
	16	______	______
	8	______	______
	17	______	______
Distributing rewards equitably	9	______	______
	18	______	______

Providing timely and straightforward performance feedback	4	______	______
	10	______	______
	19	______	______
	TOTAL SCORE	[ ]	[ ]

Comparison data

Compare your scores with three comparison standards:

1. Compare your score with the maximum possible (120).
2. Compare your scores with the scores of other students in your class.
3. Compare your scores with a norm group consisting of 500 business school students.

In comparison with the norm group, if you scored:

101 or above	you are in the top quartile
94–100	you are in the second quartile
85–93	you are in the third quartile
84 or below	you are in the bottom quartile.

Work performance assessment (pp. 275, 320)

SCORING KEY

Step 1: Enter your score from each line below, as follows:
Regular scoring: Enter the number for your response on the survey.
Reverse scoring: Subtract the number of your response from 6 and enter the result.

ITEMS		SCORE	ITEMS		SCORE
1.	Reverse	_____	8.	Regular	_____
2.	Reverse	_____	9.	Regular	_____
3.	Reverse	_____	10.	Regular	_____
4.	Reverse	_____	11.	Regular	_____
5.	Reverse	_____	12.	Regular	_____
6.	Reverse	_____	13.	Regular	_____
7.	Reverse	_____	14.	Regular	_____

Step 2: Combine your scores according to the type of performance problem. Problems with scores higher than 7 are obstacles to high performance. Total scores over 50 suggest significant, broad-based motivational deficiencies.

The Ray-Lynn Short Form Achievement Motivation Scale (p. 275)

SCORING KEY

Response options are 'Yes', (scored 3), '?' (scored 2), 'No' (scored 1). Items marked 'R' are to be reverse-scored (e.g. '1' becomes '3') before addition to get the overall score.

Minimum score: 14. Maximum score: 42.

Above average = 37.4 to 42
Average = 25.7 to 37.3
Below average = 19.9 to 25.6
Very low = 14 to 19.8

Sydney participants' average score: 31.5
Standard deviation: 5.8

Type of performance problem

ITEMS	SCORES ON ITEMS		TOTAL OF TWO
Perception	1:________	8:________	__________
Training	2:________	9:________	__________
Aptitude	3:________	10:________	__________
Resources	4:________	11:________	__________
Expectations	5:________	12:________	__________
Incentives	6:________	13:________	__________
Reward salience	7:________	14:________	__________
		TOTAL SCORE	

Changing unacceptable behaviours (p. 320)

Observer's feedback form

Rating	*Action*
1	Low
5	High

REDIRECT

________ 1. Identified the specific inappropriate behaviour. Gave examples. Indicated that the action must stop.

________ 2. Pointed out the impact of the problem on the performance of others, the unit's mission and so forth.

________ 3. Asked questions about causes and explored remedies.

REFLECT

________ 4. Described the behaviours or standards expected. Made sure the individual understood and agreed that these are reasonable.

________ 5. Asked if the individual would comply.

________ 6. Was appropriately supportive; for example, praised other aspects of the person's work, identified personal and group benefits of compliance, and made sure there were no legitimate obstacles in the way of meeting stated expectations.

RECOGNISE

________ 7. Identified rewards that were salient to the individual.

________ 8. Linked the attainment of desirable outcomes with incremental, continuous improvement.

________ 9. Rewarded (including using praise) all improvements in performance in a timely and honest manner.

Comments:

References

Accor 2009, *Reward to Engage: Rewards, Benefits and Employee Engagement in Today's Organisations*, <http://engagement.accorservices.co.uk/website/employee engagement-whitepaper-form.html>, accessed 1 July 2009.

Adams, J. S. 1963, 'Toward an understanding of inequity', *Journal of Abnormal and Social Psychology*, 67, pp. 422–36.

Ainslie, G. 1992, *Picoeconomics: The Strategic Interaction of Successive Motivational States within the Person* (New York: Cambridge University Press).

Alderfer, C. P. 1977, 'A critique of Salancik and Pfeffer's examination need-satisfaction theories', *Administrative Science Quarterly*, 22, pp. 658–72.

Andrewartha, G. 1995, *Managing Human Resources* (Melbourne: Deakin University).

Andrewartha, G. 1996, *The Recognition Grid* (Adelaide: McPhee Andrewartha Pty Ltd).

Andrewartha, G. 2002, 'Costs and consequences of poor performance mismanagement', unpublished review paper.

Argyris, C. 1992, *On Organisational Learning* (Cambridge, UK: Blackwell).

Ariely, D. 2008, *Predictably Irrational: The Hidden Forces That Shape Our Decisions* (New York: HarperCollins).

Ariely, D., U. Gneezy, G. Loewenstein and N. Mazar 2009, 'Large stakes and big mistakes', *Review of Economic Studies*, 76(2), pp. 451–69.

Armstrong, K. and A. Ward 2006, 'What makes for effective performance management?', The Work Foundation in the Corporate Partners Research Programme.

Ashton, R. and M. Roberts 2011, 'Effects of dispositional motivation on knowledge and performance in tax issue identification and research', *Journal of the American Taxation Association*, 33(1), pp. 25–50.

Atkinson, J. W. and J. O. Raynor 1974, *Motivation and Achievement* (Washington, DC: V. H. Winston).

Baird, T. S., J. E. Post and J. F. Mahon 1990, *Management: Functions and Responsibilities* (New York: Harper & Row).

Barbuto, J. E., Jr. 2006, 'Four classification schemes of adult motivation: Current views and measures', *Perceptual and Motor Skills*, 102, pp. 563–75.

Bartol, K. M. and D. C. Martin 1998, *Management* (New York: McGraw-Hill).

Bennis, W. 1984, 'The four competencies of leadership', *Training and Development Journal*, 38, pp. 15–19.

Birch, D. and J. Veroff 1966, *Motivation: A Study of Action* (Monterey, CA: Brooks-Cole).

Bove, R. 1987, 'Retraining the older worker', *Training and Development Journal*, March, pp. 77–78.

Brown, D. and P. Reilly 2008, 'Employee engagement: What is the relationship with reward management?', *World at Work Journal*, 17(4).

Butler, T. and J. Waldroop 1999, 'Job sculpting: The art of retaining your best people', *Harvard Business Review*, September–October, pp. 144–52.

Correll, M. 1999, *Four Steps to Motivational Self-management* (Adelaide: McPhee Andrewartha Pty Ltd).

Deci, E. L. and R. M. Ryan 1985, *Intrinsic Motivation and Self-determination in Human Behavior* (New York: Plenum).

Deming, W. E. 1982, *Quality, Productivity, and Competitive Position* (Cambridge, MA: Massachusetts Institute of Technology Press).

Di Cesare, J. and G. Sadri 2003, 'Do all carrots look the same? Examining the impact of culture on employee motivation', *Management Research News*, 26(1), pp. 29–40.

Dollard, J. and N. E. Miller 1950, *Personality and Psychotherapy: An Analysis in Terms of Learning, Thinking, and Culture* (New York: McGraw-Hill Book Co.).

Drucker, P. 2001, *Management Challenges for the 21st Century* (New York: HarperCollins).

Dysvik, A. and B. Kuvaas 2011, 'Intrinsic motivation as a moderator on the relationship between perceived job autonomy and work performance', *European Journal of Work & Organizational Psychology*, 20(3), pp. 367–87.

Ebrahimi, B. P. 1997, 'Motivation to manage in Hong Kong: Modification and test of Miner Sentence Completion Scale-H', *Journal of Managerial Psychology*, 12(6), pp. 401–14.

Eisenberg, J. and W. Thompson 2011, 'The effects of competition on improvisers' motivation, stress, and creative performance', *Creativity Research Journal*, 23(2), pp. 129–36.

Fellner, D. J. and B. Sulzer-Azaroff 1984, 'A behavioral analysis of goal-setting', *Journal of Organizational Behavior Management*, 6, pp. 33–51.

Festinger, L. and J. M. Carlsmith 1959, 'Cognitive consequences of forced compliance', *Journal of Abnormal and Social Psychology*, 58, pp. 203–10.

Fish, A. 1999, 'Cultural diversity: Challenges facing the management of cross-border business careers', *Career Development International*, 4(4), pp. 196–205.

Frey, B. S. and M. Osterloh (eds) 2002, *Successful Management by Motivation: Balancing Intrinsic and Extrinsic Incentives* (London: Springer-Verlag).

Friedlander, F. 1966, 'Motivations to work and organizational performance', *Journal of Applied Psychology*, 50(2), pp. 143–52.

Galbraith, J. 1967, 'An empirical investigation of the motivational determinants of task performance: Interactive effects between instrumentally—valence and motivation—ability', *Organizational Behavior & Human Performance*, 2(3), pp. 237–57.

Glasser, W. 1998, *Choice Theory: A New Psychology of Personal Freedom* (New York: HarperCollins).

Gray, R. 2008, 'Generation Y—time to grow up', *Management Today*, October.

Greenberg, J. 1990, 'Organizational justice: Yesterday, today and tomorrow', *Journal of Management*, 16, pp. 606–13.

Greenberg, J. and R. A. Baron 1997, *Behavior in Organizations: Understanding and Managing the Human Side of Work* (Englewood Cliffs, NJ: Prentice Hall).

Greenberg, J. and S. Ornstein 1984, 'Motivation in organizations', in R. G. Geen, W. W. Beatty and R. M. Arkin (eds), *Human Motivation: Physiological, Behavioral and Social Approaches* (Boston: Allyn & Bacon).

Greene, C. N. 1972, 'The satisfaction–performance controversy', *Business Horizons*, 15, pp. 31–41.

Halkos, G. and B. Dimitrios 2010, 'The effect of stress and satisfaction on productivity', *International Journal of Productivity and Performance Management*, 59(5), pp. 415–31.

Hallowell, E. M. 2005, 'Overloaded circuits: Why smart people underperform', *Harvard Business Review*, January, pp. 2–10.

Hallowell, E. 2011, *Shine: Using Brain Science to Get the Best from Your People* (Boston: Harvard Business School Press).

Hamner, W. C. 1974, 'Reinforcement theory and contingency management in organizational settings', in H. L. Tosi and W. C. Hamner (eds), *Organizational Behavior and Management: A Contingency Approach* (Chicago: St Clair Press).

Hamori, M. 2010, 'Who gets headhunted—and who gets ahead? The impact of search firms on executive careers', *The Academy of Management Perspectives*, 24(4), November, pp. 46–59.

Hatcher, N. 2009, *Work USA Survey*, A Watson Wyatt study.

Herzberg, F. 1968, 'One more time: How do you motivate employees?', *Harvard Business Review*, 46(1), pp. 53–62.
Higgins, E. T. 1989, 'Self-discrepancy theory: What patterns of self-beliefs cause people to suffer?', in L. Berkowitz (ed.), *Advances in Experimental Social Psychology* (San Diego, CA: Academic Press).
Hofstede, G. 1991, *Cultures and Organizations: Software of the Mind: Intercultural Cooperation and its Importance for Survival* (Cambridge, UK: McGraw-Hill).
House, R. J. 1971, 'A path–goal theory of leader effectiveness', *Administrative Science Quarterly*, 16, pp. 19–31.
House, R. J. and T. R. Mitchell 1974, 'Path-goal theory of leadership', *Journal of Contemporary Business*, 3, pp. 81–97.
Ilies, R., T. Judge and D. Wagner 2006, 'Making sense of motivational leadership: The trail from transformational leaders to motivated followers', *Journal of Leadership & Organizational Studies*, 13, Fall, pp. 1–22.
Irala, L. R. 2007, *Performance Measurement Using Balanced Score Card*, <http://ssrn.com/abstract=980691>, accessed 10 April 2007.
Ittner, C. D., D, F. Larcker and M. W. Meyer 2003, *Subjectivity and the Weighting of Performance Measures: Evidence from a Balanced Scorecard*, <http://ssrn.com/abstract=395241>.
Ivengar, S. 2010 *The Art of Choosing* (New York: Hachette Book Group).
Jawahar, I. M. 2006, 'An investigation of potential consequences of satisfaction with appraisal feedback', *Journal of Leadership & Organisational Studies*, 13, Winter, pp. 14–28.
Jeffries, F. L. and T. L. Hunte 2004, 'Generations and motivation: A connection worth making', *Journal of Behavioral and Applied Management*, 6(1), September pp. 37–70.
Jordan, P. C. 1986, 'Effects of extrinsic rewards on intrinsic motivation: A field experiment', *Academy of Management Journal*, 27, pp. 405–12.
Kaplan, R. S. and D. P. Norton 1992, 'The Balanced Scorecard—measures that drive performance', *Harvard Business Review*, January–February, pp. 71–79.
Kellogg, M. S. 1979, *Talking with Employees: A Guide for Managers* (Houston, TX: Gulf Publishing Co.).
Kerr, S. 1995, 'On the folly of rewarding A, while hoping for B', *Academy of Management Executive*, 9(1), pp. 7–14.
Kipnis, D. 1976, *The Powerholders* (Chicago: University of Chicago Press).
Kopelman, R. E. 1985, 'Job redesign and productivity: A review of evidence', *National Productivity Review*, Summer, pp. 237–55.
Kotter, J. P. 1996, *Leading Change* (Boston: Harvard Business School Press).
Kuo, T-H., L-A. Ho, C-H. Lin and K-K. Lai 2010, 'Employee empowerment in a technology advanced work environment', *Industrial Management & Data Systems*, 110(1), pp. 24–42.
Larkin, T. J. and S. Larkin 1992, *Communicating Change to Employees* (Melbourne: Australian Human Resources Institute).
Latham, G., M. Erez and E. Locke 1988, 'Resolving scientific disputes by the joint design of crucial experiments by the antagonists: Application to the Erez–Latham disputes regarding participation in goal setting', *Journal of Applied Psychology*, 73, pp. 753–72.
Latham, G. P. and E. A. Locke 1979, 'Goal setting—a motivational technique that works', *Organizational Dynamics*, 8, pp. 68–80.
Lawler, E. E. 1987, 'The design of effective reward systems', in J. Lorsch (ed.), *Handbook of Organizational Behavior* (Englewood Cliffs, NJ: Prentice Hall).
Lawler, E. E. 1988, 'Gainsharing theory and research: Findings and future directions', in W. A. Pasmore and E. R. Woodman (eds), *Research in Organizational Change and Development*, vol. 2 (Greenwich, CT: JAI Press).
LeDue, A.L. Jr. 1980, 'Motivation of programmers', *ACM Database*, Quarterly Publication of SIGBOP, 11(4), Summer, pp. 4–12.
Levering, R., M. Moskovitz and M. Katz 1984, *The 100 Best Companies to Work for in America* (Reading, MA: Addison-Wesley).
Locke, E. A. and G. P. Latham 1990, *A Theory of Goal Setting and Task Performance* (Englewood Cliffs, NJ: Prentice Hall).
Logan, S., E. Medford and N. Hughes 2011, 'The importance of intrinsic motivation for high and low ability readers' reading comprehension performance', *Learning and Individual Differences*, 21(1), pp. 124–8.
Loher, B. T., R. A. Noe, N. L. Moeller and M. P. Fitzgerald, 1985, 'A meta-analysis of the relation of job characteristics to job satisfaction', *Journal of Applied Psychology*, 70, pp. 280–9.
Lunsford, S. 2010, 'Survey analysis: Employee motivation by generation factors', *Training*, April, pp. 1–6.
Lusterman, S. 1985, *Trends in Corporate Education and Training*, The Conference Board, Report No. 870.
Luthans, F. and R. Kreitner 1975, *Organizational Behavior Modification* (Glenview, IL: Scott, Foresman).
McClelland, D. 1971, *Assessing Human Motivation* (New York: General Learning Press).
McClelland, D. 1976, 'Power is the great motivator', *Harvard Business Review*, 54, pp. 100–10.
McClelland, D. C., J. W. Arkinson, R. A. Clark and E. L. Lowell 1953, *The Achievement Motive* (New York: Appleton-Century-Crofts).
Macey, W. H and B. Schneider 2008, 'The meaning of employee engagement', *Industrial and Organizational Psychology*, 1(1), pp. 3–30.
McGregor, D. 1960, *The Human Side of Enterprise* (New York: McGraw-Hill).
MacLeod, D. and N. Clarke 2009, *Engaging for Success* report (London: UK).
Maier, N. R. F. 1973, *Psychology in Industrial Organizations*, 4th ed. (New York: Houghton Mifflin).

Malina, M. A. and F. H. Selto 2001, *Communicating and Controlling Strategy: An Empirical Study of the Effectiveness of the Balanced Scorecard*, <http://ssrn.com/abstract=278939>, April 2001.

Manzoni, J. and J. Barsoux 1998, 'The set-up-to-fail syndrome', *Harvard Business Review*, 76(2), pp. 101–13.

Maslow, A. H. 1970, *Motivation and Personality*, 2nd ed. (New York: Harper & Row).

Mendelson, M. B., N. Turner and J. Barling 2011, 'Perceptions of the presence and effectiveness of high involvement work systems and their relationship to employee attitudes: A test of competing models', *Personnel Review*, 40(1), pp. 26–45.

Mercer 2007, 'Engaging employees to drive global business success', *Journal of Applied Psychology*, 87(2), pp. 268–79.

Michaelson, C. 2010, 'The importance of meaningful work', *MIT Sloan Management Review*, 512), pp. 12–13.

Michener, H. A., J. A. Fleishman and J. J. Vaske 1976, 'A test of the bargaining theory of coalition formulation in four-person groups', *Journal of Personality and Social Psychology*, 34, pp. 1114–26.

Milne, P. 2007, 'Motivation, incentives and organizational culture', *Journal of Knowledge Management*, 11(6), pp. 28–38.

Mir, P., I. Trender-Gerhard, M. Edwards, S. Schneider, K. Bhatia and M. Jahanshahi 2011, 'Motivation and movement: The effect of monetary incentive on performance speed', *Experimental Brain Research*, 209(4), pp. 551–9.

Montana, P. J. and F. P. Fordham 2008, 'Motivating and managing Generation X and Y on the job while preparing for Z: A market oriented approach', *Journal of Business & Economics Research*, 6(8), August, p. 35.

Nadler, D. E. and E. E. Lawler 1977, 'Motivation: A diagnostic approach', in J. R. Hackman, E. E. Lawler and L. W. Porter (eds), *Perspective Behavior in Organizations* (New York: McGraw-Hill).

Niven, R. 2003, *Balanced Scorecard Step-by-Step for Government and Nonprofit Agencies* (Hoboken, NJ: John Wiley & Sons).

O'Leary-Kelly, A. M., J. J. Martocchio and D. D. Frink 1994, 'A review of the influence of group goals on group performance', *Academy of Management Journal*, 37, pp. 1285–301.

Pais, C. L. A. 2010, 'Self-managed teams in the auto components industry: Construction of a theoretical model', *Team Performance Management*, 16(7/8), pp. 359–87.

Penningroth, S., W. Scott and M. Freuen 2011, 'Social motivation in prospective memory: Higher importance ratings and reported performance rates for social tasks', *Canadian Journal of Experimental Psychology*, 65(1), pp. 3–11.

Petri, H. L. 1981, *Motivation: Theory and Research* (Belmont, CA: Wadsworth).

Pink, D. 2009, *Drive: The Surprising Truth About What Motivates Us* (New York: Riverhead Books).

Quick, T. L. 1977, *Person to Person Managing* (New York: St Martin's Press).

Rabey, G. P. 2001, 'Motivation is response', *Journal of Industrial and Commercial Training*, 33(1), pp. 26–28.

Ray, J. J. 1979, 'A quick measure of achievement motivation—validated in Australia and reliable in Britain and South Africa', *Australian Psychologist*, 14(3), November, pp. 337–44.

Rodriguez, P., M. Green and M. Ree 2003, 'Leading Generation X: Do the old rules apply?', *Journal of Leadership and Organizational Studies*, 9(4), pp. 67–75.

Roesch, S. C. and J. H. Amirkham 1997, 'Boundary conditions for self-serving attributions: Another look at the sports pages', *Journal of Applied Social Psychology*, 27, pp. 245–61.

Rosenthal, R. and L. Jacobson 1968, *Pygmalion in the Classroom* (New York: Holt, Rinehart & Winston).

Ruch, W. 2000, 'How to keep Gen X employees from becoming X-employees', *Training and Development*, April, pp. 40–43.

Rudman, R. 1997, *Human Resources Management in New Zealand: Contexts and Processes* (Auckland: Longman Paul Ltd).

Saks, A. M. 2006, 'Antecedents and consequences of employee engagement', *Journal of Managerial Psychology*, 21(7), pp. 600–19.

Senge, P. 1990, *The Fifth Discipline* (Sydney: Random House).

Silverthorne, C. 2001, 'A test of the path–goal leadership theory in Taiwan', *Leadership and Organizational Development Journal*, 22(4), pp. 151–8.

Skinner, B. F. 1969, *Contingencies of Reinforcement: A Theoretical Analysis* (New York: Appleton-Century Crofts).

Snyder, M., W. Stephen and D. Rosenfield 1978, 'Attributional egotism', in J. Harvey, W. Ickes and R. Kidds (eds), *New Directions in Attributional Research*, vol. 2 (Hillsdale, NJ: Erlbaum).

Staw, B. M., P. McKechnie and S. Puffer 1983, 'The justification of organizational performance', *Administrative Science Quarterly*, 28, pp. 582–600.

Steel, P. and C. J. König 2005, *Integrating Theories of Motivation*, <www.haskayne.ucalgary.ca/research/WorkingPapers/research/media/HROD_working_papers/2003_06.pdf>, accessed 14 March 2007.

Steel, P. and C. J. König 2007, 'Integrating theories of motivation', *Academy of Management Review*, 31, pp. 889–913.

Steers, R. M., L. W. Porter and G. A. Bigley 1996, *Motivation and Leadership of Work* (New York: McGraw-Hill).

Taormina, R. J. and S. K-M. Lao 2007, 'Measuring Chinese entrepreneurial motivation: Personality and environmental influences', *International Journal of Entrepreneurial Behavior & Research*, 13(4), pp. 200–21. Thaler, R. H. and C. R. Sunstein 2008, *Nudge: Improving Predictions about Health and Wealth and Happiness* (New Haven, CT: Yale University Press).

Thaler, R. and C. Sunstein 2008, *Nudge: Improving Decisions about Health, Wealth and Happiness* (New Haven, CT: Yale University Press).

Thompson, D. W. 1978, *Managing People: Influencing Behavior* (St Louis, MI: C. V. Mosby Co.).

Towers Watson 2010, *Turbocharging Employee Engagement—The Power of Recognition from Managers.*

Trompenaars, F. 1996, 'Resolving international conflict: Culture and business strategy', *Business Strategy Review*, 7, pp. 51–68.

Tversky, A. and D. Kahneman 1992, 'Advances in Prospect Theory: Cumulative representation of uncertainty', *Journal of Risk and Uncertainty*, 5, pp. 297–323.

Vroom, V. H. 1964, *Work and Motivation* (New York: Wiley).

Wanous, J. P. 1980, *Organizational Entry* (Reading, MA: Addison-Wesley).

Ward, J. H., D. S. Vaughan, J. L. Mitchell, W. E. Driskill and H. W. Ruck 2000, 'The ultimate person–job match: A key to future worker productivity', *Ergometrika*, 1, pp. 45–50.

Wayne, S. J., L. M. Shore, W. H. Bommer and L. E. Tetrick 2002, 'The role of fair treatment and rewards in perceptions of organizational support and leader–member exchange', *Journal of Applied Psychology*, 87(3), pp. 590–8.

Weston, N., I. Greenlees and R. Thelwell 2011, 'The impact of a performance profiling intervention on athletes' intrinsic motivation', *Research Quarterly for Exercise & Sport*, 82(1), pp. 151–5.

Westover, J. H. and J. Taylor 2010, 'International differences in job satisfaction: The effects of public service motivation, rewards and work relations', *International Journal of Productivity and Performance Management*, 59(8), pp. 811–28.

Wood, R. E., A. J. Mento and E. A. Locke 1987, 'Task complexity as a moderator of goal effects: A meta-analysis', *Journal of Applied Psychology*, 72, pp. 416–25.

Zemke, R., C. Raines and B. Filipczak 2000, *Generations at Work* (New York: AMA Publications).

CHAPTER 7

MANAGING CONFLICT

OBJECTIVES

- **Assess the type and sources of conflict**
- **Select the appropriate negotiation/conflict management strategy**
- **Manage interpersonal confrontations**

7

CHAPTER OUTLINE

Skill assessment

Evaluative surveys for managing conflict

Conflict resolution questionnaire

Rate each of the following statements from 1 to 5 using the ratings below to indicate how often you do as the statement says. Answer the questions in the left-hand column to portray your most usual way of dealing with conflicts, such as those at home or at work. Do not take long on any question. Give your initial reaction.

Rating scale

1 Almost never
2 Occasionally
3 Half the time
4 Usually
5 Almost always

1.	_______ / _______	I feel that conflict is a negative experience.
2.	_______ / _______	When I resolve a conflict, it improves my relationship.
3.	_______ / _______	I am afraid to enter into confrontations.
4.	_______ / _______	I feel that in conflicts someone will get hurt.
	V _______	
5.	_______ / _______	When I prepare to meet to discuss a conflict, I try to arrange for a mutually acceptable time and setting.
6.	_______ / _______	I feel it is important where a conflict takes place.
7.	_______ / _______	I try to make people feel comfortable when meeting with them about a conflict.
8.	_______ / _______	When I start to discuss a conflict with the other party, I choose my opening statement carefully in order to establish positive, realistic expectations.
	A _______	
9.	_______ / _______	I state my true feelings when dealing with conflict.
10.	_______ / _______	During a conflict, I ask questions to clarify a statement that I'm not sure of.
11.	_______ / _______	I try to be aware of how my negative and positive self-perceptions influence the way I deal with a conflict.
12.	_______ / _______	In a conflict, my reactions are based on how I think the other party perceives me.
	C _______	
13.	_______ / _______	I feel that only my needs are important.
14.	_______ / _______	I feel that, for a relationship to last, the needs of both parties must be considered.
15.	_______ / _______	In a conflict, I strive to distinguish between real needs and desires.
16.	_______ / _______	In order not to harm the relationship, I may temporarily put aside some of my own less important personal wants.
	N _______	
17.	_______ / _______	I share my positive attitude, hoping they will do the same.
18.	_______ / _______	I find it necessary to overpower others to get my own way.
19.	_______ / _______	I am aware that the other person may need to feel in control of the conflict.
20.	_______ / _______	In a conflict, I believe there should be no upper-hand.
	P _______	

21. ______ / ______ I find it easy to forgive.
22. ______ / ______ I bring up old issues from the past during a new conflict.
23. ______ / ______ When dealing with a conflict, I consider the future of the long-term relationship.
24. ______ / ______ In a conflict, I try to dominate the other party.

F ______

25. ______ / ______ I listen with an open mind to alternative options.
26. ______ / ______ I feel there is just one way to solve a problem.
27. ______ / ______ When dealing with a conflict, I have preconceived notions about the other party that I am unwilling to let go of.
28. ______ / ______ I can accept criticism from others.

O ______

29. ______ / ______ I feel that winning the war is more important than winning the battle.
30. ______ / ______ I strive for a complete and genuine resolution of a conflict rather than settling for a temporary agreement.
31. ______ / ______ When dealing with a conflict, I have a pre-determined solution to the outcome.
32. ______ / ______ I feel the need to control an argument.

D ______

33. ______ / ______ If I had my way, I win, you lose.
34. ______ / ______ When in a conflict with someone, I ask them to explain their position.
35. ______ / ______ I bargain to resolve conflict.
36. ______ / ______ At the end of a conflict, it matters to me that the other person's needs have been met as well as my own.

M ______

37. ______ / ______ I express anger constructively.
38. ______ / ______ In difficult conflicts, I would consider requesting a third-party facilitator.
39. ______ / ______ I overlook my partner's anger in order to focus on the real issues of conflict.
40. ______ / ______ I feel that it is okay to agree to disagree on specific issues in a conflict.

X ______

Total ______________

AND answer this one further question:

Using the same 1–5 scale, how often do you feel you are effective at resolving conflicts in a way that builds your long-term relationship with the other parties?

A scoring key is on page 389.

Source: Designed by members of Jock McClellan's 1993 class on conflict resolution for use as a learning tool and with no claims of scientific evaluation. Reproduced with permission. JMcClellan@qvcc.commnet.edu. (Marcus Henning did an evaluation, which can be seen at <http://aut.researchgateway.ac.nz/bitstream/10292/49/1/HenningM.pdf>)

Managing interpersonal conflict

Step 1: Respond to the following statements by writing a number from the rating scale on the following page in the left-hand column (pre-assessment). Your answers should reflect your attitudes and behaviour as they are now, not as you would like them to be. Be honest. This instrument is designed to help you discover your level of competency in managing conflict so that you can tailor your learning to your specific needs. When you have completed the survey, use the scoring key at the end of the chapter to identify the skill areas that are most important for you to master.

Step 2: When you have completed the reading and the exercises in this chapter and, ideally, as many as you can of the skill application assignments at the end of the chapter, cover up your first set of answers. Then respond to the same statements again, this time in the right-hand column (post-assessment). When you have completed the survey, use the scoring key to measure your progress. If your score remains low in specific skill areas, use the behavioural guidelines at the end of the skill learning section to guide further practice.

Rating scale

1 Strongly disagree
2 Disagree
3 Slightly disagree
4 Slightly agree
5 Agree
6 Strongly agree

Assessment
Pre- *Post-*

When I see someone doing something that needs correcting:

______ ______ 1. I avoid making personal accusations and attributing selfish motives to the other person.
______ ______ 2. When stating my concerns, I present them as my problems.
______ ______ 3. I succinctly describe problems in terms of the behaviour that occurred, its consequences and my feelings about it.
______ ______ 4. I specify the expectations and standards that have been violated.
______ ______ 5. I make a specific request, detailing a more acceptable option.
______ ______ 6. I persist in explaining my point of view until it is understood by the other person.
______ ______ 7. I encourage two-way interaction by inviting the respondent to express his or her perspective and to ask questions.
______ ______ 8. When there are several concerns, I approach the issues incrementally, starting with easy and simple issues and then progressing to those that are difficult and complex.

When someone complains about something I have done:

______ ______ 9. I look for our common areas of agreement.
______ ______ 10. I show genuine concern and interest, even when I disagree.
______ ______ 11. I avoid justifying my actions and becoming defensive.
______ ______ 12. I seek additional information by asking questions that provide specific and descriptive information.
______ ______ 13. I focus on one issue at a time.
______ ______ 14. I find some aspects of the complaint with which I can agree.
______ ______ 15. I ask the other person to suggest more acceptable behaviours.
______ ______ 16. I strive to reach agreement on a remedial plan of action.

When two other people are in conflict and I am the mediator:

______ ______ 17. I acknowledge that conflict exists and treat it as serious and important.
______ ______ 18. I help create an agenda for a problem-solving meeting by identifying the issues to be discussed, one at a time.
______ ______ 19. I do not take sides, but remain neutral.
______ ______ 20. I help focus the discussion on the impact of the conflict on work performance.

______ ______ 21. I keep the interaction focused on problems rather than on personalities.
______ ______ 22. I make certain that neither party dominates the conversation.
______ ______ 23. I help the parties generate multiple alternatives.
______ ______ 24. I help the parties find areas on which they agree.

The scoring key is on page 392.

Managing conflict questionnaire

(From K. Thomas, 'Conflict and conflict management', in M. Dunnette (ed.), *Handbook of Industrial and Organizational Psychology*, vol. 2 (Chicago: Rand McNally, 1975.)

Choose (a) or (b) from the following paired statements based on which one *best fits* your preferred way of handling differences between you and others.

1. (a) I am usually firm in pursuing my goals.
   (b) I attempt to get all concerns and issues immediately out in the open.
2. (a) I put all my cards on the table and invite the other person to do likewise.
   (b) When conflicts arise, I try to win my case.
3. (a) Once I adopt a position, I defend it strongly.
   (b) I prefer not to argue but to look for the best solution possible.
4. (a) I sometimes sacrifice my own wishes for the wishes of the other person.
   (b) I feel the differences are not always worth worrying about.
5. (a) I accept the views of others, rather than rock the boat.
   (b) I avoid people with strong views.
6. (a) I like to cooperate with others and follow their ideas.
   (b) I feel that most things are not worth arguing about. I stick to my own views.
7. (a) I try to find some compromise situation.
   (b) I am usually firm in pursuing my goals.
8. (a) When conflicts arise I try to win my case.
   (b) I propose a middle ground.
9. (a) I like to meet the other person half-way.
   (b) Once I adopt a position, I defend it strongly.
10. (a) I feel that differences are not always worth worrying about.
    (b) I try to find a compromise solution.
11. (a) I propose a middle ground.
    (b) I avoid people with strong views.
12. (a) I feel that most things are not worth arguing about. I stick to my own views.
    (b) I like to meet the other person half-way.
13. (a) I am usually firm in pursuing my goals.
    (b) I sometimes sacrifice my own wishes for the wishes of the other person.
14. (a) I accept the views of others, rather than rock the boat.
    (b) When conflicts arise, I try to win my case.
15. (a) Once I adopt a position I defend it strongly.
    (b) I like to cooperate with others and follow their ideas.
16. (a) I try to find a compromise solution.
    (b) I sometimes sacrifice my own wishes for the wishes of the other person.
17. (a) I would accept the views of others, rather than rock the boat.
    (b) I propose a middle ground.
18. (a) I like to meet the other person half-way.
    (b) I like to cooperate with others and follow their ideas.
19. (a) I feel that differences are not always worth worrying about.
    (b) I am usually firm in pursuing my goals.

20. (a) When conflicts arise, I try to win my case.
    (b) I avoid people with strong views.
21. (a) I feel that most things are not worth arguing about. I stick to my own views.
    (b) Once I adopt a position, I defend it strongly.
22. (a) I attempt to get all concerns and issues immediately out in the open.
    (b) I feel that differences are not always worth worrying about.
23. (a) I avoid people with strong views.
    (b) I put my cards on the table and invite the other person to do likewise.
24. (a) I prefer not to argue, but to look for the best solution possible.
    (b) I feel that most things are not worth arguing about. I stick to my views.
25. (a) I attempt to get all concerns and issues immediately out in the open.
    (b) I try to find a compromise solution.
26. (a) I put my cards on the table and invite the other person to do likewise.
    (b) I propose a middle ground.
27. (a) I prefer not to argue, but to look for the best solution possible.
    (b) I like to meet the other person half-way.
28. (a) I sometimes sacrifice my own wishes for the wishes of the other person.
    (b) I attempt to get all concerns and issues immediately out in the open.
29. (a) I put my cards on the table and invite the other person to do likewise.
    (b) I would accept the views of others, rather than rock the boat.
30. (a) I like to cooperate with others and follow their ideas.
    (b) I prefer not to argue, but to look for the best possible solution.

The scoring key is on page 393. Together with your scores, there is also a detailed description of the benefits and limitations of your own unique conflict management profile.

Skill learning

Interpersonal conflict management

The inability to manage agreement—not the inability to manage conflict—is the essential symptom (of the Abilene Paradox).... In fact this is the single most pressing issue of modern organizations. (Harvey 1988: 14)

One of the leading causes of business failure among major corporations is too much agreement among top management. They have similar training and experience, which means they tend to view conditions the same way and pursue similar goals. This problem is compounded by Boards of Directors failing to play an aggressive oversight role. They avoid conflict with the internal management team who appear unified on key issues and very confident of their positions. (Argenti 1976)

I'm sick of all the conflict. I wish it would go away so I could just get on with my job. (Manager, aged 36, in an engineering firm)

Most senior managers ... are less than fully in control of their companies' future, and this is due in large measure to their preoccupation with reacting to day to day things. (Hamel & Prahalad 1994: 122–8)

The origin of all conflict between me and my fellow man is that I do not say what I mean, and that I do not do what I say. (Buber 1958)

It infuriates me to be wrong when I know I'm right. (Molière)

As reflected in these brief quotes, interpersonal conflict is challenging, but it is a normal, essential and manageable part of organisational life. Given globalisation, diversity, constant change and team-based approaches in today's workplaces, conflicts are inevitable. When people with differing approaches and backgrounds work together, misunderstandings and disagreements are to be expected. Many managers tend to be uncomfortable with conflict at work, but it is part of our essential humanity. What is learned from the study of business failures is that the absence of disagreement is often viewed by managers as a sign of good leadership, when in reality it is a leading indicator of being out of touch with significant changes in the marketplace (Argenti 1976). Interpersonal conflict is a ubiquitous part of organisational life, and how managers from different organisations and cultures deal with conflict is an increasingly important predictor of organisational success (Seybolt, Derr & Nielson 1996; Tjosvold 1991).

Pony (1967) is one of the earliest scholars, who argued that conflict is a process, rather than a specific factor and/or phenomenon. Most definitions agree that conflict is a process involving two or more parties (Fink 1968). Chronic conflict can also infect the culture of an organisation. (See Chapter 3 on the toxic workplace.)

Considerable evidence suggests that a foundation of trust, matched verbal and non-verbal communication, and effective team development is a necessary precursor for minimising or resolving conflict in organisations. Trust (or lack of it) at the executive group level has an impact upon the conflict response culture of the whole organisation. At all levels, relationship distrust tends to lead to conflict over task allocation. Overall, the more trust there is, the better the inclination will be to seek conflict resolution options. Moreover a lack of effective conflict resolution strategies, rather than of conflict itself, also lowers satisfaction and productivity (Andrewartha 2011; Bekmeier-Feuerhahn & Eichenlaub 2010; Cox 2003; Dayan 2010; Han & Harms 2010; Parayitam, Olson & Bao 2010).

Organisations in which there is little disagreement about important matters generally fail in competitive environments. Members are either so homogeneous that they are ill equipped to adapt to changing environmental conditions, or so complacent that they see no need to improve the status quo. Some conflict is the lifeblood of vibrant, progressive, stimulating organisations. It sparks creativity, stimulates innovation and encourages personal improvement (Goleman 2001; Pascale 1990; Wanous & Youtz 1986).

This view was clearly in line with the management philosophy of Andrew Grove (1984), president of Intel:

> *Many managers seem to think it is impossible to tackle anything or anyone head-on, even in business. By contrast, we at Intel believe that it is the essence of corporate health to bring a problem out into the open as soon as possible, even if this entails a confrontation. Dealing with conflicts lies at the heart of managing any business. As a result, confrontation—facing issues about which there is disagreement—can be avoided only at the manager's peril. Workplace politicking grows quietly in the dark, like mushrooms; neither can stand the light of day.*

It is also true that not all conflict produces beneficial results. Many people have a very low tolerance for disagreement. Whether this is the result of family background, cultural values or personality characteristics, a high level of interpersonal conflict saps their energy and demoralises their spirit. Also, some types of conflict, regardless of frequency, generally produce dysfunctional outcomes. These include petty personality conflicts and arguments over things that cannot be changed. When conflict becomes chronic and splits teams, it reduces morale and directly reduces productivity. This is especially the case when conflict is stimulated for self-serving purposes. For example, some managers feel so unsure of their qualifications and support that they continually stir up conflicts between employees. This reduces the threat of a coalition forming to challenge the boss's rule and creates situations that reaffirm the boss's superior position. This is a classic case of using a natural, legitimate organisational process for contrived, illegitimate personal purposes. Fortunately, this tends to be the exception, not the rule, in management practice.

As Figure 7.1 shows, most scholars agree that some conflict is both inevitable and beneficial in effective organisations (Brown 1983).

However, a well-known psychologist, Abraham Maslow (1965), has observed a high degree of ambivalence regarding the value of conflict. On the one hand, he notes that managers intellectually

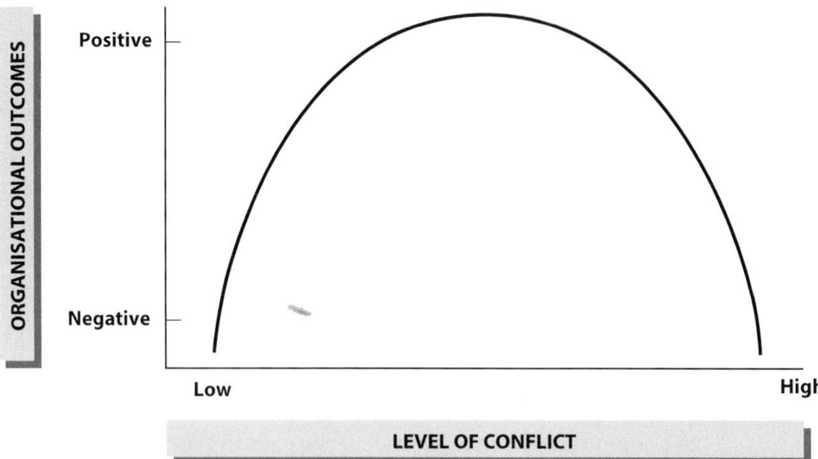

FIGURE 7.1 Relationship between level of conflict and organisational outcomes

appreciate the value of conflict and competition. They agree it is a necessary ingredient of the free-enterprise system. However, even allowing for the differences between cultures, most managers around the globe tend to demonstrate a personal preference for avoiding conflicts whenever possible.

The tension between intellectual acceptance of a principle and emotional rejection of its enactment was illustrated in a classic study of decision making (Boulding 1964). Several groups of managers were formed to solve a complex problem. They were told their performance would be judged by a panel of experts in terms of the quantity and quality of solutions generated. The groups were identical in size and composition, with the exception that half of them included a 'confederate'. Before the experiment began, the researcher instructed this person to play the role of 'devil's advocate'. This person was to challenge the group's conclusions, competing with the others to examine critically their assumptions and the logic of their arguments. At the end of the problem-solving period, the recommendations made by both sets of groups were compared. The groups with the devil's advocates had performed significantly better on the task. They had generated more alternatives and their proposals were judged as superior.

After a short break, the groups were reassembled and told that they would be performing a similar task during the next session. However, before they began discussing the next problem, they were given permission to eliminate one member. In every group containing a confederate, he or she was the one asked to leave. The fact that every high-performance group expelled their unique competitive advantage because that member made others feel uncomfortable demonstrates a widely shared reaction to conflict: 'I know it has positive outcomes for the performance of the organisation as a whole, but I don't like how it makes me feel personally.' (See also Argyris 1992.)

Much of the ambivalence towards conflict stems from a lack of understanding of the causes of conflict and the variety of modes for managing it effectively, and from a lack of confidence in our personal skills for handling the tense, emotionally charged environment typical of most interpersonal confrontations. It is natural for an untrained or inexperienced person to avoid threatening situations, and it is generally acknowledged that conflict represents the most severe test of a manager's interpersonal skills. The task of the effective manager, therefore, is to manage a normal level of conflict, while keeping conflicts focused on productive purposes (Karpin 1995; Kelly 1970; Robbins 1974; Thomas 1975).

A good manager invests time in anticipating and managing conflict. This requires two sets of skills. First, managers must be able to assess the causes of conflict accurately and select an appropriate conflict management strategy. Second, skilful managers must be able to use counselling skills to settle interpersonal disputes effectively so that underlying problems are resolved and the interpersonal relationship between disputants is strengthened. The LETS (Leadership Enhancement Team Style) questionnaire and other similar instruments (see Chapter 2) are potentially useful in this context.

Assessing the type of interpersonal conflict

Because interpersonal conflicts come in assorted lots, our first skill-building task involves the art of diagnosis. In any type of clinical setting, from medicine to management, it is common knowledge that effective intervention is based on accurate diagnosis. Figure 7.2 presents a categorising device for diagnosing the type of conflict, based on two critical identifying characteristics: focus and source. By understanding the focus of the conflict, we gain an appreciation for the substance of the dispute (what is fuelling the conflict), and by learning more about the origins, or source, of the conflict, we understand better how it began (the igniting spark).

SOURCE OF CONFLICT	FOCUS OF CONFLICT: Issues	FOCUS OF CONFLICT: People
Personal differences		
Informational deficiencies		
Incompatible roles		
Environmental stress		

FIGURE 7.2 Categorising different types of conflict

Conflict focus

It is helpful to categorise conflicts in organisations in terms of whether they are primarily focused on *people* or on *issues* (Amason et al. 1995; Eisenhardt, Kahwajy & Bourgeois 1997; Guetzkow & Gyr 1954). In other words, is this a negotiation-like conflict over competing ideas, proposals, interests or resources? Or is it a dispute-like conflict stemming from what has transpired between the parties?

One of the nice features of the distinction between people-focused and issue-focused conflicts is that it helps us understand why some managers believe that conflict is the lifeblood of their organisation, while others believe that every conflict episode sucks blood from their organisation. Research has shown that people-focused conflicts threaten relationships, whereas issue-based conflicts enhance relationships, provided that people are comfortable with them and feel able to manage them effectively (Jehn 1997). Therefore, in general, when we read about the benefits of 'productive conflict', the authors are referring to issue-focused conflict.

Although, by definition, all interpersonal conflicts involve people, people-focused conflict refers to the 'in your face' kind of confrontations in which the affect level is high and the intense emotional heat is likely to be fuelled by moral indignation. Accusations of harm, demands for justice and feelings of resentment are the common markers of personal disputes. Hence, personal disputes are extremely difficult to resolve, and the long-term effects of the dispute on interpersonal relations can be devastating. The longer this type of dispute goes on, the larger the gulf between the parties becomes and the more supporters begin showing up, arm in arm, on either side.

You might wonder how likely it is that you will actually become embroiled in a nasty, interpersonal confrontation. Isn't this something that just gets stirred up by cantankerous, insecure crackpots and gets under the skin of only defensive, closed-minded people? Although effective application of the skills covered in this book should lessen the likelihood of your interpersonal relationships becoming entangled in the web of personal disputes, the following information is sobering.

In response to the question, 'In general, what percentage of management time is wasted on resolving personality conflicts?', Max Messmer, chairman of Accountemps, reported an average response of 18 per cent from a large sample of organisations, compared with 9.2 per cent a decade earlier. He lamented the fact that approximately nine weeks of management time each year is consumed by this non-productive activity (Messmer 2006).

Coming at the subject from a different angle, a recent article, entitled 'Is having partners a bad idea?', reported the results of an *Inc.* magazine poll in which nearly two-thirds of the small business owners surveyed said that, notwithstanding the potential benefits, they preferred not adding a partner because of the increased potential for interpersonal conflict. In a second poll reported in this article, researchers at the University of Minnesota uncovered similar misgivings in family businesses. About half of the second-generation family members working in such companies were having second thoughts about the wisdom of joining the firm, because they were worried about their business careers being marred by interpersonal conflicts (Gage 1999).

Whereas people-focused conflicts have been characterised as emotional disputes, issue-focused conflicts are more like rational negotiations, which can be thought of as 'an interpersonal decision-making process by which two or more people agree how to allocate scarce resources' (Thompson 2001: 2). In issue-based conflicts, manager-negotiators are typically acting as agents, representing the interests of their department, function or project. Although negotiators have conflicting priorities for how the scarce resource should be used, in most day-to-day negotiations within an organisation the negotiators recognise the need to find an amicable settlement that appears fair to all parties. Because the negotiation outcome, if not the process itself, is generally public knowledge, the negotiators recognise that there is no such thing as one-time-only negotiations. One veteran manager observed that he uses a simple creed to govern his dealings with others—'It's a small world and a long life'—meaning that there is no long-term personal advantage to short-term gains won through unfair means.

Although the discussion of conflict management here draws liberally on the negotiations literature, the objective is to prepare you for highly charged emotional confrontations, where untrained initiators attempt to transfer their frustrations to someone else, by alleging that great harm has been caused by the offender's self-serving motives or incompetent practices. Being on the receiving end of a 'surprise personal attack' is debilitating, and so the unskilled respondent is likely to fight back, escalating the conflict with counter-accusations or defensive retorts. That is why experienced mediators agree that when a disagreement 'gets personal' it often becomes intractable.

Conflict source

The diagnostic lens now shifts from understanding the focus, or content, of a conflict ('What's this about?') to the source, or origin, of the conflict ('How did it get started?'). Managers often react as though serious interpersonal confrontations are the result of personality defects. They label people who are frequently involved in conflicts 'trouble makers' or 'poor performers', and attempt to ignore, transfer or dismiss them as a way of resolving conflict. While some individuals seem to have a propensity for making trouble and appear to be reactive under even the best of circumstances, 'personality problems' actually account for only a small percentage of organisational conflicts (Hines 1980; Schmidt & Tannenbaum 1965).

This proposition is supported by research on performance reviews (Latham & Wexley 1981). It has been shown that managers generally attribute poor performance to personal deficiencies in employees, such as laziness, lack of skill or lack of motivation. However, when staff are asked the causes of *their* poor performance, they generally explain them in terms of problems in their environment, such as poor management, insufficient support or uncooperative co-workers. While some face-saving may be involved here, this line of research suggests that managers need to guard against the assumption that bad behaviours imply bad people. In fact, the aggressive or harsh behaviours sometimes observed in interpersonal confrontations often reflect the frustrations of people who have good intentions but are unskilled in handling intense emotional experiences.

In contrast to the personality-defect theory of conflict, Table 7.1 proposes four explanations for the cause of interpersonal conflict.

TABLE 7.1 Conflict source/resolution grid

SOURCE OF CONFLICT	FOCUS OF RESOLUTION
Personal differences	Perceptions and expectations
Information deficiencies	Misinformation and misrepresentation
Role incompatibility	Goals and responsibilities
Environmental stress	Resource scarcity and uncertainty

Personal differences

Individuals bring different backgrounds to their roles in organisations. Their values and needs have been shaped by different socialisation processes, depending on their cultural and family values and beliefs, level of education, breadth of experience, gender, age and so forth. As a result, their interpretations of events and their expectations about relationships with others in the organisation will vary considerably. Conflicts stemming from incompatible personal values and needs are some of the most difficult (and challenging) to resolve. They often become highly emotional and take on moral overtones. A disagreement about who is factually correct easily turns into a bitter argument over who is morally right. In fact, being 'wrong' is a highly charged matter for humans and is itself a philosophical source of conflict (Schulz 2010).

Schulz's whole book is about the positive value of wrongness. She argues that being wrong is connected to the best qualities of empathy, optimism, imagination, conviction and courage. 'It is a vital part of how we learn and change. ... It is ultimately wrongness, not rightness, that can teach us who we are' (2010: 32).

Conflicts about right and fact also arise out of people's different non-verbal behaviours, as well as their internal mind-sets and expectations. The sense of rightness and reality has full-grown adult managers acting as if their own tastes and beliefs are the truth. This inability to distinguish 'taste' from 'truth' displays a lack of flexibility and is an EQ limitation that impacts negatively upon effective management skills. The ladder of inference is based on this premise. We are often blind to our own errors, and so 'we accept [that] fallibility is a universal phenomenon but are constantly startled by our own mistakes' (Shulz 2010: 45). Precisely because we tend to be blind to our own errors, we need to increase our self-awareness, engage in 360-degree feedback and receive other information about our managerial behaviours. 'The ability to grasp what minds do, to understand that people can hold beliefs that are mistaken or different from our own, subtends a vast swath of mature thinking' (Schulz 2010: 55). (See the discussion of this whole area in Chapter 2.)

However, parties to a dispute still have choices regarding what path their dispute will take, in terms of focusing on the issues (for example, conflicting points of view reflecting different values and needs) or the people (for example, questioning competence, intent, acceptance, understanding, and so on). It is precisely because conflicts stemming from personal differences tend to become person-focused that effective conflict managers need to understand this analytical distinction so that they can help disputants frame their conflict in terms of offending (troublesome) issues, not offensive (trouble-making) people.

This observation is particularly relevant for managers working in an organisational environment characterised by broad demographic diversity. Why? It has been observed that (1) a diverse workforce can be a strategic organisational asset, and (2) very different people tend to engage in very intense conflicts—which can become an organisational liability (Lombardo & Eichinger 1996). On the positive side, the more heterogeneous the demographic profile of an employee population is, the more diversity of experience and perspective contained in the organisation (Cox 1994).

Poor information processes

Conflicts may also result from deficiencies in the organisation's communication systems. An important message may not be received, a boss's instructions may be poorly presented or misinterpreted, or decision makers may arrive at different conclusions because they use different databases. Conflicts based on misinformation or misunderstanding can be minimised by clarifying previous messages or obtaining additional information. This generally resolves the dispute. It might entail rewording the boss's instructions, reconciling contradictory sources of data or redistributing copies of misplaced messages. This type of conflict is common in organisations, but it is also fairly easy to resolve. Once the breakdown in the information system is repaired, disputants are generally able to resolve their disagreement with a minimum of resentment.

Diversity in our backgrounds can greatly add to informational difficulties. The use of email brings another complexity to this area. The speed of email and ease of copying material to others magnifies small misunderstandings very quickly. Managers can also help reduce the source of conflict by proactively establishing effective protocols for email usage.

Role incompatibility

The complexity inherent in most organisations tends to produce conflict between members whose tasks are interdependent but whose roles are incompatible. This type of conflict is exemplified by the classic goal conflicts between line and staff, production and sales, marketing, and research and development. Each unit has different responsibilities in the organisation and, as a result, each places different priorities on organisational goals (for example, customer satisfaction, product quality, production efficiency, compliance with government regulations). It is also typical of firms whose multiple product lines compete for scarce resources. Role confusion and conflict is also inherent in de-layered organisations and in the development of work teams.

Role incompatibility conflicts may overlap with those arising from personal differences or information difficulties. The personal differences that staff bring to an organisation generally remain dormant until they are triggered by an organisational catalyst, such as interdependent task responsibilities. One reason members often perceive that their assigned roles are incompatible is that they are operating from different bases of information. They communicate with different sets of people, are tied into different reporting systems and receive information from different team leaders.

In another twist on the incompatible roles category, Shafer, Park and Liao (2002) identified a role clash between a profession and the organisation. Employees who had very strong professional identities were less committed to the organisation and more readily perceived and engaged in higher levels of organisational conflict than their non-professional colleagues.

Environmental stress

Another major source of conflict is environmentally induced stress. Conflicts stemming from personal differences and role incompatibilities are greatly exacerbated by a stressful environment. When an organisation is faced with rapid change, downsizing and disruption, its members are more likely to become embroiled in disputes over domain claims and resource requests. Scarcity and job uncertainty tends to lower trust, increase selfishness and reduce participation in decision making. These are ideal conditions for incubating interpersonal conflict (Cameron, Kim & Whetten 1987). The toxic workplace (see Chapter 3) with poor working conditions and unsafe work practices also produces stress and injury. When a large Singaporean bank recently announced a major downsizing, the threat to employees' security was so severe that it disrupted long-time, close working relationships. Even friendships were not immune to the effects of the scarcity-induced stress.

Another environmental condition that fosters conflict is uncertainty. When individuals find it difficult to predict what is going to happen to them from month to month, they become very anxious and prone to conflict. This type of 'frustration conflict' often stems from rapid, repeated change. If task assignments, management philosophy, accounting procedures and lines of authority are changed frequently, employees find it difficult to cope with the resulting stress, and sharp, bitter conflicts can easily erupt over seemingly trivial problems. This type of conflict is generally intense, but it dissipates quickly once a change becomes routine and individuals' stress levels are lowered.

When a major pet-food manufacturing factory announced that one-third of its managers would have to support a new third shift but provided no details and information about how this would work, the feared disruption of personal and family routines prompted many managers to think about looking for other jobs. In addition, the uncertainty of who was going to be required to work at night was so great that even routine management work was disrupted by posturing and infighting.

The conflict triangle

The conflict triangle (Figure 7.3) is adapted from a model of game theory called the 'drama triangle' (Karpman 1968). It is reflected in Senge's (1992) work on system archetypes. This model is another way of looking at conflict in the workplace. It helps you to understand and identify the roles that people adopt when they begin to get into potential conflict. Let us examine the model more closely.

- *The critic role.* The critic role is the position that employees (and managers) adopt when they personalise a criticism or when they wish to criticise without any dialogue or consideration of other points of view. It is a one-up, one-down authority position. The hidden (usually unconscious) intention is to maintain distance and control and to avoid responsibility.
- *The helper role.* The helper role represents the situation in which managers attempt to give assistance and support to others without their requesting it. In this role, they not only give support but also take responsibility for the other person. They implicitly assume that the person is incapable without their help. The hidden motive is to show how good they are or to avoid their own concerns or fears by reducing the emotion of the person who is experiencing difficulties. They also gain some pride from being 'helpful'.
- *The victim role.* The last position in the triangle is usually the most visible. This is the role adopted by the person who is in need. Unlike a person who is in genuine need, people in the victim role do not ask for help directly. In fact, they act helplessly, as if they have no resources of their own to solve the problem. The victim role is adopted because of a lack of self-confidence and/or a need to blame other people for their circumstances. In this role, people are very skilful at seducing helpers to help them, only later to turn on the helper. None of these three roles of critic, helper or victim is particularly responsible or mature.

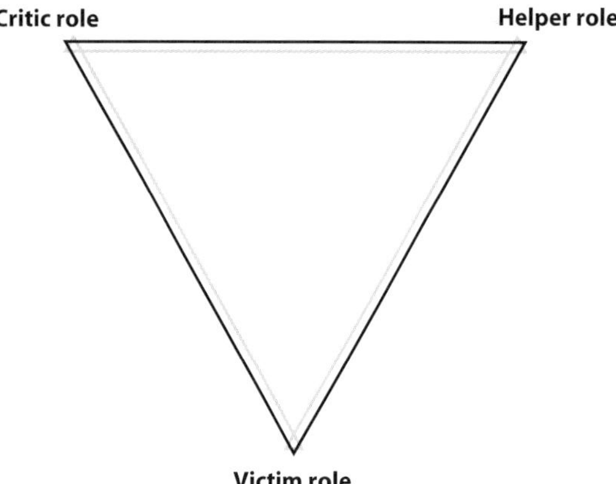

FIGURE 7.3 The conflict triangle

On the conflict triangle, adoption of any one of the roles tends to induce or encourage another person to adopt one of the complementary roles. Then a repetitive or conflict routine is established. Such a routine, by its very nature, ensures a conflict situation develops with recognisable manoeuvres that are repeated regularly between the same employees. One example of such a repetitive routine is as follows.

Geoff: (Looking really miserable) I was given a bad performance review by Bill again yesterday and it's just not fair.

Maureen: You poor thing! Maybe I can have a word to Bill for you, to see if I can get him to change his mind.

Geoff: I don't know. I've thought of that, but then Bill will blame me for talking to you.

Maureen: Well, maybe you can talk to me about what areas of your performance he has criticised and we'll see if we can help you improve those.

Geoff: I don't think there's much use in doing that; his criticism is so vague.

Maureen: (A little more impatient now) Well, why don't you go and have a discussion with Bill to clarify exactly what behaviours he wants you to change?

Geoff: (Looking quite helpless) Oh, I have tried that, but it never seems to go anywhere.

Maureen: (Even more frustrated by now) Well, maybe you just need to improve your performance then.

Geoff: (With a sharper tone in his voice) It seems like you agree with Bill!

Maureen: Oh, not again. (Feeling like she's been in this spot with Geoff several times before)

As this dialogue indicates, the routine continues until at some point there is a switch in roles. At this point, all the people in the triangle feel the shift and in some way end up losing in the exchange. Because it is a repetitive psychological routine, there is no satisfactory outcome. So, in the paradoxical manner of human beings, the routine is repeated in another time and place in order to achieve a satisfactory resolution, only to have a similar switch and disappointing outcome yet again. Ways to avoid the conflict triangle include only using objective data, not taking responsibility for others, noticing a routine when you are in it and bailing out quickly, and being as self-aware as possible (see Chapter 2). Later sections of this chapter offer some further strategies.

Mobbing

A distinct type of conflict that crosses over each of the four conflict sources discussed above is the recent phenomenon called 'mobbing'. This text defines mobbing as 'the improper sharing of group-developed perceptions of bullying behaviour of another party in such a way that credibility is given to the complainants by weight of numbers and the required confidentiality of the group action'. Mobbing is a process that avoids responsibility and denies the victim natural justice. (See also Davenport et al. 1999; Westhues 2006; Zapf 1999. And for Australian examples, see Shallcross, Ramsay & Barker 2010; Shallcross, Sheehan & Ramsay 2008.)

A typical mobbing scenario involves a staff member (the complainant) who is upset by the behaviour of a boss or a colleague (the respondent). The staff member does not bring his concern to the person causing offence. He endures several instances of the same behaviour before taking any action. He shares his upset with a trusted friend or a group of friends in the workplace. The friends inevitably support the complainant and make similar observations about the respondent and their experiences with the respondent. Fortified by group solidarity, the group of three or five staff members approaches the manager of the respondent. They demand (and receive) complete confidentiality before they discuss their complaint. They share the details of their complaint about the respondent and ask the manager not to identify them or raise the matter with the respondent. They often (and it is now a collective class-action rather than an individual complaint) state directly or imply that the situation is so serious that it is damaging the workplace and that they may have to take stress leave or even resign, or preferably the respondent should be removed.

A management-level example of this same mobbing behaviour involves private discussions between several managers (often at different levels of seniority) about the poor behaviour of a staff member. The staff member is not included in these discussions but decisions are made in relation to his or her placement elsewhere in the organisation or his or her unsuitability for promotion.

This mobbing process is based on gossiping, which is any conversation about someone without that person being present. Understandably, people may feel vulnerable and threatened when they perceive they are being intimidated. Vulnerability is worth respecting, but that is not an excuse for non-accountability. Most people do not engage in mobbing maliciously. People do not have to be malicious or mischievous to be mistaken. Often it is a misplaced but genuine belief that they have been wronged and that it is unsafe to address the issue directly. A large number of bullying complaints are based on misperceptions and misunderstandings about the behaviour, rather than on an accurate experience of intimidating behaviour. Managerial mishandling of these perceptions creates an entrenched and chronic conflict situation. Universities are particularly excellent breeding grounds for mobbing (see Westhues 2006).

Mobbing is encouraged by the following misleading managerial beliefs:

- Where there's smoke, there's fire.
- The larger the mob, the more likely there is some element of truth in the complaint.
- 'Safety in numbers' is an acceptable and responsible way to behave.
- Alleged intimidating behaviour is so frightening that it can only be dealt with by a third party and not dealt with directly.
- Without complete confidentiality, no one would ever come forward and complain about improper behaviour.
- When people complain in a group, they all want the same solution.
- When people use the same words—for example, 'intimidating' or 'bullying'—they are all referring to the same behaviour.
- A group complaint absolves each individual of individual responsibility for the complaint.

A manager who empathises with the complainants and is attempting to avoid conflict and offer protection based on the above beliefs is actually colluding in the irresponsible behaviour. Paradoxically, the consequences of mobbing actually increase negative outcomes and sustain a toxic work environment. Conflicts are exacerbated, honourable managers or staff members are labelled by implication as bullies, with no chance of correcting the perception, real bullies are not dealt with fairly or appropriately, the emotional and actual costs to the organisation and its employees are extremely high, and the ethical values and organisational culture are debased.

So, how should managers handle this complex situation? The following managerial approaches have proved effective:

- Ensure that all your staff are trained in, understand and are personally committed to the organisation's code of conduct.
- Publicly and consistently proclaim that all complaints of intimidation or bullying will be treated seriously because they *are* serious.
- Guarantee that any complainant will be protected from being punished for making a complaint.
- Identify that blanket confidentiality is not acceptable.
- Affirm that the first step in a complaint is to raise the complaint with the manager or staff member being complained about. Offer to support the complainant in this step if required.
- State that any complaints will be acted on in some manner or other, whether or not the complainant wishes it.
- Identify precisely what action or remedy the complainant considers appropriate given the nature of the complaint.
- Respond directly so that wildly unrealistic remedies are defined as such.

Westhues (2006: 241) suggests the following ten management measures to reduce the conflict potential of mobbing in an academic context, which we have adapted for general management:

1. Focus on the situation, issue or behaviour, not the person.
2. Use managerial decision-making, rather than quasi-formal investigations.
3. Avoid emotionally charged words such as 'investigation', 'bullying', and so on.
4. Have a simple, clear, fair policy and procedures manual, and use it.
5. Ensure procedural fairness and open-mindedness.
6. Only accept specific, evidence-based explanations.
7. Understand the organisational and cultural context in which mobbing occurs.
8. Defend free expression and encourage discussion with the manager or staff member concerned.
9. Keep administration (especially human resource management) open and loose.
10. Answer internal mail.

Four possible management responses to mobbing have been identified in the mobbing management grid shown in Figure 7.4. This grid displays the features of each management style in response to mobbing behaviour.

In the 'Reactive' cell, managers are open in their response and subjective in their judgment. They publicly berate the complainants for being troublemakers and report them for their actions, or they immediately side with the complainants and publicly criticise, discipline or even remove the respondent from his or her position without getting all the facts.

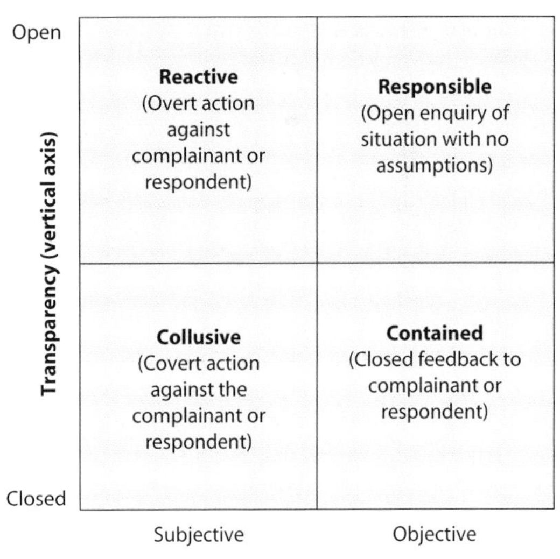

FIGURE 7.4 Mobbing management grid

Source: G. Andrewartha, Unpublished paper, McPhee Andrewartha (Adelaide: 2009).

The 'Collusive' response is both closed and subjective. Managers listen and give no indication of their future intentions and ask that the matter remain closed for now. They may believe the complaint and covertly discuss the respondent with other managers to limit, or in some subtle way punish, the respondent for the presumed offence. Alternatively, managers may side with the respondent, not indicate this to the complainants, and confidentially discuss their actions with the respondent or other managers. No open action or discussions take place.

The 'Contained' response is closed, but objective. Managers keep the matter quiet and do not reveal their strategy. They hear the complaint, quietly ask others in confidence about the matter, and with or without a confidential discussion with the respondent they form a considered view of the situation and take quiet and undeclared action based on the evidence.

The fourth alternative, the 'Responsible' approach, is the only healthy managerial response. It is both open and objective. In this approach, the manager engages in the thoughtful responses described above. Both complainants and respondent are treated respectfully and transparently. Independent data are collected, and efforts of resolution and mediation are engaged. All parties are held accountable, and appropriate and open actions are taken based on due process and fairness. All parties are protected and the matter is resolved in a timely manner.

Such mobbing workplace behaviour may be a reflection of a recent disturbing Western public culture trend in which, it is suggested, 'we think in labels and hunt in packs' (Krygier 2006).

Impact of culture and diversity on managing conflict

Increased interdependence and interactions across national, organisational and departmental borders create multiple opportunities not only for improved decision making, creativity and innovation, but also for miscommunication, misunderstanding, misperceptions and loss of productivity. In resolving conflicts, a diversity of conflict management styles leads to a variety of approaches and resolutions that have the potential for both conflict escalation and conflict de-escalation (Rubin, Pruitt & Kim 1991; Seybolt, Derr & Nielson 1996; Tjosvold 1991; Wei 2000). One feature of employing teams in cross-cultural settings is the common need to resort to virtual communication and conflict resolution methods.

Montoya-Weiss, Massey and Song (2001) found that virtual teams that operate asynchronously must do without mechanisms that synchronous teams have available to coordinate their activity and manage conflict. They found that the management of conflict was even more crucial than in synchronous teams and that temporal coordination has some significant moderating effects.

As the overview model of managing conflict presented in Figure 7.9 (later in the chapter, on page 370) suggests, before alternative conflict strategies can be considered, managers must recognise the disputants' personal preferences for handling conflict, as well as the context in which the conflict occurs. In the business environment of the 21st century, culture and workforce diversity are critical elements of the context and influencing factors of preferences for managing conflict.

Managing diversity has become an important component of managerial activities. 'Managing diversity' can be defined as the planning and implementation of organisational systems, policies and practices to manage people so that the potential advantages of diversity are maximised, while the potential disadvantages are minimised (Cox 1994). Diversity theorist Taylor Cox Jr posits that, by managing diversity in their workforces, organisations are satisfying three types of goals: (1) ethical or social responsibility goals; (2) legal obligations; and (3) economic performance goals (Cox 1994). First, managing diversity demonstrates organisational willingness to provide equal opportunities and fairness for all employees regardless of gender, race, age or any other differentiating characteristic other than performance. Second, in some countries certain aspects of managing diversity are mandated by law. Neglect of these laws often results in significant lawsuits and financial losses to settle cases of discrimination. Third, managing diversity actually affects an organisation's bottom-line results of economic performance.

The adoption of a particular conflict style is related to one's culture. (Kozan 1997) and other cross-cultural studies found that employees of different cultural backgrounds utilised all of the conflict resolution styles described in this chapter. In general, Asian employees (Chinese, Korean) and European employees (Germans, Americans) differed in their conflict resolution styles in a manner congruent with Hofstede's individualism–collectivism theory discussed in Chapter 2. Europeans used a competing style more often than their Asian colleagues, who more commonly endorsed avoidance or compromise. The studies clearly indicate that the competing style (that is, high assertiveness, low cooperativeness) is more favoured by members of individualistic cultures (the United States) than by members of collectivistic cultures (Korea, China), and that the opposite pattern occurs for the avoiding (that is, low assertiveness, low cooperativeness) and accommodating (that is, low assertiveness, high cooperativeness) styles. Most cultures displayed discomfort with confronting conflict directly; however, Americans were more likely to confront conflict than Chinese or Koreans (Holt & DeVore 2005; Kim-Jo, Benet-Martínez & Ozer 2008; Rahim & Blum 1994; Seybolt, Derr & Nielson 1996; Ting-Toomey et al. 1991; Weldon & Jehn 1995; Yuan 2010).

As discussed in Chapter 2, differing motivations may still lead to the utilisation of a common conflict management strategy. Cox developed a model—the Interactional Model of Cultural Diversity (IMCD), shown in Figure 7.5—that supplies the rationale for how diversity influences organisational effectiveness.

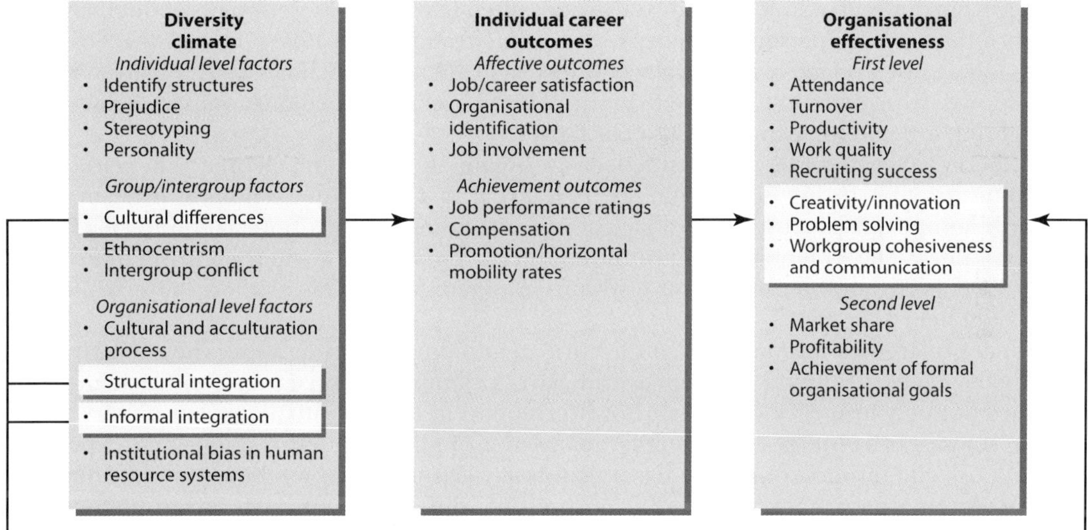

FIGURE 7.5 A model of the impact of diversity on career outcomes and organisational effectiveness

Source: Reprinted with permission of the publisher. From Taylor Cox, Jr, *Cultural Diversity in Organizations: Theory, Research and Practice*. Copyright © 1994 Berrett-Koehler Publishers Inc., San Francisco, CA. All rights reserved. <www.bkconnection.com>

The main points of the IMCD model are the following: (1) the model demonstrates the influence of diversity on multiple levels—the individual, the group and the organisation; (2) the diversity climate of the organisation is determined by the extent to which differences are valued in the workplace and the extent to which members of minority groups are respected and integrated into both the formal and informal power structure of the organisation; (3) the diversity climate affects individual career outcomes, both affective (for example, job satisfaction) and tangible (for example, promotions); and (4) organisational outcomes are affected directly by the nature of the diversity climate and indirectly by the way individuals feel about their careers and the organisation.

Cox and other scholars who adhere to the 'value in diversity' perspective offer considerable evidence for the performance benefits of a diverse workforce when managed effectively (for example, Cox, Lobel & McLeod 1991; Mandell & Kohler-Gray 1990; Morrison 1996; Thomas & Ely 1996). From recent studies of diversity (Cox & Blake 1991; Morrison 1996), some of the consistently cited economic benefits of managing diversity include:

- obtaining and maintaining increased market share
- cost savings from reducing turnover rates among minority employees

- improved creativity and problem-solving capabilities due to the broader range of perspectives and cultural mind-sets
- perceptions of fairness and equity in the workplace
- increased flexibility that positively affects motivation and minimises conflict between work and non-work demands (for example, family, personal interest, leisure).

After this relatively brief discussion of the impact of diversity on business organisations, let us consider how diversity and cultural differences influence the management of conflict. Cox's IMCD model suggests that both interpersonal and intergroup conflict can affect the diversity climate in the organisation, with subsequent implications for the overall effectiveness of the organisation.

One factor to consider in conflict management is the cultural differences of the participants involved. Are both participants from the majority culture of the organisation? If one is from a minority culture, to what extent is the diversity climate in the organisation positive or negative? Has this particular minority group or individual had a history of conflict within the organisation? These questions are important in evaluating the context of the conflict situation.

People from different ethnic and cultural groups often have very different views about the value of, and justifications for, interpersonal disputes (Adler 1991; Trompenaars 1998). To state this observation more broadly, conflict is largely a culturally defined event (Hocker & Wilmot 1991; Sillars & Weisberg 1987; Weldon & Jehn 1995) in the sense that our cultural background colours our views about what is worth 'fighting for' and what constitutes 'a fair fight'.

In addition, when the everyday business of an organisation requires people with very different demographic profiles to interact frequently, it is likely that their interactions will be marred by misunderstandings and mistrust due to a lack of understanding of, and appreciation for, each other's needs and values. The potential for harmful conflict is even greater when confrontations involve members of majority and minority groups within an organisation. This is where 'diversity-sensitive' managers can help out.

Personal preferences for handling conflict are an additional consideration when thinking about conflict management. Cultural differences can have a significant impact on conflict management styles. They not only influence choices of how to respond in conflict situations, but culture can also affect the sources of conflicts. For example, many of an individual's perceptions and expectations related to work and business organisations are culturally learned. Conflicts between individuals from different cultural groups frequently stem from personal differences inherent in not understanding one another's cultural values.

Another example is the role of uncertainty as an environmental source of stress and conflict. One of the four primary dimensions revealed in the seminal cultural research by Geert Hofstede (1980) is the extent to which uncertainty is tolerated or avoided. Some cultures, such as Japan, have a high uncertainty avoidance, whereas other cultures, such as the United States, are much more tolerant of uncertainty. Extrapolating from these findings, if an American firm and a Japanese firm create a joint venture in an industry known for highly volatile sales (for example, short-term memory chips), it might be expected that the Japanese managers would experience a higher level of uncertainty-induced conflict than their American counterparts. In contrast, because American culture places an extremely high value on individualism (another of Hofstede's key dimensions of cultural values), the US managers in this joint venture could be expected to experience a higher level of conflict stemming from their role interdependence with their Japanese counterparts.

To illustrate how various types of conflict are actually played out in an organisation, and how devastating their impact on a firm's performance can be, let us take a look at the troubles encountered by First Boston, one of the top seven investment banks dominating the New York capital market. This venerable firm became embroiled in a conflict between two important revenue divisions: trading and investment banking. After the stock-market crash in 1987, the investment banking division, which accounted for the bulk of First Boston's profits in the 1980s through mergers and acquisitions, asked that resources be diverted from trading (an unprofitable line) to investment banking. They also asked for the allocation of computer costs to be on the basis of usage, rather than splitting the costs 50:50, since investment banking made less use of computers. A review committee, including the CEO (a trader by background), reviewed the problem and finally decided to reject the investment banking division's proposals. This led to the resignations of the head of its investment division and several of its senior staff, including seven leveraged-buyout specialists.

This interdepartmental conflict was exacerbated by increasing friction between competing subcultures within the firm. In the 1950s, when First Boston began, it was 'WASPish' in composition, and its business came chiefly through the 'old-boy network'. In the 1970s, First Boston recruited a number of innovative 'whiz kids'—mostly from Jewish, Italian and Cuban backgrounds. These new employees generated innovative ways to package mergers and acquisitions, which were now the mainstay of business in the investment area. They were less 'aristocratic', and more casual in style (for example, preferring to wear jeans to the office), than their more traditional colleagues. The tension between the new 'high-flyers' and the 'old guard' appeared to colour many decisions at First Boston.

As a result of these conflicts, First Boston lost a number of key personnel. 'The quitters claim that as the firm has grown, it has become a less pleasant place to work in, with political infighting taking up too much time' (*The Economist* 1998).

Buttery and Leung (1998) argued that it is unrealistic to suggest that one negotiation style fits all cultures. In contrasting Western and Eastern approaches to negotiation, they postulated that in the West there are two main negotiation approaches: 'hard line' and 'soft line'. The hard line is when negotiators take up an initial position and then make concessions until a compromise is achieved. It is argued that their initial position forces negotiators on both sides to develop their positions. The soft-line approach involves relationship maintenance and can provide a richer approach where negotiators focus on mutual interests and not on predetermined positions. Each approach, however, is still focused on contracting rather than being part of an ongoing relationship. Indeed, research has identified that Australian firms consider strategic alliances, a form of enduring relationship, the last strategic resort (Buttery & Buttery 1994: 372).

The Eastern methods of negotiation are based on the foundation of Confucian thought, which is focused on harmony, hierarchy, the development of moral potential and kinship. These four tenets of Confucian values drive three interpersonal norms:

- basic communication patterns
- social obligation
- relationships among different life domains (Shenkar & Ronen 1987).

These norms are strongly relationship-based and involve Chinese concepts such as *guanxi*, which comes down to having access to the required influence to make things happen. It is all about storing up political capital and building relationships with a network of people through which influence is brokered. *Guanxi* requires the exchange of favours and the giving of 'face', or enhancing of someone's social status. It is not about returning one favour with another, or winning one negotiation; rather, it is about building a life-long relationship.

To be more effective in business organisations of the future, managers must take into account diversity and culture when managing conflict situations. Cross-cultural conflict management is an important consideration in any discussion of conflict management. Differences in culture, gender or other areas of diversity cannot be separated out as isolated topics. These areas must be seen as parts of an integrated whole in a global economy. Much more could have been said here about the impact of culture on conflict in business organisations, but sufficient information has been included to underscore the main points. Other books (for example, Adler 1991; Trompenaars 1998) provide more comprehensive insights into the role of culture in important management activities. (See also Chapter 2.)

Conflict response alternatives

Having examined some typical causes of conflict, the discussion now focuses on common responses. As revealed in the assessment survey, people's responses to interpersonal confrontations tend to fall

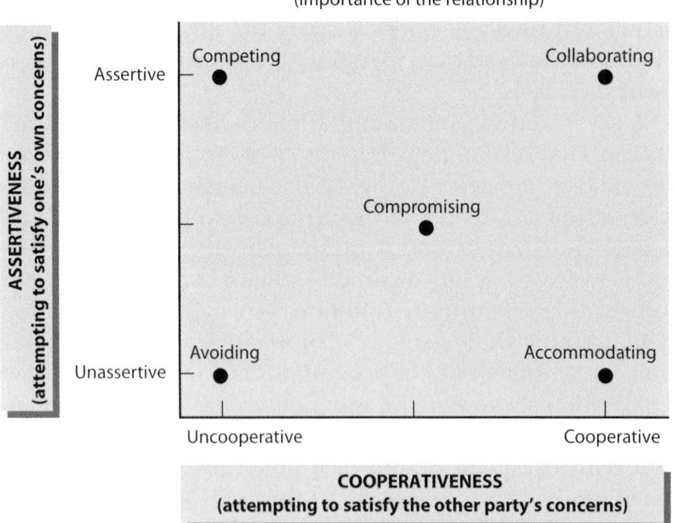

FIGURE 7.6 Two-dimensional model of conflict behaviour

Source: T. Ruble and K. Thomas, 'Support for a two-dimensional model of conflict behavior', in *Organizational Behavior and Human Performance*, 16, 1976, p. 145. Reproduced with permission from Elsevier.

into five categories: competing, accommodating, avoiding, compromising and collaborating (Filley 1975, 1978; Robbins 1974). These five aspects can also be seen as management and leadership styles. You may wish to contrast your conflict style with your LETS leadership style discussed in Chapter 2. They can be organised along two dimensions, as shown in Figure 7.6.

The five approaches to conflict reflect different degrees of cooperativeness and assertiveness. A cooperative response is intended to satisfy the needs of the other party, whereas an assertive response focuses on the needs of the dominant or initiating party. The cooperativeness dimension reflects the importance of the relationship, whereas the assertiveness dimension reflects the importance of the issue.

The competing response

The competing response (assertive, uncooperative) is an attempt to satisfy our own needs at the expense of the needs of the other individual. This can be done by using formal authority, physical threats, manipulation ploys, or by ignoring the claims of the other party. The blatant use of the authority of office ('I'm the boss, so we'll do it my way') or a related form of intimidation is generally evidence of a lack of tolerance or self-confidence. The use of manipulation or feigned ignorance is a much more subtle reflection of a self-centred leadership style. Manipulative leaders often appear to be democratic by suggesting that conflicting proposals be referred to a committee for further investigation. However, they ensure that the composition of the committee reflects their interests and preferences, so that what appears to be a selection based on merit is actually an authoritarian act.

A related ploy that some managers use is to ignore a proposal that threatens their personal interests. If the originator enquires about the disposition of his or her memo, the manager pleads ignorance, blames the mail clerk or new secretary, and then suggests that the proposal be redrafted. After several of these encounters, employees generally get the message that the boss is not interested in their ideas. This is often the critic role on the conflict triangle.

The problem with the repeated use of this conflict management approach is that it breeds resentment and lowers morale. While some observers may admire authoritarian or manipulative leaders because they appear to accomplish a great deal, their management styles generally produce a backlash in the long run as people become unwilling to absorb the emotional costs. (See the recognition grid in Chapter 6.)

The accommodating approach

The accommodating approach (obliging, cooperative, unassertive) satisfies the other party's concerns while neglecting one's own. Unfortunately, managers' neglect of their firm's interests and responsibilities to accommodate the wishes of others generally results in both parties 'losing'. The difficulty with the habitual use of the accommodating approach is that it emphasises preserving a friendly relationship at the expense of critically appraising issues, protecting personal rights and focusing on productivity. This may result in others taking advantage of the 'accommodators', which lowers their self-esteem as they observe themselves being used by others to accomplish their objectives while they fail to make any progress towards their own. This is commonly the helper role on the conflict triangle.

The avoiding response

The avoiding response (uncooperative, unassertive) neglects the interests of both parties by sidestepping the conflict or postponing a solution. This is often the response of managers who are emotionally ill prepared or poorly trained to cope with the stress associated with confrontations. Or it might reflect recognition that a relationship is not strong enough to absorb the fallout of an intense conflict. The repeated use of this approach causes considerable frustration for others because issues never seem to get resolved, really tough problems are avoided because of their high potential for conflict, and employees engaging in conflict are reprimanded for undermining the harmony of the workgroup.

Sensing a leadership vacuum, people from all directions rush to fill it, creating considerable confusion and animosity in the process. Inevitably, the conflict becomes worse. This often coincides with the victim role on the triangle.

The compromising response

The compromising response is intermediate between assertiveness and cooperativeness. A compromise is an attempt to obtain partial satisfaction for both parties, in the sense that both receive the proverbial 'half loaf'. To accommodate this, both parties are asked to make sacrifices to obtain a common gain. While this approach has considerable practical appeal to managers, its indiscriminate use is counterproductive. If employees are continually told to 'split the difference', they may conclude that their managers are more interested in resolving disputes than solving problems. This creates a climate of expediency that encourages game playing, such as asking for twice as much as you need.

The collaborating approach

The collaborating approach (cooperative, assertive) is an attempt to address fully the concerns of both parties. It is often referred to as the 'problem-solving' mode. In this mode, the intent is to find solutions to the cause of the conflict that are satisfactory to both parties, rather than find fault or assign blame. In this way, both parties can feel that they have 'won', or at least the outcome is agreed. This is the only win–win strategy among the five. The avoiding mode results in a lose–lose outcome and the compromising, accommodating and competing modes all represent win–lose outcomes.

Although the collaborative approach is not ideal for all situations, it has the most beneficial effect on the involved parties, when used appropriately. It encourages collaboration and trust, while acknowledging the value of assertiveness. It encourages individuals to focus their disputes on problems and issues, rather than on personalities. Finally, it cultivates the skills necessary for self-management, so that effective problem solvers feel empowered.

The collaborative approach to problem solving and conflict resolution works best in a positive environment that supports openness, directness and equality. Scott's (1990) ERI (emotions, reason, intuition) model of conflict resolution has merit as a quick, collaborative approach to resolving conflict. With this method, the manager needs first to manage his or her emotions (like the work involved in raising one's EQ), before using reason and intuition to make choices about how to react in different conflict situations.

Table 7.2 shows a comparison of the five conflict management approaches.

TABLE 7.2 A comparison of five conflict management approaches

Approach	Objective	Your posture	Supporting rationale	Likely outcome
1. Competing	Get your way.	'I know what's right. Don't question my judgment or authority.'	I don't get paid to be popular.	You feel vindicated, but the other party feels defeated and possibly humiliated.
2. Avoiding	Avoid having to deal with conflict.	'I'm neutral on that issue.' 'Let me think about it.' 'That's someone else's problem.'	I don't want to know about it.	Interpersonal problems do not get resolved, causing long-term frustration manifested in a variety of ways.
3. Compromising	Reach an agreement quickly.	'Let's search for a solution we can both live with so we can get on with our work.'	Let's just fix it up as quickly as possible.	Participants become conditioned to seek expedient, rather than effective, solutions.
4. Accommodating	Do not upset the other person.	'My position isn't so important that it is worth risking bad feelings between us.'	Maintaining harmonious relationships should be our top priority.	Other person is likely to take advantage of you.
5. Collaborating	Solve the problem together.	'This is my position. What is yours?' 'How can we resolve it?'	The positions of both parties are equally important.	The problem is most likely to be resolved and both parties feel satisfied that they have been treated fairly.

Conflict resolution: Gender, teams and psychology

Managers who understand procedural fairness and individual grievance psychology are likely to reduce or manage conflict more effectively than managers who do not understand these concepts. There is support that the collaboration style of conflict management is most successful in most situations. Managers under stress, or who focus more on procedures than on fairness and openness, handle conflict less satisfactorily than other managers (Tatum & Eberlin 2008). High-performing teams tend to use collaborative and compromising styles, in contrast to poorly formed teams or employees who operate independently. The latter tend to prefer the avoiding or competing style (Boros et al. 2010). Finally, there is a suggestion that although collaborative and compromising approaches are the most effective in reducing or resolving conflict, they may come at some psychosocial cost to the manager concerned. This may have certain implications for training managers in how to manage conflict (Chung-Yan & Moeller 2010). Recent research by Aquino (2000: 183–4) showed a relationship between certain types of conflict styles and employees' perceptions of victimisation: 'An obliging (accommodating) style was positively related to perceived indirect victimization, whereas avoiding was positively related to perceived direct victimization. … Further, the use of an obliging style was more strongly related to perceived victimization among low status employees.' This research has implications for the conflict style best adopted by employees and for the organisation's management of workplace mobbing (discussed above).

Most cross-cultural research of conflict management strategies has involved Asian and American cultures. (For more comprehensive reviews, see Rahim & Blum 1994 and Weldon & Jehn 1995.) A frequent criticism of much of this line of research is that most of the studies have applied Western conflict models to non-Western cultures. The five response alternatives discussed in this section are likely to be relevant in other cultures, but the balance between the elements is likely to shift significantly according to the culture.

There is additional debate about the impact of gender on conflict management responses. Some studies report that males prefer a competing response, while females tend to prefer a compromising response (Kilmann 1977). For example, a study by Golesorkhi (2006: 207) found:

> *... when it comes to judging co-worker trustworthiness, male and female employees from the same culture have more in common, despite their gender difference. On the other hand, significant differences emerge between males and females, and within each gender group, once the cultures of origin are taken into consideration. These results suggest that, as organisations become more multicultural, the need to understand how trust, gender and culture interact will become even more critical.*

Sorenson, Hawkins and Sorenson (2002) conducted research on the effect of gender on interpersonal conflict. Results indicated that gender was related to psychological type: male respondents were predominantly 'thinkers', and female respondents were predominantly 'feelers'. Psychological type influenced conflict management for only one of five conflict style preferences. 'Feelers' were more likely to choose an accommodating style than were 'thinkers'. Overall, however, the results indicated that neither psychological type nor gender accounted for a substantial amount of variance in conflict style preference.

Other studies have found gender to have little influence on a person's preferred responses to conflict (Korabik, Baril & Watson 1993). From a review of the growing literature on conflict styles and gender, Keashly (1994) draws five conclusions:

1. There is little evidence of gender differences in abilities and skills related to conflict management.
2. Evidence suggests that sex-role expectations appear to influence behaviour and perceptions of behaviour in particular conflict situations.
3. Influences and norms other than sex-role expectations may affect and influence conflict and behaviour.
4. The experience and meaning of conflict may differ for women and men.
5. There is a persistence of beliefs in gender-linked behaviour even when these behaviours are not found in the research.

So, despite recent research findings to the contrary, perceptions still exist that gender differences do occur in conflict management styles within and between cultures.

Group culture and conflict

Given that there is more demographic diversity due to globalisation, it is to be expected that there will be more conflict in our organisations.

Chatman et al. (1998) reported that individuals in collectivistic-oriented organisations tended to have more beneficial conflicts than did individualistic-oriented organisations.

As discussed earlier, conflict can have positive and negative outcomes. The two types of conflict, task-related and relationship conflict, contribute to these different outcomes. Task-related conflict is more likely to have positive effects on group functioning (Jehn 1997; Shah & Jehn 1993). It focuses on challenging various aspects of the task, which encourages positive group outcomes. Top management teams that engaged in complex tasks were shown to make better decisions with more task conflict (Amason 1996; Shah & Jehn 1993). On the other hand, relationship conflict tends to have detrimental effects on group functioning.

Further, organisational cultural congruence has been found to be positively associated with organisational performance (for example, Schein 1985; Sorensen, Hawkins & Sorenson 2002). Chuang, Church and Zikic (2004: 26–34) propose that the strength of organisational culture has a direct reverse impact on intra-group conflict.

Seven organisational cultural dimensions that influence conflict were assessed by O'Reilly, Chatman and Caldwell (1991): innovativeness, stability, respect for people, outcome orientation, attention to detail, team orientation and aggressiveness.

Knapp, Putnam and Davis (1988) are critical of the conflict literature for focusing on disagreements rather than on incompatibilities, and for failing to consider interpersonal conflict within the organisational system. They also suggest that it is important to include non-verbal and contradictory messages, multiple meanings, linkages between message tactics and strategic behaviour, and inconsistencies between intentions and communicative tactics as conflict develops.

Farmer and Roth (1998) found that larger and more cohesive groups show less competing and more avoidance, compromise and accommodation styles in response to conflict.

Conflict management styles have been related to the quality of agreement reached during negotiations (Pruitt & Carnevale 1993), and Friedman et al. (2000) indicated that individual conflict styles might shape an employee's social environment, which in turn might affect the level of ongoing work conflict and therefore his or her experience of stress. They found that those who use a more integrative style experience lower levels of conflict. Those who use a more competing or avoiding style experience higher levels of conflict and stress. To this extent, they concluded that an employee's work environment is, in part, of his or her own making:

> *Thus, a person's 'situation' depends not only on external conditions, but also on his or her own approach to people and problems. Similarly, experience of conflict is not just a function of external conditions, but also of the conflict management styles that people bring to bear on problems at work. (2000: 3)*

Negotiation strategies

Eman and Shena (2010) confirmed the importance of investing in providing a high level of negotiation training for managers and investing time in making it a routine practice for top executives. Bekmeier-Feuerhahn and Eichenlaub (2010) show that similarity in language (and implicit body language) creates the perception of similarity, which enhances trustworthiness and promotes understanding and a good negotiation atmosphere.

A number of organisational scholars have noted the similarities between conflict management and negotiation strategies (for example, Savage, Blair & Sorenson 1989).

Maddux (1988) developed a six-step negotiation process:

1. Getting to know one another.
2. Statement of goals and objectives.
3. Starting the process.
4. Expressions of disagreement and conflict are not a test of power but an opportunity to reveal what people need.
5. Reassessment and compromise.
6. Agreement in principle or settlement.

Negotiation strategies are commonly divided into two types: integrative and distributive. Negotiators who focus on dividing up a 'fixed pie' use distributive bargaining techniques, whereas parties interested in integrative outcomes search for collaborative ways of 'expanding the pie' by avoiding fixed, incompatible positions (Bazerman & Neale 1992). Distributive negotiators assume an adversarial, competitive posture. They assume that one of the parties can improve only at the other party's expense. In contrast, integrative bargainers use problem-solving techniques to find win–win outcomes. They are interested in finding the best solution rather than competing for a choice between the parties' preferred solutions (Bazerman 1986; Fisher & Brown 1988; Pruitt 1983).

As Table 7.3 shows, four of the five conflict management strategies are distributive in nature. One or both parties must sacrifice something for the conflict to be resolved. Compromising, competing, accommodating and avoiding are considered distributive solutions.

Compromise occurs when both parties make sacrifices in order to find a common ground. Compromisers are generally more interested in finding an expedient solution than an integrative solution. Competing and accommodating demand that one party give up its position in order for the conflict to be resolved. When parties to a conflict avoid resolution, they do so because they assume that

TABLE 7.3 Comparison between negotiation and conflict management strategies

Negotiation strategies	Distributive	Integrative
Conflict management strategies	Compromising Competing Accommodating Avoiding	Collaborating

the costs of resolving the conflict are so high that they are better off not even attempting resolution. The 'fixed pie' still exists, but the individuals involved view attempts to divide it as threatening, so they avoid decisions regarding the allocation process altogether.

Unfortunately, distributive negotiation strategies are consistent with the natural inclination of many individuals to approach conflicts from a 'tough-guy' or an 'easy-touch' or a 'split-the difference' perspective. The problem with the frequent use of these negotiation strategies is that they engender competition, exploitation or irresponsibility. The competing approach to negotiations, in particular, has intuitive appeal. Many observers equate effective negotiators with a tough, highly combative and even ruthless approach. Research has clearly demonstrated, however, that this 'end-justifies-the-means' view of negotiation is generally ineffective and frequently counterproductive.

Later we discuss the limited circumstances under which all forms of conflict management are appropriate. As a general purpose strategy, the integrative approach is far superior.

Effective negotiation strategies

When adopted as an organising framework, the following integrative negotiation strategies have been shown to foster collaboration (Fisher & Ury 1984).

- *Establish shared goals.* To foster a climate of collaboration, both parties need to focus on what they have in common. Making more salient their shared goals of increased productivity, lower costs, reduced design time or improved relations between departments sensitises the parties to the merits of resolving their differences to avoid jeopardising their mutual goals. The step is characterised by the general question: 'What common goals provide a context for these discussions?' Customer service is often an obvious place to start.
- *Separate the people from the problem.* Having clarified the mutual benefits to be gained by successfully concluding a negotiation, it is useful to focus attention on the real issue at hand: solving a problem. Negotiations are more likely to result in mutual satisfaction if the parties depersonalise the discussions. Integrative negotiators suppress their personal desires for revenge or one-upmanship. The other party is viewed as the advocate of a point of view, rather than a rival. The integrative bargainee would say 'That is an unreasonable position', rather than 'You are an unreasonable person'.
- *Focus on interests, not positions.* 'Positions' are demands the negotiator makes. 'Interests' constitute the reason behind the demands. Experience shows that it is easier to establish agreement on interests, because they tend to be broader and multifaceted. This step involves redefining and broadening problems to make them more tractable. When a variety of issues is examined, parties are better able to understand each other's point of view and to place their own views in perspective. A characteristic integrative statement is: 'Help me understand why you advocate that position.'
- *Invent options for mutual gains.* This step also involves creativity, but this time it is focused on generating unusual solutions. Although it is true that some negotiations may necessarily be distributive, it is a mistake for negotiators to adopt a win–lose posture automatically. By focusing both parties' attention on brainstorming alternative, mutually agreeable solutions, the negotiation dynamics naturally shift from competitive to collaborative. In addition, the more options and combinations there are to explore, the greater the probability of reaching an integrative solution. The integrative negotiator proposes: 'Now that we better understand each others' concerns and objectives, let's brainstorm ways of satisfying both our needs.'

- *Use objective criteria.* No matter how integrative both parties are, there are bound to be some incompatible interests. Rather than seizing on these as opportunities for testing wills, it is far more productive to determine what is fair. This requires both parties to examine how fairness should be judged. A shift in thinking from 'getting what I want' to 'deciding what makes most sense' fosters an open, reasonable attitude. It encourages parties to avoid over-confidence or over-commitment to their initial position. This approach is characterised by asking: 'What sense can we make out of our arguments?'
- *Define success in terms of gains, not losses.* If a manager seeks a 10 per cent raise and receives only 6 per cent, that outcome can be viewed as either a 6 per cent improvement or a 40 per cent shortfall. The first interpretation focuses on gains, the second on losses (in this case, unrealised expectations). The outcome is the same, but the manager's satisfaction with it varies substantially. It is important to recognise that people's satisfaction with an outcome is affected by the standards they use to judge it. Recognising this, the integrative negotiator facilitates resolution by judging the value of proposed solutions against reasonable standards. The integrative approach to assessing proposals is: 'Does this outcome constitute a meaningful improvement over current conditions?'

The integrative negotiation strategy can also be seen as part of a process known as reframing (Watzlawick, Weakland & Fisch 1974). The first element of *reframing* involves the process of matching, using the LETS model described in Chapter 2. The second element is to begin to change the other person's understanding of the matter without treading on their deeper values. As Epictetus said in the first century: 'It is not the things themselves which trouble us, but the opinions that we have about those things.' Reframing changes the labels or opinions we have about things without changing the things themselves. The label (or classification) we give to the facts of reality defines our reaction to these facts.

Reframing changes our label of the facts and therefore creates a new reaction. It changes the emphasis and creates new opportunities. Reframing changes the conceptual and emotional perspective or position about a situation and gives it another frame of reference that fits the 'facts' of the situation equally well, and thereby changes its entire meaning. Reframing makes unfamiliar or uncomfortable change more recognisable and more comfortable.

> *What makes reframing such an effective tool of change is that once we do perceive the alternative we cannot so easily go back to the trap and the anguish of a former view of reality. … It is almost impossible to revert to our previous helplessness about the possibility of a solution. (Watzlawick, Weakland & Fisch 1974: 95)*

In negotiation situations, it is useful to review the guidelines for resisting inappropriate influence attempts, as well as the initiator's guidelines presented later in this chapter. In essence, these guidelines suggest shifting the focus of the discussion from 'content' to 'process' in these situations. By presenting your frustration, you are able to draw attention to the unsatisfactory negotiation process. In the course of this type of conversation, the other party's underlying reasons for using a particular negotiation style often surface and the resulting information about time pressure, lack of trust, or unrealistic constituent expectations can be used to build a more collaborative mode of interaction. ('How can we work together to resolve our concerns about process so they don't impair the outcome of our discussion?')

Selecting the appropriate approach

A comparison of alternative approaches inevitably leads to the question: 'Which one is best?' While the collaborative approach produces the fewest negative side effects, each approach has its place. The appropriateness of a management strategy depends on its congruence with both personal style and situational demands. The five modes of handling conflict discussed here are not equally attractive to all individuals. People tend to have a preferred strategy that is consistent with the value they place on conflict and with their dominant personality characteristics (Porter 1973; Scott & Cummings 1973).

While there appears to be a strong link between dominant personality characteristics and preferred modes of handling conflict, managers who can adopt different strategies depending on the nature of the conflict are likely to be most effective (Block 1993; Rossi 1980; Savage, Blair & Sorenson 1989; Senge 1992). This general principle has been borne out in research on conflict management.

In one study, 25 executives were asked to describe two conflict situations, one with bad results and one with good (Phillips & Cheston 1979). These incidents were then categorised in terms of the conflict management approach used. As Figure 7.7 shows, there were 23 incidents of competing, 12 incidents of problem solving, 5 incidents of compromise and 12 incidents of avoidance.

While this was a very small sample of managers, it is noteworthy that there were almost twice as many incidents of competing as there were of problem solving, and nearly five times as many as compromising. It is also interesting that the executives indicated that competing and compromising were equally as likely to produce good results as bad results, whereas problem solving was always linked with positive outcomes and avoidance generally led to negative results.

It is striking that, despite being just as likely to produce bad results as good results, competing was by far the most commonly used conflict management mode. Since this approach is clearly not superior in terms of results, one wonders why these senior executives reported a propensity for using it. A likely answer is expediency. Evidence for this belief is provided by a study of the preferred influence strategies of more than 300 managers in three countries (Kipnis & Schmidt 1983). This study reports that when employees refuse or appear reluctant to comply with a request, managers become directive. When resistance in employees is encountered, managers tend to fall back on their superior power and insist on compliance.

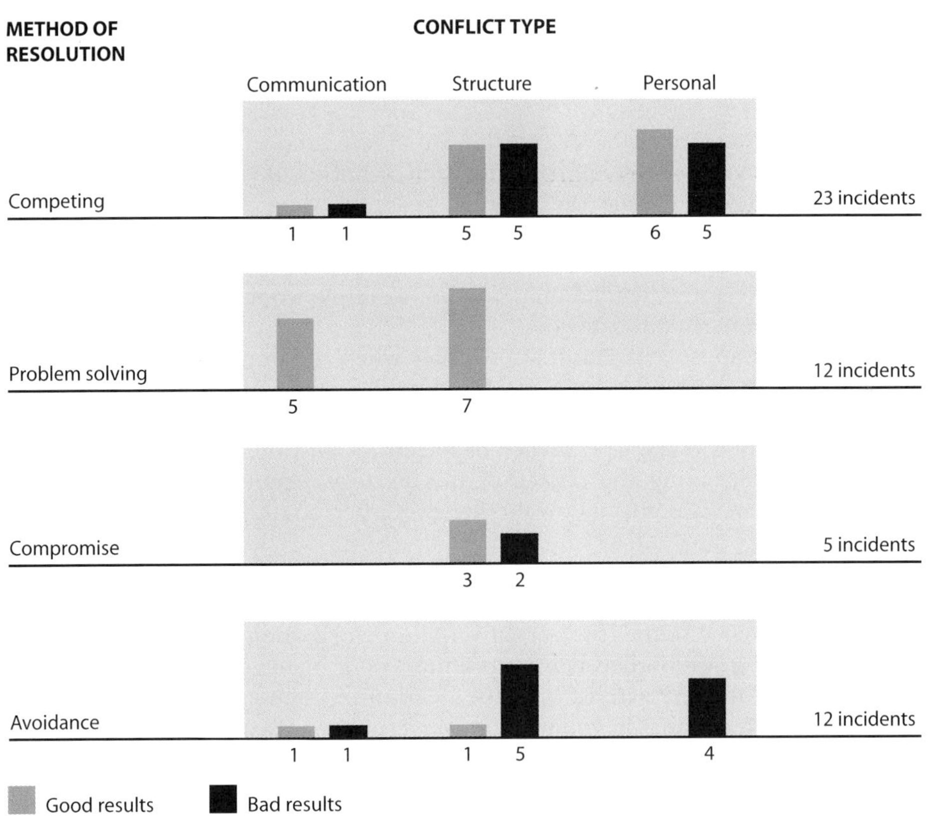

FIGURE 7.7 Outcomes of conflict resolution by conflict type and method of resolution

Source: E. Phillips and R. Cheston, *Conflict Resolution: What Works*, copyright © 1979 by the Regents of the University of California. Reproduced from the *California Management Review*, 21(4), p. 79, with permission of the Regents.

So pervasive was this pattern that the authors of this study proposed an 'Iron Law of Power: the greater the discrepancy in power between influence and target, the greater the probability that more directive influence strategies will be used' (Kipnis & Schmidt 1983: 7). This is a significant feature of managers under pressure and is connected to control issues as part of the parenting behaviour we all acquire during our development (see Andrewartha 1992).

A second striking feature of Figure 7.7 is that some conflict management approaches were never used for certain types of issues. In particular, the managers did not report a single case of problem solving or compromising when personal problems were the source of the conflict. These approaches were used primarily for managing conflicts involving incompatible goals and inconsistent reward systems between departments.

Two conclusions can be drawn from this study. First, no one approach is most effective for managing every type of conflict. Second, managers are more effective in dealing with conflicts if they feel comfortable using a variety of approaches. These conclusions point to the need to understand the conditions under which each conflict management technique is most effective. This knowledge allows managers to match the characteristics of a conflict incident with the techniques best suited for those characteristics. The salient situational factors to consider are summarised in Table 7.4.

TABLE 7.4 Matching the conflict management approach with the situation

SITUATIONAL CONSIDERATIONS	CONFLICT MANAGEMENT APPROACH				
	Competing	*Accommodating*	*Compromising*	*Collaborating*	*Avoiding*
Issue importance	High	Low	Med	High	Low
Relationship importance	Low	High	Med	High	Low
Relative power	High	Low	Equal–High	Low–High	Equal–High
Time constraints	Med–High	Med–High	Low	Low	Med–High

The competing approach is most appropriate when a conflict of values or perspectives is involved and people feel compelled to defend the 'correct' position: when a boss–employee relationship is involved; when maintaining a close, supportive relationship is not critical; and when there is a sense of urgency. An example of such a situation might be a manager's insisting that a temporary staff member follow important company safety regulations. Another example would be a manager enforcing legal compliance in a harassment situation at work.

The accommodating approach is most appropriate when the importance of maintaining a good working relationship outweighs all other considerations. While this could be the case regardless of a person's formal relationship with the other party, it is often perceived as being the only option for employees of powerful bosses. The nature of the issues and the amount of time available play a secondary role in determining the choice of this strategy. Accommodation becomes especially appropriate when the issues are not vital to the person's interests and the problem must be resolved quickly.

Trying to reach a compromise is most appropriate when the issues are complex and moderately important, there are no simple solutions, and both parties have a strong interest in different facets of the problem. The other essential situational requirement is adequate time for negotiation. The classic case is a bargaining session between representatives of management and the union to avert a threatened strike. While the characteristics of the relationship between the parties are not essential factors, experience has shown that negotiations work best between parties with equal power who are committed to maintaining a good long-term relationship.

The collaborating approach is most appropriate when the issues are critical, when maintaining an ongoing supportive relationship between peers is important and when time constraints are not pressing. Although collaboration can also be an effective approach for resolving conflicts between a manager and an employee, it is important to point out that when a conflict involves peers the collaborative mode is more appropriate than either the competing or the accommodating approach.

The avoidance approach is most appropriate when a person's stake in an issue is not high and there is no strong interpersonal reason for getting involved, regardless of whether the conflict involves a superior, an employee or a peer. A severe time constraint becomes a contributing factor because it increases the likelihood of using avoidance, by default. While the person might prefer other strategies that have a good chance of resolving a problem without damaging relationships—such as compromise and collaboration—these are ruled out because of time pressure.

Resolving interpersonal confrontations using the collaborative approach

Why put energy and time into resolving these issues at all? The reason is that work conflicts occur regularly as a normal part of working life and if ignored or forced underground they cost the organisation dearly in terms of time and reduced productivity. Clearly, part of the skill of effective conflict management is choosing an appropriate approach based on a thoughtful assessment of the situation. One characteristic of unsuccessful conflict managers is their habitual reliance on one or two strategies, regardless of changing circumstances. A second characteristic of ineffective conflict managers is their inability to implement the collaborative approach effectively. In the study by Kipnis and Schmidt (1983) discussed earlier, most managers expressed general support for the collaborative approach, but, when it appeared things were not going their way, they reverted to a directive approach (see also Argyris 1992).

One reason for this pattern is that the collaborative approach to conflict management is not easy to implement successfully. It requires much more skill than accommodating or competing, for example. It is a fairly simple matter for managers either to give in or to impose their will, but resolving differences in a truly collaborative manner is a complicated and taxing process. As a result, when situational conditions indicate that the collaborative approach is most appropriate, unskilled managers will often opt for less-challenging approaches. To help readers gain proficiency in using the collaborative approach, the remainder of this chapter describes behavioural guidelines for effectively resolving interpersonal confrontations.

These guidelines are derived from principles presented in this chapter and Chapters 2 and 6: general principles relating to the interplay between language and influence, the merits of a collaborative problem-solving process, the long-term negative effects of specific acts of exploitation or unreasonableness, and the value of increasing information inputs in order to improve the quality of decision making. The behavioural guidelines discussed next constitute specific applications of these proven management principles.

The guidelines for collaborative conflict management also draw on the negotiation literature discussed earlier. Because interpersonal confrontations involving complaints and criticisms have been shown to be the most difficult to manage in a collaborative manner, they are the focus of this section.

Four phases of conflict management

Conflict management is treated as a problem-solving process with four phases:

- problem identification
- solution generation
- action plan formulation and agreement
- implementation and follow-up.

In the midst of a heated discussion, the first two phases are the most critical steps, as well as the most difficult to manage effectively. In addition, they are the only ones a party to a dispute can control. If you initiate a complaint, you can control how you state it and whether you request a change in behaviour. However, you cannot control whether the other party agrees to change or, having agreed, actually follows up. Thus, the focus is primarily on phases one and two during the skill training. And, because disputants' perceptions are different during the early phases of a confrontation, the role of each participant is examined separately.

At a minimum, a confrontation involves two actors: an initiator and a responder. For example, an employee might complain about not being given a fair share of opportunities to work overtime; or the head of production might complain to the head of sales about frequent changes in order specifications. A two-sided conflict represents a greater challenge for responders because they have responsibility for transforming a complaint into a problem-solving discussion. This requires considerable patience and self-confidence, since unskilled initiators generally begin the discussion by blaming the responder for the problem. In this situation, an unskilled responder will naturally become defensive and look for an opportunity to 'even the score'.

If these lose–lose dynamics persist, a mediator is generally required to cool down the participants, to re-establish constructive communication and to help the parties reconcile their differences. The presence of a mediator removes some pressure from the responder, because an impartial referee provides assistance in moving the confrontation through the problem-solving phases.

The following guidelines provide a model for acting out the initiator, responder and mediator roles in such a way that problem solving can occur. In the discussion of each role, it is assumed that other participants in the conflict are not behaving according to their prescribed guidelines.

Initiator: Problem identification

Maintain personal ownership of the problem

When you are upset and frustrated, it is important to recognise that this is your problem, not the other person's. You may feel that your boss or co-worker is the source of your problem, but resolving your frustration is your immediate concern. The first step in addressing this concern is acknowledging accountability for your feelings. Effective conflict resolution requires self-responsibility about our own actions and feelings.

Suppose someone enters your closed office without asking if it is all right to do so. The fact is that entry without asking might trouble you, but the casual entry does not present a problem for your visitor. One way to determine ownership of a problem is to identify whose needs are not being met. In this case, your need for a knock on the door is not being met, so the impromptu entry is your problem.

The advantage of acknowledging ownership of a problem when registering a complaint is that it reduces defensiveness (Adler 1977). For you to solve a problem, the respondent must not feel threatened by your initial statement of that problem. By beginning the conversation with a request that the responder help solve your problem, you immediately establish a problem-solving atmosphere. For example, you might say: 'Bill, do you have a few minutes? I have a problem I need to discuss with you.'

Succinctly describe your problem in terms of behaviours, consequences and feelings

A useful model for remembering how to state your problem effectively has been prescribed by Gordon (1970): 'I have a problem. When you do X, Y results and I feel Z.' While the memorisation of set formulas for improving communication skills is not advocated, keeping this model in mind will help you to implement three critical guidelines.

First, describe the specific behaviours (X) that present a problem for you. This will help you to avoid the reflexive tendency when you are upset to give feedback that is evaluative and not specific. One way to do this is to specify the expectations or standards that have been violated. For example, an employee may have missed a deadline for completing an assigned task, your boss may gradually be taking over tasks previously delegated to you, or a colleague in the accounting department may have repeatedly failed to provide you with data required for an important presentation.

Second, outline the specific, observable consequences (Y) of these behaviours. Simply telling others that their actions are causing you problems is often sufficient stimulus for change. In fast-paced work environments, people generally become insensitive to the impact of their actions. They do not intend to cause offence, but they become so busy meeting deadlines associated with 'getting the product out the door' that they tune out subtle negative feedback from others. When this occurs, bringing to the attention of others the consequences of their behaviours will often prompt them to change.

Unfortunately, not all problems can be resolved this simply. At times, offenders are aware of the negative consequences of their behaviours, yet they persist in them. In such cases, this approach is still useful in stimulating a problem-solving discussion, because it presents concerns in a non-threatening manner. Possibly the responders' behaviours are constrained by the expectations of their boss or by the fact that the department is currently understaffed. Responders may not be able to change these constraints, but this approach will encourage them to discuss the constraints with you so that you can work on the problem together.

Third, describe the feelings (Z) you experience as a result of the problem. It is important that the responder understands that the behaviour is not just inconvenient. You need to explain how it is affecting you personally by engendering feelings of frustration, concern or insecurity. Explain how these feelings are interfering with your work. They may make it more difficult for you to concentrate, to be congenial with customers, to be supportive of your boss or to be willing to make needed personal sacrifices to meet deadlines.

Use this three-step model as a guide rather than a formula. The order of the components may vary and you should not use the same words every time. Obviously, it would get pretty monotonous if everyone in a workgroup initiated a discussion about an interpersonal issue with the words 'I have a problem'. Observe how the key elements in the model are used in different ways in the following examples:

> *I have to tell you that I get upset [feelings] when you make jokes about my bad memory in front of other people [behavior]. In fact, I get so angry that I find myself bringing up your faults to get even [consequences].*
>
> *I have a problem. When you say you'll be here at six and don't show up until after seven [behaviour], the dinner gets ruined, we're late for the show we planned to see [consequences] and I feel hurt because it seems as though I'm just not that important to you [feelings].*
>
> *The employees want to let management know that we've been having a hard time lately with the short notice you've been giving when you need us to work overtime [behavior]. That probably explains some of the grumbling and lack of cooperation you've mentioned [consequences]. Anyhow, we wanted to make it clear that this policy has got a lot of the workers feeling pretty resentful [feeling].* (Adler 1977: 223)

This approach helps to reduce the likelihood of becoming involved in the conflict triangle (as seen in Figure 7.3 on p. 343).

Avoid drawing evaluative conclusions and attributing motives to the respondent

When exchanges between two disputing parties become a little heated, each side often has a different perspective about the justification of the other's actions. Typically, each party believes they are the victim of the other's behaviour. In international conflicts, opposing nations often believe they are acting defensively rather than offensively. Similarly, in small-scale conflicts, each side may have a distorted view of its own hurt and the motives of the 'offender' (Kim & Smith 1993). Therefore, in presenting your problem, avoid the pitfalls of making accusations, drawing inferences about motivations or intentions, or attributing the responder's undesirable behaviour to personal inadequacies. Statements such as 'You are always interrupting me', 'You haven't been fair to me since the day I disagreed with you in the board meeting' or 'You never have time to listen to our problems and suggestions because you manage your time so poorly' are good for starting arguments but ineffective for initiating a problem-solving process. This process is known as *mind-reading*.

Another key to reducing defensiveness is to delay proposing a solution until both parties agree on the nature of the problem. When you become so upset with someone's behaviour that you feel it is necessary to initiate a complaint, it is often because the person has seriously violated your expected role model. For example, you might feel that your manager should have been less dogmatic and listened more during a goal-setting interview. Consequently, you might express your feelings in terms of prescriptions for how the other person should behave and suggest a more democratic, or sensitive, style.

Besides creating defensiveness, the principal disadvantage to initiating problem solving with a suggested remedy is that it hinders the problem-solving process. Before completing the problem-articulation phase, you have immediately jumped to the solution-generation phase, based on the assumption that you know all the reasons for and constraints on the other person's behaviour. You will jointly produce better, more acceptable solutions if you present your statement of the problem and discuss it thoroughly before proposing potential solutions.

Persist until understood

There are times when the respondent will not clearly receive or acknowledge even the most effectively expressed message. Suppose, for instance, that you share the following problem with a co-worker:

> *I've been bothered by something lately and I want to share it with you. To be honest, I'm uncomfortable [feeling] when you swear so much [behavior]. I don't mind an occasional 'damn' or 'hell', but the other words are hard for me to accept. Lately I've found myself avoiding you [consequences] and that's no good either, so I wanted to let you know how I feel. (Adler 1977: 228)*

When you share your feelings in this non-evaluative way, it is likely that the other person will understand your position and possibly try to change their behaviour to suit your needs. On the other hand, there are several less-satisfying responses that could be made to your comment: 'Listen, these days everyone talks that way. And besides, you've got your faults, too, you know!' (Your co-worker becomes defensive, rationalising and counter-attacking.) 'Yeah, I suppose I do swear a lot. I'll have to work on that some day.' (Your co-worker gets the general drift of your message but fails to comprehend how serious the problem is to you.) 'Listen, if you're still angry about my forgetting to tell you about that meeting the other day, you can be sure that I'm really sorry. I won't do it again.' (They totally misunderstand you.) 'Speaking of avoiding, have you seen Chris lately? I wonder if anything is wrong with him?' (Your co-worker is uncomfortable with your frustration and changes the subject.)

In each case, the co-worker does not understand or does not wish to acknowledge the problem. In these situations, you must repeat your concern until it has been acknowledged as a problem to be solved. Otherwise, the problem-solving process will terminate at this point and nothing will change. Repeated assertions can take the form of restating the same phrase several times or reiterating your concern with different words or examples that you feel may improve comprehension. To avoid introducing new concerns or shifting from a descriptive to an evaluative mode, keep in mind the XYZ formula for feedback. Persistence is most effective when it consists of 'variations on a theme' rather than 'variation in themes'.

Encourage two-way discussion

It is important to establish a problem-solving climate by inviting the respondent to express his or her opinions and ask questions. There may be a reasonable explanation for another's disturbing behaviour; the person may have a radically different view of the problem. The sooner this information is introduced into the conversation, the more likely it is that the issue will be resolved. As a rule of thumb, the longer the initiator's opening statement, the longer it will take the two parties to work through their problem.

Manage the agenda

Approach multiple or complex problems incrementally. This is one way of shortening your opening statement. Rather than raising a series of issues all at once, focus initially on a simple or rudimentary problem. Then, as you gain greater appreciation for the other party's perspective and share some problem-solving success, you can discuss more challenging issues. This is especially important when trying to resolve a problem with a person who is important to your work performance but does not have a longstanding relationship with you.

The less familiar you are with the other's opinions and personality, the more you should approach a problem-solving discussion as a fact-finding and rapport-building mission. This is best done by focusing your introductory statement on a specific issue and presenting it in such a way that it encourages the other party to respond expansively. You can then use this early feedback to shape the remainder of your agenda. For example: 'Bill, we had difficulty getting that work order processed on time yesterday. What seemed to be the problem?'

Initiator: Solution generation

Focus on commonalities as the basis for requesting a change

Once a problem is clearly understood, the discussion should shift to the solution-generation phase. Most disputants share at least some personal and organisational goals, believe in many of the same fundamental principles of management and operate under similar constraints. These commonalities can serve as a useful starting point for generating solutions.

The most straightforward approach to changing another's offensive behaviour is making a request. The legitimacy of a request will be enhanced if it is linked to common interests. This approach is particularly effective when the parties have had difficulty getting along in the past. In these situations, pointing out how a change in the respondent's behaviour would positively affect your shared fate will reduce defensiveness:

> *Jane, one of the things we have all worked hard to build in this audit team is mutual support. We are all pushed to the limit getting this job completed by the third-quarter deadline next week and the rest of the team members find it difficult to accept your unwillingness to work overtime during this emergency. Because the allocation of next quarter's assignments will be affected by our current performance, would you please reconsider your position?*

Responder: Problem identification

The problem-identification phase is now examined from the viewpoint of the person who is supposedly the source of the problem. In a work setting, this could be a manager who is making unrealistic demands, a new employee who has violated critical safety regulations, or a co-worker who is claiming credit for ideas you generated. The following guidelines for dealing with a complaint show how to shape the initiator's behaviour so that you can have a productive problem-solving experience.

Establish a climate for joint problem solving by showing genuine interest and concern

When a person complains to you, do not treat the complaint lightly. While this might seem self-evident, it is often difficult to focus your attention on someone else's problems when you are in the middle of writing an important project report or are concerned about preparing for a meeting scheduled to begin in a few minutes. Consequently, unless the other person's emotional condition necessitates dealing with the problem immediately, it is better to set up a time for another meeting if your current time pressures make it difficult to concentrate.

In most cases, the initiator will be expecting you to set the tone for the meeting. You will quickly undermine collaboration if you overreact or become defensive. Even if you disagree with the complaint and feel it has no foundation, you need to respond empathetically to the initiator's statement of the problem. This is done by conveying an attitude of interest and receptivity through your posture, tone of voice and facial expressions.

One of the most difficult aspects of establishing the proper climate for your discussion is responding appropriately to the initiator's emotions. Sometimes you may need to let a person blow off steam before trying to address the substance of a specific complaint. In some cases, the therapeutic effect of being able to express negative emotions to the boss will be enough to satisfy an employee. This occurs frequently in high-pressure jobs where irritations flare easily as a result of the intense stress.

However, a sustained emotional outburst can be very detrimental to problem solving. If an employee begins verbally attacking you or someone else and it is apparent that the individual is more interested in getting even than in solving an interpersonal problem, you may need to interrupt and provide some ground rules for collaborative problem solving. By explaining calmly to the other person that you are willing to discuss a genuine problem, but that you will not tolerate personal attacks or scapegoating, you can quickly determine the initiator's true intentions. In most instances, they will apologise, emulate your emotional tone and begin formulating a useful statement of the problem.

Seek additional information about the problem

Untrained initiators typically present complaints that are both general and highly evaluative. They make generalisations about your motives, and your personal strengths and weaknesses, from a few

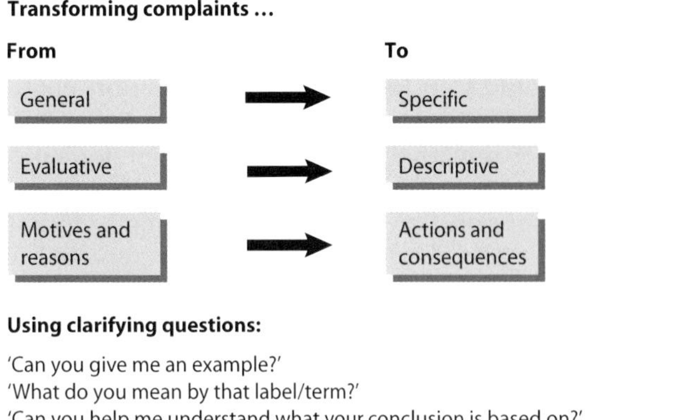

Using clarifying questions:

'Can you give me an example?'
'What do you mean by that label/term?'
'Can you help me understand what your conclusion is based on?'
'When did this first become a problem for you?'
'How often has this occurred?'
'What specific actions have led you to believe that I'm taking sides in this issue?'
'What were some of the harmful consequences of my decision?'

FIGURE 7.8 Respondents' effective use of clarifying questions

specific incidents. If the two of you are going to transform a personal complaint into a joint problem, you must redirect the conversation from general and evaluative accusations to descriptions of specific behaviours (see Figure 7.8).

To do this, ask for details about specific actions that form the basis for the evaluation. You might find it useful to phrase your questions so that they reflect the XYZ model described in the initiator's guidelines: 'Can you give me a specific example of my behaviour that concerns you?', 'When I did that, what were the specific consequences for your work?', 'How did you feel when that happened?' When a complaint is both serious and complex, it is especially critical for you to understand it completely. In these situations, check your level of understanding by summarising the initiator's main points and asking if your summary is correct.

If the initiator is seriously concerned about improving your relationship, and you suspect that they are holding back and not talking about the really serious issues, you should probe deeper. Sometimes it is useful to ask for additional complaints: 'Are there any other problems in our relationship you'd like to discuss?' Often, people begin by complaining about a minor problem to 'test the water'. If you blow up, the conversation is terminated and the critical issues are not discussed. However, if you are responsive to a frank discussion about problems, the more serious issues are likely to surface.

Agree with some aspect of the complaint

This is an important point that is difficult for some people to accept because they wonder how it is possible to agree with something they do not believe is true. They may also be worried about reinforcing complaining behaviour. In practice, this step is probably the best test of whether a responder is committed to using the collaborative approach to conflict management rather than the avoiding, competing or accommodating approaches. People who use the competing mode will grit their teeth while listening to the initiator, just waiting to find a flaw they can use to launch a counterattack. Or they will simply respond: 'I'm sorry, but that's just the way I am. You'll simply have to get used to it.' Accommodators will apologise profusely and ask for forgiveness. People who avoid conflicts will acknowledge and agree with the initiator's concerns, but only in a superficial manner because their only concern is to terminate the awkward conversation quickly.

In contrast, collaborators will demonstrate their concern for both cooperation and assertiveness by looking for points in the initiator's presentation with which they can genuinely agree. Following the principles of supportive communication, you will find it possible to accept the other person's viewpoint without conceding your own position. Even in the most blatantly malicious and hostile verbal assault (which may be more a reflection of the initiator's insecurity than evidence of your inadequacies), there is generally a grain of truth.

There are a number of ways you can agree with a message without accepting all of its ramifications (Adler 1977). You can find an element of truth, as in the incident related above. Or you can agree in principle with the argument: 'I agree that managers should set a good example' or 'I agree that it is important for sales clerks to be at the store when it opens'. If you can't find anything substantive with which to agree, you can always agree with the initiator's perception of the situation: 'Well, I can see how you would think that. I have known people who deliberately shirked their responsibilities.' Or, you can agree with the person's feelings: 'It is obvious that our earlier discussion greatly upset you.'

In none of these cases are you necessarily agreeing with the initiator's conclusions or evaluations and you are not conceding your position. You are trying to understand—to foster a problem-solving, rather than an argumentative, discussion.

Generally, initiators prepare for a complaint session by mentally cataloguing all the evidence supporting their point of view. Once the discussion begins, they introduce as much evidence as necessary to make their argument convincing; that is, they keep arguing until you agree. The more evidence that is introduced, the broader the argument becomes and the more difficult it is to begin investigating solutions. Consequently, establishing a basis of agreement is the key to culminating the problem-identification phase of the problem-solving process.

Responder: Solution generation

Ask for suggestions of acceptable alternatives

Once you are certain you fully understand the initiator's complaint, move on to the solution-generation phase by asking the initiator for recommended solutions. This triggers an important transition in the discussion by shifting attention from the negative to the positive and from the past to the future. It also communicates your regard for the initiator's opinions. This step is a key element in the joint problem-solving process.

Some managers listen patiently to an employee's complaint, express appreciation for the feedback, say they will rectify the problem and then terminate the discussion. This leaves the initiator guessing about the outcome of the meeting. Will you take the complaint seriously? Will you really change? If so, will the change resolve the problem? It is important to eliminate this ambiguity by agreeing on a plan of action.

If the problem is particularly serious or complex, it is useful to write down specific agreements, including assignments and deadlines, as well as providing for a follow-up meeting to check progress. For example:

Team leader: Okay. It seems as if Indira was a bit hasty in placing that order. I agree you must have felt excluded and I believe we need to act on this. Do you have a particular suggestion?

Team member: Yes, I do. Well, I'm not sure really, but it shouldn't happen again like that.

Team leader: So, you don't want any further action over this incident, but you want Indira not to repeat that action ever again?

Team member: Yeah, exactly.

Team leader: Okay. How about you and I meet with Indira in the next two days? I'll go through the issues, you confirm your view and I'll endorse it?

Team member: Yes, I can do that.

Team leader: Good. I'll follow up with you over the next month to see if it is progressing well.

Mediator: Problem identification

Frequently, it is necessary for managers to mediate a dispute (Karambayya & Brett 1989; Kressel & Pruitt 1989; Northcraft & Neale 1994). While this might occur for a variety of reasons, it is assumed in this discussion that the manager has been invited to help the initiator and responder resolve their differences. While assuming that the mediator is the manager of both disputants, this is not a necessary condition for the guidelines proposed. The following guidelines are intended to help mediators avoid the common pitfalls associated with this role, as shown in Box 7.1.

Acknowledge that a conflict exists and propose a problem-solving approach for resolving it

It is vital for the mediator to take seriously the problems between conflicting parties. If they feel they have a serious problem, the mediator should not belittle its significance. Remarks such as 'I'm surprised that two intelligent people like you haven't been able to work out your disagreement. We have more important things to do here than get all worked up over such petty issues' will make both parties defensive and interfere with any serious problem-solving efforts. While you might wish that

BOX 7.1 Ten ways to fail as a mediator

1. After listening to the argument for a short time, begin to communicate your discomfort with the discussion non-verbally (for example, sit back, begin to fidget).
2. Communicate your agreement with one of the parties (for example, through facial expressions, posture, chair position, reinforcing comments).
3. Say that you should not be talking about this kind of thing at work or where others can hear you.
4. Discourage the expression of emotion. Suggest that the discussion would be better held later after both parties have cooled off.
5. Suggest that both parties are wrong. Point out the problems with both points of view.
6. Suggest part-way through the discussion that you might not be the person who should be helping solve this problem.
7. See if you can get both parties to attack you.
8. Minimise the seriousness of the problem.
9. Change the subject (for example, ask for advice to help you solve one of your problems).
10. Express displeasure that the two parties are experiencing conflict (for example, imply that it might undermine the solidarity of the workgroup).

Source: Adapted from W. C. Morris and M. Sashkin, *Organization Behavior in Action: Skill Building Experience* (St Paul, MN: West Publishing Company, 1976).

your employees could have worked out their disagreement without bothering you, this is not the time to lecture them on self-reliance. Inducing guilt feelings by implying personal failure during an already emotional experience tends to distract the participants from the substantive issues at hand. Seldom is this conducive to problem solving.

One early decision a mediator has to make is whether to convene a joint problem-solving session or meet separately with the parties first. The assessment criteria shown in Table 7.5 should help you weigh the trade-offs. First, what is the current position of the disputants? Are both aware that a problem exists? Are they equally motivated to work on solving the problem? The more similar the awareness and motivation of the parties, the more likely it is that a joint session will be productive. If there is a serious discrepancy in awareness and motivation, the mediator should work to reduce that discrepancy through one-on-one meetings before bringing the disputants together.

TABLE 7.5 Choosing a format for mediating conflicts

FACTORS	HOLD JOINT MEETINGS	HOLD SEPARATE MEETINGS FIRST
Awareness and motivation		
• Both parties are aware of the problem.	Yes	No
• They are equally motivated to resolve the problem.	Yes	No
• They accept your legitimacy as a mediator.	Yes	No
Nature of the relationship		
• The parties hold equal status.	Yes	No
• They work together regularly.	Yes	No
• Their relationship is good overall.	Yes	No
Nature of the problem		
• This is an isolated (not a recurring) problem.	Yes	No
• The complaint is substantive in nature and easily verified.	Yes	No
• The parties agree on the root causes of the problem.	Yes	No
• The parties share common values and work priorities.	Yes	No

Second, what is the current relationship between the disputants? Does their work require them to interact frequently? Is a good working relationship critical for their individual job performance? What has been their relationship in the past? What is the difference in their formal status in the organisation? As discussed earlier, joint problem-solving sessions are most productive between individuals of equal status who are required to work together regularly. This does not mean that joint meetings should not be held between a supervisor and an employee, only that greater care needs to be taken in preparing for such a meeting. Specifically, if a department head becomes involved in a dispute between a staff member and a supervisor, the department head should make sure that the employee does not feel that the meeting will serve as an excuse for two managers to gang up on the employee.

Separate fact-finding meetings with the disputants prior to a joint meeting are particularly useful when the parties have a history of recurring disputes, especially if these disputes should have been resolved without a mediator. Such a history often suggests a lack of conflict management or problem-solving skills on the part of the disputants, or it might stem from a broader set of issues that are beyond their control. In these situations, individual coaching sessions prior to a joint meeting will increase your understanding of the root causes and improve the individuals' ability to resolve their differences. Following up these private meetings with a joint problem-solving session, in which the mediator coaches the disputants through the process for resolving their conflict, can be a positive learning experience.

Third, what is the nature of the problem? Is the complaint substantive in nature and easily verifiable? If the problem stems from conflicting role responsibilities and the actions of both parties in question are common knowledge, then a joint problem-solving session can begin on a common information and experimental base. However, if the complaint stems from differences in managerial style, values, personality characteristics and so forth, bringing the parties together immediately following a complaint may seriously undermine the problem-solving process. Complaints that are likely to be interpreted as threats to the self-image of one or both parties (Who am I? What do I stand for?) warrant considerable individual discussion before a joint meeting is called. To avoid individuals feeling as though they are being ambushed in a meeting, you should discuss serious personal complaints with them ahead of time, in private.

In seeking out the perspective of both parties, maintain a neutral posture regarding the disputants, if not the issues

Effective mediation requires impartiality. If a mediator shows strong personal bias in favour of one party in a joint problem-solving session, the other party may simply walk out. However, such personal bias is more likely to emerge in private conversations with the disputants. Statements such as 'I can't believe he really did that!' or 'Everyone seems to be having trouble working with Lee these days' imply that the mediator is taking sides and any attempt to appear impartial in a joint meeting will seem like mere window-dressing to appease the other party. No matter how well intentioned or justified these comments might be, they destroy the credibility of the mediator in the long run. In contrast, effective mediators respect both parties' points of view and make sure that both perspectives are expressed adequately.

Occasionally, it is not possible to be impartial on issues. One person may have violated company policy, engaged in unethical competition with a colleague or broken a personal agreement. In these cases, the challenge of the mediator is to separate the offence from the offender. If a person is clearly in the wrong, the inappropriate behaviour needs to be corrected; but it needs to be done in such a way that the individual doesn't feel that his or her image and working relationships have been permanently marred. This can be done most effectively when correction occurs in private.

Manage the discussion to ensure fairness

Keep the discussion issue-oriented, not personality-oriented. It is important for the mediator to maintain a problem-solving atmosphere throughout the discussion. This is not to say that strong emotional statements do not have their place. People often associate effective problem solving with a calm, highly rational discussion of the issues and associate a personality attack with a highly emotional outburst. However, it is important not to confuse affect with effect. Placid, cerebral discussions may not solve problems, and impassioned statements do not have to be insulting. The critical point about process is that it should be centred on the issues and the consequences of continued conflict on performance.

Even when behaviour offensive to one of the parties obviously stems from a personality quirk, the discussion of the problem should be limited to the behaviour. Attributions of motives or generalisations from specific events to personal biases distract participants from the problem-solving process. It is important for the mediator to establish and maintain these ground rules.

It is also important for a mediator to ensure that neither party dominates the discussion. A relatively even balance in the level of inputs improves the quality of the final outcome. It also increases the likelihood that both parties will accept the final decision, because there is a high correlation between feelings about the problem-solving process and attitudes about the final solution. If one party tends to dominate a discussion, the mediator can help balance the exchange by asking the less-talkative party direct questions: 'Now that we have heard Fatima's view of that incident, how do you see it?', 'That's an important point, Peter, so let's make sure Fatima agrees. How do you feel, Fatima?'

Mediator: Solution generation

Facilitate exploration of solutions rather than assessing responsibility for the problem

When parties must work closely together and have a history of chronic interpersonal problems, it is often more important to teach problem-solving skills than to resolve a specific dispute. This is done best when the mediator adopts the posture of facilitator. The role of judge is to render a verdict regarding a problem in the past, not to teach people how to solve problems in the future. While some disputes obviously involve right and wrong actions, most interpersonal problems stem from differences in perspective. In these situations it is important that the mediator avoids being seduced into 'rendering a verdict' by comments such as 'Well, you're the boss; tell us which one is right' or, more subtly, 'I wonder if what I did was right?'

The problem with mediators assuming the role of judge is that it sets in motion processes antithetical to effective interpersonal problem solving. The parties focus on persuading the mediator of their innocence and the other party's guilt, rather than striving to improve their working relationship with the assistance of the mediator. The disputants seek to establish facts about what happened in the past, rather than to reach an agreement about what ought to happen in the future. Therefore, a key aspect of effective mediation is helping disputants explore multiple alternatives in a non-judgmental manner.

Explore options by focusing on interests, not positions

Often, conflict resolution is hampered by the perception that incompatible positions necessarily entail irreconcilable differences. Mediation of such conflicts can best be accomplished by examining the interests (goals and concerns) behind the positions. These interests are the driving force behind the positions and are ultimately what people want satisfied.

The job of the mediator is to discover where interests meet and where they conflict. Interests often remain unstated because they are unclear to the participants. In order to flesh out each party's interests, ask 'why' questions: 'Why have they taken this position?', 'Why does this matter to them?' Understand that there is probably no single, simple answer to these questions. Each side may represent a number of constituents, each with a special interest.

After each side has articulated its underlying interests, help the parties to identify areas of agreement and reconcilability. It is common for participants in an intense conflict to feel that they are on opposite sides of all issues, that they have little in common. Helping them to recognise that there are areas of agreement and reconcilability often represents a major turning point in resolving longstanding feuds.

Make sure all parties fully understand and support the solution agreed upon and establish follow-up procedures

The last two phases of the problem-solving process are agreement on an action plan and follow-up. These are discussed here in the context of the mediator's role, but they are equally relevant to the other roles.

A common mistake of ineffective mediators is terminating discussions prematurely, on the supposition that, once a problem has been solved in principle, the disputants can be left to work out the details on their own. Or a mediator may assume that, because one party has recommended a solution that appears reasonable and workable, the second disputant will be willing to implement it. It is important when serving as a mediator to insist on a specific plan of action that both parties are willing to implement. If you suspect any hesitancy on the part of either disputant, this needs to be explored explicitly: 'Tom, I sense that you are somewhat less enthusiastic than Sue about this plan. Is there something that bothers you?' When you are confident that both parties support the plan, check to make sure they are aware of their respective responsibilities and then propose a mechanism for monitoring progress. You might schedule another formal meeting, or you might stop by both individuals' offices to get a progress report.

The expectant attitude

Expectation in management is a vastly overlooked and underused strategic technique of conflict resolution in particular, and successful management in general (Bennis 1985; Manzoni & Barsoux 1998). The expectant attitude is often confused with mere 'positive thinking'.

A major exponent of the expectant attitude was Milton Erickson (Rossi 1980). Erickson wrote about its importance quite extensively and conducted experiments to prove its potency. The expectant attitude registers itself in minimal non-verbal cues, which is clearly demonstrated in one of the experiments conducted by Erickson. This exercise involved a group of 20 students who were placed in pairs in separate cubicles. Person A was told that a stranger would enter the room and hand them a 20-cent piece. Person B was told they would be handed a dollar note. In a separate room, the stranger was handed ten 20-cent pieces and ten one-dollar notes and was instructed to enter the cubicles and, without speaking, approach the two people and give one person (either one) a 20-cent piece and the other person a dollar, and then leave the booth. This was done with each of the ten pairs of students. The experiment was conducted many times over 15 years. The results were always the same: in about 80 per cent of the trials, Group A members got the 20-cent piece and Group B members got the dollar.

This result is significantly greater than chance. It illustrates how the expectant attitude of the students greatly influenced, through minimal body cues, the behaviour of the provider of the money. Erickson's statements define the crucial role of the expectant attitude as a management skill:

> *Your expectant attitude immediately changes the atmosphere so that it is strikingly different. It places the person in a new frame of reference charged with an expectancy that he is familiar with ... You should be utterly confident. You are going to accomplish your purpose, your goal. And I am very confident. I look confident. I act confident. I speak in a confident way. (Rossi 1980: 61)*

In the 'Skill Practice' section of this chapter, a method is presented for developing the expectant attitude as part of your management development. When a manager defines task goals and procedures to achieve those goals, confidently expects them to be achieved and confirms that the goal has been achieved, then leadership potency naturally follows.

Summary

Conflict is a difficult and controversial topic. In most cultures it has negative connotations because it runs counter to the notion that we should get along with people by being kind and friendly. Although many people intellectually understand the value of conflict, they feel uncomfortable when confronted by it. Their discomfort may result from a lack of understanding of the conflict process, as well as from a lack of training in how to handle interpersonal confrontations effectively. This chapter has addressed these issues by introducing both analytical and behavioural skills.

A summary model of conflict management, shown in Figure 7.9, contains four elements: (1) diagnosing the sources of conflict and the associated situational considerations; (2) selecting

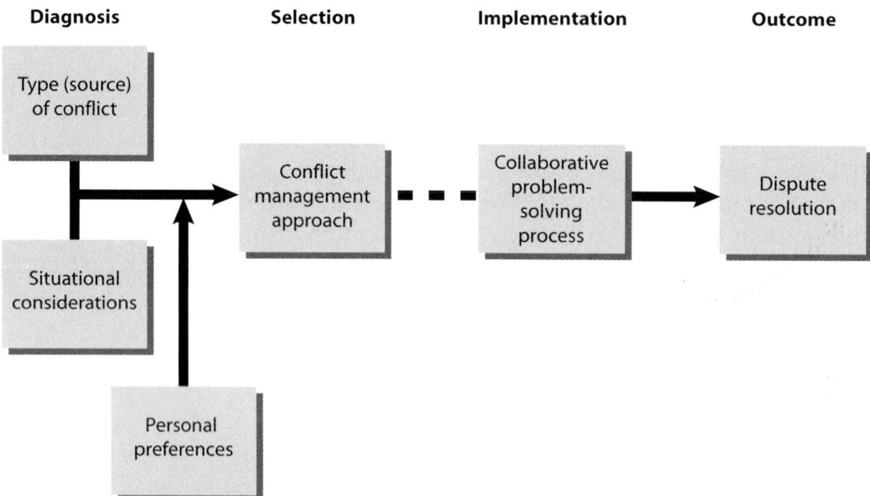

FIGURE 7.9 Summary model of conflict management

an appropriate conflict management strategy, based on the results of the diagnosis combined with personal preferences; (3) effectively implementing the strategy—in particular, the collaborative problem-solving process; which should lead to (4) a successful resolution of the dispute. Note that the final outcome of the model is successful dispute resolution. Given the claim that conflict plays an important role in organisations, the concluding observation is that the objective of effective conflict management is the successful resolution of disputes, not the elimination of conflict altogether.

The diagnostic element of the summary model contains two important components. First, assessing the source or type of conflict provides insights into the 'whys' behind a confrontation. Conflict can be caused by a variety of circumstances. Four of these have been considered: (1) irreconcilable personal differences; (2) discrepancies in information; (3) role incompatibilities; and (4) environmentally induced stress. These types of conflict differ in both frequency and intensity. For example, information-based conflicts occur frequently, but they are easily resolved because disputants have low personal stakes in the outcome. In contrast, conflicts grounded in differences of perceptions and expectations are generally intense and difficult to defuse.

The second important component of the diagnostic process is assessing the relevant situational considerations, so as to determine a feasible set of responses. Important contextual factors that were considered include the importance of the issue, the importance of the relationship, the relative power of the disputants and the degree to which time was a limiting factor.

The purpose of the diagnostic phase of the model is to choose wisely between the five conflict management approaches: avoiding, compromising, collaborating, competing and accommodating. These reflect different degrees of assertiveness and cooperativeness, or the priority given to satisfying one's own concerns versus the concerns of the other party.

Personal preferences, reflecting a person's ethnic culture, gender and personality, play a key role in our conception of effective conflict management. Our personal comfort level with using the various conflict management approaches is both an enabling and a limiting factor. If we feel comfortable with an approach, we are likely to use it effectively. Because effective problem solvers need to feel comfortable using a variety of tools, however, we should not pass over an appropriate tool because its use might be discomforting. For this reason, it is important for conflict managers to stretch their natural 'comfort zone' through skill development activities.

That is why, as shown in the figure, people elect to focus on the effective implementation of the specific conflict management approach that is both the most effective, all-purpose tool and the most difficult to use comfortably and skilfully—collaborative problem solving. It takes little skill to impose your authority on another person, to withdraw from a confrontation, to split the difference between opponents or to abandon your position at the slightest sign of opposition. Therefore, the behavioural guidelines for resolving an interpersonal confrontation involving complaints and criticisms by using a problem-solving approach were described in detail.

Behavioural guidelines

Effective conflict management involves both analytical and behavioural elements. First, it is important to understand the true causes of a conflict and to select the appropriate conflict management or negotiation approach. Second, it is necessary to implement the approach effectively.

Behavioural guidelines for the evaluative aspects of conflict management include the following:

1. Collect information on the sources of conflict. Identify the source by examining the focus of the dispute. The four sources (and their respective focuses) are personal differences (perception and expectations), poor information processes (misinformation and misinterpretation), role incompatibility (goals and responsibilities) and environmental stress (resource scarcity and uncertainty).
2. Use the *collaborative approach* for managing conflict, including integrative negotiation tactics, unless specific conditions dictate the use of an alternative approach.
3. Use the *competing approach* only when the issue is extremely important to you, a close, ongoing relationship is not necessary, you have much more power than the other person, and there is a high sense of urgency.
4. Use the *accommodating approach* only when the issue is not important to you, a close, ongoing relationship is critical, you have no other option (low power), and time is not a factor.
5. Use the *compromising approach* only when the issue is very complex and of moderate importance to both parties (and the parties feel strongly about different aspects of the issues), the relationship is of moderate importance, the parties have relatively equal power, and time constraints are low.
6. Use the *avoiding approach* only when the issue is not important to you, the relationship is not critical, your relative power is equal to, or greater than, that of the other person, and time is not a significant factor.

Behavioural guidelines for effectively implementing the collaborative (problem-solving) approach to conflict management are summarised below. These are organised according to three roles. Guidelines for the problem-identification and solution-generation phases of the problem-solving process are specified for each role. Guidelines for the action plan and follow-up phases are the same for all three roles.

Initiator

Problem identification

1. Succinctly describe your problem in terms of behaviours, consequences and feelings: 'When you do X, Y happens and I feel Z.'
   - Maintain personal ownership of the problem.
   - Use a specific incident to illustrate the expectations or standards violated.
   - Stick to the facts. Avoid drawing evaluative conclusions and attributing motives to the respondent.
2. Persist until understood; encourage two-way discussion.
   - Restate your concerns or give additional examples.
   - Avoid introducing additional issues or letting frustration sour your emotional tone.
   - Invite the respondent to ask questions and express another perspective.
3. Manage the agenda carefully.
   - Approach multiple problems incrementally, proceeding from simple to complex, easy to difficult, concrete to abstract.
   - Do not become fixated on a single issue. If you reach an impasse, expand the discussion to increase the likelihood of an integrative outcome.

LEARNING

Solution generation

4. Make a request.
   - Focus on those things you have in common (principles, goals, constraints) as the basis for recommending preferred alternatives.

Responder

Problem identification

1. Establish a climate for joint problem solving.
   - Show genuine concern and interest. Respond empathetically, even if you disagree with the complaint.
   - Respond appropriately to the initiator's emotions. If necessary, let the person 'let off steam' before addressing the complaint.
2. Seek additional information about the problem.
   - Ask questions that channel the initiator's statements from general to specific and from evaluative to descriptive.
3. Agree with some aspect of the complaint.
   - Signal your willingness to consider making changes by agreeing with facts, perceptions, feelings or principles.

Solution generation

4. Ask for recommendations.
   - To avoid debating the merits of a single suggestion, brainstorm multiple alternatives.

Mediator

Problem identification

1. Acknowledge that a conflict exists.
   - Select the most appropriate setting (one-on-one conference versus group meeting) for coaching and fact finding.
   - Propose a problem-solving approach for resolving the dispute.
2. Maintain a neutral posture.
   - Assume the role of facilitator, not judge. Do not belittle the problem or berate the disputants for their inability to resolve their differences.
   - Be impartial towards disputants and issues (provided policy has not been violated).
   - If correction is necessary, do it in private.
3. Manage the discussion to ensure fairness.
   - Focus discussion on the conflict's impact on performance and the detrimental effect of continued conflict.
   - Keep the discussion issue-oriented, not personality-oriented.
   - Do not allow one party to dominate the discussion. Ask directed questions to maintain balance.

Solution generation

4. Explore options by focusing on the interests behind stated positions.
   - Explore the 'whys' behind disputants' arguments/claims.
   - Help disputants see commonalities among their goals, values and principles.
   - Use commonalities to generate multiple alternatives.
   - Maintain a non-judgmental manner.

All roles

Action plan and follow-up

1. Ensure that all parties support the agreed-upon plan.
   - Verify understanding of, and commitment to, specific actions.
2. Establish a mechanism for follow-up.
   - Create benchmarks for measuring progress and ensuring accountability.
   - Encourage flexibility in adjusting the plan to meet emerging circumstances.

The expectant attitude is a more general way to approach conflict situations and to manage them effectively.

Skill analysis

Case study involving interpersonal conflict

Personal Investments Pty Ltd

Personal Investments (PI), located in Sydney, invests funds for institutions. In 2004 it employed approximately 75 people, 25 of whom were responsible for actual investment activities. The company managed about $1.2 billion worth of assets and derived an income of about $2.5 million.

Since its inception, PI has weathered rapid social and technological changes as well as economic volatility. Through it all, it has resisted opportunities to 'make it big' and instead stayed with less profitable, but relatively secure, investments.

Dan Richardson has an economics degree from Melbourne University and is one of the original founders of PI. He started out working in the research department and has worked in every department since then. The other partners, comfortable with Dan's conservative yet flexible nature, elected him to the position of CEO in 1995. After that, Dan became known as 'the great equaliser'. He worked hard to make sure that all the partners were included in decisions and that strong relations were maintained. Over the years he became the confidant of the other seniors and the mentor of the next generation. He took pride in his 'people skills', and PI's employees looked to Dan for leadership and direction.

Dan's management philosophy is built on the concept of loyalty—loyalty to the organisation, loyalty to its members and loyalty to friends. Bolstered by the support of the other founding members of PI, Dan continued the practice of consistent and safe investing. This meant maintaining low-risk investment portfolios with moderate income. However, PI's growth has increasingly not kept pace with other investment opportunities. As a result, Dan has reluctantly begun to consider the merits of a more aggressive investment approach. This consideration was further strengthened by the expressions of several of the younger analysts who were beginning to refer to PI as 'stodgy'. Some of them were leaving PI for positions in more aggressive firms.

One evening, Dan talked about his concerns with his tennis partner and long-time friend, Tabitha Rose. Tabitha also happened to be an investment broker. After receiving her economics degree from the University of Adelaide, Tabitha went to work for a brokerage firm in New York, beginning her career in the research department. Her accomplishments in research brought her recognition throughout the firm. Everyone respected her for her knowledge, her work ethic and her uncanny ability to predict trends. Tabitha knew what to do and when to do it. After only two years on the job, she was promoted to the position of portfolio manager. However, she left that firm for greener pastures and has spent the last few years moving from firm to firm, finally returning to Sydney.

When Tabitha heard Dan's concerns about PI's image and need for an aggressive approach, she suggested to her friend that what PI needed was some fresh blood, someone who could infuse

ANALYSIS

enthusiasm into the organisation. Someone like her. She told Dan, 'I can help you get things moving. In fact, I've been developing some concepts that would be perfect for PI.'

Dan brought up the idea of hiring Tabitha at the next staff meeting, but the idea was met with caution and scepticism. 'Sure, she's had a brilliant career on paper,' said one senior partner, 'but she's never stayed in one place long enough to really validate her success. Look at her résumé. During the past seven years she's been with four different firms, in four different positions.'

'That's true,' said Dan, 'but her references all check out. In fact, she's been described as a rising star, aggressive, productive. She's just what we need to help us explore new opportunities.'

'She may have been described as an up-and-comer, but I don't feel comfortable with her apparent inability to settle down,' said another. 'She doesn't seem very loyal or committed to anyone or anything.'

Another partner added: 'A friend of mine worked with Tabitha a while back and said that, while she is definitely good, she's a real maverick in terms of both investment philosophy and lifestyle. Is that what we really want at PI?'

Throughout the discussion, Dan defended Tabitha's work record. He repeatedly pointed out Tabitha's impressive performance. He deflected concerns about her reputation by saying that she was a loyal and trusted friend. Largely on Dan's recommendation, the other partners agreed, although somewhat reluctantly, to hire Tabitha. When Dan offered Tabitha the job, he promised her the freedom and flexibility to operate a segment of the fund as she desired.

Tabitha took the job and performed her responsibilities at PI in a superior manner. Indeed, she was largely responsible for increasing the managed assets of the company by 150 per cent. However, a price was paid for this increase. From the day she moved in, the junior analysts enjoyed working with her very much. They liked her fresh, new approach and were encouraged by the spectacular results. This caused jealousy among the other partners, who thought Tabitha was pushing too hard to change the tried-and-true traditions of the firm. It was not uncommon for sharp disagreements to erupt in staff meetings, with one or another partner coming close to storming out of the room. Throughout this time, Dan tried to soothe ruffled feathers and maintain an atmosphere of trust and loyalty.

Tabitha seemed oblivious to all the turmoil she was causing. She was optimistic about potential growth opportunities. She believed that biotechnology and laser engineering were the 'waves of the future'. Because of this belief, she wanted to direct the focus of her portfolio towards these emerging technologies. 'Investments in small firm stocks in these industries, coupled with an aggressive market timing strategy, should yield a 50 per cent increase in performance,' she argued. She rallied support for this idea, not only among the younger members of PI but also from the pension fund managers who invested with PI. Tabitha championed her position and denigrated the merits of the traditional philosophy. 'We should compromise on safety and achieve some real growth while we can,' she argued. 'If we don't, we'll lose the investors' confidence and ultimately lose them.'

Most of the senior partners disagreed with Tabitha, stating that the majority of their investors emphasised security above all else. They also disagreed with the projected profits: 'We could go from 8 to 12 per cent ROI; then again, we could drop to 4 per cent. A lot depends on whose data you use.' They reminded Tabitha: 'The fundamental approach of the company is to provide a safe investment. That's the philosophy we used to solicit the investments originally and that's the approach we are obligated to maintain.'

Many months passed and dissension among the managers grew. Tabitha's frustration over the lack of support she felt from the senior partners began to undermine the day-to-day operations of PI. She began to criticise her detractors in discussions with younger PI employees. In addition, she assigned research department employees tasks related to technological investments, distracting them from investigating more traditional alternatives. She gradually implemented her ideas within her portfolio, which accounted for approximately 35 per cent of PI's revenues. This disrupted the operations of other managers in PI, because the performance of their funds relied on the timely input of the researchers and other support staff. The other managers bristled when the research staff began tracking the ROI of the various investments on a chart prominently displayed on the conference room wall.

Amidst a rapidly spreading undercurrent of tension, one of the founding partners, Susan Watson, approached Dan one day. Conservative in her ways, Susan is the partner who walks the office and always has time to stop and chat. She began the conversation.

'Dan, I speak for most of the senior staff when I say that we are very troubled by Tabitha's approach. We've expressed ourselves well enough for Tabitha to understand, but her actions defy everything we've said. She's a catastrophe just waiting to happen.'

'I can understand your concern, Susan,' replied Dan. 'I'm troubled, too. We have an opportunity to attract new business with some of Tabitha's new ideas. And the younger staff love working on her projects. But she has stirred up a lot of turmoil.'

Susan agreed. 'The real issue is that PI is no longer presenting a unified image. Tabitha is wilfully defying the stated objectives of our organisation. And some of our oldest clients don't like that.'

'That's true, Susan. On the other hand, some of our newer clients are really encouraged by Tabitha's approach and her track record is extremely impressive.'

'Come on, Dan. You and I both know that many experts feel the market is overheating. Tabitha's paper profits could quickly be incinerated if the budget and trade deficits don't turn around. We can't stake the reputation of the firm on a few high-flying technology stocks. Dan, the other senior partners agree. Tabitha must either conform to the philosophy and management practices of this organisation or else resign.'

Reflecting on the situation, Dan realised he faced the most difficult challenge of his career. He felt a strong personal investment in helping Tabitha succeed. Not only had he hired Tabitha over the objections of several colleagues, he had personally helped her to 'learn the ropes' at PI. Beyond that, Dan was haunted by his promise to Tabitha that she would have the freedom and flexibility to perform the requirements of the position as she pleased. However, this flexibility had clearly caused problems within PI.

Finally, bowing to the pressure of his peers, Dan called Tabitha in for a meeting, hoping to find some basis for compromise.

Dan: I gather you know the kinds of concerns the senior partners have expressed regarding your approach.

Tabitha: I guess you've talked with Susan. Well, we did have a small disagreement earlier this week.

Dan: The way Susan tells it, you're wilfully defying corporate objectives and being troublesome.

Tabitha: Well, it's just like Watson to see progressive change as an attempt to take away her power.

Dan: It's not quite that simple, Tabitha. When we founded PI, we all agreed that a conservative stance was best. And right now, with the economic indicators looking soft, many experts agree that it may still be the best alternative.

Tabitha: Dan, what are you going to rely on—predictions or performance? These concerns are just smokescreens to deflect attention away from the sub-par records of other portfolio managers. Old views need to be challenged and ultimately discarded. How else are we going to progress and keep up with our competitors?

Dan: I agree we need to change, Tabitha, but gradually. You have great ideas and terrific instincts, but you can't change a longstanding firm overnight. You can help me promote change, but you're pushing so fast, others are digging in their heels. The rate of change is just as important as the direction.

Tabitha: You're telling me. And at this rate, it doesn't make much difference which direction we're headed.

Dan: Come on, Tabitha. Don't be so cynical. If you'd just stop rubbing people's noses in your performance record and try to see things from their perspective, we could calm things down around here. Then maybe we could start building consensus.

Tabitha's emotions betray her impatience with the pace of the organisation; she becomes agitated.

Tabitha: I've always admired your judgment and I value your friendship, but I honestly think you're kidding yourself. You seem to think you can get this firm to look like it's progressive—shrugging off its stodgy image—without taking any risks or ruffling any feathers. Are you interested in appearance or substance? If you want appearance, then hire a good PR person. If you want substance, then back me up and we'll rewrite the record book. Get off the fence, Dan.

Dan: Tabitha, it simply isn't that easy. I'm not PI, I'm simply its caretaker. You know we make decisions around here by consensus; that's the backbone of this organisation. To move ahead, the confidence of the others has to be won, especially the confidence of the seniors. Frankly, your reputation as a maverick makes it hard to foster confidence in and loyalty to your plans.

Tabitha: You knew my style when you hired me. Remember how you made it a point to promise me flexibility and autonomy? I'm not getting that anymore, Dan. All I'm getting is grief, even though I'm running circles around your conservative cronies.

Dan: Well, that may be true. But your flamboyance …

Tabitha: Oh, yeah. The sports car, the singles lifestyle, the messy office. But, again, that's appearance, Dan, not substance. Performance is what counts. That's what got me this far and that's my ticket out. You know I could walk into any firm in town and write my own plan.

Dan: Well, there's no reason to be hasty.

Tabitha: Do you honestly believe this can be salvaged? I think not. Maybe it's time for me to be moving on. Isn't that why you called me in here anyway?

Dan, feeling uncomfortable, breaks eye contact and shifts his gaze to the Sydney skyline. After a long pause, he continues, still gazing out of the window.

Dan: I don't know, Tabitha. I feel I've failed. My grand experiment in change has polarised the office; we've got two armies at war out there. On the other hand, you really have done a good job here. PI will no doubt lose a good part of its customer base if you leave. You have a loyal following, with both customers and staff. If you go, so do they, along with our shot at changing our image.

Tabitha: It's just like you, Dan, to take this problem personally. Blast it, you take everything personally. Even when I beat you at tennis. Your heart's in the right place: you just can't ever seem to make the cut-throat hit. You know and I know that PI needs a change in image. But it doesn't appear to be ready for it yet. And I'm certainly not willing to move slowly.

Dan: Yeah. Maybe. It's just hard to give up … [*long pause*]. Well, why don't we talk more about this after the reception tonight? Come on over and see Joanie and the kids. Besides, I'm dying to show off my new boat.

Tabitha: What you see in sailing is beyond me. It's a waste of time, lazily drifting on gentle breezes …

Dan: Save it for later, 'Speed Queen'. I've got to get ready for tonight.

DISCUSSION QUESTIONS

1. *What are the sources of conflict in this case?*
2. *What approaches to conflict management are used by the actors in this situation? How effective was each?*
3. *Based on the behavioural guidelines for the collaborative approach, how could Dan have managed this conflict more effectively?*

Skill practice

Exercises in managing complex conflict situations

Managing mobbing

Consider this case study. An employee, Mary, comes to you in your role as her manager/director. She begins the discussion with a request that what she is about to say be kept in confidence. She then begins to share her concerns about her team leader, John, who she feels has been harassing her. Each time you ask her for some specific details or a description of what she considers as John's inappropriate behaviour, she becomes teary and apologises for bothering you. Mary then proceeds to say that she is aware that other people have also experienced John behaving in a harassing or bullying manner. She suggests that John's behaviour is the reason why Frank and Jo left the workgroup to take on new appointments. She says that this has caused major problems for the team because Frank and Jo were terrific contributors, and that it has been hard to fill their vacancies because it is common knowledge in the organisation that John is difficult to work with.

If nothing is done, Mary says, she and others will leave the work team because it is a toxic work environment when John is around. She says that she loves working in the unit but cannot take being around John anymore. She adds that she does not want to have to put in a WorkCover claim as her doctor has indicated she should.

Mary suggests that you might want to talk with John's last manager, because she has heard that John left that position 'just in time' before serious allegations were made about him.

At the end of the discussion, Mary again confirms that she will not talk to John directly even if you accompany her, and that she does not want you to discuss her concerns with John either. She does, however, suggest that you might want to speak with other team members to gain confirmation that others also experience John as a bully. Finally, she reiterates that she does not want you to breach confidentiality because she is afraid of what John may do to her. She bursts into tears when you ask her what she is afraid that John may do if he becomes aware of her concerns. She does not provide you with any more detail about her concerns.

On reflection, you are aware that John does not seem to engage with any of the workgroup in the 'normal' social manner of other group members. You think that you may have observed his team members wanting to avoid contact with him. You are also aware that John is often direct and sometimes blunt in response to questions or when he provides feedback on project developments in his team meetings, and this is also his way of communicating in other group situations. You have always liked his 'no nonsense' approach to getting on with his work, but you wonder whether he behaves differently with you because he reports to you. You also know that John is going through some difficulties in his personal life and you wonder whether that has particularly 'soured' his attitude to women.

The next day, Chris, another member of the workgroup, comes to see you and says that Mary has confided in the members of the group, and that what she has said is true: everyone in the group experiences John as a bully. Chris also states that his health has been affected by John's ongoing harassment and he is thinking of lodging a WorkCover claim.

- What would be your response to Mary and Chris's discussion with you? Specifically, how would you handle Mary's request for confidentiality and Chris's comments about his potential WorkCover claim?
- As John's line manager, what action will you take as a result of Mary and Chris's discussions with you?
- Who, if anyone, would you consult to seek advice in addressing the concerns raised by Mary and Chris? What would you expect them to do, if anything?
- What are the responsibilities of your organisation? What are your responsibilities? What are the responsibilities of the employee(s) concerned?
- How would you describe 'duty of care' as it applies to this situation?
- What principles of 'natural justice' would you consider?
- What are the potential aspects of 'mobbing' that this case study highlights, and what would you do to ensure that this does not eventuate?

PRACTICE

Developing the expectant attitude

Seven steps (Andrewartha 1992) have been effective for managers in developing an expectant attitude in themselves and their staff. When these steps are incorporated, managers show their expectation in their faces and their whole demeanour. They know that what they expect to happen is going to happen. This sets the framework for potency as a manager and is the hallmark of a leader. This model is designed to build up a mind-set for the manager that is useful in overcoming the occasional doubts and setbacks in problem solving. It is a mechanism for improving self-confidence and sureness about outcomes. Use the following example of this process as a guide.

1. *Plan several stages to achieve your goal.* The goal determined by the manager might be to have supervisors effectively delegate work to their employees, rather than trying to handle it all alone. The manager might establish the following six stages:

   Stage 1: Discuss the situation with the supervisor.
   Stage 2: Identify tasks that can/should be delegated.
   Stage 3: Discuss obstacles to such delegation.
   Stage 4: Agree on strategies to implement delegation.
   Stage 5: Review the process in two weeks.
   Stage 6 (outcome): Congratulate the supervisor on effective delegation of tasks.

   Even though these stages have been 'created' in a planning process by the manager, they assume their own reality very rapidly. As each stage occurs, it becomes a benchmark which, in turn, confirms the progress towards the expected goal. The expectation begins to confirm itself.
2. *Relate each outcome (or behaviour), whatever it is, to the goal.* Expectation is in the eyes of the beholder, and one person's frown may be another person's concentrated thought. Whatever occurs is fitted into the expectant plan and utilised. All employees therefore build their own steps towards the goal. Possible negative reactions are redefined as probable evidence of progress.
3. *Define stages flexibly.* Staff are unique and your stage three may occur before stage two in their way of thinking. That is fine. A stage might be missed out altogether as the employee proceeds towards the expected goal. Flexible stages ensure the process is self-confirming.
4. *Define time flexibly.* Allow time for expectancy to succeed. Chemical treatments take time to have effect; so do subtle management strategies. Peter Senge (1992: 63) comments on this in his seventh law: cause and effect are not closely related in time and space. Sometimes, people need time to 'resist' before being ready. Time limits created by impatient managers often spell failure. The process might take four months, not two, but the expectant attitude will eventually occur. With enough time, most doubts become very elastic.
5. *Assume that any doubts are due to lack of information.* Sometimes, managers begin to doubt themselves when they do not achieve their goals as quickly as planned and in the precise way they determined. These doubts have an impact on the expectant attitude. Step 5's technique lets you assume that your plan is right on target but you are lacking all the information at this time. Step 5 is an effective way of softening doubts. With more information it would be possible to see how successful you were. Natural doubts are used to further the expectant attitude.
6. *Remember you do not really know everything about your employees' internal models or thought processes.* Employees may look irritable or seem to lack interest in the planned goal. If a manager treats these reactions at face value, the expectant process may easily be diminished. Step 6 allows the manager to be unsure about the real internal motivation of the employee. You can assume the process is working, despite appearances to the contrary. What you really do not know cannot affect the expectancy. As Argyris (1992) and others have established, we do not always do what we say, or say what we mean.
7. *Be really curious about the process.* Curiosity allows the manager to become fascinated with the process now and the outcome is assumed. Interest in what is happening now shifts the reliance and focus away from a more distant goal. It is taken for granted and is therefore more certain. Curiosity automatically confirms expectation.

This process is more successful the more closely you match the employees' non-verbal communication. The single most effective technique with employees is to confirm the 'rightness' of the goal in all your words and actions. If you totally believe in it and demonstrate that belief, it is compelling.

Assignment

Select three problem situations at work and practise the expectant attitude process over the next three months.

1. Observe the steps you have most difficulty with.
2. Concentrate on these steps in future practice.
3. Review your success after three months.

Exercise in assessing sources of conflict

Asian Electronics' management problems

To manage conflict between others effectively, it is important to be aware of early warning signs. It is also important to understand the underlying causes of disagreements. Conflict that is unmanaged, or managed ineffectively, interferes with workgroup performance. The keys to managing conflict effectively are recognising it in its early stages and understanding its roots.

Assignment

Reread the memos, faxes, voice mail and email messages in the Asian Electronics exercise in Chapter 1, page 33. As you examine each of these documents, look for evidence of organisational conflicts. Identify the two conflicts that you think are most significant for you to address in your role as Chris Pearson. Begin your analysis of these conflicts by identifying their likely sources or causes. Use the list below to guide your thinking. Prepare to present your analysis, along with supporting evidence from the memos. Also, share your ideas regarding how this analysis of the causes of conflict would influence your approach to resolving the conflict.

SOURCE OF CONFLICT	FOCUS OF CONFLICT
1. Personal differences	Perception and expectations
2. Poor informational processes	Misinformation and misinterpretation
3. Role incompatibility	Goals and responsibilities
4. Environmental stress	Resource scarcity and uncertainty

Exercises in selecting an appropriate conflict management strategy

Not all conflicts are alike, so they cannot all be managed in exactly the same way. Effective managers are able to assess accurately the true causes of conflict and to match each type of conflict with an appropriate management strategy.

For each of the following brief scenarios, select the most appropriate conflict management strategy. Refer to Table 7.4 (on page 358) for assistance in matching situational factors with strategies.

Difficult conversations

Imagine you are Jason, the divisional manager of a large financial services organisation. Read through the email from Jennifer (below) very carefully, then respond to the questions that follow. Feel free to make any other comments. Write down your responses in no more than one page.

Background information

Jennifer, director of the Business Support Unit, sent the email below to Bill, a project officer in the divisional office. Jason, the divisional manager, was copied into the email.

Email
Hello, Bill

I wish to remind you that all requests for administrative support and assistance for the eight administrative staff within the division's Business Support Unit must be brought to my attention, and it is recommended in future that you copy me into all such tasks and requests for information.

The administrative staff report to me and as such I need to be aware of the tasks they are performing, deadlines, etc. that may conflict with other duties, as I may need to reallocate resources to suit and meet statutory responsibilities.

Planning will negate the need for all requests to have urgent or short deadlines. It is recommended that this pressure not be put on the administrative staff to avoid conflicting with their other responsibilities.

I request in future that you demonstrate courtesy in all communications instead of the dismissive, non-inclusive, rude, bullying and challenging manner you currently display to me and also that you respect me both personally and professionally.

As the manager of the Business Support Unit and a senior staff member of the division, I would appreciate your attention to this matter and seek your cooperation and contribution to the team values.

Furthermore, as the person assigned responsibility by the director for implementing, monitoring and reporting on the systems and processes required to comply with legislative, audit and government standards, I am reminding you that you must abide by them as stated in the policies and procedures manual. Evidence exists of recurrent lapses in your compliance with these directions, along with excuses and reminders. They are mostly commonsense and in place for a reason. Your blatant and frequent disregard has direct impact on the business and results in limited staff resources taking on additional tasks to fit in with you, or to rectify your repeated transgressions and oversights.

You have been with the organisation for a considerable period of time and as such it is expected that you have read and understood the documented requirements to be adhered to and had ample opportunity to seek clarification. Future non-compliances will be documented and the general manager will be informed.

I am not alone in my frustration in working with you, Bill. I have previously gone through a mediation session with you that wasn't successful, and I do not intend to repeat the experience. I would welcome a transformation from you to achieve a healthier, improved and cooperative work environment. I am willing to meet you halfway, but I do not envisage anything more than a respectful working relationship.

I will not debate or be challenged by you on the contents of this instruction. Nor will you enter into discussion with my staff on these matters. I have included Jason in this email to ensure he is aware of the contents and consequences that may arise in the future.

Regards
Jennifer

Questions

1. As Jason, the general manager of this division who was copied into this email, what would you do and in what order?
2. What points do you specifically need to address?
3. Who would you need to talk to, and how would you plan the conversations?
4. What would you be seeking as an outcome?

After completing your notes, consider the 'ideal' manager conflict resolution responses and outcomes listed below.

Ideal conflict resolution responses

General comments

- A real positive would be that the participants did not get into a knee-jerk response of an email exchange with Jennifer.

- Read the email again and make notes of concerns and issues to deal with.
- Immediately email Bill and tell him not to take any action until you see him, as you are now managing this matter.
- Make a time to see Jennifer as soon as possible.
- Confirm what was meant by 'previous mediation' and get the facts, including who conducted it, reports or summary documents, and check for any written agreements and monitoring arrangements.

What points do you specifically need to address?
- The inappropriateness of both the content and tone of Jennifer's email and her lack of authority to direct. Jennifer is not Bill's manager.
- Explore the current specific concerns that Jennifer has about Bill's behaviour and what she has done to address these before sending the email.
- What were the barriers to Jennifer approaching Bill directly at the time of the first incident?
- What were the barriers to Jennifer discussing the problem with Jason and seeking help?
- What outcome did Jennifer expect from the email?
- Explore Bill's reaction to the email. Does he agree that some of the points raised are accurate?
- What would he like to happen from this point?
- What in all of the allegations needs to be addressed?
- Is there any negative effect on other staff or external customers?
- What personal support for each person can be arranged (for example, Employee Assistance Program)?

Who would you need to talk to, and how would you plan the conversations?
- Decide the optimum outcome and have a Plan B. Consider long-term and shorter-term outcomes and allow time for change.
- Depending on your (Jason's) previous involvement, you may need to get independent advice.
- Arrange meetings with Jennifer and Bill that can be private and with no interruptions, and arrange adequate time for each meeting.
- Provide an explanation and lead time to Jennifer and Bill so that they understand the topic of the discussion and have some planning time.
- Write down the points for discussion and consider your point of view as general manager, as well as the points of view of other staff in the workplace, when making decisions.

What would you be seeking as an outcome?
- A more respectful relationship within the workplace and compliance with the organisation's code of conduct.
- An acknowledgment of the different roles and responsibilities within the division all contributing towards service to customers.
- An agreement by Jennifer and Bill that would lead to behaviour change, and steps in place for the general manager to monitor compliance with that agreement.
- A clear statement of action that may be taken if change does not occur.

Sizzlers

You have decided to take your family out to the local Sizzlers to celebrate your son's birthday. You are a single parent, so getting home from work in time to prepare a special dinner is very difficult. On entering the restaurant, you ask the waiter to seat you in a quiet area of the restaurant because your daughter, Mary, is quite shy and is sensitive to loud noise. On your way to your seat, you notice that the restaurant seems crowded for a Monday night. After you and your children are seated and have placed your orders, your conversation turns to family plans for the approaching New Year holidays. Interspersed in the general conversation is light banter with your son about whether he is going to be top goal scorer next weekend.

Suddenly you become aware that your daughter is looking uncomfortable and holding her ears. You look around and notice a lively group of business people seated at the table behind you, all of whom are talking loudly and using inappropriate language. Your impression is that they are celebrating some type of special occasion. You realise that something has to be done. You ask your son to escort Mary outside while you go and find the manager.

1. What are the salient situational factors?
2. What is the most appropriate conflict management strategy?

Phelps Pty Ltd

You are Philip Ming, head of sales for an office products firm, Phelps. Your personnel sell primarily to small businesses in Taiwan. Phelps is doing about average for this rapidly growing market. The firm's new CEO, Sarasvati Danpasar, is putting a lot of pressure on you to increase sales. You feel that a major obstacle is the firm's policy on extending credit. Cathy, head of the credit office, insists that all new customers fill out an extensive credit application. Credit risks must be low; credit terms and collection procedures are tough. You can appreciate her point of view, but you feel it is unrealistic. Your competitors are much more lenient in their credit examinations: they extend credit to higher risks, their credit terms are more favourable, and they are more lenient in collecting overdue payments. Your sales personnel frequently complain that they are not 'playing on a level field' with their competition.

When you bring this concern to Sarasvati, she says she wants you and Cathy to work things out. Her instructions do not give many clues to her priorities on this matter. 'Sure, we need to increase sales, but the small business failure in this area is the highest in the country, so we have to be careful we don't make bad credit decisions.'

You decide it is time to have a serious discussion with Cathy. A lot is at stake.

1. What are the important situational factors?
2. What is the most appropriate conflict management strategy?

Exercises in resolving interpersonal disputes

The heart of conflict management is resolving intense, emotionally charged confrontations. The chapter discussed guidelines for using the collaborative (problem-solving) approach to conflict management in these situations. Assuming that the collaborative approach is appropriate for a particular situation, the general guidelines can be used by an initiator, a responder or a mediator.

PRACTICE

Assignment

Following are three situations involving interpersonal conflict and disagreement. When you have finished reading the assigned roles, review the appropriate behavioural guidelines. (See the observer's feedback form on page 398.) Do not read any of the role descriptions except those assigned to you.

In the first exercise, practise applying the guidelines for the initiator's role. In the second incident, which focuses on proper responses to emotional accusations, you will play the respondent's role. In the third exercise, you will practise mediating conflicts between employees. An observer will be assigned to give you feedback on your performance, using the observer's form as a guide.

Where's my paper?

Jan, director of human resources

You have been director of HR for State Power for ten years. Just when you thought you had your job perfectly under control, the sky fell in. The union has been trying to organise your factory; the federal government recently named your company as failing to submit a satisfactory affirmative action report; two senior directors were forced to resign last month because of the company's poor performance; and, on top of all that, your long-time personal assistant just died of a heart attack.

You have been asked to give a keynote address at a national convention on a new productivity program your company has pioneered, and you are looking forward to getting away from the office for a few days to catch your breath. You gave your talk to your new assistant, Chris, a couple of days ago so she would have plenty of time to get it keyed in and reproduced.

This morning you have come into the office to proofread and rehearse your talk prior to catching a plane this evening and you are shocked to find a note saying your assistant called in sick. You rush over to her desk and begin frantically searching for your paper. You find it mixed in with some material for the quarterly report that should have been sent in two weeks ago, a stack of overdue correspondence and two days' unopened mail.

As you dial Chris's home phone number, you realise that you are perspiring heavily and your face is flushed. This is the worst mess you can remember happening in years.

Chris, personal assistant

You hear the phone ring and it is all you can do to get out of bed and limp into the kitchen to answer it. You feel really rotten. On the way home last night, you slipped on your child's bicycle in the driveway and sprained your knee. You can hardly move today and the pain is excruciating. You are also a bit hesitant about answering the phone because you figure it is probably your boss, Jan, calling because you are getting behind in your work. You know you deserve some of the blame, but it wasn't all your fault.

Since you began working for Jan a month ago, you have asked several times for a thorough job description. You find you do not really understand either Jan's priorities or your specific responsibilities. You replaced a woman who died suddenly after working for Jan for ten years. You were hired to pick up the pieces, but you have found working with Jan extremely frustrating. She has been too busy to train you properly and she assumes you know as much about the job as your predecessor. This is particularly a problem since you have not worked as a PA for three years and you feel your skills are a bit rusty.

Jan's talk is a good example of the difficulties you have experienced. She gave you the talk a couple of days ago and said it was urgent, but that was on top of a quarterly report that was already overdue, a backlog of correspondence, filing and more. You have never filled out a report like this before and every time you asked Jan a question she said she'd discuss it with you later, as she ran off to a meeting. When you asked if it would be possible to get some additional help to catch up on the overdue work, Jan said the company could not afford it because of poor sales. This irked you because you knew you were being paid far less than your predecessor. You knew Jan faced some urgent deadlines, so you had planned to return to the office last night to type Jan's speech and try to complete the report, but two hours in the emergency room at the hospital put an end to that plan. You tried calling Jan to explain the problem only to find she has an unlisted number.

As you sit down and prop up your leg, you wince with pain as you pick up the phone.

Is Barry suitable?

Melissa, office manager

You are the manager of an auditing team sent to Bangkok, Thailand, to represent a statutory authority based in Brisbane. You and Barry, one of your auditors, were sent to Bangkok to set up an auditing operation. Barry is about seven years older than you and has five more years' seniority in the firm. Your relationship has become very strained since you were recently designated as the office manager. You feel you were given the promotion because you have established an excellent working relationship with the Thai staff as well as with a broad range of international clients. In contrast, Barry has told other members of the staff that your promotion simply reflects the firm's heavy emphasis on affirmative action. He has tried to isolate you from the all-male accounting staff by focusing discussions on sports, local night spots and so forth.

You are sitting in your office reading some complicated new reporting procedures that have just arrived from the office. Your concentration is suddenly interrupted by a loud knock on your door. Without waiting for an invitation to enter, Barry bursts into your office. He is obviously very upset and it is not difficult for you to surmise why he is in such a nasty mood.

You recently posted the audit assignments for the coming month and you scheduled Barry for a job you knew he would not like. You had set up a time to discuss the assignments with him, but he is quite early. Barry is one of your senior auditors and the company norm is that they get the choice assignments. This particular job will require him to spend two weeks away from Bangkok in a remote town, working with a company whose records are notoriously messy.

Unfortunately, you have had to assign several of these less desirable audits to Barry recently because you are short of personnel. But that is not the only reason. You have received several complaints recently from the junior staff (all Thais) that Barry treats them in a condescending manner. They feel he is always looking for an opportunity to boss them around, as if he were their supervisor rather than an experienced, supportive mentor. As a result, your whole operation works more smoothly when you can send Barry out of town on a solo project for several days. It stops him from coming into your office and telling you how to do your job and the morale of the rest of the auditing staff is significantly higher.

Barry slams the door and proceeds to express his anger over this assignment.

Barry, senior auditor

You are really upset! Melissa is deliberately trying to undermine your status in the office. She knows that the authority's norm is that senior auditors get the better jobs. You have paid your dues and now you expect to be treated with respect. And this is not the first time this has happened. Since she was made office manager, she has tried to keep you out of the office as much as possible. It is as if she does not want her rival for leadership of the office around. When you were asked to go to Bangkok, you assumed that you would be made the office manager because of your seniority in the firm. You are certain that the decision to pick Melissa is yet another indication of affirmative action practices.

In staff meetings, Melissa has talked about the need to be sensitive to the feelings of the office staff as well as the clients in this multicultural setting. 'Where does she get off preaching about sensitivity! What about my feelings, for heaven's sake?' you wonder. This is nothing more than a straightforward power play. She is probably feeling insecure about being the only female accountant in the office and being promoted over someone with more experience. You decide: 'Sending me out of town is a clear case of "out of sight, out of mind".'

Well, it is not going to happen that easily. You are not going to roll over and let her treat you unfairly. It is time for a showdown. If she does not agree to change this assignment and apologise for the way she has been treating you, you are going to register a formal complaint with her boss. You are prepared to submit your resignation if the situation does not improve.

Meeting at BI Manufacturing Company

BI Manufacturing Company is the largest company of its kind, established in 1947. Its sales currently average $25 million a year, with an annual growth of approximately 6 per cent. There are over 550 employees in production, sales and marketing, accounting, engineering and management.

Tommy Chan is general manager. He has held his position for a little over two years and is well respected by his employees. He has a reputation for being firm but fair. Tommy's training was in engineering, so he is technically minded and he frequently likes to walk around the production area to see for himself how things are going. He has also been known to roll up his sleeves and help work on a problem on the shop floor. He is not opposed to rubbing shoulders with even the lowest-level employees. On the other hand, he tries to run a tight company and employees generally stick to their assigned tasks. He holds high expectations for performance, especially from individuals in management positions.

Richard Hooton is director of production at BI Manufacturing. He has been with the company since he was 19 years old, when he worked in the loading dock. He has worked his way up through the ranks and now, at age 54, is the oldest of the management personnel. Hooton has his own ideas of how things should be run in production and he is reluctant to tolerate any intervention from anyone, even Tommy Chan. Because he has been with the company so long, he feels he knows it better than anyone else and he believes he has had a hand in making it the success that it is. His main goal is to keep production running smoothly and efficiently.

Barbara Price is director of sales and marketing. She joined the company about 18 months ago. Before that, she held the position of assistant manager of marketing at NHM Steel. Price is a very conscientious employee and is anxious to make a name for herself. Her major objective, which she has never hesitated to make public, is to be a general manager some day. Sales at BI Manufacturing have increased in the past year to near record levels under her guidance.

Charles Lin is regional sales director for the southeastern region. He reports directly to Barbara Price. This region represents the largest market for BI Manufacturing and Charles is considered the most competent salesperson in the company. He has built personal relationships with several major clients in his region. He has been with the company for 12 years, all of them in sales.

It is Friday afternoon and tomorrow at noon Tommy Chan leaves for New Delhi to attend an important meeting with potential overseas investors. He will be gone for two weeks. Before he leaves, there are several items in his in-basket that must receive attention. He calls a meeting with Richard Hooton and Barbara Price in his office. Just before the meeting begins, Charles Lin calls and asks if he may join the meeting for a few minutes, since he is in town and has something important to discuss that involves both Tommy Chan and Richard Hooton. Chan gives permission for him to join the meeting, since there may not be another chance to meet with Lin before the trip. The meeting convenes, therefore, with Chan, Hooton, Price and Lin all in the room.

Assignment

Form groups of four. Each person should take the role of one of the characters in the management staff of BI Manufacturing Company. Assign a fifth person to serve as an observer and provide feedback at the end of the meeting, using the observer's feedback form on page 398 as a guide. No one should read the instructions for another staff member's role. (The memos will be introduced by Tommy Chan during the meeting.)

Tommy Chan, general manager

Three memos arrived today and you judge them to be sufficiently important to require your attention before you leave on your trip. Each memo represents a problem that requires immediate action. You need commitments from key staff members to resolve these problems. You are concerned about this meeting because these individuals do not work as well together as you would like.

For example, Richard Hooton is very difficult to pin down. He always seems suspicious of the motives of others and has a reputation for not making tough decisions. You sometimes wonder how a person could become the head of production in a major manufacturing firm by avoiding controversial issues and blaming others for the results.

In contrast, Barbara Price is very straightforward. You always know exactly where she stands. The problem is that sometimes she does not take enough time to study a problem before making a decision. She tends to be impulsive and anxious to make a decision, whether it is the right one or not. Her general approach to resolving disagreements between departments is to seek expedient compromises. You are particularly disturbed by her approach to the sales incentive problem. You felt strongly that something needed to be done to increase sales during the winter months. You reluctantly agreed to the incentive program because you did not want to dampen her initiative. But you are not convinced this is the right answer, because, frankly, you are not yet sure what the real problem is.

Charles Lin is your typical aggressive, 'take no prisoners' sales manager. He is hard-charging and uncompromising. He is great in the field because he gets the job done, but he sometimes ruffles the feathers of the corporate staff with his 'black-and-white' style. He is also fiercely loyal to his sales staff, so you are sure he will take the complaint from an important customer (memo 1) about the poor behaviour of Sam Jones, a senior salesperson in Charles's team, very badly.

- Memo 1 requires a decision about how to respond to the complaint about Sam Jones.
- Memo 2 is from the firm's accountant recommending that it is risky but a good investment to purchase the small factory over the road. This matter also needs to be resolved today.
- Memo 3 is also from the accountant and concerns the figures in Barbara's area, which confirm that the sales incentive scheme is not working. Action needs to be taken either to drop the sales incentive scheme or put more resources into making it work.

In contrast to the styles of your staff, you have tried to use an integrative approach to problem solving: focusing on the facts, considering everyone's inputs equally and keeping conversations about controversial topics problem-focused. Since taking over this position two years ago, one of your goals has been to foster a team approach among your staff.

Note: For more information about how you might approach the issues raised by these memos in your staff meeting, review the collaborating approach in Table 7.2 (on page 352) as well as the mediator's behavioural guidelines on page 372.

Richard Hooton, director of production

The backbone of BI Manufacturing is production. You have watched the company grow from a small, struggling shop to a firm with a real impact on the region because of its outstanding production processes. Your own reputation among those who know manufacturing is a good one and you are confident that you have been a major factor in the success of BI Manufacturing. You have passed up several job offers over the years because you feel loyal to the company, but sometimes the younger employees do not seem to afford you the respect that you think you deserve.

The only times you have had major problems in production are when the young know-it-alls fresh from university have come in and tried to change things. With their scientific management concepts coupled with soft human relations training, they have more often made a mess of things than helped to improve matters. The best production methods have been practised for years in the company and you have yet to see anyone who could improve on your system.

On the other hand, you respect Tommy Chan as general manager. Because he has experience, the right kind of training and is involved in the production part of the organisation, he has often given you good advice and shown special interest. He mostly lets you do what you feel is best, however, and he seldom dictates specific methods for doing things.

Your general approach to problems is to avoid controversy. You feel uncomfortable when production is made the scapegoat for problems in the company. Because this is a manufacturing business, it seems as if everyone tries to pin the blame for problems on the production department. You have felt for years that the firm was getting away from what it does best: mass-producing a few standard products. Instead, the trend has been for marketing and sales to push for more and more products, shorter lead times and greater customisation capability. These actions have increased costs and caused significant production delays as well as higher rejection rates.

Note: During the forthcoming meeting, you should adopt the avoidance approach shown in Table 7.2. Defend your turf, place blame on others, defer taking a stand and avoid taking responsibility for making a controversial decision.

PRACTICE

Barbara Price, director of sales and marketing

You are anxious to impress Tommy Chan because you have your eye on a position that is opening up at the end of the year in the parent company. It would mean a promotion for you. A positive recommendation from Tommy Chan would carry a lot of weight in the selection process. Given that both BI Manufacturing and the parent company are largely male-dominated, you are pleased with your career advancement so far and you are hoping it will continue.

One current concern is Tommy Chan's suggestion some time ago that you look into the problem of slow sales during the winter months. You implemented an incentive plan that was highly recommended by an industry analyst at a recent trade conference. It consists of three separate incentive programs:

- competition among regions: the salesperson in the top region would have his or her picture in the company newsletter and receive an engraved plaque
- a holiday in Hawaii for the top salesperson in the company
- cash bonuses for salespeople who obtained new customer orders.

Unfortunately, these incentives have not worked. Not only have sales not increased for the company as a whole, but sales for two regions are down an average of 5 per cent. You have told the sales force that the incentives will last through this quarter, but if sales do not improve, your budget will be in the red. You have not budgeted for the prizes, since you expected the increased sales to more than offset the cost of the incentives.

Obviously, this was a bad idea; it is not working and it should be dropped immediately. You are a bit embarrassed about this aborted project. But it is better to cut your losses now and try something else than continue to support an obvious loser.

In general, you are very confident and self-assured. You feel that the best way to get work done is through negotiation and compromise. What is important is making a decision quickly and efficiently. Maybe everyone does not get exactly what they want, but at least they can get on with their work. There are no black and whites in this business, only 'greys' that can be traded off to keep the management process from bogging down with 'paralysis by analysis'. You are impatient over delays caused by intensive studies and investigations of detail. You agree with Tom Peters: Action is the hallmark of successful managers.

Note: During this meeting, use the compromise approach shown in Table 7.2. Do whatever is necessary to help the group make a quick decision so that you can get on with the pressing demands of your work.

Charles Lin, regional sales director

You do not get back to company headquarters often, because your customer contacts take up most of your time. You regularly work 50–60 hours a week and you are proud of the job you do. You also feel a special obligation to your customers to provide them with the best product available in the timeliest fashion. This sense of obligation comes not only from your commitment to the company but also from your personal relationship with many of the customers.

Lately, you have been receiving more and more complaints from your customers about late deliveries of BI Manufacturing's products. The time between their ordering and delivery is increasing and some customers have been greatly inconvenienced by the delays. You have made a formal inquiry of the production department to find out what the problem is. They replied that they are producing as efficiently as possible and they see nothing wrong with past practices. Richard Hooton's assistant even suggested that this was just another example of the sales force's unrealistic expectations.

Not only will sales be negatively affected if these delays continue, but your reputation with your customers will be damaged. You have promised them that the problem will be quickly solved and that products will begin arriving on time. Since Richard Hooton is so rigid, however, you are almost certain that it will do no good to talk with him. His employee probably got his negative attitude from Hooton.

In general, Hooton is a 1970s production worker who is being pulled by the rest of the firm into the 21st century. Competition is different, technology is different and management is different, but Richard is reluctant to change. You need shorter lead times, a wider range of products and the capacity to do some customised work. Certainly, this makes the production department work harder, but other firms are providing these services with the use of just-in-time management processes, robots and so forth.

Instead of getting down to the real problems, head office, in their typical high-handed fashion, announced an incentives plan. This implies that the problem is in the field, not the factory. It made some of your people angry to think they were being pressed to increase their efforts when they were not receiving the back-up support needed to get the job done. Sure, they liked the prizes, but the way the plan was presented made them feel as if they were not working hard enough. This is not the first

PRACTICE

time you have questioned the judgment of Barbara, your boss. She is certainly intelligent and hard-working, but she does not seem very interested in what is going on out in the field. And she does not seem very receptive to 'bad news' about sales and customer complaints.

Note: During this meeting, use the competing approach to conflict management and negotiations, shown in Table 7.2. However, do not overplay your part, because you are the senior regional sales manager and, if Barbara continues to move up fast in the organisation, you may be in line for her position.

Skill application

Suggested assignments

1. Select a specific conflict with which you are very familiar. Using the framework for identifying the sources of conflict discussed in this chapter, analyse this situation carefully. It might be useful to compare your perceptions of the situation with those of informed observers. What type of conflict is this? Why did it occur? Why is it continuing? Next, using the guidelines for selecting an appropriate conflict management strategy, identify the general approach that would be most appropriate for this situation. Consider both the personal preferences of the parties involved and the relevant situational factors. Is this the approach that the parties have been using? If not, attempt to introduce a different perspective into the relationship and explain why you feel it would be more productive. If the parties have been using this approach, discuss with them why it has not been successful thus far. Share information on specific behavioural guidelines or negotiation tactics that might increase the effectiveness of their efforts.
2. Using the same situation as in 1, analyse the conflict using the influence dimensions and the five matching skills described in Chapter 2. How were the participants mismatched on these factors? In what way might this have contributed to the conflict? Describe how matching on the influence dimensions and the five factors may assist in achieving a resolution to the conflict.
3. Identify a situation where another individual is doing something that needs to be corrected. Using the respondent's guidelines for collaborative problem solving, construct a plan for discussing your concerns with this person. Include specific language designed to state your case assertively without causing a defensive reaction. Role-play this interaction with a friend and incorporate any suggestions for improvement. Make your presentation to the individual and report on your results. What was the reaction? Were you successful in balancing assertiveness with support and responsibility? Based on this experience, identify other situations you feel need to be changed and follow a similar procedure.
4. Volunteer to serve as a mediator to resolve a conflict between two individuals or groups. Using the guidelines for implementing the collaborative approach to mediation, outline a plan of action prior to your intervention. Be sure to consider carefully whether or not private meetings with the parties prior to your mediation session are appropriate. Report on the situation and your plan. How did you feel? What specific actions worked well? What was the outcome? What would you do differently? Based on this experience, revise your plan for use in related situations.
5. Identify a difficult situation involving negotiations. This might involve transactions at work, at home or in the community. Review the guidelines for integrative bargaining and identify the specific tactics you plan to use. Write down specific questions and responses to probable initiatives from the other party. In particular, anticipate how you might handle the possibility of the other party's using a distributive negotiation strategy. Schedule a negotiation meeting with the party involved and implement your plan. Following the session, debrief the experience with a co-worker or friend. What did you learn? How successful were you? What would you do differently? Based on this experience, modify your plan and prepare to implement it in related situations.

Application plan and evaluation

The intent of this exercise is to help you apply this cluster of skills in a real-life, out-of-class setting. Now that you have become familiar with the behavioural guidelines that form the basis of effective skill performance, you will improve most by trying out those guidelines in an everyday context. Unlike a classroom activity, in which feedback is immediate and others can assist you with their evaluations, this skill application activity is one you must accomplish and evaluate on your own. There are two parts to this activity. Part 1 helps to prepare you to apply the skill. Part 2 helps you to evaluate and improve on your experience. Be sure to write down answers to each item. Do not short-circuit the process by skipping steps.

Part 1: Planning

1. Write down the two or three aspects of this skill that are most important to you. These may be areas of weakness, areas you most want to improve, or areas that are most salient to a problem you face right now. Identify the specific aspects of this skill that you want to apply.
2. Now identify the setting or the situation in which you will apply this skill. Establish a plan for performance by actually writing down a description of the situation. Who else will be involved? When will you do it? Where will it be done?
3. Identify the specific behaviours you will engage in to apply this skill. Set action plans for your skill performance.
4. What are the indicators of successful performance? How will you know that you have been effective? What will indicate that you have performed competently?

Part 2: Evaluation

5. When you have completed your implementation, record the results. What happened? How successful were you? What was the effect on others?
6. How can you improve? What modifications can you make next time? What will you do differently in a similar situation in the future?
7. Looking back on your whole skill practice and application experience, what have you learned? What has been surprising? In what ways might this experience help you in the long term?

Scoring keys and supplementary materials

Conflict resolution questionnaire (p. 332)

SCORING KEY

1. Reverse the scores for the following questions: 1, 3, 4, 13, 18, 22, 24, 26, 27, 31, 32, 33 and 35. Reverse those questions by looking at the response given in the left-hand column (p. 332) and writing in a reversed score in the right-hand column as follows:

Answer:		Score:
5	becomes	1
4	becomes	2
3	remains	3
2	becomes	4
1	becomes	5

2. For the questions that do not need to be reversed, write the same number given in the left-hand answer column in the right-hand score column.
3. Calculate subtotals and the total. The 40 questions are in groups of four, based on topics in Dudley Weeks' book *The Eight Essential Steps to Conflict Resolution* (Los Angeles: Jeremy Tarcher, 1992). Add the scores for each group of four and put the result in the blank. (The letter is just an abbreviation for the topic of that group.) Then add the subtotals and enter the result in the 'Total' blank.
4. Interpret the results and learn from them. The higher your scores, the more effective you are likely to be at finding resolutions that meet everyone's real needs and that build your long-term relationships. Of the ten subtotals, which were the highest? These are probably areas where you are effective. Which subtotals were the lowest? These are probably areas where you might try a different approach. Pick two or three of the questions with the lowest scores and try out behaviours that might make you more effective at resolving conflicts productively.

Learning from the survey

The higher your score on any question or section of the survey, the more likely you are to be effective at arriving at resolutions that meet both people's needs and build the relationship. Low scores may indicate areas where you could increase your effectiveness.

For each question on the survey, some advice is given below. The advice was compiled by the Conflict Resolution class and is based primarily on Weeks' book, but also includes ideas from other sources, including *Getting to Yes* by Roger Fisher and William Ury (1984). The guidelines are given in groups of four, corresponding to the ten lettered groups in the survey, which are in turn based on the topics or steps in Weeks' book.

For the questions or sections on which you got the lowest scores, read the guidelines and consider trying them. They may help you to be more effective.

V. VIEW conflict as natural and positive

View conflict as a natural outgrowth of diversity among people, which can be addressed in a win–win way that strengthens your relationships. Remember the value of building your long-term relationship. View the resolution of the conflict and the building of the relationship as interrelated parts. Prevention works best.

1. View conflicts as opportunities for growth, for you and the other person, and for your relationship.
2. Handle the differences in a way that strengthens your relationship; together you will find more satisfying resolutions for this and future conflicts.
3. Address differences directly, realising that you are more likely to meet both your concerns and the other's if you discuss issues openly.
4. Separate the people from the problem, so you can protect the relationship while addressing the problem.

A. ATMOSPHERE

Start by establishing an effective atmosphere that promotes partnership and problem solving.

5. Meet with the other at a mutually satisfactory time, when you both have plenty of time and are free from distractions.
6. Meet in an equally acceptable place that is tranquil and gives you equal power.
7. Help the other feel comfortable and safe, affirming the importance of the relationship.
8. Start by saying that you know the two of you can invent some solutions together that are mutually acceptable.

C. CLARIFY perceptions

Work with the other so you both are very clear about what the conflict is really about. Eliminate ghost issues that arise from misperceptions. Separate the people from the problem. Acknowledge emotions as legitimate. Then face the problem together.

9. Be clear with yourself and with the other about how you feel and how you perceive the problem. Use 'I' statements to tell the other how you feel, rather than 'You' statements that blame. Assert your needs without attacking the other.
10. Ask questions to clarify your perception of the other's perceptions. Listen actively. Acknowledge what the other says.
11. Look at yourself honestly, clarifying your needs and misperceptions.
12. Clear up misperceptions and stereotypes. Avoid 'pushing buttons'.

N. Note NEEDS, not wants

Identify the needs that are essential to you, the other person and your relationship.

13. Acknowledge the legitimate needs of the other, as well as those of your own. Recognise that there are usually multiple interests. Fractionate the problem.
14. Recognise that sustaining your relationship requires meeting needs of both.
15. Distinguish between real needs and secondary desires. Identify the other's core goals that you can support.
16. Postpone contentious demands that might damage the relationship until you and the other have worked on meeting needs of the relationship first.

P. Produce positive partnership POWER

Build 'power with', shared power that enables lasting resolutions and relations.

17. Be positive; be clear about yourself and your values. Keep reaching for the other's positive power and potential for constructive action. Recognise the power of effectiveness that comes from having the skills to develop the relationship, understand interests, invent options, and agree based on objective criteria.
18. Avoid negative 'power over', which wastes energy in seesaw battles and which may backfire and prevent you achieving your lasting goals. Treat others as you want to be treated.
19. Do not stereotype the other only by their negative power; keep options open for the other's constructive power. Do not ask who is more powerful; be optimistic about outcomes.
20. Work as a team, realising you need each other's positive power to act effectively. Be unconditionally supportive of the relationship.

F. Focus on the FUTURE first, then learn from the past

21. Forgive (which does not mean you approve). Acknowledge that all fall short. Move beyond the negative past; look to the positive potential. Be hard on the problem and soft on the people.
22. Focus on the current issue. Do not pick at old wounds. Learn from the past; recall good resolutions.
23. Remember the importance of the long-term relationship. Create images of an improved relationship resulting from effective resolution of the conflict.
24. Work as partners for mutually beneficial agreements that will nurture your relationship.

O. Open up OPTIONS for mutual gain

25. Listen with an open mind to alternative options. Ask for the other's options first; learn from them.
26. Prepare for discussions by inventing several specific new options that meet shared needs. Do not view these as final goals but as starting points. Together, brainstorm new possibilities. Separate inventing from deciding. Postpone critical discussion.

27. Beware preconceived answers. Look for common ground behind seeming oppositions. Avoid stereotypes.
28. Listen actively and acknowledge what is being said (which does not mean agreeing with it).

D. Develop 'DOABLES', stepping-stones to action

29. Develop small steps that lead you closer to a mutually healthy decision on larger issues. Choose ones that meet shared needs and that you have the shared power to implement.
30. Do not rest with temporary fixes that are not sufficient to meet the long-term problem. As the three little pigs learned, solid construction will last.
31. View this as a cooperative process whose best outcome cannot be foreseen alone at the beginning.
32. You will have a more satisfactory outcome if all factions participate as equals. Understand that the others have interests and needs too.

M. Make MUTUAL-BENEFIT agreements

33. Avoid win–lose solutions, which damage the long-term relationship. Consider the needs of the other, you, and your relationship, and you both will win. Avoid a contest of wills. Yield to reason, not pressure. Do not be a 'door-mat'.
34. Ask the other to clarify his or her interests; clarify your own.
35. Avoid bargaining, posturing, demands and threats, which kill cooperative problem solving. Acknowledge non-negotiable elements. Focus on interests, not positions, but do build large agreements on small 'doables'.
36. Be caretaker of the other's welfare as well as your own. Make agreements that meet objective, reasonable standards of fairness. Make agreements that meet the needs of both and that build the relationship.

X. EXTRA considerations

37. Express anger constructively. Emotions are legitimate and communicate. Channel anger's energy. Focus on the angering behaviour, not the person.
38. Define your best alternative to a negotiated agreement. Seek a third-party facilitator when you and the other lack the needed skills or when there seem to be intractable differences.
39. Hear the other's anger non-defensively. Do not react to emotional outbursts. Look for what you can do about the situation together.
40. Agree to disagree on specific value differences. Do not feel you have to agree on everything.

Managing interpersonal conflict (p. 333)

SCORING KEY		ASSESSMENT	
Skill area	*Items*	*Pre-*	*Post*
Initiating a complaint	1	______	______
	2	______	______
	3	______	______
	4	______	______
	5	______	______
	6	______	______
	7	______	______
	8	______	______
Responding to a criticism	9	______	______
	10	______	______
	11	______	______
	12	______	______

	13	______	______
	14	______	______
	15	______	______
	16	______	______
Mediating a conflict	17	______	______
	18	______	______
	19	______	______
	20	______	______
	21	______	______
	22	______	______
	23	______	______
	24	______	______
	TOTAL SCORE	☐	☐

Comparison data

Compare your scores with three comparison standards:

1. Compare your score with the maximum possible (144).
2. Compare your scores with the scores of other students in your class.
3. Compare your scores with a norm group consisting of 500 practising managers and business school students. In comparison to the norm group, if you scored:

120 or above	you are in the top quartile
116–119	you are in the second quartile
98–115	you are in the third quartile
97 or below	you are in the bottom quartile.

Managing conflict questionnaire (p. 335)

Scoring and interpreting

The alternative statement pairs are listed on the left. The alternatives, (a) or (b), are arranged in the columns. Ring (a) or (b) as chosen and total the number of items/column.

The **Thomas-Kilmann Conflict Mode inventory** (adapted from Thomas 1975) lets you 'chart' your perception of your behaviour in conflict situations where the concerns of you and others seem to be incompatible. The inventory observes five types of behaviour in handling conflict:

A = Competing *B* = Accommodating *C* = Avoiding *D* = Collaborating *E* = Compromising

The columns represent the five styles. Column scores indicate, through your reaction to the statements, preferred styles as you perceived the statements in relation to yourself. The maximum score per column is 12. More than 6 indicates a leaning to that style; less than 6, a relative dislike.

1. **Competing**

- We are assertive and uncooperative.
- We pursue our own concerns, not the other's.
- A power-oriented mode; we find and use power to win our position.
- We argue, we use our position, we apply economic sanctions.
- It may mean 'standing up for our rights', defending a position that we believe is correct, or simply trying to win.

STATEMENT PAIR	A = Competing (forcing)	B = Accommodating (soothing)	C = Avoiding (withdrawal)	D = Collaborating (problem solving)	E = Compromising (sharing)
1		(b)	(a)		
2		(a)	(b)		
3		(b)	(a)		
4	(b)			(a)	
5	(b)			(a)	
6	(b)			(a)	
7			(b)		(a)
8			(a)		(b)
9			(b)		(a)
10	(a)				(b)
11	(b)				(a)
12	(a)				(b)
13			(a)	(b)	
14			(b)	(a)	
15			(a)	(b)	
16				(b)	(a)
17				(a)	(b)
18				(b)	(a)
19	(a)		(b)		
20	(b)		(a)		
21	(a)		(b)		
22	(b)	(a)			
23	(a)	(b)			
24	(b)	(a)			
25		(a)			(b)
26		(a)			(b)
27		(a)			(b)
28		(b)		(a)	
29		(a)		(b)	
30		(b)		(a)	
TOTALS	A	B	C	D	E

2. **Accommodating**
- We are unassertive and cooperative—the opposite of competing.
- We forego our own concerns in order to satisfy the concerns of the other.
- There are elements of self-sacrifice and altruism.
- It may take the form of selfless generosity or charity, obeying another person's order when one would prefer not to, or yielding to another's point of view.

3. **Avoiding**
- We are unassertive and uncooperative.
- We do not immediately pursue our own concerns or those of the other.
- We do not address a potential conflict.
- It may take the form of diplomatic sidestepping, postponing until a better time, or simply withdrawing from a threatening situation.

4. **Collaborating**
- We are assertive and cooperative—the opposite of avoiding.
- We attempt to work with the other to find a solution that optimises the concerns of both.

- We dig into an issue to identify the underlying concerns and find alternatives to meet both sets of concerns.
- It might involve exploring a disagreement, learning from each other's insights, concluding to resolve a condition that might be the source of competition.
- Or it might involve confronting and trying to find a creative solution.

5. Compromising

- We are intermediate in both assertiveness and cooperativeness.
- The objective is to find an expedient, mutually acceptable solution that partially satisfies both.
- It falls on a middle ground between competing and accommodating.
- It gives up more than competing but less than accommodating.
- It addresses an issue more directly than avoiding, but doesn't explore it in as much depth as collaborating.
- It means splitting the difference, making a compromise, exchanging concessions, or seeking the expedient middle ground.
- It may leave both partially dissatisfied—a sub-optimal position.

There are no right answers from the inventory. The five modes are useful for descriptive and 'model' purposes—to reflect on useful social skills. We may say that 'two heads are better than one' (*collaborating*), but we might also think 'soothe your enemies with kindness' (*accommodating*), 'Split the difference' (*compromising*), 'Leave well enough alone' (*avoiding*) and 'Might makes right' (*competing*).

A mode's effectiveness depends on the situation and the skill in adopting the behaviours associated with it. We may each be capable across all five, but our temperament might lean us towards one or two in a 'dominant' sense. It is unlikely that we have just one (rigid) style of dealing with conflict. We may use some modes better than others—relying on these more heavily, because of temperament or practice.

The conflict behaviours we use will stem from our personal predispositions and the demands of the situations we are in.

A. Competing

Uses:

- When quick, decisive action is vital—for example, in emergencies.
- On important issues where unpopular courses of action need implementing—for example, when cost cutting, enforcing unpopular rules, imposing discipline.
- On issues vital to company welfare when you know you are right.
- To protect yourself against people who take advantage of non-competitive behaviour.

If you scored high:

- Perhaps people have learned that it is unwise to disagree with you, or have given up trying to influence you. This closes you off from information.
- Are subordinates afraid to admit ignorance and uncertainties? In competitive climates, we fight for influence and respect. This means acting more certain and confident than one feels. People are less able to ask for information and opinions, and thus are less able to learn.

If you scored low:

- Do you often feel powerless in situations? Are you unaware of the power you do have, unskilled in its use, or uncomfortable with the idea of using it? This may hinder your effectiveness by restricting your influence.
- Do you have trouble taking a firm stand, even when you see the need? Sometimes concerns for others' feelings or anxieties about using power cause us to vacillate. Postponing may mean delay and adding to suffering and/or resentment of others.

B. Accommodating

Uses:

- When you realise that you are wrong—to allow a better position to be heard, to learn from others, and to show that you are reasonable.

- When the issue is much more important to the other person than to yourself—to satisfy the needs of others, and as a goodwill gesture to help maintain a cooperative relationship.
- To build up social credits for later issues which are important to you.
- When continued competition would only damage your cause—when you are outmatched and losing.
- When preserving harmony and avoiding disruption are especially important.
- To aid in the managerial development of subordinates by allowing them to experiment and learn from their own mistakes.

If you scored high:
- Do you feel that your own ideas and concerns are not getting the attention they deserve? (Deferring too much to the concerns of others can deprive you of influence, respect and recognition. It also deprives the organisation of your potential contributions.)
- Is discipline lax? (Although discipline for its own sake may be of little value, there are often rules, procedures and assignments whose implementation is crucial for you or the organisation.)

If you scored low:
- Do you have trouble building goodwill with others? (Accommodation on minor issues that are important to others are gestures of goodwill.)
- Do others often seem to regard you as unreasonable?
- Do you have trouble admitting it when you are wrong?
- Do you recognise legitimate exceptions to rules?
- Do you know when to give up?

C. Avoiding

Uses:
- When an issue is trivial, of only passing importance, or when other more important issues are pressing.
- When you perceive no chance of satisfying your concerns—for example, when you have low power or you are frustrated by something which would be very difficult to change (national policies, someone's personality, etc.).
- When the potential damage of confronting a conflict outweighs the benefits of its resolution.
- To let people cool down—to reduce tensions to a productive level and to regain perspective and composure.
- When gathering more information outweighs the advantages of an immediate decision.
- When others can resolve the conflict more effectively.
- When the issue seems tangential or symptomatic of another more basic issue.

If you scored high:
- Does your coordination suffer because people have trouble getting your inputs on issues?
- Does it often appear that people are 'walking on eggshells'? (Sometimes a dysfunctional amount of energy can be devoted to caution and the avoiding of issues, indicating that issues need to be faced and resolved.)
- Are decisions on important issues made by default?

If you scored low:
- Do you find yourself hurting people's feelings or stirring up hostilities? (You may need to exercise more discretion in confronting issues or more tact in framing issues in non-threatening ways. Tact is partially the art of avoiding potentially disruptive aspects of an issue.)
- Do you often feel harried or overwhelmed by a number of issues? (You may need to devote more time to setting priorities—deciding which issues are relatively unimportant and perhaps delegating them to others.)

D. Collaborating

Uses:

- For an integrative solution where both concerns are important and not to be compromised.
- When the objective is to learn—for example, testing assumptions, understanding others' views.
- To merge insights from different perspectives.
- To gain commitment by incorporating others' views into a consensual decision.
- To work through hard feelings that interfere with an interpersonal relationship.

If you scored high:

- Do you spend time discussing issues in depth that do not seem to deserve it? (Collaboration takes time and energy—perhaps the scarcest organisational resources. Trivial problems do not require optimal solutions, and not all personal differences need to be hashed out. The overuse of collaboration and consensual decision making sometimes represents a desire to minimise risk by diffusing responsibility for a decision or by postponing action.)
- Does your collaborative behaviour fail to elicit collaborative responses from others? (The exploratory and tentative nature of some collaborative behaviour may make it easy for others to disregard collaborative overtures; or the trust and openness may be taken advantage of. You may be missing some cues which would indicate the presence of defensiveness, strong feelings, impatience, competitiveness or conflicting interests.)

If you scored low:

- Is it hard for you to see differences as opportunities for joint gain—as opportunities to learn or solve problems? (Although there are often threatening or unproductive aspects of conflict, indiscriminate pessimism can prevent you from seeing collaborative possibilities and thus deprive you of the mutual gains and satisfactions which accompany successful collaboration.)
- Are subordinates uncommitted to your decisions or policies? (Perhaps their own concerns are not being incorporated into those decisions or policies.)

E. Compromising

Uses:

- When goals are moderately important, but not worth the effort or potential disruption of more assertive modes.
- When two opponents with equal power are strongly committed to mutually exclusive goals—are in labour–management bargaining.
- To achieve temporary settlements to complex issues.
- To arrive at expedient solutions under time pressure.
- As a backup mode when collaboration or competition fails to be successful.

If you scored high:

- Do you concentrate so heavily upon the practicalities and tactics of compromise that you sometimes lose sight of larger issues—principles, values, long-term objectives, company welfare?
- Does an emphasis on bargaining and trading create a cynical climate of gamesmanship? (Such a climate might undermine interpersonal trust and deflect attention away from the merits of the issues discussed.)

If you scored low:

- Do you find yourself too sensitive or embarrassed to be effective in bargaining situations?
- Do you find it hard to make concessions? (Without this safety valve, you may have trouble getting gracefully out of mutually destructive arguments, power struggles, etc.)

Resolving interpersonal disputes

'Where's my paper?' (p. 382), 'Is Barry suitable?' (p. 383) and 'Meeting at BI Manufacturing Company' (p. 384)

Observer's feedback form

Rating action

1 Low
5 High

INITIATOR

_________ Maintained personal ownership of the problem, including feelings.
_________ Avoided making accusations or attributing motives.
_________ Succinctly described the problem (behaviours, outcomes, feelings).
_________ Specified expectations or standards violated.
_________ Persisted until understood.
_________ Encouraged two-way interaction.
_________ Approached multiple issues incrementally (proceeded from simple to complex, easy to hard).
_________ Appealed to what the disputants had in common (goals, principles, constraints).
_________ Made a specific request for change.

RESPONDER

_________ Showed genuine concern and interest.
_________ Responded appropriately to the initiator's emotions.
_________ Avoided becoming defensive or overreacting.
_________ Sought additional information about the problem (shifted general to specific, evaluative to descriptive).
_________ Focused on one issue at a time, gradually broadening the scope of the discussion, searching for an integrative solution.
_________ Agreed with some aspect of the complaint (facts, perceptions, feelings or principles).
_________ Asked for suggestions for making changes.
_________ Proposed a specific plan of action.

MEDIATOR

_________ Treated the conflict and disputants seriously.
_________ Broke down complex issues, separated the critical from the peripheral.
_________ Began with a relatively easy problem.
_________ Helped disputants avoid entrenched positions by exploring underlying interests.
_________ Remained neutral (facilitator, not judge).
_________ Pointed out the effect of the conflict on performance.
_________ Kept the interaction issue-oriented.
_________ Made sure that neither party dominated the conversation.
_________ Kept conflict in perspective by emphasising areas of agreement.
_________ Helped generate multiple alternatives.
_________ Made sure that both parties were satisfied with and committed to the proposed resolution.

Comments:

References

Adler, N. J. 1991, *International Dimensions of Organizational Behavior*, 2nd ed. (Boston: PWS-KENT Publishing).

Adler, R. B. 1977, 'Satisfying personal needs: Managing conflicts, making requests and saying no', in *Confidence in Communication: A Guide to Assertive and Social Skills* (New York: Holt, Rinehart & Winston).

Amason, A. C. 1996, 'Distinguishing the effects of functional and dysfunctional conflict on strategic decision making: Resolving a paradox for top management teams', *Academy of Management Journal*, 39, pp. 123–48.

Amason, A. C., W. A. Hochwarter, K. R. Thompson and A. W. Harrison 1995, 'Conflict: An important dimension in successful management teams', *Organizational Dynamics*, Autumn, pp. 20–34.

Andrewartha, G. 1992, *The Expectant Attitude as a Management Skill* (Adelaide: McPhee Andrewartha Pty Ltd).
Andrewartha, G. 2011, *Leadership Enhancement Team Style (LETS)* (Adelaide: McPhee Andrewartha).
Aquino, K. 2000, 'Structural and individual determinants of workplace victimization: The effects of hierarchical status and conflict management style', *Journal of Management*, 26, pp. 171–92.
Argenti, J. 1976, *Corporate Collapse: The Causes and Symptoms* (New York: John Wiley & Sons).
Argyris, C. 1992, *On Organizational Learning* (Cambridge, UK: Blackwell).
Bazerman, M. 1986, 'Why negotiations go wrong', *Psychology Today*, June, pp. 54–58.
Bazerman, M. H. and M. A. Neale 1992, *Negotiating Rationally* (New York: The Free Press).
Bekmeier-Feuerhahn, S. and A. Eichenlaub 2010, 'What makes for trusting relationships in online communication?', *Journal of Communication Management*, 14(4), pp. 337–55.
Bennis, W. 1985, *Leaders: The Strategies for Taking Charge* (New York: Harper & Row).
Block, P. 1993, *Stewardship* (San Francisco: Berrett Koehler Publications).
Boros, S., N. Meslec, P. L. Curseu and W. Emons 2010, 'Struggles for cooperation: Conflict resolution strategies in multicultural groups', *Journal of Managerial Psychology*, 25(5), pp. 539–54.
Boulding, E. 1964, 'Further reflections on conflict management', in R. L. Kahn and E. Boulding (eds), *Power and Conflict in Organizations* (New York: Basic Books).
Brown, L. D. 1983, *Managing Conflict at Organizational Interfaces* (Reading, MA: Addison-Wesley).
Buber, M. 1958, *I and Thou* (New York: Charles Scribner).
Buttery, A. and E. Buttery 1994, *Business Networks: Reaching New Markets with Low-cost Strategies* (Melbourne: Pitman Publishing).
Buttery, A. and T. K. P. Leung 1998, 'The difference between Chinese and Western negotiations', *European Journal of Marketing*, 32(3/4), pp. 374–89.
Cameron, K. S., M. U. Kim and D. A. Whetten 1987, 'Organizational effects of decline and turbulence', *Administrative Science Quarterly*, 32, pp. 222–40.
Chatman, J. A., J. T. Polzer, S. G. Barsade and M. A. Neale 1998, 'Being different yet feeling similar: The influence of demographic composition and organizational culture on work process and outcomes', *Administrative Science Quarterly*, 43, pp. 749–80.
Chuang, Y. T., R. Church and J. Zikic 2004, 'Organizational culture, group diversity and intra-group conflict', *Team Performance Management*, 10(1/2), pp. 26–34.
Chung-Yan, G. A. and C. Moeller 2010, 'The psychosocial costs of conflict management styles', *International Journal of Conflict Management*, 21(4), pp. 382–99.
Cox, K. B. 2003, 'The effects of intrapersonal, intragroup, and intergroup conflict on team performance effectiveness and work satisfaction', *Nursing Administration Quarterly*, 27(2), April/June, pp. 153–63.
Cox, T. H. 1994, *Cultural Diversity in Organizations: Theory, Research and Practice* (San Francisco: Berrett-Koehler).
Cox, T. H. and S. Blake 1991, 'Managing cultural diversity: Implications for organizational competitiveness', *Academy of Management Executive*, 5(3), pp. 45–56.
Cox, T. H., S. Lobel and P. McLeod 1991, 'Effects of ethnic group cultural difference on cooperative versus competitive behavior in a group task', *Academy of Management Journal*, 34, pp. 827–47.
Davenport, N., R. Schwartz and G. Elliot 1999, *Mobbing: Emotional Abuse in the American Workplace* (Ames, IA: Civil Society Publishing).
Dayan, M. 2010, 'Managerial trust and NPD team performance: Team commitment and longevity as mediators', *Journal of Business & Industrial Marketing*, 25(2), pp. 94–105.
Economist, The 1998, 'Risk management: Too clever by half', *The Economist*, 14 November.
Eisenhardt, K. M., J. L. Kahwajy and L. J. Bourgeois 1997, 'How management teams can have a good fight', *Harvard Business Review*, July–August, pp. 77–85.
Eman, I. E. and W. Y. Shena 2010, 'Does negotiation training improve negotiators' performance?', *Journal of European Industrial Training*, 34(3), pp. 192–210.
Farmer, S. M. and J. Roth 1998, 'Conflict-handling behavior in work groups', *Small Group Research*, 29(6), pp. 669–713.
Filley, A. C. 1975, *Interpersonal Conflict Resolution* (Glenview, IL: Scott, Foresman).
Filley, A. C. 1978, 'Some normative issues in conflict management', *California Management Review*, 71, pp. 61–66.
Fink, C. F. 1968, 'Some conceptual difficulties in the theory of social conflict', *Journal of Conflict Resolution*, 12, pp. 412–60.
Fisher, R. and S. Brown 1988, *Getting Together: Building a Relationship that Gets to Yes* (Boston: Houghton Mifflin).
Fisher, R. and W. Ury 1984, *Getting to Yes* (Boston: Houghton Mifflin).
Friedman, R. A., S. T. Tidd, S. C. Currall and J. Tsai 2000, 'What goes around comes around: The impact of personal conflict style on work conflict and stress', *International Journal of Conflict Management*, 11(1), pp. 32–55.
Gage, D. 1999, 'Is having partners a bad idea?', *Industry Week Growing Companies Edition*, December, pp. 46–47.
Goleman, D. 2001, 'An EI-based theory of performance', in C. Chernis and D. Goleman (eds), *The Emotionally Intelligent Workplace* (San Francisco: Jossey-Bass).

Golesorkhi, B. 2006, 'Gender differences and similarities in judgments of trustworthiness', *Women in Management Review*, 21(3), pp. 195–210.

Gordon, T. 1970, *Parent Effectiveness Training* (New York: Wyden).

Grove, A. S. 1984, *High Output Management* (London: Souvenir Press).

Guetzkow, H. and J. Gyr 1954, 'An analysis of conflict in decision making groups', *Human Relations*, 7, pp. 367–81.

Hamel, G. and C. Prahalad 1994, 'Competing for the future', *Harvard Business Review*, July–August, pp. 122–8.

Han, G. and B. D. Harms 2010, 'Team identification, trust and conflict: A mediation model', *International Journal of Conflict Management*, 21(1), pp. 20–43.

Harvey, J. 1988, *The Abilene Paradox* (San Diego, CA: Lexington Books).

Hines, J. S. 1980, *Conflict and Conflict Management* (Athens, GA: University of Georgia Press).

Hocker, J. L. and W. W. Wilmot 1991, *Interpersonal Conflict* (Dubuque, IA: W. C. Brown).

Hofstede, G. 1980, 'Motivation, leadership, and organization: Do American theories apply abroad?', *Organizational Dynamics*, Summer, pp. 42–63.

Holt, J. L. and C. J. DeVore 2005, 'Culture, gender, organizational role, and styles of conflict resolution: A meta-analysis', *International Journal of Intercultural Relations*, 29, pp. 165–96.

Jehn, K. A. 1997, 'A qualitative analysis of conflict types and dimensions of organizational groups', *Administrative Science Quarterly*, 41, pp. 530–57.

Karambayya, R. and J. M. Brett 1989, 'Managers handling disputes: Third party roles and perceptions of fairness', *Academy of Management Journal*, 32, pp. 687–704.

Karpin, D. S. 1995, *Enterprising Nation: Report of the Industry Task Force on Leadership and Management Skills* (Canberra: Australian Government Publishing Service).

Karpman, S. B. 1968, 'Fairy tales and script drama analysis', *Transactional Analysis Bulletin*, 26, April, pp. 36–42.

Keashly, L. 1994, 'Gender and conflict: What does psychological research tell us?', in A. Taylor and J. B. Miller (eds), *Conflict and Gender* (Cresskill, NJ: Hampton Press).

Kelly, J. 1970, 'Make conflict work for you', *Harvard Business Review*, 48, July–August, pp. 103–13.

Kilmann, R. H. 1977, 'Developing a forced-choice measure of conflict-handling behavior: The "mode" instrument', *Educational and Psychological Measurement*, 37(2), pp. 309–25.

Kim, S. H. and R. H. Smith 1993, 'Revenge and conflict escalation', *Negotiation Journal*, 9, pp. 37–44.

Kim-Jo, T., V. Benet-Martínez and D. J. Ozer 2008, *Culture and Interpersonal Conflict Resolution Styles: Role of Acculturation, Culture & Interpersonal Conflict*, vol. 1 (MCB UP Ltd), pp. 38–54.

Kipnis, D. and S. Schmidt 1983, 'An influence perspective in bargaining within organizations', in M. H. Bazerman and R. J. Lewicki (eds), *Bargaining Inside Organizations* (Beverly Hills, CA: Sage Publications).

Knapp, M. L., L. L. Putnam and L. J. Davis 1988, 'Measuring interpersonal conflict in organizations', *Management Communication Quarterly*, 1(3), pp. 414–29.

Korabik, D., G. L. Baril and C. Watson 1993, 'Managers' conflict style and leadership effectiveness: The moderating effects of gender', *Sex Roles*, 29(5/6), pp. 405–20.

Kozan, K. 1997, 'Culture and conflict management: A theoretical framework', *International Journal of Conflict*, 8(4), pp. 338–60.

Kressel, K. and D. G. Pruitt 1989, *Mediation Research: The Process and Effectiveness of Third Party Intervention* (San Francisco: Jossey-Bass).

Krygier, M. 2006 'Four puzzles about the Rule of Law', *The Monthly*, July.

Latham, G. and K. Wexley 1981, *Increasing Productivity through Performance Appraisal* (Reading, MA: Addison-Wesley).

Lombardo, M. M. and R. W. Eichinger 1996, *The Career Architect, Development Planner* (Minneapolis, MN: Lominger Limited).

Maddux, R. 1988, *Successful Negotiation* (London: Kogan Page).

Mandell, B. and S. Kohler-Gray 1990, 'Management development that values diversity', *Personnel*, 67, pp. 41–7.

Manzoni, J. and J. Barsoux 1998, 'The set-up-to-fail syndrome', *Harvard Business Review*, 76(2), pp. 101–13.

Maslow, A. H. 1965, *Eupsychion Management: A Journal* (Chicago: Irwin).

Messmer, M. 2006, *CMA Accounting Magazine*, April.

Montoya-Weiss, M. M., A. P. Massey and M. Song 2001, 'Getting it together: Temporal coordination and conflict management in global virtual teams', *Academy of Management Journal*, 44, pp. 1251–62.

Morris, W. C. and M. Sashkin 1976, *Organization Behavior in Action: Skill Building Experience* (St Paul, MN: West Publishing Company).

Morrison, A. M. 1996, *The New Leaders: Leadership Diversity in America* (San Francisco: Jossey-Bass).

Northcraft, G. and M. Neale 1994, *Organization Behavior: A Management Challenge* (Chicago: Dryden Press).

O'Reilly, C. A., J. Chatman and D. F. Caldwell 1991, 'People and organizational culture: A profile comparison approach to assessing person–organization fit', *Academy of Management Journal*, 34, pp. 487–516.

Parayitam, S., B. J. Olson and Y. Bao 2010, 'Task conflict, relationship conflict and agreement-seeking behavior in Chinese top management teams', *International Journal of Conflict Management*, 21(1), pp. 94–116.

Pascale, R. T. 1990, *Managing on the Edge: How Successful Companies Use Conflict to Stay Ahead* (London: Viking).
Phillips, E. and R. Cheston 1979, 'Conflict resolution: What works', *California Management Review*, 21, pp. 76–83.
Pony, L. R. 1967, 'Organization conflict: Concepts and models', *Administrative Science Quarterly*, 12, pp. 296–320.
Porter, E. H. 1973, *Manual of Administration and Interpretation for Strength Deployment Inventory* (La Jolla, CA: Personal Strengths Assessment Service).
Pruitt, D. G. 1983, 'Integrative agreements: Nature and consequences', in M. H. Bazerman and R. J. Lewicki (eds), *Negotiating in Organizations* (Beverly Hills, CA: Sage Publications).
Pruitt, D. G. and P. J. Carnevale 1993, *Negotiation in Social Conflict* (Buckingham, UK: Open University Press).
Rahim, M. A. and A. A. Blum 1994, *Global Perspectives on Organizational Conflict* (Westport, CT: Praeger).
Robbins, S. P. 1974, *Managing Organizational Conflict: A Nontraditional Approach* (Englewood Cliffs, NJ: Prentice Hall).
Rossi, E. L. (ed.) 1980, *The Collected Papers of Milton H. Erickson* (New York: Irvington).
Rubin, J. Z., D. G. Pruitt and S. H. Kim 1991, *Social Conflict: Escalation, Stalemate and Settlement* (New York: McGraw-Hill).
Ruble, T. and K. Thomas 1976, 'Support for a two-dimensional model of conflict behavior', *Organizational Behavior and Human Performance*, 16, p. 145.
Savage, G. T., J. D. Blair and R. L. Sorenson 1989, 'Consider both relationships and substance when negotiating strategically', *Academy of Management Executive*, 3, pp. 37–48.
Schein, E. 1985, *Organizational Culture and Leadership* (San Francisco: Jossey-Bass).
Schmidt, W. H. and R. Tannenbaum 1965, 'Management of differences', *Harvard Business Review*, 38, November–December, pp. 107–15.
Schulz, K. 2010, *Being Wrong: Adventures in the Margin of Error* (New York: HarperCollins).
Scott, G. G. 1990, *Resolving Conflict* (Oakland, CA: New Harbinger Publications, Inc.).
Scott, W. E. and L. L. Cummings 1973, *Readings in Organizational Behavior and Human Performance* (Burr Ridge, IL: Irwin).
Senge, P. 1992, *The Fifth Discipline* (Sydney: Random House).
Seybolt, P. M., C. B. Derr and T. R. Nielson 1996, 'Linkages between national culture, gender, and conflict management styles', working paper, University of Utah.
Shafer, W. E., L. J. Park and W. M. Liao 2002, 'Professionalism, organizational-professional conflict and work outcomes: A study of certified management accountants', *Accounting, Auditing & Accountability Journal*, 15(1), pp. 46–68.
Shah, P. P. and K. A. Jehn 1993, 'Do friends perform better than acquaintances? The interaction of friendship, conflict, and task', *Group Decision and Negotiation*, 2, pp. 149–65.
Shallcross, L., S. Ramsay and M. Barker 2010, 'A proactive response to the mobbing problem: A guide for HR managers', *New Zealand Journal of Human Resource Management*, 10(1), pp. 27–37.
Shallcross, L., M. Sheehan and S. Ramsay 2008, 'Workplace mobbing: Experiences in the public sector', *International Journal of Organizational Behavior*, 13(2), pp. 56–70.
Shenkar, O. and S. Ronen 1987, 'The cultural context of negotiations: The implications of Chinese interpersonal norms', *Journal of Applied Behavioral Science*, 23(2), pp. 263–75.
Sillars, A. and J. Weisberg 1987, 'Conflict as a social skill', in M. E. Roloff and G. R. Miller (eds), *Interpersonal Processes: New Directions in Communication Research* (Beverly Hills, CA: Sage).
Sorensen, J. B., K. Hawkins and R. L. Sorenson 2002, 'The strength of corporate culture and the reliability of firm performance', *Administrative Science Quarterly*, 47, pp. 70–91.
Tatum, C. and R. J. Eberlin 2008, 'The relationship between organizational justice and conflict style', *Business Strategy Series*, 9(6), pp. 297–305.
Thomas, D. and R. Ely 1996, 'Making differences matter: A new paradigm for managing diversity', *Harvard Business Review*, 74(5), pp. 79–91.
Thomas, K. 1975, 'Conflict and conflict management', in M. Dunnette (ed.), *Handbook of Industrial and Organizational Psychology*, vol. 2 (Chicago: Rand McNally).
Thompson, L. 2001, *The Mind and Heart of the Negotiator*, 2nd ed. (Upper Saddle River, NJ: Prentice Hall).
Ting-Toomy, S., G. Gao, P. Trubisky, Z. Yang, H. Kim, S. Lin and T. Nishida 1991, 'Culture, face maintenance, and strategies of handling interpersonal conflict: A study in five cultures', *International Journal of Conflict Management*, 2(4), pp. 275–96.
Tjosvold, D. 1991, *The Conflict Positive Organization* (Reading, MA: Addison–Wesley.
Trompenaars, F. 1998, *Riding the Waves of Culture: Understanding Diversity in Global Business* (New York: Irwin).
Wanous, J. P. and A. Youtz 1986, 'Solution diversity and the quality of group decisions', *Academy of Management Journal*, 1, pp. 149–59.
Watzlawick, P., J. Weakland and R. Fisch 1974, *Change: Principles of Problem Formation and Problem Resolution* (New York: W. W. Norton).
Weeks, D. 1992, *The Eight Essential Steps to Conflict Resolution* (Los Angeles: Jeremy Tarcher).

Wei, H-C. 2000, 'Chinese-style conflict resolution: A case of Taiwanese business immigrants in Australia', *Intercultural Communication Studies*, 9, p. 289.

Weldon, E. and K. A. Jehn 1995, 'Examining cross-cultural differences in conflict management behavior: A strategy for future research', *International Journal of Conflict Management*, 6, pp. 387–403.

Westhues, K. 2006, 'The Waterloo Strategy for prevention of mobbing in higher education', in *The Remedy and Prevention of Mobbing in Higher Education* (Lewiston, NY: The Edwin Mellen Press).

Yuan, W. 2010, 'Conflict management among American and Chinese employees in multinational organizations in China', *Cross Cultural Management: An International Journal*, 17(3), pp. 299–311.

Zapf, D. 1999, 'Organizational, work group related and personal causes of mobbing/bullying at work', *International Journal of Manpower*, 20(1/2), pp. 70–85.

PART 3

GROUP SKILLS

CHAPTER 8

EMPOWERING AND DELEGATING

OBJECTIVES

- **Empower others**
- **Delegate effectively**
- **Share power**

8

CHAPTER OUTLINE

Skill assessment

Evaluative surveys for empowering and delegating

Effective empowerment and delegation

Step 1: Before you read the material in this chapter, respond to the following statements by writing a number from the rating scale below in the left-hand column (pre-assessment). Your answers should reflect your attitudes and behaviour as they are now, not as you would like them to be. Be honest. This instrument is designed to help you discover your level of competency in empowering and delegating so that you can tailor your learning to your specific needs. When you have completed the survey, use the scoring key at the end of the chapter to identify the skill areas discussed in this chapter that are most important for you to master.

Step 2: When you have completed the reading and the exercises in this chapter and, ideally, as many as you can of the skill application assignments at the end of the chapter, cover up your first set of answers. Then respond to the same statements again, this time in the right-hand column (post-assessment). When you have completed the survey, use the scoring key on page 445 to measure your progress. If your score remains low in specific skill areas, use the behavioural guidelines at the end of the skill learning section to guide further practice.

Rating scale

1 Strongly disagree
2 Disagree
3 Slightly disagree
4 Slightly agree
5 Agree
6 Strongly agree

Assessment

Pre-	*Post-*	
		In situations where I have an opportunity to empower others:
______	______	1. I help people develop personal mastery in their work by involving them first in less complex tasks and then in more difficult ones.
______	______	2. I help people feel competent in their work by recognising and celebrating their small successes.
______	______	3. I try to demonstrate successful task accomplishment.
______	______	4. I point out other successful people who can serve as role models.
______	______	5. I frequently praise, encourage and express approval of other people.
______	______	6. I provide regular feedback and needed support.
______	______	7. I try to foster friendships and informal interaction.
______	______	8. I highlight the important impact that a person's work will have.
______	______	9. I try to provide all the information that people need to accomplish their tasks.
______	______	10. As I become aware of it, I pass along relevant information to people on a continuous basis.
______	______	11. I ensure that people have the necessary resources (equipment, space and time) to succeed.
______	______	12. I help people get access to needed resources that I may not have available personally.

______ ______ 13. I help people become involved in teams in order to increase their participation.
______ ______ 14. I let teams make decisions and implement their own recommendations.
______ ______ 15. I foster confidence by being fair and equitable in my decisions.
______ ______ 16. I exhibit caring and personal concern for each person with whom I have dealings.

When delegating work to others:

______ ______ 17. I specify clearly the results I desire.
______ ______ 18. I specify clearly the level of initiative I want others to take (for example, wait for directions, do part of the task and then report, do the whole task and then report).
______ ______ 19. I allow participation by those accepting assignments regarding when and how the work will be done.
______ ______ 20. I make certain that the amount of authority I give matches the amount of responsibility I give for producing results.
______ ______ 21. I work within existing organisational structures when delegating assignments and never bypass someone without informing them.
______ ______ 22. I identify constraints and limitations that people will face but also provide needed support.
______ ______ 23. I maintain accountability for results, not for methods used.
______ ______ 24. I delegate consistently, not just when I am overloaded.
______ ______ 25. I avoid upward delegation by asking people to recommend solutions, rather than merely asking for advice or answers, when a problem is encountered.
______ ______ 26. I make clear the consequences of success and failure.

The scoring key is on page 445.

Personal empowerment

This instrument helps to identify the extent to which you are empowered in your own work. You should respond to the items based on your own job or, if you are at university or college, the work you do as a student. The items listed below describe different orientations people can have with respect to their work roles. Using the following rating scale, indicate the extent to which you believe each is true of you.

Rating scale

1 Very strongly disagree
2 Strongly disagree
3 Disagree
4 Neutral
5 Agree
6 Strongly agree
7 Very strongly agree

______ 1. The work that I do is very important to me.
______ 2. I am confident about my ability to do my work.
______ 3. I have significant autonomy in determining how I do my job.
______ 4. I have a significant impact on what happens in my work unit.
______ 5. I trust my co-workers to be completely honest with me.
______ 6. My work activities are personally meaningful to me.
______ 7. My work is within the scope of my competence and capabilities.
______ 8. I can decide how to go about doing my own work.

______ 9. I have a great deal of control over what happens in my work unit
______ 10. I trust my co-workers to share important information with me.
______ 11. I care about what I do in my work.
______ 12. I am confident in my capabilities to perform my work successfully.
______ 13. I have considerable opportunity for independence and freedom in how I do my work.
______ 14. I have a significant influence over what happens in my work unit.
______ 15. I trust my co-workers to keep the promises they make.
______ 16. The work I do has special meaning and importance to me.
______ 17. I have mastered the skills necessary to do my work.
______ 18. I have a chance to use personal initiative in carrying out my work.
______ 19. My opinion counts in my work unit's decision making.
______ 20. I believe that my co-workers care about my well-being.

The scoring key is on page 446.

Skill learning

What is empowerment?

Although the 1990s have been referred to as the empowerment era (Hardy & Leiba-O'Sullivan 1998; Leach, Wall & Jackson 2003), empowerment initiatives and research are still going strong across the globe (cf. Barton & Barton 2011; Charbonnier-Voirin & El Akremi 2011) in a broad range of industries (Heger 2007; Lawrence 2007) such as media (O'Hare & Kudrle 2007), education (Burnett 2011) and health care (Benson 2007; Wagner et al. 2010). Empowerment sometimes means delegating responsibility, giving employees increased decision-making authority, and providing information for people so that they can decide what to do and how it should be done, within the boundaries defined by an organisation's strategy, vision and mission. For example, according to Deans (2002: 76):

> *In 1996 Fantastic Furniture was hovering on the brink of oblivion. The private chain of furniture stores was in administration. Julian Tertini and partners, Peter Brennan and Peter Draper, saw a future for the Australian company, based on the empowerment of staff. Previously staff had been given no clue as to the success or otherwise of the company. Now store managers run their own show and it is head office that has to justify its costs. Store staff keep 25 per cent of all profits above budget while workers in Fantastic's factories receive bonuses. All staff also qualify for an employee share scheme. Fantastic was floated three years ago and in the period to late 2002 net earnings have trebled to $A6.8 million.*

Managers who empower people frequently remove controls, constraints and boundaries. For example, Bill Wawn, a divisional director in charge of client service with Macquarie Investment Management (MIM), says a key element in effective client service is empowerment of employees. MIM's client service staff are given budgets that they can spend at their own discretion. 'They have a certain amount of money they know they can spend,' he says. 'They could, say, spend $40 on a courier, waive a fee or initiate something more than they have been asked for, to get the job done' (Hoyle 1995). Another example of removing controls, constraints and boundaries is the RBC (Royal Bank of Canada) Financial Group, which has empowered its customer service employees by giving them discretion to spend up to $1000 per customer in order to solve any problem and 'make it right' (Milligan & Smith 2002).

Rather than being a 'push' strategy, in which managers try to induce employees to respond in desirable ways through incentives and influence techniques, empowerment is a 'pull' strategy. It focuses on ways that managers can design a work situation so that it energises people and provides intrinsic encouragement to employees to learn and perform better (Leach, Wall & Jackson 2003). In the context of such a strategy, people accomplish tasks because they are attracted by them, not because of an external reward system or influence technique.

Studies have illustrated that empowering management–employee approaches can lead to world-class performance and better customer service (cf. Barton & Barton 2011; Bea 1999; Berdahl 2003; Cane 1994; Fassel 2003; Hernan 1999; Mader 2003; Milligan & Smith 2002). Heller's (1999) review of the Tavistock Institute's 25-year program of research on organisational influence sharing illustrates several things:

1. Employees at the 'coal face' have, on average, almost no influence on the decision process.
2. Particularly at middle and senior levels, participative practices varied significantly for different types of decisions (for example, strategic decisions versus problems close to their work).
3. Participation varies significantly between the phases of a decision cycle, with lower-level employees usually having more influence over implementation than over initiation or the process of development and alternative choices.
4. Where employed properly and involving people with relevant experience and skill, empowerment is associated with a better quality and effectiveness of decisions, a significant reduction in the underutilisation of human resources and, ultimately, improved organisational performance.

Empowerment processes tacitly acknowledge that the survival of many businesses rests not with plant and equipment or management skills, but with the ideas and talents of employees. Although people undoubtedly make the difference in an organisation, it must be realised that empowerment is not a solution to all management problems (cf. Tulgan 2007; Vidal 2007).

Empowering others, for example, can lead to dilemmas. On the one hand, research has illustrated for years that empowered employees are frequently more productive, more satisfied and more innovative, and that they create higher-quality products and services than non-empowered employees (Greenberger & Stasser 1991; Kanter 1983; Sashkin 1982, 1984; Spreitzer 1992). Organisations are often more effective when an empowered workforce exists (Conger & Kanungo 1988; Gecas 1989; Schulze 2000; Thomas & Velthouse 1990). On the other hand, empowerment means giving up control and letting others make decisions, set goals, accomplish results and receive rewards. It means that other people will probably get the credit for success. Managers with high needs for power and control (see McClelland 1975) face a challenge when they are expected to sacrifice their needs for someone else's gain. They may ask themselves: 'Why should others get the credit when I am in charge? Why should I allow others to exercise power, and even facilitate their acquiring more power, when I want to receive rewards and recognition myself?'

Fortunately, you do not need to sacrifice desired rewards, recognition or effectiveness in order to be a skilful and empowering manager. On the contrary, through real empowerment managers actually multiply their own power. They and their organisations become more effective than they could have been otherwise. For most managers, empowerment is a skill that must be developed and practised, because, despite the high visibility of the concept of empowerment in popular literature, its actual practice is all too rare in modern management.

It is also important to remember that employee empowerment does not mean management's abdication of responsibility. As Minett (2000) states in relation to the hospitality industry in Australia:

> *... the issue of management responsibility and employee empowerment is an important one for Australian hotels. The trend towards employee empowerment can sometimes lead to managers abrogating their responsibilities, but empowerment should mean helping staff to make their own decisions, not leaving them to it. Management is [about] providing guidance rather than expecting employees to blindly follow. Managers should also remember new technologies and management theories are only tools.*

This chapter begins by discussing the core dimensions of empowerment and, in particular, how to effectively accomplish empowerment. The second part of the chapter discusses a special situation in which empowerment is essential: the delegation of responsibility. The chapter concludes with a summary model of empowerment and delegation and a list of behavioural guidelines for successfully empowering and delegating to others.

According to Professor Lex Donaldson at the Australian Graduate School of Management, one of the most well-researched findings in organisation and management science over the last four decades is that, when environments are predictable and stable, organisations can function well as routine, controlled, mechanistic units (Donaldson 1985, 1995, 2001). Under such conditions, employees can be expected to follow rules and procedures and to engage in standardised, formalised behaviour. Managers can maintain control and issue top-down mandates regarding the strategy and direction to be pursued by the organisation. There is little need for empowerment in these types of situations (cf. Tulgan 2007; Vidal 2007).

However, the modern business environment is often described using such terms as hyper-turbulence, hyper-complexity, hyper-speed, hyper-competition and transformational change. Under such conditions, prescriptions for organisation and management effectiveness call for a flexible, autonomous, entrepreneurial, empowered workforce (Drucker 1988, 2003a, 2003b; Peters 1992) rather than one that relies on top-down direction and control. Less centralised decision making, less top-down direction and less autocratic leadership are all suggested as prerequisites for high-performing modern organisations operating in these 'hyper' conditions.

When environments are unstable and unpredictable (that is, when they change a great deal or in unpredictable ways), managers, employees and organisational structures, policies and procedures must be more flexible and organic in order to be successful (Anonymous 2002; Ashby 1956; Eisenhardt & Galunic 1993; Lawrence & Lorsch 1967). For example, in a study of 40 installations of computerised technology, flexibility (that is, a greater amount of work done outside traditional job classifications and more people available that routinely perform a given task) was a significant predictor of success (that is, greater productivity, cost reduction, quality improvement and lower response time) (Carlopio, Fleischer & Roitman 1988).

Similarly, in many service industries, flexibility is critical. According to Peter Ellwood, group CEO of the British bank and insurance firm Lloyd's of London, which employs 80 000-plus staff, 'employee empowerment and autonomy are vital to the bank's fortunes and [are] of more importance than technological tools' (Anonymous 2002: 21). According to Ellwood, these flexible human resource practices have helped to retain staff and lower recruitment costs.

Unfortunately, other research has shown that, instead of becoming adaptable, flexible, autonomous and self-managing, some individuals in rapidly changing, complex environments behave in ways opposite to what is needed to succeed. Cameron, Whetten and Kim (1987) found in their studies that both managers and employees tended to become less flexible, less adaptable, less autonomous, less self-managing, more stable, more rigid and more defensive when they faced turbulence and change. Based on their research on how organisations were managed when they faced decline, turbulence, downsizing and change, 12 negative attributes or attitudes have been identified and are summarised in Table 8.1.

How can we ever expect a workforce in a changing environment to develop the prescribed characteristics for effectiveness (that is, to be adaptable, flexible, autonomous and self-managing) if people become more dependent on top managers in uncertain times rather than more independent? If managers are skilled at empowering employees, the inertia that drives organisations towards dysfunctional attitudes is counteracted; people become more effective, even in the face of trying times.

Empowerment is a key to unlocking the potential of a successful workforce in an era of chaotic change and escalating competitive conditions. But what is empowerment? What does it mean to be an empowered employee? What is the set of management skills associated with empowerment?

To empower means to enable; it means to help people develop a sense of self-efficacy, or to feel successful or effective at a particular task (Geller 2003); it means to overcome causes of powerlessness or helplessness; it means to energise people to take action; it means to mobilise intrinsic excitement factors in work. Empowerment not only involves the capacity to accomplish a task but also includes a way of defining oneself. Empowered people possess the wherewithal to accomplish something, but they also think differently of themselves after empowerment.

Historical roots of empowerment

The word 'empowerment' was in vogue in the 1980s and 1990s. The concept of empowerment has been referred to in many books and articles in the last two decades, and it has become popular to use

TABLE 8.1 Reactions to change

ATTRIBUTE	EXPLANATION
Centralisation	Decision making is pulled towards the top of the organisation. Less power is shared.
Threat-rigidity response	Conservative, self-protective behaviours predominate. Old habits persist. Change is resisted.
Loss of innovativeness	Trial-and-error learning stops. Low tolerance for risk and creativity.
Decreasing morale	In-fighting and a mean mood permeate the organisation. *It isn't fun.*
Politicised environment	Special-interest groups organise and become vocal. Everything is negotiated.
Loss of trust	Leaders lose the confidence of employees. Distrust predominates among employees.
Increased conflict	In-fighting and competition occur. Self-centredness predominates over the good of the organisation.
Restricted communication	Only good news is passed upwards. Information is not widely shared and is held close to the vest.
Lack of teamwork	Individualism and disconnectedness inhibit teamwork. Lack of coordination occurs.
Loss of loyalty	Commitment to the organisation and to the leader erodes. Focus is on defending oneself.
Scapegoating leaders	Leadership anaemia occurs as leaders are criticised, priorities become blurred and a siege mentality occurs.
Short-term perspective	A crisis mentality is adopted. Long-term planning and flexibility are avoided.

Source: Adapted from K. S. Cameron, D. A. Whetten and M. U. Kim, 'Organizational dysfunctions of decline', *Academy of Management Journal*, 30, 1987, pp. 126–38.

LEARNING

the term to refer to everything from team building to decentralised organisational structures. In fact, the word has been so overused that its precise meaning may have become obscured. To help you avoid confusing empowerment with other related management behaviours, a brief background to the roots of empowerment is provided, because it is by no means a new concept.

Empowerment has its roots in the disciplines of psychology, sociology and theology, dating back decades, even centuries. In the field of psychology, Adler (1927) developed the concept of 'mastery motivation', emphasising the striving that people have for competence in dealing with their world. Similar concepts introduced several decades ago include 'effectance motivation', an intrinsic motivation to make things happen (White 1959); 'psychological reactance', which refers to seeking freedom from constraints (Brehm 1966); 'competence motivation', a striving to encounter and master challenges (Harter 1978); and 'personal causation', a drive to experience free agency (DeCharms 1979). In each of these studies, the root concepts are similar to the notion of empowerment discussed in this chapter: that is, the inclination of people to experience self-control, self-importance and self-liberation.

In sociology, notions of empowerment have been fundamental to most 'rights' movements (for example, civil rights, women's rights, gay rights) (see Bookman & Morgan 1988; Solomon 1976), in which people campaign for freedom and control of their own circumstances. Moreover, much of the writing about attacking societal problems through social change has centred fundamentally on the empowerment of groups of people (Alinsky 1971; Marx 1844). That is, people seek social change in order to increase their empowerment.

In theology, ideas about free will versus determinism, self-will versus submissiveness, predestination versus faith, and humanism versus positivism have been hotly debated for centuries. At their root, they are all variations on a theme of empowerment versus helplessness. The more contemporary literature on 'liberation theology' (Freire & Faundez 1989) emphasises the empowerment of individuals to take charge of their own destinies, rather than relying on the dictates of an all-controlling, supernatural force. This does not mean that people who believe in a supreme being cannot feel empowered;

rather, it implies that they couple a sense of self-mastery and self-determination with their faith in a higher power.

Empowerment, then, is not a new concept. It has appeared in various forms throughout modern management literature. In the 1950s, for example, management literature was filled with prescriptions that managers should be friendly to employees (human relations); in the 1960s, that managers should be sensitive to the needs and motivations of people (sensitivity training); in the 1970s, that managers should ask employees for help (employee involvement); and, in the 1980s, that managers should form teams and hold meetings (quality circles) (see Byham 1988). The continuation of these themes in the 1990s suggested that managers should empower people. But despite the continuing emphasis on various versions of employee involvement and empowerment, the ability to empower employees is still not common in most managers' repertoires of skills. Empowerment is more rarely seen than prescribed.

Inhibitors to empowerment

In his book on managerial empowerment, Peter Block (1987: 154) noted that empowerment is sometimes difficult to accomplish:

> *Many, increasingly aware of the price we pay for too many controls, have had the belief that if some of these controls were removed, a tremendous amount of positive energy in service of the organisation would be released. While in many cases this has happened, too often our attempts at giving people more responsibility have been unwelcomed and met with persistent reluctance. Many managers have tried repeatedly to open the door of participation to their people, only to find them reluctant to walk through it. [In a study of managers who were offered total responsibility for their work areas] about 20 percent of the managers took the responsibility and ran with it, about 50 percent of the managers cautiously tested the sincerity of the offer and then over a period of six months began to make their own decisions. The frustrating part of the effort was that the other 30 percent absolutely refused to take the reins. They clutched tightly to their dependency and continued to complain that top management did not really mean it, they were not given enough people or resources to really do their job, and the unique characteristics of their particular location made efforts at participative management unreasonable.*

As Block noted, managers and employees are sometimes reluctant to accept empowerment, and they are even more reluctant to offer it. One reason for this is the personal attitudes of managers. Several management surveys have examined the reasons that managers have not been willing to empower their employees (Byham 1988; Newman & Warren 1977; Preston & Zimmerer 1978). These reasons can be organised into three broad categories:

1. *Attitudes about employees.* Managers who avoid empowering others often believe that their employees are not competent enough to accomplish the work, are not interested in taking on more responsibility, are already overloaded and unable to accept more responsibility, would require too much time to train, or should not be involved in tasks or responsibilities typically performed by the boss. They feel that the problem of non-empowerment lies with the employees, not with themselves. The rationale is: 'I'm willing to empower my people, but they just won't accept the responsibility.'
2. *Personal insecurities.* Some managers fear they will lose the recognition and rewards associated with successful task accomplishment if they empower others. They are unwilling to share their expertise or 'trade secrets' for fear of losing power or position. They have an intolerance for ambiguity that leads them to feel that they personally must know all the details about projects assigned to them. They prefer working on tasks by themselves rather than getting others involved, or they are unwilling to absorb the costs associated with employees making mistakes. The rationale is: 'I'm willing to empower people, but when I do they either mess things up or try to grab all the glory.'
3. *Need for control.* Non-empowering managers often have a high need to be in charge and to direct and govern what is going on. They presume that an absence of clear direction and goals from the boss and a slackening of controls will lead to confusion, frustration and failure on the part of employees. They feel that direction from the top is mandatory. Moreover, they often see short-lived,

disappointing results from pep talks, work teams, suggestion systems, job enrichment programs and other fix-it activities ('We tried that and it didn't work'). The rationale is: 'I'm willing to empower people, but they require clear directions and a clear set of guidelines; otherwise, the lack of instructions leads to confusion.'

The rationale associated with each of these inhibitors may be partially true. They nevertheless inhibit managers from achieving the success associated with skilful empowerment. Even if managers demonstrate the willingness and courage to empower others, success still requires skilful implementation. Incompetent empowerment, in fact, can undermine, rather than enhance, the effectiveness of an organisation and its employees.

For example, incompetent empowerment such as giving employees freedom without clear directions or resources has been found to lead to psychological casualties among individuals, as manifested by increased depression (Alloy et al. 1984), heightened stress (Averill 1973), decreased performance and job satisfaction (Greenberger et al. 1989), reduced alertness and even increased mortality (Langer & Rodin 1976). Of course, these negative consequences are not associated solely with incompetent empowerment. They have been noted, nevertheless, in situations where attempted empowerment was ineffective and unskilful.

This evidence suggests that when managers associated empowerment with behaviours such as 'simply letting go', refusing to clarify expectations, abdicating responsibility, having an absence of ground rules, or giving inflexible or inconsistent directions—none of which is consistent with skilful empowerment—the results were not only unsuccessful but even harmful. Because of the negative psychological and physiological consequences for employees, resulting from non-empowerment or from incompetent empowerment, Sashkin (1984) labelled skilful empowerment 'an ethical imperative' for managers.

LEARNING

Dimensions of empowerment

In one of the best empirical studies of empowerment to date, Spreitzer (1992) identified four dimensions of empowerment. One dimension has been added to her model here, based on the research of Mishra (1992). The importance of these dimensions is also supported by a number of more recent studies (Axtell & Parker 2003; Hemric, Eury & Shellman 2010; Holdsworth & Cartwright 2003; Sibthorp 2003; Siegall & Gardner 2000). This section explains these five dimensions of empowerment. For managers to empower others successfully, they must engender these five qualities in those they intend to empower. Skilful empowerment means producing in other people a sense of:

- self-efficacy
- self-determination
- personal control
- meaning
- trust (see Table 8.2).

TABLE 8.2 Five core dimensions of empowerment

DIMENSION	EXPLANATION
Self-efficacy	A sense of personal competence
Self-determination	A sense of personal choice
Personal control	A sense of having impact
Meaning	A sense of value in activity
Trust	A sense of security

When managers are able to foster these five attributes in others, they have successfully empowered them. It was suggested earlier that not only can empowered people accomplish tasks, but they also think differently about themselves. These five dimensions describe that difference. After explaining the five dimensions, guidelines are provided for engendering each of them.

Self-efficacy

When people are empowered, they have a sense of self-efficacy, or the feeling that they possess the capability and competence to perform a task successfully. Empowered people not only feel competent; they feel confident that they can perform adequately. They feel a sense of personal mastery and believe they can learn and grow to meet new challenges (Bandura & Wood 1989; Bennis & Nanus 1985; Conger & Kanungo 1988; Gecas 1989; Zimmerman 1990). Many believe that this is the most important element in empowerment, because having a sense of self-efficacy determines whether people will persist in attempting to accomplish a difficult task.

For example, Robert Wood, from the Australian Graduate School of Management, in a series of studies conducted with a number of colleagues, found that self-efficacy had both a direct effect on organisational performance (that is, production efficiency on a computerised organisational simulation) and an indirect effect, through its influence on analytic strategies (for example, systematically testing various managerial options). Individuals with a good sense of self-efficacy seem to be better able to cope with the setbacks and short-term problems that frequently accompany the implementation of a plan. They seem more able to test and revise their plans. On the other hand, those with low perceived self-efficacy become more self-doubting, set themselves lower goals, and become less systematic in their appraisal and selection of plans (Bandura & Wood 1989; Wood & Bandura 1989; Wood, Bandura & Bailey 1990; Wood & Locke 1990).

> *The strength of people's conviction in their own effectiveness is likely to affect whether they would even try to cope with given situations. ... They get involved in activities and behave assuredly when they judge themselves capable of handling situations that would otherwise be intimidating. ... Efficacy expectations determine how much effort people will expend and how long they will persist in the face of obstacles and aversive experiences. (Bandura 1977: 193–4)*

A great deal of research has been done on the consequences of self-efficacy and its opposite, powerlessness, especially in relation to physical and psychological health. For example, self-efficacy has been found to be a significant factor in predicting health management and the indexes measuring health-promoting and health-monitoring behaviours (Loeb, Steffensmeier & Kassab 2011), the developmental benefits of an adventure education experience (Sibthorp 2003) and in overcoming phobias and anxieties (Bandura 1986), alcohol and drug abuse (Seeman & Anderson 1983), eating disorders, smoking addiction and depression (Seligman 1975), as well as in increasing tolerance for pain (Neufeld & Thomas 1977). Recovery from illness and injury, and coping with job loss or disruptions, is more effective and more rapid among people who have developed a strong sense of self-efficacy, because they are more physically and psychologically resilient and are better able to change negative behaviours (Gecas, Seff & Ray 1988; Schwalbe & Gecas 1988).

Bandura (1977) suggested that three conditions are necessary for people to feel a sense of self-efficacy—a belief that:

- they have the ability to perform a task
- they are capable of putting forth the necessary effort
- no outside obstacles will prevent them from accomplishing the task.

In other words, people feel empowered when they develop a sense of self-efficacy by having a basic level of competence and capability, a willingness to put forth effort to accomplish a task, and the absence of overwhelming inhibitors to success.

Self-determination

Empowered people also have a sense of self-determination. Whereas self-efficacy refers to a sense of competence, 'self-determination' refers to the feeling of having a choice. 'To be self-determining means to experience a sense of choice in initiating and regulating one's own actions' (Deci, Connell & Ryan 1989: 580). People feel self-determined when they can voluntarily and intentionally involve themselves in tasks, rather than being forced or prohibited from involvement. Their actions are a consequence of personal freedom and autonomy. Empowered individuals have a sense of responsibility for and ownership of their activities (Rappoport, Swift & Hess 1984; Rose & Black 1985; Staples 1990; Zimmerman 1990). They see themselves as proactive self-starters. They are able to take initiative on their own accord, make independent decisions and try out new ideas (Conger & Kanungo 1988; Thomas

& Velthouse 1990; Vogt & Murrell 1990). Rather than feeling that their actions are predetermined, externally controlled or inevitable, they experience themselves as the locus of control.

Chapter 2 discusses the difference between an internal and an external locus of control. People who feel a sense of empowerment are most likely to have an internal locus of control: that is, they feel that they control what happens to them.

Research shows that a strong sense of self-determination is associated with less alienation in the work environment and more work satisfaction (Holdsworth & Cartwright 2003; Organ & Greene 1974), higher levels of work performance (Anderson, Hellreigel & Slocum 1977), more entrepreneurial and innovative activity (Hammer & Vardi 1981), high levels of job involvement (Runyon 1973) and less job strain (Gennill & Heisler 1972). In medical research, the negative effects of stress on health have been shown to be mitigated by having high control, high empowerment (that is, meaning, competence (or self-efficacy), self-determination and impact) and high work commitment (Nyssen et al. 2003), while recovery from severe illness has been found to be associated with having the patient 'reject the traditional passive role and insist on being an active participant in his own therapy' (Gecas 1989: 298). People who are helped to feel that they can have a personal impact on what happens to them, even with regard to the effects of disease, are more likely to experience positive outcomes than those who lack this feeling.

Self-determination is associated most directly with having choices about the methods used to accomplish a task, the amount of effort to be expended, the pace of the work and the time-frame in which it is to be accomplished. Empowered individuals have a feeling of ownership of tasks because they can determine how they are accomplished, when they are accomplished and how quickly they are completed. Having a choice is the critical component of self-determination.

LEARNING

Personal control

Empowered people have a sense of personal control over outcomes. They believe that they can make a difference by influencing the environment in which they work or the outcomes being produced. Personal control is 'an individual's beliefs at a given point in time in his or her ability to effect a change in a desired direction' (Greenberger et al. 1989: 165). It is the conviction that, through our own actions, we can influence what happens. 'Personal control', then, refers to a perception of impact.

Empowered people do not believe that obstacles in the external environment control their actions; rather, they believe that those obstacles can be controlled. They have a feeling of 'active control'—which allows them to bring their environment into alignment with their wishes—as opposed to 'passive control'—in which their wishes are brought into alignment with environmental demands (see Greenberger & Stasser 1991; Rappoport, Swift & Hess 1984; Rothbaum, Weisz & Snyder 1982; Thomas & Velthouse 1990; Zimmerman & Rappoport 1988). Instead of being reactive to what they see around them, people with a sense of personal control try to maintain command over what they see and do.

Medical research on childbirth has illustrated, for example, that women who chose to deliver with a spinal anaesthetic had higher fear of childbirth, an external locus of control for childbirth, and a desire for passive compliance in the childbirth process; while women who laboured without spinal anaesthetic had lower fear of childbirth, an internal locus of control for childbirth, and a desire to actively participate in the childbirth process (Anonymous 2004). In other words, women with a high sense of personal control (internal locus of control) rejected the spinal anaesthetic and had a greater desire to participate actively in the childbirth process. Women with a lower sense of personal control (external locus of control) chose to be more passive in the process.

According to Geller (2003: 33):

> *Personal control has been widely researched. … more than 2000 studies have investigated the relationship between perceptions of personal control and other variables. Internals are more achievement-oriented and health-conscious than externals.*

'Internals' are also less prone to distress and more likely to seek medical treatment when needed. In addition, having an internal locus of control helps to reduce chronic pain, facilitates psychological and physical adjustment to illness and surgery, and hastens recovery from some diseases. Internals perform better at jobs that allow them to set their own pace, whereas externals work better when a machine controls the pace.

Having a sense of personal control is related to, but distinct from, having power and influence. These last two concepts emphasise external sources of control and are associated with such factors as an individual's position, appearance, skills and visibility. Usually, obtaining power is desirable in order to influence or control the behaviour of others. In contrast, personal control is focused internally and the emphasis is on controlling one's own life, space and results. Control of self and the situations in which we place ourselves, more than control of others, is the objective.

Research suggests that people are intrinsically motivated to seek personal control (White 1959). They fight to maintain a sense of control of themselves and their situations. Prisoners of war, for example, have been known to do strange things, such as refusing to eat certain foods, not walking in a certain place, or developing secret communication codes, in order to maintain a sense of personal control. A certain amount of personal control is necessary for people to maintain psychological and physical well-being. When people lose personal control completely, they are usually labelled insane or psychopathic.

Even small losses of personal control can be harmful physically and emotionally. For example, loss of control has been found to lead to depression, stress, anxiety, low morale, loss of productivity, burnout, learned helplessness and even increased death rates (Greenberger & Stasser 1991; Langer 1983; Shapiro et al. 2011). The major predictor of suicide is also the sense of loss of personal control. Having a sense of personal control, then, is necessary for health as well as for empowerment. But even the most empowered people are not able to control totally everything that happens to them; no one is in complete control of their life. But empowerment helps people increase the number of personal outcomes they can control. Often, this is as much a matter of identifying areas in which personal control is possible as it is of manipulating or changing the external environment to increase control.

Meaning

Empowered people have a sense of meaning. They value the purpose or goals of the activity in which they are engaged. Their own ideals and standards are perceived as consistent with what they are doing. The activity 'counts' in their own value system. Empowered individuals believe in, and care about, what they produce. They invest psychic or spiritual energy in the activity and they feel a sense of personal significance from their involvement. They experience personal connectedness and personal integrity as a result of engaging in the activity (Bennis & Nanus 1985; Block 1987; Conger & Kanungo 1988). 'Meaningfulness', then, refers to a perception of value.

Activities infused with meaning create a sense of purpose, passion or mission for people. They provide a source of energy and enthusiasm, rather than draining energy and enthusiasm from people. Merely getting paid, helping an organisation earn money or just doing a job does not create a sense of meaning for most people. Something more fundamental, more personal and more value-laden must be linked to the activity. It must be associated with something more human.

Acquiring personal benefit does not guarantee meaning. For example, service to others may bring no personal reward, yet it may be far more meaningful than work that produces a hefty pay cheque. Involvement in activities without meaning, on the other hand, creates dissonance and annoyance, and produces a sense of disengagement from the work. People become bored or exhausted. Other incentives—such as rules, supervision or extra pay—are required to get people to invest in the work. Unfortunately, these extra incentives are costly to organisations and represent non-value-added expenses that constrain organisational efficiency and effectiveness. It costs companies a lot of money to require work that has little or no meaning to employees. Self-estrangement results from lack of meaning; vigour and stimulation result from meaningful work (Hackman & Oldham 1980; Kahn 1990; Thomas & Velthouse 1990).

Research has found that, when individuals engage in work they feel is meaningful, they are more committed to it and more involved in it. They have a higher concentration of energy and are more persistent in pursuing desired goals than when a sense of meaning is low. People feel more excitement and passion for their work and have a greater sense of personal significance and self-worth because of their association with activity that is meaningful. Individuals empowered with a sense of meaning have also been found to be more innovative, upwardly influential and personally effective than those whose sense of meaning is low (Bramucci 1977; Deci & Ryan 1987; Kanter 1968; Nielson 1986; Spreitzer 1992; Vogt & Murrell 1990).

Trust

Finally, empowered people have a sense of trust. Covey (1999) suggests that you cannot successfully compete globally without trust. Trust gives you the ability to make meaningful partnerships inside and outside an organisation. Empowered people are confident that they will be treated fairly and equitably. They have an assurance that, when they are in employee situations, they will not be taken advantage of by those in positions of authority or power. They believe that principles of justice will guide the behaviour of those who control valuable resources (for example, money, information, time). Even though trust implies being in a position of vulnerability (Zand 1972), empowered individuals have faith that no harm will come to them (Barber 1983; Deutsch 1973; Luhmann 1979; Mishra 1992). When they are at the mercy of someone else's decisions, empowered individuals believe that they will not deliberately be injured. 'Trust', then, refers to a sense of security.

Research on trust has found that trusting individuals are more apt to replace superficiality and facades with directness and intimacy; they are more apt to be open, honest and congruent, rather than deceptive or shallow. They are more search-oriented and self-determining, more self-assured and willing to learn. They have a larger capacity for interdependent relationships and they display a greater degree of cooperation and risk-taking in groups than do those with low trust. Trusting people are more willing to try to get along with others and to be a contributing part of a team. They are also more self-disclosing, more honest in their own communication and more able to listen carefully to others. They have less resistance to change and are better able to cope with unexpected traumas than those with low levels of trust. Individuals who trust others are more likely to be trustworthy themselves and to maintain high personal ethical standards (Gibb & Gibb 1969).

Because 'trusting environments allow individuals to unfold and flourish' (Golembiewski & McConkie 1975: 134), empowerment is closely tied to a sense of trust. Having a feeling that the behaviour of others is consistent and reliable, that information can be held in confidence and that promises will be kept are all a part of developing a sense of empowerment in people. Trusting others allows people to act in a confident and straightforward manner, without wasting energy on self-protection, trying to uncover hidden agendas or playing politics. In brief, a sense of trust empowers people to feel secure.

Review of empowerment dimensions

The main point of the discussion thus far is to show that fostering the five attributes of empowerment in individuals—self-efficacy (a sense of competence), self-determination (a sense of choice), personal control (a sense of impact), meaningfulness (a sense of value) and trust (a sense of security)—produces very positive outcomes. Research findings associated with each of the five dimensions of empowerment indicate that both personal and organisational advantages result when people feel empowered. Negative consequences occur, on the other hand, when people experience the opposite of empowerment, such as powerlessness, helplessness and alienation. Helping people feel a certain way about themselves and their work helps them to be more effective in the behaviours they display. Some authors have gone so far as to claim that helping others develop this feeling of empowerment is at the very root of managerial effectiveness. Without it, they claim, neither managers nor organisations can be successful in the long term (Bennis & Nanus 1985; Block 1987; Conger 1989; Kanter 1983).

As a psychological state, however, empowerment is never under the complete control of a manager. Individuals can refuse to feel empowered. Still, a sense of empowerment can be influenced significantly by the conditions in which people find themselves. For that reason, the next section of this chapter discusses specific actions managers can take to empower others.

LEARNING

How to develop empowerment

People are most in need of empowerment when they are faced with situations they perceive to be threatening, unclear, overly controlled, coercive or isolating; when they experience inappropriate feelings of dependency or inadequacy; when they feel stifled in their ability to do what they would like to do; when they are uncertain about how to behave; when they feel that some negative consequence is imminent; and when they feel unrewarded and unappreciated.

Ironically, most large organisations engender these kinds of feelings in people because, as we have known for many years (cf. Block 1987), bureaucracy encourages dependency and submission. Rules, routines and traditions define what can be done, stifling and supplanting initiative and discretion. In such circumstances, the formal organisation—not the individual—is the recipient of empowerment. Therefore, in large organisations, empowerment is especially needed. Empowerment is also vital in environments outside corporate bureaucracies. For example, studies demonstrate the positive effects of empowerment on education, child development, learning in school, coping with personal stress and changing personal habits (Burnett 2011; Ozer & Bandura 1990).

Despite the applicability of empowerment in many different contexts, the discussion here concentrates on ways in which managers can empower their employees. The focus is on empowerment mainly as a management skill, even though people in other roles, such as parents, teachers, coaches, tutors and friends, can also benefit by developing the skills of empowerment.

Research by Kanter (1983), Bandura (1986), Hackman and Oldham (1980) and others have produced at least nine specific prescriptions for fostering empowerment—that is, producing a sense of competence, choice, impact, value and security:

- articulating a clear vision and goals
- fostering personal mastery experiences
- modelling
- providing support
- creating emotional arousal
- providing necessary information
- providing necessary resources
- connecting to outcomes
- creating confidence.

Each of these prescriptions is discussed on the following pages. Figure 8.1 illustrates their relationships to the five core dimensions of empowerment. Some of these prescriptions are similar to the guidelines found in Chapters 5 and 6. The skills involved with communication, influence, motivation and empowerment are all related, but the context of empowerment sheds a different light on some of the guidelines you have read before.

Articulating a clear vision and goals

Creating an environment in which individuals can feel empowered requires that they be guided by a clearly articulated vision of where the organisation is going and how they can contribute as individuals. Most of us desire to know the purpose of the activities in which we engage, what the ultimate objective is and how we fit into that objective. One of the worst circumstances we can experience in our work life is an organisation with a total lack of direction or where no common objective or goal is evident. This is the classic condition—called *anomie*—that leads to anarchy, chaos and even death (Durkheim 1964). To avoid such anarchic conditions, a clear vision and an established set of goals must be articulated so that behaviour remains congruent with organisational purposes.

Many authors and studies confirm that the most effective way to articulate a vision in a clear and energising way is by using word pictures, stories, metaphors and real-life examples (Berry 2004; Cameron & Quinn 1999; Hallman 2011; Hattersley 1997; McKee 2003; Martin et al. 1983; Swap et al. 2001; Wiles 2003). That is, individuals are more likely to understand a vision if it has right-brain

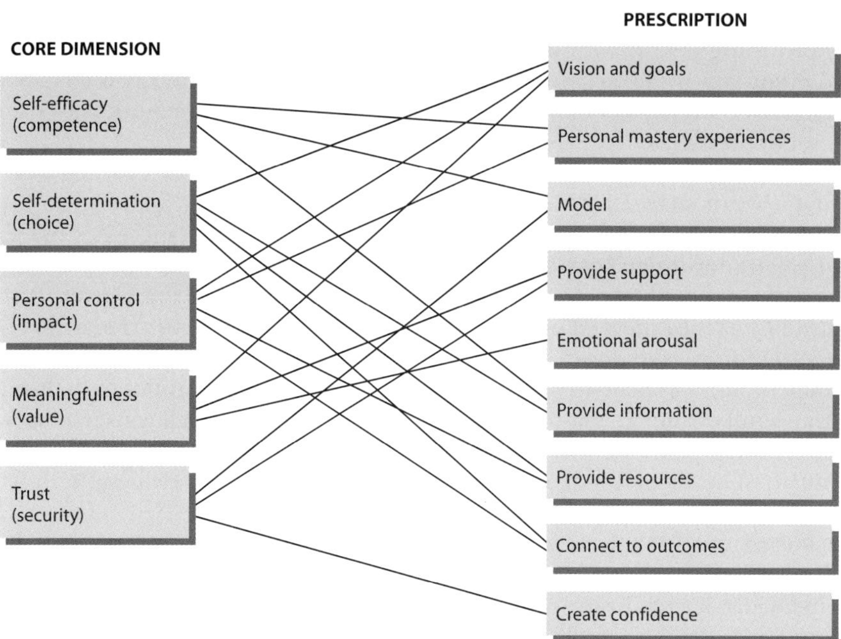

FIGURE 8.1 Relationship between satisfaction and performance

(intuitive, pictorial, story-based) as well as left-brain (logical, reasonable, performance-based) elements associated with it. Not only do people understand communication more clearly when it contains stories and examples as well as descriptions, but they develop more of a sense of self-determination ('I can see the alternatives available'), a sense of personal consequence ('I can see how I can influence the outcomes') and a sense of meaning ('I can see why this is so important').

Empowerment is also enhanced as specific behavioural goals are identified that help to guide individuals' behaviour as they work on their tasks. Goals specify desired outcomes as well as accountability. Locke and Latham (1990) identified the attributes of the most effective goals, and the acronym 'SMART goals' best summarises these attributes:

- *Specific goals*—those that are identifiable, behavioural and observable.
- *Measurable goals*—those that have outcome criteria associated with them, that can be assessed objectively, and for which the degree of successful accomplishment can be determined. The accomplishment of measurable goals can be evaluated.
- *Aligned goals*—those that are congruent with the overall purposes and vision of the organisation. Their accomplishment contributes to the broader good.
- *Reachable goals*—realistic goals, those that are not so far above the capacity of the individual that they become discouraging at best and considered nonsense at worst. 'Reachable' does not mean easily achieved, because research is clear that difficult goals—'stretch goals'—are better motivators of behaviour and predict higher levels of accomplishment than easy goals (Locke & Latham 1990).
- *Time-bound goals*—that is, a time for accomplishing the goals is specified. Goals that have no ending point are not effective; a clear deadline for achievement is needed.

Individuals are empowered because they are provided with a clear vision of the future, and some specific, behavioural goals that help to clarify how they can get there.

Fostering personal mastery experiences

Bandura (1986) found that the single most important thing a manager can do to empower other people is to help them experience personal mastery over some challenge or problem. By successfully accomplishing a task or resolving a problem, people develop a sense of mastery. Personal mastery can be fostered by providing people with the opportunity to accomplish successively more difficult tasks, which will lead eventually to the accomplishment of desirable goals. The key is to start with easy tasks and then progress by small steps to more difficult tasks until the person experiences a sense of mastery over an entire set of problems.

Managers can help employees to feel increasingly empowered by helping them develop an awareness that they can succeed. One way to do this is by breaking apart large tasks and giving employees only one part at a time. The manager watches for small successes achieved and then highlights and celebrates them. Jobs can be expanded incrementally so that tasks become broader and more complex as people master the basic elements. Employees are given further problem-solving responsibility as they succeed in resolving rudimentary difficulties. Managers can also provide opportunities for employees to direct or lead others in a project, task force or committee.

When managers adopt a small-wins strategy, individuals get opportunities to succeed in small ways, even though an overall challenge may be formidable (Weick 1979). Small wins may seem insignificant by themselves, but they generate a sense of movement, progress and success (Amabile & Kramer 2011; Wilson 2010). The recognition and celebration of small wins leads people to feel empowered and capable.

Lee Iacocca used this strategy to turn around a failing Chrysler Corporation in the early 1980s. An analysis of his speeches to the top management team at Chrysler over a period of five years reveals that, even though Chrysler was losing money, its costs were too high and quality was a major problem, Iacocca continued to celebrate small successes. For example, he regularly announced that a certain amount of money was saved, a particular improvement was produced, a certain executive was hired away from the competition or a compliment was received from a Wall Street analyst, even though the firm was losing a billion dollars a year. A great deal of emphasis was placed on succeeding at small things, all of which were aimed at eventually toppling the much larger challenge of company survival. In this case, continual small wins (minor personal mastery experiences) led to a big achievement.

Modelling

A third way to empower people is to model or demonstrate the correct behaviour they are to perform. Observing someone else succeed at challenging activities, Bandura (1977) found, provides a forceful impetus for others to believe that they, too, can succeed. It helps people realise that a task is do-able, that a job is within their capabilities and that success is possible (cf. Duyilemi 2008).

The manager may serve as the role model by demonstrating desired behaviours, although it may not be possible for a manager to model desired behaviours personally for every single employee. The manager may not see an employee often enough to show him or her how to accomplish work or to demonstrate success. Alternatively, however, managers may be able to draw their employees' attention to other people who have been successful in similar circumstances. They might make it possible for employees to associate with senior or visible people who could serve as role models, and they could provide opportunities for employees to be coached by these successful people. They can partner employees with mentors who can discuss their own past experiences that were similar to the employee's.

In other words, empowering people involves making available examples of past success. This is consistent with the learning model on which this book is based. The skill analysis step of the learning model exemplifies appropriate and inappropriate behaviour engaged in by others. It provides a model of people who have succeeded in accomplishing the desired skill. This modelling function helps to foster a sense of empowerment in individuals who are trying to develop and improve their management skills by showing ways in which such skills can be showcased successfully.

Think of what happens when a barrier is broken. In track and field athletics, for example, once John Thomas broke the seven-foot high-jump mark and Roger Bannister broke the four-minute mile record, a host of other athletes quickly exceeded that standard. But before the first person broke those barriers, they were considered insurmountable. It took someone to demonstrate that the standard could be exceeded in order for others to experience the empowerment necessary to replicate the accomplishment themselves.

Providing support

A fourth technique for helping others experience empowerment is providing them with social and emotional support. If people are to feel empowered, managers should praise them, encourage them, express approval of them, back them and reassure them. Kanter (1983) and Bandura (1986) both found that a crucial part of empowerment is having responsive and supportive managers. Managers seeking to empower their employees should find ways to praise their performance regularly. They can write letters or notes to employees, to members of their unit, or even to their family, indicating that the employee's good work has been noticed. They can provide feedback to employees about their abilities and competencies. They can arrange for opportunities where employees can receive social support from others by becoming part of a team or social unit. They can express confidence in employees by supervising them less closely or by allowing longer time intervals to elapse before requiring them to report results. Managers can hold regular ceremonies where employees' achievements are recognised. It may simply be a matter of listening to employees and trying to understand their feelings and points of view. Simply matching the non-verbal aspect of employee behaviour is further subtle, strong support (see Chapter 2).

Managers can empower others, then, by engendering a feeling that they are accepted, that they are a valued asset, and that they are an integral part of the overall organisational mission or objective. This support can come from either the manager or co-workers.

Cameron, Freeman and Mishra (1991), for example, described a variety of support activities undertaken by a highly effective manager who was forced to retrench employees due to a corporate downsizing mandate. Understandably, the retrenchments undermined employee trust, increased scepticism and escalated a sense of powerlessness. Because the announcement came down from the parent company, employees felt that they had lost the ability to control their own destinies. In short, they felt disempowered.

Following the lay-offs, the manager held personal meetings with each remaining employee to reaffirm his or her value to the organisation. People were told in a straightforward manner that they were considered to be valuable human resources, not human liabilities, to the company. A special 'Build with Pride' week was held in which outsiders—the press, government officials, family members, school classes—were invited to tour the facility and provide feedback (which, by the way, consistently took the form of praise) to the employees for the products and services they were producing. An impromptu barbecue was held one lunch hour to recognise and celebrate the extra-mile efforts of one group of employees in the facility. People were assured that counselling, training and assistance would be provided when job assignments changed or positions were merged as a result of the downsizing.

In general, this notable manager attempted to re-empower his workforce by providing social and emotional support in a variety of ways. He helped to provide the assistance people needed to cope with the uncertainty resulting from this uncontrollable event. Predictably, both organisational and individual performance results did not deteriorate after downsizing. Instead, contrary to what happens in most organisations that downsize, performance actually improved.

Creating emotional arousal

Emotional arousal means replacing negative emotions such as fear, anxiety or crabbiness with positive emotions such as excitement, passion or anticipation. To empower people, managers can make the work environment fun and attractive (see Firth 1995 and von Oech 1990 for suggestions). They ensure that the purpose behind the work is clear. They ensure that people's right brain (the side that controls emotions and passions) is involved in the work, as well as their left brain (the side that controls logic and analysis). Bandura (1977) found that the absence of positive emotional arousal makes it difficult, if not impossible, for individuals to feel empowered.

Managers need to clearly identify their organisation's vision and mission. Empowerment without vision leads to chaos. Managers must have a clear picture of what employees are empowered to do and where they are going. This vision and mission must be linked, not only to a desirable future but also to personal values. Employees must see how what they are doing every day is associated with their basic beliefs. Employees can get more excited, for example, about working for the betterment of humankind, for the improvement of the quality of people's lives, and for personal growth and development than they can for a 10 per cent return to institutional investors. This is not to say that revenue for shareholders is unimportant. Emotional arousal is, however, associated more with personal values than with organisational profitability.

The following is an example of a poor mission statement, taken from the 1994 annual report of a local company: 'To contribute to the progress of society with superior quality products and excellent service for each of our constituents—consumers, dealers, employees, shareholders and the community.' A lovely sentiment, indeed. But what does it mean? Is this company selling cars or condoms, or is it a new casino? We cannot tell from this statement. It does not help employees to make day-to-day decisions, or excite anyone who works in the firm.

A better example comes from the 1994 annual report of another local firm (involved with nutritional supplements) that has chosen to provide a series of philosophical statements that are then turned into grounded actions. For example, the firm states that it:

- guarantees cruelty free—'No animal has suffered in the creation of this quality product'
- has a quality commitment—the company ensures 'complete labelling of its products'
- informs consumers—the company 'has an ongoing commitment to provide responsible, authoritative information to enable the general public to make informed decisions about their health'.

These types of statements let all 'constituents' know what they can expect from the company in a specific, actionable manner. An employee of this firm would probably know how to respond to a customer request for product information. A manager would be likely to know the types of products in which to invest. This second mission clearly allows people to see how what they are doing every day is associated with their basic beliefs and values.

Managers can also increase employees' sense of empowerment by holding periodic social gatherings to foster friendships among co-workers. In their official communications, they can occasionally include a joke or light-hearted message to relieve tension. They can use superlatives in providing feedback or describing successes (for example, say 'terrific' once in a while instead of 'good'). They can make sure that employees are clear about how their work will affect the company's customers. Managers can schedule regular events where employees can hear compelling motivational messages. They can help to identify external threats or challenges that need to be met.

In the late 1980s, Avis Australia began an employee participation program. The company used a series of groups and spent massive amounts of money (that is, 10 per cent of the payroll) on training (Roberts 1996a). Sydney airport staff developed a switch that turned off an automatic car wash once the car has passed through and saved $4000 worth of water per year. Avis depots made an exhaustive 48-point check of all vehicles, with random quality checks made nationally. They deducted any faults from a possible 100 points. A smeared windscreen resulted in the loss of five points, a deflated tyre lost two. Avis originally set a score of 95 as the passing rate. Later, with staff consistently reaching that goal, the pass rate was increased to 98. Adelaide staff persuaded local car dealers to conduct their own 48-point check. This meant that Adelaide Avis staff did not have to do it and could rent out a new car within 30 minutes of taking delivery of it. Staff were fully empowered to make decisions in their area of work. Reservations staff could offer rebates, upgrades and even free rentals to dissatisfied customers. Information about financial results and the company's market position were shared with all staff, who earned bonuses if the company met and exceeded its profit plan. Since 1991, $2 million has been paid into the staff employee performance participation program.

Why does what Avis has done produce such energy, commitment and a sense of empowerment? This is related to what happens when people play sport. First off, there is a clear goal (for example, winning, exceeding a personal best) and the goal is pitted against a standard that people care about (for example, winning the Grand Final, a century at Lord's). In recreation, the score-keeping and feedback systems are objective, self-administered and continuous. In a basketball game, for example, everyone knows that a free throw always counts for one point, that the winner is the team that makes the most baskets, and that there is never a time when everyone cannot find out the exact score of the game. In the Avis example, goals and standards were clearly defined, information was collected and shared, and measures were objective.

It can be seen, therefore, that managers can help to empower people through emotional arousal, not just by being a cheerleader, delivering charismatic speeches and keeping the work climate fun, but also by capitalising on some of the principles of recreation that create excitement: clear goals, objective, self-administered and continuous score keeping, and feedback.

Providing necessary information

Kanter (1983) identified information as one of the most crucial managerial 'power tools'. Australians are increasingly using information as a source of power and a means of reducing their anxiety (Mackay 1993). Information, particularly information that is viewed as central or strategic in an organisation, can be used to build a power base and to make oneself indispensable and influential in that organisation. In contrast, when managers provide their people with more rather than less information, those employees gain a sense of empowerment and are more likely to work productively, successfully and in harmony with the manager's wishes. The manager actually enhances his or her power base by involving others in the pursuit of desirable outcomes. With more information, people tend to experience more self-determination, personal control and trust. The resulting sense of empowerment enhances the probability that they will not resist the manager's wishes or work at protecting themselves. Rather, they are likely to collaborate with the empowering manager.

Empowering managers keep employees informed about what is happening in other areas of the organisation that might affect what they are doing. Managers will keep employees informed of policy-making meetings and senior-level discussions related to their area of responsibility. Employees can be given access to sources closest to the information they need, such as senior-level people in the organisation, customers or the market research staff. Historical or 'context' information can be shared, to give employees as broad a background as possible. Managers should make certain that employees have information about the effects of their own behaviour on others and on the organisation's goals.

Therefore, a manager who wishes to increase employees' sense of empowerment will make sure that they are given all the task-relevant information needed to carry out an assignment. The empowering manager will make available, on an ongoing basis, pertinent technical information and data collected by others.

To be sure, it is possible to overload people with information and create anxiety and burnout with too much data. But experience has shown that most people suffer from too little information, rather than too much. Furthermore, if the operative term 'relevant information' is applied in this context, overload is less likely to occur. Spreitzer (1992) found, for example, that people who received relevant information about costs, customers and strategy felt significantly more empowered than those who did not. Block (1987: 90) argued:

> *Sharing as much information as possible is the opposite of the military notion that only those who 'need to know' should be informed. Our goal is to let people know our plans, ideas and changes as soon as possible. … If we are trying to create the mind-set that everyone is responsible for the success of this business, then our people need complete information.*

Research by Cameron, Freeman and Mishra (1993) further confirms the importance of providing information to enhance empowerment. In one study, for example, they interviewed CEOs of large, well-known companies every six months to assess the organisational changes and strategies the CEOs were using to cope with declining revenues. In one firm, not much progress was being made in improving the financial outlook. The CEO was very careful to share information on financial, productivity, cost and climate indicators in the company only with his senior management team. No one else in the firm had access to that information. A change of CEO, however, led to a dramatic change in information-sharing policy. The new CEO began to provide information to every single employee in the firm who desired it. No data were treated as the sole possession of senior management. The cleaners had the same access as the senior management team. The resulting empowerment that employees experienced led to dramatic results. Employee-initiated improvements increased markedly, morale and commitment surged, and the resulting financial turnaround made the CEO look like a genius. He attributed his success to his willingness to empower employees by sharing the information they needed to know to improve.

Providing necessary resources

In addition to providing information, empowerment is also fostered by providing people with other kinds of resources that help them accomplish their tasks. Empowering managers are less directors and commanders than they are resource providers and obstacle eliminators. One of the primary missions of empowering managers, then, is to help others to accomplish their objectives.

Managers attempting to enhance employees' empowerment by providing them with needed resources will ensure that the employees receive adequate and ongoing training and development experiences. Sufficient technical and administrative support will be provided to ensure success. Managers will give employees space, time or equipment that may not be readily available otherwise. They will ensure that employees have access to communication and/or interpersonal networks that will make their jobs easier. Employees can also be given discretion to spend monies or commit resources to activities that they consider important.

It is unrealistic, of course, to assume that everyone can have everything they desire. Very few successful organisations have excess resources to be distributed at will. The most important resources that empowering managers can provide are those that help people to achieve control over their own work and lives: that is, to foster a sense of self-efficacy and self-determination. When individuals feel that they have what they need to be successful and the freedom to pursue what they want to accomplish, performance is significantly higher than when these types of resources are not available (Spreitzer 1992).

Southcorp Wines' huge Karadoc winery in northwestern Victoria spent 6–7 per cent of its payroll on training to prepare its 250 staff for greater involvement and responsibility (Roberts 1996b). They increasingly devolved responsibility for day-to-day decision making to the people with the knowledge and responsibility for putting decisions into action. Bob Baxter, Karadoc's chief executive, set the parameters for the winery's capital-spending budget in line with overall strategy and allowed departmental heads to negotiate the split-up of the investment dollars among themselves. One of the biggest benefits, according to Roberts' article, was the freeing of managers from routine decision making. This allowed time to develop the site's first strategic plan. Departmental and team plans 'cascaded' down from that overall strategic plan, ensuring that all levels measured their performance against agreed-upon goals. Former management responsibilities that have been devolved relate to issues such as safety, quality, process improvement, rostering and training. Their focus, therefore, changed from controlling people to controlling business systems. Improvements were seen in a 7 per cent productivity increase, inventory reductions of over 50 per cent and improved safety performance (a drop from 1500 hours of lost time per year to less than 80 hours).

When people are given discretion and control over their work lives, when they have what they need to be successful in terms of information, goals and administration, performance is significantly higher than when these resources are not available. In summary: resources lead to empowerment.

Connecting to outcomes

One of the important lessons learned by US manufacturing companies as a result of the Japanese invasion of the North American automobile and consumer electronics industries in the late 1970s and 1980s is that workers experience more empowerment when they can see the outcomes of their work. It was often a surprise to US companies, for example, that their Japanese counterparts regularly visited customers in their homes or places of business, regularly observed how the products that the workers produced were used, and regularly received feedback directly from end-users. This connection with the ultimate customer helped workers to feel more empowered as well as providing a valuable source of improvement ideas. The importance of connecting workers with customers was confirmed by Hackman and Oldham's (1980) now classic research on job design and job enrichment. These investigators found that people are motivated at work when they can interact with their ultimate customers and see the effects of their work.

A related idea is to provide employees with the authority to resolve problems on the spot. Studies at IBM, Ford Motor Company, motor vehicle dealerships and other companies indicated that allowing employees to address customer concerns at the time the complaint was registered affected both employees and customers positively. When employees were given discretion to resolve a problem, respond immediately to a customer's complaint, fix the error instantly, or commit a certain level of company resources in pursuing customer satisfaction, not only was customer satisfaction dramatically increased (an average improvement of 300 per cent) but workers felt far more empowered as well. Employees were given the necessary authority to go along with their responsibility for customer satisfaction, and they were provided with an opportunity to affect outcomes directly.

Hackman and Oldham (1980) suggested that another highly effective way to enhance employee motivation and satisfaction is to create task identity—that is, the opportunity to accomplish a whole task. Individuals become frustrated and lack a sense of empowerment when they work on only part of a task, never see the end result of their work, and are blocked from observing the impact that their job creates. A worker who had a very lucrative job in a prestigious Wall Street firm quit because he became frustrated with his inability to see the results of his work. He was regularly asked to accomplish the first few steps in a complicated job and then to hand the work over to a senior executive who completed the work and received most of the recognition. Not only was this man denied deserved rewards, but, more important to him, he was unable to feel he had completed a whole job. Task identity and the resulting sense of empowerment were completely lacking.

Having task identity implies that individuals can plan, implement and evaluate the success of their efforts. The effects of what is accomplished can be assessed as well as the outcome. To feel empowered, in other words, people want to know whether they successfully completed their assigned job, as well as whether that job made any difference to the overall success of their work unit. The clearer that connection is, the more they will feel empowered.

In sum, clarifying the connections between individuals' work and the outcomes and effects fosters empowerment by helping individuals to develop a sense of self-efficacy (they feel more capable and competent) and of personal consequence (a sense of having personal impact).

Creating confidence

The final technique for engendering empowerment is to create a sense of confidence among employees in the trustworthiness of the manager. Rather than being on guard and suspicious, employees are secure in their feeling that the manager and the organisation are honourable. This confidence helps to drive out uncertainty, insecurity and ambiguity in the relationships between employees and the manager.

There are at least two reasons why individuals feel more empowered as they develop greater confidence in their manager. First, the wasteful, unproductive behaviours associated with mistrust and suspicion are avoided. When people distrust one another, they do not listen, communicate clearly, try hard or collaborate. In contrast, when trust exists, individuals are free to experiment, to learn and to contribute without fear of retribution. Second, individuals who are admirable and honourable always create positive energy for others and make them feel more capable. It is not without reason that universities trumpet the number of Nobel Prize winners in their faculties, the number of outstanding faculty members in their business schools and the notable achievements of their best students. Although other members of the university may have nothing to do with the achievements being publicised, they gain an enhanced self-image and a sense of empowerment because they are affiliated with the same organisation. For these reasons, creating confidence in a manager helps employees to develop a sense of empowerment.

In creating such a sense of confidence and trustworthiness, five factors are especially important: reliability, fairness, caring, openness and competence. Managers create confidence and thereby engender empowerment in others as they display these five characteristics, which are associated with being honourable.

1. *Reliability*. Managers who wish their employees to develop confidence in them need to exhibit reliability. The managers' behaviour must be consistent, dependable and stable. Their actions are congruent with their words and attitudes.
2. *Fairness*. Good managers also need to be fair and must not take wrongful advantage of anyone. They are equitable in their actions. Employees are clear about the criteria used by the manager in making judgments, as well as about how the manager applies those criteria. Managers must make clear the standards by which employees will be judged and ensure that those standards are applied in an unbiased way.
3. *Caring*. Managers must show a sense of personal concern for employees and help each one to feel important to the manager. Managers validate the points of view of their employees and avoid denigrating them as individuals. When correction is needed, caring managers focus on the mistake or the behaviour, not on the individual's personal characteristics.
4. *Openness*. Confidence-building managers are open in their relationships. No harmful secrets exist, and relevant information is shared openly and honestly with employees. This does not suggest that a manager cannot keep confidences. It does mean that employees do not have to worry about hidden agendas that could negatively affect them, because their manager is straightforward and honest.
5. *Competence*. Employees should be made aware of their manager's competence. They need to be assured that their manager has the necessary ability, experience, and knowledge to perform tasks and solve problems. Without flaunting their expertise, skilful managers inspire employees to feel that their confidence in the expertise and proficiency of their leader is not misplaced.

The power of creating confidence in employees is illustrated by several CEOs who were interviewed about the key to successful organisational change. Each CEO had managed a downsizing or redesign of the organisation, and was attempting to maintain a healthy, productive workforce in the midst of turmoil. The key role of trust and confidence in management is hard to miss (see Cameron, Freeman & Mishra 1993; Mishra 1992).

> *If they don't believe what I'm telling them, if they think it's all a bunch of bull, don't expect them to go out there and work a little harder. They won't work a little different. They're not going to be receptive to change unless they understand and trust the things that we're talking about are true. I think trust is the biggest single issue …*
>
> *I had a boss one time who said, 'What you do speaks so much louder than what you say.' I've always stuck that in the back of my mind. I believe that. The people watch very closely what you do. And boy, you cannot underestimate that.*
>
> *What's most important in my organisation is this: being truthful. Don't 'BS' anyone. Tell them what it is. Right or wrong or different. Tell them the truth.*
>
> *My people are all 150 per cent dedicated to helping one another. Because no one of them can do it alone, they need each other badly. But here comes the openness and trust. You have to talk about those things. I don't think you can go in and accomplish things without talking about what the barriers are going to be in trying to make a change or set a new direction. …*

Successful managers create confidence in themselves among their employees. They are authentic, honourable and trustworthy.

Review of empowerment principles

Box 8.1 summarises the actions discussed in relation to the prescriptions for empowerment, providing a list of things managers can do to empower their employees. Not all these suggestions are relevant in every circumstance or with every person, of course, but developing the skill of empowerment depends partly on knowing what alternatives are available to empower people as well as knowing how to implement them. This list is not comprehensive; other activities may be equally effective in empowering people. But these prescriptions represent actions that you will want to practise as you try to improve your competence in the skill of empowerment. The skill practice section of this chapter provides an opportunity for you to do this.

BOX 8.1 Practical suggestions for empowering others

Articulate a clear vision and goals
- ❑ Create a picture of a desired future.
- ❑ Use word pictures and emotional language to describe the vision.
- ❑ Identify specific actions and strategies that will lead to the vision.
- ❑ Establish SMART goals.
- ❑ Associate the vision and goals with personal values.

Foster personal mastery experiences
- ❑ Break apart large tasks and assign one part at a time.
- ❑ Assign simple tasks before difficult tasks.
- ❑ Highlight and celebrate small wins.
- ❑ Incrementally expand job responsibilities.
- ❑ Give increasingly more responsibility to solve problems.

Model successful behaviours
- ❑ Demonstrate successful task accomplishment.
- ❑ Point out other people who have succeeded.
- ❑ Facilitate interaction with other role models.
- ❑ Find a coach.
- ❑ Establish a mentor relationship.

Provide support
- ❑ Praise, encourage, express approval for and reassure.
- ❑ Send letters or notes of praise to co-workers or family members.
- ❑ Regularly provide feedback.
- ❑ Foster informal social activities to build cohesion.
- ❑ Supervise less closely and provide down time.
- ❑ Hold recognition ceremonies.

Arouse positive emotions
- ❑ Foster activities to encourage friendship formation.
- ❑ Periodically send light-hearted messages.
- ❑ Use superlatives in giving feedback.
- ❑ Highlight compatibility between important personal values and organisational goals.
- ❑ Clarify the impact on the ultimate customer.
- ❑ Foster attributes of recreation in work: clear goals, effective score-keeping and feedback systems, and out-of-bounds behaviour.

Provide information
- ❑ Provide all task-relevant information.
- ❑ Continuously provide technical information and objective data.
- ❑ Pass along relevant cross-unit and cross-functional information.
- ❑ Provide access to information or people with senior responsibility.
- ❑ Provide access to information from its source.
- ❑ Clarify effects of actions on customers.

Provide resources
- ❑ Provide training and development experiences.
- ❑ Provide technical and administrative support.
- ❑ Provide needed time, space or equipment.
- ❑ Ensure access to relevant information networks.
- ❑ Provide more discretion to commit resources.

Organise teams
- ❑ Assign the team an important task or problem.
- ❑ Let the team solve the problem and implement the solution.
- ❑ Assign team facilitators, not team leaders.
- ❑ Foster information sharing and learning.
- ❑ Provide rewards for effective team membership.
- ❑ Help team members teach one another.

Create confidence
- ❑ Exhibit reliability and consistency.
- ❑ Exhibit fairness and equity.
- ❑ Exhibit caring and personal concern.
- ❑ Exhibit openness and honesty.
- ❑ Exhibit competence and expertise.

Research suggests that empowered individuals are most inclined to empower others. Knowing what provides a sense of empowerment for you can be helpful as you consider ways in which you, in turn, can empower others. The instrument that you completed in the skill assessment section ('Effective empowerment and delegation') identifies the extent to which you behave in ways that empower the people with whom you work and the extent to which you delegate work effectively. How much you actually engage in the behaviours discussed is assessed, as well as the extent to which you are an effective delegator. We now turn to the topic of delegation.

Delegating work

Consider the following familiar story of an entrepreneur reaching crisis point:

> *I was working from 5 am and getting home after my children had gone to bed, but I still had to examine every letter that left the office and change something, even if the letter was perfect. I was becoming a control freak. My management training company for senior executives had grown rapidly, passing the one million turnover mark within three years. My diary was crammed, my desk overflowing, and there were never enough hours in the day to complete the many projects I started. I only realised there was a problem when my employees criticised communication within the company in a staff survey. I knew we wouldn't grow further unless I relaxed my grip. I had to learn to delegate and empower the people around me. (Adapted from Gracie 1999.)*

According to Thomson (2003: 116):

> *Australian entrepreneurs leading fast-growing firms must learn how to delegate. This is especially true as the business matures, when the entrepreneur needs to guide it into new markets. Tas Zorbas, the MD of Kresta, says he wanted to do everything during the early stages of his business. Zorbas says he was freed to focus on expansion after finding a trusted 'right-hand man'.*

Mapletoft (2003: 20) concurs:

> *It takes a commitment from the owner to handle the growing pains of change, to give up some control and to delegate. The act of remanaging one's schedule begins with identifying one item daily that can be delegated to others and following through on it.*

Obviously, if a person is doing a task alone, knowing how to empower others is largely irrelevant. In the vast majority of work situations, however, it is impossible for one person to perform all the work needed to carry out an organisation's mission, so the work and the responsibility to carry it out must be shared with others. All managers need to delegate work and empower their employees if they are to accomplish the tasks of the organisation and succeed (cf. Klein et al. 2006). Delegation involves the assignment of work to other people and it is an activity inherently associated with all managerial and leadership positions. Without delegation and the empowerment that must accompany it, no organisation and no manager can enjoy long-term success.

In a *Harvard Business Review* interview, Carl Holmes, a firefighter in the United States for almost 30 years and a fire chief for eight, related how he found a battalion chief down on the ground 'slinging water' when the far side of the building was collapsing (Maruca 1999). This lack of oversight can cost lives and money. Battalion chiefs are now required to remain in their command vehicles, which are outfitted with the most sophisticated information and communications equipment available. From this vantage point, they are responsible for the big picture, while firefighters on the ground are empowered and responsible for local operational decisions at the point of action.

This section discusses the nature of delegation as well as ways in which delegation can be most effectively empowered. 'Delegation' normally refers to the assignment of a task. It is work-focused. Empowerment, on the other hand, focuses on people, and on the way people think and feel about themselves. The earlier discussion focused on ways in which managers can affect people's sense of being empowered. We now look at ways in which managers can get work accomplished effectively through empowered delegation.

Although delegation is commonly practised by managers, it is by no means always performed competently. In fact, it has been recognised for years that the 'lack of courage to delegate properly, and of knowledge of how to do it, is one of the most general causes of failures in organisations' (Urwick 1944: 51). (See Berman 2003 for a more recent example.) Management educators and researchers have paid little attention to delegation, and less is known about the relationships between delegation and management effectiveness than many other common management skills (Hackman & Dunphy 1990; Locke & Schweiger 1979).

Advantages of empowered delegation

Learning to become a competent delegator who can simultaneously empower others has several important advantages for managers. It obviously helps managers to accomplish more work than they could do otherwise and can be used as a time-management tool to free up discretionary time. On the other hand, if delegation occurs only when managers are overloaded, those receiving the delegated tasks may feel resentful and sense that they are being treated only as objects to meet the managers' ends. In such cases, they will experience a sense of disempowerment. However, skilful use of empowered delegation can provide significant benefits to organisations, managers and the individuals receiving the assigned tasks. Table 8.3 summarises these advantages.

Empowered delegation can help to develop employees' capabilities and knowledge so that their effectiveness is increased. It can be a technique to encourage personal mastery experiences. Delegation can also be used to demonstrate trust and confidence in the person receiving the assignment. Mishra (1992) summarised research showing that individuals who felt trusted by their managers were significantly more effective than those who did not feel that way. Empowered delegation can be used to enhance the commitment of individuals receiving work. Beginning with the classic study of participation by Coch and French (1948), research has consistently demonstrated a positive relationship between having an opportunity to participate in work and subsequent satisfaction, productivity, commitment, acceptance of change and desire for more work.

Empowered delegation can also be used to improve the quality of decision making by bringing to bear more information, closer to the source of the problem, than the manager has alone. Delegating tasks to those who have direct access to relevant information can enhance efficiency (that is, require less time and fewer resources) as well as effectiveness (that is, result in a better decision). Finally, empowered delegation can increase the coordination and integration of work by funnelling information and final accountability through a single source. Empowering managers, in other words, can ensure that no cross-purposes occur in delegation and that different tasks are not producing contradictory effects. Competently administered, empowered delegation can produce all five dimensions of empowerment: a sense of competence, choice, impact, value and security.

When delegation is ineffectively performed, however, negative consequences can result that not only inhibit empowerment but also subvert the ability to get work accomplished at all. For example, instead of freeing up time, ineffective delegation may require even more time to supervise, evaluate, correct and arbitrate disagreements among employees. Employees may find themselves spending a longer time to accomplish a task because of a lack of know-how, experience or information. Stress levels and interpersonal conflict may increase when tasks, accountability or expectations are unclear. Managers may find themselves out of touch with what is really going on with employees, and they may lose control and find that the goals being pursued are incompatible with the rest of the organisation. Chaos, rather than coordination, can result. Employees may also begin to expect that they

TABLE 8.3 Advantages of delegation

ADVANTAGE	EXPLANATION
Time	Increases the manager's discretionary time
Development	Develops delegates' knowledge and capabilities
Trust	Demonstrates trust and confidence in delegates
Commitment	Enhances commitment of delegates
Information	Improves decision making with better information
Efficiency	Enhances efficiency and timeliness of decisions
Coordination	Fosters work integration by manager coordination

should be involved in all decisions and that any decision the manager makes alone is autocratic and unfair.

This section identifies ways in which the positive outcomes of delegation can be cultivated and the potential negative outcomes of poor delegation avoided. Empowerment and delegation must be linked in the accomplishment of work. Guidelines are now presented for deciding when to delegate, to whom to delegate and, finally, how to delegate.

Deciding when to delegate

Empowered delegating involves deciding, first of all, when to delegate tasks to others and when to perform them yourself. When should employees be assigned to design and perform work or make decisions? To determine when delegation is most appropriate, managers should ask five basic questions (Vroom & Jago 1974; Vroom & Yetton 1973). Research indicates that when delegation occurs based on these questions, successful results are almost four times more likely than when these questions are not considered. The questions are equally applicable whether assigned work is to be delegated to a team or to a single employee.

1. *Do employees have the necessary (or superior) information or expertise?* In many cases, employees may actually be better qualified than their managers to make decisions and perform tasks because they are more familiar with customer preferences, hidden costs and work processes, due to being closer to day-to-day operations.
2. *Is the commitment of employees critical to successful implementation?* Participation in the decision-making process increases commitment to the final decision. When employees have some latitude in performing a task (that is, what work they do and how and when they do it), they must usually be involved in the decision-making process to ensure their cooperation. While participation will generally increase the time required to make a decision, it will substantially decrease the time required to implement it.
3. *Will employees' capabilities be expanded by this assignment?* Delegation quickly gets a bad name in a work team if it is viewed as a mechanism used by the boss to get rid of undesirable tasks. Therefore, delegation should be consistent, not just when overloads occur. It should reflect an overall management philosophy emphasising employee development. Enhancing the abilities and interests of employees should be a central motive in delegating tasks.
4. *Do employees share with management and each other common values and perspectives?* If employees do not share a similar point of view with one another and with their manager, unacceptable solutions, inappropriate means and outright errors may be perpetrated. This produces a need for closer supervision and frequent monitoring. Articulating a clear mission and objective for employees is crucial. In particular, managers must be clear about why the work is to be done. Coonradt (1985) found that important people are always told why, but less important people are merely told what, how or when. Telling employees why the work is meaningful creates a common perspective.
5. *Is there sufficient time to do an effective job of delegating?* It takes time to save time. To avoid misunderstandings, managers must spend sufficient time explaining the task and discussing acceptable procedures and options. Time must be available for adequate training, for questions and answers, and for opportunities to check on progress.

Empowered delegation depends on a positive answer to each of these questions. If any of these conditions is not present when delegation is being considered, the probability is greater that it will not be effective. More time will be required, lower quality will result, more frustration will be experienced and less empowerment will occur. However, a negative answer to any of the questions does not necessarily mean that effective delegation is forever precluded; managers can change situations so that employees get more information, develop common perspectives and have adequate time to receive delegation.

Deciding to whom to delegate

Having decided to delegate a task, managers must then consider whether to involve only a single individual or a team of employees. If the decision is made to form a team, it is important to decide how much authority to give the members of the team. For example, managers should determine whether the team will only investigate the problem and explore alternatives, or whether it will make the final decision. Managers must also outline whether or not they will participate in the team's deliberations.

Figure 8.2 presents a model to help managers decide who should receive delegated tasks—individuals or teams—and whether the manager should be an active participant in a team if it is formed. The figure is constructed as a 'tree diagram', allowing a manager to ask questions and, as a result of the answer to each question, move along a path until a final alternative is selected (Huber 1980; Vroom & Jago 1974). Here is how it works.

If you were a manager determining whether to involve others in accomplishing a task or making a decision, look over the considerations below the question: 'Should I involve others in the task or the decision?' If you decide that your employees do not possess the relevant information or skills, that their acceptance is not important, that no personal development can occur for members of the team, that time is tight or that conflicts will arise among the employees, you should answer 'no' to this question. The tree then prescribes that you perform the task or make the decision yourself. However, if you answer 'yes' to this question, you move on to the next question: 'Should I direct my employees to form a group?' Look over the five considerations below that question and then continue through the

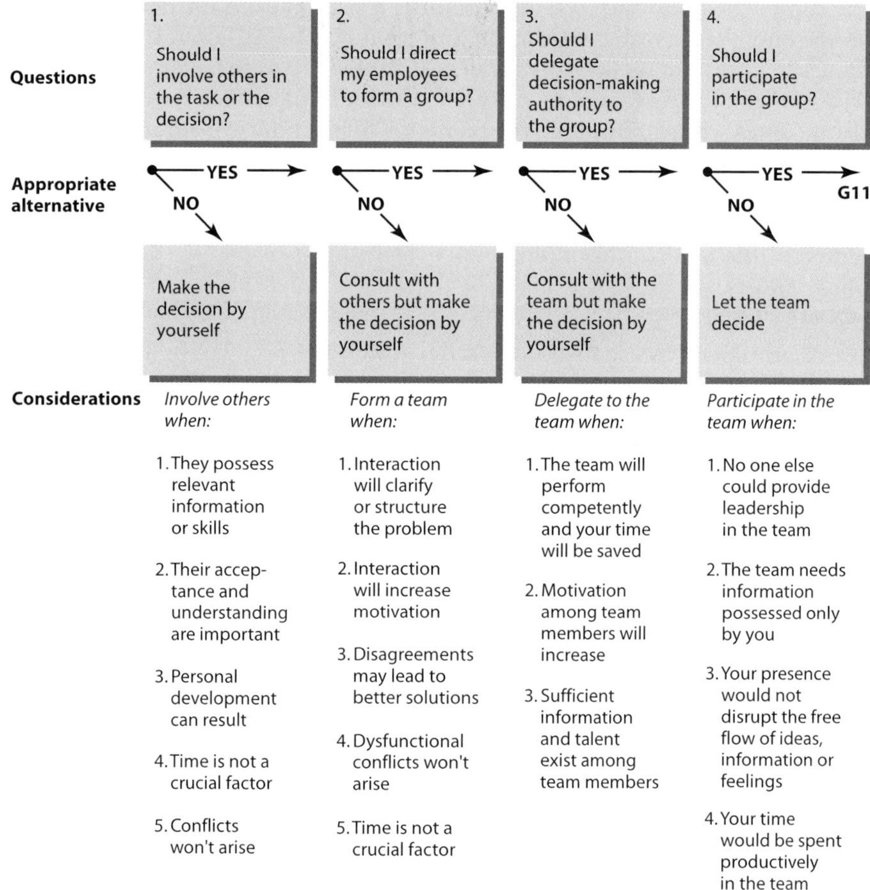

FIGURE 8.2 Relationship between satisfaction and performance

model. Any of the considerations below a question can result in a 'no' answer. The most participative and empowering alternative is to delegate work to a team and then participate as an equal member of the team. The least empowering response, of course, is to do the work yourself.

Deciding how to delegate effectively

Delegation may be seen as a cyclical, three-phase process during which a task is passed from the manager to an employee, the employee completes the task, and the employee then passes the completed task back to the manager (Hackman 1994; Hackman & Dunphy 1990). The three phases are as follows:

1. *Delegation of discretion*—where managers decide how much responsibility and authority they are willing to give to the employee.
2. *Supervision of the employee*—involving discussions about the task, monitoring of the employee while he or she is working on the task, and monitoring of the results achieved.
3. *Employee accountability to the manager*—where a decision is made regarding the degree to which the employee is answerable to the manager for his or her actions and the outcomes.

Positive outcomes of empowered delegation are contingent on managers following ten proven principles throughout the process. (See Anonymous 2003 for a longer list of similar principles.)

Begin with the end in mind

Managers must articulate clearly the results that are desired from the delegated task. Being clear about what is to be accomplished and why it is important is a prerequisite for empowered delegation. In fact, unless people know why a task is important and what is to be achieved by performing it, they are unlikely to act at all. No voluntary action ever persists unless these two elements are present. People do not stick with work, study, assignments or other activities unless they have an idea of the purpose and intended outcomes. At a minimum, recipients of delegation will infer or fabricate a purpose or desired outcome, or the task will not be performed at all. To ensure that the ends desired by the manager are perceived as desirable by others, the manager should point out the personal benefits to be achieved, the connection of task accomplishment to the organisation's mission, or the important values represented by the task (for example, service, learning, growth).

Delegate completely

Managers must clearly specify the constraints under which the task will be performed. Every organisation has rules and procedures, resource constraints or boundaries that limit the kind of action that can be taken. These should be clarified when the task is delegated. In particular, managers must be clear about deadlines and the time-frame for reporting back. When should the task be completed, who should receive the report and to whom is accountability being assigned? No empowerment can occur without employees knowing what these boundaries are.

Managers must also specify precisely the level of initiative expected. No other oversight in the delegation process causes more confusion than the failure to delineate expectations about the level of initiative expected or permitted. At least five levels of initiative are possible, each of which may vary in terms of the amount of empowerment available to employees. These initiative levels differ in the amount of control permitted over the timing and content of the delegated task. The five alternatives are:

1. *Wait to be told what to do.* Take action only after specific directions are given. This is the least empowering form of delegation because it permits no initiative on the part of the employee. There is no control over timing (that is, when the task is to be accomplished) or content (that is, what is to be done).
2. *Ask what to do.* Some discretion is provided to employees in that they have some control over the timing of the task, but not its content. Employees may formulate ideas for approaching the task, but because no action can be taken until the manager gives approval, empowerment is highly constrained.

3. *Recommend, then take action.* This alternative is more empowering because employees are given some freedom over both the timing and the content of the delegated task. However, at least three different types of recommendations are possible, each with a different level of empowerment. One is for employees simply to gather information, present it to the manager and let the manager decide what needs to be done. Another is for employees to determine alternative courses of action for each part of the task, leaving the manager to choose which course will be followed. Still another possibility is to outline a course of action for accomplishing the entire task and have the whole package approved at once. Progressively more empowerment is associated with each of these three recommendation types.
4. *Act, then report results immediately.* Employees are given the freedom to act on their own initiative, but they are required to report to the manager immediately on completion to ensure that their actions are correct and compatible with other organisational work. Employees may be permitted to perform only one part of a task at a time, reporting the results of each individual step. Or they may be given the discretion to perform the entire task, reporting only when the final result has been accomplished. The second alternative, of course, is the most empowering. But it may not be possible unless employees possess the necessary ability, information, experience or maturity.
5. *Initiate action and report only routinely.* Employees receive complete control over timing and over content of the tasks assigned. Reporting occurs only in a routine fashion to maintain coordination. With sufficient ability, information, experience and maturity among employees, this level of initiative is not only the most empowering but also the most likely to produce high satisfaction and motivation among employees (Hackman & Oldham 1980).

The important point for managers to remember is that they must be very clear about which of these levels of initiative they expect of their employees.

Allow participation in the delegation of assignments

Employees are more likely to accept delegated tasks willingly, perform them competently, and experience empowerment when they help to decide what tasks are to be delegated to them and when. Often, managers cannot give employees complete choice about such matters, but providing opportunities to decide when tasks will be completed, how accountability will be determined, when work will begin, or what methods and resources will be used in task accomplishment increases employees' empowerment. Such participation should not be manipulative; that is, opportunities for participation should not be provided merely to convince employees of decisions already made. Rather, managers should promote participation when task requirements allow it and when acceptance and personal development can result.

Bernard (1938) formulated an 'acceptance theory of authority' in which he proposed that people will accept and fulfil assignments only if four conditions are met. First, employees must understand what they are being asked to do. Second, employees must perceive that the assignment is consistent with the purpose of the organisation. Third, employees must believe that the assignment is compatible with their own interests. Fourth, employees must be able to perform the assignment.

Bernard's theory underscores the importance of two-way communication during the delegation process. Employees should not only be encouraged to ask questions and seek information about delegated assignments, but also should feel free to express ideas about the parameters of the work to be delegated. Expecting employees to seek answers to questions, or providing guidance on every aspect of the delegated assignment, can produce overdependence if the manager answers every detailed question or provides continual advice. On the other hand, managers who remain available for consultation and ideas interchange, foster two-way communication and encourage a climate of openness and sharing make the delegation process empowering.

Establish parity between authority and responsibility

The oldest and most general rule of thumb in delegation is to match the amount of responsibility given with the amount of authority provided. Commonly, managers assign responsibility for work to employees without furnishing a corresponding amount of discretion to make decisions and authority to implement those decisions. If employees are to be successful, they must have as much authority as they need to accomplish the tasks assigned to them. An important part of developing a sense of self-determination and a sense of personal control—both critical dimensions of empowerment—is ensuring this match. Of course, managers must also take care not to delegate more authority than responsibility, thereby giving employees more authority, discretion, resources or information than they can use. Such a mismatch leads to a lack of accountability, potential abuses of power, and confusion on the part of employees. For example, without the necessary responsibility, providing a child with a loaded gun or a $50 note in a sweet shop could result in actions that would lead to undesirable outcomes.

Although managers cannot delegate ultimate accountability for delegated tasks, they can delegate prime accountability. This means that 'the buck stops', eventually, at the manager's desk. Final blame for failure cannot be given away. This is ultimate accountability. But managers can delegate *prime accountability*, which means that employees can be given responsibility for producing desired short-term results. Their accountability is to the manager who delegated to them. Giving employees prime accountability is an important part of empowered delegation.

Work within the organisational structure

Another general rule of empowered delegation is to delegate to the lowest organisational level at which a job can be done. The people who are closest to the actual work being performed or the decision being made should be involved. They are usually the ones with the largest, most accurate fund of information. By definition, this increases efficiency (lower labour and information collection costs) and it frequently increases effectiveness (better understanding of problems). Whereas managers have a broader overall view of problems, the detailed knowledge needed to accomplish many tasks is most likely to reside with those who are lower in the organisational hierarchy.

In delegating a task down more than one level in an organisation, it is important that the organisational chain of command be followed. In other words, delegation must occur through employees, not around them. If a senior manager circumvents the formal hierarchy, bypassing a manager to communicate directly with that manager's employee, the manager becomes disempowered. The employee now becomes accountable to the senior manager, not the manager with direct responsibility for the employee. The entire accountability system is thus destroyed. Following the chain of command by involving those at affected levels of the hierarchy in delegation is important for empowered delegation.

All individuals affected by a decision must be informed that it has been delegated. This applies to cross-functional coordination as well as hierarchical coordination. If an employee has been delegated responsibility, others who may have needed information, who may influence the results or who may implement the recommendations must be notified of the delegation. If delegation occurs but no one knows about it, authority is essentially nullified.

Provide adequate support for delegated tasks

When authority is delegated to employees, managers must provide as much support to them as possible. As discussed earlier, this involves making public announcements and presenting clearly stated expectations. It also means continuously providing relevant information and resources to help employees accomplish tasks. Reports, recent news clippings, customer data, articles, and even random thoughts that pertain to the delegated task should be passed on as they become available. This support not only aids task accomplishment but also communicates interest and concern for employees. Managers should help employees learn where to acquire needed resources, since the manager alone cannot be the sole source of all the support that employees will need.

Agreeing on the limits of resource use is also important. Since unlimited access to resources is never possible, managers must be clear about the limit beyond which no further resources can be used. Formulating a budget or establishing a set of specifications is a common way to specify limits.

Another form of support that managers can provide is to bestow credit—but not blame—publicly. Even though prime accountability has been delegated, pointing out mistakes or faults in front of others embarrasses people, creates defensiveness and fosters the impression that the manager is trying to pass the buck and get rid of final accountability. This guarantees that employees will be less willing to initiate action on their own in the future.

Correcting mistakes, critiquing work and providing negative feedback on task performance of employees should be done in private, where the probability of problem solving and training can be enhanced.

Focus accountability on results

Once tasks are delegated and authority is provided, managers should generally avoid closely monitoring the way in which employees accomplish the tasks. Excessive supervision of methods destroys the five dimensions of empowerment: self-efficacy, self-determination, personal control, meaningfulness and trust. Successful accomplishment of a task, rather than use of the manager's preferred procedures, is, after all, the primary goal of delegation. To be sure, harmful or unethical means for accomplishing tasks cannot be tolerated, and methods that obstruct other employees or subvert organisational rules cannot be used. For the most part, though, managers should focus primarily on the results achieved by employees rather than on the techniques used to achieve those results.

For accountability to be maintained, there must be agreement on acceptable levels of performance. Managers must clearly specify what level of performance is expected, what constitutes unacceptable performance and what requirements are associated with the result. Without such specifications, it becomes difficult for managers not to worry about means as well as ends. By allowing employees to exercise initiative regarding how to tackle a task, their sense of empowerment is enhanced, and innovation and originality are more likely as well.

Delegate consistently

The time for managers to delegate is before they have to. Sometimes, when managers have time to do work themselves, they do just that, even though that work could and should be delegated. Two problems result. First, delegation becomes simply a method for relieving the manager's workload and stress. A primary reason for delegation—empowering employees—is forgotten. Employees begin to feel that they are merely 'pressure valves' for managers rather than valued team members. Second, when delegation occurs only under pressure, there is no time for training, providing needed information or engaging in two-way discussions. Clarity of task assignments may be impaired. Employees' mistakes and failures increase and managers are tempted to perform tasks alone, to ensure quality. When managers delay delegating until they are overloaded, they create pressure on themselves to perform delegatable tasks personally, thereby increasing their own overload.

Another key to consistent delegation is for managers to delegate both pleasant and unpleasant tasks. Sometimes, managers keep for themselves the tasks they like to perform and pass less desirable work along to employees. It is easy to see the detrimental consequences this has on morale, motivation and performance. When individuals feel that they are being used only to perform 'dirty work', follow-through on delegated tasks is less likely. On the other hand, managers must not be afraid to share difficult or unpleasant tasks with employees. Playing the role of martyr by refusing to involve others in disagreeable tasks or drudgery creates unrealistic expectations for employees and isolates managers. Consistency of delegation, then, means that managers delegate tasks continuously, not just when overworked, and that they delegate both pleasant and unpleasant tasks.

Avoid upward delegation

Although it is crucial for employees to participate in the delegation process in order to become empowered, managers must conscientiously resist all so-called upward delegation, in which employees seek to shift responsibility for delegated tasks back on to the shoulders of the superior who did the initial delegating. Managers who fail to forestall upward delegation will find their time being tied up doing employees' work rather than their own.

Suppose an employee comes to a manager after delegation has occurred and says: 'We have a problem. This assignment just isn't turning out very well. What do you suggest I do?' If the manager replies, 'Gee, I'm not sure. Let me think about it and I'll get back to you', the original delegated task has now been shifted from the employee back to the manager. Note that the manager has promised to report to the employee—that is, to maintain prime accountability—and the employee is now in a position to follow up on the manager's commitment—that is, supervising the manager. Thus, the employee has become the manager and the manager the employee. Managers, in the hope of being helpful to and supportive of their employees, often get caught in the trap of upward delegation.

One way to avoid upward delegation is to insist that employees always take the initiative of developing their own solutions. Instead of promising the employee a report on the manager's deliberations, a more appropriate response would have been: 'What do you recommend?', 'What alternatives do you think we should consider?', 'What have you done so far?', 'What do you think would be a good first step?' Rather than sharing problems and asking for advice, employees should be required to share proposed solutions or to ask permission to implement them. Managers should refuse to solve delegated tasks. That is why specifying the expected level of initiative is so important (see 'Delegate completely', page 432). It not only avoids upward delegation, but also helps managers train employees to become competent problem solvers and to avoid working on tasks for which someone else has prime accountability. Yielding to upward delegation does not empower employees; rather, it makes them more dependent.

Clarify consequences

Employees should be made aware of the consequences of the tasks being delegated to them. They are more likely to accept delegation and be motivated to take the initiative if it is clear what the rewards for success will be, what the opportunities might be, or what the impact on the ultimate customer or the organisation's mission can be. In particular, managers should help employees understand the connection between successful performance and financial rewards, opportunities for advancement, learning and developmental opportunities, and informal recognition. Most specific delegated assignments do not result in a direct pay-off from the formal reward system, of course. But associating some desirable consequence—as minor as a pat on the back or a congratulatory mention in a staff meeting, or as major as a financial bonus or incentive—enhances successful delegation.

Clarifying consequences also helps to ensure an understanding that delegation implies not only task accomplishment but enhancement of interpersonal relationships as well. Relationships with others in the organisation, on the team or with the manager individually should be strengthened as a result of task accomplishment. Accomplishing assignments in the course of damaging or destroying relationships creates more long-term costs than any organisation can bear. Therefore, a desirable consequence of any delegation experience is the enhancement of interpersonal relationships and a strengthening of the organisation.

Review of delegation principles

The ten principles summarising how to delegate, preceded by the five criteria for determining when to delegate and the four questions for identifying to whom to delegate, provide guidelines for ensuring not only that employees will experience a sense of empowerment but that other positive consequences will result as well. In particular, research results clearly show that empowered delegation leads to the following consequences:

- Delegated tasks are readily accepted by employees.
- Delegated tasks are successfully completed.
- Morale and motivation remain high.
- Employees' problem-solving abilities are increased.
- Managers have more discretionary time.
- Interpersonal relationships are strengthened.
- Organisational coordination and efficiency are enhanced.

Figure 8.3 summarises the relationships between these principles.

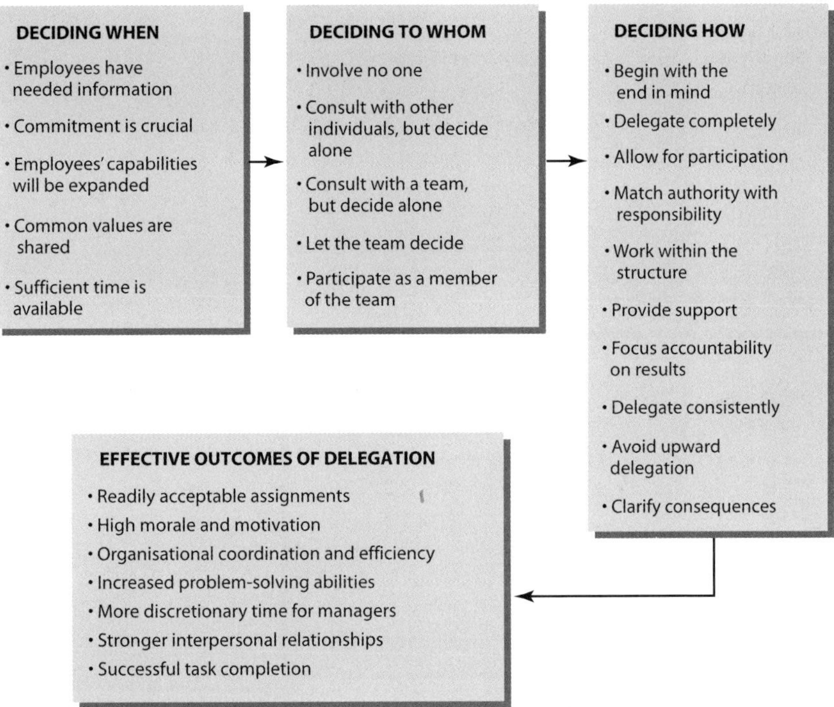

DECIDING WHEN
• Employees have needed information
• Commitment is crucial
• Employees' capabilities will be expanded
• Common values are shared
• Sufficient time is available
DECIDING TO WHOM
• Involve no one
• Consult with other individuals, but decide alone
• Consult with a team, but decide alone
• Let the team decide
• Participate as a member of the team
DECIDING HOW
• Begin with the end in mind
• Delegate completely
• Allow for participation
• Match authority with responsibility
• Work within the structure
• Provide support
• Focus accountability on results
• Delegate consistently
• Avoid upward delegation
• Clarify consequences
EFFECTIVE OUTCOMES OF DELEGATION
• Readily acceptable assignments
• High morale and motivation
• Organisational coordination and efficiency
• Increased problem-solving abilities
• More discretionary time for managers
• Stronger interpersonal relationships
• Successful task completion

FIGURE 8.3 Relationships among principles of effective delegation

Summary

Empowerment means helping to develop in others a sense of self-efficacy, self-determinism, personal control, meaning and trust. Unfortunately, because of the turbulent, complex, competitive circumstances that many organisations face, managers frequently react with the tendency to be less, rather than more, empowering. When managers feel threatened, they can become rigid and seek more control over their employees. However, without empowered employees, organisations cannot adapt, survive or succeed in the long run.

There are nine prescriptions that managers can use to empower others. There are also principles and criteria for ensuring empowered delegation, which results in better acceptance of delegated tasks by employees, enhanced motivation and morale, improved coordination and efficiency, better development of employees, increased discretionary time, strengthened relationships and successful task performance. Producing a sense of empowerment in others and delegating in a way that empowers employees also bring desirable outcomes for organisations as well as employees. Empowered employees are more productive, psychologically and physically healthy, proactive and innovative, persistent in work, trustworthy, interpersonally effective and intrinsically motivated; they have higher morale and commitment than employees who are not empowered. Figure 8.4 illustrates the relationships between the various elements of empowerment and delegation.

Behavioural guidelines

As you practise empowering others and carry out empowered delegating, you will want to use the following guidelines as cues. To ensure empowerment in others, follow these guidelines.

1. Foster personal mastery experiences for others by:
   - breaking apart large tasks and helping the person do one part at a time
   - involving people in simple tasks before difficult tasks

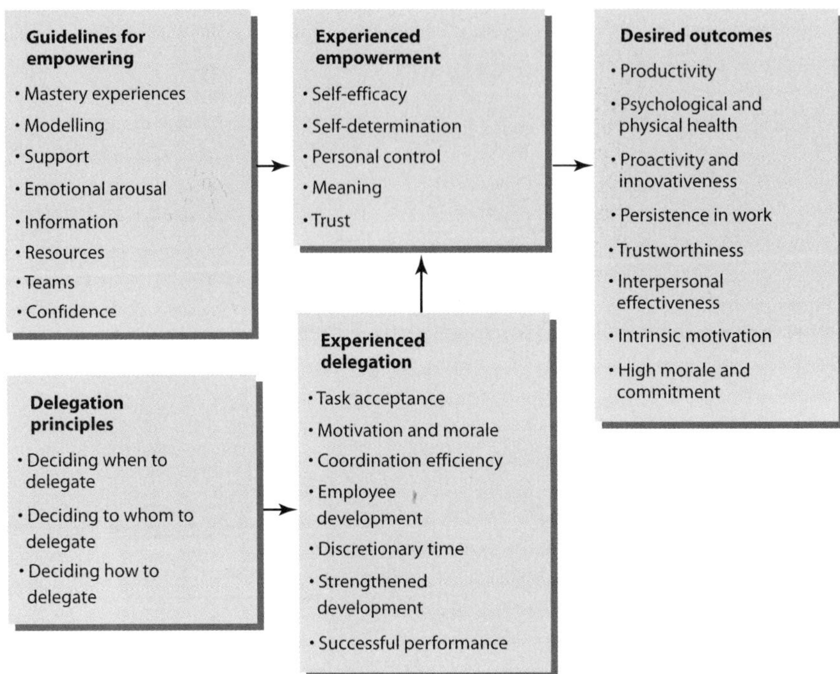

FIGURE 8.4 Relationships between the elements of empowerment and empowered delegation

- highlighting and celebrating small wins that others accomplish
- incrementally expanding others' job responsibilities
- giving increasingly more responsibility to others to solve problems.

2. Successfully model the behaviours you want others to achieve by:
   - demonstrating successful task accomplishment
   - pointing out other people who have succeeded at the same task
   - facilitating interaction with other people who can serve as role models
   - finding a coach or tutor for the person
   - establishing a mentor relationship with the person.
3. Provide needed support to other people by:
   - praising, encouraging, expressing approval for and reassuring others when they perform well
   - writing letters or notes of praise to employees, as well as to their family members and co-workers, in recognition of noteworthy accomplishments
   - providing regular feedback to people
   - fostering informal social activities in order to build cohesion among people
   - supervising less closely and providing more time between reports on results
   - holding formal and informal recognition ceremonies.
4. Arouse positive emotions among others by:
   - fostering activities to encourage the formation of friendships
   - periodically sending light-hearted messages to people to keep the climate fun and interesting
   - using superlatives in giving positive feedback
   - highlighting compatibility between important personal values held by your employees and the organisation's goals
   - clarifying the impact of outcomes on ultimate customers
   - fostering attributes of recreation in work by clarifying goals, instituting effective score-keeping and feedback systems, and specifying out-of-bounds behaviour.

5. Provide information needed by others to accomplish their work by:
   - providing all the information relating to the accomplishment of a task
   - continuously providing technical information and objective data that may come to you from time to time
   - passing along relevant cross-unit and cross-functional information to which others may not have access
   - providing access to information or to people with senior responsibility in the organisation
   - providing access to first-hand rather than second-hand information
   - clarifying the effects of employees' actions on customers.
6. Provide resources needed for others to accomplish their work by:
   - providing training and development experiences, or information about where they can be obtained
   - providing technical and administrative support, or information about where they can be obtained
   - providing needed time, space or equipment, or information about where they can be obtained
   - ensuring access to relevant information networks
   - providing discretion to others to commit resources that will help accomplish ultimate objectives.
7. Involve others in teams and task forces by:
   - assigning a team an important task or problem
   - letting a team not only solve a problem but implement the solution as well
   - assigning facilitators rather than leaders for the team, in order to foster equal participation and involvement
   - fostering information sharing and learning among team members
   - basing reward systems at least partly on effective team membership, not just on individual performance
   - helping team members teach and develop one another.
8. Create confidence among others by:
   - being reliable and consistent in your behaviour towards others
   - being fair and equitable in all your decisions and judgments
   - exhibiting caring and personal concern for others
   - being open and honest in your communications
   - exhibiting competence and expertise with regard to objectives to be achieved.

To effectively achieve empowered delegation, follow these guidelines.

1. Determine when to delegate work to others by addressing five key criteria:
   - Do employees have the information or expertise necessary to perform a task? Are they closer to the relevant information than you are?
   - Is the commitment of employees critical to successful implementation? Can employees subvert task accomplishment?
   - Will employees' capabilities be expanded by this assignment? Will it help others to develop themselves?
   - Do employees share a set of common values and perspectives? Are there likely to be conflicting points of view?
   - Does sufficient time exist to do an effective job of delegating? Can adequate information and training be provided?
2. Determine to whom work should be delegated by using the decision tree in Figure 8.2 (on page 431). Decide whether you should do the task yourself, consult with individual employees, consult with a team of employees, or participate as an equal member of a team of employees, by analysing the characteristics of the employees listed in the figure.
3. To delegate work effectively, follow these ten rules of thumb:
   - Begin with the end in mind. Specify desired results.
   - Delegate completely. Identify the level of initiative to be taken by employees.
   - Allow participation, especially regarding how and when tasks will be accomplished.

LEARNING

- Match levels of authority with levels of responsibility. Maintain balance.
- Work within the structure. When delegating work at lower levels, delegate through employees, not around them.
- Provide support for tasks being delegated. Identify resource limitations.
- Maintain accountability for results. Avoid overly close monitoring of methods.
- Delegate consistently. Do not delegate merely because you are overloaded.
- Avoid upward delegation. Ask employees to recommend solutions, rather than asking for assistance or advice.
- Clarify consequences. Identify important effects of successful task accomplishment.

Skill analysis

Case studies involving empowerment and delegation

Minding the store

On 1 February, Ruth Cummings was formally named branch manager for a leading department store in an up-market Sydney suburb. Her boss, Ken Hoffman, gave her this assignment on her first day: 'Ruth, I'm putting you in charge of this store. Your job will be to run it so that it becomes one of the best stores in the system. I have a lot of confidence in you, so don't let me down.'

One of the first things Ruth did was to hire an administrative assistant to handle inventories. Because this was such an important part of the job, she agreed to pay her assistant slightly more than the top retail clerks were making. She felt that having an administrative assistant would free her to handle marketing, sales and personnel matters—areas she felt were crucial if the store was to be a success.

Within the week, however, she received a call from Hoffman: 'Ruth, I heard that you hired an administrative assistant to handle inventories. Don't you think that's a bit risky? Besides, I think paying an assistant more than your top sales clerk is damaging to morale in the store. I wish you had cleared this with me before you made the move. It sets a bad precedent for the other stores and it makes me look like I don't know what is going on in the branches.'

Three weeks later, Ruth appeared on a local day-time talk show to discuss new trends in fashion. She had worked hard to make contact with the hosts of the show and she felt that public exposure like this would increase the visibility of her store. Although the TV spot lasted only ten minutes, she was pleased with her performance and with the chance to get public exposure.

Later that night at home, she received a phone call from Hoffman: 'Don't you know our policies? Any TV appearances made on behalf of the store are to be cleared through head office. Normally, we like to have representatives from the main store appear on these kinds of shows because they can do a better job of plugging our merchandise. It's too bad that you didn't notify someone of your intentions. This could be very embarrassing for me.'

Ruth was approached in the store by one of the sales staff. A customer had asked to charge approximately $3000 worth of china as a gift for his wife on his in-store account. He had been a customer of the store for several years and Ruth had seen him on several occasions, but store rules indicated that no in-store charge could be made for more than $1000 for any reason. She told the customer that she was not authorised to okay a charge of that amount but that, if he would like to use his credit card or to contact head office, maybe arrangements could be made.

Later in the day an irate Hoffman called: 'What in the world are you thinking about, Ruth? Today we had a customer ring and say that you wouldn't make a sale to him because the charge was too much. Do you know how long he has been a customer of ours? And do you know how much he spends in the store every year? I certainly hope we haven't lost him as a customer because of your blunder. This makes me very upset. You've just got to learn to use your head.'

Ruth thought about the conversation for several days and finally decided that she needed to see Ken Hoffman. She called his secretary to schedule an appointment for the following day.

DISCUSSION QUESTIONS

1. *What rules of thumb related to empowerment were violated by Ken Hoffman? By Ruth Cummings?*
2. *What rules of thumb related to delegation were violated by Ken Hoffman? By Ruth Cummings?*
3. *What should Ruth Cummings and Ken Hoffman discuss in their meeting? Identify specific agenda items that should be raised.*
4. *What are the questions that Ruth should ask Ken to help her acquire the necessary elements of empowerment? What questions should Ken ask Ruth to be better able to ensure her success?*
5. *If you were an outside consultant attending the meeting, what advice would you give Ken? What advice would you give Ruth?*

Changing the portfolio

You are head of a staff unit reporting to the general manager of finance. He has asked you to provide a report on the firm's current portfolio, including recommendations for changes in the current selection criteria. Doubts have been raised about the efficiency of the existing system, given current market conditions, and there is considerable dissatisfaction with prevailing rates of return.

You plan to write the report, but at the moment you are perplexed about the approach to take. Your own specialty is the bond market and it is clear to you that detailed knowledge of the equities market, which you lack, would greatly enhance the value of the report. Fortunately, four members of your staff are specialists in different segments of the equities market. Together, they possess a vast amount of knowledge about the intricacies of investment. However, they seldom agree on the best way to achieve anything when it comes to investment philosophy and strategy.

You have six weeks before the report is due. You have already begun to familiarise yourself with the firm's current portfolio and have been provided by management with a specific set of constraints that any portfolio must satisfy. Your immediate problem is to come up with some alternatives to the firm's present practices and to select the most promising for detailed analysis in your report.

DISCUSSION QUESTIONS

1. *Should this decision be made by you alone? Why or why not?*
2. *If you answer the question 'Should I involve others?' affirmatively, which alternative in Figure 8.2 should be used in making a decision? Justify your choice.*
3. *What are the most important considerations in deciding who should be involved in this task?*
4. *If others are to become involved, how much empowerment should they have? What would you do specifically to achieve the appropriate level of empowerment?*

Skill practice

Exercises for empowering and delegating

Executive Development Associates

Assume that you are Mary O'Connell, general manager at Executive Development Associates. Your firm provides outplacement, training and development, career planning and head-hunting services for a large number of big, successful companies. You have been at the corporate board meeting for the last three days in the Blue Mountains, and you have relied on your assistant to screen out all but the most important or urgent messages. You slip into the office on the way home from the airport on Monday evening, just to check your electronic messages and your mail. Aside from a host of phone calls to return, here is the collection of messages that your assistant retrieved from your email file and mailbox.

Interoffice Memorandum
Data Processing Centre
DATE: 15 June 2012
TO: Mary O'Connell, General Manager
FROM: Deborah Gobits, for the Data Processing Staff

After looking over last quarter's audit, it is clear that the number of complaints our group is receiving from individuals throughout the company is escalating. The problem is an obvious one to us. It is, simply, that several incompatible software systems have evolved over the last several years in various departments and it is becoming increasingly difficult to coordinate across units. As you know, some data have to be retyped two or three times into different systems because of these incompatibilities.

Our own employees, not to mention our customers, are becoming increasingly impatient with our slow turnaround time. They focus squarely on our group as the bottleneck. We think the rising complaint numbers in the quarterly audit are misleading, however, and divert us from the real cause of the problem.

We're writing this memo to you collectively to urge you to address this issue as soon as possible. At a minimum, it should be discussed at our staff meeting on Tuesday. So far, the data processing staff is taking the blame for not getting data processed fast enough, yet it is really the fault of the system, not our unit.

We'll look forward to hearing from you on Tuesday.

Interoffice Memorandum
Human Resources Department
DATE: 15 June 2012
TO: Mary
FROM: Lucy

I was excited by your speech at the senior management meeting last week in which you established a new challenge for all senior executives. With the new competitive environment that we face, the vision that you articulated for our future is both exciting and challenging and, I think, an important step forward. It really makes clear the key success factors that should drive our business.

In particular, I think your directive for all senior executives to disseminate the vision to their own employees throughout the organisation is a good way to get the message delivered. However, in your speech you made a statement that troubled me. You said: 'We used to pay you on the basis of new accounts generated, quarterly earnings, customer satisfaction ratings and new product designs. Our new barometer is going to be how you're doing in disseminating the vision throughout your own units.'

Frankly, I'm perplexed as to how we'll ever measure this directive. As the person responsible for administering the appraisal and reward systems, I'm not sure what criteria we'll look for or what indicators we'll use to determine success. I'm afraid that we'll create dissatisfaction if we don't have something specific outlined. Our people, especially those who may not perform, will think it is purely arbitrary. Do you really mean to have us change the appraisal and compensation systems to include this new criterion? How do you propose that we measure effective performance? What would you like me to do to support your statement? Did you mean to make the statement that you did?

This is rather urgent because I have a staff meeting Tuesday afternoon and I promised to have a response by then. I've already stalled until I had a chance to talk to you.

Australia University
24 May 2012
Dear Ms O'Connell

I am happy to be joining Executive Development Associates after several years at Australia University. As you know, leaving Australia University has been quite traumatic for me and that is what motivated me to make a request of you. I'm convinced that the reason I didn't receive tenure at Australia University is because the expectations were never clear about what my responsibilities were and what the criteria for success were.

I know your company is very professional and employees are pretty much on their own, but I'm feeling a need to get some specific performance requirements outlined for me. I'm sure that I can be a good addition to your company, but I want to be clear about what your expectations are.

I have set a meeting with you on Tuesday through your secretary. Would you please outline a specific set of responsibilities and expectations for my job as instructor in the training and development department? If possible, I'd like it in writing to avoid any misunderstanding. Regardless, I'll look forward to talking to you on Tuesday.

Thank you for your consideration.

Sincerely

Lester Frost

Interoffice Memorandum
Training and Development
DATE: Monday, a.m.
TO: Mary
FROM: Robert
RE: Tom Kinnir's jury duty

I know you're just getting back, but we've got an emergency on our hands.

I was just notified this morning by Tom that he has been selected for jury duty and that (can you believe it) he is being sequestered! Mary, this couldn't have come at a worse time. As our expert on activity-based costing, Tom's the only person we have who can teach the topic. So what's the trouble, you say? The trouble is that we have more than 100 corporate trainers showing up here for a seminar on Friday and the seminar isn't prepared yet. Tom said that he has some notes and a few transparencies on his desk, but he had planned to spend this entire week designing and preparing it. None of us knows the topic very well—but we're not even sure what information we need, what data still needs to be gathered, who's got what and how we go about filling in. Help! We're counting on this seminar to make budget this quarter and we're feeling a little ticked-off at Tom for waiting until the last minute. What do we do next?

By the way, how were the Blue Mountains?

Interoffice Memorandum Outplacement Department
DATE: Monday, a.m.
TO: Mary O'Connell
FROM: Rajan Mishra
RE: Pending plant closure

You may have missed the news over the weekend. It was announced in the paper that Consolidated Manufacturing is closing its plant in town. That means that about 2000 people will be out of work.

If we want the business, we've got to get moving right away. They will be looking at proposals from outplacement firms next week. We've got to get our proposal together, identify staff, determine a budget and prepare a presentation in the next day or two.

Sounds like a great opportunity. I'll stop by tomorrow when you get back.

Assignment

1. For each message, outline specifically the plan you will implement to empower others effectively to solve these problems. Determine who should be involved, what level of initiative should be taken, what actions you can take to ensure empowerment, how accountability should be maintained, and so on.
2. Write out the actions you would take in response to each item. A worksheet has been provided to remind you of what you should consider as you record your responses.
3. When you have completed your own responses, form a team of fellow students and share your plans. Provide feedback to one another on what is especially good, what could be improved and what could be added to each action plan. In particular, which principles of empowerment are included, which are omitted and which are contradicted?

Worksheet: Executive Development Associates

For each message, write out your plan of action, taking into consideration the questions listed below. Most, but not all, questions are relevant to each message and they can guide your action plan.

1. Who should be involved in resolving this issue? Will you form a team?
2. What kinds of personal mastery experiences can be provided for those who will be involved? Can you model successful behaviour?
3. What kinds of support, information and resources can be given?
4. How will you create emotional arousal and create confidence in others?
5. What are the main considerations in deciding if you should delegate each task?
6. If you opt for delegation, what will you do to include the following:
   - begin with the end in mind
   - delegate completely
   - allow participation
   - match authority with responsibility
   - work within the structure
   - provide support
   - maintain accountability
   - ensure consistency of delegation
   - avoid upward delegation
   - clarify consequences?

Skill application

Suggested assignments

1. Teach someone else (your spouse, a colleague, your boss) how to empower others and delegate effectively. Include the principles in Box 8.1 in your discussion. Use your own examples and illustrations.
2. Interview a manager about his or her empowerment practices. Try to determine what is especially effective, what does not work, what comes over as condescending and what motivates people to perform. Identify the extent to which the manager knows and uses the principles discussed in the skill learning section of this chapter.
3. Think of a situation you now face with which you would like some help. It may be a task you want to accomplish, a tough decision you need to make or a team you want to form. Make sure you think of something that requires the involvement of other people. Write down specific things you can do to empower other people to help you. How can you help them do what they want to do, while simultaneously having them do what you want them to do?
4. Schedule a meeting with a manager who is not very good at empowerment. As a student who has learned about and practised empowerment and delegation, share what you have learned and offer suggestions that could help this manager improve.

Application plan and evaluation

This exercise is intended to help you apply this cluster of skills in a real-life, out-of-class setting. Now that you have become familiar with the behavioural guidelines that form the basis of effective skill performance, you will improve most by trying out those guidelines in an everyday context. Unlike a classroom activity, in which feedback is immediate and others can assist you with their evaluations, this skill application activity is one you must accomplish and evaluate on your own. There are two parts to this activity. Part 1 assists in preparing you to apply the skill. Part 2 helps you to evaluate and improve on your experience. Be sure to write down answers to each item. Do not short-circuit the process by skipping steps.

Part 1: Planning

1. Write down the two or three aspects of this skill that are most important to you. These may be areas of weakness, areas you most want to improve, or areas that are most salient to a current problem. Identify the specific aspects of this skill that you want to apply.
2. Now identify the setting or the situation in which you will apply this skill. Establish a plan for performance by writing down a description of the situation. Who else will be involved? When will you do it? Where will it be done?
3. Identify the specific behaviours you will engage in to apply this skill. Operationalise your skill performance.
4. What are the indicators of successful performance? How will you know that you have been effective? What will indicate that you have performed competently?

Part 2: Evaluation

5. When you have completed your implementation, record the results. What happened? How successful were you? What was the effect on others?
6. How can you improve? What modifications can you make next time? What will you do differently in a similar situation in the future?
7. Looking back on your whole skill practice and application experience, what have you learned? What has been surprising? In what ways might this experience help you in the long term?

Scoring keys and supplementary materials

Effective empowerment and delegation (p. 406)

SCORING KEY

Skill area	*Items*	**ASSESSMENT** *Pre-*	*Post*
Personal mastery experiences	1, 2	_______	_______
Modelling	3, 4	_______	_______
Providing support	5, 6	_______	_______
Arousing positive emotions	7, 8	_______	_______
Providing information	9, 10	_______	_______
Providing resources	11, 12	_______	_______
Organising teams	13, 14	_______	_______
Creating confidence	15, 16	_______	_______
Delegating work	17–26	_______	_______
	TOTAL SCORE	☐	☐

Comparison data

Compare your scores with three comparison standards:

1. Compare your score against the maximum possible (156).
2. Compare your scores with the scores of other students in your class.
3. Compare your scores with a norm group consisting of 500 business school students. In comparison to the norm group, if you scored:

above 122	you are in the top quartile
109 to 122	you are in the second quartile
95 to 108	you are in the third quartile
94 or below	you are in the bottom quartile.

Personal empowerment (p. 407)

SCORING KEY

Skill area	*Items*	*Mean (Total/4)*
Self-efficacy (competence)	2, 7, 12, 17	________
Self-determination (choice)	3, 8, 13, 18	________
Personal control (impact)	4, 9, 14, 19	________
Meaningfulness (value)	1, 6, 11, 16	________
Trust (security)	5, 10, 15, 20	________

Comparison data

Scores from approximately 3000 middle managers in manufacturing and service organisations:

	Mean	*Top 1/3*	*Bottom 1/3*
Self-efficacy	5.76	>6.52	<5.00
Self-determination	5.50	<6.28	<4.72
Personal control	5.49	>6.34	<4.64
Meaningfulness	5.88	>6.65	<5.12
Trust	5.33	>6.03	<4.73

References

Adler, A. 1927, *Understanding Human Nature* (Garden City, NY: Garden City Publishing Co.).

Alinsky, S. D. 1971, *Rules for Radicals: A Pragmatic Primer for Realistic Radicals* (New York: Vintage Books).

Alloy, L. B., C. Peterson, L. Y. Abrahamson and M. E. P. Seligman 1984, 'Attributional style and the generality of learned helplessness', *Journal of Personality and Social Psychology* 46, pp. 681–7.

Amabile, T. and S. Kramer 2011, 'The power of small wins', *Harvard Business Review*, 89(5), pp. 70–80.

Anderson, C., D. Hellreigel and J. Slocum 1977, 'Managerial response to environmentally induced stress', *Academy of Management Journal*, 20, pp. 260–72.

Anonymous 2002, 'Harnessing talents and skills and Lloyds TSB', *HR Monthly*, 1 May, p. 21.

Anonymous 2003, '18 tips for better delegation', *HR Focus*, 80(4), p. 11.

Anonymous 2004, 'Pain medicine: A woman's beliefs about childbirth rules labor anesthesia choices', *Drug Week*, 23 January, p. 386.

Ashby, R. 1956, *Design for the Brain* (London: Science Paperbacks).

Averill, J. R. 1973, 'Personal control over aversive stimuli and its relationship to stress', *Psychological Bulletin*, 80, pp. 286–303.

Axtell, C. M. and S. K. Parker 2003, 'Promoting role breadth self-efficacy through involvement, work redesign and training', *Human Relations*, 56(1), p. 113.

Bandura, A. 1977, 'Self-efficacy: Toward a unifying theory of behavioral change', *Psychological Review*, 84, pp. 191–215.

Bandura, A. 1986, *Social Foundations of Thought and Action: A Social Cognitive Theory* (Englewood Cliffs, NJ: Prentice Hall).

Bandura, A. and R. Wood 1989, 'Effect of perceived controllability and performance standards on self-regulation of complex decision making', *Journal of Personality and Social Psychology*, 56, pp. 805–14.
Barber, B. 1983, *The Logic and Limits of Trust* (New Brunswick, NJ: Rutgers University Press).
Barton, H. and L. Barton 2011, 'Trust and psychological empowerment in the Russian work context', *Human Resource Management Review*, 21(3), pp. 201–8.
Bea, J. R. 1999, 'Getting excellent results', *Health Forum Journal*, 42(6), pp. 40–1.
Bennis, W. and B. Nanus 1985, *Leaders: The Strategies for Taking Charge* (New York: Harper and Row).
Benson, J. 2007, 'A different beat', *Broadcasting & Cable*, 137(17), p. 34.
Berdahl, J. 2003, 'In search of power equilibrium', *Canadian HR Reporter*, 16(7), p. 7.
Berman, E. L. 2003, 'Delegation: Responsibility and authority', *Industrial Management*, 45(4), p. 6.
Bernard, C. I. 1938, *The Functions of the Executive* (Cambridge, MA: Harvard University Press).
Berry, J. 2004, 'Road deaths 15,000, shark attack deaths 1', *The Age*, 18 December.
Block, P. 1987, *The Empowered Manager: Positive Political Skills at Work* (San Francisco: Jossey-Bass).
Bookman, A. and S. Morgan 1988, *Women and the Politics of Empowerment* (Philadelphia: Temple University Press).
Bramucci, R. 1977, 'A factorial examination of the self-empowerment construct', PhD dissertation, University of Oregon.
Brehm, J. W. 1966, *Response to Loss of Freedom: A Theory of Psychological Reactance* (New York: Academic Press).
Burnett, C. 2011, 'Medium for empowerment or a "centre for everything": Students' experience of control in virtual learning environments within a university context', *Education & Information Technologies*, 16(3), pp. 245–58.
Byham, W. C. 1988, *Zapp! The Lightning of Empowerment* (New York: Harmony Books).
Cameron, K. S., S. J. Freeman and A. K. Mishra 1991, 'Best practices in white-collar downsizing: Managing contradictions', *Academy of Management Executive*, 5, pp. 57–73.
Cameron, K. S., S. J. Freeman and A. K. Mishra 1993, 'Organization downsizing and redesign', in G. P. Huber and W. Glick (eds), *Organizational Change and Design* (New York: Oxford University Press).
Cameron, K. S. and R. E. Quinn 1999, *Diagnosing and Changing Organizational Culture* (Reading, MA: Addison-Wesley).
Cameron, K. S., D. A. Whetten and M. U. Kim 1987, 'Organizational dysfunctions of decline', *Academy of Management Journal*, 30, pp. 126–38.
Cane, A. 1994, 'People in business—Getting the best out of people is the buzz, empowerment the word', *Australian Financial Review*, 29 December.
Carlopio, J., M. Fleischer and D. Roitman 1988, 'Computerized manufacturing technology and work organization's effects on labor relations and satisfaction', in W. Karwoski, H. M. Parsons and H. R. Parsaei, *Ergonomics of Hybrid Automated Systems* (New York: Elsevier).
Charbonnier-Voirin, A. and A. El Akremi 2011, 'The effect of empowerment on employees' adaptive performance', *Industrial Relations*, 66(1), pp. 122–49.
Coch, L. and J. R. P. French 1948, 'Overcoming resistance to change', *Human Relations*, 11, pp. 512–32.
Conger, J. A. 1989, 'Leadership: The art of empowering others', *Academy of Management Executive*, 3, pp. 17–24.
Conger, J. A. and R. N. Kanungo 1988, 'The empowerment process', *Academy of Management Review*, 13, pp. 471–82.
Coonradt, C. A. 1985, *The Game of Work* (Salt Lake City, UT: Shadow Mountain Press).
Covey, S. 1999, 'Trust and transformation', *Incentive*, 173(11), p. 10.
Deans, A. 2002, 'Julian Tertini', *Bulletin*, 26 November, pp. 76–77.
DeCharms, R. 1979, 'Personal causation and perceived control', in L. C. Perlmuter and R. A. Monty, *Choice and Perceived Control* (Hillsdale, NJ: Erlbaum).
Deci, E. L., J. P. Connell and R. M. Ryan 1989, 'Self-determination in a work organization', *Journal of Applied Psychology*, 74, pp. 580–90.
Deci, E. L. and R. M. Ryan 1987, 'The support of autonomy and control of behavior', *Journal of Personality and Social Psychology*, 53, pp. 1024–37.
Deutsch, M. 1973, *The Resolution of Conflict: Constructive and Destructive Processes* (New Haven, CT: Yale University Press).
Donaldson, L. 1985, *In Defence of Organizational Theory* (Cambridge, UK: Cambridge University Press).
Donaldson, L. 1995, *American Anti-management Theories of Organization* (Cambridge, UK: Cambridge University Press).
Donaldson, L. 2001, *The Contingency Theory of Organizations* (Thousand Oaks, CA: Sage).
Drucker, P. 1988, 'The coming of the new organization', *Harvard Business Review*, January–February.
Drucker, P. F. 2003a, 'Future of management', *Executive Excellence*, 20(5), p. 3.
Drucker, P. F., 2003b, 'New trends in management, *Executive Excellence*, 20(8), p. 8.
Durkheim, E. 1964, *The Division of Labor in Society* (New York: Macmillan).
Duyilemi, A. 2008, 'Role modelling as a means of enhancing performance of Nigerian girls in science, technology and mathematics education', *International Journal of Learning*, 15(3), pp. 227–34.
Eisenhardt, K. M. and D. C. Galunic 1993, 'Renewing the strategy-structure-performance paradigm', *Research in Organizational Behavior*, 15.
Fassel, D. 2003, 'Building better performance', *Health Forum Journal*, 46(2), Spring, p. 44.
Firth, D. 1995, *How to Make Work Fun* (London: Gowler).
Freire, P. and A. Faundez 1989, *Learning to Question: A Pedagogy of Liberation* (New York: Continuum Publishing Company).
Gecas, V. 1989, 'The social psychology of self-efficacy', *Annual Review of Sociology*, 15, pp. 291–316.
Gecas, V., M. A. Seff and M. P. Ray 1988, 'Injury and depression: The mediating effects of self concept', paper presented at the Pacific Sociological Association Meetings, Las Vegas.

Geller, E. 2003, 'People-based safety', *Professional Safety*, 48(12), p. 33.
Gennill, G. R. and W. J. Heisler 1972, 'Fatalism as a factor in managerial job satisfaction', *Personnel Psychology*, 25, pp. 241–50.
Gibb, J. R. and L. M. Gibb 1969, 'Role freedom in a TORI group' in A. Burton (ed.), *Encounter Theory and Practice of Encounter Groups* (San Francisco: Jossey-Bass).
Golembiewski, R. T. and M. McConkie 1975, 'The centrality of trust in group processes', in Cary Cooper (ed.), *Theories of Group Processes* (New York: Wiley).
Gracie, S. 1999, 'Delegate don't abdicate', *Management Today*, March, p. 92.
Greenberger, D. B. and S. Stasser 1991, 'The role of situational and dispositional factors in the enhancement of personal control in organizations', *Research in Organizational Behavior*, 13, pp. 111–45.
Greenberger, D. B., S. Stasser, L. L. Cummings and R. B. Dunham 1989, 'The impact of personal control on performance and satisfaction', *Organisational Behavior and Human Decision Processes*, 43, pp. 29–51.
Hackman, B. K. 1994, 'Reconceptualizing managerial delegation behaviour', *Asia Pacific Journal of Human Resources*, 32, pp. 33–52.
Hackman, B. K. and D. C. Dunphy 1990, 'Managerial delegation', *International Review of Industrial and Organizational Psychology*, 5, pp. 35–57.
Hackman, J. R. and G. R. Oldham 1980, *Work Design* (Reading, MA: Addison-Wesley).
Hallman, J. 2011, 'Storytelling is a compass in trying times', *Quill*, 99(2), p. 24.
Hammer, T. H. and Y. Vardi 1981, 'Locus of control and career self-management among non-supervisory employees in industrial settings', *Journal of Vocational Behavior*, 18, pp. 13–29.
Hardy, C. and S. Leiba-O'Sullivan 1998, 'The power behind empowerment: Implications for research and practice', *Human Relations*, 51(4), pp. 451–84.
Harter, S. 1978, 'Effectance motivation reconsidered: Toward a developmental model', *Human Development*, 21, pp. 34–64.
Hattersley, M. 1997, 'The managerial art of telling a story', *Harvard Management Update*, January, pp. 3–4.
Heger, B. 2007, 'Linking the employment value proposition (EVP) to employee engagement and business outcomes: Preliminary findings from a linkage research pilot study', *Organization Development Journal*, 25(2), pp. 121–33.
Heller, F. 1999, 'Influence at work: A 25-year program of research', *Human Relations*, 51(12), pp. 1425–56.
Hemric, M., A. Eury and D. Shellman 2010, 'Correlations between perceived teacher empowerment and perceived sense of teacher self-efficacy', *AASA Journal of Scholarship & Practice*, 7(1), pp. 37–50.
Hernan, P. 1999, 'The untrained, unempowered masses', *Industry Week*, 248(22), pp. 94–6.
Holdsworth, L. and S. Cartwright 2003, 'Empowerment, stress and satisfaction: An exploratory study of a call centre', *Leadership and Organization Development Journal*, 24(3), p. 131.
Hoyle, S. 1995, 'Australia: Client service the priority—managed funds', *Australian Financial Review*, 15 August.
Huber, G. P. 1980, *Managerial Decision Making* (Glenview, IL: Scott, Foresman).
Kahn, W. A. 1990, 'Psychological conditions of personal engagement and disengagement at work', *Academy of Management Journal*, 33, pp. 692–724.
Kanter, R. 1983, *The Change Masters* (New York: Simon and Schuster).
Kanter, R. M. 1968, 'Commitment and social organization: A study of commitment mechanisms in utopian communities', *American Sociological Review*, 33, pp. 499–517.
Klein, K., J. Ziegert, A. Knight and X. Yan 2006, 'Dynamic delegation: Shared, hierarchical, and deindividualized leadership in extreme action teams', *Administrative Science Quarterly*, 51(4), pp. 590–621.
Langer, E. J. 1983, *The Psychology of Control* (Beverly Hills, CA: Sage).
Langer, E. J. and J. Rodin 1976, 'The effects of choice and enhanced personal responsibility', *Journal of Personality and Social Psychology*, 34, pp. 191–8.
Lawrence, K. 2007, 'Winning at "employee moments of truth" through HR products and services', *Organization Development Journal*, 25(2), pp. 159–62.
Lawrence, P. and J. Lorsch 1967, *Organizations and Environments* (Homewood, IL: Irwin).
Leach, D. J., T. D. Wall and P. R. Jackson 2003, 'The effect of empowerment on job knowledge: An empirical test involving operators of complex technology', *Journal of Occupational and Organizational Psychology*, 76(1), p. 27.
Locke, E. and G. Latham 1990, *A Theory of Goal Setting and Task Performance* (Upper Saddle River, NJ: Prentice Hall).
Locke, E. A. and D. M. Schweiger 1979, 'Participation in decision making: One more look', *Research in Organizational Behavior*, 1, pp. 265–340.
Loeb, S. J., D. Steffensmeier and C. Kassab 2011, 'Predictors of self-efficacy and self-rated health for older male inmates', *Journal of Advanced Nursing*, 67(4), pp. 811–20.
Luhmann, N. 1979, *Trust and Power* (New York: Wiley).
McClelland, D. 1975, *Power: The Inner Experience* (New York: Irvington).
Mackay, H. 1993, *Re-inventing Australia: The Mind and Mood of Australia in the 90s* (Sydney: Angus & Robertson).
McKee, R. 2003, 'Storytelling that moves people', *Harvard Business Review*, June, pp. 51–5.
Mader, R. P. 2003, 'To keep your crew happy, let them steer the ship', *Contractor*, 50(4), April, p. 7.
Mapletoft, T. L. 2003, 'Don't let the tank run down to empty: Delegate tasks to balance the personal and professional', *Nation's Restaurant News*, 6 October, 37(40), p. 20.
Martin, J., M. Feldman, M. J. Hatch and S. Sitkin 1983, 'The uniqueness paradox of organizational stories', *Administrative Science Quarterly*, 28, pp. 438–52.
Maruca, R. 1999, 'Fighting the urge to fight fires', *Harvard Business Review*, 77(6), p. 30.

Marx, K. 1844, *Early Writings*, edited and translated by T. B. Bottomore (New York: McGraw-Hill).
Milligan, A. and S. Smith 2002, 'Uncommon practice: People who deliver a great brand experience', *Financial Times*, 10 July.
Minett, D. 2000, 'The two sides of management responsibility', *Hospitality*, 1 May, p. 45.
Mishra, A. K. 1992, 'Organizational response to crisis: The role of mutual trust and top management teams', PhD dissertation, University of Michigan.
Neufeld, R. W. J. and P. Thomas 1977, 'Effects of perceived efficacy of a prophylactic controlling mechanism on self-control under painful stimulation', *Canadian Journal of Behavioral Science*, 9, pp. 224–32.
Newman, W. H. and K. Warren 1977, *The Process of Management* (Englewood Cliffs, NJ: Prentice Hall).
Nielson, E. H. 1986, 'Empowerment strategies: Balancing authority and responsibility', in S. Scrivastiva et al. (eds), *Executive Power* (San Francisco: Jossey-Bass).
Nyssen, A. S., I. Hansez, P. Baele, M. Lamy and V. De Keyser 2003, 'Occupational stress and burnout in anaesthesia', *British Journal of Anaesthesia*, 90(3), March, p. 333.
O'Hare, D. and V. Kudrle 2007, 'Increasing physician engagement', *Physician Executive*, 33(3), pp. 38–45.
Organ, D. and C. N. Greene 1974, 'Role ambiguity, locus of control and work satisfaction', *Journal of Applied Psychology*, 59, pp. 101–12.
Ozer, E. M. and A. Bandura 1990, 'Mechanisms governing empowerment effects: A self-efficacy analysis', *Journal of Personality and Social Psychology*, 58, pp. 472–86.
Peters, T. 1992, *Liberation Management* (New York: Ballantine Books).
Preston, P. and T. W. Zimmerer 1978, *Management for Supervisors* (Englewood Cliffs, NJ: Prentice Hall).
Rappaport, J., C. Swift and R. Hess 1984, *Studies in Empowerment: Steps Toward Understanding and Action* (New York: Haworth Press).
Roberts, P. 1996a, 'Avis still leading from the front', *Australian Financial Review*, 5 September.
Roberts, P. 1996b, 'Giving change another chance', *Australian Financial Review*, 18 July.
Rose, S. M. and B. L. Black 1985, *Advocacy and Empowerment: Mental Health Care in the Community* (Boston: Routledge and Kegan Paul).
Rothbaum, F., J. R. Weisz and S. S. Snyder 1982, 'Changing the world and changing the self: A two-process model of perceived control', *Journal of Personality and Social Psychology*, 42, pp. 5–37.
Runyon, K. E. 1973, 'Some interaction between personality variables and management style', *Journal of Applied Psychology*, 57, pp. 288–94.
Sashkin, M. 1982, *A Manager's Guide to Participative Management* (New York: American Management Association).
Sashkin, M. 1984, 'Participative management is an ethical imperative', *Organizational Dynamics*, 12, pp. 4–22.
Schulze, H. 2000, 'Paths to top service', *Asiaweek*, 21 April, p. 61.
Schwalbe, M. L. and V. Gecas 1988, 'Social psychological consequences of job-related disabilities', in J. T. Mortimer and K. M. Borman, *Work Experience and Psychological Development through Life Span* (Boulder, CO: Westview).
Seeman, M. and C. S. Anderson 1983, 'Alienation and alcohol', *American Sociological Review*, 48, pp. 60–77.
Seligman, M. E. P. 1975, *Helplessness: On Depression, Development and Death* (San Francisco: Freeman).
Shapiro, J., J. Astin, S. Shapiro, D Robitshek and D. Shapiro 2011, 'Coping with loss of control in the practice of medicine', *Families, Systems & Health: The Journal of Collaborative Family Healthcare*, 29(1), pp. 15–28.
Sibthorp, J. 2003, 'An empirical look at Walsh and Golins' adventure education process model: Relationships between antecedent factors, perceptions of characteristics of an …', *Journal of Leisure Research*, 35(1), p. 80.
Siegall, M. and S. Gardner 2000, 'Contextual factors of psychological empowerment', *Personnel Review*, 29(6), p. 703.
Solomon, B. B. 1976, *Black Empowerment: Social Work in Oppressed Communities* (New York: Columbia University Press).
Spreitzer, G. M. 1992, 'When organizations dare: The dynamics of individual empowerment in the workplace', PhD dissertation, University of Michigan.
Staples, L. H. 1990, 'Powerful ideas about empowerment', *Administration in Social Work*, 14, pp. 29–42.
Swap, W., D. Leonard, M. Shields and L. Abrams 2001, 'Using mentoring and storytelling to transfer knowledge in the workplace', *Journal of Management Information Systems*, 18(1), pp. 95–114.
Thomas, K. W. and B. A. Velthouse 1990, 'Cognitive elements of empowerment: An interpretive model of intrinsic task motivation', *Academy of Management Review*, 15, pp. 666–81.
Thomson, J. 2003, 'Step back to move forward', *Business Review Weekly*, 23 October, pp. 116–17.
Tulgan, B. 2007, 'Empowerment myth', *Leadership Excellence*, 24(4), p. 9.
Urwick, L. 1944, *Elements of Administration* (New York: Harper and Brothers).
Vidal, M. 2007, 'Manufacturing empowerment? "Employee involvement" in the labour process after Fordism', *Socio-Economic Review*, 5(2), p. 197.
Vogt, J. F. and K. L. Murrell 1990, *Empowerment in Organizations* (San Diego, CA: University Associates).
von Oech, R. 1990, *A Whack on the Side of the Head* (New York: Warner Books).
Vroom, V. H. and A. G. Jago 1974, 'Decision making as social process: Normative and descriptive models of leader behavior', *Decision Sciences*, 5, pp. 743–69.
Vroom, V. H. and P. W. Yetton 1973, *Leadership and Decision Making* (Pittsburgh, PA: University of Pittsburgh Press).
Wagner, J., G. Cummings, D. Smith, J. Olson, L. Anderson and S. Warren 2010, 'The relationship between structural empowerment and psychological empowerment for nurses: A systematic review', *Journal of Nursing Management*, 18(4), pp. 448–62.

Weick, K. 1979, *The Social Psychology of Organising* (Reading, MA: Addison-Wesley).

White, R. W. 1959, 'Motivation reconsidered: The concept of competence', *Psychological Review*, 66, pp. 297–333.

Wiles, C. 2003, 'Take your speech cues from the actor's trade', *Harvard Management Communication Letter*, July, pp. 3–4.

Wilson, T. 2010, 'The small wins really count', *Ultra-Fit Magazine*, 20(7), p. 67.

Wood, R. E. and A. Bandura 1989, 'Impact of conceptions of ability on self-regulatory mechanisms and complex decision making', *Journal of Personality and Social Psychology*, 56, pp. 407–15.

Wood, R. E., A. Bandura and T. Bailey 1990, 'Mechanism governing organizational performance in complex decision-making environments', *Organizational Behavior and Human Decision Processes*, 46, pp. 181–201.

Wood, R. E. and E. A. Locke 1990, 'Goal setting and strategy effects on complex tasks', *Research in Organizational Behavior*, 12, pp. 73–109.

Zand, D. E. 1972, 'Trust and managerial problem solving', *Administrative Science Quarterly*, 17, pp. 229–39.

Zimmerman, M. A. 1990, 'Taking aim on empowerment research: On the distinction between individual and psychological conceptions', *American Journal of Community Psychology*, 18, pp. 169–77.

Zimmerman, M. A. and J. Rappaport 1988, 'Citizen participation, perceived control and psychological empowerment', *American Journal of Community Psychology*, 16, pp. 725–50.

CHAPTER 9

BUILDING EFFECTIVE TEAMS

OBJECTIVES

- **Diagnose stages of team development**
- **Build high-performance teams**
- **Foster effective teamwork**
- **Plan and conduct effective team meetings**

9

CHAPTER OUTLINE

Skill assessment

Evaluative surveys for building effective teams
- Team development behaviours
- Diagnosing the need for team building

Skill learning

The need for teams and teamwork

The advantages and disadvantages of teams

Stages of team development

Virtual teams

Conducting effective team meetings

Summary

Behavioural guidelines

Skill analysis

Case study involving building effective teams
- The cash register incident

Skill practice

Exercise in team building
- Preparing and conducting a team meeting at Asian Electronics

Skill application
- Suggested assignments
- Application plan and evaluation

Scoring keys and supplementary materials

References

Skill assessment

Evaluative surveys for building effective teams

Team development behaviours

Step 1: Before you read the material in this chapter, respond to the following statements by writing a number from the rating scale that follows in the left-hand column (pre-assessment). Your answers should reflect your attitudes and behaviour as they are now, not as you would like them to be. Be honest. This instrument is designed to help you discover your level of competency in building effective teams so that you can tailor your learning to your specific needs. When you have completed the survey, use the scoring key at the end of the chapter to identify the skill areas discussed in this chapter that are most important for you to master.

Step 2: When you have completed the reading and the exercises in this chapter and, ideally, as many as you can of the skill application assignments at the end of this chapter, cover up your first set of answers. Then respond to the same statements again, this time in the right-hand column (post-assessment). When you have completed the survey, use the scoring key to measure your progress. If your score remains low in specific skill areas, use the behavioural guidelines at the end of the skill learning section to guide your further practice.

Rating scale

1 Strongly disagree
2 Disagree
3 Slightly disagree
4 Slightly agree
5 Agree
6 Strongly agree

Assessment

Pre- *Post-*

When I am in the role of leader in a team:

______ ______ 1. I know how to establish credibility and influence among team members.
______ ______ 2. I behave congruently with my stated values and I demonstrate a high degree of integrity.
______ ______ 3. I am clear and consistent about what I want to achieve.
______ ______ 4. I create positive energy by being optimistic and complimentary of others.
______ ______ 5. I build a common base of agreement in the team before moving forward with task accomplishment.
______ ______ 6. I encourage and coach team members to help them improve.
______ ______ 7. I share information with team members and encourage participation.
______ ______ 8. I articulate a clear, motivating vision of what the team can achieve along with specific short-term goals.

When I am in the role of team member:

______ ______ 9. I know a variety of ways to facilitate task accomplishment in the team.
______ ______ 10. I know a variety of ways to help build strong relationships and cohesion among team members.
______ ______ 11. I confront and help to overcome negative, dysfunctional or blocking behaviours by others.

______ ______ 12. I shift roles from facilitating task accomplishment to helping build trusting relationships among members, depending on what the team needs to move forward.

When I desire to make my team perform well, regardless of whether I am a leader or member:

______ ______ 13. I am knowledgeable about the different stages of team development experienced by most teams.

______ ______ 14. I help establish clear expectations and purpose as well as help team members feel comfortable with one another at the outset of a team.

______ ______ 15. I encourage team members to become as committed to the success of the team as to their own personal success.

______ ______ 16. I help team members become committed to the team's vision and goals.

______ ______ 17. I help the team avoid 'groupthink' by making sure that sufficient diversity of opinions is expressed in the team.

______ ______ 18. I can diagnose and capitalise on my team's core competencies or unique strengths.

______ ______ 19. I encourage the team to improve continuously, as well as to seek dramatic innovations.

______ ______ 20. I encourage exceptionally high standards of performance and outcomes that far exceed expectations.

The scoring key is on page 497.

Diagnosing the need for team building

Teamwork has been found to affect organisational performance dramatically. Some managers have credited teams with helping them to achieve incredible results. However, teams do not work all the time in all organisations, so managers must decide when teams should be organised. To determine the extent to which teams should be built in your organisation, complete the instrument below.

Think of an organisation in which you participate (or will participate) that produces a product or service. Answer these questions with that organisation in mind. Write a number from a scale of 1 to 5 in the blank at the left: 1 indicates there is little evidence; 5 indicates there is a lot of evidence.

______ 1. Output has declined or is lower than desired.

______ 2. Complaints, grievances or low morale are present or are increasing.

______ 3. Conflict or hostility between members is present or is increasing.

______ 4. Some people are confused about assignments, or their relationships with other people are unclear.

______ 5. Lack of clear goals and lack of commitment to goals exist.

______ 6. Apathy or lack of interest and involvement by members is in evidence.

______ 7. Insufficient innovation, risk taking, imagination or initiative exists.

______ 8. Ineffective and inefficient meetings are common.

______ 9. Working relationships across levels and units are unsatisfactory.

______ 10. Lack of coordination among functions is apparent.

______ 11. Poor communication exists; people are afraid to speak up; listening is not occurring; and information is not being shared.

______ 12. Lack of trust exists among members and between members and senior leaders.

______ 13. Decisions are made that some members do not understand or with which they do not agree.

______ 14. People feel that good work is not rewarded or that rewards are unfairly administered.

______ 15. People are not encouraged to work together for the good of the organisation.

______ 16. Customers and suppliers are not part of organisational decision making.

______ 17. People work too slowly and there is too much redundancy in the work being done.

______ 18. Issues and challenges that require the input of more than one person are being faced.
______ 19. People must coordinate their activities in order for the work to be accomplished.
______ 20. Difficult challenges that no single person can resolve or diagnose are being faced.

Source: W. G. Dyer, *Team Building: Issues and Alternatives* (Reading, MA: Addison-Wesley, 1987). Reproduced with permission.

The scoring key is on page 497.

LEARNING

Skill learning

The need for teams and teamwork

Teams have made their way into almost every area of private and public sector business (Harrison et al. 2003; May 2002). In health care (Buljac-Samardzic et al. 2011; Lewin & Reeves 2011), law firms (Anonymous 2002a), politics (James 1999a, 1999b), universities (Illing 1999; New Zealand Press Association 1999), construction (Cave 1999; Wright 1999), manufacturing (Anonymous 2002b; Siegel 2003), the high-technology sector (Barczak & Wilemon 2003; Lander et al. 2004), chemical and pharmaceutical production (Ainsworth 1999) and financial services (Higgins 2003; Unkles 2002) teams are being used to increase quality, cost efficiency, productivity, service levels, cross-functional coordination, innovation, learning and more.

There are numerous circumstances that create the need for more teams and teamwork in organisations. Two of these are the continuing growth of service industries and the globalisation of markets and competition. Service industries often require team-based skills from employees, such as communication skills, flexibility and initiative. Because customer satisfaction is the key to success, and because in service industries customers have a role to play in ensuring their own satisfaction, customers can become part of the team.

For example, the Australian Taxation Office introduced a Tax Pack to improve the overall quality of the work that customers experience in their dealings with the Tax Office. Similarly, the University of New South Wales Centre for Safety Science and the WorkCover Authority developed a HAZPAK. A self-help guide to risk assessment, HAZPAK was designed to help small and medium-sized businesses identify and evaluate hazards and risks in the workplace. By systematically creating such close relationships with customers, the Tax Office blurred the traditional distinction between customers and employees and created a team that included both.

Due to the deregulation of Australia's financial markets and the increasing deregulation of many other formerly protected industries, such as textiles, clothing and footwear, Australia must now be more competitive internationally. Complex problems arise that require innovation, creativity and a diversity of inputs for success. On a strategic level, this has led to the creation of joint ventures, partnerships and mergers (for example, AMPOL and Woolworths, BlueScope Steel and Pioneer, Shell Oil and Coles, AMP Capitol and Heatley) to unite the necessary skills, products and services to meet local and international demands (Attaran & Attaran 2003). On a more operational level, deregulation has led to the pooling of talent within organisations, often in the form of cross-functional teams, in order to create the specialised yet flexible skill base required to compete in global markets.

Teams are important to managers, not only because there are many new opportunities for the application of teams but because there are times when the dysfunction of existing teams can cost money and lives. For example, consider the following:

> *Because one of our major clients was a large airline ... we read the transcripts of what the 'black box' recorders showed to be the last few minutes of [other airlines'] flights that did not make it. Many showed lack of teamwork to be a significant contributory factor in many accidents and crashes. Overall it has been estimated that over 70 per cent of all airline accidents and crashes are a function of communication rather than technical factors. (Margerison & McCann 1990: 3)*

Successful teams, whether at work, home or play, have several distinct characteristics. For example:

- Effective teams have interdependent members. The productivity and efficiency of an entire unit is determined by the coordinated, interactive efforts of all its members.
- Effective teams help members to be more efficient working together than alone.
- Effective teams can outperform even the best individual's performance.
- Effective teams function so well that they create their own magnetism. Team members desire to affiliate with a team because of the advantages they receive from membership.
- Effective teams do not always have the same leader. Leadership responsibility can rotate and sometimes is shared broadly.
- In effective teams, members care for and support one another. No member is devalued or unappreciated. All are treated as an integral part of the team.
- In effective teams, members cheer for and bolster the leader, and vice versa. Mutual encouragement is given and received by each member.
- In effective teams, there is a high level of trust among members. Members are interested in others' success as well as their own.

These eight points, which are the focus of this chapter, are among the important attributes of teams. Learning how to foster effective team processes, team roles, team leadership and positive relationships among team members is an important team-building skill. The intention in this chapter is to help you improve your skill in managing teams, both as a leader and as a team member.

The advantages and disadvantages of teams

Teams have captured the attention of many managers because of the large amounts of data that show that the use of teams brings improvements in productivity, quality and morale. For example, a noted management consultant Tom Peters (1987: 306) asserted:

> *Are there any limits to the use of teams? Can we find places or circumstances where a team structure does not make sense? Answer: No, as far as I can determine. That's unequivocal, and meant to be. Some situations may seem to lend themselves more to team-based management than others. Nonetheless, I observe that the power of the team is so great that it is often wise to violate apparent common sense and force a team structure on almost anything.*

Although many companies have attributed their improvements in performance directly to the institution of teams in the workplace (Brunelli 1999; Evans & Wolf 2006; Triolo et al. 2002; Wellins, Bynam & Wilson 1991), not everyone agrees with Tom Peter's unequivocal enthusiasm for teams. There is a time and place for everything—including groups and teams.

Advantages of teams

Many firms are counting on teams, for various reasons:

> *Even routine work, such as food production at a McDonald's, can be made enjoyable when done in a team. Consider this comment about the avant-garde performance artist Laurie Anderson who spent some time working in Maccas: '... But the most interesting thing which delighted and astonished her was that she found it a very happy experience to work among a team. She reported that, mundane though the work was, the joy of being in a small group of people working to strict and speedy deadlines and bonding together as a team was something which made her surprisingly happy.' (Bruce 2003: 1)*

> *Cross-functional teams are at the heart of every motorcycle produced by Harley-Davidson Motor Co., all the way from conception and design of the motorcycle to its production and product launch—teams of buyers, suppliers, manufacturing engineers and beyond will all have their voices heard, says Leroy Zimdars, Harley-Davidson's director of supply chain management. (Brunelli 1999)*

In a bid to improve its product quality and manufacturing efficiency, the implementation of more in-depth teamwork in the factory is part of Volvo's $4 million investment in their truck assembly factory at Wacol, Brisbane. (Lynch 1995)

Mrs Shipley, the former prime minister of New Zealand, reshaped the cabinet in 1998 into teams of ministers. These were intended to identify the Government's true priorities and improve cross-portfolio co-ordination. (James 1999b)

Other more scientific and systematic studies of the impact of teams have also reported impressive results. Literally thousands of studies have been conducted on groups and teams and their impact on various performance outcomes. One of the first and most well-known studies ever conducted on teams was undertaken by Coch and French (1948) in the Harwood Company, a manufacturer of men's shirts, shorts and pyjamas. Faced with the need to respond to competitors' lower prices, Harwood decided to speed up the line and make other process changes. Employees had responded badly, however, to previous changes in the production process, and they resisted the threat of further changes. To implement these planned changes, Harwood's management used three different types of strategies.

One group of employees received an explanation of the new standards to be imposed, the proposed changes in the production process to be implemented and why the changes were needed. A question-and-answer period followed the explanation. A second group of employees was presented with the problem, asked to discuss it and reach agreement on solutions, and then elect representatives to generate the new standards and procedures. In a third group, every member was asked to discuss and become involved in establishing and implementing the new standards and procedures. All members participated fully as a team.

The results of this comparison were dramatic. Despite having their jobs simplified, members of the first group showed almost no improvement in productivity; hostility towards management escalated; and within 40 days 17 per cent of the employees had left the company. Members of the second group regained their previous levels of productivity within 14 days and improved slightly thereafter. Morale remained high and no employees left the company. Members of the third group, however, who participated fully as a team, regained earlier productivity levels by the second day and improved 14 per cent over that level within the month. Morale remained high and no one left the company.

Other classic studies of coal mines and pet food and car manufacturers revealed similar advantages of teams (for example, Trist 1969; Walton 1965). More recently, one of the most comprehensive surveys ever conducted on employee involvement in teams was carried out among the *Fortune* 1000 companies by Lawler, Mohrman and Ledford (1992). They found that employee involvement in teams had a strong positive relationship with several dimensions of organisational and employee effectiveness. In general, Lawler and his colleagues found that, among firms that were actively using teams, both organisational and individual effectiveness were above average and improving in virtually all categories of performance. In firms without teams, or in which teams were infrequently used, effectiveness was average or low in all categories.

In studies of self-directed teams, Near and Weckler (1990) found that individuals in self-directed teams scored significantly higher than individuals in traditional work structures on innovation, information sharing, employee involvement and task significance. Macy et al. (1990) reported that the use of self-directed teams correlated highly with increases in organisational effectiveness, heightened productivity and reduced defects. Wellins, Bynam and Wilson (1991) reported that two-thirds of companies that implemented self-directed work teams could run their companies with fewer managers and, in 95 per cent of the cases, a reduced number of managers was reported to be beneficial to company performance. The results of many other studies have produced similar outcomes (Ancona & Caldwell 1992; Hackman 1990; Janz 1999).

Many of the reasons for the positive outcomes of teams have been known for years. Maier (1967), for example, in a classic description of the conditions under which teams are more effective than individuals acting alone, and vice versa, pointed out that teams can:

- produce a greater number of ideas and pieces of information than individuals acting alone, so decision making and problem solving are more informed and are of higher quality

Our team needs one good multi-skilled Maintenance Associate

Our team is down one good player. Join our group of multi-skilled Maintenance Associates who work together to support our assembly teams at Australian Automotive Manufacturing.

We are looking for a versatile person with skills in one or more of the following: ability to set up and operate various welding machinery, knowledge in electric arc and MIG welding, willingness to work on detailed projects for extended time periods and general overall knowledge of the automobile manufacturing process. Willingness to learn all maintenance skills a must. You must be a real team player, have excellent interpersonal skills and be motivated to work in a highly participative environment.

Send qualifications to:

AAM

Australian Automotive Manufacturing
PO Box 616
Port Wayne, WA 6987
Include phone number. We respond to all applicants.

Maintenance Technician/Welder

Leading automotive manufacturer looking for Maintenance Technician/Welder. Position requires the ability to set up and operate various welding machinery and a general knowledge of the automobile production process. Vocational school graduate or 3–5 years' on-the-job experience required. Competitive salary, full benefits and tuition reimbursement offered.

Interviews Monday, May 6, at the Holiday Inn South, 3000 Semple Road, 9:00 a.m. to 7:00 p.m. Please bring pay stub as proof of last employment.

NMC

National Motors Corporation
5169 Blane Hill Centre
Springfield, SA 5712

FIGURE 9.1 A team-oriented advertisement and a traditional advertisement for a position

- improve understanding and acceptance among individuals involved in problem solving and decision making due to team members' participation in the process
- have higher motivation and performance levels than individuals acting alone because of the effects of 'social facilitation'; that is, people are more energised and active when they are around other people
- offset personal biases and blind spots that inhibit effective problem analysis and implementation but that are not noticed by single individuals
- are more likely to engage in a 'risky shift'—that is, to entertain risky alternatives and to take innovative action—than individuals acting alone.

In addition, teams are frequently more fun. Consider, for example, two advertisements that appeared next to one another in a metropolitan newspaper, both seeking to fill the same type of position. They are reproduced in Figure 9.1. While neither advertisement is negative or inappropriate, they are substantially different. Which job would you rather take? Which firm would you rather work for?

Disadvantages of teams

Teams are not a panacea for everything that ails organisations; they do not represent a magic potion that managers can apply to help them accomplish their objectives (cf. DeChurch & Zaccaro 2010). Just getting people together and calling them a team by no means makes them a team. A leading expert on teams, Richard Hackman (1993), pointed out that mistakes are common in team building and team management. Rewarding and recognising individuals instead of the team, not maintaining stability of membership over time, not providing teams with autonomy, not fostering interdependence among team members, using the team to make all decisions instead of having individuals make decisions when appropriate, failing to orient all team members, having too many members on the team, not providing appropriate structure for the team and not providing the team with needed resources are all common mistakes Hackman found in his studies of teams. Moreover, a team is not always an appropriate mechanism for dealing with a challenge facing an organisation. For example, simple, routine or highly formalised work (for example, stuffing pimentos into olives) is not well-suited to teams.

According to some, there is even a covert and sinister side to the use of teams (Sinclair 1989, 1992). For example, Amanda Sinclair (1989: 2), at the University of Melbourne Graduate School of Management, has suggested that:

> *The team ideology tyrannises because, under the banner of benefits to all, teams are frequently used to camouflage coercion with the appearance of cohesion, conceal conflict with the appearance of consensus, convert conformity into an appearance of creativity, to give unilateral decisions a co-determinist seal of approval, to delay action in the supposed interests of consultation, to legitimate lack of leadership and to disguise expedient arguments and personal agendas.*

Sinclair (1989) suggested that all individuals experience substantial and continuing internal tensions as group members, and that participation in groups is usually stressful and only occasionally, for some, satisfying. This tension derives from individual needs to establish a special relationship with the leader, a need that groups inevitably frustrate, and from the inevitable conflict between individual and group/organisational goals and values. Still others, Sinclair (1989) reminds us, would describe all group activity as the consuming and irresolvable struggle for power. Teams, therefore, do not necessarily provide fulfilment of individual needs, or unequivocally contribute to individual or organisational satisfaction, performance or effectiveness.

In other words, although teams can be powerful tools for producing organisational success under certain circumstances, they are by no means an easy answer to all our organisational ills. Teams can take too long to make decisions; they may drive out effective action with 'groupthink' (discussed later in the chapter); and they can create confusion and frustration for their members. Many of us have been irritated by being members of an inefficient committee, a team dominated by one member, or having to take responsibility for the output of a team that compromised on excellence in order to get agreement from everyone. To rephrase an old saying: 'A camel is a horse designed by a team.'

If team failure is common, how can success in teams be assured? How can managers help ensure the effectiveness of the teams in which they are involved? What should one learn to become a skilful team leader and team member? Because of the rapid growth of teams, as well as the potential positive impact teams can have on an organisation's success, it is clear that understanding teams and teamwork is a prerequisite for any effective manager in modern organisations. We now turn, therefore, to the key management skills of team development, team building and teamwork.

Stages of team development

A team is defined as two or more individuals who work together towards a common objective. Team members' behaviour is interdependent and their personal goals are subservient to the accomplishment of the team goal. A certain degree of commitment to and desire for team membership is present. Even though individuals may be formally designated a team, if they act to bring exclusive credit to themselves, to accomplish their own objectives instead of the team's objective or to maintain independence from others, they are not truly a team, regardless of their name. A key challenge, then, is determining how to build the elements of a team into an independent group of individuals who have no prior commitment to one another or to a common task (Harrison et al. 2003; Knouse 2007).

To build, lead or participate in a team effectively requires us to understand the stages of development that teams follow as they form and carry out their functions. Effective managers are skilful at helping teams to be successful as they progress from the early stages of development, when a team is still struggling to become a coherent entity, to a more mature stage of development, when the team has become a highly effective, smoothly functioning organism. This chapter focuses on helping you improve your skill in each phase of team development.

Evidence of a predictable pattern of team development has been available since the early part of the 20th century. Beginning with Dewey's (1933) emphasis on the five (cognitive) stages of learning and Freud's (1921) analysis of children's (affective) responses to authority figures, research has proliferated on the cognitive and affective changes that occur in groups and teams over time. In fact, several thousand studies of groups and teams have appeared in just the last decade. Researchers have studied a wide variety of types of groups and teams with varying compositions and attributes. Problem-solving teams, quality circles, therapy groups, task forces, interpersonal growth groups, student project teams and many other types have been studied extensively.

Studies have ranged from teams meeting for just one session to teams with working lives extending over several years. Membership in teams has varied widely, ranging from children to aged people, top executives to line employees, students to instructors, volunteers to prison inmates, professional athletes to playground children. The analyses have focused on dynamics such as team-member roles, unconscious cognitive processes, group dynamics, problem-solving strategies, communication patterns, leadership actions, interpersonal needs, decision-making quality, innovativeness and productivity.

Despite the variety in composition, purpose and longevity across teams being investigated, the stages of group and team development emerging from these studies have been strikingly similar. For a review and summary of a dozen or so team-stage development models, see Cameron and Whetten (1981, 1984). Teams tend to develop through four separate stages. These stages were first labelled by Tuckman (1965) as 'forming', 'storming', 'conforming' and 'performing'. Because of their rhyme and simplicity, these labels are still widely used today. Table 9.1 summarises the four main stages of team development.

TABLE 9.1 Typical attributes of the four stages of team development

STAGE	CATEGORY	CHARACTERISTICS
Forming	Team member questions	• Who are these other people? • What is going to happen? • What is expected of me? • Where are we headed and why? • Who is the leader? • What are our goals? • How do I fit in? • How much work will this involve?
	Interpersonal relationships	• Silence • Self-consciousness • Dependence • Superficiality • Reactivity • Uncertainty
	Task issues	• Orient members • Become comfortable with team membership • Establish trust • Establish relationships with the leaders • Establish clarity of purpose • Deal with feelings of dependence

TABLE 9.1 *Continued*

STAGE	CATEGORY	CHARACTERISTICS
	Effective leader behaviours	• Make introductions • Answer questions • Establish a foundation of trust • Model expected behaviours • Clarify goals, procedures, rules and expectations
Storming	Team member questions	• How will we handle disagreements? • How will we communicate negative information? • Can the team be changed? • How can we make decisions amidst disagreement? • Do we really need this leader? • Do I want to maintain my membership in the team?
	Interpersonal relationships	• Polarisation of team members • Coalitions or cliques being formed • Competition among team members • Disagreement with the leader • Challenging others' points of view • Violating team norms
	Task issues	• Manage conflict • Legitimise productive expressions of individuality • Overcome groupthink • Examine key work processes of the team • Turn counter-dependence into interdependence
	Effective leader behaviours	• Identify a common enemy and reinforce the vision • Generate commitment among team members • Turn students into teachers • Be an effective mediator • Provide individual and team recognition • Foster win–win thinking
Conforming	Team member questions	• What are the norms and expectations? • How much should I conform? • What role can I perform? • Will I be supported? • Where are we headed? • How much should I invest and commit?
	Interpersonal relationships	• Cooperativeness • Ignoring disagreements • Conformity to standards and expectations • Obedience to leader directions • Heightened interpersonal attraction • Commitment to a team vision
	Task issues	• Maintain unity and cohesion • Differentiate and clarify roles • Determine levels of personal investment • Clarify the future • Decide on levels of commitment to the team's future
	Effective leader behaviours	• Facilitate role differentiation among team members • Show support to team members • Provide feedback • Articulate a vision of the future for the team • Help generate commitment to the vision

STAGE	CATEGORY	CHARACTERISTICS
Performing	Team member questions	• How can we continuously improve? • How can we foster innovativeness and creativity? • How can we build on our core competence? • What improvements can be made to our processes? • How can we maintain a high level of energy and commitment to the team?
	Interpersonal relationships	• High mutual trust • Unconditional commitment to the team • Multifaceted relationships among team members • Mutual training and development • Entrepreneurship • Self-sufficiency
	Task issues	• Capitalise on core competence • Foster continuous improvement • Anticipate needs of customers and respond in advance of requests • Enhance speed and timeliness • Encourage creative problem solving
	Effective leader behaviours	• Foster innovation and continuous improvement simultaneously • Advance the quality culture of the team • Provide regular, ongoing feedback on team performance • Play sponsor and orchestrator roles for team members • Help the team avoid reverting to earlier stages

For teams to be effective and for team members to get the most benefit from team membership, teams must progress through the first three stages of development to achieve stage four. In each separate stage, particular challenges and issues predominate, and it is by successfully managing these issues and overcoming the challenges that a team matures and becomes more effective. Skilful managers, whether serving as team leaders or team members, help the team progress to the next stage of development.

To explain each stage and identify ways in which skilled managers assist teams in moving towards increasingly high performance and effectiveness, the discussion focuses on the dominant team member questions, interpersonal relationships, task issues and effective leader behaviours that characterise each stage. Being able to diagnose the stage of a team's development and adopt the appropriate leader behaviours is a skill that separates the most effective managers from those who are less effective.

The forming stage

Team member questions, interpersonal relationships and task issues

Most performers know that at the beginning of a concert the audience is 'cold'. Because the audience is not initially very responsive, major performers use a warm-up act to get the audience 'in tune' or to 'become one' with the performer. Similarly, when team members first come together, they are much like an audience at the outset of a concert. They are not a team, but an aggregation of individuals sharing a common setting. Something must happen for them to feel that they are a cohesive unit. Recall an instance in which you met a group of people for the first time. It may have been at the outset of a semester in university, in a committee or task-force meeting, in a church or professional group, or on a sports team. When you first came together with other potential team members, you probably did not feel integrated into a cohesive unit. In fact, you may have had several questions in your mind:

- Who are these other people?
- What is going to happen?
- What is expected of me?

- Where are we headed and why?
- Who is the leader?
- What are our goals?
- How do I fit in?
- How much work will this involve?

The questions uppermost in the minds of participants in a new team have to do with establishing a sense of security and direction, getting oriented and becoming comfortable with the new situation. Sometimes, new team members can articulate these questions, while at other times they are little more than general feelings of discomfort or disconnectedness. Uncertainty and ambiguity tend to predominate as individuals seek some type of understanding and structure. Because there is no shared history with the team, there is no unity among members. Thus, the typical interpersonal relationships that predominate in this stage are:

- silence
- self-consciousness
- dependence
- superficiality
- reactivity
- uncertainty.

Individuals cannot begin to feel like a team until they become familiar with the rules and boundaries of their setting. They do not know who to trust, who will take the initiative, what constitutes normal behaviour or what kinds of interactions are appropriate. The individuals are not yet a real team, only a collection of individuals. Therefore, the task of the team in this stage is less focused on producing an output than on developing the team itself. Helping team members become comfortable with one another takes precedence over task accomplishment. A team faces the following kinds of task issues in its first stage of development:

- orienting members
- becoming comfortable with team membership
- establishing trust
- establishing relationships with the leader
- establishing clarity of purpose
- dealing with feelings of dependence.

Effective leader behaviours

Teams can remain in the first stage for an extended period, and many do when no clear direction is provided about what the team is to accomplish, what the rules are or what each member's responsibilities entail. Some teams never move past this stage of development but remain a loose aggregation of individuals without the magnetism or the commitment that characterise high-performing teams. The lifespan of such a team is likely to be short. Unless a skilful person takes time to deal with the issues and anxieties of team members, it will become progressively harder for the team to develop beyond this stage. Such teams eventually dissolve. On the other hand, this stage can be relatively brief if a leader of the team takes the following actions:

- makes introductions
- answers questions
- establishes a foundation of trust
- models expected behaviours
- clarifies goals, procedures, rules and expectations.

In this stage, skilful team leaders act more like directors than facilitators. This stage is not a time for team leaders to rely on free and open discussion and consensus decision making to accomplish an outcome; rather, direction, clarity and structure are needed. The first task is to ensure that all team members know one another and that their questions are answered (even unasked questions that are on the minds of team members). Because relatively little participation may occur during this stage, the temptation is for team leaders to rush ahead or to short-circuit introductions and instructions. Skilful team leaders leave time for questions, however, and they urge team members to reveal their uncertainties. Guidelines, boundaries and expectations are clarified so that team members understand how they fit in, how much will be required of them and how much trust they can have in the team.

Chapter 2 identified how trust is built on matching others, and Chapter 8 discussed five dimensions on which trust and confidence are built: reliability, fairness, caring, openness and competence. Team leaders must model these attributes in their own behaviour in order to establish the foundation of trust. This means being consistent and dependable in actions and congruent in communication. It means being equitable and fair and showing personal concern for all team members. It means sharing information openly, honestly and clearly, while exhibiting sensitivity to the needs of all team members. Finally, it means helping team members to become aware of the competence and resources available to them.

According to Evans and Wolf (2006), the best teams focus on three things:

1. They focus on providing a common work discipline and are concerned with how individuals and small groups work together. They are disciplined and rigorous in their approach to work. They pay attention to small details, eliminate problems at the source and strive for efficiency, removing waste and excess wherever possible.
2. They focus on communication. Information about problems and solutions is shared widely, frequently and in small increments. Feedback is critical to success and learning.
3. Leaders focus on guiding their teams towards a common goal. Leaders are connectors. They articulate clear and simple goals for each project based on their strategic vision, and they connect people to others who can help achieve those goals.

One of the crucial responsibilities of a team leader is to help clarify to all team members the structure of the team. Without a structure in place and clearly understood by everyone, a team will have a difficult time progressing past the forming stage of development. When the team leader successfully provides the necessary clarity and structure, however, the team can progress to the second stage.

The storming stage

Team member questions, interpersonal relationships and task issues

Virtually every team goes through a stage where team members question the legitimacy of the team's direction, the leader, the roles of other team members, the opinions or decisions being espoused and the task objectives. This is a natural phase of development in the team, because, up to now, the team has largely been characterised by harmony and consensus. However, such a condition will not last forever. The team members have not yet learned how to cope with conflict, differences and disruptions. The team's long-term success, however, will depend on how well it manages this storming stage of development. The team can disintegrate if this stage is not managed well. Typical questions that arise in team members' minds during this stage are:

- How will we handle disagreements?
- How will we communicate negative information?
- Can the team be changed?
- How can we make decisions amidst disagreement?
- Do we really need this leader?
- Do I want to maintain my membership in the team?

An old proverb states: 'All sunshine makes a desert.' Similarly, team growth implies that some struggles must occur, some discomfort must be experienced and some obstacles must be overcome for the team to prosper in the long term. The team must learn to deal with adversity, especially that produced by its own members. If team members are more interested in keeping the peace than in solving problems and accomplishing tasks, the team will never become effective and its long-term viability will be threatened. Consequently, harmony is sometimes sacrificed as the team attacks problems and accomplishes objectives.

Team members in this stage of development do not cease to care about one another, and they remain committed to the team and its success. But they do begin to take sides on issues, to find that they are more compatible with some team members than with others, and to agree with some points of view more than with others. This differentiation in roles and perspectives creates interpersonal relationships characterised by:

- polarisation of team members
- coalitions or cliques being formed
- competition among team members
- disagreement with the leader
- challenging others' points of view
- violating team norms.

The storming stage does not necessarily imply that the team becomes chaotic, self-destructive or mean-spirited. Rather, the same results occur as when teenagers begin to separate from their parents, when junior managers in companies begin to break away from their mentors and when pupils begin to challenge their teachers. Separation anxiety, competition and even resentment may arise, mainly because the old pattern of relationships has changed. The unquestioned authority of the leader is challenged and is no longer inviolate. Independence and interdependence replace dependence. Disagreements are common. Therefore, effective conflict management strategies take on added importance, as team members are required sometimes to adopt an initiator role, sometimes a responder role and sometimes a mediator role in addressing inevitable conflicts.

It is also common in the storming stage for team members to test and challenge the boundaries and norms of the team. This might include small aberrations such as coming in late, holding side conversations in team meetings or interrupting the team's work. It might also encompass more significant challenges, such as trying to oust the team leader, generating new rules to replace the original ones, or building a coalition to alter the team's goals and objectives significantly.

The testing of norms and boundaries is sometimes merely an expression of a need for individuality, while in other instances it is a product of strong feelings that the team can be improved. The main task issues to be addressed by the team in this stage include:

- managing conflict
- legitimising productive expressions of individuality
- overcoming groupthink
- examining the key work processes of the team
- turning counter-dependence into interdependence.

Conflict, coalition formation and counter-dependence create conditions that may lead to the norms and values of the team being questioned. For example, team members may challenge the legitimacy of the team's reward system, the way work is organised or the amount of time being spent. Rather than being stifled, resisted or shut off, team members should be encouraged to turn those challenges into constructive suggestions for improvement. Do not just identify problems—anyone can do that. Identify solutions.

The team must be careful during this stage to restate and reinforce the overall vision for the team and not to confuse it with more specific, short-term goals or processes. Abandoning the core vision will not help the team progress beyond this stage of development; rather, the team will become mired in debates about key values. Coalitions must be reminded of the common vision and principles that bond the overall team, even though different subgroups may take different positions on issues.

It is important for team members to feel that they can legitimately express their personal uniqueness and idiosyncrasies, so long as they are not destructive to the overall team. It is clear from research on teams that they are more effective if membership is heterogeneous than if all team members act, believe and see things in the same way (Murnigham 1981). Maintaining flexibility in the team implies that tolerance for individuality is acceptable and that changes and improvements are promoted.

Expressing individuality does not mean, of course, that commitment to the overall team's success need be abandoned. In fact, it is important during this stage to reinforce constantly the need for team members to focus on the welfare of the overall group and the achievement of the vision. One of the best ways for this to happen is for the team to make certain that a win–win philosophy permeates the team's activities.

As discussed in Chapters 5 and 7, a win–win philosophy means that team members try to ensure that everyone benefits from their actions. All changes, challenges or suggestions are pursued for the good of the team, not for self-aggrandisement at the expense of the team. Team members should understand that they win only if all team members win. Losing and causing others to lose (for example, not getting rewarded, not accomplishing the objective, not feeling good about oneself) is not acceptable.

One of the potential problems with a win–win philosophy in a team, however, is that it can lead to the emergence of a phenomenon called 'groupthink' (Janis 1972). *Groupthink* occurs when the cohesiveness and inertia developed in a group or team drive out good decision making or problem solving. The preservation of the team takes precedence over accurate decisions or high-quality task accomplishment. Not enough conflict occurs.

Irv Janis (1972) conducted research in which he chronicled several high-performing teams that in one instance performed in a stellar fashion but performed disastrously in another instance. What was the difference? Why did the same team do so well in one circumstance and so poorly in another? The answer is groupthink. Groupthink typically occurs when the following attributes arise in teams:

- *Illusion of invulnerability.* Members feel assured that the team's past success will continue. ('Because of our track record, we cannot fail.')
- *Shared stereotypes.* Members dismiss disconfirming information by discrediting its source. ('Engineers just don't understand these things.')
- *Rationalisation.* Members rationalise away threats to an emerging consensus. ('The reason they don't agree with us is ...')
- *Illusion of morality.* Members believe that they, as moral individuals, are not likely to make wrong decisions. ('We would never knowingly make a bad decision.')
- *Self-censorship.* Members keep silent about misgivings and try to minimise doubts. ('I must be wrong if others think this way.')
- *Direct pressure.* Sanctions are imposed on members who explore deviant viewpoints. ('If you don't agree, why don't you leave the team?')
- *Mind-guarding.* Members protect the team from being exposed to disturbing ideas. ('Don't listen to them. They're way-off base.')
- *Illusion of unanimity.* Members conclude that the team has reached a consensus because the most vocal members are in agreement. ('If Dave, Melissa and Pam agree, there must be a consensus.')

The problem with groupthink is that it leads teams to commit more errors than normal. As an example, consider the following commonly observed scenario. Not wanting to make a serious judgment error, a leader convenes a meeting of his team. In the process of discussing an issue, the leader expresses a preference for one option. Other team members, wanting to appear supportive, present arguments justifying the decision. One or two members tentatively suggest alternatives, but they are strongly overruled by the majority. The decision is carried out with even greater conviction than normal because everyone is in agreement, but the consequences are disastrous. How did this happen? While the leader brought the team together to avoid making a bad decision, the presence of groupthink actually made a bad decision more likely. Without the social support provided by the team, the leader may have been more cautious in implementing a personally preferred but uncertain decision.

To avoid groupthink, each team should make certain that the following characteristics are present:

- *Critical evaluators.* At least one team member should be assigned the role of critic or evaluator of the team's decisions.

- *Open discussion.* The team leader should not express an opinion at the outset of the team meeting but should encourage open discussion of differing perspectives by team members.
- *Subgroups.* Multiple subgroups in the team may be formed to develop independent proposals.
- *Outside experts.* Invite outside experts to listen to the rationale for the team's decision and critique it.
- *Devil's advocate.* Assign at least one team member to play devil's advocate during the discussion if it seems that too much homogeneity exists in the team's discussion.
- *Second-chance meetings.* Sleep on the team's decision and revisit it afresh the next day. The expression of team members' second thoughts should be encouraged.

Effective leader behaviours

All team members must be involved in avoiding groupthink and in reinforcing the vision of the team, but the leader has a special responsibility to ensure that the two things occur. In addition to these two key factors, other leader behaviours that are most effective in this stage are:

- identify a common threat or enemy to increase feelings of cohesion
- generate commitment among team members
- turn students into teachers
- be an effective mediator
- provide individual and team recognition
- foster win–win thinking.

When survival is at stake, internal conflict and individual differences in a team are set aside in favour of the needs of the larger team. For example, R. G. Menzies galvanised Australians when he informed them that Great Britain had declared war on Germany and that as a result Australia was also at war. In the United States, Franklin D. Roosevelt was accused of allowing the bombing of Pearl Harbor in 1941 in order to mobilise the American people to stop debating among themselves and enter the war.

Effective team leaders can overcome resistance and conflict by identifying factors outside the organisation that threaten its welfare. If threats originating inside the organisation are pointed out, conflict and rigidity are reinforced. Members tend to blame one another, find scapegoats and try to reduce their discomfort (Cameron, Kim & Whetten 1987). On the other hand, when threats are external, cooperation increases and individuals mobilise to overcome resistance. Managing the storming stage, therefore, involves raising the consciousness of people inside the organisation to the presence of external threats.

Another way to manage storming behaviour is to enhance the commitment of team members by turning students into teachers. To increase the commitment of newly hired engineers, one division within Dow Corning Corporation requires its engineers to spend time recruiting new employees on university campuses. Every other year, engineers are sent to campuses to attract the best graduating students for positions at Dow Corning. However, recruiting occurs not just in engineering schools but in business schools, law schools, and maths and chemistry departments. Those trained to recruit students stay at home and the engineers are assigned to the task.

Why would Dow Corning do such a thing? Why leave the experts at home and send engineers to do a job for which they have not been trained? One reason for this strategy is that it helps to increase the commitment of the newly hired engineers. To recruit students, the engineers must publicly praise Dow Corning, restate the corporate vision and point out its merits. After making such public pronouncements, individuals become committed to what they have espoused. In other words, new engineers are traditionally treated as students in the company, being recipients of the corporate vision and values. By becoming teachers of others outside the company, however, engineers convert themselves. Since a core competence of Dow Corning is chemical engineering, the intent is to increase the commitment of this crucial group by turning them into teachers of others.

Figure 9.2 illustrates a similar system used by Xerox Corporation to institutionalise a major change in the company's culture. Resistance to change, conflict and differences in perspective were all

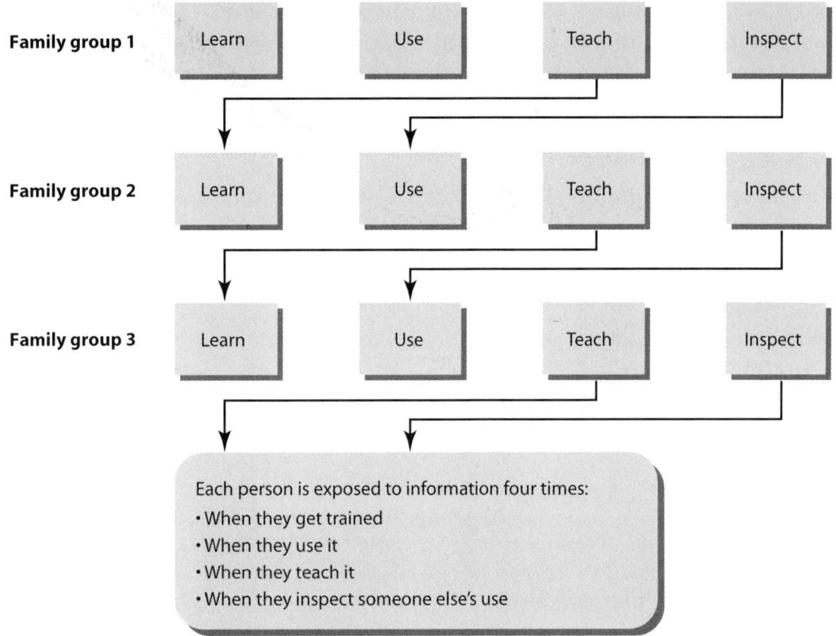

FIGURE 9.2 The Xerox dissemination process

effectively managed by forming teams across the company, labelled 'family groups'. Each family group engaged in four activities to generate commitment and implement the change:

- *Learn.* Principles were taught and discussed.
- *Apply.* Action plans were formed and an improvement agenda was implemented.
- *Teach.* The principles and successful experiences were taught to others.
- *Inspect.* The performance and action plans of others were measured and monitored.

Teams were exposed to the desired information four times: when they learned it, when they applied it, when they taught it and when they inspected it. More importantly, team members' commitment to both the information and the team was ensured because of their involvement in each of these four steps.

Throughout this and other stages of team development, the team leader also needs to ensure that rewards and recognition are provided to the team, not just to individuals. A common mistake in teams is for individuals to be singled out for praise or awards rather than the team. 'Employee of the month', 'top salesperson' and 'high scorer' are all awards that can destroy team cohesion and perpetuate team member competition and divisiveness. Team members are motivated to work for individual recognition rather than the good of the team. Consequently, team leaders need to ensure that the team itself is recognised and rewarded for achievement, not just individuals. This might be done, for example, with team-recognition ceremonies, T-shirts or trophies for all team members, or team pictures published in the newspaper. The point is to build commitment and unity in the team in order to counteract the tendency of the team to become fragmented during the storming stage. By so doing, the team is made ready to enter the third stage of development: conforming.

The conforming stage

Team member questions, interpersonal relationships and task issues

Once a team has resolved the issues of the forming and storming stages, those issues are replaced by others that lead the team into a new stage of development. When a team begins to function as a unit and team members become comfortable in their setting, they experience pressure to conform to the emerging norms. For example, recall a time when you became a member of an ongoing team. Chances are that you almost immediately felt pressure to conform. That is because team members become inclined to behave consistently with other team members' expectations. The more team members interact with one another, the more they develop common behaviours and perspectives. This conformity may affect the amount of work done by the team, styles of communicating, approaches to problem solving and even dress.

The major focus of team members shifts from overcoming uncertainty and increasing clarity in the forming and storming stages to becoming unified and identifying roles that can be played by each member in the conforming stage. Typical questions in team members' minds during this stage include:

- What are the norms and expectations?
- How much should I conform?
- What role can I perform?
- Will I be supported?
- Where are we headed?
- How much should I invest and commit?

During the conforming stage, team members become contented with team membership and begin to value the team's goals more than their own personal goals. Individual needs begin to be met through the team's accomplishments. The team, rather than the leader or a single person, takes responsibility for solving problems, confronting and correcting mistakes, and ensuring success. Agreement and willingness to go along characterise the climate of the team, since members are willing to put aside personal biases for the good of the group. Individuals experience feelings of loyalty to the team, and the interpersonal relationships that most characterise team members include:

- cooperativeness
- ignoring disagreements
- conformity to standards and expectations
- obedience to the leader's directions
- heightened interpersonal attraction
- commitment to a team vision.

In this stage, however, tension arises between forces pushing the team towards cohesion and forces pushing the team towards differentiation. At the same time as strong bonds of team unity are being formed, individuals try to differentiate themselves from one another and adopt unique roles in the team. They seek to become complementary to one another rather than duplicative. The presence of differentiated roles in the team may actually foster team cohesion and unity. But the potential tension gives rise to the following task issues that must be addressed in this stage of development:

- maintaining unity and cohesion
- differentiating and clarifying roles
- determining levels of personal investment
- clarifying the future
- deciding on levels of commitment to the team's future.

In identifying which roles to perform in order to contribute the most to the success of the team, members have two main categories of roles from which to choose: task-facilitating roles and relationship-building roles. It is difficult for team members to emphasise both types of roles equally, and most people tend to contribute in one area more than the other. That is, some team members tend to be more task-focused, whereas others tend to be more relationship-focused. Task-facilitating roles are those that help the team accomplish its outcome objectives—for example, to produce a product or service, solve a problem or generate a new idea. Among the common task-facilitating roles are:

- *Direction giving*—identifying ways to proceed or alternatives to pursue and clarifying goals and objectives.
- *Information seeking*—asking questions, analysing knowledge gaps, requesting opinions, beliefs and perspectives.
- *Information giving*—providing data, offering facts and judgments, and highlighting conclusions.
- *Elaborating*—building on the ideas expressed by others; providing examples and illustrations.
- *Coordinating*—pulling ideas together and helping others examine each other's suggestions and comments; helping members work together.
- *Monitoring*—developing measures of success and helping to maintain accountability for results.
- *Process analysing*—analysing processes and procedures used by the team in order to improve efficiency and timeliness.
- *Reality testing*—exploring whether ideas presented are practical or workable.
- *Enforcing*—keeping the team focused on the task at hand and driving out all side issues.
- *Summarising*—combining ideas and summing up points made in the team; helping members understand the conclusions that have been reached.

Relationship-building roles are those that emphasise the interpersonal aspects of the team. They focus on assisting team members to feel good about one another, to enjoy the team's work and to maintain a tension-free climate. Among the common relationship-building roles are:

- *Supporting*—praising the ideas of others and pointing out others' contributions.
- *Harmonising*—mediating differences between others and finding a common ground in disputes and conflicting points of view.
- *Tension relieving*—using jokes and humour to reduce tension and put others at ease.
- *Confronting*—challenging unproductive or disruptive behaviours; helping to ensure proper behaviour in the team.
- *Energising*—motivating others towards greater effort and accomplishment; exuding enthusiasm.
- *Developing*—assisting others to learn, grow and achieve; orienting and coaching members of the team.
- *Facilitating*—helping to build solidarity among team members and smoothing interactions.
- *Processing*—reflecting group feelings and helping to smooth out the team's functioning.

Without both types of roles being played, a team does not advance past the second stage of development. Some members must ensure that the team accomplishes its tasks, while others must ensure that members remain bonded together interpersonally. These are usually not the same individuals. Each team member begins to play different roles, with some roles becoming more dominant than others. The key is to have a balance between task-oriented roles and relationship-building roles displayed in the team. The downfall of many teams is that they become unidimensional (for example, they emphasise task accomplishment exclusively) and do not give equal attention to both types of roles.

The next time you are in a team setting, try keeping track of the behaviours displayed by each team member. See if you can identify the 'task masters' and the 'relationship builders'. Which roles do you most naturally play yourself? The advantage of being able to recognise different roles is that team development cannot progress unless many of these roles are present and effectively performed. Knowing which roles are needed and being able to play multiple roles helps to perpetuate team effectiveness.

Of course, each role can also have a down-side if performed ineffectively or in inappropriate circumstances. For example, elaborating may be disruptive if the team is trying to reach a quick decision; tension relieving may be annoying if the team is trying to be serious; enforcing may create resistance when the team is already experiencing high levels of pressure; facilitating may mask real differences of opinion and tension between team members. However, even more likely is the presence of other unproductive roles that team members play. These roles inhibit the team or its members from achieving what they could have achieved, and they destroy morale and cohesion. They are called *blocking roles*. A few of them are pointed out here because, as you analyse the teams to which you belong, you may recognise these roles being performed and be able to confront them. Among common blocking roles are:

- *Overanalysing*—splitting hairs and examining every detail excessively.
- *Overgeneralising*—blowing something out of proportion and drawing unfounded conclusions.
- *Fault finding*—being unwilling to see the merits of others' ideas or behaviours.
- *Premature decision making*—making decisions before goals are stated, information is shared, alternatives are discussed or problems are defined.
- *Presenting opinions as facts*—failing to examine the legitimacy of proposals and labelling personal opinions as truth.
- *Rejecting*—rejecting ideas based on the person who stated them rather than on their merits.
- *Pulling rank*—using status, expertise or title to get ideas accepted rather than discussing and examining their value.
- *Dominating*—excessive talking, interrupting and/or cutting others off.
- *Stalling*—not allowing the group to reach a decision or finalise a task by side-tracking the discussion, being unwilling to agree or repeating old arguments.

Effective leader behaviours

Each of these blocking roles has the potential to inhibit a team from efficiently and successfully accomplishing its task, by crushing morale, destroying consensus, creating conflict and encouraging ill-informed decisions. Team leaders must work with team members to avoid blocking roles while at the same time ensuring that task-facilitating and relationship-building roles are adequately represented on the team. Maintaining a balance of role emphasis and ensuring that roles being performed are not disruptive or destructive is an important responsibility of the team leader. In addition, the following leader behaviours are required in this stage of the team's development:

- facilitate role differentiation among team members
- show support to team members
- provide feedback
- articulate a vision of the future for the team
- help to generate commitment to the vision.

Helping a team to develop cohesion relies at least partly on providing feedback to team members. This means giving them information about how they are doing as individuals, as well as how the team is doing as a unit. In providing feedback to others, team leaders and team members should use the following guidelines:

- *Focus feedback on behaviour rather than people.* Individuals can control and change their behaviour. They cannot change their personalities or physical characteristics.
- *Focus feedback on observations rather than inferences, and on descriptions rather than judgments.* Facts and objective evidence are more trustworthy and acceptable than opinions and conjectures.
- *Focus feedback on behaviour related to a specific situation, preferably to the 'here-and-now', rather than on abstract or past behaviour.* It will merely frustrate people if they cannot pinpoint a specific incident or behaviour to which you are referring. Similarly, people cannot change something that has already happened and is 'water under the bridge'.
- *Focus feedback on sharing ideas and information rather than giving advice.* Explore alternatives together. Unless requested, avoid giving directive feedback and demands; instead, help recipients identify changes and improvements themselves.
- *Focus feedback on the amount of information that the person receiving it can use, rather than on the amount you might like to give.* Information overload causes people to stop listening. Not enough information leads to frustration and misunderstanding.
- *Focus feedback on the value it may have to the receiver, not on the emotional release it provides for you.* Feedback should be for the good of the recipient, not merely for you to let off steam.

- *Focus feedback on time and place so that personal data can be shared at appropriate times.* The more specific feedback is, or the more it can be anchored in a specific context, the more helpful it can be.

In addition to providing feedback to help team members become a cohesive unit, the most important thing a team leader can do is to articulate a vision of the future for the team. Peter Senge (1991) asserted that every effective, high-performing team and organisation has a clear, inspirational vision. The difficult part is not for any individual to develop a vision but for individual members to go through the processes of enrolment and commitment to a shared vision.

In one of the best studies published on high-performing teams, Katzenbach and Smith (1993a: 50) stated:

> *The best teams invest a tremendous amount of time and effort exploring, shaping, and agreeing on a [vision] that belongs to them collectively and individually. ... With enough time and sincere attention, one or more broad, meaningful aspirations invariably arise that motivate teams to provide a fundamental reason for their extra effort.*

All teams have specific goals and objectives to achieve, but a vision is something different. It helps to illuminate the core values and principles that will guide the team in the future. It gives a sense of direction. It provides a glimpse of possibilities, not just probabilities. It evokes deeper meaning and deeper commitment than task or goal statements. It is intended to help team members think differently about themselves and their future. It serves as a glue to bind the team together. It does all this by way of at least three characteristics:

1. *Left-brained and right-brained.* An effective vision statement contains objective targets, goals and action plans (left-brain components) as well as metaphors, colourful language and emotion (right-brain components). It captures the head (left-brain) as well as the heart and imagination (right-brain) of team members. The most motivating vision statements (for example, Martin Luther King's speech 'I Have a Dream', Winston Churchill's 'Never Give Up' and 'Blood, Toil, Tears and Sweat' speeches, Paul Keating's 'Banana Republic' reference) contain both left-brained elements (specific objectives) and right-brained elements (emotional imagery).
2. *Interesting.* Many years ago, Murray Davis (1971) pointed out that what people judge to be interesting and energising has little to do with truth or legitimacy. Rather, what is interesting is information that contradicts weakly held assumptions and challenges the status quo. If a vision is consistent with what is already believed or known (for example, 'We will accomplish our work'), people tend to dismiss it as common sense. They do not remember it and it does not motivate them. If a vision is contradictory to strongly held assumptions, or if it blatantly challenges the core values of team members (for example, 'Every team member will become rich'), it is labelled ridiculous, silly or blasphemous. A vision that helps to create a new way to view the future, on the other hand, that challenges the current state of things, is viewed as interesting and energising. For example, 'We will land on the moon in ten years' was just contradictory enough, just outlandish enough, just enough of a stretch to be interesting. It not only made people think, it provided something new to think about.
3. *Passion and principles.* Effective visions are grounded in core values that team members believe in, and about which they feel passionate. Even if a team's task objective were to vanish, for example, members might still desire to affiliate with the team because of the core principles associated with its vision. Therefore, the principles in the vision must be personal. A vision focused on 'increasing productivity' is less magnetic than a vision based on 'personal growth'. 'Achieving profitability' is less magnetic than 'building a better world'. Furthermore, such principles are best phrased using superlatives. Notice the difference in how you feel about the following comparisons: 'exceptional performance' versus 'good performance'; 'passionately involved' versus 'committed'; 'explosive growth' versus 'substantial growth'; 'awesome products' versus 'useful products'. Visions based on the former phrases engender more enthusiasm and passion than those based on the latter phrases.

Once a vision of the future has been articulated, it is important for leaders to ensure that team members commit to it. Although a vision may exist, if team members do not accept the vision as their own, it is worthless and may, in fact, tear apart rather than solidify a team. Team leaders can foster commitment to their vision and hence to team cohesion in three principal ways: public commitment, consensus through participation and frequent communication.

Public commitment

When people state their commitments in public, they are motivated to behave consistently with those public declarations (Salancik 1977). The internal need for congruence enhances the probability that public statements will be followed by consistent actions. For example, during the Second World War good cuts of meat were in short supply. Lewin (1951) found a significant difference between the commitment level of shoppers who promised aloud to buy more plentiful but less desirable cuts of meat (for example, liver, kidneys, brains) compared with those who promised to do so in private. In another study, students in a college class were required to set goals for how much they would read and what kinds of marks they would get in exams. Only half the students were allowed to state these goals publicly to the rest of the class. By mid-semester, the students who had stated their goals publicly averaged an 86 per cent improvement, compared with a 14 per cent improvement for the other students. These findings suggest that effective team leaders should provide opportunities for team members to represent the team in public so that they can reiterate and represent the vision themselves. This fosters commitment.

Consensus through participation

Having the opportunity to be involved in formulating plans to accomplish the vision also engenders commitment to it. Effective team leaders, therefore, foster commitment by involving team members in reaching consensus about various aspects of the vision.

One way to enhance the participation and agreement of all team members is to use a technique such as the *nominal group technique* (NGT). This technique ensures that everyone on the team is heard and that consensus is reached. The technique consists of six steps:

1. Team members are presented with a challenge or issue—for example, how to accomplish the vision.
2. Individual team members silently and independently write down their ideas. This is the nominal (non-interacting) phase.
3. Each team member (one at a time, in round-robin fashion) presents an idea to the group. No discussion of the ideas occurs. All ideas are recorded for the team to see.
4. After all individuals have presented their ideas, a discussion of the merits of the ideas occurs. Ideas are merged, eliminated, expanded and modified.
5. Team members privately vote on their preferred ideas. This might be done by having each team member select the top two or three ideas, dividing ten points among the alternatives, rank-ordering the alternatives, or other decision-making alternatives.
6. A revised list of the best ideas is presented to team members for discussion. If a consensus emerges, the team is finished. If not, the procedure returns to the second step and continues through more rounds until the best ideas are identified and agreement is reached.

The point is to help all team members participate and express opinions while still building team consensus.

Frequent communication

Commitment is enhanced if the vision is communicated frequently. If leaders stop communicating the vision or if they change themes in their interactions with the team, members tend to think that the vision is not important. Unless leaders continually and consistently articulate, rehearse and reinforce the vision, it loses its power and the team's commitment erodes. Leaders must also serve as models of the principles in the vision. No question should exist in the minds of those who interact with team leaders as to what the vision is. A leader who exemplifies this principle is Jan Carlzon, former CEO of Scandinavian Airlines (SAS), a highly thought-of team leader and executive. Carlzon (1987: 88, 92) stated:

Good leaders spend more time communicating than anything else. From my first day at SAS I've made communicating, particularly with our employees, a top priority. In fact, during the first year I spent exactly half my working hours out in the field talking to SAS people. The word going around was that any time three employees gathered, Jan Carlzon would probably show up and begin talking with them. ... When we began reorganising SAS, our critics scoffed at our efforts as mere promotional gimmicks. They claimed we had become too marketing oriented, but in fact we hadn't increased our marketing budget one cent. Rather, we were spending our money more effectively on messages that were easily understood.

In summary, skilful managers in the conforming stage of development help to build cohesion and unity, help team members to engage in productive but differentiated roles and help to create commitment to a motivating vision. When this is achieved, the team can then move on to the next stage of development.

The performing stage

Team member questions, interpersonal relationships and task issues

When a team reaches the performing stage of development, it is able to function as a highly effective and efficient unit. Because it has worked through the issues embedded in each of the previous stages of development, the team is able to work at a high level of performance. The team has overcome issues of lack of trust, uncertainty, unclear expectations, non-participativeness, dependence and self-centredness typical of the first, or forming, stage of development. It has overcome tendencies towards counter-dependence, conflict, polarisation and disharmony typical of the storming stage. It has clarified a vision, team member roles, the degree of personal commitment to the team and the leader's direction typical of the conforming stage. It now has the potential to develop the attributes of a high-performing team.

A list of attributes of high-performance teams is provided in Box 9.1, based on the research of Katzenbach and Smith (1993a, 1993b) and Petrock (1991). These attributes are those that produce

BOX 9.1 Some attributes of high-performing teams

PRODUCE PERFORMANCE OUTCOMES
High-performing teams *do* things. They *produce* something; they do not just discuss it. Without accomplishment, teams dissolve and become ineffective over time.

SPECIFIC, SHARED PURPOSE AND VISION
The more specific the purpose, the more commitment, trust and coordination can occur. Individuals do not work for themselves; they work for one another in pursuit of the shared purpose. The shared purpose can also be the same as a motivating vision of what the team should achieve.

MUTUAL, INTERNAL ACCOUNTABILITY
The sense of internal accountability is far greater than any accountability imposed by a boss or outsider. Self-evaluation and accountability characterise a high-performing team.

BLURRING OF FORMAL DISTINCTIONS
Team members do whatever is needed to contribute to the task, regardless of previous positions or titles. Team membership and team roles are more predominant than outside status.

COORDINATED, SHARED WORK ROLES
Individuals always work in coordination with others on the team. The desired output is a single group product, not a set of individual products.

INEFFICIENCY LEADING TO EFFICIENCY
Because teams allow for lots of participation and sharing, mutual influence about purpose and blurring of roles, they are initially inefficient. Later, because they come to know one another so well and can anticipate each other's moves, they become much more efficient than single people working alone.

Sources: J. R. Katzenbach and D. K. Smith, 'The discipline of teams', *Harvard Business Review*, 71(2), 1993, pp. 111–20; and F. Petrock, 'Team dynamics: A workshop for effective team building', presentation at the University of Michigan Management of Managers Program, 1991.

the benefits mentioned earlier in the chapter (for example, productivity improvements, quality achievements and cost reductions). By and large, teams produce dramatic successes in organisations only if they reach the performing stage of development.

The team in the performing stage is not, of course, free of issues. Team members still face a set of questions that tend to predominate in this stage:

- How can we continuously improve?
- How can we foster innovativeness and creativity?
- How can we build on our core competence?
- What further improvements can be made to our processes?
- How can we maintain a high level of energy and contribution to the team?

Team members' questions in this stage change from being static to being dynamic. They shift in focus from building the team and accomplishing objectives to fostering change and improvement. Continuous improvement replaces accomplishment as a key objective. Up to this point, the team has been trying to manage and resolve issues that lead to three key results in the team: accomplishing tasks or objectives, coordinating and integrating team members' roles, and assuring the personal well-being of all team members. A process was necessary to ensure the collective responsibility and involvement of all team members in the team's tasks and goals. By successfully managing the issues that dominate the first three stages of development, however, the team does not need to continue to focus exclusively on making itself a competent unit. Instead, it can now turn to achieving a level of performance above the ordinary. This leads interpersonal relationships to be characterised by:

- high mutual trust
- unconditional commitment to the team
- multifaceted relationships among team members
- mutual training and development
- entrepreneurship
- self-sufficiency.

Team members in this stage are confident that they have an important role to play in the team and that they are competent enough to perform it and contribute to the team's success. They are self-sufficient. On the other hand, they are also closely connected to other members of the team in terms of their commitment and personal concern for them. This does not mean that all high-performing team members are close personal friends. Rather, they exhibit a sense of mutual responsibility and concern for one another as they carry out their work. Their relationships are not limited merely to accomplishing a task together but also extend to ensuring that each team member is learning, developing and improving. Coaching and assisting one another is common.

In addition to multifaceted relationships and unconditional, two-way commitment to one another, team members also take responsibility individually for continuously improving the team and its processes. Unlike the storming stage, however, this improvement is not based on counter-dependence or on the need to display individuality. Rather, it is based on a genuine commitment to seeing the team perform better than it is currently performing. Therefore, experimentation, trial-and-error learning, freewheeling discussions of new possibilities and personal responsibility by everyone for upgrading performance is typical. The major task issues in this stage include:

- capitalising on core competence
- fostering continuous improvement
- anticipating the needs of stakeholders and responding in advance of requests
- enhancing speed and timeliness
- encouraging creative problem solving.

In this stage of development, the team becomes more aware of its core competence (see Prahalad & Hammel 1990). Over time, teams develop particular areas of expertise or proficiency. Team members' styles, individual skills and patterns of interaction, and the team's vision, help to produce certain areas of specialty that the team develops as its own. It might be playing defence for a basketball team, solving complicated problems on a group accounting assignment in class, or producing new ideas in a research and development team.

Team core competence refers not only to an aggregation of individual team members' skills but also includes knowledge, styles, communication patterns and ways of behaving that come to characterise a team. They are unique features that are difficult to duplicate and give the team a special strength. By knowing its own core competence, a team can capitalise on these strengths and focus its energies on activities in which it can excel.

In addition to clarifying core competence, the performing stage is also characterised by a focus on the pursuit of both continuous improvement and innovation. *Continuous improvement* refers to small, incremental changes that team members initiate. It can be represented by a hundred 1 per cent changes. *Innovation*, on the other hand, represents large, visible, discontinuous changes. Innovations are breakthroughs that can be represented by a single 100 per cent change. Traditionally, people in Eastern cultures have been thought to be continuous-improvement oriented, whereas people in Western cultures have been thought to be innovation-oriented:

> *We find that the West has been stronger on the innovation side and Japan stronger on the Kaizen [the Japanese word for continuous improvement] side. These differences in emphasis are also reflected in the different social and cultural heritages, such as the Western educational system's stress on individual initiative and creativity as against the Japanese educational system's emphasis on harmony and collectivism. (Imai 1986: 32. Reproduced with permission of The McGraw-Hill Companies.)*

Table 9.2 summarises the differences between a continuous-improvement approach and an innovation approach to team development. Contrary to Imai's claim, high-performing teams in this stage of development emphasise both types of improvement: small and continuous as well as large and dramatic. A discussion of how to foster creative breakthroughs and innovation is contained in Chapter 4. The implementation of a continuous-improvement approach, on the other hand, depends mostly on team members' orientation or the culture developed in the team. To illustrate this point, we share with you a conversation one of the authors had with a Japanese executive who indicated that, as far as he was concerned, the United States had 'lost the war'. When asked what he meant, the executive said it was the economic war that had been lost. The United States was still ahead in economic productivity

TABLE 9.2 Characteristics of innovation and continuous improvement (Kaizen)

ELEMENT	KAIZEN	INNOVATION
Effect	Long-term, long-lasting, undramatic	Short-term, dramatic
Procedure	Small steps	Large steps
Time-frame	Continuous, incremental	Intermittent, non-incremental
Change	Gradual, constant, predictable	Abrupt, unpredictable
Involvement	Everyone	A few champions
Approach	Collectivism, group effort, systems approach	Rugged individualism, individual ideas and effort
Mode	Maintenance and improvement	Scrap and rebuild
Spark	Conventional know-how and state of the art	Technological breakthroughs, new inventions, new theories
Requirements	Little up-front investment, large effort to maintain it	Large up-front investment, little effort to maintain it
Orientation	People	Technology
Evaluation	Process, efforts, systems	Profits, outcomes
Training	Generalist	Specialist
Goal	Adaptability	Creativity
Information	Widely shared, open communication	Not widely shared, proprietary

Source: M. Imai, *Kaizen: The Key to Japan's Competitive Success* (New York: McGraw-Hill, 1986). Reproduced with permission of The McGraw-Hill Companies.

and size, he said, but Japan was catching up fast. And when Japan overtook the United States, the war would be over. He was challenged to justify this conclusion and his rationale is noteworthy. He said:

> *When you in the West receive a new product or technology, you assume that is the best it will ever be. Durability is at the highest level, no defects are present, and no repairs are needed. On the other hand, when we in the East receive a new product or technology, we assume that is the worst it will ever be, because we haven't had a chance to improve it yet. From now on it gets better.*

This statement illustrates the culture that is needed in high-performing teams to develop a continuous-improvement approach coupled with an innovation approach to team performance. Addressing this challenge, as well as others noted as follows, is one of the main tasks of the team leader.

Effective leader behaviours

Teams functioning in the performing stage do not require strong, directive leadership in the traditional sense. They become more and more like a self-managing team, able to manage their own processes, training, rewards and membership. On the other hand, an important role for a leader does exist that relates more to the cultural or cognitive aspects of the team than to its task performance or relationship building. Prescriptions for effective leader behaviours in this stage include:

- foster innovation and continuous improvement simultaneously
- advance the quality culture of the team
- provide regular, ongoing feedback on team performance
- play sponsor and orchestrator roles for team members
- help the team to avoid reverting to earlier stages.

Having moved through the first three stages of development, teams frequently move into a stage characterised by innovation and continuous improvement. The main task of the leader during this high-performance stage of development is to help team members expand their focus from merely accomplishing their work and maintaining good interpersonal relationships to seeking to upgrade and elevate the team's performance.

One way to do that is to help the team's approach to quality become more advanced. Box 9.2 summarises three different phases of quality culture in which teams and organisations can operate. Few reach the third, most advanced level of quality culture, but, if they are to be most successful, teams should do so. High-performing teams strive for this third phase. The three phases and how they relate to this stage of team development are briefly explained (Cameron 1992).

BOX 9.2 Phases of quality culture development

ERROR DETECTION

Regarding products
- Inspect and detect errors
- Reduce waste, cost of failure and rework
- Correct mistakes
- Focus on the *output*

Regarding customers
- Avoid doing things that could annoy customers
- Respond to complaints quickly and accurately
- Reduce dissatisfaction
- Focus on customers' *needs* and requirements

ERROR PREVENTION

Regarding products
- Prevent errors
- Expect zero defects
- Design and produce it right the first time
- Focus on *processes* and root causes

Regarding customers
- Satisfy and exceed customers' expectations
- Help customers to avoid future problems
- Obtain customers' preferences in advance and follow up
- Focus on customers' *preferences*

CREATIVE QUALITY AND CONTINUOUS IMPROVEMENT

Regarding products
- Improve and escalate on current standards of performance
- Create new alternatives
- Concentrate on things-gone-right
- Focus on improving *suppliers* and *customers* as well as *processes*

Regarding customers
- Surprise and delight customers
- Engage in extra-mile restitution
- Anticipate customers' expectations
- *Create customers' preferences*

Error detection

Most teams and organisations operate in the first phase of quality culture: error detection. In producing a product or service, they try to avoid mistakes and reduce waste (for example, minimise rework, repair, scrap). They produce an outcome and then check to make certain that the work has been done correctly. In other words, they 'inspect-in' quality. In their relationships with customers, they try to avoid annoying or dissatisfying them by responding to complaints in a timely and accurate manner. They focus on what customers need or require and, after the product or service has been delivered, they ask customers how satisfied they are with it. By and large, this is a reactive or defensive approach to quality. It assures that the team meets basic requirements, but errors are identified after the fact.

Error prevention

In the second phase of quality—error prevention—the team shifts its emphasis towards avoiding mistakes by producing a product or service right the first time. Errors are prevented by focusing on how the task is accomplished (that is, the process) and by holding all team members, not just inspectors or checkers, accountable for quality. Finding out why mistakes occurred is more important than finding individual errors. In relationships with customers, the emphasis moves from mere customer requirements to preferences and expectations. The team strives to exceed expectations and to help customers reach a high level of satisfaction with the product or service, not just non-annoyance. One way this happens is by training customers to know what to expect before a product or service is delivered, and to share their preferences and expectations before the product or service is produced. That way, customisation can occur.

Innovation with continuous improvement

The third phase of quality—innovation coupled with continuous improvement—focuses on improvement rather than preventing errors. The team's standard changes from hitting a target to improving performance. Its objective is to achieve levels of quality in the product or service that are not only unexpected but unrequested. Problems are solved for customers and benefits provided that they do not expect anyone to deliver. New standards are actually created for customers because the team surprises and delights them. It is this third phase of quality culture that characterises the world's best companies and its highest-performing teams. The role of the leader in the performing stage of development is to help the team achieve this way of approaching the quality of its work.

Team members are encouraged to:

- strive continuously to improve their own and the team's work processes
- deliver extra-mile restitution to customers when mistakes do occur
- anticipate requests and respond in advance of receiving them
- help solve problems for customers, and for other team members, that they do not expect anyone to solve for them.

Research is clear that the highest levels of commitment and loyalty from customers and team members result from such an approach (Cameron 1992).

Figure 9.3 illustrates these three phases of quality in the form of a graph. The vertical axis on the graph represents satisfaction, ranging from high satisfaction ('love it') on the top to low satisfaction ('hate it') on the bottom. The horizontal axis represents performance and ranges from low performance ('awful') on the left to high performance ('great') on the right. To understand the figure, consider the experience of purchasing a car. If we were to ask you what features are of most interest to you when buying a new car, you might list fuel consumption, having four doors, roominess, a responsive engine and good handling. If the dealer showed you a car that exactly met your expectations, we would position you at the intersection of the two axes at point A; that is, in the middle of the satisfaction axis and in the middle of the performance axis. However, if you discovered that the car performed much better than you expected—say, fuel consumption was better and the engine

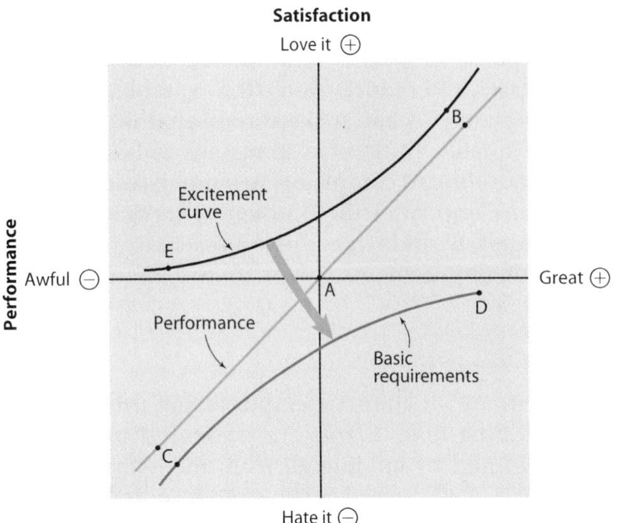

FIGURE 9.3 Basic performance and excitement factors

was more powerful—satisfaction would increase to point B in the figure. If, however, the fuel consumption was terrible and the car rattled and leaked—that is, it performed lower than expected—satisfaction would decrease to point C on the graph. Connecting points B, A and C results in a performance curve. These are the features that the team tries to improve continuously, to drive satisfaction up by finding ways to push performance to the right side of the axis. These features are identifiable and easily recognised.

If, when you got into your new car, however, you discovered that, although the features you requested were satisfactory, the car had no carpet and no shock absorbers, you would no doubt be dissatisfied. But we could ask you for a comprehensive list of features you are looking for in a car and you would probably never list carpet and shock absorbers. That is because you assume that these items are basic features of all new cars. If such basic features are missing, people are dissatisfied. However, no one cares much about whether the shock absorbers are painted red or black, cost $15 or $35, or whether there are one or two on each tyre, so long as the ride is smooth. This illustrates the fact that a basic curve also exists in the figure. If certain basic features are absent, people are upset (point C). But the presence of additional basic features does not lead to a rise in satisfaction (point D). Having more of a basic feature simply does not add value.

Now assume that when you got into the car the seat automatically adjusted itself to fit your height and leg length, the mirrors automatically adjusted themselves, and the seat became heated almost immediately on cold winter days. You were given something that you did not expect—a delightful surprise. Satisfaction would go up to point B. On the other hand, if no such features were present in the car, satisfaction would not decrease because these features were not expected in the first place (point E). Connecting points B and E creates an excitement curve that shows what happens when innovation and breakthroughs occur. Loyalty and commitment are products of receiving features on the excitement curve.

The point of this figure is simple. Every team must perform its basic work competently and accomplish its basic, required tasks (the basic curve). It should also continuously improve its task accomplishment and strive to generate higher performance and satisfaction with its products or services (the performance curve). However, it can become a high-performance team by producing innovations, delightful surprises, and breakthroughs in task accomplishment and service delivery (the excitement curve). An important task of the team leader in this stage of development is to help the team accomplish all three kinds of activities.

As in previous stages of development, another important task of the team leader is to provide constant feedback to the team on its performance and make certain that adequate information is circulated among team members. Praise and pats on the back cannot be too frequent, but they should not be targeted primarily at individuals. The team as a unit needs to be recognised and kept informed. A common prescription of high-performing team leaders, in fact, is 'communicate, communicate, communicate'. Most team leaders suggest that this is the key to their success (see Katzenbach & Smith 1993b). Communicating praise and feedback should occur at regularly scheduled intervals (consistency) and should be frequent.

We have pointed out thus far that teams progress through four different stages of development. The fourth, or final, stage is the one achieved by high-performing teams and the one towards which all teams should aspire. The issues that must be resolved along the way, however, and the changes that team leaders must make to push the team along to the next stage of development are significant. Leaders of effective teams do not become so by accident.

They are able to diagnose which stage a team is in and identify the main issues facing the team. They can therefore answer team members' questions, facilitate effective interpersonal relationships in the team, resolve task issues and display effective leadership behaviours.

Virtual teams

Virtual teams have become increasingly popular in organisations in recent years. A *virtual team* is a group of people who never meet face to face, or meet only very rarely, and interact on work-related tasks via communications technologies such as email, the internet or some type of computer-supported cooperative work (CSCW) software (for example, Lotus Notes or First Class). Lipnack and Stamps (1999) define a virtual team as those 'with a common purpose that use technology to cross time zones, distance and the boundaries of organisations'. Are virtual teams really teams? Katzenbach and Smith (1993a) define a team as a specific type of group, particularly relevant for organisations, that consists of 'a small number of people with complementary skills who are committed to a common purpose, performance goals and approach for which they hold themselves mutually accountable'. Earlier in the chapter a team was defined as two or more individuals who work together towards a common objective. According to either of these definitions, even if the members never meet face to face they can still be considered a team.

Are virtual teams likely to be as important and widespread as face-to-face teams? Virtual teams are being used in many industries, from international finance and investing to manufacturing (Attaran & Attaran 2003; Barreta 2000; Chase 1999; Kimble 2011; Knouse 2007). Many factors are driving modern organisations from traditional face-to-face teams towards virtual teams and workplaces (adapted from Bergiel, Bergiel & Balsmeier 2008; Cascio 2000; Harris 2003; Townsend, DeMarie & Hendrickson 1998: 18):

- In today's competitive global economy, organisations capable of rapidly creating virtual teams of talented people can respond quickly to changing business environments, thus providing an important form of competitive advantage.
- Advances in mobility and communications technology allow people to change locations and jobs, or to contribute to teams working anywhere in the world via the internet and teleconferencing.
- Organisations can save a great deal of money by reducing the overheads associated with maintaining offices.
- The increasing use of flat, or horizontal, organisational structures, in response to intensifying competitive environments, results in the decentralisation of decision making and in structurally and geographically distributed human resources. Recent advances in both information and transportation technologies allow organisations to take advantage of the benefits of teams of people working together even when separated by time zones and geography.
- Environments are emerging that require interorganisational cooperation. Strategic partnering, downsizing and/or outsourcing have increased in popularity as organisations have eliminated their non-core processes to concentrate on their core, value-added processes. The resulting interrelationships require high levels of interorganisational cooperation and teamwork, sometimes among traditionally competitive firms. Virtual teams provide the links between these cooperating organisations.
- There is a continued shift from production to service/knowledge work environments. 'This trend was made clear in 1993, when *Fortune* merged its traditionally separate Top 500 rankings of industrial and service companies into a single list, implicitly admitting it could not distinguish between the two groups' (Dawson 2000: 8–9). Service activities are often less structured and less defined than manufacturing processes and require the cooperation of team members in dynamic work situations that evolve according to customer requirements. 'Virtual teams enable this organisational flexibility because they integrate the effectiveness of traditional teamwork

with the power of advanced communication and information technologies, allowing them to accommodate increased dynamism in both team membership and task structure' (Townsend, DeMarie & Hendrickson 1998: 19–20).

The increasing globalisation of trade and corporate activity has radically altered the competitive environment of many organisations. Technological advances have enabled many firms to compete in the global marketplace. 'Multinational operations require high levels of cooperation and collaboration across broad geographical boundaries. Turning these networks of collaborators into fully connected virtual teams has the potential to increase both the efficiency and quality of communications in this challenging environment' (Townsend, DeMarie & Hendrickson 1998: 20). Solomon (1998: 13) suggests that virtual teams 'help global companies, preventing them from needing to reinvent the game with each new project. They enable organisations to realise 24-hour productivity via the latest in technology. They allow cross-pollination between cultures as well as business units, adding depth of knowledge and experience to the endeavor.' Cascio (2000) wrote:

> *John Brown Engineers & Constructors Ltd, a member of the engineering division of Trafalgar House, the world's third largest engineering and construction organisation, with 21,000 employees around the globe, was able to access local pharmaceutical engineering talent at a project site in India. Using virtual work arrangements, the firm was able to traverse national boundaries, enabling it to work with and present a local face to its global clients. This enhanced its global competitiveness.*

Virtual teams are real and they are here to stay. Depending on your particular organisational circumstances and industry, of course, virtual teams may be more or less important and widespread than face-to-face teams in the long run. It should be obvious, however, that regardless of your particular industry and circumstances virtual teams are likely to be a part of your future.

Will virtual teams proceed through the same phases of development as face-to-face teams? Are virtual teams likely to be subject to the same dynamics (based on homogeneity, heterogeneity, size, roles, norms and contingency factors) as face-to-face teams? There is no evidence to suggest that virtual teams are any different from face-to-face teams in terms of their developmental and operational dynamics (Roebuck & Britt 2002). More research will inevitably surface over the next few years that will further examine these issues. It seems clear, however, that the technology involved in virtual team communication will have a significant impact on team dynamics.

For example, research done by Harvard Business School professor Kathleen Valley, who was interviewed in a *Harvard Business Review* article (Maruca 2000), suggests that, compared with face-to-face interactions, less information is shared via email and it is much more likely to be exaggerated or altered in some way. People lie more readily when they interact through email. Online negotiations seem to be more rigid and formal. When the entire exchange is documented on a computer screen, negotiators are less flexible and less willing to 'give and take'. With email, people are more likely to be rude and to escalate conflict, so negotiations are considerably more likely to degenerate into an unpleasant exchange. Ultimately, the whole email dynamic makes it much more difficult to reach an agreement. Professor Valley's research showed that more than 50 per cent of email negotiations ended in an impasse, while in face-to-face negotiations the most frequent outcome was a mutually beneficial agreement and only 19 per cent ended in an impasse.

Duarte and Snyder (1999) seem to agree with Professor Valley. They suggest that, while email is useful for generating ideas and plans and for collecting data, it is less useful for solving problems without answers, or for negotiating technical or interpersonal conflicts. They believe that it is subject to misuse for messages requiring high symbolism, and has low social presence and information richness. The work by Duarte and Snyder also suggests that virtual teams reliant on telecommunications may have difficulty when the issues under consideration are highly emotional or ambiguous, or when the team is newly formed or short-lived.

The technologically induced differences in the communication processes of virtual teams have the potential to create a radically different work environment for the virtual team participant (Townsend, DeMarie & Hendrickson 1998). These changes affect the way that team members conduct their work and how they communicate and express themselves. According to Townsend, DeMarie and Hendrickson (p. 28), therefore:

> *Virtual team members must learn new ways to express themselves and to understand others in an environment with a diminished sense of presence.*
>
> *Virtual team members will be required to have superior team participation skills. Because team membership will be somewhat fluid, effective teams will require members who can quickly assimilate into the team.*
>
> *Virtual team members will have to become proficient with a variety of computer-based technologies.*
>
> *In many organisations, virtual team membership will cross national boundaries, and a variety of cultural backgrounds will be represented on the team. This will complicate communications and work interactions, and will require additional team member development in the areas of communication and cultural diversity.*

Because of the technologically induced difficulties common among virtual team members, leaders must do everything to facilitate communication and trust among them (Chase 1999; Fan et al. 2011; Kimble 2011; Montoya-Weiss, Massey & Song 2001; Morris, Marshall & Rainer 2002). Team leaders must continually consider issues such as who needs to talk to whom, about what, through what medium, how often, and who else needs to be informed. This will go a long way towards ensuring that rapport is not broken, that trust does not break down due to unintentional misunderstandings, and that everybody has a clear idea of the team process and objectives (Chase 1999). Here are some communication tips for virtual teams (adapted from Chase 1999):

- *Getting acquainted.* If you have the finances and the time, let team members meet face to face for an initial strategic team-development planning session. Otherwise, try to get members acquainted virtually through chat rooms or video-conferencing. It is important to allow people to get to know something about other team members outside their work roles. This helps to make people, and their relationships, more alive and multi-dimensional.
- *Communication skills.* When you are communicating only by telephone and email, it is easy for misunderstandings to occur. Without the non-verbal cues of eye contact, vocal tone and body language, an email message can sometimes sound much harsher than was intended. A refresher session on basic email and voice-mail etiquette can help reduce miscommunication.
- *Conflict management.* As part of the normal process of team development, conflict of one sort or another will eventually become an issue. In a virtual environment, because team members do not have to deal with one another face to face, they may tend to sweep a problem under the carpet until it becomes so large it can no longer be ignored. Make a special effort to catch conflicts early and deal with them fairly.
- *Technology tools.* Although there are many simple technology tools for facilitating communication, feedback and timely workflow, people will be hesitant to use tools with which they are unfamiliar. Take the time to ensure that everyone is well trained on whatever type of technology the virtual team is using.

Keeping in mind these technologically induced differences in the communication processes of virtual teams, the keys to virtual team success must finally be considered. Are they any different from the keys to success for more traditional face-to-face teams? In many ways, a virtual team is just like any other team. Members do not have to be best friends, but there must be reasonable rapport, respect and confidence in one another's competency (Chase 1999). Team success depends on effective communication and knowledge sharing among members (Townsend, DeMarie & Hendrickson 1998). This is even more important in a virtual environment because there is no day-to-day, face-to-face interaction. With virtual teams the conditions under which effective communication, rapport, respect and confidence can develop must be intentionally created (Chase 1999).

Finally, consider the following excerpts from Townsend, DeMarie and Hendrickson (1998: 24, 26):

> *The traditional factors identified with high team performance come into play in the virtual environment as well. Effective communication skills, clarity of goals, and a performance orientation will continue to be critical*

attributes for virtual team members. To fully exploit the advantages of the new environment, virtual team members will require basic teamwork training and development, and will also need training to enhance team workers' facility with the new information and communication technologies. Effective training in such virtual function skills as how to best use telecommunicative capability and collaborative systems may ultimately result in teams that function as naturally in a technologically empowered, virtual environment as teams currently do around a conference table.

Training and developing virtual team members is in many ways no different from training and developing good team members in general; developing skills in communication, goal setting, planning, and task proficiency are all as important for the virtual team as for the traditional team. What is different about the virtual team is the amount of technical training that is required to empower the team member to function in the virtual environment.

Recent research (Knouse 2007) suggests that virtual team performance is enhanced when virtual teams are more task-focused than interpersonally focused. Ensuring that virtual teams have the skills mix, the task training and the task leadership they need will help to provide task cohesion, rather than interpersonal cohesion, and will lead to better task-oriented outcomes.

Working with, and in, teams, whether face-to-face or virtual, is not natural, easy or effortless. It requires discipline and focus. It needs special effort to ensure that communication works and that rapport, trust and a shared understanding develop over time among team members. Team members must be aware of their roles and group norms to ensure that the positive consequences of these factors win out over their potential downsides. Team leaders must attend to the balance between homogeneous and heterogeneous memberships to ensure the proper levels of cohesion and diversity. Teams must have clearly established and measurable objectives, and regular performance feedback. With these issues in mind, organisational leaders can help to ensure that their enterprises reap the benefits, and minimise the problems, of working with teams.

Conducting effective team meetings

In addition to building a team and enhancing its development, the commonplace tasks associated with planning and holding effective team meetings are also crucial for team leaders. Unfortunately, because these activities seem so mundane and unglamorous, planning and conducting a simple meeting is often the undoing of what would otherwise be highly effective teams. If a team's meetings are ineffective, the team will never capitalise on its potential. This chapter concludes with a discussion of how to manage and conduct effective team meetings.

Not only is it important to be a skilful planner and conductor of meetings to foster team effectiveness, but management effectiveness in general depends on this skill. A study by the 3M company showed that meetings occupy a large percentage of the typical manager's workweek. The study found that the number of meetings had doubled over the previous decade and their cost had nearly tripled. About 15 per cent of the personnel budget of most companies is spent on meetings. In addition, the amount of time spent in meetings is positively associated with the manager's hierarchical level: the more senior the manager, the more meetings they attend (3M 1994).

The four Ps of effective meetings

Effective meeting managers and team leaders keep in mind four steps in preparing for and conducting meetings: purpose, participants, planning and process.

Purpose

'Purpose' refers to the reason for which a meeting is held. When information can be conveyed by a memo or a phone call, when people are not prepared, when key people cannot attend, when the cost of a meeting is higher than the potential pay-off, and when there is no advantage to holding a meeting even if scheduled, no meeting should be called. Four main guidelines for determining when to hold meetings are:

- *Information sharing.* When all the needed information is not held by any single person, when ideas will be stimulated by getting people together, and when it is not clear what information is needed or available, a meeting should be called.
- *Commitment building.* Because individuals become committed to a course of action when they are involved in its planning and implementation, meetings should be called to foster such participation.
- *Information disseminating.* When many people must receive the same message in the same way, or when updated information must be disseminated quickly, sharing information in a meeting is more efficient than in multiple one-on-one sessions. Furthermore, in a meeting, individuals have a chance to provide feedback and to discuss the information being shared.
- *Problem solving and decision making.* Groups outperform the best individuals in accomplishing complex tasks and making high-quality decisions where various pieces of information are needed. Therefore, meetings should be called to solve complex problems and make difficult decisions.

Participants

Participants are the individuals invited to attend a meeting. In conducting an effective meeting, it is important to determine the size and composition of the group to be invited. Meetings can fail because too many or too few participants attend or because the wrong mix of people is present. If a meeting is too large, for example, discussion may be superficial and diffuse, and few people will be able to participate. If a meeting is too small, not enough information will be shared and problems will not be adequately solved. Therefore, certain guidelines should be followed when deciding who to invite to a meeting. Table 9.3 identifies the types of meetings and recommended number of participants in each type. The appropriate size depends primarily on the purpose of the meeting.

TABLE 9.3 Recommended meeting size

PURPOSE OF THE MEETING	RECOMMENDED NUMBER OF PARTICIPANTS
Decision making and problem solving	5
Problem identification or brainstorming	10
Interactive seminars and training sessions	15
Informational meetings	30
Formal presentations	Unlimited

'Meeting composition' refers to three main dimensions: homogeneity–heterogeneity, competition–cooperation and task–process. A homogeneous group is composed of members with similar backgrounds, personalities, knowledge and/or values. In general, homogeneous groups produce less conflict and disagreement, but their outcomes may be mundane and unimaginative. Heterogeneous groups, on the other hand, produce more differences among individuals, which lead to criticisms and disputes but potentially more novel and complex solutions to problems as well.

With regard to the competition–cooperation dimension, the result of research on its effect in problem-solving meetings is compelling. Studies have consistently shown that groups whose members are working towards a common goal and who adopt a cooperative stance towards one another perform more effectively, and produce higher levels of member satisfaction, than groups whose members are striving to fulfil individual needs or are pursuing competing goals. Cooperative groups demonstrate more effective interpersonal communication, more complete division of labour, higher levels of involvement and better task performance.

On the task–process dimension, meetings are more effective if they have participants who generate a balance of both. Task-oriented participants are 'all business'. They have little tolerance for joking or for discussions of feelings and friendships. The task is accomplished efficiently, but satisfaction may be low. Process-oriented participants, on the other hand, emphasise *esprit de corps* and participation. They are sensitive to participants' feelings and satisfaction. Accomplishment may be sacrificed in favour of members' enjoyment.

Planning

'Planning' refers to preparation for the meeting agenda. Often, the justification for a meeting is clear (for example, we need to determine how to get fuel to troops at the front) and the appropriate individuals are in attendance, but the meeting still seems to flounder, wandering aimlessly and unable to produce a final decision. Such meetings often begin with the leader saying, 'We have a problem that I think we all need to sit down and discuss.' The leader's erroneous assumption is that, because a problem exists and all participants understand it, the meeting will be successful. Unfortunately, participants may come to the meeting unprepared, may be unaware of critical information, may be unclear about their specific role, may be confused about how the decision will be made and may be unmotivated to achieve the objective. Conversely, the meeting planner may try to cram too much into a single meeting, schedule too many presentations, handle too many documents or cover too much business. Tropman (1985) proposed the following rules and guidelines for planning meetings effectively:

1. *The rule of halves.* All agenda items for an upcoming meeting must be in the hands of the person scheduling the agenda no later than one-half of the time interval between the last meeting and the upcoming meeting. Thus, if meetings are held weekly, agenda items for the next meeting should be gathered by the person constructing the agenda by the halfway mark in the week. This allows time to sort and cluster items, handle some items one-on-one outside the meeting, and produce and distribute an agenda in advance of the meeting.
2. *The rule of three-fourths.* Packets of information, including minutes from the past meeting and an agenda, should be sent to meeting participants at the three-quarter point between meetings. For example, if a weekly meeting is scheduled, the packet should be sent out approximately two days before the next meeting.
3. *The agenda rule.* Agendas for meetings should be written with action verbs and/or sentence summaries, not with single words. Rather than saying 'Minutes', for example, use: 'Approve minutes.' Rather than 'Production report', use: 'Determine production schedule.' This provides clarity and impetus for what the meeting should accomplish.
4. *The rule of sixths.* Approximately two-thirds of the meeting should be focused on current agenda items. The remaining third should be subdivided into two sixths. One of those sixths of meeting time should be spent on past agenda items and follow-up. The remaining sixth of the meeting should be spent on future agenda items (that is, planning or preparation). Continuity is thus maintained and agenda items do not slip through the cracks.
5. *The rule of thirds.* All meetings are divided into three parts: (1) a start-up period in which less difficult items are covered, latecomers arrive and people get on-board; (2) a heavy work period in which the most difficult items are considered; and (3) a decompression period in which the meeting begins to wind down. Instructional items should be handled in the first period, items for decision should be handled in the second period, and items for discussion should be handled in the third period.
6. *The reports rule.* Reports circulated to meeting participants should always contain executive summaries and/or options memos. An *executive summary* highlights key points and conclusions of the report. An *options memo* summarises alternatives to be discussed and decided upon. This eliminates the need to sift through many pages to find relevant information and to spend meeting time shuffling through the report.
7. *The agenda bell rule.* This rule is a more specific statement of several previous rules about when certain types of agenda items should be covered. Agenda items should be considered in order of ascending controversiality; attention should then be turned to discussion and decompression items. Figure 9.4 shows a typical agenda bell for a meeting.
8. *The agenda integrity rule.* All items on the agenda should be discussed, and items not on the agenda should not be discussed. This rule helps to ensure that participants do not sidetrack the meeting with items that are tangential, for which no one has prepared or for which insufficient information is available.

9. *The temporal integrity rule.* This rule is simple: start on time and end on time. Follow a time schedule in the meeting itself. This ensures that all agenda items are given adequate time, that latecomers are not rewarded by having the meeting wait for them and that people can count on finishing at a certain point.
10. *The minutes rule.* Minutes of meetings should have three characteristics: agenda relevance (information recorded is related to an agenda item), content relevance (minutes should be written in a form that follows the agenda so that it is easy to find pertinent material) and decision focus (minutes should reflect decisions, conclusions and actions agreed upon, rather than the processes by which the decisions were reached).

These ten rules of meeting preparation help to ensure that, when individuals arrive for a meeting and the meeting begins, a structure and plan will be in place to make the meeting productive and efficient.

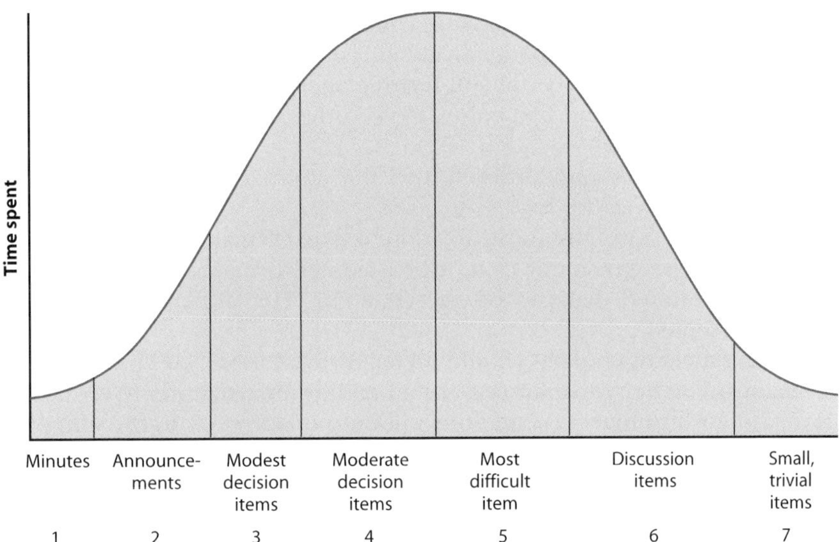

FIGURE 9.4 The agenda bell

Process

The fourth P in meeting preparation is process. 'Process' refers to the actual conduct of meetings and the methods used to ensure that meetings are effective. Huber (1980) outlined seven steps for conducting a meeting.

1. *Review.* At the beginning of the meeting, review the agenda and the tasks to be accomplished as well as progress made to date in previous meetings. This helps participants know precisely what is expected and encourages them to stay focused on the task at hand. It also makes controlling time in the meeting much easier.
2. *Introductions.* Meeting participants should be introduced to each other and helped to feel comfortable together, especially if controversial issues are to be considered. The critical nature of this step is illustrated by an incident in which faculty representatives on the board of a major athletics conference met several times with representatives of a university administration to discuss the eligibility of a star athlete. Both sides were suspicious of the others' motives, and several previous meetings had failed to resolve the dispute. Then, before the next meeting, the participants were invited to attend a social gathering featuring an outdoor barbecue. During this event, participants got to know one another on a more personal basis, and in the meeting the next day a breakthrough was achieved to resolve the dispute. Several participants credited the social gathering with playing a major role in breaking down barriers between the two factions.

3. *Ground rules.* It should be made clear what kind and amount of participation is expected, what variations from the agenda will be tolerated, what the time-frame will be, and so on. Establishing a structure for the meeting at the outset helps keep it on track.

   The manner in which decisions are to be made should also be determined. For example, will everyone in the meeting have to agree in order to reach a conclusion? Will a majority rule? Will everyone have a vote? Several options exist for making decisions and reaching a conclusion, and it should be determined which will be used in the meeting. Among the options are:
   - *Majority rule.* Each meeting participant votes on alternatives, and the alternative with a majority of the votes wins.
   - *Highest total.* When more than two alternatives are being considered, none might get a majority of the votes. The alternative with the highest number of votes is therefore adopted.
   - *Straw vote.* A non-binding vote is taken to get a sense of the feelings of participants towards various alternatives. This may happen several times before a decision is reached, in order to eliminate non-supported alternatives from consideration.
   - *Weighted rating.* Meeting participants divide 100 points between the alternatives, so that the strength of their support can be tallied. If three alternatives exist, for example, a participant can give 90 points to one and five points to two others. The alternative with the most points wins.
   - *Ranking.* Alternatives are rank-ordered and the alternative receiving the highest average ranking is adopted.
   - *Consensus.* All participants must agree to adopt one particular alternative.
   - *In principle.* Although agreement cannot be obtained on all specific details, certain general principles are identified that can be agreed upon. The principles, rather than the entire proposal, are accepted.
4. *Reports.* Early in the meeting, reports should be heard from those who have been pre-assigned to make presentations. This helps to maintain accountability for assignments, reduces the presenters' apprehension and ensures that presentations will not be tacked on to the end of the meeting. It also allows the presenter to concentrate on other agenda items after the presentation—something that will probably not occur before the presenter has made his or her report.
5. *Displays.* To maintain the interest of participants, use various media to present information. Handouts, overhead transparencies, slides, flip charts, videos and whiteboard diagrams are all helpful in maintaining interest and increasing the efficiency with which information is presented. In general, participants should be able to use at least two of their senses during a meeting (for example, seeing and hearing).
6. *Participation.* Participation in a meeting should be equitable among participants, which does not mean that everyone must make exactly the same number of comments. Those with more information will participate more, as will those with vested interests in the topic. However, it is important to control the over-participator or the person who dominates the discussion, as well as to encourage those who may have something to contribute but are not inclined to share it. Equity should also be maintained among different points of view, so that representatives of one side of an argument do not dominate the discussion. Ways to promote discussion among participants include the following:
   - Ask open-ended questions rather than questions that can be answered with a 'yes' or a 'no'.
   - Ask questions using the language of the participants rather than jargon or obscure terminology.
   - Encourage participants to share personal experiences that relate to the topic being considered.
   - Use examples from your own experience to clarify points.
   - Make eye contact with those you are talking to and summarise their points when they finish their statements.
   - Ask group members for their reactions to points made by other meeting participants.
   - When appropriate, involve others in answering a question asked of you.
   - Make certain that, as the leader, you facilitate the discussion rather than dominate it.

7. *Summarise.* Close the meeting by summarising the decisions reached, tasks assigned, progress accomplished, key points discussed and what was learned in the meeting. Review action items that will be reported on at the next meeting. Help meeting participants feel a sense of accomplishment at what has been achieved during the meeting. This may also be a good time to anticipate the next meeting by identifying when minutes and the next meeting's agenda will be distributed and what preparation will be required.

Handling difficult team members

Despite the best efforts of a team leader or the conductor of a meeting, some participants will not always behave in ways that help the team meeting to be successful. Some people may be more interested in self-aggrandisement than in team success. They may criticise other team members or try to dominate the meeting agenda. Sometimes, they do not pull their weight and do not take responsibility. This tendency towards 'social loafing' is especially common. It has been observed that when three people pull together on a rope, they achieve only two and a half times the power of an individual acting alone. In fact, the larger the group, the less effort is put forth by any single individual member (Latane, Williams & Harkins 1979). Four factors account for this:

- *Equity of effort.* 'No one else is working to their potential, so why should I?'
- *Loss of accountability.* 'I am an insignificant part of this large group, so no one will notice or care what I do.'
- *Sharing of rewards.* 'Why should I work harder than others when we will all get the same reward?'
- *Coordination loss.* 'The more people involved, the more I have to wait for others, talk to others and coordinate my work with others, so I am less efficient.'

How do effective team leaders and meeting managers cope with disruptive, difficult or loafing team members? When students are writing a report together during a semester, how do they ensure that all team members will take equal responsibility for the report? How do business task forces ensure that when team members enter a meeting they will not use it as a forum to impress the boss? If everyone on the team gets the same reward, what is to keep some members from getting a reward they did not earn? Table 9.4 identifies 11 disruptive behaviours that are common in meetings, along with suggested responses. The two generic types of difficult team members—dominating and reluctant participants—are discussed in more detail next.

TABLE 9.4 Suggestions for handling difficult team members

TYPE	BEHAVIOUR	SUGGESTED RESPONSE
Hostile	'It'll never work.' 'That's a typical engineering viewpoint.'	'How do others here feel about this?' 'You may be right, but let's review the facts and evidence.' 'It seems we have a different perspective on the details, but we agree on the principles.'
Know-it-all	'I have worked on this project more than anyone else in the room …' 'I have a PhD in Economics, and …'	'Let's review the facts.' (Avoid theory or speculation.) 'Another noted authority on this subject has said …'
Loudmouth	Constantly blurts out ideas or questions. Tries to dominate the meeting.	*Interrupt:* 'Can you summarise your main point/question for us?' 'I appreciate your comments, but we should also hear from others.' 'Interesting point. Help us understand how it relates to our subject.'
Interrupter	Starts talking before others have finished.	'Wait a minute, Jim. Let's allow Jane to finish what she was saying.'

continues

TABLE 9.4 *Continued*

TYPE	BEHAVIOUR	SUGGESTED RESPONSE
Interpreter	'What John is really trying to say is . . .' 'John would respond to the question by saying . . .'	'Let John speak for himself. Go ahead, John, finish what you were saying.' 'John, how would you respond?' 'John, do you think Jim correctly understood what you said?'
Gossiper	'Isn't there a regulation that you can't . . .' 'I thought I heard the financial controller say . . .'	'Can anyone here verify this?' (Assuming no response.) 'Let's not take up the time of the group until we can verify the accuracy of this information.'
Whisperer	Irritating side conversation going on between two people.	Walk up close to the guilty parties and make eye contact. Stop talking and establish dead silence. Politely ask the whisperers to wait until the meeting is over to finish their conversation.
Silent distractor	Reads newspapers, rolls their eyes, shakes heads, fidgets.	Ask questions to determine their level of interest, support and expertise. Try to build an alliance by drawing them into the discussion. If that doesn't work, discuss your concerns with them during a break.
Busy-busy	Ducks in and out of the meeting repeatedly, taking messages, dealing with crises.	Preventive measures include scheduling the presentation away from the office, checking with common offenders before the meeting to ask if the planned time is okay for minimum interruptions.
Latecomer	Comes late and interrupts the meeting.	Announce an odd time (8:46) for the meeting to emphasise the need for promptness. Make it inconvenient for latecomers to find a seat and stop talking until they do. Establish a 'latecomers' kitty' for refreshments.
Early leaver	Announces, with regrets, that they must leave for another important activity.	Before starting, announce the ending time and ask if anyone has a scheduling conflict.

Source: Adapted from D. A. Peoples, *Presentations Plus* (New York: Wiley, 1988).

Dominating participants

Some interactions can be dominated by people who contribute a disproportionate amount to the conversation. It is very difficult to tell someone that they talk too much. It is a bit easier to assert yourself and to say: 'There is something I would like to say about that when you've finished.' This alerts the person that you too would like to contribute and that you are willing to listen to what they have to say until they have finished. Many people find it difficult, if not impossible, to bring themselves to interrupt someone in this type of situation. We are often afraid of interrupting because we think it is rude. However, it is the other person who is being rude by dominating the conversation. At the same time, you may be contributing to that rudeness by not really listening to what the person is saying. It is better to assert yourself by acting as a competent supportive communicator.

Reluctant participants

Some people are reluctant to speak in certain circumstances. It is sometimes difficult to relate to these reluctant communicators and to get to know them or what is on their minds. This can be a great loss. Sandy Plunkett (1992: 77) had this to say about the problem:

> *Have you ever been to a meeting, listened closely to what was being discussed and thought you had a good idea but did not speak out for fear of ridicule, or worse? Many business managers would admit that this is an all too common barrier to generating good ideas and making sound decisions. With statistics showing the typical business manager spends between 35% and 70% of his or her day in meetings, that means a lot of potentially good ideas have gone unheard and a lot of productivity wasted.*

Reflect, for a moment, on a recent meeting in which there were one or more reluctant participants. How was this handled? Did the reluctant participants eventually contribute to the meeting or was their potential contribution overlooked? How might this have affected the outcome of the meeting? What might have been done to help these reluctant participants to contribute?

Sometimes these people need to be asked directly to contribute to the meeting or conversation (for example, 'What do you think?'). Another strategy is to find ways of making these people more comfortable in contributing, by breaking down into smaller groups, by using structured techniques such as brainstorming, or by somehow making it possible for people to contribute anonymously. Another technique is just sitting in silence while directing your attention their way. This may bring them out. Silence is an interesting part of a meeting or a group conversation. Typically, we think that four or five seconds of silence is a very long time. If you intentionally let it build for 10 or 15 seconds, quite frequently even the quietest of people will speak up to fill the void. Unfortunately, some of the more outspoken of the group might jump in first and will need to be quieted.

The general rule of thumb is to avoid embarrassing or intimidating meeting participants, regardless of their disruptive behaviour. The way difficult team members are handled not only sets the tone for the kind of discussion that will ensue in the meeting but also helps to determine what kind of feelings will characterise team members. It sets the tone and the culture of the team. Instead of attacking and being defensive, therefore, use supportive communication, collaborative conflict management and techniques of empowerment, as discussed in Chapters 5, 7 and 8, in these situations. Discuss concerns in an open, direct, problem-oriented and supportive manner.

Summary

Because almost everyone is a member of at least one team at work or in non-work activities, because teams are becoming increasingly prevalent in the workplace, and because teams have been shown to be powerful tools in improving the performance of individuals and organisations, it is important to become proficient in leading and participating in teams. But merely putting people together with an assigned task does not make them into a team. Because teams develop through different stages—each with its unique challenges and issues—it takes skill to help a team to become a high-performing unit. Different behaviours are required in each of the four stages of team development. The chapter described the different attributes of each of these stages and provided guidelines for managing the issues that characterise them. It also addressed some of the pros and cons of virtual teams and discussed ways to make them more effective.

Behavioural guidelines

1. Determine the stage in which your team is operating by identifying the major questions, interpersonal relationships and task issues that characterise the team. Use Table 9.1 (on page 461) for a comprehensive listing. Adopt the appropriate leadership behaviours that correspond to that stage of development.
2. Become familiar with the attributes of high-performing teams and make certain that these attributes characterise your team. In particular, ensure that goals are clear, known by everyone and can be achieved in small steps; that standards of excellence, rather than mere acceptability, are applied; that feedback on results is provided; that team members can use all their skills and knowledge and are continuously trained; that adequate equipment and facilities, performance measures and rules and penalties are available; that performance-based rewards and praise and recognition are prevalent; that team members have autonomy; that plans and tactics to beat a specific competitor are in place; and that team members have a sense of commitment to the team.
3. When a team is in the forming stage of development:
   - Make certain that all team members are introduced to one another.
   - Answer team members' questions, even those they do not ask aloud.

   - Work to establish a foundation of trust and openness between yourself and team members, and among team members themselves.
   - Model the behaviours that you expect from all team members, such as honesty, openness and friendliness.
   - Clarify the goals, procedures and expectations of the team.
4. When a team is in the storming stage of development:
   - Adopt a mediator role when conflict is encountered.
   - Encourage a win–win philosophy in the team: if a single team member wins, everyone wins.
   - Re-emphasise the vision for the team and its core principles in order to maintain a strong team bond.
   - Avoid groupthink by encouraging open discussion, having at least one team member critically evaluate the team's decisions, forming subgroups in the team, formally designating a devil's advocate in the team, having important decisions reviewed by an outside expert and holding second-chance meetings to review the team's decisions.
   - Encourage the team to assess, analyse and improve its processes by identifying the sequence of steps used to accomplish each task, mapping those steps, and identifying ways to improve the process by making it faster, more efficient and of higher quality.
   - To enhance team cohesion and commitment, identify a common enemy for the team and reinforce the vision.
   - Turn students into teachers by having team members represent team values and goals to outsiders.
   - In addition to providing recognition to individuals in the team, make certain that rewards and recognition are given to the team as a unit.
5. When a team is in the conforming stage of development:
   - Facilitate role differentiation among team members by helping them learn to perform various task-facilitating and relationship-building roles.
   - Show support to team members by complimenting and recognising them.
   - Provide feedback to individuals on the team and to the team as a unit. Feedback may be positive or negative, but make certain that it focuses on behaviour rather than people, on observations rather than inferences, on the here-and-now situation rather than the past, on sharing information rather than giving advice, on the amount of information that can be useful to the team members rather than the amount you might like to give, on the value it will have to team members rather than just letting off steam, and on a specific time and place.
   - Articulate a vision of the future for the team that is both left-brain and right-brain oriented, interesting to team members and that expresses passion regarding core principles.
   - Help generate commitment to the vision by encouraging team members to express public approval of the vision, participate in articulating and implementing it, and communicating it frequently.
6. When a team is in the performing stage of development:
   - Capitalise on its core competence by articulating clearly what that competence is and building on those strengths.
   - Foster both innovation (or dramatic breakthrough changes) and continuous improvement (or small incremental changes) among all team members.
   - Advance the quality culture of the team by moving from an error-detection approach through error-prevention to creative quality. Work towards 'excitement' in the team's products and services.
   - Provide regular, ongoing feedback on team performance.
   - Play sponsor and orchestrator roles for team members so that their ideas and changes are integrated with those of others and receive adequate support.
   - Help the team to avoid reverting to earlier stages of development by continuing to emphasise the attributes of high-performance teams.

7. When preparing for and conducting team meetings, keep in mind the four Ps of managing meetings: preparation, participants, planning and process.
8. Make certain that the purpose of meetings is clear. Is the meeting for information sharing, information dissemination, building commitment, or solving problems and making decisions?
9. Ensure that the proper number and mix of people are invited to the meeting. Make certain that the number of participants is not too large or too small, and that participants represent an appropriate variety of perspectives.
10. In preparing a meeting agenda, follow the ten rules for meeting planning: the rule of halves, the rule of three-fourths, the rule of sixths, the rule of thirds, the agenda rule, the reports rule, the agenda bell rule, the agenda integrity rule, the temporal integrity rule and the minutes rule.
11. In conducting meetings, follow the seven rules of good meeting process: review past information at the beginning of the meeting, make introductions, establish ground rules for how decisions will be made, hear reports early in the meeting, use informational displays, encourage participation among team members, and summarise commitments and action items at the end of the meeting.
12. Handle difficult team members not by embarrassing or intimidating them but by helping them to become more productive contributors to the team's effort through supportive communication, conflict management and empowerment.

Skill analysis

Case study involving building effective teams

Think about a group of which you are a part. If you are not currently in any group, think back to the most recent time you were. Write a brief history of your experience on that team in light of the four stages of team development discussed in this chapter.

1. Were the stages of development of your team roughly analogous to the stages discussed here? Can you identify specific examples of each of the four stages of development in your case?
2. How did your team perform? Explain why you think your team performed the way it did. What were the main predictive factors?
3. Why was your team needed? What was your team lacking?
4. Make some recommendations about what you should do now—or could have done, in the case of a non-current team—to capitalise on what you know about teams. If you were to become a consultant to your team, what advice would you give about how to capitalise on team building?

The cash register incident

Read the following incident description once and only once. Do not take notes. Then proceed with the remainder of the exercise.

> *A store owner had just turned off the lights in the store when a man appeared and demanded money. The owner opened a cash register. The contents of the cash register were scooped up and the man sped away. A member of the police force was notified promptly.*

This exercise is accomplished in two steps, the first by yourself and the second in a team with four or five other people.

Step 1: Assume that you observed the incident described in the paragraph above. Later, a journalist asks you questions about what you observed in order to write an article for the local newspaper. Answer the questions from the journalist by yourself. Do not talk with anyone else about your answers. Do not go back to reread the paragraph above.

Answer

Y	yes
N	no
DK	don't know

Step 2: The journalist wants to interview your entire team together. Do not go back and reread the paragraph. As a team, discuss the answers to each question and reach a consensus decision—that is, one with which everyone on the team agrees. Do not vote or engage in 'horse-trading'. The journalist wants to know what you all agree upon.

Statements about the incident

Now, as a journalist, I am interested in what happened here. Can you tell me just what occurred? I would like to see if you can confirm or deny the following statements that I have picked up by talking to other people.

Alone	*Team*	
______	______	1. Did a man appear after the owner turned off his store lights?
______	______	2. Was the robber a man?
______	______	3. Is it true that the man didn't demand money?
______	______	4. The man who opened the cash register was the owner, right?
______	______	5. Did the store owner scoop up the contents of the cash register?
______	______	6. Okay, so someone opened the cash register, right?
______	______	7. Let me get this straight: after the man who demanded the money scooped up the contents of the cash register, he ran away?
______	______	8. The contents of the cash register contained money, but do you know how much?
______	______	9. Did the robber demand money from the owner?
______	______	10. Okay, by way of summary, the incident concerns a series of events in which only three persons are involved: the owner of the store, a man who demanded money and a member of the police force?
______	______	11. Let me be sure I understand. The following events occurred: someone demanded money, the cash register was opened, its contents were scooped up and a man dashed out of the store?

When you have finished your team decision making and mock interview with the journalist, go back and examine the original incident description. Calculate how many answers you got right as an individual, then calculate how many correct answers your team achieved.

DISCUSSION QUESTIONS

1. *How many individuals did better than the team as a whole? Why?*
2. *How could your team discussion have been improved?*
3. *What roles did different members of the team play? Who was most helpful? Who was least helpful?*

Skill practice

Exercise in team building

Preparing and conducting a team meeting at Asian Electronics

Part 1

Refer back to the Asian Electronics' in-basket exercise in Chapter 1, page 33. Assume the role of Chris Pearson. Since you are new to your position, you decide to hold a meeting with some or all of your direct reports tomorrow afternoon (Tuesday). You want to be brought up to date as well as handle the items of business introduced in your email, phone messages and memos.

1. Review each of the 16 items in the Asian Electronics' in-basket exercise. This will remind you again of the tasks to be addressed.
2. Determine the purpose of the meeting, the participants (who should attend) and the plan (agenda). Also determine how long the meeting should last.
3. Generate an actual meeting agenda showing all items of business that you want to cover, using the ten rules and guidelines earlier in this chapter.
4. Determine the meeting process you will use, following the seven guidelines discussed in the skill learning section—namely, review, introductions, ground rules, reports, displays, participation and summarise.

Part 2

5. Now form a team in which each member is assigned to play one of the roles in the Health and Financial Services Group. The team should consist of:

   Chris Pearson, Director of Operations
   Janet Meow, Group 1 Manager
   Narida Idris, Group 2 Manager
   William Chen, Group 3 Manager
   Jeremy Fernandez, Group 4 Manager
   Mark McIntyre, Group 5 Manager
   John Small, Group 6 Manager
   Sivar Kumar, Group 8 Manager
   Armand Marke, Customer Service Manager
   Michelle Harrison, Office Administrator

6. Select an agenda for the meeting that was generated by one of the team members in Part 1. Work through the agenda with all the staff members. Determine a preset time limit, but do not make the meeting so short that it is superficial. Each team member should realistically play the role assigned to them, even if not much specific information exists for the role in the memos. Team members should play the roles as though they were beginning a new team meeting with a new leader. What do you recommend that Chris do about each of the items on the meeting agenda?
7. This meeting could be held as a 'fish bowl' in the class, or multiple meetings could be conducted at once with several different teams. If the meeting is a fish bowl, observers should (a) analyse the roles being played by different team members, and (b) critique the effectiveness of the meeting itself and identify ways in which the meeting could have been improved. If multiple meetings are held at once, have team members critique the meeting after it concludes.
8. At the conclusion of the meeting, analyse the roles played by each team member. Observe who played task-initiating roles, relationship-building roles and blocking roles in the team meeting.

Skill application

Suggested assignments

1. Teach someone else how to determine which stage of development a team is in and what leader behaviours are most effective in each separate stage.
2. Analyse the characteristics of a team in which you are a member. Use the Influence Dimensions in Chapter 2 to analyse the behaviours and styles of team members and determine in what ways the team's functioning could be improved. Based on the attributes of high-performance teams discussed earlier, identify what could be done to improve its performance.
3. Conduct a role analysis of a real team meeting that is trying to make a decision, solve a problem or examine an issue. Who performed what roles? Which team members were most helpful? Which team members were least helpful? Provide feedback to the team on what roles you saw being played, what roles were missing and what improvements could have made the team more effective.
4. Write out a formal vision statement for a team you are leading. Make certain that the vision possesses the attributes of effective, energising vision statements discussed in the chapter. Identify specifically what you can do to get team members to commit to that vision.
5. Use the nominal group technique in a team meeting to reach a consensus decision. Follow precisely the steps outlined in the text.
6. Select a team assigned to perform a task or produce an outcome. Do a formal process assessment and analysis by listing the activities involved in the process and constructing a process map. Then generate ways to improve the process by eliminating redundancies, cutting out time or finding ways to prevent mistakes.
7. For a team in which you participate, identify the basic services that it must deliver, the performance services that it should deliver, and the excitement services that it could deliver to its customers if it were not only to satisfy them but also to surprise and delight them.

Application plan and evaluation

The aim of this exercise is to help you apply this cluster of skills in a real-life, out-of-class setting. Now that you have become familiar with the behavioural guidelines that form the basis of effective skill performance, you will improve most by trying out those guidelines in an everyday context. Unlike a classroom activity, in which feedback is immediate and others can assist you with their evaluations, this skill application activity is one you must accomplish and evaluate on your own. There are two parts to this activity. Part 1 helps to prepare you to apply the skill. Part 2 helps you to evaluate and improve on your experience. Be sure to write down answers to each item. Do not short-circuit the process by skipping steps.

Part 1: Planning

1. Write down the two or three aspects of this skill that are most important to you. These may be areas of weakness, areas you most want to improve or areas that are most salient to a problem you face right now. Identify the specific aspects of this skill that you want to apply.
2. Now identify the setting or the situation in which you will apply this skill. Establish a plan for performance by writing down a description of the situation. Who else will be involved? When will you do it? Where will it be done?
3. Identify the specific behaviours you will engage in to apply this skill. Operationalise your skill performance.
4. What are the indicators of successful performance? How will you know that you have been effective? What will indicate that you have performed competently?

Part 2: Evaluation

5. When you have completed your implementation, record the results. What happened? How successful were you? What was the effect on others?
6. How can you improve? What modifications can you make next time? What will you do differently in a similar situation in the future?
7. Looking back on your whole skill practice and application experience, what have you learned? What has been surprising? In what ways might this experience help you in the long term?

Scoring keys and supplementary materials

Team development behaviours (p. 454)

SCORING KEY		ASSESSMENT	
Skill area	*Items*	*Pre-*	*Post*
Personal mastery experiences	1, 2	______	______
Leading the team	1–8	______	______
Being an effective team member	9–12	______	______
Diagnosing and facilitating team development	13–20	______	______
	TOTAL SCORE	☐	☐

Comparison data

Compare your scores against three standards:

1. against the maximum possible scores (120)
2. against the scores of other students in your class
3. against a norm group consisting of 500 graduate business school students. In comparison to the norm group, if you scored:

95 or above	you are in the top quartile
82 to 94	you are in the second quartile
68 to 81	you are in the third quartile
below 68	you are in the bottom quartile.

Diagnosing the need for team building (p. 455)

Comparison data (N = 1500 students)

Mean score:	54.22
Top quartile:	70 or above
Third quartile:	53–69
Second quartile:	39–52
Bottom quartile:	38 or below

References

3M Meeting Management Team 1994, *Mastering Meetings*, (New York: McGraw-Hill).
Ainsworth, S. J. 1999, 'Teamwork 2000', *Chemical and Engineering News*, 77(46), pp. 54–59.
Ancona, D. G. and D. Caldwell 1992, 'Bridging the boundary: External activity and performance in organizational teams', *Administrative Science Quarterly*, 27, pp. 459–89.
Anonymous 2002a, 'Teams score goals', *Law Institute Journal*, 1 August, p. 47.
Anonymous 2002b, 'Successful teams', *Manufacturers' Monthly*, August, p. 12.
Attaran, M. and S. Attaran 2003, 'The coming age of virtual teaming: Guidelines for managers', *International Journal of Management*, June 20(2), p. 171.
Barczak, G. and D. Wilemon 2003, 'Team member experiences in new product development: Views from the trenches', *R and D Management*, 33(5), pp. 463–79.
Barreta, S. 2000, 'Real managers make up virtual team', *Pensions and Investments*, 28(1), p. 8.
Bergiel, B., E. Bergiel and P. Balsmeier 2008, 'Nature of virtual teams: A summary of their advantages and disadvantages', *Management Research News*, 31(2), January, pp. 99–110.
Bruce, R. 2003, 'Opinion: Robert Bruce—More than the sum of its parts', *Accountancy*, 1, September, p. 1.
Brunelli, M. A. 1999, 'How Harley-Davidson uses cross-functional teams', *Purchasing*, 127(7), p. 148.
Buljac-Samardzic, M., J. van Wijngaarden, K. van Wijk and N. van Exel 2011, 'Perceptions of team workers in youth care of what makes teamwork effective', *Health & Social Care in the Community*, 19(3), pp. 307–16.
Cameron, K. S. 1992, 'Ways in which TQM is implemented', presentation at the Academy of Management Meetings, Atlanta, GA.
Cameron, K. S. and D. A. Whetten 1981, 'Perceptions of organizational effectiveness in organizational life cycles', *Administrative Science Quarterly*, 27, pp. 524–44.
Cameron, K. S. and D. A. Whetten 1984, 'Organizational life cycle approaches: Overview and applications to higher education', *Review of Higher Education*, 6, pp. 60–102.
Cameron, K. S., M. Kim and D. Whetten 1987, 'Organizational effects of decline and turbulence', *Administrative Science Quarterly*, 32, pp. 222–40.
Carlzon, J. 1987, *Moments of Truth* (Cambridge, MA: Ballinger).
Cascio, W. 2000, 'Managing a virtual workplace', *The Academy of Management Executive*, 14(3), pp. 81–90.
Cave, M. 1999, 'Team building', *Australian Financial Review*, 24 September, p. 56.
Chase, N. 1999, 'Learning to lead a virtual team', *Quality*, 38(9), p. 76.
Coch, L. and J. R. P. French 1948, 'Overcoming resistance to change', *Human Relations*, 1, pp. 512–33.
Davis, M. 1971, 'That's interesting!', *Philosophy of the Social Sciences*, 1, pp. 309–44.
Dawson, R. 2000, *Developing Knowledge-based Client Relationships: The Future of Professional Services*, Butterworth-Heinemann, Woburn, MA.
DeChurch, L. and Zaccaro, S. 2010, 'Teams won't solve this problem', *Human Factors*, 52(2), pp. 329–34.
Dewey, J. 1933, *How We Think* (Boston: Heath).
Duarte, D. L. and N. T. Snyder 1999, *Mastering Virtual Teams* (San Francisco: Jossey-Bass).
Dyer, W. G. 1987, *Team Building: Issues and Alternatives* (Reading, MA: Addison-Wesley).
Evans, P. and B. Wolf 2006, 'Collaboration rules', in *Harvard Business Review on the High-performance Organization* (Boston: Harvard Business School Publishing), pp. 89–112.
Fan, Z., W. Suo, B. Feng and Y. Liu 2011, 'Trust estimation in a virtual team: A decision support method', *Expert Systems with Applications*, 38(8), pp. 10240–51.
Freud, S. 1921, *Group Psychology and the Analysis of the Ego* (London: Hogarth Press).
Hackman, J. R. 1990, *Groups that Work (and Those that Don't)* (San Francisco: Jossey-Bass).
Hackman, J. R. 1993, 'Teams and group failure', presentation at the Interdisciplinary College on Organization Studies, University of Michigan, October.
Harris, C. 2003, 'Building innovative teams' (London: Palgrave).
Harrison, D. A., S. Mohammed, J. E. McGrath, A. T. Florey and S. W. Vanderstoep 2003, 'Time matters in team performance: Effects of member familiarity, entrainment, and task discontinuity on speed and quality', *Personnel Psychology*, 56(3), p. 633.
Higgins, B. 2003, 'Sources of sales team conflicts under study', *National Underwriter*, 107(36), p. 12.
Huber, G. P. 1980, *Managerial Decision Making* (Glenview, IL: Scott, Foresman).
Illing, D. 1999, 'Talking business is simply plain sailing', *Australian*, 15 September, p. 35.
Imai, M. 1986, *Kaizen: The Key to Japan's Competitive Success* (New York: McGraw-Hill).
James, C. 1999a, 'Young ministers out to loosen Treasury's grip', *New Zealand Herald*, 21 April.
James, C. 1999b, 'State shake-up in wake of Cave Creek', *New Zealand Herald*, 7 September.
Janis, I. 1972, *Victims of Groupthink* (Boston: Houghton Mifflin).
Janz, B. D. 1999, 'Self-directed teams in IS: Correlates for improved systems development work outcomes', *Information & Management*, 35(3), p. 171.
Katzenbach, J. R. and D. K. Smith 1993a, *The Wisdom of Teams* (Boston: Harvard Business School Press).
Katzenbach, J. R. and D. K. Smith 1993b, 'The discipline of teams', *Harvard Business Review*, 71(2), pp. 111–20.

Kimble, C. 2011, 'Building effective virtual teams: How to overcome the problems of trust and identity in virtual teams', *Global Business & Organizational Excellence*, 30(2), pp. 6–15.
Knouse, S. 2007, 'Building task cohesion to bring teams together', *Quality Progress*, 40(3), pp. 49–53.
Lander, M. C., R. L. Purvis, G. E. McCray and W. Leigh 2004, 'Trust-building mechanisms utilized in outsourced IS development projects: A case study', *Information and Management*, 41(4), pp. 509–28.
Latane, B., K. Williams and S. Harkins 1979, 'Many hands make light of the work: The causes and consequences of social loafing', *Journal of Personality and Social Psychology*, 37, pp. 822–32.
Lawler, E. E., S. A. Mohrman and G. E. Ledford 1992, *Employee Involvement and Total Quality Management* (San Francisco: Jossey-Bass).
Lewin, K. 1951, *Field Theory in Social Science* (New York: Harper).
Lewin, S. and S. Reeves 2011, 'Enacting "team" and "teamwork": Using Goffman's theory of impression management to illuminate interprofessional practice on hospital wards', *Social Science and Medicine*, 72(10), pp. 1595–602.
Lipnack, J. and J. Stamps 1999, 'Virtual teams', *Executive Excellence*, 16(5), pp. 14–15.
Lynch, M. 1995, 'Volvo puts $4m into truck plant', *Australian Financial Review*, 14 June, p. 13.
Macy, B. A., J. J. Norton, P. O. Bliese and H. Izumi 1990, 'The bottom line impact of new design and the design: North America from 1961–1990', paper presented at the International Conference on Self-Managing Work Teams, Denton, TX, September.
Maier, N. R. G. 1967, 'Assets and liabilities of group problem solving: The need for an integrative function', *Psychological Review*, 74, pp. 239–49.
Margerison, C. J. and D. J. McCann 1990, *Team Management Index* (Brisbane: Team Management Resources).
Maruca, F. R. 2000, 'The electronic negotiator', *Harvard Business Review*, 78(1), p. 16.
May, J. 2002, 'Team building for a successful business', *Grocers' Review (NZ)*, 1 July, p. 54.
Montoya-Weiss, M., A. Massey and M. Song 2001, 'Getting it together: Temporal coordination and conflict management in global virtual teams', *Academy of Management Journal*, 44(6), pp. 1251–62.
Morris, S. A., T. E. Marshall and R. K. Rainer 2002, 'Impact of user satisfaction and trust on virtual team members', *Information Resources Management*, 15(2), pp. 22–30.
Murnigham, K. 1981, 'Group decision: What strategies to use?', *Management Review*, 70, pp. 55–61.
Near, R. and D. Weckler 1990, 'Organizational and job characteristics related to self-managing teams', paper presented at the International Conference on Self-Managing Work Teams, Denton, TX, September.
New Zealand Press Association 1999, 'Thirty-three polytech staff told of job losses', 23 April.
Peters, T. 1987, *Thriving on Chaos* (New York: Knopf).
Petrock, F. 1991, 'Team dynamics: A workshop for effective team building', presentation at the University of Michigan Management of Managers Program.
Plunkett, S. 1992, *Business Review Weekly*, 17 April.
Prahalad, C. K. and G. Hammel 1990, 'The core competence of the corporation', *Harvard Business Review*, 90, pp. 79–91.
Roebuck, D. B. and A. B. Britt 2002, 'Virtual teaming has come to stay', *Southern Business Review*, 28(1), pp. 29–39.
Salancik, G. R. 1977, 'Commitment and control of organizational behavior and belief', in B. M. Staw and G. R. Salancik (eds), *New Directions in Organizational Behavior* (Chicago: St Clair Press).
Senge, P. 1991, *The Fifth Discipline* (New York: Doubleday).
Siegel, J. J. 2003, 'Rheem Team contractors work together', *Air Conditioning, Heating and Refrigeration News*, 29 September, 220(5), p. 22.
Sinclair, A. 1989, *The Tyranny of the Team*, Working Paper no. 4, Graduate School of Management, University of Melbourne, Melbourne.
Sinclair, A. 1992, 'The tyranny of a team ideology', *Organizational Studies*, 13(4), pp. 611–26.
Solomon, C. M. 1998, 'Building teams across borders', *Global Workforce*, November, pp. 13–17.
Townsend, A. M., S. M. DeMarie and A. R. Hendrickson 1998, 'Virtual teams: Technology and the workplace of the future', *The Academy of Management Executive*, 12(3), pp. 17–29.
Triolo, P., P. Hansen, Y. Kazzaz, H. Chung and S. Dobbs 2002, 'Improving patient satisfaction through multidisciplinary performance improvement team', *Journal of Nursing Administration*, 32(9), pp. 448–54.
Trist, E. 1969, 'On sociotechnical systems', in W. G. Bennis, K. D. Benne and R. Chin (eds), *The Planning of Change* (New York: Holt Rinehart and Winston), pp. 269–82.
Tropman, J. E. 1985, *Meetings: How to Make Them Work for You* (New York: Van Nostrand Reinholdt).
Tuckman, B. W. 1965, 'Developmental sequence in small groups', *Psychological Bulletin*, 63, pp. 384–99.
Unkles, J. 2002, 'Flat earth or flat management?', *Journal of Banking and Financial Services*, 1 June, p. 4.
Walton, R. E. 1965, 'Two strategies for social change and their dilemmas', *Journal of Applied Behavioral Science*, 1, pp. 167–79.
Wellins, R. S., W. C. Bynam and J. M. Wilson 1991, *Empowered Teams* (San Francisco: Jossey-Bass).
Wright, G. 1999, 'Collaborative dividends', *Building Design and Construction*, 40(11), pp. 50–52.

CHAPTER 10

MANAGING CHANGE

OBJECTIVES

- **Diagnose the need for personal and organisational change**
- **Build a repertory of change-invoking behaviours and skills**
- **Foster an environment conducive to change**
- **Plan and conduct personal and organisational change**

10

CHAPTER OUTLINE

Skill assessment

Evaluative surveys for organisational change

Organisational change behaviours

Step 1: Before you read the material in this chapter, respond to the following statements by writing a number from the rating scale below in the left-hand column (pre-assessment). Your answers should reflect your attitudes and behaviour as they are now, not as you would like them to be. Be honest. This instrument is designed to help you discover your level of competency in personal and organisational change so that you can tailor your learning to your specific needs.

Step 2: When you have completed the reading and the exercises in this chapter and, ideally, as many as you can of the skill application assignments at the end of the chapter, cover up your first set of answers. Then respond to the same statements again, this time in the right-hand column (post-assessment).

Rating scale

1 Strongly disagree
2 Disagree
3 Slightly disagree
4 Slightly agree
5 Agree
6 Strongly agree

Assessment
Pre- *Post-*
When preparing for and conducting personal change:

______ ______ 1. I am aware that organisations are made up of people in relationships with other people.
______ ______ 2. I help change the people-related and people-perpetuated systems that are involved in our work.
______ ______ 3. I focus on affecting the behaviour and mind-sets of myself and others.
______ ______ 4. I remember that personal change occurs at an intellectual as well as an emotional level.
______ ______ 5. I am sensitive to how assumptions and paradigms limit the way people view the world.
______ ______ 6. I have a clear idea that it takes time, effort and persistence to achieve and maintain significant personal and organisational growth and development.
______ ______ 7. I appreciate the fact that, before we can change, there has to be the motivation to do so.
______ ______ 8. I diagnose areas of likely resistance to change and prepare to manage our natural resistance to change.
______ ______ 9. I ensure that people practise new behaviours, receive feedback, and see the effects and consequences of these new ways of thinking and behaving.
______ ______ 10. I ensure that the three essential elements of awareness, resource and facilitating structures are available before attempting to make personal change happen.
______ ______ 11. I prepare for the fact that people naturally resist change.

When using teams for organisational change:

______ ______ 12. I am aware that teams are becoming the unit of organisation responsible for the implementation of significant changes in work practices and organisation.

______ ______ 13. I have a clear idea of what it means to combine tasks, create natural work units, establish client relationships, expand jobs vertically and open feedback channels.

When attempting to make change in an organisational setting:

______ ______ 14. I help people articulate implicit models in their minds regarding the functioning of an organisation.

______ ______ 15. I prepare for the fact that an organisation influences, and is influenced by, the world outside its four walls.

______ ______ 16. I think and plan in terms of making changes in the five main organisational subsystems: (a) production or technical, (b) boundary spanning, (c) maintenance, (d) adaptive, and (e) managerial.

______ ______ 17. I prepare different intervention strategies for deep interventions as compared with more shallow interventions.

______ ______ 18. I make certain that change agents are in frequent contact and communication with employees, see their point of view, perceive their project as critical to their own success, and understand the business and the firm.

______ ______ 19. I appreciate that change agents can play strategic, facilitating, operational and/or training roles.

______ ______ 20. I have a clear idea that the four basic steps in collective behavioural change are sensitivity, signalling, enabling and reinforcement.

Skill learning

Change in organisations

This chapter focuses on the most common activity that demonstrates leadership in organisations—leading change. Despite the often-heroic image of leaders, every person can develop the skills needed to lead change. On the other hand, effectively leading change involves a complex and difficult-to-master set of skills, so assistance is often required in order to do it successfully.

It is not news that we live in a dynamic, turbulent and chaotic world. No one can predict with any degree of certainty what the world will be like in five or ten years. Things change too fast. We know that the technology currently exists, for example, to put the equivalent of a full-size computer in a wristwatch, or to inject the equivalent of a laptop computer into the bloodstream. New computers are beginning to be etched on molecules instead of silicone wafers. The half-life of any technology you can name—from complex computers to nuclear devices to software—is less than six months.

The mapping of the human genome is probably the greatest source for change, for not only can we now change a banana into an agent to inoculate people against malaria, but new organ development and physiological regulation promise to dramatically alter population lifestyles. As at the time of writing, hundreds of animals have been patented. It took ten years to produce a generic alternative to a normal pharmaceutical drug in 1965, whereas that time was halved by 1980, halved again by 1990, and by the year 2000 generic alternatives were able to be produced for almost any pharmaceutical compound in about a week. In 1980 it took a year to assemble 12 000 DNA base pairs; by 1999 it took less than a minute, and by the end of 2000, 1000 base pairs could be assembled in less than one second. Currently, computers are being configured that can sequence every major disease in a single day. Who can predict the changes that will result?

Organisations do not change—people do

Change, therefore, seems to be inevitable in most organisations. In these days of new technology, reengineered business processes, learning organisations, and massive organisational and social change, it is important for managers to remember that organisations do not change, as organisations do not exist. Organisations are not commodities or things. They do not exist in the sense that this book exists. No one can show us an organisation in the way they can show us their car. Organisations are social processes; they are made up of people in relationships with other people. That is all there really is. Of course, we formalise and legalise some of those relationships. We come to agreements and establish rules, regulations, policies and procedures. But we must remember that organisations are nothing more than social contracts and relationships between people. Therefore, when we refer to 'organisational change', we need to realise that we are using the term as a form of shorthand for 'personal change in an organisational context'.

Why does this matter to managers at work? Remembering that organisations are relational processes, not things, helps managers to remain aware that if they want to change the organisation there is actually no organisation there for them to change. They can change themselves and the relationships, habits, expectations, agreements, rules, regulations, policies and procedures that have been established in the past. What managers are talking about when they consider changing their organisations is changing the behaviour and mind-sets of people, and changing the people-related and people-perpetuated systems that are involved in their work.

Because of this, the discussion of organisational change in this chapter begins by looking at the topic of personal change. All organisational change requires personal change in an organisational setting. This means that every individual in an organisation, from the chief executive down, must be willing and able to grow, learn and adapt (Champy 2003; Jayne 2003; Rotella 2003). For example, 'Earnest W. Deavenport Jr, chairman and CEO of Eastman Chemical, doesn't like heights. ... He joined an Outward Bound trip where he climbed up and rappelled down cliffs in the High Sierras. He attacked the task like the engineer that he is, learning the technical aspects to better reach his goals' (Howard 1999). Another example is former General Electric CEO Jack Welch who spent 'a full 30 per cent of his time teaching in both formal and informal settings and attending to other people's development activities' (Cohen & Tichy 1999: 136).

Although it may be true that organisational change is actually personal change in an organisational context, it is important to remember that there are other levels of analysis with which successful change managers must concern themselves. Therefore, the second section of this chapter deals with organisational-level change.

What is personal change?

Personal change can come from skills-based learning of the type provided in this text, or it can come more dramatically, as in the following case. In either situation, people perceive themselves to be different after the experience(s). Although this is far from being fully understood, in terms of either the process or its outcomes, once you have been through it, it is easier to appreciate.

Personal change occurs at an intellectual and an emotional level. That is why it is hard to define it solely in verbal or intellectual terms. We do not have a vocabulary to communicate the emotional experiences involved. To facilitate the discussion of this topic, read the following case:

Geoff is an accountant by training. Now, in his mid-thirties, he has taken on more general management responsibilities. Over the past couple of years he has discovered administrative and managerial skills he never suspected he possessed. A special project he has recently completed proved highly profitable for his company and has given him a bright future.

With his career finally starting to take off, Geoff expected he would feel on top of the world. However, he feels increasingly dissatisfied with the way his life is going. He has always worked long hours and been driven to work hard and succeed. Until recently, the drama of fighting to surmount business challenges was exciting, and more than compensated for the sacrifices and stress involved in the struggle. As a matter of fact, that struggle seemed to be what life was all about. Now he has begun to tire of the endless battles and feels he is losing sight of whatever goal or pay-off all this effort was supposed to be aimed at.

Geoff has always been a competitive individual. He tends to be impatient with himself and with others. He likes to see things done quickly and well. He dislikes laziness or inefficiency. He is a bit intolerant of people who, from his point of view, seem to worry fruitlessly or just mark time in the face of some difficulty. He prefers to solve the problem, or at least get control of the situation, as quickly as possible. Geoff is a friendly and generous person whose critical feelings about others have rarely shown, until lately. As his own frustration has grown, he finds it more and more difficult to restrain his impatience with others. He has become visibly irritated more and more often with his wife, with 'pointless, bloody meetings at work', and with friends and colleagues for 'whingeing' about their problems. Geoff has special difficulty restraining his impatience with his older son, aged 11, who is becoming noticeably fearful and inhibited in the face of his father's frequent criticism and who perceives Geoff's disapproval even when it is not expressed in words.

Weeks and months have passed, one very much like another, with no real pleasure in living for Geoff. His feelings of frustration have mounted. Uncharacteristically, one morning, when caught in traffic on the way to the office, Geoff lost his temper, pounded the steering wheel and cursed out loud at no one in particular. After the outburst, feeling some relief for a moment, he thought to himself: 'I used to fight problems; now I seem to be fighting the world and time itself, and I'm losing.'

The other night at a party, Geoff fell into a heated discussion with (as he thinks of them) two 'intellectual snobs' who criticised several of his political beliefs. They had him out-gunned in terms of facts and, he felt, had tried to make a fool of him in front of the other people present. Geoff went home furious. He hadn't felt so completely helpless for years. What little sleep he got that night was marred by dreams of being publicly ridiculed while unable to retaliate or protect himself in any way. He woke up several times with intense feelings of panic and shame; they passed, but were acutely painful while they lasted.

The following morning, feeling rather drained and lost, Geoff did something quite uncustomary for him. He wandered into his four-year-old daughter's room and played on the floor with her, relaxed and idle, for over an hour. After a while, painful thoughts about the previous night's incident came to mind again, bringing tears to his eyes. Despite his efforts to hold them back, his daughter noticed the tears. She didn't seem disturbed at all, but, to his utter surprise, immediately walked over to him, put her hand on his cheek to comfort him, looked into his eyes and said: 'Oh, Daddy, you don't have to cry. I love you.' Then he really began to cry, and the two of them rolled on the floor crying and laughing for a long time.

Later that day Geoff went for a walk by himself. He reflected on his family, his career, his past. He pictured himself at 20, an idealistic young man, full of hope and conviction. What had happened to that young man? 'What do I want from my life?' Geoff blurted aloud. He realised that he had no ready answer to his question. He felt lost. It seemed certain to him that something was fundamentally wrong with his basic attitude towards life.

Source: Adapted from D. Burns, *Feeling Good: The New Mood Therapy* (New York: Bantam, 1981).

How can we describe what has happened to Geoff? Something seems to have changed for him very slowly over time. And now, in a relatively short period of time, more noticeable changes are occurring. One way that people have begun to talk about these processes is in terms of changes in the way we view the world, changes in our perceptions of reality or shifts in our personal paradigms. Paradigm shifts have been discussed for years in many different contexts. For example, when humans shifted from the belief that the Earth was the centre of the universe to the current view that the sun is the centre, they shifted paradigms. When the world 'became' round—that is, when Europeans after the year 1492 decided that the world was no longer flat—the collective paradigm shifted and the world was no longer flat. Our paradigms shift as well on a more personal and individual level. If you are married and/or you have children, think about how the world completely changed after these events.

The word 'paradigm' comes from the Greek root *parádeigma*, meaning 'model' or 'pattern'. A paradigm, therefore, may be defined as a set of assumptions; as the thoughts, perceptions and values that form a particular version of reality. Our paradigm is the way we view the world. It is the water to the fish. Paradigms explain the world to us and help us to predict its behaviour. An example of a personal perceptual paradigm shift occurs if you look at the black arrow in the upper right corner of Figure 10.1 and then look at the straight black line on the left edge. What else do you see?

Most of us have been perceptually trained to look at the 'black ink' in Figure 10.1, both by our experiences of reading and because of the initial directions to look at the black arrow and the straight line. With this perceptual bias we tend to look at the ink, and we see an arrow, the line and some strange shapes. However, if we look at what artists talk about as 'negative space' and try to

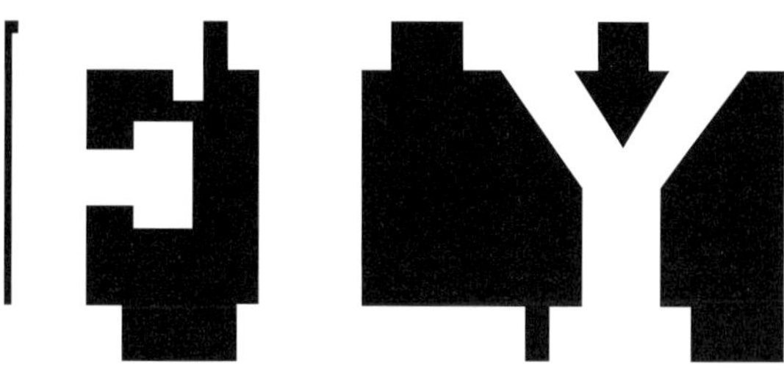

FIGURE 10.1 Visual paradigm

see the word that is spelled out in the white space framed by the black ink, we should be able to see the word 'FLY'. You may not see the word at first; at the moment when you can, you experience a paradigm shift or an 'Ah ha!' experience. The word 'FLY' was there all along. Until our perceptual paradigm changed, it did not exist for us. It is these shifts in the way we view the world that provide significant and lasting personal and organisational change. Quick fixes, within our personal lives and applied to our problems at work, do not make the fundamental shifts necessary for profound and enduring change.

Why personal change is difficult

Personal change is difficult because it takes time and effort, yet many people tend to think that it should be quick and effortless. If it took us 30 years to become the people we are now, why do we think we can change in 30 minutes? You would not expect to become physically fit after a single three-kilometre run. As part of a fitness program, you would start off slowly and work consistently, performing a number of different exercises, routines and distances over a long period of time. This is the best way to approach personal growth and change, as if it were some form of intra-personal fitness program. A second thing to remember is that personal change happens in stages. We do not change from acting, thinking and feeling one way to being the person we would like to be without passing through a number of intermediate forms. In other words, we will not achieve all our personal change goals at once. Again, this process takes time and we may not always be able to see the series of small successes as clearly as when something dramatic happens, as in Geoff's case.

Growth, change and skills development seem to follow cyclical patterns. There are periods in our lives in which we are growing and changing very much, and other periods in which, regardless of what we do, we do not seem to be making any headway. This is important to remember so that you do not become discouraged during periods of little or no change. Another thing to remember is that personal change and organisational change, as with skills development, take effort and activity. That is to say, we cannot learn by sitting around doing nothing. Of course, thinking and self-reflection are integral parts of the process. However, thought and intention without behavioural practice get us nowhere.

There are no 'five easy steps' to personal change and fulfilment. By definition, change requires energy and therefore effort. A basic principle of physics is that things at rest tend to stay at rest and things in motion stay in motion. It requires energy to make objects at rest move or to change the direction of moving things. The same is true for learning and change. It takes time, effort and persistence to achieve and maintain significant personal and organisational growth and development. However, learning and change are not completely linear processes. That is, one unit of effort does not always result in one unit of change. Especially at the outset, you may see significant change once you begin to really apply yourself. Conversely, there may be times when you are investing tremendous effort and energy and seeing only minimal gains. At these times, it is important not to become discouraged.

The process of personal change

A four-stage model (see Figure 10.2) of personal change will be explored here, based on the work of Kurt Lewin, who is arguably the founder of the processes now referred to as organisational development (see Dunphy 1981).

It is important that personal change is viewed as a process of stages for several reasons. First, it helps us to identify where we are so that we can plan to change, as well as mark progress or periods of stagnation. It helps us to align strategy and activities and to allow the process the time it needs. For example, if we are very early on in our personal change process, we should not be expecting to have

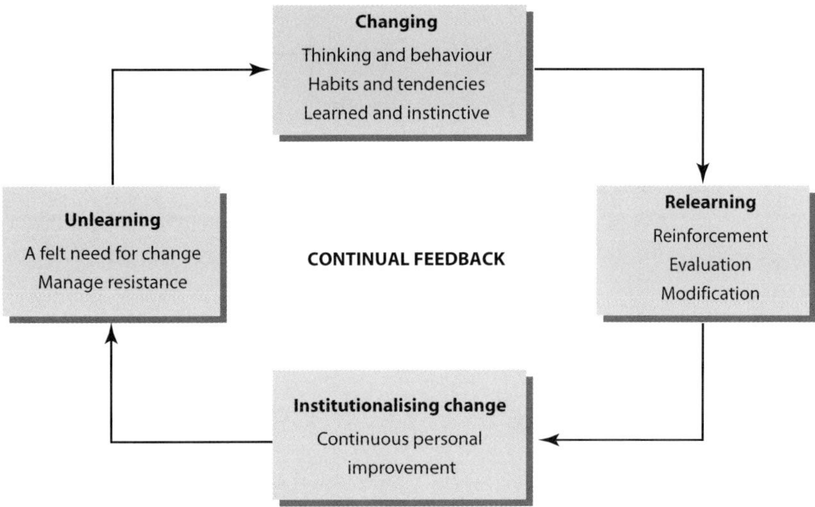

FIGURE 10.2 A model of the personal change process

got it all right; we should be reminding ourselves that change takes time and effort, and we should be working hard at our exercises and the change technologies to be discussed in the next section. Finally, viewing personal change as a process over a number of different stages reminds us that our incentives may change over time. This is important, as the things that motivate us early on in the process may be very different from what drives us towards the end.

The stages considered here are unlearning, changing, relearning and institutionalising change.

Unlearning: The motivation to action

Before we can change, there has to be the motivation to do so. Because personal transformation takes effort and time, it requires great energy. We have to feel a need to change in order to generate the necessary activity and momentum to do so. We also have to manage our natural resistance to change. It is during this first stage of the process that we are beginning to feel dissatisfied with what is going on in our lives and we sometimes start to think that what we are doing, thinking and feeling is somehow not 'right', as was the case with Geoff. We also begin to realise the need to actually unlearn some of what we have learned in the past, because it no longer seems to be working for us.

Changing: The process of transformation

This second stage in the overall personal change process is itself a process that has a number of phases within it.

Figure 10.3 illustrates that for us to make significant personal change, we must do more than just understand and learn new concepts and ideas; we need the opportunity to practise the new behaviours, we have to get feedback and see the effects and consequences of these new ways of thinking and behaving, and we must practise the new patterns often enough so that they become integrated and we eventually consider these new patterns to be 'the way we are'. This model is consistent with social learning theory (Bandura 1977; Bandura & Locke 2003). It emphasises that the process of personal change depends on observation, feedback and practice, and it is the basis on which the design of this textbook is built.

The process starts as we gain self-awareness and self-knowledge. Once we know where we are, we can begin the process of going elsewhere. We then have to begin learning new concepts and ideas, and we need to begin practising new ways of thinking and behaving. We discuss this stage in more detail in the next section. The process ends with our incorporating these new thoughts and behaviours into our formulations of 'the way we are' so that we can complete the cycle and see a change from 'the way we used to be'. This last aspect is also discussed further below.

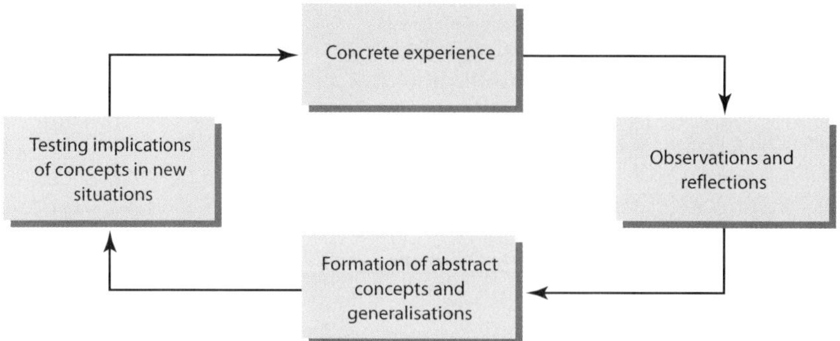

FIGURE 10.3 An experiential learning model

Source: Adapted from D. A. Kolb, I. M. Rubin and J. M. McIntyre, *Organizational Psychology: An Experiental Approach*, 3rd ed. (1979). Adapted with permission of Pearson Education Inc., Upper Saddle River, NJ.

Relearning: Practising new thoughts and behaviour

Once we have felt the need to change, unlearned old habits and patterns, managed the inevitable resistance, and begun to change our thinking and behaviour, we must continue to practise and eventually to institutionalise these new responses. At this relearning stage of the process—and at the fourth stage, institutionalising change—the tools of personal change become critical. Two tools for personal change are briefly discussed: journalling and the day of difference.

Journalling is simply writing down our thoughts, feelings and impressions. When we journal, we reflect on things that have happened to us and we write something about our reflections. Personal journals may be used to keep account of the main events of the day, insights, ideas, critical incidents, feelings, patterns of behaviour, quotes, stories, jokes and names, particularly as they relate to your skills development program. You will get better at listening to your inner self as you do more of this. (See <www.davethefox.com/innerjourney/innerjourney.htm> and <www.momscape.com/articles/journaling.htm> for applications and exercises related to journalling.)

There are several ways you can chronicle things in your journal. One of the first things people consider doing in their diary is to reflect on things that have happened during the day. This can be done as a more or less random process of recording what happened, what you thought, how you felt, what you wanted to do, what you actually did, what you should have done, who was involved, and what you think they thought, felt, wanted to do, actually did, and so on. It is also valuable to recognise the interconnections among the elements and how they affected each other. Others who prefer more structure may record a backward or forward review of the day, starting or ending with waking up and what happened before they began the review exercise.

Two other possibilities for journalling are to record critical incidents such as conflicts, successes, failures, decisions, interpretations and hunches, and to write a story as if you were an unbiased third party, a witness or an observer. The benefits of this type of discipline include not only the exercise of the will and self-discipline, but also the insights provided about yourself, your reactions and behaviours. It is suggested that this type of exercise sharpens your thinking abilities and helps to improve your memory (Boydell 1985).

A *day of difference* is a day where you establish the intention to do certain things differently, simply for the sake of change. You attempt to unfreeze your thinking and behaviour, and try to break old behavioural and thought patterns. We have a great associative memory between our muscles and our thoughts. If we change our activities, we stimulate some new thoughts. Consider the worst thing that could happen if you tried something new. We often think that if we do something new we will look stupid or make someone angry. Frequently, however, these are merely habitual thought patterns and are not really applicable to what you have in mind. If we take the time to look at the situation realistically, we may find that we would not look stupid, just different. We would not make someone angry; they really would not care very much one way or the other.

New behaviours and thoughts can range from quite simple and private to more complex and public. For example, you could change the location in which you get dressed in the morning or where you eat breakfast, or you could vary what you eat or the sequence of clothing you put on. You can take a different road to work or use a different mode of transport. You can start your workday by conversing with colleagues or by ploughing into your work, whichever you normally do not do. You could rearrange your schedule if it is in a distinct pattern. You could take a day off to stay home and play, with or without the kids, if you have any. You could go to work on Saturday and/or Sunday, if you never do, just to see what it is like and to rearrange the office or do that filing or organising you have been meaning to do for ages. You can change the style of your clothing, change the food you eat, deliberately confront someone you have been avoiding, listen to the radio, read a book or just sit and talk at night instead of watching television. You could say 'hello' and talk to a complete stranger.

On your day of difference, you can also practise keeping an open mind. You can practise believing something that you normally would not believe. You can attempt to see someone else's point of view or agree with them and try to argue for their opinions when you would normally simply dismiss them. You can use your journal to help you with this. Try playing the 'devil's advocate' with yourself. You may be surprised by how you begin to appreciate that the world is not how you first thought it was—there may be shades of grey to the black and white.

Institutionalising change: Making personal development a habit

Rather than thinking that all we have to do is make a few changes and then be done with it, personal growth and development is best seen as a continuous process. In the same way that many firms are involving their employees in decision making, problem solving and quality improvement groups towards the goal of continuous improvement, so too can we as individuals. You can think of this process of personal transformation as paralleling an organisation's total quality management (TQM) and continuous improvement programs. Personal transformation can be viewed as TQM for the individual.

Requirements for personal change

For any personal change to happen, three essential elements must be present. The first element is awareness. It is often said that getting an alcoholic to admit to their problem—that is, become aware of it—is the beginning of their road to recovery. Similarly, if we do not have a good idea of who we are and where we are within the context of our personal journey, there is little hope of our making significant progress.

The second major prerequisite for significant personal change is resources. There is no way to make personal change without a significant investment of such resources as time, money, and energy or effort. People who expect to see major life, or organisational, changes within a few days or weeks are bound to be disappointed. Human beings are the way they are because of a series of factors—both environmental and genetic—that cannot be altered without significant investment.

A third prerequisite for personal growth and development is what is referred to as facilitating structures. Going back to the analogy of alcoholics, once they admit that they have a problem, they need a great deal of support to stay off alcohol. They attend regular meetings and have lists of names and phone numbers they can call to provide support during the times of inevitable crisis. These facilitating structures are often neglected in organisational settings. The importance of rites, rituals, processes, discussions and support people is hard to exaggerate. These facilitating structures provide an element usually missing in unsuccessful personal and organisational change efforts.

Another model of the requirements for change in organisations, for those who are more mathematically oriented in their thinking, is adapted from work done by Beckhard (1969). This model reminds us of several things. It states that three conditions must be fulfilled before we can expect any personal or organisational change to begin. There must be:

- dissatisfaction with the present situation
- a vision of what is possible or possibly different in the future
- clear and achievable first steps to reach the vision.

If the conditions are all positive values (that is, they are all present), then their product will fulfil the following equation:

$$D \times V \times F > R$$

where D = dissatisfaction with the current state
V = a vision of the future and what is possible
F = the first steps towards the vision are clear
R = our natural resistance to change.

If any element is not present (that is, has a zero value), the equation is not solved and we have no possibility of overcoming the natural resistance to change.

Therefore, to motivate people to begin the process of change you need to focus their attention on:

- the way they see their past and current situations not living up to their expectations and causing high levels of dissatisfaction with the way they now do business
- a positive image of their future, a vision of what it could be like, and the confidence that this vision can and will be followed through on and achieved
- the specific actions they could all agree would move them in the right direction (that is, the first steps on the long road of change)
- an awareness that change is a slow, long-term process, and not something we do once and then forget about.

Reactions to change

People naturally resist change. Generally speaking, humans are good learners. They find something that seems to work and they stick with it. This is a generalised coping strategy. Once we have found our 'favourite' way to drive to work, what benefit could there be in trying a new route each day? Many of us find comfort in our familiar patterns and routines. When we are confronted with the need to change, therefore, we naturally experience some resistance. Change requires effort and a re-evaluation of our behaviour and thinking.

Elisabeth Kübler-Ross (1969) studied death and dying for many years. She discussed a model of the psychological adjustment process that many individuals seem to go through when confronted with the loss of a loved one. The model seems to apply equally well to how many people adjust to organisational change. When someone dies, we must adjust to life without them. We must reconfigure our view of the world. Similarly, when asked to make personal change at work, we must also get used to life being different and to the need to alter our attitudes, beliefs and views about the world.

The first stage of the model is concerned with denial and isolation. It is at this point that a person might say: 'I can't believe it. They really can't be thinking of doing that.' During this first stage, people often think the need to change does not relate to them. They think that, if they ignore it, it will go away. The changes are considered to be just another management fad—the 'flavour of the month'. If the changes persist, however, people may become angry. Feelings of fear, of being out of control or frustrated, are not unusual at this second stage in the adjustment process. Still further down the road, some people may begin to bargain about the required changes. Feelings of panic, and attempts to place blame and to engage in avoidance behaviour are not uncommon.

Once people have begun to move towards acceptance of the seemingly inevitable, they may begin to experience depression. They may become lethargic and lose motivation and initiative. Unfortunately, this often results in reduced communication and interaction at the very time in the overall change process when increases in effort, communication and interaction are needed. Finally, people move into the phase of acceptance. Negative acceptance results in a state of resignation. 'I guess we are stuck with this new system. We'll have to learn to get around it.' Positive acceptance results in the perception of new possibilities. 'It was hard to get used to this new system, but now I can see the potential benefits.'

This model of our process of adjusting to change does not suggest that the phases are linear or unequivocal. People can skip stages, move forwards and backwards through them, or be in several stages simultaneously. Like all models, this one is useful only as an aid to our thinking.

Personal change in an organisational context

It is important to remember that we live and work within social contexts and environments that support and influence our patterns of thought and behaviour. We do not make personal changes in a void. If a person tries to change, it will have an effect on everyone with whom the person regularly has contact. As you experiment with the concepts and skills in this text, you may find that your family and co-workers notice some changes. Some of these changes will be very much appreciated; others might be resisted because they threaten the status quo and force people to tread on unfamiliar ground. It is very much easier to change if the 'significant others' who may be affected are aware, involved and supportive of your efforts.

An important part of your personal planning about skill acquisition should be a consideration of these issues and how you plan to gain the support of those who influence your behaviour and management success. The elements depicted in Figure 10.4 may be thought of as a guide to identify the significant factors that must be involved if you are to bring about significant and sustained personal change in an organisational context.

Another issue regarding personal change in an organisational context is that the prevailing organisational structure will affect your ability and willingness to change. A great deal is known about the structures of organisational environments in which people are best able to change and to innovate. The basic distinction is between firms with organic versus mechanistic forms. Although the organic and mechanistic forms do not represent a simple dichotomy, it has been found that firms with more organic structural forms tend to be more innovative. More mechanistically structured firms are usually less innovative and more resistant to change. Following are several structural characteristics of organisations that seem to be associated with the promotion or inhibition of behavioural innovation, flexibility and change.

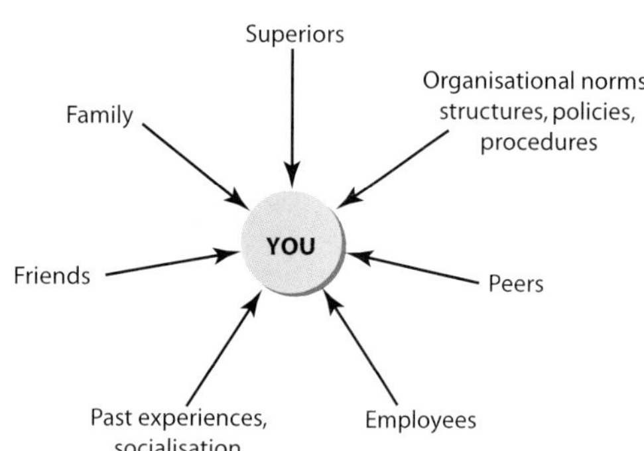

FIGURE 10.4 Factors influencing your behaviour and personality

1. Some specific characteristics of organic forms of organisation are:
   - informal definitions of jobs
   - lateral, network-like communication patterns
   - consultative, rather than authoritative, communication styles
   - diffusion of knowledge-seeking throughout the firm
   - greater prestige and importance attached to extraorganisational knowledge and activities than to internal knowledge or activities.
2. Some specific characteristics of mechanistic organisational forms are:
   - rigid breakdowns of roles and jobs into functional specialities
   - precise definitions of duties, responsibilities and power
   - hierarchical control, authority and communication
   - belief that the managers at the top know what is best
   - reliance on vertical, top-down interactions
   - greater prestige and importance attached to internal than to extraorganisational knowledge or activities.
3. Related general structural features are that firms with more flexible, organic forms of organisation tend to be flatter (that is, have fewer hierarchical levels), to be less formalised (that is, have

fewer rules and regulations), and have greater professional variance (that is, a greater diversity of professions is represented), less centralisation of power and decision making, and more slack resources.

The structure of an organisation does not operate independently of its managers (Ambrose & Schminke 2003; Leavitt 2003). Structure shapes the behaviour of managers and, in turn, is shaped by their behaviour. For example, organisations that are mechanistic select and reward managers with values and behaviours consistent with this form of organisation. These managers then perpetuate the system, while more flexible, change-oriented managers never get ahead or choose to leave the organisation. Of course, the reverse is also true. Many people believe intuitively that organisational size should be related to change orientation and innovativeness. Research has shown consistently, however, that organisation size is a surrogate for several other variables such as total resources, slack resources and organisational structure (Donaldson 2001).

The structural variables discussed above do not cause people to be more innovative. These variables have been shown either to inhibit or facilitate change, not cause it. In other words, an organisation that has a great deal of extra resources will not necessarily provide a more innovative environment than an organisation with less. Research consistently shows, however, that having more slack resources makes it easier for people trying to encourage personal change and flexibility to do so successfully. Similarly, the fact that an organisation is very low on formalisation does not mean that it will necessarily stimulate change. What can be implied is that it is easier to innovate and change in an organisation that is less formalised than it is to innovate and change in a highly formalised organisation.

Organisational change

This conversation about how the organisational context and structure will affect people's ability and willingness to change brings us directly to the topic of organisational-level change. Scores of books and articles have been written on the topic of organisational change. A summary or review of this literature will not be attempted, as it has been done before (see Adizes 1992; Dunphy 1981; Morgan 1993). Instead, a unique conceptual perspective will be provided that will enable the reader to develop some new thinking skills to help in leading positive organisational change.

Leading positive change is a management skill that focuses on unlocking positive human potential. Positive change enables individuals to experience appreciation, collaboration, vitality and meaningfulness in their work. It focuses on creating abundance and human well-being. It fosters positive deviance. It acknowledges that positive change engages the heart as well as the mind.

There are five key management skills and activities required to effectively lead positive change: (1) establishing a climate of positivity; (2) creating readiness for change; (3) articulating a vision of abundance; (4) generating commitment to the vision; and (5) institutionalising the positive change. Figure 10.5 summarises these steps, and they are discussed below.

Leaders of positive change are not all CEOs, of course, nor are they in titled or powerful positions. On the contrary, the most important leadership demonstrated in organisations usually occurs in departments, divisions and teams, and by individuals who take it upon themselves to enter a temporary state of leadership (Quinn 2004; Meyerson 2001). These principles apply as much to the first-time manager as to the experienced executive.

Establishing a climate of positivity

The first and most crucial step in leading positive organisation-level change is to set the stage for change by establishing a climate of positivity. Because constant change is typical of all organisations, most managers most of the time focus on the negative or problematic aspects of change. A leader who will focus on positive change is both rare and valuable. Not everyone masters it, although everyone can.

Baumeister et al. (2001) pointed out that negative occurrences, bad events and disapproving feedback are more influential and longer lasting in people than positive, encouraging and upbeat

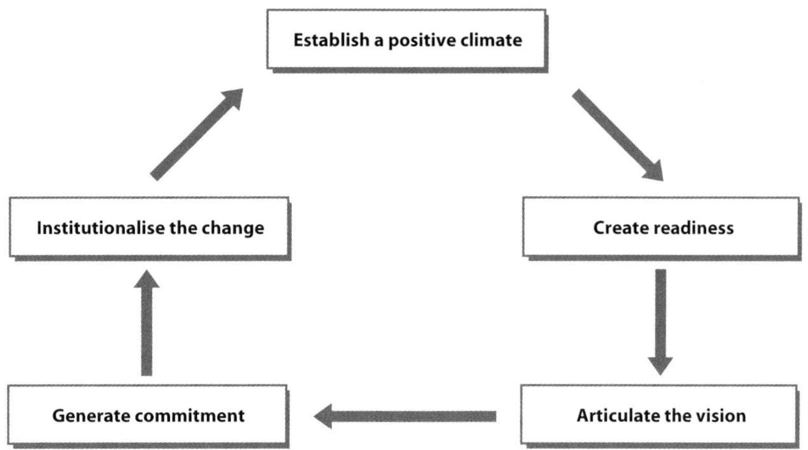

FIGURE 10.5 A framework for positive change

occurrences. For example, if someone breaks into your home and steals $1000, it will affect you more, and will be more long-lasting in its effects, than if someone were to send you a $1000 gift. In other words, according to Baumeister's review of the literature, people tend to pay more attention to negative than to positive phenomena, and for good reason. Ignoring a negative threat could cost you your life. Not attending to negative events could prove dangerous. Ignoring a positive, pleasant experience, on the other hand, would only result in regret. Consequently, managers and organisations—constantly confronted by problems, threats and obstacles—have a tendency to focus on the negative much more than the positive. Managers must consciously choose to pay attention to the positive, uplifting and flourishing aspects of the organisation, otherwise negative tendencies will overwhelm the positive. Leading positive change, in other words, is going against the grain. It is not necessarily a natural thing to do. It requires skill and practice.

Mahatma Gandhi's statement (Gold 2002) illustrates the necessity of positivity even though it is difficult:

> *Keep your thoughts positive, because your thoughts become your words. Keep your words positive, because your words become your behavior. Keep your behavior positive, because your behavior becomes your habits. Keep your habits positive because your habits become your values. Keep your values positive, because your values become your destiny.*

In order to establish a climate of positivity in an organisation, managers must help establish at least three necessary conditions: (1) positive energy networks; (2) a climate of compassion, forgiveness and gratitude; and (3) attention to strengths and the best self.

Create positive energy networks

Have you ever been around a person who just makes you feel good—you leave every interaction with this person happier, more energised and uplifted? In contrast, do you know people who are constantly critical, negative and discouraging—they seem to deplete your reserve of positive energy? Recent research has suggested that people can be identified as 'positive energisers' or 'negative energisers' in their relationships with others (Baker, Cross & Wooten 2003) and this conceptualisation has been more recently applied in leadership, education and business (cf. Karakas 2011; Kunze & Bruch 2010; Searle & Barbuto 2011). Positive energisers are those who strengthen and create vitality and liveliness in others. Negative energisers are people who deplete the good feelings and enthusiasm in people and make them feel diminished, devalued or drained. Research shows that positive energisers are higher performers, enable others to perform better and help their organisations succeed more than do negative energisers (Baker, Cross & Wooten 2003). People who drain energy from others tend to be critical, express negative views, fail to engage others, and are more self-centred than positive energisers.

Being a positive energiser is associated with being sensitive in interpersonal relationships, trustworthy, supportive to others in comments, actively (not passively) engaged in social interactions, flexible and tolerant in thinking, and unselfish. Positive energy creators are not necessarily charismatic or just Pollyannaish. Rather, they are optimistic and giving, and others feel better by being around them.

Here is why these qualities are so important in leading positive change. Research by Wayne Baker (2001) has investigated the kinds of networks that exist in organisations. Most research investigates two kinds of networks—information networks and influence networks. If you are at the centre of an information network, more information and communication flow through you than through anyone else. You have access to a greater amount of information than others. Predictably, people at the centre of an information network have higher performance and are more successful in their careers than people on the periphery. The same can be said for people at the centre of influence networks. Influential people are not always people with the most prestigious titles; rather, they tend to be people who can influence others to get things done. Recent research has discovered, however, that positive energy networks are far more powerful in predicting success than information or influence networks. In fact, being a positive energiser in an organisation is four times more predictive of success than being at the centre of an information network or even being the person with an important title or senior position. Displaying positive energy, in other words, tends to be a very powerful predictor of personal as well as organisational success.

Effective managers identify positive energisers and then make certain that networks of people are formed who associate with these energisers. Positive energisers are placed in positions where others can interact with them and be influenced by them. The research findings are clear that people who interact with positive energisers perform better, as well as do the positive energisers themselves, in fact. In addition to forming positive energy networks, effective managers will also foster positive energy in other people by: (1) exemplifying or role modelling positive energy themselves; (2) recognising and rewarding people who exemplify positive energy; and (3) providing opportunities for individuals to form friendships at work (which are usually positive energy creators).

Ensure a climate of compassion, forgiveness and gratitude

A second aspect of a climate of positivity in organisations is the appropriate display of compassion, forgiveness and gratitude. These terms may sound a bit saccharine and soft—even out of place in a serious discussion of developing management skills for the competitive world of business. Yet recent research has found them to be very important predictors of organisational success. Companies that scored high on these attributes performed significantly better than others (Cameron 2003). That is, when managers fostered compassionate behaviour among employees, forgiveness for missteps and mistakes, and gratitude resulting from positive occurrences, their firms excelled in profitability, productivity, quality, innovation and customer retention. Managers that reinforced these virtues were more successful in producing bottom-line results.

Paying attention to these concepts simply acknowledges that employees at work have human concerns; they feel pain, experience difficulty, and encounter injustice in their work and personal lives. Think of people you know, for example, who are currently managing a severe family illness, experiencing a failed relationship, coping with hostile and unpleasant co-workers or associates, or facing overload and burnout. Many people and organisational systems do not allow personal problems to get in the way of getting the job done; human concerns take a back seat to work-related concerns; and, regardless of what is happening personally, responsibilities and performance expectations remain the same. To lead positive change, however, managers must build a climate in which human concerns are acknowledged and where healing and restoration can occur. Because change always creates pain, discomfort and disruption, leaders of positive change are sensitive to the human concerns that can sabotage change efforts. Without a reserve of goodwill and positive feelings, almost all change fails. Therefore, unlocking people's inherent tendency to feel compassion, to forgive mistakes and to express gratitude helps build the human capital and reserve needed to successfully lead positive change. How might that occur?

Compassion

Kanov et al. (2003) found that compassion is built in organisations when managers foster three things: collective noticing, collective feeling and collective responding. When people are suffering or experiencing difficulty, the first step is to notice or simply become aware of what is occurring. An iron-clad rule exists at Cisco Systems, for example, where CEO John Chambers must be notified within 48 hours of the death or serious illness of any Cisco employee or family member. People are on the lookout for colleagues who need help.

The second step is to enable the expression of collective emotion. Planned events where people can share feelings (such as grief, support or love) help build a climate of compassion. For example, a memorial service for a recently deceased executive at which the CEO shed tears was a powerful signal to organisation members that responding compassionately to human suffering was important to the organisation (Kanov et al. 2003).

The third step is collective responding, meaning that the manager ensures that an appropriate response is made when healing or restoration is needed. In the aftermath of the tragic events in New York on 11 September 2001, many examples of compassion—and non-compassion—were witnessed in organisations around the United States. While some leaders modelled caring and compassion in the responses they fostered, others stifled the healing process (see Dutton et al. 2002).

Forgiveness

Many managers assume that forgiveness has no place in the work setting. Because of high quality standards, the need to eliminate mistakes and a requirement to 'do it right the first time', some managers assume that they cannot afford to let errors go unpunished. They believe that forgiving mistakes will just encourage people to be careless and unthinking. However, forgiveness and high standards are not incompatible (Rego et al. 2011). That is because forgiveness is not the same as pardoning, condoning, excusing, forgetting, denying, minimising or trusting (Enright & Coyle 1998). To forgive does not mean relieving the offender of a penalty (that is, pardoning) or saying that the offence is not serious, or forgotten (that is, condoned, excused, denied, minimised). The memory of the offence need not be erased for forgiveness to occur. Rather, forgiveness in an organisation involves the capacity to abandon justified resentment, bitterness and blame, and instead to adopt positive, forward-looking approaches in response to harm or damage (Cameron & Caza 2002).

Because minor offences and disagreements occur in almost all human interactions, especially in close relationships, most people are practised forgivers. Without forgiveness, relationships could not endure and organisations would disintegrate into squabbles, conflicts and hostilities (cf. Goodstein & Aquino 2010 on restorative justice). One explanation for the successful formation of the European Economic Union is forgiveness (Glynn 1994). Collectively speaking, the French, the Dutch and the British forgave the Germans for the atrocities of the Second World War, as did other damaged nations. Likewise, the reciprocal forgiveness demonstrated by the United States and Japan after the war helps explain the flourishing economic and social interchange that developed in subsequent decades. On the other hand, the lack of peace in certain war-torn areas of the world can be at least partly explained by the refusal of organisations and nations to forgive one another for past trespasses (Helmick & Petersen 2001).

The importance of forgiveness in organisations, and societies, is illustrated by Nobel laureate Desmond Tutu (1999: 155) in his description of post-apartheid South Africa:

> *Ultimately, you discover that without forgiveness, there is no future. We recognize that the past cannot be remade through punishment. … There is no point in exacting vengeance now, knowing that it will be the cause for future vengeance by the offspring of those we punish. Vengeance leads only to revenge. Vengeance destroys those it claims and those who become intoxicated with it. … Therefore, forgiveness is an absolute necessity for continued human existence.*

Forgiveness is enhanced in organisations when managers do the following things.

1. Acknowledge the trauma, harm and injustice that their organisation members have experienced, but define the occurrence of hurtful events as an opportunity to move forward towards a new goal.

2. Associate the outcomes of the organisation (for example, its products and services) with a higher purpose that provides personal meaning for organisation members. This higher purpose replaces a focus on self (for example, retribution, self-pity) with a focus on a higher objective.
3. Maintain high standards and communicate the fact that forgiveness is not synonymous with tolerance for errors or lowered expectations. Use forgiveness to facilitate excellence by refusing to focus on the negative; instead, focus on achieving excellence.
4. Provide support by communicating that human development and human welfare are as important in the organisation's priorities as the financial bottom line. This kind of support helps employees catch sight of a way to move past the injury.
5. Pay attention to language, so that terms such as 'forgiveness', 'compassion', 'humility', 'courage' and 'love' are acceptable; this language provides a humanistic foundation upon which most forgiveness occurs.

An analysis of several organisations' successful turnarounds after the trauma of downsizing reveals these five steps being demonstrated in institutionalising forgiveness.

Gratitude

Observing acts of compassion and forgiveness—not to mention being the recipient of them—creates a sense of gratitude in people. Gratitude is crucial in organisations, because it leads to reciprocal behaviour, equity and justice (for example, returning a favour, doing good in return for receiving good, being fair). Simmel (1950: 388) referred to gratitude as 'the moral memory of mankind ... if every grateful action ... were suddenly eliminated, society (at least as we know it) would break apart'.

Feelings of gratitude have been found to have a dramatic effect on individual and organisational performance. For example, Emmons (2003) induced feelings of gratitude in students by assigning them to keep journals as part of a semester-long assignment. Some of the students were required to keep 'gratitude journals' on a daily or weekly basis. That is, they wrote down events or incidents that happened during the day (or week) for which they were grateful. Other students were assigned to write down events or incidents that were frustrating, and still other students were assigned to write down events or incidents that were merely neutral. Students keeping gratitude journals, compared with the frustrated students and the neutral students, experienced fewer physical symptoms such as headaches and colds; felt better about their lives as a whole; were more optimistic about the coming week; had higher states of alertness, attentiveness, determination and energy; reported fewer hassles in their lives; engaged in more helping behaviour towards other people; experienced better sleep quality; and had a sense of being more connected to others. In addition, they were absent and tardy less often and had higher average marks. Feelings of gratitude had significant impact on student classroom performance as well as people's personal lives.

McCraty and Childre (2004) helped explain one reason why the positive effect of gratitude occurs in people's lives. They studied the heart rhythms of people when they experienced frustrating or stressful work conditions, and compared those rhythms with changes that occurred when people were induced into a gratitude condition. Figure 10.6 shows the differences. For the first 200 seconds, the

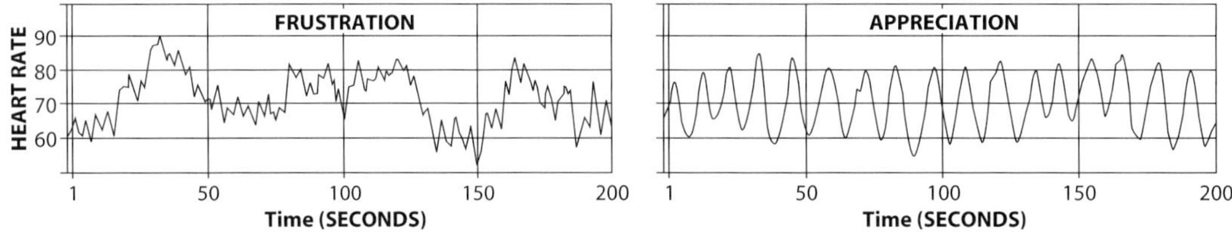

FIGURE 10.6 Heart rhythms in frustration and in gratitude conditions

These are actual heart rhythm patterns resulting from an induced state of frustration followed by an induced gratitude condition.

Source: R. McCraty and D. Childre, 'The grateful heart', in R. Emmons and M. McCullough (eds), *The Psychology of Gratitude* (New York: Oxford University Press, 2004), pp. 230–55. Reproduced with permission of Institute of HeartMath.

erratic and disordered heart pattern shows a condition of frustration and stress, whereas for the next 200 seconds the heart-beat pattern shows a condition of appreciation and gratitude. It is easy to see why performance and health are enhanced by gratitude.

Emmons also found that expressions of gratitude by one person tend to motivate others to express gratitude, so a self-perpetuating, virtuous cycle occurs when gratitude is expressed. Gratitude elicits positive behaviours on the part of other people. (They are more likely to lend money, provide compassionate support, and to behave reciprocally.) For example, a hand-written 'thank you' on a restaurant bill by the server elicits about 11 per cent higher tips, and visits by case workers and social workers is 80 per cent higher if they are thanked for coming (McCullough, Emmons & Tsang 2002). People respond positively to expressions of gratitude. Thus, not only does gratitude help people feel good but it helps them to do good as well.

Managers engender gratitude in an organisation simply by expressing gratitude frequently and conspicuously themselves, even for small acts and small successes, and by keeping track of things that go right (not just things that go wrong) and expressing gratitude for them. Elaborate programs are not needed, just frequent 'thank you's.

Pay attention to strengths and the best self

Identifying people's strengths (or what they do right) and then building on them creates more benefit than identifying weaknesses (or what people do wrong) and trying to correct them. For example, managers who spend more time with their strongest performers (rather than their weakest performers) achieved double the productivity. In organisations where workers have a chance to 'do what they do best everyday', productivity is one-and-a-half times greater than in normal organisations. People who are given feedback on their strengths are significantly more likely to feel highly engaged and to be more productive than people who are given feedback on their weaknesses. Students who are given feedback on their talents have fewer days of absenteeism, are late less often and have higher grade-point averages than those who get no feedback on their talents. The strongest readers make more improvement in a speed-reading class designed to improve reading than the poor readers (Clifton & Harter 2003).

A dramatic finding resulted from a study of top management teams engaged in strategic planning for their organisations. Losada and Heaphy (2003) studied 60 teams of senior executives who met to set objectives, refine budgets and identify plans for the coming year. The research focused on investigating why some teams and their organisations performed better than others. The teams used in the research were executives and top managers in well-recognised companies.

The teams were categorised into three groups based on six measures of performance, such as firm profitability, productivity, managerial capability, and so on. The three groups were: (1) those that performed well; (2) those that performed about average; and (3) those that performed poorly. To explain the differences between the groups, the communication patterns of the teams were carefully monitored and analysed. The single most important factor in predicting success—which was four times more powerful in predicting success than any other factor—was the ratio of positive comments to negative comments. Positive comments are those that express appreciation, support, helpfulness or compliments. Negative comments express criticism, disapproval or blame. The results of the research were dramatic. In high-performing teams, the ratio of positive to negative comments was 5:1. Five times more positive comments were made than negative comments. In medium-performing teams, the ratio was 1:1. In low-performing teams, the ratio was 0.36:1. In other words, in low-performing teams, there were three negative comments for every positive comment.

What these results show is that high-performing teams have an abundance of positive comments compared with negative comments. Effective teams are far more complimentary and supportive than ineffective teams. It is not that correction and criticism are entirely absent, but the positive comments far outweigh the negative comments. Teams that performed moderately well had about an equal number of positive and negative comments, and teams that performed poorly had many more negative comments than positive ones. The same ratios, by the way, have been found in successful marriages. Marriages that are strong have a ratio of 5:1 positive interactions. Marriages that end in divorce have more negative than positive comments (Gottman 1994).

Obviously, the management skill demonstrated by effective leaders of positive change is to bias their communication towards positive, supportive comments rather than negative and corrective comments. Remember, however, that the ratio is not 100:1 or 5:0. That is, critical, confrontational and corrective comments need to be present and cannot be ignored. It is just that effective managers are, by and large, more focused on positive than negative communication.

Reflected best-self feedback

One technique that managers can use to enhance positivity and focus on strengths is called reflected best-self feedback (Quinn, Dutton & Spreitzer 2003). This is a technique developed and used extensively at the University of Michigan Business School and recently adopted at the Harvard Business School, MIT and several major corporations in the United States. It is designed to provide people with feedback on their strengths and unique capabilities. This kind of information is not given to people frequently, if ever, but receiving it allows individuals to build on their unique strengths in a positive way. Figure 10.7 illustrates the kind of feedback resulting from this exercise.

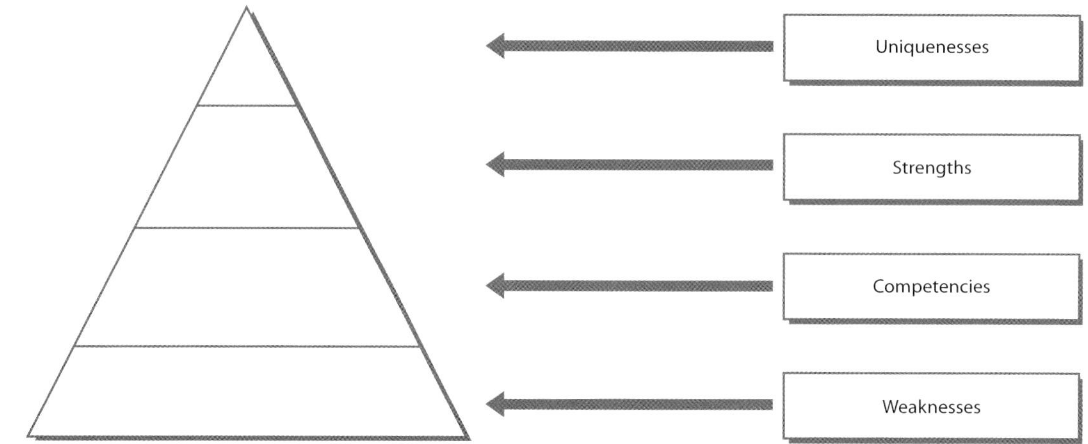

FIGURE 10.7 Personal weaknesses, competencies, strengths and uniquenesses

Begin at the bottom of the figure. Most of us have a lot of weaknesses—areas that are underdeveloped, areas in which we are uninformed, areas in which we have little skill. Most feedback systems provide information on what those areas are and how we compare with other people's capabilities in the same areas. These areas are labelled weaknesses in Figure 10.7. We also all have areas in which we perform competently. We do fine—not stellar, but good enough. Those are areas of competence. A third category is areas of well-developed skill. We are outstanding performers in some areas. We have special capabilities or talents, and we do better than most people. These are areas of strength. Finally, we all have areas that are unique to us. If we do not contribute what we have, or if we do not share our capacities and gifts, no one else has the ability to do so. Our talent or skill is special. This area is referred to as uniquenesses. Research indicates that capitalising on our strengths and uniquenesses produces more success than trying to work on and overcome weaknesses—even though weaknesses may be more numerous and more obvious (Clifton & Harter 2003).

Summary

Not everyone, and maybe even very few people, live or work in a positive organisational climate in which people flourish and experience positive energy. The role of the leader of positive change, therefore, is to facilitate and engender these characteristics. Box 10.1 summarises some specific behaviours that can be implemented.

Being a source of positive energy and building positive energy networks lead to higher levels of personal success and organisational success. Similarly, the expression of compassion, forgiveness

BOX 10.1 Establishing a climate of positivity

1. Create positive energy networks.
   - Place positive energisers in places where others can interact with them and be influenced by them.
   - Model positive energy yourself.
   - Recognise and reward positive energisers.
   - Provide opportunities for people to form close friendships at work.
2. Ensure a climate of compassion, forgiveness and gratitude.
   - Enable collective noticing of human concerns.
   - Enable the expression of collective emotion.
   - Enable the collective responding to difficulty, pain or distress.
   - Publicly and personally acknowledge trauma and harm.
   - Identify higher-purpose outcomes that people can point towards.
   - Maintain high standards and look towards the future after mistakes.
   - Provide personal support to people who have been harmed.
   - Pay attention to languages so that virtuous words are acceptable.
   - Express gratitude frequently and conspicuously, even for small acts.
   - Keep track of things that go right (not just those that go wrong).
3. Identify and give people feedback on their strengths and unique competencies.
   - Implement a reflected best-self feedback process.
   - Spend the most time with the strongest performers.
   - Work to capitalise on strengths, rather than focusing on overcoming weaknesses.
   - Use five positive comments for every negative comment in your interactions with others.

and gratitude in organisations is also associated with superior performance, both personally and organisationally. And focusing on strengths and talents (celebrating successes, complimenting on what is going right, recognising what people do well) produces superior performance as well. Therefore, as the first step in leading positive change, establishing a positive climate is a crucial prerequisite. Without it, resistance and negativity are almost certain to present major obstacles. The tendency of most people is to focus on the problems, challenges and negative issues associated with change. With a positive climate, however, positive change is much more likely to be successful. Figure 10.8 shows the relationship between these three aspects of positive climate.

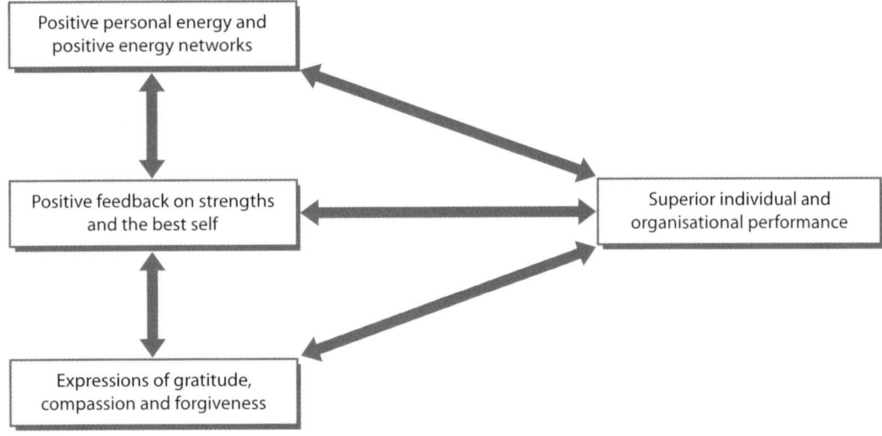

FIGURE 10.8 Relationships between factors in a climate of positivity

Receiving feedback on strengths and successes produces feelings of gratitude and compassion, which, in turn, leads to being positively energised. Each factor, in turn, affects performance directly as well as in combination with the other factors.

Creating readiness for change

In addition to establishing a climate of positivity, individuals must feel a need for the change and must understand its importance and urgency. A positive climate is a crucial foundation, but leading positive change requires engaging individuals in the actual process of change. The second step in leading positive change, therefore, is to create readiness among those to be involved in the change (Choi & Ruona 2011). Many techniques are available, but three are mentioned here.

Benchmark best practice, and compare current performance with the highest standards

One way to create readiness for change is to compare current levels of performance with the highest standards you can find. Identifying who else performs at spectacular levels helps set a standard towards which people can aspire. It identifies a target of opportunity. This is referred to as benchmarking, and it involves finding best practice, studying it in detail, and then planning to exceed that performance. Identifying best practice does not mean copying it. It means learning from it and exceeding it. Planned performance goes beyond the best practice, otherwise benchmarking is merely mimicking. Several different kinds of best practice standards are available for comparison.

- *Comparative standards*, or comparing current performance with similar individuals or organisations (for example, 'Here is how we are doing relative to our best competitors').
- *Goal standards*, or comparing current performance with the publicly stated goals (for example, 'Here is how we are doing compared with the goals we have established').
- *Improvement standards*, or comparing current performance with improvements made in the past (for example, 'Here is how we are doing compared with our improvement trends of the past year').
- *Ideal standards*, or comparing current performance with an idea or perfect standard (for example, 'Here is how we are doing relative to a zero defect standard').
- *Stakeholder expectations*, or comparing current performance with the expectations of customers, employees or other stakeholders (for example, 'Here is how we are doing in meeting customer demands').

The standard of comparison that is most appropriate depends, of course, on what opportunities exist, which standard has the most legitimacy with organisation members, and which standard is perceived to be reachable. The purpose of these comparisons is to highlight the opportunities available by finding a higher level of performance and showing the possibility of achieving it.

Identifying benchmark standards also helps to ensure that new information, new ideas and new perspectives will be imported, and that standards not considered possible before may become realistic. To study others who may be doing the same job better than you, you can sponsor visitors, hold learning events (symposia and colloquia) or conferences, create study teams and schedule visits to other sites. The objective is to unfreeze people from a reliance on past practices by learning that there may be a better way.

Institute symbolic events

Leaders of positive change must signal the end of the old way of doing things and the beginning of a new way of doing things by means of symbols. This means that an event is used to signify a positive change or a new future. The symbolic event should be tangible and clearly identified with the positive change.

For example, during the 1980s Chrysler Motors in the United States was experiencing very dark days. The company was bankrupt and no one knew for sure if it would survive. Lee Iacocca was hired to be the new CEO. Tens of thousands of cars sat idle in the 'sales bank' (Chrysler's term for cars parked in vacant lots) waiting to be sold. In his first closed-door speech to senior executives, Iacocca announced that the sales bank would be abolished. All cars in the sales bank would be sold at 'distressed prices'. 'But,' he said, 'I want to keep one. You know what people do when they pay off the mortgage; they burn it on the front lawn. I want to burn that last car on the front lawn of headquarters, so the whole world knows it's over!' (Cameron 1985). A symbolic event was held, in fact, in which the last car in the sales bank was burned, symbolising a new future under Iacocca.

In the same speech, Iacocca asked all top managers to write down on a piece of paper all they had achieved in Chrysler during the past 12 months. After they had done so, they were instructed to tear up the paper and throw it away. They were to take out another piece of paper and write down all the things they were going to achieve for the company in the next 12 months. That was the document Iacocca instructed them to hang on their wall and explain to their co-workers. Symbolically, Iacocca was communicating the message: 'You may have succeeded in the past, but the future is where we will now put our emphasis.' The symbolic imagery communicated that message far more powerfully than merely stating it in a speech. The point is, symbolic images capture hearts as well as heads and that resource is required for positive change to occur.

Create a new language

Another way to create readiness for change is to help organisation members begin to use different language to describe old realities. When new language is used, perspectives change. For example, a key goal for the theme park division at Disney Corporation is to provide the best service in the world. The trouble is, most of Disney's theme park employees in the summer months are college students working at temporary jobs and not particularly invested in being a park sweeper or a concession stand cashier. Disney addresses this challenge by making sure that all new employees at Disneyland are taught that they have been hired by central casting, not the personnel department. They are cast members, not employees. They wear costumes, not uniforms. They serve guests and audience members, not tourists. They work in attractions, not rides or arcades. They have roles in the show and play characters (even as grounds-keepers), not merely work in a job. During working hours, they are on-stage and must go off-stage to relax, eat or socialise.

The intent of this alternative language is to change the way these employees think about their work, to place them in a mind-set that they would not have considered otherwise. At Disney, summer employees are in show business—on stage, playing a role, performing for an audience. Changing language helps unfreeze old interpretations and helps create new ones. Another example is CNN. When the network was first formed, employees were fined $100 if they spoke the word 'foreign'. The reason: at a worldwide news organisation, no one is foreign. Thinking globally requires that language change, and 'foreign' became a forbidden word. Leading positive change requires that optimistic words replace pessimistic words, and language that blocks progress is shunned. Intel, for example, forbids phrases such as 'It can't be done', 'It won't work', 'It's just like an idea we already tried' and 'It will never get approved'. These phrases are all 'creativity killers', and they inhibit positive change, innovation and improvement.

Bennis and Nanus (1985) observed that the most successful leaders in education, government, business, the arts and the military are those who have developed a special language. Most notable is the absence in their vocabularies of the word 'failure'. These individuals simply have not allowed themselves, or others around them, to accept the possibility of failure. Alternative descriptors are used, such as 'temporary slowdown', 'false start', 'miscue', 'error', 'blooper', 'stumble', 'foul-up', 'obstacle', 'disappointment' or 'non-success'. These leaders use an alternative language in order to interpret reality for their organisations, to foster a willingness to try again, and to foster an inclination towards positive change. This language communicates the fact that failure is not an option. Success is just around the corner.

Summary

Creating readiness is a step designed to mobilise individuals in the organisation to actively engage in the positive change process. It involves more than merely unfreezing people. Making people uncomfortable is a frequent prescription for getting them ready for change, and it often works. Making people uncomfortable, however, usually involves creating fear, crisis or negative conditions. There is no doubt, of course, that change also creates its own discomfort. Interpersonal relationships, power and status, and routine ways of behaving are disrupted by change, so change is usually interpreted as anything but a positive condition. Leading positive change, on the other hand, focuses on ways to create readiness that unlock positive motivations rather than resistance and provide optimistic alternatives rather than fear. Benchmarking best practice, positive symbols and new language are three practical ways to do it, as summarised in Box 10.2.

BOX 10.2 Creating readiness in others to pursue positive change

1. Benchmark best practice and compare current performance with the highest standards.
   - Use comparable others as standards.
   - Use stated goals as standards.
   - Use past improvement as a standard.
   - Use an ideal as a standard.
   - Use others' expectations as a standard.
2. Institute symbolic events to signal the positive change.
   - Interpret events or activities as indicators of the beginning of a new era.
   - Manage people's interpretations and mental images of incidents so that they reinforce the intended change.
   - Pay as much attention to the meaning of the change as the substance of the change.
3. Create a new language that illustrates the positive change.
   - Use words associated with the change that capture people's imagination.
   - Use passionate and inspiring language.
   - Use words that communicate and reinforce a new direction.

Establishing a climate of positivity and creating readiness for change does little good, of course, if there is not a clear idea of where the positive change is heading. That is why the third step in the framework refers to articulating a clear, motivating vision of abundance.

Articulating a vision of abundance

Positive change seldom occurs without a leader articulating a vision of abundance. By 'abundance' we mean a vision of a positive future, a flourishing condition and a legacy about which people care passionately. This kind of vision helps unleash human wellsprings of potential, since it addresses a basic human desire—to do something that makes a difference, something that outlasts one's own life, and something that has enduring impact. Visions of abundance are different from visions of goal achievement or effectiveness, such as earning a certain percentage profit, becoming number one in the marketplace or receiving personal recognition. Rather, these are visions that speak to the heart as well as the head.

Most organisations have some kind of mission statement or have established goals, but a vision statement is something different. Visions include the universalistic values and principles that will guide behaviour. They provide a sense of direction. They help identify what the future holds. They provide glimpses of possibilities, not just probabilities. They evoke deeper meaning than mission statements or goals. They provide optimism and hope.

For example, goals that call for a 20 per cent increase in return on investment (ROI), an improvement in product quality, timelier responses to customers or lower costs are all valuable and important to organisations, but they are not visions. They are examples of targets that the organisation wants to achieve. Visions, on the other hand, are focused on helping individuals think differently about themselves and about their future. The most motivating vision statements (for example, Churchill's 'Never give in' speech, Kennedy's 'Ask not what your country can do for you' speech, Mandela's 'A dream for which I am prepared to die' speech, Martin Luther King's 'I have a dream' speech) are more than specific goals.

Inspiring vision statements are interesting. They contain challenges and prods that confront and alter the ways people think about the past and the future. They are not outlandish or cavalier in their message, just provocative. For example, Ralph Peterson, CEO of CH2MHill (a large environmental and engineering firm), indicated that 'corporate immortality' was the ultimate objective of the company, meaning that the firm was in business to create outcomes that would last well beyond the lifetime of any individual. Jeffrey Schwartz, CEO of shoe and clothing company Timberland, espoused a vision related to doing good in order to do well—organisational virtuousness is equally as important as organisational profitability. Tom Gloucer, CEO of Reuters, espoused the vision that Reuters would become 'the fastest company in the world'.

These examples are not intended to illustrate the best vision statements, of course, nor even vision statements that energise you personally. But, in each case, they carried a strong and motivating message for those in the organisation. They helped paint a mental picture. One of the chief reasons is that these vision statements are interesting. They identify a message that people care about, but which challenges the normal perception of things. The statements confront the status quo and provide a new way to think about what people do in the organisation every day. The fact that they are interesting is what captures attention and positive energy.

Attach the vision to a symbol

Effective vision statements are associated with a symbol. This is more than a symbolic event that helps create readiness for change. Rather, people must associate the vision with something tangible they see or hear. They should be reminded of the vision regularly by the presence of a symbol. That symbol could be a logo, a phrase from a speech, a flag, a physical structure, or any number of things that can serve as a reminder of where the vision is taking the organisation. For example, Maulden Mills reconstructed a plant that had been devastated by fire on the same property to symbolise human commitment and corporate compassion. The replacement structures for the World Trade Center towers in New York are targeted specifically to symbolise a positive and uplifting future after the devastating September 11 tragedy.

Box 10.3 summarises some specific behaviours you can use in articulating a high-impact vision of abundance.

BOX 10.3 Articulating a vision of abundance

1. Focus on creating positive deviance, rather than correcting negative deviance.
   - Focus on possibilities more than probabilities.
   - Focus on extraordinary, spectacular achievement, rather than just winning or being seen as successful.
2. Include left-brain images by asking questions such as:
   - What are our most important strengths as an organisation?
   - Where do we have a strategic advantage?
   - What major problems and obstacles do we face?
   - What stands in the way of significant improvement?
   - What are the primary resources that we need?
   - What information is required?
   - Who are our key customers?
   - What must be done to respond to customers' expectations?
   - What measureable outcomes will we accomplish?
   - What are the criteria to be monitored?

continues

BOX 10.3 *Continued*

3. Include right-brain images by asking questions such as:
   - What is the best we can achieve?
   - What represents peak performance?
   - What stories or events can we tell that characterise what we stand for?
   - What metaphors or analogies can we use that will identify what the future of our organisation will look like?
   - What symbols are appropriate for helping capture people's imaginations?
   - What colourful and inspirational language can exemplify what we believe in?
4. Make the vision interesting by challenging weakly held assumptions.
5. Ensure credibility of the vision through demonstrating:
   - Integrity in adhering to a consistent set of principles.
   - Knowledge regarding the implications of the vision.
   - Enthusiasm and personal passion for the vision.
   - Association with core personal values.
   - A straightforward and simple message.
   - Exciting and energising language.
6. Attach the vision to a symbol to constantly remind people of the vision.
   - Create visual images such as logos, flags or signs.
   - Make certain that the visual symbol is closely associated with the vision so that it remains a constant reminder.

Generating commitment to the vision

Once this vision of abundance has been articulated, it is necessary for leaders to help organisation members commit to that vision, to sign-up, to adopt the vision as their own, and to work towards its accomplishment. The whole intent of a vision is to mobilise the energy and human potential of individuals who are to implement it and will be affected by it. Four ways to generate commitment to a vision are discussed below. Others are discussed in depth in the chapters on motivation, empowerment and teamwork.

Apply the principles of recreation

An interesting truism was identified by Chuck Coonradt (1985): 'People will pay for the privilege of working harder than they will work when they are paid.' Think about that for a minute. In other words, under certain circumstances individuals are more committed to doing work that actually costs them money than they are to doing work for which they receive remuneration. Sometimes people will pay to work, when they will not work when they are paid. How can that be? In what circumstances might that be the case?

Consider the following hypothetical example. Suppose you live in a cold climate and one day in the winter, as you arrive at work, you find that the heating is out of order. As the temperature falls to 10 degrees, you put on a coat. At 5 degrees you complain that it is too cold to work. At 0 degrees you leave, confident that no one could expect you to perform in such adverse conditions. Then you put on your $300 ski outfit, grab your $750 skis and boots, and race off to the slopes, in order to pay $75 for a lift ticket, $25 for petrol and $30 for a junk-food lunch. You will spend all day in –2 degree weather working much harder skiing than you would have worked at the organisation where you could have been paid. If this sounds unusual, consider the skyrocketing absenteeism rates in companies and universities when the first big snow falls in ski areas or when the surf is up in cities close to the beach. People regularly choose to pay to work harder than they would consider working when they are paid.

'Well,' you say. 'That's because it's fun. It's recreation.' And you are right. But there is no reason why the work performed in a regular job cannot be characterised by the same principles that characterise recreation. In other words, what causes people to want to engage in recreational work can also be what causes them to be equally committed to their occupational work. At least five characteristics are typical of recreational work (Coonradt 1985):

1. Goals are clearly defined.
2. Scorekeeping is objective, self-administered, peer-audit and compared with past performance.
3. Feedback is frequent.
4. Personal choice is present; rules are consistent and do not change until the season is over.
5. A competitive environment is present.

Despite the inherent motivation and commitment associated with these principles, many leaders behave inconsistently with them. Their vision is not stated clearly and precisely. There is no objective, self-administrated evaluation system. The scorekeeping system is controlled hierarchically, by managers one step above, instead of being peer-audited and continuous, as in recreation. Criteria of evaluation are vague and inconsistently administered. Organisation feedback often comes only when quarterly earnings statements are tabulated, and then it is often focused on what went wrong. Personal freedom is too often constrained, as evidenced by the elaborate bureaucratic structures that typify most large organisations. It is not unusual to have the criteria of success change in the middle of the game, especially if a new manager takes over. And most employees never see how what they do makes any difference at all in obtaining the ultimate goal, or winning against a competitor.

The way for leaders to generate commitment to the vision is to identify clear, consistent goals associated with the vision; to identify the criteria that will indicate progress towards reaching the vision, which each organisation member can monitor; to provide mechanisms for frequent feedback to organisation members; to give individuals personal choice and the maximum discretion possible; to maintain a consistency and stability of the rules of the game and expectations; and to identify a competitive standard against which performance can be evaluated. Like commitment to recreation, commitment to visions, if based on similar principles, will also become strong and long-lasting.

Institute a small-wins strategy

People become committed to change when they see progress being made or success being achieved. We are all more committed to winners than to losers. Fans attend more games when the team has a good record than when it has a poor record. The number of people claiming to have voted for a winning candidate always exceeds by a large margin the actual number of votes received. In other words, when we see success, or progress being made, we are more committed to respond positively, to continue that path and to offer our support.

Leaders of positive change create this kind of support by identifying small wins (Carlopio 1998, 2003; Kotter 1996), a strategy that was discussed in sections on managing stress as well as in discussions on problem solving and empowerment. This small-wins strategy is applicable in a variety of skill-building activities, so part of the discussion is repeated here. The key message is that publicising small wins creates commitment and builds momentum for desired change (Weick 1981). For example, when beginning a major change initiative, leaders might begin with small things such as a new coat of paint, abolishing reserved parking spaces, adding a display case for awards, flying a flag, holding regular social events, instituting a suggestion system, and so on. These small changes (and hundreds more) are each designed to create commitment to the visualised change.

A small-wins strategy, in other words, is designed to create a sense of momentum by creating minor, quick changes. The basic rule of thumb for small wins is: Find something that is easy to change. Change it. Publicise it, or recognise it publicly. Then find a second thing that is easy to change and repeat the process.

Small wins create commitment for many reasons (Weick 1993):

- They reduce the importance of any one change. ('It's no big deal to make this change.')
- They reduce demands on any group or individual. ('There isn't a lot to do.)
- They improve the confidence of participants. ('At least I can do that.')
- They help to avoid resistance or retaliation. ('Even if they disagree, it's only a small loss.')

- They attract allies and create a bandwagon effect. ('I want to be associated with this success.')
- They create the image of progress. ('Things seem to be moving forward.')
- If they do not work, they create only a small flop. ('No major harm is done and no long-lasting effects occur.')
- They provide initiatives in multiple arenas. ('Resistance cannot be coordinated or organised in a single area.')

Communicate the vision

Effective leaders of positive change communicate the vision, then they communicate it again, then again, and then again. If leaders stop communicating the vision, or if they change themes as they address organisation members, the members tend to think that the vision is no longer important. Unless leaders continually and consistently articulate and re-articulate the vision, it loses its power and commitment erodes. Being accused of repetition is much less serious than being accused of neglect. Persistent and continuous delivery of the vision message is required, but, surprisingly, this is a frequent shortcoming of leaders. They give a speech or hand out a sheet of paper on which the vision is written, then they think their job is complete. In reality, it has only begun. Nelson Mandela did not ever speak in South Africa, for example, without re-articulating his vision of human dignity and equal treatment for all persons.

Creating commitment is enhanced, in other words, by applying principles of recreational work, providing opportunities for public statements of commitment, instituting small wins, and communicating the vision frequently, consistently and broadly. In essence, as summarised in Box 10.4, leaders will achieve commitment to that which they say, that which they do and that which they reward, but, without consistency and frequency, not necessarily to that which they want.

BOX 10.4 Generating commitment to the vision

1. Apply principles of recreation to the work associated with the vision:
   - Clearly define goals.
   - Ensure that scorekeeping is objective, self-administered, peer-audited and compared with past performance.
   - Ensure frequent (or continuous) feedback.
   - Provide opportunity for personal choice.
   - Ensure that rules are consistent and do not change.
   - Provide a competitive environment.
2. Provide opportunities for people to publicly commit to the vision.
   - Hold events where people can verbalise their commitment.
   - Ask people to teach others about, or recruit others to sign up for, the vision.
3. Institute a strategy of small wins.
   - Find something easy to change.
   - Change it.
   - Publicise it.
   - Repeat the process multiple times.
4. Communicate the vision frequently.
   - Never give a public speech or presentation without mentioning the vision.
   - Make certain that all your written messages contain references to the vision.
   - Avoid changing messages.

Institutionalising the positive change

The final challenge for leaders of positive change is to make the change a part of ongoing organisational life. The challenge is to separate the vision from the visionary, to get others to own and become champions of the change, to create processes that reinforce the positive change without having to continually rely on the leader. The objective is to ensure that, even if the leader leaves, the positive change will continue because of the sustainable impetus put in place. If Bill Gates had been incarcerated for unfair business competition, Jan Carlzon had been in a plane crash, Lee Iacocca had been run over by a car or Jack Welch had been electrocuted by a faulty refrigerator wire, Microsoft, SAS, Chrysler and General Electric would not have missed a step. The positive changes championed by these leaders would still have been pursued, because they had become embedded in their organisations' cultures. They were institutionalised and had gained irreversible momentum.

Institutionalising change does not happen quickly, of course, and the four previous steps in positive change—establishing a climate of positivity, creating readiness, articulating a vision, and generating commitment—must all be successfully accomplished first. However, institutionalisation is the necessary final step if the organisation is to successfully achieve positive change. How do leaders institutionalise their positive changes? Three hints are provided.

Turn students into teachers

Often it is assumed that it is the leader's responsibility to articulate the vision of abundance, and everyone else listens to it and accepts it. Teachers teach what students need to know and students learn it for the exam. The CEO gives direction and the rest of the employees follow.

The most effective leaders, however, provide an opportunity for everyone in the organisation to articulate the vision, or to teach others about the desired positive change. This process requires that every person develop 'a teachable point of view' (Tichy 1993). Developing one's own teachable point of view means that individuals come to believe in something and they can clearly explain what it is and why. In other words, people get to the point where they can articulate the vision in their own words. They are given opportunities to teach others what they understand the positive change to be. They are required to develop their own perspective on the positive change in a way that it can be explained and illustrated to someone else. They are transformed from students or listeners into teachers or visionaries.

Researchers at the National Training Laboratories in Maine in the United States developed a 'learning stair' (see Figure 10.9). Their studies found that people remember only 5 per cent of what they hear in a lecture, 10 per cent of what they read, 20 per cent of what they view in a video, 30 per cent of what they observe being demonstrated, 50 per cent of what they discuss in a group, 75 per cent of what they apply, and 90 per cent of what they teach to others. That is, by teaching someone else about the vision or the intended positive change, individuals remember it, become committed to it, and make it a part of their own personal agenda.

One manifestation of this principle was at Xerox under Rex Kern, a remarkable leader who turned around that company in the late 1980s and early 1990s. Kern's focus was on rapidly institutionalising a

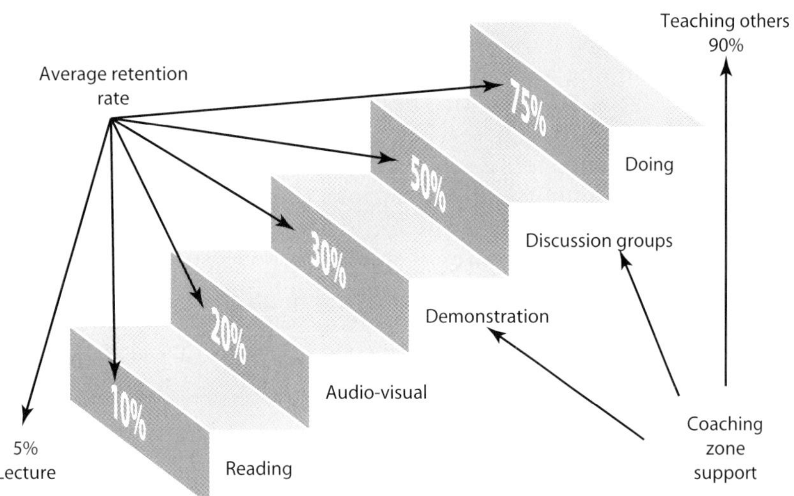

FIGURE 10.9 The learning stairs

Source: The Learning Stairs, NTI Institute, Bethel, Maine.

positive change process by turning students into teachers. He spent time sharing his vision of positive change with his top leadership team. Then these leaders were required to apply what they had heard—that is, to implement personal action agendas and make personal changes. Then, most importantly, they were required to teach the positive change vision to someone else. Who would they teach? They taught the next level of leaders in the firm. They were also required to assess or monitor the positive change. This was in order to identify measurable indicators, milestones and hard data to ensure that the positive change was really taking place. It was a way to guard against lip service with no real substance. What did they assess? It was the action agendas and managerial experiments implemented by the leaders they taught. The process continued down through all the organisational levels. Each person, in other words, was exposed to the vision four times: when they learned it from their leader, when they applied it, when they taught it, and when they assessed it. Within a year, Xerox had achieved stunning results. It is widely acknowledged that this process was key in turning Xerox around as a company and in labelling Rex Kern as one of the great corporate leaders of the 20th century.

This process is similar to the one used by certain divisions within Hewlett Packard. These divisions require engineers to spend time recruiting on university campuses. Having engineers actually recruit students—from disciplines in business, mathematics, physical sciences, arts and humanities, as well as engineering—is highly risky, since engineers are not trained recruiters. However, the strategy pays off because the engineers are required to articulate the vision, publicly praise Hewlett Packard and teach interested job candidates about the company. Former Hewlett Packard 'students' are required to become the 'teachers'. These engineers may not convince many rookie recruits, but by articulating the H-P Way they internalise it themselves. They become inoculated. As a result, Hewlett Packard has the lowest turnover rate in the industry among engineers, one of its stated core competencies.

Build human capital

For positive change to have staying power, for it to last beyond the lifetime of the leader, people throughout the organisation must have developed the capability to lead the vision themselves, to institute positive change and to carry on under their own initiative. In other words, well-developed human capital is always the chief predictor of growth in financial capital. The skill set of the people is the bedrock on which organisational success is built. No company can make money over time without well-developed human capital (capable and skilful employees). Institutionalising positive change occurs as individuals throughout the organisation develop the capacity to lead positive change themselves.

Metrics, measurement, milestones

A third aspect of institutionalisation is the establishment of metrics (or specific indicators of success), measures (or methods for assessing levels of success) and milestones (or benchmarks to determine when detectable progress will have occurred). These three factors help to ensure accountability for change, make it clear whether or not progress is being made, provide visible indicators that the change is successful, and help make change more successful (Lingle & Schiemann 1996). The adage 'You get what you measure' is an illustration of this principle. Change becomes institutionalised when it becomes a part of what people are held accountable to achieve. When it is clear what the measures are, people tend to respond to those measures. If students are measured on their test scores but not on the extra reading they do, they will certainly spend more effort and time studying for the exams than reading extra materials. It is only when people are measured on different criteria that they shift their focus. Consequently, institutionalising positive change means that clear metrics are identified, a measurement system is put into place, and a milestone is identified for when the change must have been accomplished.

As an illustration of these points is Jan Carlzon's (1987: 108–9) approach to institutionalising his vision in the once-struggling Scandinavian Airlines:

> *... employees at all levels must understand exactly what the target is and how best to achieve it. Once the frontline personnel ... have taken on the responsibility of making specific decisions, these employees must have an accurate feedback system for determining whether the decisions they are making are, in fact, the ones that*

will accomplish the company's overall goals. ... The necessity of measuring results is particularly crucial for those employees who affect customer service but don't have face-to-face contact with these customers. Ticket agents get immediate feedback on their job performance hundreds of times a day from the customers they serve. However, other workers such as baggage handlers have no such advantages. In fact, loading and unloading cargo is probably the most thankless job we have at SAS. ... The baggage handlers never come into contact with the passenger, and so they never get positive or negative feedback from them. Lacking this, they need clear targets and other means of measuring how well they are meeting their goals.

The keys to establishing effective metrics, measures and milestones for positive change are:

- Identify two or three metrics or indicators that specify the result that is to be achieved. (A common mistake is to measure too many things. The key is to focus on a few core items.) These should not be metrics associated with effort or methods, but should focus on results or outcomes. Specifically, they should address the outcomes desired from the vision of abundance. At SAS Airlines, one metric includes the elapsed time between the plane pulling up to the gate and the first bag being delivered on the carousel.
- Determine a measurement system. Data should be collected at certain time intervals in particular ways. This may be reports, surveys or face-to-face meetings. At SAS, daily logs are kept of baggage-handler performance. These measures do not focus on hours worked or how many bags are handled. They focus on the key outcomes desired—namely, speed and accuracy of delivery.
- Milestones are specified, meaning that at a certain point in time a measurable amount of progress will have been achieved. For example, by the end of the month baggage-handler timeliness will have improved 1 per cent. By the end of the year, it will have improved 15 per cent. Milestones simply create a time-frame for keeping track of real progress.

Institutionalising a vision of abundance and positive change, in sum, depends on making it a part of daily life and the habitual behaviour displayed by individuals throughout the organisation. No positive change can survive if it depends solely on the leader. Therefore, helping people to develop a teachable point of view about the positive change and providing opportunities for them to teach, building human capital through developing others' leadership skills, and instituting metrics, measurements and milestones to ensure accountability are all actions that can help to ensure successful institutionalisation of positive change. Specific behaviours associated with these strategies are summarised in Box 10.5.

BOX 10.5 Institutionalising the vision and creating irreversible momentum

1. Turn students into teachers.
   - Provide opportunities for people to develop a teachable point of view.
   - Make certain that others are required to articulate the vision themselves.
2. Build human capital.
   - Ensure training and development opportunities for others so they can be leaders of positive change.
   - Encourage the formation of networks and friendships that support.
3. Identify metrics, measures and milestones.
   - Identify when measureable progress will be achieved.
   - Identify what the specific criteria will be for evaluating success.
   - Determine how successful achievement of the vision will be ascertained.
   - Maintain accountability for the success of the positive change.

Summary

There are a multitude of changes taking place in many Australian organisations and they are driven by various factors. Although organisational change is often discussed as if organisations were objects that could be moulded and bent, as a blacksmith transforms a bar of iron, it is more functional to conceive of organisations as social processes, especially when trying to introduce significant change into the system. The first level of change—personal change—is difficult to describe or achieve. A four-stage model of the personal change process involves:

- unlearning
- changing existing behaviours and thoughts
- relearning, reinforcing, and modifying a new set of behaviours and thought patterns
- making change a habit and thus institutionalising personal growth and development.

Two tools useful for personal change are journalling and the day of difference. Several reactions to change can be experienced, such as denial, anger, bargaining, depression and acceptance.

The prevailing organisational structure will affect the organisation's ability and willingness to change. Although the organic and mechanistic forms do not represent a simple dichotomy, firms with more organic structural forms tend to be more innovative. More mechanistically structured firms are usually less innovative and more resistant to change. Organic firms are characterised by:

- low centralisation of power and decision making
- low organisational formalisation
- high organisational complexity
- high organisational interconnectedness
- high organisational slack.

Mechanistic firms are characterised by:

- high centralisation of power and decision making
- high organisational formalisation
- low organisational complexity
- low organisational interconnectedness
- low organisational slack.

The five key management skills and activities required to effectively lead positive change are: (1) establishing a climate of positivity; (2) creating readiness for change; (3) articulating a vision of abundance; (4) generating commitment to the vision; and (5) institutionalising the positive change.

Behavioural guidelines

To begin thinking about how this material can be applied in an organisational setting, reference is made to another model developed by Roger Collins of the Australian Graduate School of Management in 2004. Professor Collins suggests four basic steps in collective behavioural change: sensitivity, signalling, enabling and reinforcement. This model is used here as a way of integrating and applying what has been covered so far.

1. *Sensitivity*. Create awareness of the need for and readiness to change. Whether it is individuals or entire organisational systems that are changing, awareness of the need and intention to change is a necessary first step. At the organisational level of analysis, this impetus may come from any of the following:
   - information about competitors
   - client feedback
   - market research
   - staff attitude surveys
   - benchmarking and comparative performance information
   - stakeholder 'mirrors'
   - organisational trauma.
2. *Signalling*. Decide on and then clearly communicate the direction and means of travelling. Relevant individuals must set a direction, goal, mission or vision, and then clearly and continuously communicate this information to others. These signals must be loud enough to be perceived

above the background of everyday information and consistent enough to provide a unified field of vision. At the organisational level, a number of mechanisms may be relevant:
- mission and vision processes
- corporate and business-level planning processes
- definition of core values
- speeches, visits, information
- new organisation structures
- new performance indicators and levels
- new sources of performance feedback.

3. *Enabling*. Provide new skills, new structures and resources to motivate people to behave in new ways. At the organisational level of consideration, there are so many forces reinforcing the status quo that enabling processes must be well funded and well supported. These activities include such things as:
   - job and/or process redesign
   - new technology
   - team building
   - goal setting
   - personal growth and development
   - new physical environments
   - access to new information
   - training
   - changes in leadership and/or leadership styles.
4. *Reinforcement*. Behaviour that is reinforced is more likely to recur. This has been shown to work in the case of rats and children, and it even works with people in organisational settings. You must continually and intelligently manage the consequences of behaviour to encourage people to continue to behave in new ways. If you reward individual performance, for example, and you want to change to a team-based work environment, you had better change the reward structure to reinforce successful group-oriented behaviour and success. Three issues become critical at this stage:
   - *Early successes*. If people attempt to change and those early attempts are failures or the successes go unnoticed, the change process will suffer. Early on, therefore, make sure that people take on small projects with a high likelihood of success and be sure to actively reward both success and effort.
   - *Client and other performance feedback*. Be sure to measure progress and give feedback on results. Without baseline data, and subsequent information on progress, there is no way to modify effort, direct progress or reward success.
   - *Recognition and rewards*. Most people will not do something for nothing, and those that do will not do it for long. Remember that positive reinforcement can come in many forms besides money. Recognition, appreciation and acknowledgement are powerful motivators.

ANALYSIS

Skill analysis

Case study involving organisational change

Globe Maintenance Pty Ltd

Mr Burns founded Globe in 1991 as a spin-off of a family company, taking a $220 000 client with him as part of the arrangement. The contract with the customer called for the cleaning of ashtrays, the emptying of wastepaper baskets, and the vacuuming of offices and hallways. The company expanded as a result of the hard work of Mr Burns and a small, dedicated workforce. Soon Globe offered additional services, including window cleaning, gardening, and mechanical maintenance of heating and air-conditioning. In 2000 Globe won a contract to provide ramp services for an airline in Globe's home city. This included the cleaning of aircraft while at the terminal, some baggage handling and other labour-intensive non-mechanical services. These ramp services accounted for half of Globe's sales and 60 per cent of profit, due to fewer competitors, higher capital investment and higher risk.

The company grew by taking advantage of any opportunity that came along. By 2006 Globe was a medium-sized maintenance company, employing 1800 people in various departments that all directly reported to Mr Burns (that is, sales and marketing, accounting and debt collection, personnel and training, equipment purchase and maintenance, scheduling, general cleaning staff and specialist staff). As a result of having grown without acquisitions or mergers, all departments and storerooms were on the same property.

Although a simple, flat organisation in terms of structure, the operations were extremely complex and fluid as there was a great deal of two-way communications needed between the departments to complete any one contract. For example, the sales department needed to know what staff and equipment were available before selling contracts, the equipment department needed to know the types of sales anticipated as well as the training requirements of the cleaning staff allocated to use some equipment types, and the personnel department needed to know anticipated sales and current staff capabilities and levels. As each department depended on the others, the barriers between the departments tended to break down. This effect was heightened by the minimal number of rules Mr Burns had put in place. Mr Burns felt that the 'can do' attitude and strong work ethic that had typified the employees were more important in achieving Globe's goals.

Mr Burns had engaged two consulting firms over the past three years. Each had spent days interviewing staff and management, and had recommended a reorganisation of the company structure and processes, and suggested that more sophisticated strategy, planning, budgeting and accounting systems were necessary. Currently, pricing of services is done in line with the competition, and profit is used to pay salaries and buy supplies and equipment. The consultants also felt that there needed to be a clear structure with formalised work procedures, as well as the establishment of a formal system of interdepartmental information flow. The managers of the departments had attempted to implement some of the rule and procedure changes, but both times their efforts appeared to get lost in the more pressing aspects of business and in the resistance of the staff. However, the resistance to change did not indicate underlying labour–management hostility as much as a lack of appreciation of the need for change. The employees were quite proud of the company they had built and did not see the limitations on further expansion. While the actual cleaners were unionised, the union had been cooperative during the past ten years and the staff felt their allegiance lay with Globe.

In early 2007, Mr Burns announced his retirement and the sale of Globe to a large conglomerate holding company. The strategic planning unit of the new holding company studied Globe and its environment. They concluded that the ramp service market was going to become more competitive, but they thought they had an advantage with their expertise and cost efficiency. Although there were quite a few small operators competing successfully on the smaller jobs and a near monopoly of a few very big operators on the big jobs, the basic building maintenance market was tight but viable. Therefore, they determined that the following strategy was necessary to allow the long-term survival and expansion of Globe:

1. The firm is to be broken up into two divisions, Aircraft Ramp Services and Globe Building Maintenance. Aircraft Ramp Services is to consist of those staff already having expertise in aircraft servicing, while the rest of the staff will form Globe Building Maintenance. An office will be maintained with resource staff to oversee and provide assistance to the two divisions.
2. Ramp Services is to become as cost efficient and as quality conscious as possible to ensure continued renewal of its contracts, while also bidding for other contracts on a cost basis. Given that labour is the major cost, most changes will need to be productivity-based.

3. Globe's building maintenance operations will move to a quality service focus for up-market offices such as legal chambers and consultancy offices, offering many extras such as porter/maid service, furniture polishing, carpet care such as spot treatment and shampooing, and hand-towel and soap service. This is to be an efficient operation, although the major emphasis is to be on the provision of top-quality services and the monitoring of customer needs and competitors' actions to ensure that Globe Building Maintenance retains its quality edge. Thus, it is expected that Globe will constantly be innovating with new services and 'extras'. It is envisaged that Globe will move from a 'business as usual' culture to a customer-driven culture of quality performers and innovators.

Source: This case was written by Robert Waldersee and has been adapted by James Carlopio.

Managing the changes

You have been hired as managing director to head the implementation of these changes during the next three years. Globe is expected to be profitable at the end of this time. You have examined Globe's situation and agree that the recommended strategy is the best for the organisation. The holding company has allocated 25 per cent of Globe's 2006 profits for this reorganisation (that is, $750 000, not including equipment costs, which are to be funded by the divisions).

You know that you have four main questions to ask yourself: (1) Where are we? (2) Where do we want to go? (3) How can we get there? (4) How will we get there? Since you have been given the answer to the second question (that is, the strategic planning unit of the conglomerate holding company has outlined the answer to 'Where do you want to go?' in the three points on the previous page), your task is to address the remaining points.

1. *Where are we?* Start out by quickly assessing the answer to the first question. What can you gather about the culture, structure, operations, organisation, finances and so on of the firm?
2. *Where do we want to go?* Review the three strategy points in the case.
3. *How can we get there?* Roughly outline some actions that you could take to implement these changes, ways you might influence your division managers and employees, and what you think are some of the key aspects of the organisation and its people that need to be changed and why. How might different stakeholder groups perceive the changes? What are some of the most likely effects of these changes on people at the 'coalface', on people in the 'middle', on 'support' staff, and on management?
4. *How will we get there?* Make some decisions. On your first day at work, what is the most significant step you would take to implement your strategy? What will you do to begin the process of 'unfreezing' and preparing the organisation for change?

Be sure to draw on what has been discussed in this chapter.

Skill practice

PRACTICE

Exercises in process redesign and change

Process assessment exercise

Using the information in Figure 10.10 as an example, generate a formal process assessment, analysis and improvement strategy. Select a process in which you are involved that could be improved through process assessment, analysis and improvement procedures. If none comes readily to mind, you may select one of the following:

1. The process used to make decisions by your team.
2. The process used for course registration in your university.
3. The process used to serve a meal at the university cafeteria.

4. The process used to evaluate students and teachers in your university or training facility.
5. The process used to repair and service your car.
6. The process used to rent a car at an airport.
7. The process involved in obtaining a university degree.
8. The process used to restock food on supermarket shelves.

Do this activity in your team, using the following steps:

1. Agree on a process that all group members are familiar with.
2. Identify all the activities involved in the process. Organise them into a sequential flow.
3. Map the activities to show how they are connected to one another, who is involved in the activities, what coordination occurs and what communication lines are operative.
4. Now generate an ideal process map. That is, generate the same process where time, waste and errors are cut in half. Design it from scratch as a 'perfect' process.
5. Based on the ideal map, refine the process map you generated in step 2 and show the improvements you can make in it.
6. Make a presentation of your process assessment analysis and improvement strategy to the class. They should critique it in terms of its realism, the accuracy of the assessment and the map, and the amount of improvement you identified.

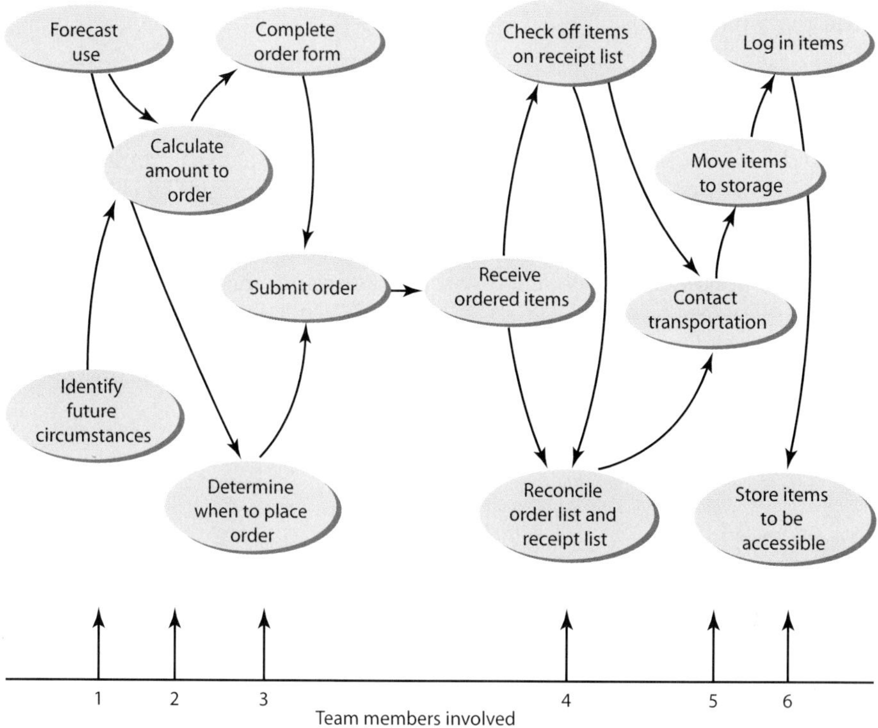

FIGURE 10.10 A simplified process map: Replenishing supplies

Skill application

Suggested assignments

1. Use one of the tools of personal change (that is, journalling or the day of difference) to generate some motivation and direction for personal change.
2. Use the following as a guide to personal values clarification. This can also help to generate some motivation and direction for personal change.

Values clarification exercise

1. **Values** (What do I stand for?)

   Our values are what we believe to be important and worthwhile. They are guidelines for living that influence our thoughts, feelings and behaviour. They represent who we are and what we stand for. Everyone has a set of values. Our values help us to make decisions on whether a course of action is right or wrong. It is useful not only to write down our values but to carry them around with us as a guide during these turbulent times.
   a. List the important aspects in your life down the left-hand side of a page.
   b. Think about the relative importance of these aspects and rank them from 'most important' to 'least important'.
   c. Now rank the aspects in terms of the amount of time you actually spend on, or with, each of them. If there are discrepancies between the rankings and the amount of time you are spending on each one, this is a good opportunity for thought and assessment. If you are spending the most time on aspects that are not of greatest importance to you, you may want to consider making some adjustments in your life. Of course, we may make sacrifices in the short term (for example, spending more time on study and less with family) for a longer-term gain (for example, getting a job that we want).
   d. Now list the major stakeholders to whom you feel you should be accountable in your life and state how you are going to be accountable to them. You are being asked to make some values-based commitments or values-based action statements. Ideally, they should:
      - be actionable (that is, begin with the words 'I will …')
      - be consistent with one another
      - be performance-enhancing
      - be in writing
      - be few in number.

   Alternatively, you may wish to write one or more statements to cover the values you uphold with respect to one or more of your stakeholders.
2. **Vision** (Where or what would I like to be in five years' time?)
   a. What is your dream for your life? What would you like to do with the rest of your life? Write down your answer(s).
   b. Next, think about your wishes and desires. They can be such things as recognition, love, new experiences or security. Write down a list of your wishes and dreams. This is your 'wouldn't it be nice to do or have' list.
   c. Now separate your wishes from your desires. For example, climbing Mt Everest involves years of planning and discipline and we may not desire it sufficiently to devote the time and energy necessary to accomplish it.
   d. Consider the items you desire to include in your vision (that is, the light on the hill you would like to aspire to in the next five years). Consider the various facets of your life before finalising your list (for example, family, self, spiritual, recreational, financial, social, educational). Now write your 'impossible' dream, your big goals for the next five years. This should be a bold statement of your ultimate vision for your self.

3. **Mission** (What am I about? What business am I in?)
Invent your future from the limitless future, rather than based on your past and what you think is reasonable or possible. Think and dream about the impossible. That is where success lives. Now write your personal mission statement.
4. Develop an **implementation plan** for making some form of organisational change. Consider as many of the potentially relevant issues as you can. Be sure to cover activities such as the structures needed to make the changes happen, changes to reporting relationships, creation of working groups and steering committees, changes to reward systems and performance indicators, creation and modification of communication systems and procedures, education and training, the alignment of sponsors, champions and project managers, and an analysis of critical aspects of the existing organisational culture and system (for example, norms regarding change and risk, likely barriers and resistors, identification of likely sponsors and champions).

Application plan and evaluation

The aim of this exercise is to help you apply this cluster of skills in a real-life, out-of-class setting. Now that you have become familiar with the behavioural guidelines that form the basis of effective skill performance, you will improve most by trying out those guidelines in an everyday context. Unlike a classroom activity, in which feedback is immediate and others can assist you with their evaluations, this skill application activity is one you must accomplish and evaluate on your own. There are two parts to this activity. Part 1 helps to prepare you to apply the skill. Part 2 helps you to evaluate and improve on your experience. Be sure to write down answers to each item. Do not short-circuit the process by skipping steps.

Part 1: Planning

1. Write down the two or three aspects of this skill that are most important to you. These may be areas of weakness, areas you most want to improve, or areas that are most salient to a problem you face right now. Identify the specific aspects of this skill that you want to apply.
2. Now identify the setting or the situation in which you will apply this skill. Establish a plan for performance by writing down a description of the situation. Who else will be involved? When will you do it? Where will it be done?
3. Identify the specific behaviours you will engage in to apply this skill. Operationalise your skill performance.
4. What are the indicators of successful performance? How will you know that you have been effective? What will indicate that you have performed competently?

Part 2: Evaluation

5. After you have completed your implementation, record the results. What happened? How successful were you? What was the effect on others?
6. How can you improve? What modifications can you make next time? What will you do differently in a similar situation in the future?
7. Looking back on your whole skill practice and application experience, what have you learned? What has been surprising? In what ways might this experience help you in the long term?

References

Adizes, I. 1992, *Mastering Change* (Santa Barbara, CA: Adizes Institute).

Ambrose, M. L. and M. Schminke 2003, 'Organization structure as a moderator of the relationship between procedural justice, interactional justice, perceived organizational support, and supervisory trust', *Journal of Applied Psychology*, 88(2), p. 295.

Baker, W. 2001, *Achieving Success through Social Capital* (San Francisco: Jossey-Bass).

Baker, W., R. Cross and M. Wooten 2003, 'Positive organizational network analysis and energizing relationships', in K. Cameron, J. Dutton and R. Quinn (eds), *Positive Organizational Scholarship: Foundations of a New Discipline* (San Francisco: Berrett-Koehler).

Bandura, A. 1977, 'Self-efficacy: Toward a unifying theory of behavioral change', *Psychological Review*, 84, pp. 191–215.

Bandura, A. and E. A. Locke 2003, 'Negative self-efficacy and goal effects revisited', *Journal of Applied Psychology*, 88(1), p. 87.

Baumeister, R., E. Bratslavsky, C. Finkenauer and K. Vohs 2001, 'Bad is stronger than good', *Review of General Psychology*, 5, pp. 323–70.

Beckhard, R. 1969, *Organization Development: Strategies and Models* (Reading, MA: Addison-Wesley).

Bennis, W. and B. Nanus 1985, *Leaders: The Strategies for Taking Charge* (New York: Harper & Row).

Boydell, T. 1985, *Management Self-development* (Geneva: International Labour Office).

Burns, D. 1981, *Feeling Good: The New Mood Therapy* (New York: Bantam).

Cameron, K. 1985, 'Iacocca's transformation of Chrysler: Excerpts from Lee Iacocca's speeches to his top management team, 1979–1984' (in possession of the author).

Cameron, K. 2003, 'Organizational virtuousness and performance', in K. Cameron, J. Dutton and R. Quinn (eds), *Positive Organizational Scholarship: Foundations of a New Discipline* (San Francisco: Berrett-Koehler).

Cameron, K. and A. Caza 2002, 'Organizational and leadership virtues and the role of forgiveness', *Journal of Leadership and Organizational Studies*, 9, pp. 33–48.

Carlopio, J. 1998, *Implementation: Making Workplace Innovation and Technical Change Happen* (Sydney: McGraw-Hill).

Carlopio, J. 2003, *Changing Gears: The Strategic Implementation of New Technology* (London: Palgrave Macmillan).

Carlzon, J. 1987, *Moments of Truth* (Cambridge, MA: Ballinger).

Champy, J. 2003, 'The hidden qualities of great leaders', *Fast Company*, 76, November, p. 135.

Choi, M. and W. Ruona 2011, 'Individual readiness for organizational change and its implications for human resource and organization development', *Human Resource Development Review*, 10(1), pp. 46–73.

Clifton, D. and J. Harter 2003, 'Investing in strengths', in K. Cameron, J. Dutton and R. Quinn (eds), *Positive Organizational Scholarship: Foundations of a New Discipline* (San Francisco: Berrett-Koehler).

Cohen, E. and N. Tichy 1999, 'Leadership beyond the walls begins with leadership within', in F. Hesselbein, M. Goldsmith and I. Somerville (eds), *Leading Beyond the Walls* (San Francisco: Jossey-Bass).

Coonradt, C. 1985, *The Game of Work* (Salt Lake City: Shadow Mountain Press).

Donaldson, L. 2001, *The Contingency Theory of Organizations* (Thousand Oaks, CA: Sage).

Dunphy, D. 1981, *Organizational Change by Choice* (New York: McGraw-Hill).

Dutton, J., P. Frost, M. Worline, J. Lilius and J. Kanov 2002, 'Leading in times of trauma', *Harvard Business Review*, January, pp. 54–61.

Emmons, R. 2003, 'Acts of gratitude in organizations', in K. Cameron, J. Dutton and R. Quinn (eds), *Positive Organizational Scholarship: Foundations of a New Discipline* (San Francisco: Berrett-Koehler).

Enright, R. and C. Coyle 1998, 'Researching the process model of forgiveness within psychological interventions', in E. Worthington (ed.), *Dimensions of Forgiveness* (Philadelphia: Templeton Foundation Press).

Glynn, P. 1994, 'Toward a politics of forgiveness', *American Enterprise*, 5, pp. 48–53.

Gold, T. 2002, *Open Your Mind, Open Your Life* (Springfield, IL: Andrews McNeel Publishing).

Goodstein, J. and K. Aquino 2010, 'And restorative justice for all: Redemption, forgiveness, and reintegration in organizations', *Journal of Organizational Behavior*, 31(4), pp. 624–8.

Gottman, J. 1994, *Why Marriages Succeed and Fail* (New York: Simon & Schuster).

Helmick, R. G. and R. L. Petersen 2001, *Forgiveness and Reconciliation: Religion, Public Policy, and Conflict* (Philadelphia: Templeton Foundation Press).

Howard, K. 1999, 'Reeling in the change', *Chief Executive*, 149, November, p. 24.

Jayne, V. 2003, 'MBAs: Do MBAs deliver?', *New Zealand Management*, June, p. 51.

Kanov, J., S. Maitlis, M. Worline, J. Dutton and P. Frost 2003, 'Compassion in organizational life', *American Behavioral Scientist*, pp. 1–54.

Karakas, F. 2011, 'Positive management education: Creating creative minds, passionate hearts, and kindred spirit', *Journal of Management Education*, 35(2), April, pp. 198–226.

Kolb, D. A., I. M. Rubin and J. M. McIntyre 1979, Org*anizational Psychology* (Englewood Cliffs, NJ: Prentice Hall).

Kotter, J. 1996, *Leading Change* (Cambridge, MA: Harvard Business Press).

Kübler-Ross, E. 1969, *On Death and Dying* (New York: Macmillan).

Kunze, F. and H. Bruch 2010, 'Age-based faultlines and perceived productive energy: The moderation of transformational leadership', *Small Group Research*, 41(5), pp. 593–620.

Leavitt, H. J. 2003, 'Why hierarchies thrive', *Harvard Business Review*, 81(3), p. 96.

Lewin, K. 1951, *Field Theory in Social Science* (New York: Harper & Row).

Lingle, J. and W. Schiemann 1996, 'From balanced scorecard to strategic gauges: Is measurement worth it?', *Management Review*, 85(3), pp. 56–61.

Losada, M. and E. Heaphy 2003, 'The role of positivity and connectivity in the performance of business teams: A nonlinear dynamics model', *American Behavioral Scientist*, 47, pp. 740–65.

McCraty, R. and D. Childre 2004, 'The grateful heart', in R. Emmons and M. McCullough (eds), *The Psychology of Gratitude* (New York: Oxford University Press), pp. 230–55.

McCullough, M., R. Emmons and J. Tsang 2002, 'The grateful disposition: A conceptual and empirical topography', *Journal of Personality and Social Psychology*, 82, pp. 112–27.

Meyerson, D. 2001, *Tempered Radicals* (Cambridge, MA: Harvard Business School Press).

Morgan, M. 1993, *Creating Workforce Innovation* (Sydney: Business and Professional).

Quinn, R. 2004, *Building the Bridge as You Walk on It* (San Francisco: Jossey Bass).

Quinn, R., J. Dutton and G. Spreitzer 2003, 'The reflected best-self feedback exercise', University of Michigan Business School.

Rego, A., N. Ribeiro, M. Cunha and J. Jesuino 2011, 'How happiness mediates the organizational virtuousness and affective commitment relationship', *Journal of Business Research*, 64(5), pp. 524–32.

Rotella, K. 2003, 'Creating a winning team: Ferguson's culture', *Supply House Times*, April, p. 10.

Searle, T. and J. Barbuto 2011, 'Servant leadership, hope, and organizational virtuousness: A framework exploring positive micro and macro behaviors and performance impact', *Journal of Leadership & Organizational Studies*, 18(1), pp. 107–17.

Simmel, G. 1950, *The Sociology of Georg Simmel* (Glencoe, IL: The Free Press).

Tichy, N. M. 1993, *Control Your Destiny or Someone Else Will* (New York: Doubleday).

Tutu, D. 1999, *No Future Without Forgiveness* (New York: Doubleday).

Weick, K. 1981, 'Small wins: Redefining the scale of social problems', *American Psychologist*, 39, pp. 40–49.

Weick, K. 1993, 'Small wins in organizational life', *Dividend*, Winter, pp. 20–24.

Glossary

ability: the product of aptitude multiplied by training and opportunity.

accommodating approach: a response to conflict that tries to preserve a friendly interpersonal relationship by satisfying the other party's concerns while ignoring one's own. It generally ends with both parties losing.

achievement orientation: an emphasis on personal accomplishment and merit as the basis for getting ahead, used in contrast to an ascription orientation. One of the key dimensions that identifies international culture differences.

advising response: a response that provides direction, evaluation, personal opinion or instructions.

affectivity orientation: an emphasis on open displays of emotion and feeling as being acceptable, used in contrast to a neutral orientation. One of the key dimensions that identifies international culture differences.

alarm stage: initial response to stress characterised by increases in anxiety, fear, sorrow or depression.

ambidextrous thinking: the use of both the left and right sides of the brain, indicative of the most creative problem solvers.

analytical problem solving: a method of solving problems that involves four steps: (1) defining the problem; (2) generating alternative solutions; (3) evaluating and selecting an alternative; and (4) implementing and following up on the solution.

anticipatory stressor: the anxious expectation of unfamiliar, uncertain or disagreeable events.

artificial constraints: arbitrary boundaries placed around a problem that restrict possible alternative approaches and make the problem impossible to solve creatively.

ascription orientation: an emphasis on attributes such as age, gender or family background as the basis for getting ahead, used in contrast to achievement orientation. One of the key dimensions that identifies international culture differences.

attraction: also referred to as personal attraction 'likability' stemming from agreeable behaviour and attractive physical appearance; a combination of behaviours normally associated with friendships that have been shown to contribute to managerial success.

autonomy: the freedom to choose how and when to do a particular task; one of the characteristics of an intrinsically satisfying job.

avoiding response: an unassertive, uncooperative reaction to conflict that neglects the interests of both parties by side-stepping the issue. The resulting frustration may engender power struggles as others rush to fill the leadership vacuum.

Balanced Scorecard: a strategic performance management system involving four perspectives—customer, internal processes, people and growth, and financial.

basic curve: representing basic, required work of a team.

bias against thinking: the inclination to avoid mental work, one indication of the conceptual block, complacency.

bipolar question: question that gives interviewees only two limited options to choose from in answering. The result may be inaccurate information.

blocking roles: behaviours that stand in the way of or inhibit the effective performance of a team or that subvert team member effectiveness.

brainstorming: a technique designed to help people solve problems by generating alternative solutions without prematurely evaluating and rejecting them.

centrality: the attribute of a position in which the occupant is a key member of informal networks of task-related and interpersonal relationships. The resulting access to information, resources and the personal commitment of others is an important source of power.

challenging goals: one of the factors affecting the motivating potential of stated goals—hard goals tend to be more motivating than easy goals.

clarification probe: question(s) designed to clarify information given by the interviewee.

closed questions: interview questions designed to elicit specific information from interviewees by restricting the possible answers the interviewee can give. Useful when time is limited and/or when answers to open questions need clarifying.

coaching: a one-on-one process of professional and personal support, guidance, challenge and development.

cognitive dissonance reduction: individuals strive to reduce inconsistencies between their own beliefs and behaviours and their expectations of others.

cognitive style: the manner in which an individual gathers and evaluates information he or she receives.

collaborating approach: the cooperative, assertive, problem-solving mode of responding to conflict. It focuses on finding solutions to the basic problems and issues that are acceptable to both parties, rather than on finding fault and assigning blame. Of the conflict management approaches, this is the only win-win strategy.

collectivism orientation: an emphasis on the predominance of groups, families or collectives over individuals, used in contrast to individualism orientation. One of the key dimensions that identifies international culture differences. Also referred to as communitarianism.

commitment: the conceptual block that results when an individual endorses a particular point of view, definition or solution.

competition–cooperation: studies consistently show that groups whose members are working towards a common goal perform more effectively and produce higher levels of member satisfaction than groups whose members seek to fulfil individual needs or pursue competing goals.

complacency: the conceptual block that occurs not because of poor thinking habits or inappropriate assumptions but because of fear, ignorance, self-satisfaction or mental laziness.

compression: the conceptual block that results from an individual's looking at a problem too narrowly, screening out too much relevant data, or making assumptions that inhibit solving the problem.

compromising response: a reaction to conflict that attempts to find satisfaction for both parties by 'splitting the difference'. If overused, it sends the message that settling disputes is more important than solving problems.

conceptual blocks: mental obstacles that restrict the way a problem is defined and limit the number of alternative solutions that might otherwise be considered.

conformity level: the second level of values maturity, at which moral reasoning is based on agreement with and support of society's conventions and expectations.

congruence: exactly matching the communication, verbally and non-verbally, to what an individual is thinking and feeling.

conjunctive communication: connection of responses to previous messages in such a way that conversation flows smoothly.

consistent goals: one of the factors affecting the motivating potential of stated goals—it is difficult to pursue goals that are inconsistent or incompatible.

constancy: the conceptual block that results from using only one way to look at a problem—to approach, define, describe or solve it.

continuous improvement: small, incremental changes team members initiate.

core competence: an aggregation of individual team member skills, including knowledge, styles, communication patterns and ways of behaving.

counselling: interpersonal communication used to help subordinates recognise their own problems rather than offering advice, direction or a right answer.

creative problem solving: a method of solving problems that involves four stages: (1) preparation, (2) incubation, (3) illumination, and (4) verification.

deep breathing: relaxation technique of taking several successive, slow deep breaths, then exhaling completely.

deep relaxation technique: an approach for use in building psychological resiliency in which both body and mind become completely relaxed.

defensiveness: focusing on self-defence rather than listening; occurs when an individual feels threatened or punished by the communication.

deflecting response: a response that switches the focus from the communicator's subject to one selected by the listener; or simply the change of subject by the listener.

delegation: assignment of responsibility for tasks to subordinates.

descriptive communication: objective description of the event or behaviour that needs modification; description of the reaction to the behaviour or its consequences; and suggestion of a more acceptable alternative.

diffuseness orientation: an emphasis on integrating work, family and personal roles in a society, used in contrast to specificity orientation. One of the key dimensions that identifies international culture differences.

dignity (and liberty): the ethical decision principle that a decision is right and proper if it preserves the basic humanity of individuals and provides the opportunity for them to have greater freedom.

direct analogies: a synectic problem-solving technique in which individuals apply facts, technology and previous experience to solving a problem.

disciplining: a motivational strategy by which a manager reacts negatively to an employee's undesirable behaviour in order to discourage further occurrences. Disciplining may be useful up to a point but does not encourage exceptional performance.

disconfirmation: a 'put-down'; or the feeling resulting from communication that demeans or belittles the recipient and threatens his or her sense of self-worth.

disjunctive communication: responses that are disconnected from what was stated before. It can result from (1) a lack of equal opportunity to speak; (2) long pauses in a speech or before a response; or (3) when one person decides the topic of conversation.

disowned communication: attribution to an unknown person, group or some external source; allows the communicator to avoid responsibility for the message and therefore avoid investing in the interaction.

distributive bargaining perspective: negotiation tactic that requires both parties to sacrifice something to resolve the conflict—to divide up a 'fixed pie'. (Contrast with the integrative approach.)

double-barrelled question: a problematic question that actually consists of two questions that should be asked separately in order to avoid confusing the interviewee.

effort: an important source of power suggesting personal commitment.

elaboration probe: question(s) designed to pursue a topic further when an interviewee has responded with superficial or inadequate information.

empowerment: the use of acquired power to give others power in order to accomplish objectives; it strikes a balance between lack of power and abuse of power.

enactive strategy: a method of managing stress that creates a new environment by eliminating the stressors.

encounter stressor: the type of stressor that results from interpersonal conflict.

environmentally induced stress: conflict-fostering tension induced by such organisational factors as budget tightening or uncertainty caused by rapid, repeated change.

equity: workers' perceptions of the fairness of rewards based on the comparison of what they are getting out of the work relationship (outcomes) to what they are putting into it (input).

ethics: the development of a principle-based knowledge of what is right and wrong, and doing what is right.

evaluative communication: a statement that makes a judgment about or places a label on other individuals or on their behaviour.

excitement curve: representing innovations and breakthroughs in task accomplishment and service delivery.

expertise: cognitive ability resulting from formal training and education or from on-the-job experience; an important source of power in a technological society.

extrinsic outcomes: rewards for performances that are controlled by someone other than the employee—usually the supervisor—such as appreciation, job security or good working conditions. (Compare with internal motivators.)

false bipolar question: a poorly worded interview question, implying the choices are mutually exclusive, when in fact the respondents are more likely to have mixed feelings (for example, do you approve or disapprove of overtime work?).

fantasy analogies: a synetic problem-solving technique in which individuals ask: 'In my wildest dreams, how would I wish the problem to be resolved?'

feedback: information regularly received by individuals from superiors about their performance on a job. Knowledge of results permits workers to understand how their efforts have contributed to organisational goals.

feeling strategy: a method of interpreting and judging information subjectively or impressionistically rather than objectively; one which defines and redefines a problem on a trial-and-error basis.

flexibility: the freedom to exercise one's judgment—an important prerequisite for gaining power in a position—particularly in tasks that are high in variety and novelty.

flexibility of thought: the diversity of ideas or concepts generated.

flexible communication: the result of the willingness of the coach or counsellor to accept the existence of additional data or other alternatives and to acknowledge that other individuals may be able to make significant contributions both to the problem solution and to the relationship.

fluency of thought: the number of ideas or concepts produced in a given length of time.

forcing response: an assertive, uncooperative response to conflict that uses the exercise of authority to satisfy one's own needs at the expense of another's.

forming stage: first stage of team development where team is oriented to each other and establishes clarity of purpose.

funnel sequence: a sequence of interview questions that begins with general questions and moves towards more and more specific questions.

goal characteristics: effective goals are specific, consistent and appropriately challenging.

goal setting: the foundation of an effective motivational program, which consists of (1) including employees in the goal-setting process; (2) setting specific, consistent and challenging goals; and (3) providing feedback.

goal-setting process: the critical consideration is that goals must be understood and accepted if they are to be effective.

groupthink: one of the pitfalls in group decision making that occurs when the pressure to reach consensus interferes with critical thinking. When the leader or the majority appears to prefer a particular solution, holders of dissenting views are reluctant to speak out.

hardiness: a combination of the three characteristics of a highly stress-resistant personality—control, commitment and challenge.

hierarchical needs model: a general theory of motivation, positing that behaviour is oriented towards need fulfilment and that human needs tend to be arranged hierarchically (that is, lower-level needs must be fulfilled before higher-order needs become salient).

homogeneity–heterogeneity: members of a homogeneous group share similar backgrounds, personalities, knowledge and values. Due to this sameness, these groups tend to produce mundane and unimaginative outcomes. Members of a heterogeneous group are dissimilar and because of their differences are apt to be better at addressing novel, complex tasks.

human capital: a person's abilities and competencies ('I know the answer to the question'). Compare with social capital.

idea champion: person who comes up with the innovative solutions to problems.

ignoring: a manager's neglect of both the performance and the job satisfaction of employees. Such a lack of effective leadership can paralyse a work unit.

ignoring commonalities: a manifestation of the commitment block—the failure to identify similarities among seemingly disparate situations or data.

illumination stage: in creative thought, the third stage, which occurs when an insight is recognised and a creative solution is articulated.

imagery and fantasy: a relaxation technique using visualisation to change the focus of one's thoughts.

imperviousness in communication: the failure of the communicator to acknowledge the feelings or opinions of the listener.

imposing: a manager's exploitation of employees by assigning tasks with the sole emphasis on performance and without regard to their job satisfaction—usually disastrous in the long term.

incongruence: a mismatch between what one is experiencing and what one is aware of, or a mismatch between what one feels and what one communicates.

incubation stage: an early stage in creative thought in which mostly unconscious mental activity combines unrelated thoughts in pursuit of a solution to a problem.

indifference: a type of communication in which the other person's existence or importance is not acknowledged.

individualism orientation: an emphasis on the self, uniqueness and individuality, used in contrast to collectivism orientation. One of the key dimensions that identifies international cultural differences.

indulging: a manager's emphasis on employee satisfaction to the exclusion of employee performance; the resulting country-club atmosphere hinders productivity.

informational deficiencies: breakdowns in inter-organisational communication. Conflicts based on the resulting misunderstandings tend to be common but easy to resolve.

initiator role: the part played in a conflict management model by the individual who first registers a complaint with another person who is the 'responder'. (See 'Behavioural Guidelines' in Chapter 7, 'Managing Conflict'.)

innovation: large, visible, discontinuous changes; breakthroughs.

innovativeness: fostering new ideas among individuals by methods such as placing them in teams and separating them at least temporarily from the normal pressures of organisational life.

instrumental values: those values that prescribe desirable standards of conduct or methods to reach a goal.

integrating: a motivation strategy that emphasises job performance and job satisfaction equally—a challenging strategy for a manager to implement, but one that can result in both high productivity and high morale of employees.

integrative perspective: negotiation tactic in which the focus is on collaborative ways of 'expanding the pie' by avoiding fixed, incompatible positions. (Contrast with distributive approach.)

interchange incompatibility: the inability of individuals to communicate effectively owing to their having different interpersonal needs.

internal locus: the viewpoint of an individual who attributes the success or failure of particular behaviour to his or her own actions.

interpersonal compatibility: the matching of individuals' needs.

interpersonal competence: the ability to manage conflict, to build and manage high-performance teams, to conduct efficient meetings, to coach and counsel employees, to provide negative feedback in constructive ways, to influence others' opinions, and to motivate and energise employees.

interpersonal orientation: the aspect of self-awareness that relates to behaviour and relationships with other people.

interview: a specialised form of communication conducted for a specific task-related purpose.

intrinsic outcomes: job characteristics inherent in the job itself, over which the manager has no control and that determine whether or not a particular employee will find that job interesting and satisfying. (Compare with external motivators.)

intuitive strategy: a type of thinking that uses preconceived notions about the sort of information that will be relevant and looks for commonalities among the various elements of data.

invalidating communication: that which denies the other person the possibility of contributing to the communication.
inverted funnel sequence: a sequence of interview questions that begins with specific questions and moves towards more and more general questions.
issue-focused conflict: interpersonal conflicts that are substantive, or content, oriented. (See people-focused conflict.)
issue selling: influence strategy characterised by being the champion or representative of an issue.
Janusian thinking: thinking contradictory thoughts at the same time; conceiving two opposing ideas to be true concurrently.
leading question: a tricky interview question that includes the desired answer in the question itself. While useful in a sales interview, it can lead to biased answers in other types of interviews.
learning style: the way in which individuals perceive, interpret and respond to information. Four main learning styles exist.
left-hemisphere thinking: brain activity concerned with logical, analytic, linear or sequential tasks.
legitimacy: conformity with an organisation's value system and practices, which increases one's acceptance and thus one's influence in that organisation.
level of initiative: the extent to which a subordinate is expected to take a task. At least five levels can be identified: (1) wait to be told; (2) ask what to do; (3) recommend, then act; (4) report after acting; and (5) act independently.
life balance: the development of resiliency in all areas of one's life in order to handle stress that cannot be eliminated.
locus of control: the second dimension of orientation towards change; the viewpoint from which an individual judges the extent to which he or she controls his or her own destiny.
management: the capacity to create a work environment in such a way that each person is uniquely motivated to achieve the organisational goals and feels recognised for doing so.
matching: the process of utilising self-awareness and acute observation to match the mood, manner and 'culture' of the other person so as to maximise influence and understanding.
mediator role: the conflict management role played by the third party who intervenes in a dispute between an 'initiator' and a 'responder'.
mentoring: process by which a senior manager takes a junior manager under their wing and guides their understanding and knowledge of the organisation.
mobbing: the improper sharing of group-developed perceptions of bullying behaviour of another party in such a way that credibility is given to the complainants by weight of numbers and the required confidentiality of the group action.
morphological forced connections: a technique to expand alternative solutions by forcing the integration of seemingly unrelated elements. The four steps are (1) writing down the problem; (2) listing its attributes; (3) listing alternatives to each attribute; and (4) combining different alternatives from the attributes list.
morphological synthesis: a four-step process intended to expand the number of creative alternatives available for solving a problem. It involves combining the different attributes of a problem together in unique ways.
motivation: a combination of desire and commitment demonstrated by effort.
muscle relaxation: technique of relaxation by easing the tension in successive muscle groups.
need for achievement: an expressed desire for accomplishment and recognition.
need for affection: the drive for close personal relationships with others while preserving one's separateness.
need for affiliation: an expressed desire for social relations.
need for control: the desire to maintain for oneself a satisfactory balance of power and influence in relationships.
need for inclusion: the basic desire of people to maintain relationships and share activities with others.
need for power: an expressed desire for control, or influence, over others.

negotiation strategies: tactics used in the bargaining phase of negotiation—collaborating, forcing and accommodating—that are consistent with the related conflict management approaches and have about the same outcomes.

negotiations: an interpersonal decision-making process used for resolving differences or allocating scarce resources.

nominal group technique (NGT): a group decision-making technique; a highly structured form of brainstorming. In an NGT session, group members (1) individually write down as many alternative solutions to a problem as they can think of; (2) report their ideas, which are transcribed on to a flip-chart; (3) discuss the ideas briefly for clarification only; and (4) vote for the alternatives they prefer. The process is repeated until a consensus is reached.

non-inquisitiveness: the failure to ask questions, obtain information or search for data; an example of the complacency block.

norming stage: the second stage of a team's development in which expectations become clear, a group identity is formed, and the norms become clear and accepted.

open questions: interview questions designed to elicit general information from interviewees—how they feel, what their priorities are and how much they know about a topic. Useful for establishing rapport, they can be time consuming.

orchestrator: person who brings together cross-functional groups and necessary political support to facilitate implementation of a creative idea.

organisational culture: the values and basic assumptions that typify an organisation. It refers to the most basic elements of an organisation, or 'just the way things are around here'.

orientation towards change: an individual's adaptability to ever-increasing levels of ambiguity and turbulence.

originator incompatibility: the stalemate that occurs when either both people want to initiate in an area or neither does.

owned communication: statements for which a person takes responsibility, acknowledging that he or she is the source of the message; an indication of supportive communication.

participants: individuals invited to attend a meeting.

participation: the actual process of meetings and the methods used to ensure that meetings involve everyone present. The involvement of individuals—in addition to a single leader—in an activity.

particularism orientation: an emphasis on relationships and close personal connections to govern behaviour, used in contrast to universalism orientation. One of the key dimensions that identifies international cultural differences.

people-focused conflict: interpersonal conflict that is personal (for example, a clash between different personalities or interpersonal styles). (See issue-focused conflict.)

perceptual stereotyping: defining a problem by using preconceptions based on past experience, thus preventing the problem from being viewed in novel ways.

performance: the product of ability multiplied by motivation.

performance curve: refers to the elements in a product or service that customers expect to be present and which they identify as preferences. The more closely the supplier's performance meets the preferences of the customer, the higher the satisfaction level of the customer.

performing stage: stage of a team where it is able to function as a highly effective and efficient unit.

personal analogies: recommended as part of synectics, whereby individuals try to identify themselves as the problem, asking the question: 'If I were the problem, what would I like? What would satisfy me?'

personal differences: variations among individuals' values and needs that have been shaped by different socialisation processes. Interpersonal conflicts stemming from such incompatibilities are the most difficult for a manager to resolve.

personal management interview program: a regularly scheduled, one-on-one meeting between a manager and his or her subordinates.

personal values: an individual's standards that define what is good/bad, worthwhile/worthless, desirable/undesirable, true/false, moral/immoral.

perspective: the evaluation of a meeting from a distance.

planning: preparation for the meeting agenda.

preparation stage: a stage in creative thought that includes gathering data, defining the problem, generating alternatives and consciously examining all available information.

principled level: the third and highest level of values maturity in which an individual judges right from wrong by following internalised principles developed from personal experience.

proactive strategy: a method of managing stress that initiates action in order to resist the negative effects of stress.

probing response: a response that asks a question about what the communicator just said or about a topic selected by the listener.

problem-solving process: an approach to conflict resolution that focuses on identifying underlying problems, or issues, and brainstorming solutions.

problem-solving teams: small groups of workers who meet for an hour or two each week to discuss ways to improve.

process: a sequential set of activities designed to lead to a specific outcome.

process analysis: step in process management used to identify a better way to perform a particular process.

process assessment: identification of the sequence of tasks, activities and individuals involved in delivering an output.

process improvement: stage in process management where process itself is changed so as to foster advancement.

process management: the assessment, analysis and improvement of sets of activities engaged in by teams.

process map: shows each of the activities in relationship to one another.

purpose: the reason a meeting is held, including information sharing, commitment building, information disseminating, and problem solving and decision making.

quality circles: problem-solving teams who meet to discuss issues and make recommendations to upper management.

reactive strategy: a method for managing stress that copes with the stressors immediately, temporarily reducing their effects.

reason: the influence strategy that relies on persuasion and appeal to rational consideration of the inherent merits of the request in order to gain compliance. It is explicit and direct, not manipulative.

reassigning: moving the poor performer to a position more consonant with his or her skill level and aptitude.

reciprocal incompatibility: the stalemate that occurs when there is no match between one person's expressed behaviour and another's wanted behaviour.

reciprocity: an influence strategy through which a manager uses bargaining as a tool for exacting a subordinate's compliance. This approach operates on the principle of self-interest and respect for the value of the interpersonal relationship.

redirection: a behaviour-shaping process that follows a reprimand and gives the offender the opportunity to receive a future reward by modifying his or her behaviour.

refitting: adapting the requirements of a job to an employee's abilities in order to improve poor performance.

reflecting response: a response that serves two purposes: (1) to confirm a message that was heard; and (2) to communicate understanding and acceptance of the other person.

reflection probe: non-directive question(s) used for either elaboration or clarification of information; it generally mirrors or repeats some aspect of the interviewee's last answer.

reflective probe: a response to a communicator by reflecting back in one's own words what the communicator said. The purpose is to clarify the message and help the communicator feel open and safe in sharing more messages.

reframing: stress-reduction technique of redefining a situation as manageable.

rehearsal: relaxation technique of trying out stressful scenarios and alternative reactions.

reinforce: when rewards are linked to desired behaviours they are said to reinforce those behaviours (that is, increase their frequency).

relational algorithm: a blockbusting technique for combining unrelated attributes in problem solving by connecting words to force a relationship between two elements in a problem.

relationship-building roles: those that emphasise the interpersonal aspects of the team.

relevance: the characteristic of a position whose tasks relate most closely to the dominant competitive goals of an organisation and therefore enhance the power of the occupant.

repetition probe: a repeated or paraphrased question used if the interviewee has not directly answered a question the first time.

reprimand: a behaviour-shaping approach used to transform unacceptable behaviours into acceptable ones; the discipline should be prompt and it should focus on the specific behaviour.

resiliency: one's capacity to cope with stress.

resistance stage: response to stress in which defence mechanisms predominate.

respectful communication: treating subordinates as worthwhile, competent and insightful by emphasising joint problem solving rather than projecting a superior position.

responder role: the part played in a conflict-management model by the person who is supposedly the source of the 'initiator's' problem.

resupplying: managerial option for overcoming an employee's lack-of-ability problem that focuses on supplying the support needed to do the job.

retraining: a management tool for overcoming the problem of an employee's poor performances, especially needed in rapidly changing technical work environments.

retribution: an influence strategy that involves a threat—the denial of expected rewards or the imposition of punishment. It usually triggers an aversive response in the subordinate and the breakdown of the interpersonal relationship.

reverse the definition: a tool for improving and expanding problem definition by reversing the way you think of the problem.

rewarding: the motivational strategy that links desired behaviours with employee-valued outcomes. Such positive reinforcement gives an employee more incentive for exceptional accomplishment than does disciplining.

right-hemisphere thinking: mental activity concerned with intuition, synthesis, playfulness and qualitative judgment.

rigidity in communication: a type of message that portrays the communication as absolute, unequivocal or unquestionable.

role incompatibility: the conflict-producing difference between workers whose tasks are interdependent but whose priorities differ because their responsibilities within the organisation differ. The mediation of a common superior is usually the best solution.

self-awareness: a knowledge of one's own personality and individuality.

self-centred level: the first level of values maturity. It contains two stages of values development, moral reasoning and instrumental values, which are based on personal needs or wants and the consequences of an act.

self-determination: feelings of having a choice.

self-disclosure: the revealing to others of ambiguous or inconsistent aspects of oneself; a process necessary for growth.

self-efficacy: empowered feeling of possessing the capability and competence to perform a task successfully.

self-managing teams: most advanced form of teamwork; maintain all responsibilities with the team that are normally spread across multiple levels and functions on an ongoing basis.

sensitive line: an invisible boundary around one's self-image, which if threatened, will evoke a strong defensive reaction.

separating figure from ground: the ability to filter out inaccurate, misleading or irrelevant information so that the problem can be defined accurately and alternative solutions can be generated.

situational stressor: the type of stressor that arises from an individual's environment or circumstances, such as unfavourable working conditions.

skill variety: an attribute of a job that uses an individual's talents and abilities to the maximum and thus makes the job seem worthwhile and important.

small-wins strategy: a strategy for individuals to use for coping with stress; it involves celebrating each small successful step in the attack on a large project.
social capital: a person's social connections ('I know someone who knows the answer to the question'). (Compare with human capital.)
social loafing: a pitfall in group decision-making performance that occurs when the effort of a large group seems to negate the importance of each member's individual contribution. The result is that each member puts out less than his or her best effort. A group leader can counteract this tendency by emphasising the importance of individual effort and by expressing positive expectations.
specific goals: goals that are measurable, unambiguous and behavioural.
specificity orientation: an emphasis on separating work, family and personal roles in a society, used in contrast to diffusion orientation. One of the key dimensions that identifies international cultural differences.
sponsor: person who helps provide the resources, environment and encouragement that the idea champion needs in order to work.
storming stage: team development stage where members question the team's direction, the leader, roles of other members' and task objectives.
stressors: stimuli that cause physiological and psychological reactions in individuals.
subdivision: the breaking apart of a problem into smaller parts.
superiority-oriented communication: a message that gives the impression that the communicator is informed while others are ignorant, adequate while others are inadequate, competent while others are incompetent, or powerful while others are impotent.
supportive communication: communication that helps managers share information accurately and honestly without jeopardising interpersonal relationships.
symbolic analogies: symbols or images that are imposed on the problem; recommended as part of synectics.
synectics: a technique for improving creative problem solving by putting something you do not know in terms of something you do know.
task-facilitating roles: those that help the team accomplish its outcome objectives.
task identity: an attribute of a job that enables an individual to perform a complete job from beginning to end.
task-process: research indicates that effective groups contain members who are highly task oriented as well as those who are concerned about maintaining the quality of the group's process. Task-oriented members are all business, focusing on outcomes and not worrying about members' feelings and attitudes; process-oriented members encourage everyone to participate and are most concerned with member satisfaction.
task significance: the degree to which the performance of a task affects the work or lives of other people. The greater its significance, the more meaningful the job is to the worker.
terminal values: those values that designate desirable ends or goals for an individual.
thinking languages: the various ways in which a problem can be considered, from verbal to non-verbal or symbolic languages as well as through sensory and visual imagery. Using only one thinking language is one indication of the constancy block.
threat-rigidity response: the tendency of almost all individuals, groups and organisations to become rigid, meaning conservative and self-protective, when faced with a threat.
time stressor: the type of stressor generally caused by having too much to do in too little time.
tolerance of ambiguity: an individual's ability to cope with ambiguous, fast-changing or unpredictable situations in which information is incomplete, unclear or complex.
two-way communication: the result of respectfulness and flexibility.
Type A personality: a hard-driving, hostile, intense, highly competitive personality.
universalism: the ethical decision principle that a decision is right and proper if everyone would be expected to behave in the same way under the same circumstances.
validating communication: a message that helps people feel recognised, understood, accepted and valued. It is respectful, flexible, two-way and based on agreement.

verification stage: the final stage in creative thought in which the creative solution is evaluated relative to some standard of acceptability.
vertical thinking: defining a problem in a single way and then pursuing that definition without deviation until a solution is reached.
visibility: the power-enhancing attribute of a position that can usually be measured by the number of influential people one interacts with in the organisation.
win–win philosophy: ensuring that everyone benefits from actions.
work design: the process of matching job characteristics and workers' skills and interests.

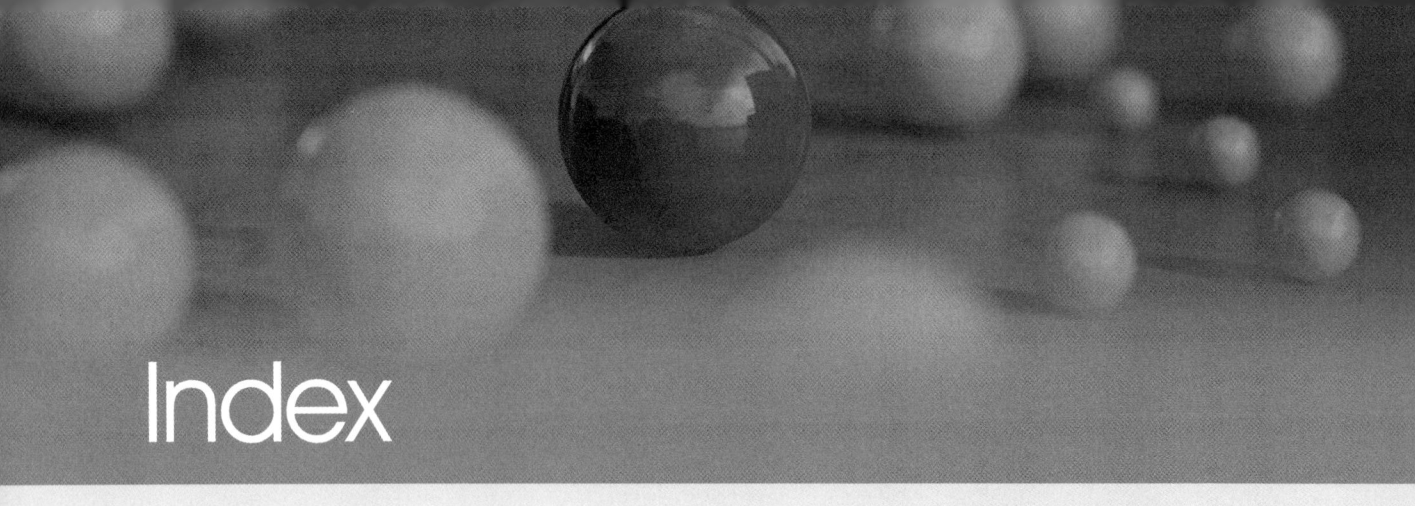

Index

Page numbers in *italics* refer to figures.